Uncle John's HEAVY DUTY BATHROOM READER®

By the Bathroom Readers' Institute

Bathroom Readers' Press
Ashland, Oregon

OUR "REGULAR" READERS RAVE!

"Keep up the good work. I love your books and have almost every one of them. I got my Mom and Dad hooked on them two years ago, and my brother and wife recently started reading as well."

—Jon

"You guys are amazing! I love fun trivia facts and history. My favorite thing about your book is that it is so random and funny."

—John

"I love your books. They're very educational and highly entertaining. I never want to set them down until I finish them. Keep them coming."

—Roland

"Just a note to tell you that I've really enjoyed all 22 editions!"

—Michael

"I love *Uncle John's Bathroom Readers*! I annoy everyone at school, my weirdo cousin, and my parents with your completely useless information. And it isn't all useless. During school we do trivia, and I answer almost all of them correctly!"

—Megan

"I just wanted to say thank you for the book. I read it every day—it's become my 'Bathroom Bible.'"

—Katherine

"You guys are so amazingly smart! How do you know all this stuff? Like, come on, all the stuff I learned in *Did You Know?* and *Facts to Annoy Your Teacher* made me look just like Einstein!"

—Bobby

UNCLE JOHN'S HEAVY DUTY
BATHROOM READER®

For information, write:
The Bathroom Readers' Institute, P.O. Box 1117,
Ashland, OR 97520
www.bathroomreader.com • 888-488-4642

Cover design by Michael Brunsfeld, San Rafael, CA
(*Brunsfeldo@comcast.net*)
BRI "technician" on the back cover: Larry Kelp

ISBN-13: 978-1-60710-183-3 / ISBN-10: 1-60710-183-1

Library of Congress Cataloging-in-Publication Data
Uncle John's heavy duty bathroom reader.
    p. cm.
ISBN 978-1-60710-183-3 (pbk.)
1. American wit and humor. 2. Curiosities and wonders.
I. Bathroom Readers' Institute (Ashland, Or.)
PN6165.U5366 2010
081.02'07—dc22

2010013077

Printed in United States of America
First Printing
1 2 3 4 5 6 7 8 14 13 12 11 10

THANK YOU!

The Bathroom Readers' Institute sincerely thanks the people whose advice and assistance made this book possible.

Gordon Javna

John Dollison

Brian Boone

Jay Newman

Thom Little

Amy Miller

Michael Brunsfeld

Angela Kern

Jolly Jeff Cheek

Jack Mingo

Erin Barrett

Jahnna Beecham

Malcolm Hillgartner

Megan Todd

Judy Plapinger

William Dooling

Jill Bellrose

Mikael Levin

Elizabeth Harvey

Michael Kerr

Christine DeGueron

James Greene Jr.

Leslie Weishar

Scarab Media

Amelia & Greta Zeve

Claudia Bauer

Geri Gale

Gary Morris

JoAnn Padgett

Melinda Allman

Monica Maestas

Amy & Annie

Ginger Winters

Maggie Javna

Matt Ofsanik

Tom "Yellow" Mustard

Sydney Stanley

David Calder

Karen Malchow

Elise Gochberg

Julie Bégin

Media Masters

Eddie Deezen

Publishers Group West

Bloomsbury Books

Raincoast Books

Porter the Wonder Dog

Thomas Crapper

Hiya, Sam! Hiya, Gideon!

CONTENTS

Because the BRI understands your reading needs, we've
divided the contents by length as well as subject.
Short—a quick read
Medium—2 to 3 pages
Long—for those extended visits, when something
a little more involved is required
* Extended—for those leg-numbing experiences

INTRODUCTION

G **REETINGS, FELLOW TRIVIA HOUNDS!**
As we scramble to finish our latest (and our favorite-ever) *Bathroom Reader*, I'm reminded of a question that I hear a lot: "Aren't you guys afraid you'll run out of stuff to write about?"

The answer is a big, fat no.

We're *more* concerned that we're not going to live long enough to write about everything we plan to write about. (For example, in next year's Bathroom Reader we're going to include an amazing article about...on second thought, why spoil the surprise?) For us, every day is another fantastic opportunity to plunge into the depths of science, history, current events, language, sports, and pop culture. To explore strange, new worlds. To seek out new life and new civilizations. To boldly go... (Oops. I got carried away again.)

But what's even more gratifying than hunting and gathering all the great information that goes into *Uncle John's Bathroom Reader* is paring it all down to its most absorbing elements and passing it along to you.

So without further ado, here are a just a few of the *Heavy Duty* duty topics you'll find in this book:

• **When Words Collide:** Pun-ishing quotes, a guide to "butt" words, phrases coined on *The Simpsons*, and Esperanto—the invented language that was supposed to bring about world peace

• **Flubs and Flops:** The best worst movie ever, the Wicked Witch who fell through the stage, and Michelangelo's dirty little secrets

• **Throne Room Tales:** Toilet mishaps (as told by ER docs), an interesting "morsel" of archaeology called the Lloyd's Bank Turd, poop that's art, and art that poops

• **Oddities Galore:** The Whopperknocker and other mythical beasties, the strange fate of Big Nose George's skull cap, some *other* famous leaning towers, and how to make prison wine

- **Pop Science:** The healing powers of witch hazel, all about anthrax, the solar system's most violent moon, what the dinosaurs ate, and the physics of breakfast cereal

- **Origins:** The Mini Cooper, the Magic 8-ball, the office cubicle, the shopping mall, and the Ch-ch-ch-chia pet!

- **History Unleashed:** Intrepid explorers who never returned, the Mohawk "skywalkers" who built New York's City's skyscrapers, and the man who made Pearl Harbor a "day that will live in infamy"

- **The Sporting Life:** The weightlifter who ate himself out of the Olympics, the dangers of watching the Super Bowl, NASCAR's most dangerous family, and Rollie Fingers' $300 mustache

- **Creature Features:** The powerful brains of birds, the complex societies of ants, a devil of a turtle, 185 uses for a pig (would you believe...train brakes?), and the secret language of dogs

And speaking of dogs, I'm going to forego the usual thanking of the inhouse and outhouse BRI staff (Great job, everyone!) and take a moment to say thanks to the *Bathroom Reader's* best friend, Porter the Wonder Dog. You've been our loyal companion since... well, before we even had an e-mail address. Thanks for your love, your cuteness, your tricks, and your sticking by my side on all those long nights of writing and editing. Porter, you give real meaning to the phrase "good dog." Oh, yes you do!

So on behalf of Porter and the entire BRI staff, Happy Reading.

And as always...

Iri kun la Fluo!*

—Uncle John

(*That's Esperanto for "Go with the Flow!")

YOU'RE MY INSPIRATION

It's always interesting to find out where the architects of pop culture get their ideas. These may surprise you.

PATRICK BATEMAN. In the 2000 movie *American Psycho*, Christian Bale portrayed Patrick Bateman, a stockbroker by day, sociopathic serial killer by night. Bale based his characterization on another actor. According to director Mary Harron, "he had been watching Tom Cruise on *David Letterman*, and he just had this very intense friendliness with nothing behind the eyes."

DONKEY KONG. When a 1981 video game called *Radar Scope* sold poorly, Nintendo suddenly had 2,000 empty arcade-game cabinets to fill. At the same time, a deal with King Features to make a Popeye Nintendo game fell apart, so staff designer Shigeru Miyamoto just used the Popeye love triangle for inspiration— Popeye, his girlfriend Olive Oyl, and brute Bluto became Mario, Pauline, and a giant ape named Donkey Kong.

BENDER AND NELSON. Cartoonist Matt Groening's two TV series are laced with references to John Bender, the teen rebel portrayed by Judd Nelson in *The Breakfast Club*, one of Groening's favorite movies. The hard-drinking, sarcastic robot Bender on *Futurama* was named for him; school bully Nelson Muntz on *The Simpsons* was named after Judd Nelson; and Bart Simpson's catchphrase "eat my shorts" was first uttered by John Bender.

OLD NAVY. Is there really a sea-based military force of elderly people? No, but there is a bar in Paris called Old Navy. In 1994 the president of the Gap, Millard Drexler, saw it while he was in France. He scrapped the name he was considering for his discount clothing store, Forklift, and decided instead to call it Old Navy.

THE SS MINNOW. The boat that took the seven castaways to *Gilligan's Island* was named after FCC chairman Newton Minow. In a 1961 speech he called television a "vast wasteland." *Gilligan's Island* creator Sherwood Schwartz named the doomed vessel after Minow as an insult.

EMBARRASSED IN THE E.R.

What's worse than a trip to the emergency room? A trip to the E.R. for something really humiliating. These are real-life E.R. reports.

"Forehead pain: Patient shot self in nose with BB gun."

"Head injury: Rolled off couch and hit telephone."

"40-year-old female using toothbrush to make herself gag, accidentally swallowed toothbrush."

"Abdominal pain. Diagnosis: tight pants and belt."

"Patient stuffed ear with toilet paper so roach wouldn't crawl in, now unable to remove."

"Patient missed punching bag, hit metal safe."

"Concussion, severe headache: Patient being pulled on a sled behind golf cart, struck a bump, launched in air."

"Pulled groin while riding mechanical bull."

"Bruised shoulder: Husband was throwing cell phone at cat, missed cat."

"Patient, 23, used a sword to cut a piece of paper. Laceration left arm."

"Accidentally swallowed guitar pick."

"Patient, 31, was playing sex games with wife, had belt around neck, jumped over something and got hung up. Also fell down stairs."

"Ankle injury from falling off stage doing karaoke."

"Swallowed toothpick while eating cabbage."

"Fell off monkey bars at police academy."

"Patient playing with pillow case, buddy put a rock in it."

"Insect bites on lips while riding a go-kart."

"Generalized body rash after being in pool and hot tub at hotel."

"Pain, swelling, blister on palm: Patient, 15, was playing video games, woke next day with swollen hand. Pain and swelling getting worse."

"Patient has wrist pain after sex and bowling."

Fewer than 1% of all patented inventions ever make money.

FOUNDING FATHERS

Three famous food origins to chew on.

ROBERT H. COBB. In the 1930s, the hot restaurant for anyone in the movie industry was the Hollywood Brown Derby, located at North Vine Street. Owner Robert Cobb claimed to have invented the restaurant's signature dish in 1935, and named it after himself: the Cobb Salad. (A more likely scenario: the chefs at the Brown Derby invented it.) The original Cobb consisted of a mixture of greens (iceberg lettuce, watercress, chicory, and romaine), topped with diced chicken breast, tomatoes, avocado, chopped bacon, hard-boiled eggs, chives, and Roquefort cheese, served with a red wine vinaigrette. The Brown Derby closed in 1985 (Cobb died in 1970), by which time they'd sold more than four million Cobb Salads.

GRANNY SMITH. Maria Sherwood Smith was 50 years old when she and her husband Thomas settled on a farm in New South Wales, Australia, and began planting fruit orchards. She liked to experiment with fruit hybrids, and in 1868, at the age of 69, she crossed a European wild apple with a common Australian apple to create a new breed—light green in color, tart in flavor, and slow to brown when cut and exposed to air. Smith died just two years later, not living to see her apple blossom. The Australian government began cultivating it in 1895. It was first exported to the U.K. in the 1930s, but didn't make it to the U.S. until 1972. Today it's one of the most popular apple varieties in the world.

GENNARO SBARRO. In 1956 Sbarro emigrated from Naples, Italy, to Brooklyn, where he found work in an Italian deli. By 1959 he'd opened his own deli in the Bensonhurst neighborhood, and five years later he owned four delis around New York. In 1977 Sbarro expanded into restaurants. The first one was located where you'd still find a Sbarro today: a shopping mall. The store in Kings Plaza Shopping Center in Brooklyn (it's still there) established the Sbarro format of pizza and pasta, served cafeteria-style. Today there are more than 1,600 Sbarro restaurants in 47 states and 43 countries. (And they're still mostly in malls.)

Makes cents: Men tend to tip female waiters more; women tend to tip male waiters more.

DREAMY FACTS

What happens to you when you sleep? Read on.

- According to experts, dreaming is a natural brain function, and all human beings do it. But some people never remember their dreams.

- People who have quit a longtime smoking habit report having very vivid reams for several weeks after stopping.

- The Old English word *dream*, which etymologists believe is the origin of our word dream, meant "'joy," "mirth," or "music."

- Psychologists say that both men and women become sexually aroused while dreaming—even if the dream has no sexual content.

- Average amount of time spent dreaming per night: 1½ to 2 hours.

- The Raramuri people of northern Mexico believe that dreams are the result of one's soul "waking" or "sobering," and seeing the world more clearly than usual. (Raramuri families often wake up and discuss their dreams during the night.)

- The longest dreams—up to 45 minutes long—usually occur in the morning.

- Negative emotions, such as anxiety, are more commonly felt during dreams than positive ones are.

- Studies show that women who experience nightmares during pregnancy have easier births than women who don't.

- Birds, like humans, experience REM (rapid eye movement) sleep, during which they experience brain wave activity similar to that of humans. This suggests that birds dream.

- Reptiles also experience brain activity during sleep that suggests they too may dream. (Fish do not.)

- Scientists believe schizophrenics suffer from irregular REM sleep, and that the hallucinations and delusions they experience may actually be "waking dreams."

- For most of his life, President Lyndon Johnson had nightmares that he was paralyzed.

Shock jock: Green Bay QB Matt Hasselbeck has been struck by lightning twice.

LITTLE THINGS MEAN A LOT

*"The devil's in the details," says an old proverb. It's true—
sometimes the littlest things can cause BIG problems.*

THE WRONG E-MAIL LIST

In April 2009, more than 30,000 applicants to the University of California San Diego received an e-mail that began: "We're thrilled that you've been admitted to UC San Diego, and we're showcasing our beautiful campus on Admit Day!" Thousands of excited students shared the good news and started booking flights and hotel rooms. But two hours later, those same applicants received a second e-mail from UCSD informing them that the first one was a mistake. "In all humility, I ask that you please accept my apologies," wrote admissions director Mae Brown, who later explained that the first e-mail was supposed to go only to the 18,000 applicants who had been accepted, but it was accidentally sent to all 47,000 who applied. "We accessed the wrong database," she admitted. Said one of the rejected applicants: "It was one of the greatest moments in my life and then, boom, it was one of the lowest."

AN AUSTRALIAN ACCENT...IN AUSTRALIA

A man, a woman, and a dog walked into the Thai Spice restaurant in Adelaide, Australia, in 2009, only to be told by a waiter: "We don't allow dogs in here!" The woman responded (in her native Australian accent), "But he's a gay dog!" Offended, the waiter—who was from Thailand—told them to leave immediately. A few days later the restaurant's owner, Hong Hoa Thi To, received a call from South Australia's Equal Opportunity Tribunal asking him why service was refused to a blind man who came in with a friend and his guide dog. "*Guide* dog?" asked Hong? He thought the woman had said "*gay* dog." The restaurant was ordered to apologize to the man and pay him $1,500. "My staff genuinely believed that it was an ordinary pet dog which had been desexed to become a gay dog," said Hong.

Only Oscar to win an Oscar: Oscar Hammerstein II, for Best Song (1941 and '45).

A TYPO

In 1987 Kamjai Thavorn, 30, was sentenced to 20 years in an Indonesian prison for heroin possession. In 2007 Thavorn, then 50, told the warden that his sentence had ended, and he should be set free. The warden's answer: No. According to the prison's paperwork, Thavorn began serving in 1997—not 1987—and still had a decade left to go. For the next three years, he pleaded to be set free...to no avail. He might still be behind bars today if not for a chance meeting in 2010 with Indonesia's justice minister, who was touring the facility. Thavorn told the minister his situation, the matter was looked into, and Thavorn was finally freed. Prison officials apologized, explaining that whoever admitted him must have accidentally typed a "9" instead of an "8."

THE WRONG ADDRESS

When real estate agent Peter Collard arrived at the six-bedroom house he was trying to sell in Brisbane, Australia, in 2010, he was horrified to discover that half of the yard was dug up and ten palm trees had been ripped out of the ground. Next to the devastation were two confused-looking workmen and a backhoe. When Collard asked them what the (blank) they were doing, the men quickly loaded the backhoe onto the trailer and, without a word, drove away. According to police, they were digging a swimming pool, but due to an address mix-up, they were at the wrong house. The workers were never located, and Collard's insurance company denied his claim for compensation. Cost of the repair: $20,000.

A PIN

An American Airlines 767 landed at the company's maintenance facility in Fort Worth, Texas, after a test flight in 2009. Standard procedure dictates that a pin be inserted into the front landing gear to prevent it from retracting while it's on the ground. Someone forgot to follow standard procedure. When workers boarded to complete their post-maintenance checklist, one of them pulled the front landing gear lever. The wheel retracted and the 767 plunked down nose-first onto the tarmac. Luckily, no one was underneath it, but according to sources from the airline, the structural damage was so extensive that the plane—which was only six years old and cost $150 million—was "beyond repair."

GIVE ME A SIGN!

Church reader boards are a great source of humor and wisdom.
Here are some real signs that we've collected.

"There are some questions
that can't be answered
by Google"

"Staying in bed shouting,
'Oh God!' does not constitute
going to church"

"Read the Bible—it will
scare the hell out of you"

"Walmart is not the
only saving place"

"Forgive your enemies—it
messes with their heads"

"Salvation guaranteed, or your
sins cheerfully refunded!"

"Do not criticize your
wife's judgment—see
who she married"

"There's no A/C
in Hell either"

"God shows no favoritism but
our sign guy does. Go Cubs!"

"Swallowing pride will never
give you indigestion"

"Cars aren't the only things
recalled by their maker"

"Come in and let us prepare
you for your finals"

"Life stinks. We have
a pew for you"

"Friends are God's way
of apologizing to us
for our families"

"Whoever stole our mower:
God will get you."

"How do we make holy water?
We boil the hell out of it"

"Now open between
Easter and Christmas!"

"Forbidden fruit creates
many jams"

"Santa Claus never died
for anyone"

"Down in the mouth?
It's time for a faith lift"

"Pessimists need a kick
in the can'ts"

"Church parking only.
Violators will be baptized"

"Too cold to change sign!
Message inside."

In the 1800s, artists used paint made from ground-up mummies.

FATAL FLIGHT FIRSTS

At least they got to be the first in the world at something.

LT. THOMAS E. SELFRIDGE

Claim to Fame: First person killed in a plane crash

Story: On September 17, 1908, Orville Wright was demonstrating his Wright Flyer at Fort Myer army base in Virginia. Along for the ride was 26-year-old First Lieutenant Tom Selfridge, a U.S. Army dirigible pilot. About 150 feet above the ground, a propeller broke. Wright was able to glide the craft to about 75 feet, but then it went into a nosedive. Selfridge suffered a fractured skull and died that evening. Wright suffered a broken thigh, pelvis, and ribs, and spent seven weeks in the hospital, but lived to fly again.

VERNON CASTLE

Claim to Fame: First celebrity plane death

Story: In the early 1900s, Vernon and Irene Castle were trend-setting superstars who appeared in Broadway productions and movies. When World War I began, Vernon returned to his native England and became a war pilot, then returned to the United States to train American pilots. On February 15, 1918, he took off from an airfield near Fort Worth, Texas—and was forced to make an emergency maneuver to avoid another plane. That caused his plane to stall, and it crashed. Castle died soon after.

ORMER LOCKLEAR

Claim to Fame: First airplane fatalities while filming a movie

Story: Locklear was a World War I pilot, then a barnstormer who flew in daredevil shows across the country. In 1920 he got the starring role as a pilot (and stunt man) in the film *The Sky-wayman*. For the movie's finale, Locklear was supposed to simulate a plane crashing into oil derricks—at night. He'd warned the lighting crew to douse their lights as he got near so he could see to pull out of the dive at the last minute. They didn't, and he crashed, killing himself and his co-pilot. However, thanks to the lights staying on, the director got vivid footage of the crash and its gruesome aftermath...and used it in the movie.

45% of Americans age 60 have at least one parent still living.

CANCELLED! WAIT...

*Life doesn't follow schedules, but TV does. So it's surprising when the
networks revive a show that's been taken off the air—especially
when they do it after broadcasting the "final episode."*

Program: *Sledge Hammer!*
The End: This dark satire-sitcom centered around a loose
cannon police officer named Sledge Hammer (David Rasche).
Sledge loved to use his gun—he slept with it, cooked with it, and
shot criminals far more often than necessary. The show was a critical success for ABC, but not a ratings hit, so it was cancelled at
the end of the 1986–87 season. *Sledge Hammer!* producers decided
to have the show go out with a bang (of course): Sledge attempts
to disable a nuclear bomb set to destroy Los Angeles. He is unsuc-
cessful, and all the characters—and the entire city—are destroyed.
But Wait: The ratings for the last episode were so high that ABC
changed its mind and renewed the show for another year. The
scriptwriters explained the post-apocalypse revival by saying the
new episodes took place "five years earlier" than the first season,
even though the story lines picked up exactly where the plot had
left off before the bomb threat. Unfortunately, ABC gave it a time
slot opposite *The Cosby Show* and reduced its budget, suggesting
that the network never really expected the show to do well. It
didn't. It was cancelled in 1988.

Program: *Family Guy*
The End: It debuted on Fox after the 1999 Super Bowl, so its
initial ratings were high. But critics dismissed the animated show
about an overweight man and his wacky, dysfunctional family as a
ripoff of *The Simpsons*, and the ratings gradually declined. Fox
stuck with the show until 2002, when it was quietly cancelled
before the fall season.
But Wait: In 2003 reruns of the show found an audience on
"Adult Swim"—the late-night block of adult-oriented cartoons on
cable TV's Cartoon Network. Suddenly, *Family Guy* was a big hit.
In the 18–49 demographic (which advertisers and networks most
want to reach), the show routinely beat *The Tonight Show* and *Late*

The production of a single chicken egg requires about 120 gallons of water.

Show with David Letterman, with an average of two million total viewers. On top of that, *Family Guy* DVD sets were the top TV sellers of 2003, moving three million copies. And so, in an unprecedented move, Fox brought the series back. *Family Guy* returned to the air in 2005, where it's been a top-20 hit ever since.

Program: *Buffy the Vampire Slayer*
The End: The critically acclaimed but little-watched show about a teenage girl who fights off pure evil aired on the teen-oriented WB network. After languishing in the ratings for five seasons, the WB cancelled *Buffy* in spring 2001. Writers wrapped up the show's extensive mythology by having Buffy (Sarah Michelle Gellar) die.
But Wait: UPN bought the series and resurrected it in fall 2001. What about the dead main character? No problem! (It's a show about the *un*dead, after all.) Buffy's friends use magic spells to raise her from the dead and pull her out of Heaven, which gives Buffy severe depression for the better part of the season. Despite a loyal cult following, the show's ratings never improved. It was cancelled in 2003.

Program: *Scrubs*
The End: This hospital sitcom ran on NBC from 2001 until 2008, when the network cancelled it due to low ratings (it ranked 115th for the year). ABC picked up the show, but ratings for the eighth season were even worse, so the network ordered the show's producers to prepare a final episode. The big ending aired in May 2009 with the on-again/off-again relationship of Drs. Dorian (Zach Braff) and Reid (Sarah Chalke) happily resolved and with every major guest star and minor character in the show's run making an appearance. Dorian and Reid move away, everyone says goodbye, show over.
But Wait: ABC needed midseason replacement shows for the 2009–10 season, so despite having aired its final show, *Scrubs* was renewed for 13 more episodes. Creator Bill Lawrence completely revamped the show, setting it in a new location (a medical school) and with an almost completely new cast. It didn't help. Only about half of the *Scrubs* viewers from the previous season returned (3.8 million vs. 5.6 million), and ABC aired all 13 episodes in just a few weeks.

All spider species make silk, but only about half spin webs to catch prey.

LOST (AND FOUND) ALBUMS

Not every album that gets recorded—even ones by the most popular musicians—gets released to the public. For a variety of reasons, a project may get shelved indefinitely...or forever. But luckily, sometimes they do get to see the light of day. Here are a few albums that once were lost, but now are found.

ALBUM: *Finian's Rainbow* soundtrack (1954)

LOST: *Finian's Rainbow* was a hit Broadway musical—it ran for nearly two years, winning two Tony Awards, and originating the standards "How Are Things in Glocca Morra?" and "Old Devil Moon." The plot: An Irish immigrant moves to the South and buries a pot of gold near Fort Knox, believing it will magically multiply, all the while trying to avoid the leprechaun from whom he stole the treasure. In 1954 a former Disney animator named John Hubley began production on an animated film version of *Finian's Rainbow* and lined up top talent to provide voices and music, including Frank Sinatra, Ella Fitzgerald, Louis Armstrong, and the Oscar Peterson Trio. Nine songs were recorded before the production's financial backers ran into tax trouble and the film project was canceled.

FOUND: In 2002 Hubley's widow, Faith Hubley, discovered a low-quality acetate copy of the *Finian's Rainbow* songs, recorded off the original master tapes (which have never surfaced). Narration was recorded in 1954, and that was on the master tapes, not on Hubley's copy. But the nine songs were, and they were released on the 2002 box set *Frank Sinatra in Hollywood (1940–1964)*.

ALBUM: Marvin Gaye, *The Ballads* (1979)

LOST: Gaye was one of Motown's top-selling artists, and a dominant soul singer in America by the late 1960s. But what he really wanted to be was a jazz and torch-song singer. Motown let him try three times: *The Soulful Moods* (1961), *When I'm Alone I Cry* (1964), and *Hello Broadway* (1964) were all jazz and show-tune albums, and all sold poorly. Another attempt in 1968 was can-

---

Guitar heroes: 20% of Americans have played in a band at some time in their lives.

celed halfway through recording. Gaye returned to his pop career until 1977, when he decided to take another shot at jazzy torch songs, recording *The Ballads* in his home studio. Included were "The Shadow of Your Smile," "She Needs Me," and "Why Did I Choose You." Gaye convinced Motown to release it in 1979, but changed his mind and released a disco-tinged gospel album instead. *The Ballads* was never released; Gaye died in 1984.

Found: Columbia, Gaye's label at the time of his death, worked with Motown to obtain Gaye's never-released jazz recordings from 1968, along with tracks from the late-'70s sessions. The cobbling of those two sets (seven songs, plus alternate takes of three of those songs) was released in 1997 as *Vulnerable*. The cover featured a simple black-and-white portrait of Gaye, a leftover from the photo shoot for his 1971 classic, *What's Going On*.

Album: The Beatles, *Get Back* (1969)

Lost: In 1969 Paul McCartney decided that after several albums full of multitracked studio wizardry (*Revolver*, *Sgt. Pepper's Lonely Hearts Club Band*, and *The White Album*), the Beatles' next record should be a return to the simple, blues-based, pared-down rock 'n' roll of their early years—songs that could even be performed live, unlike their more recent technically intricate work. So the band convened to make an album McCartney appropriately titled *Get Back*, and invited a camera crew to make a documentary film of the process, also to be titled *Get Back*. The crew caught the Beatles in what would turn out to be the band's final days. McCartney and John Lennon frequently clashed over the direction of the music, and George Harrison walked out of a session one day, vowing never to return (although he did). It was so taxing that the *Get Back* sessions went untouched for a year, until early 1970, when EMI Records forced the band to finish the album. Lennon decided to hire famed producer Phil Spector, whose first order of business was to change the name of the album (and the film) to *Let It Be*. Spector's vision contrasted sharply with McCartney's. He gave the songs an intricate, lush, sweeping orchestral sound, not the simple one McCartney had planned. McCartney hated it, and this dispute directly led to the breakup of the Beatles in April 1970, just one month before *Let It Be* was released. The original *Get Back* tapes were abandoned and locked away in a vault.

At one time, denture makers added uranium to false teeth to give them a "healthy" glow.

Found: In 2001 McCartney met with *Let It Be* film director Michael Lindsay-Hogg to discuss issuing the film on DVD for the first time, and the conversation turned to the creation of a companion album, but the way McCartney had meant to do *Get Back*, stripped of Spector's influence. After getting approval from surviving bandmates Ringo Starr and George Harrison, McCartney hired audio engineers to assemble the album from the original tapes. They were digitally cleaned up and remastered and released in 2003 as the guitar/bass/drums/piano-only *Let It Be...Naked*. The album was a hit, selling a million copies in the United States.

Album: Chicago, *Chicago XXII* (1993)

Lost: Chicago was one of the biggest rock bands of the 1970s with hits like "Colour My World," "Saturday in the Park," and "Does Anybody Really Know What Time It Is?" In the '80s, the band became even more popular when it shifted to a softer, synthesizer-driven sound—songs like "You're the Inspiration" and "Hard to Say I'm Sorry." By 1993 the band's popularity had waned, so they decided to return to their 1970s jazz-rock sound by recording *Chicago XXII*, with plans to release it in March 1994. The band loved it and considered it the best thing they'd done in years. But executives at Warner Bros. Records felt it wasn't commercial enough and pulled the album from its release schedule. At least that's what they told the band. Members of the group believe *Chicago XXII* was shelved in retaliation for the group's refusing to sign off on a deal to license its songs for use in TV commercials. Chicago left Warner in 1994, retaining the rights to *Chicago XXII*... but no other label wanted it.

Found: The album became an underground phenomenon; its mystique was boosted by Chicago doling out the unreleased music in pieces. Three band members each re-recorded songs for solo albums, a handful of finished tracks were included on a Chicago box set, and the band frequently performed the songs live, to positive response from fans. Rhino Records, which specializes in new albums by retro acts, took notice and gave *Chicago XXII*, re-titled *Stone of Sisyphus*, a proper release in 2008. The album didn't trigger the group's revival—it peaked at #122 on the album charts—but fans still called it Chicago's best work in years.

SUFFERING FOOLS

Just how hard is it to be smarter than most everyone else? We don't know, but Uncle John says it's really hard. Here are some more thoughts on the matter.

"For every person with a spark of genius, there are a hundred with ignition trouble."
—**Kurt Hanks**

"A common mistake people make when trying to design something completely fool-proof is to underestimate the ingenuity of complete fools."
—**Douglas Adams**

"Stupidity is a gift of God, but one mustn't misuse it."
—**Pope John Paul II**

"Brains are an asset, if you hide them."
—**Mae West**

"The trouble with the world is that the stupid are cocksure and the intelligent are full of doubt."
—**Bertrand Russell**

"The company of fools may first make us smile, but in the end we always feel melancholy."
—**Oliver Goldsmith**

"Before God we are all equally wise—and equally foolish."
—**Albert Einstein**

"My New Year's Resolution: To tolerate fools more gladly, provided this does not encourage them to take up more of my time."
—**James Agate**

"Talk sense to a fool and he calls you foolish."
—**Euripides**

"It's too bad that stupidity isn't painful."
—**Anton LaVey**

"The only way to comprehend what mathematicians mean by infinity is to contemplate the extent of human stupidity."
—**Voltaire**

"Always be smarter than the people who hire you."
—**Lena Horne**

"Take all the fools out of this world and there wouldn't be any fun living in it. Or profit."
—**Josh Billings**

"Just think of how stupid the average person is, and then realize half of them are even stupider!"
—**George Carlin**

As of 2000, a Canadian law still on the books placed a bounty on all Indian scalps.

BAD NEWS / GOOD NEWS

From bad news you can often get an uplifting piece of good news. As these stories will prove.

HONK IF YOU LIKE FREEDOM
Bad News: Bernard Levine, 82, found an injured goose in his Toms River, New Jersey, backyard in April 2010. It had an arrow stuck in its chest.

Good News: Lucky for the goose, Levine is a retired veterinarian. He captured the stricken bird, took it to the Toms River Animal Hospital, which he founded in 1955, and surgically removed six inches of the 26-inch arrow (as well as several air gun pellets) from its chest. He then brought the goose to the Raptor Trust, a bird rehabilitation center. Three weeks later, Levine was present as vet techs freed the bird—now four pounds heavier and in perfect health—on the trust's protected forest land. "It feels great to see him free and liberated," Levine said, "enjoying life the way a goose should."

LIFE SAVER
Bad News: In April 2010, Robert E. Smith, 48, was working as an attendant at a mental health facility in Lehigh Valley, Pennsylvania, when he was told that a 20-year-old female patient had climbed out a window onto a fire escape and was headed up to the roof of the three-story building. Smith followed her out the window and tried to convince the troubled young woman to come back inside. She refused to listen, and made a lunge to jump. Smith grabbed her arm—and she took him with her. They fell together 30 feet to the ground.

Good News: The young woman survived...and so did Smith. He actually maneuvered his body as they fell so that he would hit first, which not only saved the woman's life, but saved her from receiving any serious injuries at all. "That's just the kind of person he is," Smith's uncle, Thomas Katchisin, told the *Philadelphia Inquirer*. Smith shattered bones in both his arms, suffered a wound to his head, broke several ribs, and, after several hours of surgery, was in the hospital for nine days. But he made a full

---

Among the passengers aboard the *Mayflower*: a Mastiff and a Springer Spaniel.

recovery. "I have no regrets," he said later. "She walked away, and that's good."

DOUBLE JEOPARDY

Bad News: In April 2010, Andriej Ivanov, 26, made his way to a bridge over the Belaya River in Ufa, central Russia. He wasn't there for the view: His fiancée had recently been killed in a car crash—on the day before their wedding—and he was going to jump off the bridge and kill himself. Worse news: When he got to the bridge, he found that someone had beaten him to the spot. Maria Petrova, 21, had recently been thrown out of her parents' home after she became pregnant and was there to kill *herself*. Ivanov arrived just as she was climbing over the railing to make the 100-foot plunge into the water.

Good News: Andriej ran to Maria and yelled for her to stop. "Something in my heart snapped," he said, "and I couldn't let her do it no matter how broken my own heart was." He was able to convince her to climb back down, the two ended up talking long into the night, and then the next day, and the day after that—and in May 2010 announced to their families that they were getting married. "All that pain was worthwhile," Maria said, "because it led me to my Andriej."

＊　　＊　　＊

KARMA

In 2006 *Monty Python* and *A Fish Called Wanda* star John Cleese performed his one-man stage show in the city of Palmerston North, New Zealand. He didn't have a good time. He later reported in an audio diary on his website that the audience was unresponsive, the arena in which he performed was subpar, and that Palmerston North itself was so wretched it must be "the suicide capital of the country." The unresponsive locals did respond to Cleese: They unofficially renamed their municipal garbage dump after him when someone put up a sign reading "Mt. Cleese" at the landfill. Said Palmerston North Water and Waste Manager Chris Pepper, "It's popped up overnight, and nobody has said to pull it down."

DINO CHOW

So what did dinosaurs eat 200 million years ago?
Don't look now—it may be in your garden.

C LASSIC JURASSIC
You'll find them in flower arrangements, funeral wreaths, back yards in Arizona and Southern California, and botanical gardens around the United States. They look like a cross between a palm and a fern, with a stout trunk and a crown of feather-like leaves across the top. But these ancient plants—called *cycads*, (pronounced "SY-kads")—are closer to gingko trees and conifers. They've been growing on this planet for more than 300 million years, making them among the oldest species of any kind still living in the world.

During the Jurassic Period (200 million years ago), cycads dominated global forests. The Earth was much wetter back then, prime growing conditions for these plants. Based on fossil evidence, scientists believe cycads comprised 20 percent of all plant life at the time, so the jungles that Tyrannosaurus rex crashed around in and the brontosaurus munched on was most likely a cycad forest (which is why botanists prefer to call the Jurassic era the "Age of Cycads," not the "Age of Dinosaurs").

Cycads grow best in tropical and sub-tropical areas, but fossilized remains of the plants have been found on every continent and from Siberia to the South Pole. Scientists consider these finds proof that the Arctic and Antarctic were once much warmer.

LIVING FOSSILS

The key to the cycads' longevity is their ability to produce their own fertilizer—in essence, they feed themselves. Their roots often grow out of the ground, providing a home for photosynthetic bacteria. In exchange, the bacteria provide nitrogen to the cycad. This nitrogen-fixing ability allows cycads to flourish in extremely poor soil: Some species can grow in sand, and many can tolerate salty soil. Sadly, many cycad species are endangered today, as their favored tropical habitat is rapidly being destroyed by human activity. Once widespread across the globe, cycads today are limited to

---

Most charitable city, based on actual donations: Miami. Least: Detroit.

ranges in Australia, Japan, sub-Saharan Africa, Madagascar, South Asia, Indonesia, Central and South America, Mexico, and Florida. Also, cycads reproduce slowly, which doesn't help them survive abrupt changes to their environment. But cycads have already successfully weathered two mass extinction periods in world history, so don't count them out.

PSYCHED FOR CYCADS

• Cycads contain BMAA, a paralyzing neurotoxin. But native peoples in Australia, Africa, and North America found ways to leach out the poison and turn the starchy stems into edible flour.

• The Seminole Indians of Florida called cycads the "white bread plant." Their entire diet was based around *sofkee*, a pudding made from its starch. When Confederate soldiers garrisoned in Florida during the Civil War ran out of provisions, they tried to create their own version of sofkee. Unfortunately they skipped the soaking process that removed the plant's poison and hundreds died.

• White settlers in Florida eventually learned the Seminole process and created the first industry in the area by making a cooking powder they called arrowroot starch, or *coontie*, which was what the Florida cycad was called. During World War I, army doctors discovered that coontie mixed with beef broth was the only food that soldiers who'd been gassed could stomach. The coontie industry lasted until the 1930s, when the market collapsed due to the over-harvesting of native cycads.

• The Japanese word for cycad is *sotetsu*. Cycad nuts were eaten as a food of last resort during famines, and a particularly bad famine in the 1920s is still referred to as *sotetsu jinkoku*, or "cycad hell."

• The Japanese sago "palm" is perhaps the best-known cycad in the world (though misnamed—it isn't a palm).

• A great petrified forest of cycads lies just outside Minnekahta, in the Black Hills of South Dakota. It was once a national monument until fossil hunters stripped away all of the visible specimens and sold them to museums and collectors.

• The largest cycad alive today is the Hope's Cycad, located in Daintree, Australia. It's 1,000 years old and 65 feet high.

• Cycad seeds look like pine cones, and can weigh as much as 90 pounds.

OLYMPIC PRANKSTERS

When American snowboarder Scotty Lago was forced out of the 2010
Winter Games in Vancouver after he posed for a suggestive photo
with his bronze medal, that got us wondering: What other
silly stunts have been pulled at the Olympics?

Athletes: Dean Kent, Corney Swanepoel, and Cameron Gibson, three swimmers representing New Zealand at the 2008 Summer Games in Beijing, China

Prank: Taking photos of a young teammate—in a compromising position, in a compromising condition, in a compromising place

Details: The day after the closing ceremonies, one of the younger members of the team, 18-year-old Daniel Bell, got drunk in a Beijing nightclub where the Speedo swimsuit company was hosting an open-bar party. Kent, Swanepoel, and Gibson found Bell passed out in the restroom (on the pot), and took immediate action. After calling for medical assistance, they cleaned Bell up and dragged him home…but not before taking a picture of him semi-nude (and still passed out) in the toilet stall. Somebody posted copies of the picture around the New Zealand swimmers' quarters in the Olympic Village, and from there they spread to the rest of the team. That's how the New Zealand Olympic Committee learned of the prank.

What Happened: Kent, Swanepoel, and Gibson were thrown off the Olympic team and exiled from the Olympic Village. They had to spend their last night in China in a Beijing hotel. (Bell received no punishment.)

Athletes: Troy Dalbey and Doug Gjertsen, American swimmers who won gold medals in two relay events in the 1988 Summer Games in Seoul, South Korea

Prank: Grand Theft Lion

Details: The day after winning their medals, Dalbey and Gjertsen celebrated their victory by bar-hopping with friends. As they were leaving the bar in the Hyatt Regency Hotel, Dalbey grabbed a decorative lion's head off the wall and walked out with it. When the police caught up with them in another bar, they still had the lion and were arrested for theft (valued at $830).

What Happened: South Korean prosecutors agreed to drop the charges after Dalbey and Gjertsen admitted guilt and wrote a letter apologizing to the South Korean people. The U.S. Olympic Committee was less forgiving: Dalbey and Gjertsen were dropped from the team and confined to their Olympic Village quarters until they could leave the country. Dalbey was later suspended from competition for 18 months; Gjertsen, who was cleared of the theft charges, received a three-month suspension. (They both got to keep their gold medals.)

Athlete: Dawn Fraser, one of the greatest Australian swimmers of all time and winner of gold medals in the 1956, 1960, and 1964 Summer Games

Prank: Playing capture the flag...with the emperor's flag

Details: During the 1964 Tokyo Games, Fraser and two friends were walking by the Imperial Palace when they saw an Olympic flag on a flagpole and decided to steal it. Police caught them red-handed.

What Happened: Apparently pranks are more acceptable in Japan than they are in South Korea, because as soon as the police realized who Fraser was, they released the three without charge, *after* Fraser signed autographs for the arresting officers. Emperor Hirohito even insisted that Fraser keep the flag. But the story doesn't end there. Fraser had been making waves with the Australian Olympic Committee throughout the Games, marching in the opening ceremonies after she'd been told not to, wearing her own swimsuit instead of the one provided by the team's sponsor (hers was more comfortable), and at the closing ceremonies, wearing a friend's hat instead of the one that came with her team uniform. Small infractions all, but when Fraser got home, the Australian Swimming Union banned her from competition for 10 years, effectively ending her swimming career and shutting her out of the 1968 Summer Olympics. That, in turn, denied her a shot at becoming the first female swimmer to win gold medals in four different Olympics.

Athlete: Jim Chapin, a speed skater competing in the 1980 Winter Games in Lake Placid, New York

Prank: Boorish behavior—with an actual *boar*

Details: When Chapin learned that the Olympic Village cooks were preparing a special exotic-food dinner for the athletes, he and some friends "borrowed" the carcasses of a wild boar, a shark, and a barracuda from the kitchen. They snuck the 250-pound boar into the quarters of speed skater Beth Heiden and tucked it under the covers of her bed, lying flat on its back with its legs and snout pointing up toward the ceiling. "The boar still had the hair and everything," Chapin told the *Washington Post*. "Sure would have liked to see Heiden's face. We considered leaving the shark in the bathtub, but we thought it was too risky." (No word on what happened to the barracuda.)

What Happened: They got away with it.

Athlete: Hal Prieste, an American diver who won a bronze medal at the 1920 summer games in Antwerp, Belgium

Prank: Stealing another flag—a *very* important flag

Details: Acting on a dare from teammate Duke Kahanamoku, Prieste, 24, climbed a 15-foot flag pole at the Olympic stadium and stole the Olympic flag. Not just any Olympic flag, either: The flag he stole was the *very first* one to feature the Olympic symbol of five interlocking rings, which had been created in 1913.

What Happened: Prieste was never caught, and the fate of that famous first flag remained a mystery for decades. Then one day in 2000, Prieste, then 103, decided to return the flag he'd kept in the bottom of a suitcase for 77 years. The flag was handed over in a special ceremony during the Summer Olympics in Sydney, Australia. "Will there be a plaque with my name on it?" Prieste jokingly asked officials. Sure enough, if you ever get a chance to visit the Olympic Museum in Lausanne, Switzerland, right next to the flag display you'll see a plaque thanking Prieste for giving it back.

*   *   *

NO TAN IN MONTANA

On December 14, 1924, the temperature in Fairfield, Montana, dropped 84°F—from 63° at noon to –21° at midnight, the greatest 12-hour temperature change ever recorded in the United States.

FLUBBED HEADLINES

Whether silly, naughty, obvious, or just plain bizarre, they're all real.

UAW Elects King
as Next President

Big Ben Celebrates
150 Years of Bongs

HOMELESS MAN
UNDER HOUSE ARREST

Colleen Campbell
champions the rights
of murder victims
after being one herself

*Tight end retires
after colon surgery*

**Seven testify
toddler looked hot**

*Editor's wife
rented to 2 suspects,
FBI says*

Woman in sumo wrestler
suit assaulted her
ex-girlfriend in gay pub
after she waved at man
dressed as a Snickers bar

**Want to spell
like a champ? Read
Wenster's Dictionary**

DIANA WAS STILL ALIVE
HOURS BEFORE SHE DIED

Arson Suspect
is Held in Fire

**Ten Commandments:
Supreme Court says some
okay, some not**

*Minus shorts, banks
get breathing room*

*Black History Month
Will Be Held Feb. 23*

Teen Learns to Live
With Stutttering

*A's Hole Keeps
Getting Deeper*

Steele Pure Gold

**Death Is Nation's
Top Killer**

SOME 70,000 TURTLE EGGS
TO BE WHISKED FAR FROM OIL

POLL SAYS THAT 53%
BELIEVE MEDIA OFFEN
MAKES MISTAKES

World's largest tire manufacturer: Lego. They make 300 million toy tires every year.

HOW NOT TO ROB A BANK

These days, it's harder than ever to hold up a bank and actually get away with it, but some people do. Not these robbers, though: Each one made a key mistake. Let's see what they did wrong.

THE JOB: A 16-year-old boy handed a note to a teller at People's United Bank in Fairfield, Connecticut, in March 2010. The demand: "Put $100,000 into a bag." As the teller started filling a bag, the boy noticed the bank was being put on lockdown, so he ran out with only $900. He made it to the parking lot and started running toward his getaway car. Inside it was his accomplice, 27-year-old Albert Bailey. A swarm of cops were already there and easily apprehended the pair.

THE MISTAKE: About 15 minutes earlier, Bailey actually phoned the bank and said, "Get the money ready—we're coming!"

THE JOB: In April 2005, a group of armed men stormed into a Chicago bank and tied up several bank employees. The gang escaped with $81,000. The police had no leads and no suspects.

THE MISTAKE: Five months later, one of the robbers called a "Morning Zoo" Chicago radio show and bragged about the job. Calling himself "D," he gave details that only the robbers would know. An FBI agent on her way to work was listening to the show, so she went to the radio station and traced the call to a cell phone owned by Randy Washington, 24. He and an accomplice, William Slate, 19, were both arrested.

THE JOB: In March 2010, Robert Yoder, 55, of Fallbrook, Washington, walked into a bank and demanded the teller fill up a pouch full of money. The teller complied. Yoder walked out of the bank, got into his truck, and drove away.

THE MISTAKE: Yoder was a tow-truck driver, and the name of his company was printed on the truck, which could clearly be seen by a surveillance camera. Yoder got a call that afternoon about a broken-down vehicle, but when he showed up, there was no broken-down vehicle, only the police. He was arrested.

THE JOB: A man walked into a Chase Bank in Chicago wearing

Mongolian warrior helmets doubled as cooking pots—and inspired the Chinese wok.

a clown mask with a big red nose and red hair. He was carrying a toy machine gun. He handed a demand note to a teller, who filled up a bag with money. The clown ran out of the bank.

THE MISTAKE: His getaway vehicle was a bicycle. It took him a minute or so to get going (the mask, toy gun, and bag of money made it difficult). That was all the time that a police officer needed to chase down the clown and tackle him.

THE JOB: Jarell Paul Arnold, 34, walked into a credit union in Anchorage, Alaska, in 2009, asked the teller to check his account balance, and then handed her a holdup note. She filled a bag with about $600, and Arnold fled the scene. Police arrived at the bank a few minutes later, but the suspect was nowhere to be found.

THE MISTAKE: *He asked the teller to check his account balance—* and showed her his driver's license to verify his ID. The teller gave the information to the cops; Arnold is now serving 12 years in prison for bank robbery, with no time off for stupid behavior.

THE JOB: In 2009 a would-be bank robber in Kirchheim, Austria, approached the door of the bank, donned a Barack Obama mask, took out a gun, and went to open the door.

THE MISTAKE: The bank was closed. It had been for 35 minutes. Inside were several bank employees taking part in a training session. The frustrated bank robber banged his gun on the window. According to one of the workers, "We thought it was part of the training, some sort of initiative test, or a joke. Laughing only seemed to make him more angry." The robber gave up and left.

THE JOB: A man stuffed a knife into his front pants pocket and walked into a bank in Kumagaya, Japan, in 2010.

THE MISTAKE: He didn't really know *how* to rob a bank, so he asked a teller, "Any idea how you rob a bank?" The teller asked her supervisor what to do if someone asks how to rob a bank. The supervisor politely asked the man to leave. He did, but the worker who was escorting him out noticed blood running down the man's thigh. Somehow, he'd stabbed himself with his knife. He was taken to a hospital, treated, and arrested—but for illegal possession of a weapon, not for attempted robbery. (He didn't actually rob the bank; he only asked *how* to do it.)

Length of the average professional fireworks show in 1980: 1 hour. Today: 20 minutes.

DOT BOMBS

Today we take buying things over the Internet for granted. But the concept of e-commerce was brand new in the 1990s, as billions of dollars were invested in new Internet companies. And nearly all of them fizzled—some because they were ahead of their time, others simply because they were bad ideas. Here's a look at some of the biggest Internet busts.

COMPANY: Flooz.com
PRODUCT: Internet currency
LOADING… Most Americans do at least some online shopping or bill paying today, but in 1998 people were scared and skeptical about giving a credit card number over the Internet. So Flooz.com conceived a "safe" Internet currency. Consumers were supposed to go to Flooz.com, enter in their credit card number, and buy Internet money, or "Flooz," which could then be used to pay for purchases at online merchants. Based on that concept, Flooz secured $34 million from investors and agreements with Tower Records, Barnes & Noble, Restoration Hardware, and other retailers to accept Flooz as legal tender on their websites.
…FILE NOT FOUND: A large percentage of Flooz's budget went to TV commercials starring celebrity spokesperson Whoopi Goldberg. But the idea never quite caught on—as people became more comfortable with buying things over the Internet and as major retailers started securing credit card data with a new, nearly impenetrable data-disguising system called *encryption*, few thought it was necessary to buy special online money. Flooz flopped on August 26, 2001, after which all outstanding "flooz"—and $34 million in investors' money—turned to dust.

COMPANY: Webvan.com
PRODUCT: Groceries
LOADING… The service offered by this Internet-based company was both old and new: Home delivery of groceries, which was once common but hadn't been offered since the mid-20th century, when Americans started switching from local grocers to chain supermarkets. In Webvan's business model, groceries would be ordered off the Internet and arrive at the customer's home via a nearly fully auto-

---

It takes 50 pounds of olives to produce one gallon of olive oil.

mated process (the vans still required people to drive them). It seemed like a great idea to a lot of people: Webvan raised and spent more than $1 billion, using the funds to expand outside of its San Francisco home area to eight more cities in just over a year. Most of the money went for computerized warehouse facilities where orders were automatically boxed, sorted, and loaded onto delivery trucks. By mid-2000, Webvan.com was valued at $1.2 billion and announced plans to expand into 18 more metropolitan areas.

...FILE NOT FOUND: E-commerce may have changed many elements of business, but it did not change the fact that a company needs a certain number of customers to turn a profit. Webvan looked good to investors, but it expanded too fast. Furthermore, grocery profit margins are very slim—not enough to cover $1 billion worth of state-of-the-art distribution centers. Webvan spoiled in July 2001, its share price having dropped from $30 to 6¢ in a matter of months. The brand name—not the company—resurfaced in 2009 as "a member of the Amazon family."

COMPANY: MVP.com
PRODUCT: Sporting goods
LOADING... This company had a lot going for it at its 1999 launch: Its investors included beloved sports icons (and seasoned product endorsers) such as quarterback John Elway, basketball superstar Michael Jordan, and hockey icon Wayne Gretzky. That seemed like a big advantage for a company selling sporting goods online. Another advantage: MVP.com had a lucrative advertising deal—a four-year contract with CBS Television in which the online merchant got consistent ad time during the broadcast of CBS's highly watched NFL games. In return, CBS got an equity stake in the company, with a guaranteed annual payout of $10 million.

...FILE NOT FOUND: But just a year later, MVP.com failed to pay CBS its $10 million...because it didn't have the $10 million to pay. In fact, the company never turned a profit. (Marketing experts say the advertising deal was ill-conceived—sports spectators are not necessarily sports *participants*.) When they didn't receive their cut, CBS voided the contract...and canceled all of MVP.com's future advertising. MVP.com was KO'd at the end of 2000. Its address (www.mvp.com) was taken over by SportsLine, a new sports news service managed by...CBS.

Made guys: 27 actors from the movie *Goodfellas* also appeared on *The Sopranos*.

WHEN WORDS COLLIDE

Wii hate when someone points out that weave used the wrong word to describe something, sew we complied this list of commonly misspelled or misused wurds.

- A **capital** is a nation or state's principal city, which houses the **capitol**, the building in which lawmakers convene.

- To **flounder** is to struggle. But if you do it for long, you may **founder**, or completely unravel and come apart.

- A **hoard** is a large group of objects. A **horde** is a large group of people.

- Light can pass through a **translucent** object and become obscured. If the light goes all the way through, then the surface is **transparent**.

- **Flotsam** is cargo lost at sea, floating on the surface. **Jetsam** is jettisoned cargo that sinks to the bottom of the sea.

- To feel hostility toward something is to be **adverse.** To be completely opposed to it outright is to be **averse.**

- **Emigrants** leave their homeland to reside in another place. Once they're in the new place, they're called **immigrants**.

- An **amiable** person is cheerful and good-natured. An **amicable** person is cooperative.

- A **distinct** object is one that is clearly visible; a **distinctive** one is unique or unusual.

- A saying by a famous person is a **quotation,** not a quote. **Quote** is a verb that means to repeat somebody else's words.

- A **crevasse** is a deep, wide crack. A **crevice** is a small, narrow crack.

- **Elicit** means to draw out something through persuasion, such as secret information. That info might have been a secret because it contained evidence of illegal or **illicit** activities.

- An **eminent** person is someone who is well known and highly regarded. The word **imminent** describes an event that is about to take place.

- Your **conscience** is your moral center, your sense of right vs. wrong. **Conscious** is an adjective that means to be awake and aware.

LUCKY FINDS

*Ever stumbled across something valuable? It's an incredible feeling.
Here's the latest installment of a* Bathroom Reader *favorite.*

LET ME STAND NEXT TO YOUR FIRE
The Find: A burned guitar
Where It Was Found: Under a pile of junk in a garage
The Story: In 1967, while performing at the Finsbury Astoria, an old theater in North London, Jimi Hendrix doused his Fender Stratocaster with lighter fluid, lit a match, and set the guitar on fire. The roadies rushed in and put the fire out; Hendrix had to be taken to the hospital to be treated for minor burns. That performance was a defining moment in rock history, but the guitar itself was thought to have been lost. It changed several hands several times: Bassist Noel Redding had it at first, but it ended up with Hendrix's press officer, Tony Garland, who stored it in his parents' garage in East Sussex…and forgot about it. It remained there, untouched, for nearly 40 years, until Garland's nephew unearthed it in 2007. The guitar—one of two that Hendrix burned, and the only one that survived—was sold to an American collector for $430,000. He said he was going to put some new strings on it, plug it in, and see if any of that "Hendrix magic" is still there.

WHAT THE FUGUE?
The Find: A musical symphony
Where It Was Found: In a library basement
The Story: Heather Carbo, a librarian at the Palmer Theological Seminary in Philadelphia, had heard a rumor that a symphony written in Beethoven's own hand was stored somewhere in the seminary. But no one had ever seen it, and it was probably just that, a rumor. Then, one summer day in 2005, Carbo was cleaning out some cabinets in the library's basement and found a colorful, hardbound book. The moment she saw it, she suspected it was the Beethoven symphony, but she can't read music (or German), so she called in musical experts, who verified that it was indeed Beethoven's "Gross Fugue in B flat major." Released in 1826, less than a year before Beethoven's death, the fugue—with its frequent

use of dissonance—was panned by the critics. (It's since been called "ahead of its time.") The 80-page manuscript revealed the work of a composer who was constantly erasing and revising, and who wrote notes in the margins on everything from proper piano fingering techniques to his own dissatisfaction with the work. "This piece, more than any other, shows Beethoven striving for something beyond all human limits," said American composer Gerald Levinson. How did it get to an American seminary? In 1890 it was purchased in Germany by Cincinnati industrialist William Howard Doane. The manuscript was thought to have been a part of a collection donated to the seminary by Sloane's daughter in 1950, but everything else from that collection (including an original Mozart manuscript) had been accounted for. For decades, historians assumed that Beethoven's Gross Fugue was lost forever. In December 2005 it was sold at auction to an anonymous buyer. Sale price: $1.7 million.

GETTING A LITTLE ACTION

The Find: A comic book

Where It Was Found: In a box in the basement

The Story: A down-on-their-luck family (who wish to remain anonymous) was about to lose their home. It had been in the family since the 1950s, but by 2010 they were nearly bankrupt and facing foreclosure. With no way to meet their mortgage payments, they decided it was time to pack up and move out. When Dad and the kids were sorting though boxes of Grandpa's stuff in the basement (which hadn't been touched for decades), they found some old comic books. One of them, called *Action Comics #1*, featured Superman on the cover, holding a car over his head. It was dated June, 1938. Could this be the very first Superman comic? The father contacted Vincent Zurzolo, the owner of Metropolis Collectibles in New York. "99.9 percent of the claims I hear that someone has found *Action Comics #1* turn out be false," he later said. But this time it was the real deal—*the* most sought-after comic book in existence. Originally sold for 10 cents, less than 100 copies are known to exist. It's expected to fetch anywhere from $250,000 to $1 million for the family—more than enough to save their house. "You couldn't have asked for a happier ending," said Zurzolo. "Superman saved the day."

PINK PING PONG

Heirloom tomatoes are rare or obscure varieties of tomatoes that result from random, natural cross-pollination. There are hundreds of them, and they're often uniquely colored, shaped…and named. These are real names of real varieties.

Banana Legs	German Johnson
Ding Wall Scotty	Black From Tula
Extreme Bush	Moneymaker
Heidi	Blaby Special
Burgess Mammoth Wonder	Golden Egg
Turkey Chomp	Spoon
Arkansas Traveler	Green Zebra
Smeig Craig	Big Rainbow
Black Sea Man	Plum Tigris
Glamour	Sugar Lump
Polish Dwarf	Amish Paste
Red Stuffer	Zogola
Bloody Butcher	Beauty Queen
Mortgage Lifter	Pink Ping Pong
Snow White	Orange Fleshed Purple Smudge
Tartar of Mongolistan	Cherry-Go-Round
Delicious	Kellogg's Breakfast
Eva's Purple Ball	Stump of the World
Tommy Toe	Hank
Mr. Stripey	

Mamma mia! Average ticket price for a Broadway show in 2010: $76.

THE LAST...

It's nice to be the first, but being last can be memorable too.

...surviving American World War I veteran: Frank Buckles joined the Army at age 16 and served as an ambulance driver on the Western Front. He turned 109 in February 2010.

...major film released on VHS: The 2005 Oscar-nominated thriller *A History of Violence.*

...30-game-winning pitcher in Major League Baseball: Denny McLain of the Detroit Tigers, in 1968, amassed a 31–6 record.

...ABA player in the NBA: The NBA absorbed the failing American Basketball Association—and its top players—in 1976. The last one still playing in the NBA was Hall of Famer Moses Malone, who retired from the San Antonio Spurs in 1995.

...Soviet head of state: Mikhail Gorbachev was the General Secretary of the Communist Party when the U.S.S.R. dissolved in 1991, making him the last leader of the Soviet Union.

...U.S. president who was neither Democrat nor Republican: In 1850 Vice President Millard Fillmore—a Whig—assumed office upon the death of President Zachary Taylor and served until 1853.

...guest host of *The Muppet Show*: Roger Moore, then-portrayer of James Bond, hosted the last episode of the original show in 1981.

...person publicly executed in the guillotine: Eugene Weidmann, convicted of six murders, was beheaded on June 17, 1939, outside a prison in Versailles, France.

...black-and-white series on American television: *Mister Rogers' Neighborhood.* It didn't switch over to color until 1969.

...immigrant to enter the U.S. via New York's Ellis Island: A Norwegian man named Arne Peterssen was the last person to be processed at the facility, in 1954.

...time Coca-Cola was made with cane sugar: 1980. That year, American bottlers switched to the cheaper sweetener high-fructose corn syrup. (But Mexican and kosher bottlers still use sugar.)

Buckwheat is not related to wheat.

BIRD BRAINS, PART I

It's long been assumed that the world's most intelligent animals (after humans) are the "higher" mammals—great apes, dolphins, whales, and elephants, each of which uses tools and complex forms of communication. Over the past few decades, however, biologists have discovered that one non-mammal group also belongs to that exclusive club: birds.

WINGS
Earth's 9,000 avian species include expert toolmakers, communicators, navigators, architects, and problem solvers. Numbering at least 100 billion, birds range in size from the tiny hummingbird—which is lighter than a penny—to the ostrich, which stands nine feet tall and can weigh 300 pounds. Birds inhabit every continent; some can fly five miles high (Rüppell's vultures) and others can dive 1,000 feet below the surface of the ocean (Emperor penguins).

Birds' levels of intelligence vary greatly as well. And even the so-called "dumb" ones are smarter than previously thought. Many farmers dismiss domestic turkeys as being quite stupid, but after studying poultry for 30 years, Oregon State University biologist Tom Savage says that turkeys are misunderstood: "They have a keen awareness of their surroundings. The dumb tag simply doesn't fit." As scientists are only recently finding out, this can be said of many bird species. In fact, a more fitting insult than "bird brain" is "lizard brain": Birds' brains are very large in proportion to their bodies—6 to 11 times larger than those of similar-size reptiles.

So which bird is the most intelligent of them all? The answer (coming later) may surprise you.

GIMME SHELTER

One way that scientists define intelligence: the ability to physically alter an object to suit a specific need, such as toolmaking or elaborate nest construction. Starting with nests, here are two of the most impressive avian abodes.

• **Tailorbird:** Native to tropical Asia, this warbler is known as "nature's seamstress." After finding two suitably large leaves in the top of a tree, the female pierces holes into the opposite edges of each one with her sharp beak (the holes are so tiny that the leaf doesn't brown). Then the male brings her either spider silk, cocoon silk, or plant fibers. Using her beak as a needle, the tailor-bird threads the holes with the silk and literally sews the tops of the leaves together into a roof that that they put over the nest for camouflage and protection.

• **Bowerbird:** The male of this Australian species spends up to nine months building an attractive home (or *bower*) to serve as a "love nest." First, he gathers hundreds of stems and meticulously weaves them together into a hut on the ground with a wide opening; he uses a few larger sticks as pillars to hold up the massive roof, which can measure six feet across. Then he searches the forest for adornments to place inside and on top of his bower: colorful feathers from other birds, flower petals, autumn leaves, acorns, fruit, pebbles, shells, even human garbage. Outside, the bowerbird creates a "front lawn" using tufts of green moss and may even line the border with purple beetle wings. The final step: He performs an elaborate song-and-dance routine. When a female arrives at his colorful bower, he presents her with a flower.

HATCHING A THEORY

The big question among ornithologists (people who study birds): Do these unusual nesting skills come from mere instinct—as is the case with the nests of reptiles, fish, and insects—or is there something more intelligent at work? To find out, in 2008 a team of Scottish researchers studied African weaver birds. Because the males construct several nests each year, the team was able to study many constructions by a single weaver in a short period of time. If he was driven by instinct, then all of his nests would look roughly the same. But the weaver's nests varied significantly, suggesting that experience plays some part in nest construction.

That's significant because only the most intelligent animals can plan, improvise, and learn from their mistakes. Exactly which factor rules birds most—instinct or experience—is still being determined. However, it's becoming evident that (at least from an intelligence point of view) some bird species are more like us than even most of our fellow mammals are.

For one, we're both social animals. Biologists theorize that over time, the birds' need to maintain a high place in their group's

---

Animal with the highest ratio of brain-to-body mass: the shrew (10%).

"pecking order" has made their brains grow larger in proportion to their bodies. That's how it worked with modern humans; it helped us become expert problem solvers. According to the results of one study, some birds are better at solving problems than we are.

PIGEON-HOLED

The "Monty Hall Dilemma" (named after the *Let's Make a Deal* host) is a logic test. You are given three doors to choose from and behind one of them is a prize. Let's say you choose Door No. 1, but the tester opens Door No. 2 and says, "It's not in here. Do you want to switch to Door No. 3?" Though it sounds counterintuitive to most people, switching doors actually *doubles* the probability of finding the prize. (For a more detailed explanation, see page 480.)

In 2009 researchers decided to try this dilemma on pigeons—and then try it *again* on humans. Their finding: "The birds adjusted their probability of switching and staying to approximate the optimal strategy. Replication of the procedure with human participants showed that humans failed to adopt optimal strategies, even with extensive training." To translate (because it seems like we might need to), pigeons can be more logical than people.

WHAT A TOOL

According to legend, the ancient Greek playwright Aeschylus was told by a soothsayer that he would die when a house landed on him. Frightened, Aeschylus hid in the desert—far from any houses. Then an eagle flew over him, mistook Aeschylus's bald head for a rock, and dropped a tortoise on it, killing Aeschylus. The question among ornithologists: Was the eagle using the playwright's head as a tool with which to break open the tortoise's "house" to get to the meat inside? Probably not, because the eagle didn't manipulate Aeschylus's head in any way. Vultures, however, are different: When a vulture finds an ostrich egg, it searches for a suitable rock, then picks up the rock in its talons, flies over, and drops the rock on the egg. Because the vulture manipulated the rock, it *was* using it as a tool. And one bird—the world's smartest—takes this cracking process to a whole new level.

What is it? Turn to page 256 to find out.

Turn to page 256 to find out.

Cars traveling at 65 mph need 160 feet to come to a stop. Semi-trucks need 420 feet.

CH-CH-CH-CHIA!

*Even if you've never actually owned one, you probably know what
a Chia Pet is, thanks to the TV commercials that blanket the
airwaves each holiday season. Here's the origin of one of
America's most popular pieces of pop-culture kitsch.*

THE SEED OF AN IDEA

In 1977 a San Francisco advertising executive named
Joseph Pedott made a trip to Chicago's annual housewares
show to drum up clients for his agency. As he toured the convention, Pedott quizzed exhibitors and attendees on what products
were popular that year. One executive, a buyer for a chain of drug
stores, told him about some little animal-shaped terra-cotta
planters imported from Mexico that sold pretty well as gift items.
The planters had grooves etched into their sides and came with a
pack of *chia* seeds. When the seeds were soaked in water and
planted in the grooves, the animals grew chia "fur."

The little planters had been a part of Mayan culture for at least
200 years, but they'd been imported into the United States for
only two. A Chicago importer named Walter Houston discovered
them on a trip to Mexico in 1975 and had been selling them in
Florida and the midwestern United States under the brand name
"Chiapet." But they weren't a very profitable item, and he doubted
they ever would be.

Pedott disagreed: He thought that with the right marketing
push, Chiapets could sell very well indeed, at least for a season or
two before the novelty ran its course. Rather than recruit Houston
as a client for his ad agency, Pedott bought the rights to the Chia-
pet product line outright so that he could sell the little planters
himself. In 1982 he rolled the product out nationwide under the
slightly changed name "Chia Pet." And what kind of pet? In 1982
there was only one kind: a ram.

AS SEEN ON TV

The biggest change that Pedott made to the Chia Pet line wasn't
the way he spelled the name, it was the way he sold the product.
Walter Houston hadn't spent a lot of money on advertising—he

Actor Dan Aykroyd has webbed toes.

just pitched his product to stores, and if they liked it, they took a few and put them on their shelves. Marketed that way, the Chia-pet line didn't offer much promise to Houston *or* the retailers. Customers didn't know what Chiapets were, or even that they existed at all, so no one was exactly breaking down the door to buy them. Chiapets might sit on store shelves for weeks or months on end, taking up valuable retail space that could have been used to sell items that were in greater demand.

This was where Pedott's advertising background proved so valu-able: In just 30 seconds, the catchy TV commercials he created introduced the Chia Pets to viewers and explained what they were and how they worked. And thanks to the famous "Ch-ch-ch-Chia!" jingle, invented during a brainstorming session when someone playfully stuttered the product's name, the TV ads indeli-bly (and annoyingly) imprinted the Chia Pet name in the public mind.

Once those ads hit the airwaves, customers could walk into stores and ask for Chia Pets by name. And they did, by the tens and then by the hundreds of thousands. Whatever resistance retailers had to stocking the little rams—soon to be accompa-nied by bulls, bunnies, puppies, kittens, frogs, and countless other critters—melted away when the Chia Pets started flying off store shelves.

PERMA CHIA

About the only miscalculation Pedott made in his marketing strat-egy was that he assumed sales would drop off after a few years. They never did—nearly 30 years after the re-branded, re-marketed Chia Pets hit store shelves in 1982, his company, Joseph Enter-prises, still sells about half a million of them a year, including licensed cartoon characters (beginning in 2000) and selected American presidents, including two different versions of President Barack Obama ("Determined," with a serious look on his face, and "Happy," with a smiling "Commander in Chia" look). The Obama Chia Pets are the first to depict a living person, and they're also the most controversial Chia Pets ever: In 2009 both the Wal-greens and CVS chains pulled them from store shelves after cus-tomers complained. (No word on whether the complaints were from Democrats or Republicans.)

Bestselling fiction author of all time: William Shakespeare. #2: Agatha Christie. (Dr. Seuss is #9.)

H–H–H–HEALTHY

If you were ever tempted to taste a chia seed or sprout but didn't for fear of being p–p–p–poisoned, you needn't have worried: The seeds and sprouts are actually good for you. They were an important food crop to the Aztecs and are still grown for food in Central and South America, and now even in Australia.

• The chia seeds are from the *Salvia hispanica* plant, a member of the mint family. They're rich in omega-3 fatty acids and are also high in protein, fiber, and antioxidants.

• The seeds can be eaten raw or added to corn or wheat flour to make baked goods. The sprouts can be added to sandwiches or sprinkled on salads, just like alfalfa sprouts. In Mexico they're mixed into water or juice to make a health drink called *chia fresca*. Chia Goodness is a brand of chia/hemp-seed breakfast cereals sold in the United States and Canada.

• If you've ever owned a Chia Pet, you know that when the seeds are soaked in water, they form an oily, gelatinous paste. That's not some chemical that's added to the seeds to make them stick to the Chia Pet; that's a natural property of the seeds themselves, one that makes them useful in thickening porridge or oatmeal. That oil is also how the seeds got their name: *Chia* comes from *chian*, the Aztec (or Nahuatl) word for "oily." The southernmost Mexican state of Chiapas takes its name from the Nahuatl words *chia* and *apan*—"chia river."

• You may be eating chia seeds already, without even knowing it: They are sold in health food stores under the brand names Salba, Mila, and Sachia. Golf legend Arnold Palmer even has his own line of chia seeds, sold under the brand name Anutra.

POT–ABLE

Chia seeds can't reach their full potential when planted on a Chia Pet. (How well would you do on a diet of water and no food?) So if you want to see what a full-grown chia plant looks like, plant some seeds in potting soil. They'll grow more than three feet tall and produce clusters of purple or white flowers on long stems.

*   *   *

"Even a little dog can pee on a big building." **—Jim Hightower**

Average person's cholesterol level in China: 127. In America: 227.

RETRONYMS

It's a new way to describe an old term after a new development requires differentiation. Confused? You won't be after reading these examples.

Snail mail: It was called "mail" until e-mail. (A shorter version is beginning to catch on—"smail.")

Land line: It was just a regular telephone line until cell phones became popular.

Coca-Cola Classic: The word "classic" was added in 1985 after the release of New Coke, which flopped.

World War I: Originally called "The Great War" and "The War to End All Wars" …until World War II.

Corn on the cob: Referred to as "corn" until canned and frozen corn became popular in the 1920s.

Cloth diaper: The invention of the disposable diaper in 1949 created the need for this term.

Hardcover book: All books were hardcover until the 1930s, when paperbacks were introduced.

Silent film: Called "films" until the talkies took over in the late 1920s.

Organic farming: How farming was done for millennia before chemical fertilizers and pesticides were introduced.

Vinyl records, or vinyl: Until CDs, records were just records.

Broadcast television: Needed since the introduction of cable and satellite TV.

Acoustic guitar: From the 1600s until the 1930s, they were just "guitars." Then the electric guitar was invented.

George H. W. Bush: He rarely used his middle initials until his son became president.

Hard copy: To distinguish a printed, paper document from an e-mailed one.

Contiguous United States: Coined after Alaska and Hawaii became states in 1959.

Field hockey: The original "hockey," it's still called that in countries where ice hockey, created later, isn't as popular.

Offline: What computer users refer to as anything not computer related, such as "outside."

Moe money: Hank Azaria has voiced more than 160 characters on *The Simpsons*.

Q & A:
ASK THE EXPERTS

*Everyone's got a question or two they'd like answered—basic stuff,
like "Why is the sky blue?" Here are a few of those questions,
with answers from some of the world's top trivia experts.*

PREPARE FOR TAKEOFF

Q: *On commercial airlines, why do you have to put your seat in
the upright position before takeoff and landing?*

A: "Should an emergency occur during either of these times, passengers have a better chance of survival if they evacuate the plane
immediately. Milliseconds count in these situations, so everyone
would be in a mad rush to find an emergency exit. Coach passengers know how difficult squeezing out of a seat mid-flight just to
get to the lavatory can be; now imagine that the cabin is filled
with smoke and visibility is near zero. Reclined seats, extended
table trays, and briefcases in the aisle would cause already panicked folks to stumble and fall, and hamper the evacuation
process." (From *Mental Floss* magazine's "7 Burning Questions
About Air Travel," by Kara Kovalchik)

EAT ME...NOT!

Q: *What would happen if you ate one of those "Do not eat!" silica
gel packets found in the packaging of dry goods such as clothing and
medicine?*

A: "Silica gel absorbs and holds water vapor. While the contents
of a silica gel packet are basically harmless, consuming them
would be an unpleasant experience. The moisture would be
whisked away from the sides and roof of your mouth, your gums,
and tongue, giving an all-too-accurate meaning of the phrase 'dry
mouth.' If it did happen to get past your mouth—unlikely because
you'd probably be making every effort to spit it out—you might
suffer a few irritating side effects such as dry eyes, an irritated, dry
feeling in your throat, aggravated, dry mucous membranes and
nasal cavity, and an upset stomach." (From "Discovery Health," by
Katherine Neer)

FLUID ENTERTAINMENT

Q: *Do liquid crystal displays (LCDs) actually contain liquid?*

A: "In this case, the term 'liquid' refers to a peculiar quality of a certain type of crystal, not its physical appearance. The *twisted nematic* liquid crystal is the most common type used in LCD televisions and monitors today. It has a naturally twisted crystalline structure. A particular feature of this crystal is that it reacts to electric currents in predictable ways—i.e., by untwisting to varying degrees depending on the current to which it is exposed. Hence the 'liquid' part of the crystal's moniker: Rather than being an oxymoron (How can a solid also be a liquid?), the term refers to the relative pliability of the crystals themselves, which is to say, their twistability." (From "LCD TV Buying Guide," by Jack Burden)

CHEER UP, OFFICER!

Q: *Why do police officers wear blue uniforms?*

A: "In 1829 the London Metropolitan Police, the first modern police force, developed standard police apparel. These first police officers, the famous 'Bobbies' of London, wore a dark blue, paramilitary-style uniform. The color helped to distinguish them from the British military, who wore red and white uniforms. Based on the London police, the New York City Police Department adopted the dark blue uniform in 1853. Today, most U.S. law enforcement agencies continue to use dark uniforms for their ability to help conceal the wearer in tactical situations and for their ease in cleaning. Dark colors also help hide stains." (From "The FBI Law Enforcement Bulletin," by Richard R. Johnson)

DON'T GET TESTY!

Q: *Why do patients have to cough during a hernia exam?*

A: "A hernia occurs when soft tissue, usually part of the intestine, protrudes through a weak point or tear in your abdominal wall. This bulging is most likely to occur when there's increased pressure on your abdomen, such as when lifting, straining, sneezing, or coughing. Forcing a cough during a hernia exam causes your abdominal muscles to contract and increase pressure within your abdomen. This may force a hernia to bulge out, making it easier to detect during examination." (From the Mayo Clinic's website, by Michael Picco, M.D.)

TO TELL THE TRUTH

Truth is elusive, truth is power, truth is the subject of these quotations.

"We know the truth, not only by the reason, but also by the heart."
—**Blaise Pascal**

"The greatest enemy of knowledge is not ignorance. It is the illusion of knowledge."
—**Stephen Hawking**

"As scarce as truth is, the supply has always been in excess of the demand."
—**Josh Billings**

"The opposite of a correct statement is a false statement. But the opposite of a profound truth may well be another profound truth."
—**Niels Bohr**

"Say not, 'I have found the truth,' but rather, 'I have found a truth.'"
—**Khalil Gibran**

"There is nothing as boring as the truth."
—**Charles Bukowski**

"When something important is going on, silence is a lie."
—**A. M. Rosenthal**

"When I tell the truth, it is not for the sake of convincing those who do not know it, but for the sake of defending those that do."
—**William Blake**

"The fact that a great many people believe something is no guarantee of its truth."
—**W. Somerset Maugham**

"What people say, what people do, and what they say they do are entirely different things."
—**Margaret Meade**

"All truths are easy to understand once they are discovered; the point is to discover them."
—**Galileo**

"Truth is so rare that it is delightful to tell it."
—**Emily Dickinson**

"The truth has a million faces, but there is only one truth."
—**Hermann Hesse**

"All generalizations, including this one, are false."
—**Mark Twain**

...sleep paralysis—the inability to move for several minutes after awakening.

WHEN YOU GOTTA GO...

*Everybody dies. But few people's deaths are bizarre enough to get
a mention in one of our books. So rest in peace, dearly departed,
and know that your lives had great meaning—you've
entertained a legion of bathroom readers.*

SCHOOL'S OUT...FOREVER

For 36 years, Sharon Smith had devoted her life to teaching elementary school in Molino, Florida. On the day of her retirement in June 2008, the 57-year-old fourth-grade teacher bid a fond farewell to her final class of kids. Then, just a few minutes later, Smith had trouble breathing. She died en route to the hospital. Her retirement had lasted less than half an hour.

HEART TO HEART

Sixty-nine-year-old Sonny Graham's 2008 death in Vidalia, GA, was thought to be just another tragic case of suicide until it was revealed that, 12 years earlier, he'd received a heart transplant from a donor who had also committed suicide. Even stranger, both men died in the same manner: a self-inflicted gunshot wound. Stranger still, Graham was married to Cheryl Cottle, the widow of the man whose heart he received. "I felt like I had known her for years," he told a reporter in 2006. "I couldn't keep my eyes off her." Cottle was widowed a second time by the same sad heart.

CREAM-ATED

A French circus clown named Yves Abouchar was killed during a performance in 1995 after another clown threw a pie at his face. Abouchar choked on the foam topping.

SWAN SONG

In June 2010, rumors began circulating throughout Mexico that crooner Sergio Vega, also known as El Shaka, had been shot and killed. That's not surprising, considering that Vega was a *Grupero*, a singer who performs *narcocorridos*—ballads about Mexican drug lords. Each drug lord has his own crooner, and they are often the victims of retribution from rival drug lords. However, the rumor of

Vega's murder was false. Vega, 40, confirmed that himself in an interview to an entertainment website. An hour later, while the news was circulating that he *hadn't* been shot and killed, Vega was shot and killed.

HE BLEW IT

When investigators found the dead body of a 45-year-old Abner Kriller in his wrecked car, his glasses were covered by bubble gum. It seemed that Kriller blew such a big bubble that it popped all over his face. He couldn't see and ran off the road.

NOT A PEAK EXPERIENCE

In 1993 a French mountain climber named Gerard Hommel— who'd successfully peaked Mt. Everest six times—died in his kitchen. He fell off a step ladder while changing a light bulb.

BLACK MAGIC NUMBERS

In 2001 Vladimir Grashnov, the former CEO of Mobitel, a Bulgarian mobile phone company, died of cancer at the age of 48. Two years after that, a Bulgarian mafia boss named Konstantin Dimitrov, 31, was shot and killed by an assassin. In 2005 Konstantin Dishliev, a Bulgarian real estate agent who sold drugs, was shot and killed. How are these three deaths related? Each man had been issued the same cell phone number from Mobitel. When each man died, it was assigned to the next man, who also died. (Mobitel has discontinued issuing that phone number.)

AUGUSTUS GLOOPED

In 2002 a chocolate factory worker named Yoni Cordon didn't show up to his job in Hatfield, Pennsylvania, for three days. Then his body was found inside a 1,200-gallon vat of chocolate. No one had seen him fall in. Nor did anyone know exactly how many chocolate chips had been made and sold before he was discovered.

CHECKMATE

At a 1992 chess tournament in Moscow, Grand Chess Master Nikolai Gudkov beat a computer three times in a row. When he touched the electronic board for a fourth game, the computer electrocuted him.

PASTEUR CURED RABBIS

...and other real answers given on real tests by real students,
collected by their poor, poor teachers and passed along to us.

Sir Francis Drake circumcised the world with a 100-foot clipper."

"Ancient Egypt was inhabited by mummies and they all wrote in hydraulics."

"The Magna Carta provided that no man should be hanged twice for the same offense."

"The Civil War was between China and Pakistan."

"A myth is a female moth."

"Miguel de Cervantes wrote *Donkey Hote*."

"The colonists won the War and no longer had to pay for taxis."

"Benjamin Franklin discovered electricity by rubbing two cats backward and declared, 'A horse divided against itself cannot stand.'"

"To change centimeters to meters you take out centi."

"Lincoln's mother died in infancy, and he was born in a log cabin which he built with his own hands."

"In the Olympic games, Greeks ran races, jumped, hurled the biscuits, and threw the java."

"The sun never set on the British Empire because the British Empire is in the East and the sun sets in the West."

"Louis Pasteur discovered a cure for rabbis."

"Lincoln went to the theater and got shot in his seat by one of the actors in a moving-picture show."

"The French Revolution was accomplished before it happened and catapulted into Napoleon."

"Homer was not written by Homer but by another man of that name."

"Nero was a cruel tyranny who would torture his subjects by playing the fiddle to them."

"Gravity was invented by Isaac Walton. It is chiefly noticeable in the autumn when the apples are falling off the trees."

The German language has words to describe 30 different types of kisses.

FIGHT CLUB, STARRING RUSSELL CROWE

Some films are so closely associated with a specific actor or director that it's hard to imagine they weren't the first choices. But it happens all the time. Can you imagine, for example…

BEN AFFLECK & MATT DAMON AS JACK & ENNIS (*Brokeback Mountain*, 2005) Gus Van Sant was the first big-name director to show interest in adapting Annie Proulx's 1997 short story about the struggles of two cowboys who fall in love. Having previously directed real-life best friends Affleck and Damon in *Good Will Hunting*, Van Sant offered them the roles, but Damon declined (he'd just played a homosexual in *The Talented Mr. Ripley*). When Ang Lee took over the project, he offered the roles to Joaquin Phoenix and Mark Wahlberg (Wahlberg declined because the gay subject matter "creeped him out"). The parts ultimately went to Heath Ledger and Jake Gyllenhaal.

MARK WAHLBERG AS DONNIE DARKO (*Donnie Darko*, 2001) The first actor tapped to play the troubled teenager was Jason Schwartzman (*Rushmore*), who had to turn down the role because of scheduling conflicts. Vince Vaughn auditioned, but at 30 he was too old to play a high-school student. Mark Wahlberg was then offered the part, but reportedly told director Richard Kelly that he would only play Darko with a lisp. Kelly said no, and Wahlberg was out. The lengthy casting process came to an end as soon as Jake Gyllenhaal showed up. According to co-star and co-producer Drew Barrymore: "Jake simply *was* Donnie Darko."

RUSSELL CROWE AS TYLER DURDEN (*Fight Club*, 1999) One of the film's producers wanted Crowe to play Durden, the character who convinces the narrator to start a club for committing terrorist acts. That decision was put on hold while they looked for a director. The first choice was Peter Jackson, a fan of the original Chuck Palahniuk novel, but he'd already begun work on *The Lord of the Rings*. Bryan Singer (*The Usual Suspects*) was sent the book but he didn't even read it. The third choice, British director Danny Boyle (*Trainspotting*), was busy with other projects. When their fourth choice, David Fincher, finally signed on, he lobbied for Brad Pitt to play Durden. Leading the candidates to play the narrator were Matt Damon and Sean Penn. Instead, Fincher cast the lesser-known Edward Norton, impressed by his performance in *The People vs. Larry Flynt*. The female lead was offered to Renée Zellweger, but she declined due to the dark subject material. Cast instead: Helena Bonham Carter.

TOM CRUISE AS BENJAMIN BUTTON (*The Curious Case of Benjamin Button*, 2008) F. Scott Fitzgerald's 1922 short story about a man who ages in reverse spent decades in development. Jack Nicholson was the first actor considered for the role of Button, and that was back in the 1970s. Several director/actor teams subsequently signed on to the project but then opted out, including Frank Oz and Martin Short, Steven Spielberg and Tom Cruise, and Ron Howard and John Travolta. Reason: The makeup effects were too difficult to do convincingly. Director Spike Jonze and screenwriter Charlie Kaufman (the team behind *Being John Malkovich*) were offered a shot at it, but they also said no. Thanks to improvements in digital effects, the story finally made it to the big screen in 2008 with David Fincher directing Brad Pitt in the lead, the duo's third film together (after *Se7en* and *Fight Club*).

CAMERON DIAZ AS BRIDGET JONES (*Bridget Jones's Diary*, 2001) When the film adaptation of Helen Fielding's novel was announced, many industry-watchers in the U.K. (including Fielding herself) hoped that British actresses Helena Bonham Carter or Kate Winslet would play Bridget. Winslet was busy with other movies, and Bonham Carter wasn't interested in a romantic comedy. With those two out—and to the horror of British fans of the book—the producers picked rail-thin American Cameron Diaz to play the slightly overweight Jones. But the director, Sharon Maguire, wanted an unknown for the part. So she auditioned another American, Renée Zellweger, then best known for her roles in *Jerry Maguire* and *Nurse Betty*. "If you go with me and we get this wrong," Zellweger told the director, "we are so busted." The actress spent months perfecting her British accent and gained nearly 25 pounds for the role. It paid off: Zellweger was nominated for an Oscar and, perhaps more importantly, she received rave reviews in England.

STRANGE LAWSUITS

These days it seems that people will sue each other over practically anything. Here are some real-life examples of unusual legal battles.

The Plaintiff: Craig Clark Show, 49, from Portland, Oregon
The Defendants: The Idaho State Police
The Lawsuit: In 2009 Show was riding his motorcycle through Idaho when he was pulled over on suspicion of drunk driving. He could only watch helplessly as the cops searched through all of his stuff…including a Native American medicine bag that had been blessed by a medicine woman, who told him the bag *had* to remain closed or its powers of protection would run out. The police opened it…and Show's life started going downhill (for one thing, he *was* charged with a DUI), so he sued the police for the destruction of the bag's mystical properties, seeking $25,000 in damages.
The Verdict: Perhaps there *were* protective powers in that bag—just before the court case was to begin in early 2010, Show fell seriously ill. The trial will resume after (and if) he recovers.

The Plaintiff: Sherri Perper, 56, of Queens, New York
The Defendant: Forum Novelties, a costume store
The Lawsuit: Perper went to a Halloween party in 2008 wearing a clown costume that she bought from Forum Novelties. But she couldn't quite figure out how to walk in the oversize clown shoes. At some point, she tripped and crashed to the floor. It may have seemed funny to her fellow partygoers, but Perper wasn't laughing. In fact, she was in agony…and she blamed the shoes. According to her lawyer, she sustained "severe fracture injuries" to both of her legs. Claiming that the clown shoes were "defective and dangerous," Perper is seeking unspecified monetary damages.
The Verdict: Pending.

The Plaintiff: Gabriela Nagy, of Toronto, Canada
The Defendant: Rogers Wireless, a cellular phone company
The Lawsuit: In 2006 Nagy set up a business phone with Rogers Wireless in her maiden name. A year later, her husband (not

named in court documents) added Internet and land-line services to the account, for which he received a bill—in *his* name—that included all the calls made on *her* line. And he noticed that she'd called one particular number quite often. It turned out she was having an affair, and it was her boyfriend's number. Result: Her husband divorced her. She also claimed she was too depressed to go to her $100,000-per-year job and was fired. Nagy is suing Rogers for $600,000 for not respecting her right to privacy.

The Verdict: Pending.

The Plaintiff: John Brandrick, 62, from Cornwall, England

The Defendant: Royal Cornwall Hospital (RCH)

The Lawsuit: In 2005 Brandrick went to RCH complaining of acute abdominal pain and was told he had pancreatic cancer. He was given less than a year to live. Brandrick quit his job, stopped paying his mortgage, emptied his bank account, and bought lavish gifts and expensive meals for his loved ones. A year passed. Not only was Brandrick not dead, he felt great. He returned to RCH and was told that it wasn't cancer after all…but pancreatitis, which had cured itself. Destitute, he sued RCH for negligence, but because he couldn't afford a lawyer, he was hoping for a settlement.

The Verdict: The case never made it to court. And it's unclear whether Brandrick received any money from RCH.

The Plaintiff: Marion V., a high-school teacher in Germany

The Defendant: "Kim," one of her 16-year-old students

The Lawsuit: In early 2010, Mrs. V. walked into her classroom and saw that one of the students had drawn a bunny rabbit on the chalkboard. Deathly afraid of rabbits, Mrs. V. ran out of the room in terror. She was so upset that she couldn't work for the remainder of the school year. Claiming "infringement of general personal rights," Mrs. V. filed a civil complaint against Kim. Why Kim? Because she was the only one who knew of Mrs. V.'s phobia (she had attended another school where Mrs. V. taught, and a similar bunny-on-the-chalkboard incident occurred there in 2008).

The Verdict: Case dismissed.

The mimic octopus can change the shape and color of its body…

THE PACKERS ARE IN HIS BLOOD

Green Bay Packers fans are known for being among the most loyal and dedicated in the NFL. How dedicated? Since 1960, every game at Lambeau Field has sold out, and the waiting list for season tickets is estimated to be more than 100 years long. Here's the story of one of the most dedicated "Cheeseheads" of them all.

FAN FOR LIFE

Jim Becker, who turned 80 in 2010, has been going to Green Bay Packers games since his father took him to his first game in 1941, when he was 11. He was a Packers fan throughout his childhood, his teenage years, and into adulthood. He followed the team from afar while serving in the Korean War. Then, as soon as his military service ended, he was back at Lambeau Field. And that's when real life began to intrude upon his love for his team.

Becker married his sweetheart, Patricia, in 1952; their first child was born the following year. Another child soon followed, then another, then another. If you've ever tried to hustle up money for football tickets while raising just a couple of kids, you can imagine how difficult it must have been for Becker; he and his wife would eventually have 11 children. But Becker put his kids first: He refused to dip into the family's budget to buy his Packers tickets.

There must have been days when Becker despaired of ever seeing a game in person again, but not after he learned that blood banks paid cash to people who donated blood. Suddenly he had a source of funds: "They were paying $15 a pint, more than a game ticket," he told the *Milwaukee Journal Sentinel*. "I'd go four or five times a year and use the money to buy the tickets."

BLOOD SPORT

For Becker, the blood bank really was a bank—whenever he needed money for football tickets, he gave more blood. He bought his tickets this way for the next 20 years: He was at Lambeau Field during the so-called "wilderness years" of the mid- to late 1950s, including the 1958 season, when the Packers went 1–10–1, their worst season ever. He was there for the glory years of 1959–1967, when Vince Lombardi coached the team to five championships in seven years, including victories in the first two Super Bowls. He was at the famous "Ice Bowl" NFL Championship Game of 1967, when the Packers beat the Dallas Cowboys 21–17 in –13°F weather (and a wind chill of –48°F), the coldest air temperature ever recorded at an NFL game. And he was there for the disappointing post-Lombardi years, when the Packers averaged only one winning season every four or five years. "A fan is somebody that follows a team win or lose," he says.

IRON MAN

Buying football tickets with blood money was certainly a sign of dedication, but it seemed nothing more than that until 1975, when Becker had to give his family medical history as part of a company physical. Becker's father had died in 1950 of a disease called *hemochromatosis*, in which iron accumulates in the body until it reaches toxic levels. Sufferers often show no signs of illness until it's too late; Becker's father seemed to be in fine health before he suddenly slipped into a coma and died at age 43.

Hemochromatosis can be hereditary, the doctor explained to Becker, and tests were ordered to determine whether he had inherited the disease. Sure enough, he had. But he wasn't *sick*, not at all, even though he was 45, two years older than his father was when the disease killed him. That didn't make any sense... until the doctor explained that hemochromatosis is treated by *bloodletting*—removing blood on a regular basis to draw off the accumulated iron.

SAFETY

By then Becker had donated blood more than 145 times over the past 20 years. In so doing, he not only paid for all those Packers tickets, he saved his own life, spared his 11 children the fate of growing up without a father, and saved his wife from having to raise all those kids alone.

He also found a measure of fame: In 2010 Becker beat out nine other finalists to be named the 12th inductee into the Green Bay Packers Fan Hall of Fame. At last report he was still donating blood three to four times a month, and still going to Packers games.

BANK ERROR IN YOUR FAVOR

When you're playing Monopoly, it's always fun to pick up the card that says, "Bank Error in Your Favor, Collect $200." But what would you do if that happened to you in real life?

Customer: Benjamin A. Lovell, 48, a $600-a-week salesman living with his mother in Brooklyn, New York

Bank Error: Lovell went to his local Commerce Bank branch in December 2007 to deposit money into his account (estimated balance: $400). But the teller mistakenly accessed an account belonging to someone named Benjamin S. Lovell. And that account contained more than $5 million.

What Happened: When the teller informed Lovell that "his" account had $5 million in it, he withdrew $10,000, probably just to see if he could. Then, over the next four weeks, he withdrew more money. Prosecutors say that by the time Lovell was arrested in February 2008, he'd withdrawn $2.1 million from the account, and had blown all but $500,000 of it on "bad investments, jewelry for a girlfriend, dental implants, vitamins, and colonics."

Outcome: At last report, Lovell was still awaiting trial for grand larceny. If convicted, he faces up to 25 years in prison. "He didn't intend to steal from anyone," his attorney says. "Based on what the bank told him, he really believed the money was his."

Customer: Howard Jenkins, 31, a roofing company employee

Bank Error: In May 1994, Jenkins withdrew $10 from a Nations-Bank ATM to treat his girlfriend to lunch. According to the ATM, he had $889,437 in his account. That sounded about $889,000 too high, so Jenkins went home and rechecked his balance using the bank's telephone banking system, which told him he had $88 *million* in his account.

What Happened: Jenkins raced back to the bank and filled out a withdrawal slip for $4 million. Moments later he walked out with seven certified checks—one for $997,000 and six for $500,000

There are 2,598,960 possible hands you can be dealt in a game of Texas Hold 'Em.

each—and $3,000 in cash. Then he treated his girlfriend to lunch (price: $10). While they were eating, Jenkins showed her the checks and the cash.

Outcome: No word on who gets the credit, but when Jenkins and his girlfriend finished their lunch, they (accompanied by a lawyer) returned to the bank and gave the $4 million back. No charges were filed. "I know something happened," said NationsBank president Alex Sink, "although I don't know exactly what."

Customer: David Hickey, 49, of Dublin, Ireland
Bank Error: While Hickey was traveling in Spain in November 2001, he asked the Bank of Ireland to transfer £1,500 (about $2,150) into his Spanish bank account. With Spanish pesetas worth about 200 to the British pound, the bank should have transferred 300,000 pesetas into Hickey's account. Instead, it transferred 300,000 *euros* into his account, or nearly $270,000.

What Happened: As soon as the Bank of Ireland caught the mistake, it called in the Garda, the Irish equivalent of the FBI, and had Hickey arrested in Spain. Bad idea: Hickey didn't appreciate being treated like a criminal while on vacation. "I have broken no laws," he told a reporter, "I was unaware I had the money."

Outcome: Since Hickey really hadn't broken any laws, the bank could not take the money back out of his account without his written consent, which he refused to give. Adding insult to injury, Hickey withdrew 60,000 euros before the Bank of Ireland could get a court order freezing the account, and threatened to spend it. He never did spend it, and he had no legal grounds for keeping it either, since it clearly didn't belong to him. But he did teach the Bank of Ireland a lesson by returning the 300,000 euros slo-o-o-wly, in three installments, over the next twelve months.

Customer: Ali-Kausar Barlas, a car salesman living in East Hartford, Connecticut
Bank Error: In 1986 Barlas deposited a check for $374.03 into his bank account, but the bank mistakenly credited his account with $44,374.03.

What Happened: Barlas withdrew $43,000 and used it to travel to his native Pakistan and get ready to marry his girlfriend. He paid her parents a $10,000 dowry, spent another $10,000 entertaining his future in-laws, and then brought his fiancée back to the United States, where he was arrested.

Outcome: In a plea bargain reached with prosecutors, Barlas pleaded guilty to first-degree larceny, received a suspended five-year sentence, and agreed to pay the money back. He married his girlfriend a week later. "He could have done worse with the money," Assistant State's Attorney John Massameno told reporters. "At least some romance was involved."

Customer: Philip Stagg, 33, an itinerant carpenter in Colorado

Bank Error: In 1977 Stagg deposited $608 into his Bank of Breckinridge checking account, but when the bank failed to post it to his account, one of his checks bounced.

What Happened: At first the bank agreed that there probably had been a mistake, and Stagg was owed $608. Then a bank official decided that Stagg was trying to steal the bank's money and had him arrested for theft.

Outcome: Stagg was charged with a felony, tried...and acquitted. Afterward, he sued the Bank of Breckinridge for defamation of character and intentional infliction of emotional stress. He won that case, too, and was awarded a $70,000 judgment against the bank. He later settled for $50,000, after the bank promised not to appeal the verdict. Shortly after the deal was worked out, the bank was sold to new owners, and they were the ones who got stuck with the bill. "If it had been up to us, we damn sure would have appealed it," new bank president Dean Boyd told reporters.

*　　*　　*

TWO WEIRD FLAGS

• The Benin Empire is now part of Nigeria, but it was a nation from 1440 to 1897. Its flag depicted a man slicing another man's neck with a sword—decapitating him mid-stroke.

• Mozambique's flag is layered: On top of green, black, yellow, and white stripes is a red triangle, and top of that is a yellow star, and atop the star are the three objects that are apparently most vital to the troubled nation: a book, a hoe, and an AK-47 machine gun.

Some species of caterpillars are cannibalistic.

CELEBS' GOOD DEEDS

Sure, it's fun to knock famous folks down a peg, but sometimes they do nice things. Not as a PR stunt—simply because they felt like it.

MATTHEW McCONAUGHEY

During the 2001 Toronto International Film Festival, the actor was watching his film *13 Conversations About One Thing* when one of the characters on the screen asked, "Why do you want a doctor?" Just then, a member of the audience yelled, "Turn on the lights! We need a doctor in here!" A woman at the screening had suffered a seizure, and her heart had stopped beating. Like a true action hero, McConaughey rushed over and began performing mouth-to-mouth resuscitation. According to Toronto police, he actually saved her life. Said actor Alan Arkin, "She woke up and saw him kissing her and now we know why she had the seizure."

TOM HANKS

As bride-to-be Natalia Dearnley tried to get to her wedding in Rome in 2008, a movie crew filming *Angels and Demons* was blocking access to the church where the groom and guests were waiting. Dearnley was told that she would have to wait until the day's filming was completed to get through. Hanks, the film's star, heard about her predicament and asked director Ron Howard to stop filming. Then he escorted the starstruck bride across the road to the church. (He even held the train of her dress to keep it from getting dirty.)

DEMI MOORE

Late one night in April 2009, Moore was checking her Twitter account when she saw this post from one of her 37,000 followers: "Getting a knife, a big one that is sharp." Then she posted another one: "gbye…gonna kill myself now." Moore checked the profile and discovered it was an unemployed Silicon Valley woman. Moore quickly wrote to her: "Are you serious?" No response. Moore then reposted the message on her website alerting anyone in San Jose who might know this woman. Moore's fans flooded the police department with calls; the cops located the distraught woman and took her in for psychiatric evaluation. Two days later, the woman reappeared on Moore's Twitter page: "Going to pay it forward!!! Starting today, no more pity party!"

KEANU REEVES

In 2003 Reeves, who starred in *The Matrix* trilogy, gave away $74 *million* of his salary to the "unsung heroes" of the films—the special effects crew. The 29 people who worked for years on the project received $2.5 million each. Reeves, who has also donated millions of dollars to leukemia research, downplayed the good deed: "I could live on what I've already made for the next few centuries."

PAUL McCARTNEY

In 2003 a New Zealand singer named Glenn Aitken was performing at a restaurant in the hotel where McCartney happened to be staying. After the show, the former Beatle approached Aitken and told him how impressed he was with his vocals. Aitken thanked McCartney and explained that he'd been trying to get a record deal for years, to no avail. "I'll see what I can do," said McCartney. Not only did McCartney get a record deal for Aitken, he played bass on one of the tracks. "It was so monumentally incredible," said Aitken, who grew up idolizing the Beatles. "I find it almost impossible to put into words."

*　　*　　*

NIGHT OF THE DRIVING DEAD

Rescue crews in Portland, Oregon, were called to the scene of a single-car accident one summer evening in 2010. When they arrived, they were alarmed by the extent of the injuries. The victims' faces were all bleeding; their skin was white, as if they were dead, and blood and guts were smeared all over their clothes. It was quite gruesome.

Or was it? It turned out that, when the accident happened, the five people were on their way to a costume party, all dressed and made up like zombies. Said police Sgt. Greg Stewart, "We're glad that everyone is alive, despite being undead."

Missing link? Humans have 46 chromosomes; potatoes have 48.

KEITH MOON, BATHROOM BOMBER

More than 30 years after his death, the Who's drummer, Keith Moon, is still remembered as one of the best in rock history. And as more than one hotel chain learned to their regret, that wasn't all he was known for.

MY GENERATION
In the summer of 1967, the British rock group the Who embarked on their first concert tour of the United States. They were the opening act for Herman's Hermits, best known for their hit single "Mrs. Brown, You've Got a Lovely Daughter." The Who had played dates in the U.S. before, including their breakthrough appearance at the Monterey International Pop Festival just a few weeks earlier that June. But this was the band's first cross-country tour, and there still was much about America that was new and unfamiliar to them.

Take American fireworks, for example: In many Southern states, giant firecrackers much more powerful than the "penny bangers" sold in England were perfectly legal. They could be bought cheaply and in large quantities all over the South. The Hermits had discovered them on their first American tour in 1965, and now, on a swing through Alabama, they introduced Keith Moon, the Who's 20-year-old drummer, to his first bag of American fireworks—cherry bombs.

Cherry bombs are still sold today, but in the 1960s they contained as much as 20 times the explosive power they do now—more than enough to maim or blind anyone who was holding them when they went off, or who happened to be standing too close. The U.S. Consumer Product Safety Commission banned original-strength cherry bombs in 1966, but judging from the reign of terror on which Keith Moon was about to embark, they must have still been available.

MAGIC BUS
The Hermits' favorite prank was throwing cherry bombs out of

It took the Jivaro Indians of South America about a week to make a shrunken head.

their tour bus, taking care to hold the lit bombs for a few seconds before tossing them so that they would explode in front of the car traveling behind theirs. Moon, with a little help from Who bassist John Entwistle, came up with his own destructive trademark when the tour pulled into Birmingham, Alabama, and the band decided that the hotel's room service wasn't up to snuff: He blew up his hotel-room toilet.

Why did Moon single out his toilet for destruction? The original plan was to blow up the *plumbing* beneath the toilet, not the toilet itself. The idea was to do damage without the hotel finding out who was responsible, or whether anyone was actually responsible at all. For all the management would know, the pipe under the floor might have burst as a result of normal wear and tear.

AMAZING JOURNEY

Apparently toilets in the United States flush differently than they do in the U.K., because when Moon and Entwistle tossed their first lit cherry bomb into that hotel toilet in Birmingham, they expected it to flush right down the bowl and into the plumbing pipes. But it didn't—instead, it just swirled around and around the bowl as the fuse burned lower and lower. At the last second, Moon and Entwistle fled the bathroom, slamming the door behind them just as the bomb went off, blowing the toilet to pieces. When Moon and Entwistle opened the door, all they saw was smoke, shards of porcelain, and a hole in the floor.

The destruction must have made quite an impression on Moon, because he quickly abandoned the idea of blowing up pipes he couldn't see in favor of toilets he could, even if it meant getting caught and having to pay for the damage. "From that moment on," biographer Tony Fletcher writes in *Moon: The Life and Death of a Rock Legend*, "no toilet in a hotel or changing room was safe until the tour moved away or Keith's bomb supply ran out."

I CAN'T EXPLAIN

Some toilet bombings stood out more than others: On a trip to New York in 1968, a *very* drunk Moon blew up the toilet in his room on the ninth floor of the Gorham Hotel, a popular spot with rock bands. Then he climbed out onto the window ledge, where he tossed more cherry bombs onto the police, who responded to

How to tell whether you have a cold or the flu: Colds make you sneeze; flus don't.

the call of an explosion at the hotel. Thrown out of the Gorham, the Who moved to the Waldorf-Astoria, one of New York's swankiest hotels. Then, when the management locked the Who out of their rooms until they paid their bill in advance and in cash (probably after receiving a call from the Gorham), Moon retrieved his luggage from his locked room by blowing the door off its hinges.

Thrown out of two hotels in 24 hours, the Who tried to book rooms in a third. By then, word had gotten around to every hotel in town, though, and suddenly no rooms were available anywhere. Pete Townshend, the Who's guitarist and songwriter, stayed with friends that night; everyone else had to sleep on the tour bus.

WON'T GET FOOLED AGAIN

The Who was one of the highest-earning bands of the era, but the band was soon reduced to staying at mid-priced hotel chains like the Holiday Inn because none of the elite hotels would have them. During one trip to New York in 1971, they did manage to book rooms at the Navarro, a luxurious hotel overlooking Central Park. But that was only because the hotel was under renovation—the manager put them in rooms that hadn't been redone yet, and let Moon demolish them to his heart's content. (One night Moon bashed his way through a brick wall to retrieve a cassette tape from the locked room next door.)

Moon's reign of toilet terror ended only after his untimely death in 1978 at the age of 32, when he overdosed on the prescription medication he was taking to treat his alcoholism. It's not clear exactly how many toilets he destroyed during his 11-year love affair with cherry bombs; one estimate places the value of all that destroyed porcelain at half a million dollars.

LONG LIVE ROCK

If you watched the halftime show on Super Bowl Sunday in 2010, you know the Who are still going strong, albeit minus Moon and Entwistle, who died from a heart attack in 2002. But the band may not be around much longer: In 2010 the Who cancelled their spring touring schedule when Pete Townshend, who is partially deaf, suffered a recurrence of *tinnitus*—buzzing or ringing in the ears—brought on, no doubt, by more than 40 years of exposure to loud music...and all those exploding toilets.

LOCK AND LOAD

The origin stories of a few gun-related phrases.

L OCK AND LOAD
Meaning: Get ready
Origin: The phrase was originally "load and lock." In the early 20th century, the standard army rifle was the 1903 Springfield. The safety on that rifle couldn't be locked until the rifle was loaded, so it was "loaded" with a clip, the bolt was closed, and the safety was "locked," meaning the rifle was ready for action. When the M1 Garland replaced the Springfield as standard issue in 1936, the phrase was reversed to "lock and load," because the M1's safety could be locked *before* loading. In any case, "lock and load" in the sense of readying a rifle for use was first made famous by John Wayne in the 1949 film *Sands of Iwo Jima*. It came to mean "get ready" sometime in the late 1980s.

JUMP THE GUN
Meaning: To act before the appropriate time
Origin: The origin of this phrase dates back to 1905: Athletes in running competitions who left the starting line before the starter's pistol went off were said to have "beaten the pistol." The phrase morphed into "jump the gun" sometime over the next 15 years because it was already being used metaphorically by 1921. The earliest known use of the phrase in a nonathletic sense appeared in *The Iowa Homestead* newspaper that year in a story that said: "Give the pigs a good start; jump the gun, so to speak, and get them on a grain ration before weaning time." It's been used that way ever since.

RIDE SHOTGUN
Meaning: To sit in the front passenger seat of a car
Origin: In the 1939 film *Stagecoach*, Curly (George Bancroft) says to Ringo Kid (John Wayne), "I'm gonna ride shotgun," and proceeds to sit next to a stagecoach driver with a shotgun in his hand. The film was an enormous success and began the Western

A 2-inch square of Velcro is strong enough to suspend a 175-lb. person from a wall.

film (and later television) craze that gripped America for decades. People therefore assumed it was used back in the 1800s, but there's no evidence for that: The earliest known reference to the phrase appeared in 1919 in Utah's *Ogden Examiner*—long after the end of the stagecoach era—about a parade in which a prominent local citizen would "ride shotgun" in an antique stagecoach. It appeared only occasionally until the film made it popular.

LOCK, STOCK, AND BARREL

Meaning: The entire thing

Origin: The lock, the stock, and the barrel are the three main components of a musket, the longarm commonly used by armies until the late 1800s. The *lock* is the firing mechanism that "locks" into position and is released by pulling the trigger. The *stock* is the section to which the lock and barrel are attached and which is rested against the shoulder when firing. The *barrel* is the metal cylinder down which the musket ball travels. So if you had the lock, stock, and barrel of a musket—you had an entire musket. The phrase was in use in the way we know it today by the mid-1700s. But the earliest written reference comes from a Connecticut newspaper account of a July 4th celebration: A group of revelers with a "huge keg of rum" made several toasts, one of which was to "Patriotism—Self interest, the cock, lock, stock and barrel." (The "cock" is the hammer, a part of the lock.)

STICK TO YOUR GUNS

Meaning: Stand by your convictions

Origin: This was originally a military command, "stand to your guns," meaning "hold your position." The first known metaphorical use dates to 1769 in *The Life of Samuel Johnson*, by Scottish biographer James Bobswell: "Mrs. Thrale stood to her gun with great courage in defense of amorous ditties." The first known use in the United States was in Earl Derr Biggers's 1913 detective novel *Seven Keys to Baldpate*, where a Mr. Max advised a Mr. Peters to "stick to your guns." The phrase has been with us ever since.

WHO NEEDS BREAD?

A sandwich consists of some kind of food placed between two slices of bread, right? Technically, yes…but not necessarily, as proven by these restaurant "innovations" that can push you close to the USDA-recommended daily intake of 2,000 calories and 65 grams of fat in just a few bites.

Restaurant: Friendly's
Sandwich: Grilled Cheese Burger Melt
Details: In 2010 the ice cream and burger chain introduced this offering. It's both a cheeseburger and a grilled cheese sandwich—well, *two* grilled cheese sandwiches, actually. A beef patty, a slab of cheddar, and all the fixin's are placed in between not two halves of a bun, but rather in between two full-size grilled cheese sandwiches.
"Nutrition:" 1,500 calories, 79 grams of fat

Restaurant: Kentucky Fried Chicken
Sandwich: Double Down
Details: The Double Down is a chicken sandwich, except that instead of bread, there's chicken. Two fried boneless chicken breasts fill in for the top and bottom pieces of bread, and in between the two hunks of chicken are bacon, a slice of pepper jack cheese, a slice of Swiss cheese, and a hefty dollop of "Colonel's Sauce" (it's mostly mayonnaise). When it was test-marketed in 2009, many critics thought this bizarre, high-fat sandwich was an elaborate hoax. It wasn't. It did so well in test markets that KFC put it in every store in April 2010 for a six-week limited run. Then it did so well that the restaurant kept it around until Labor Day.
"Nutrition:" The Double Down had 540 calories and 32 grams of fat. A slightly healthier version was also available, substituting grilled chicken breasts for the fried ones. It had 60 fewer calories and seven fewer grams of fat, but a third *more* sodium.

Restaurant: Mulligan's, a Decatur, Georgia, restaurant
Sandwich: Luther Burger

Details: According to lore, soul singer Luther Vandross loved to eat at Mulligan's, so they created a burger in his honor. Result: the Luther Burger, a bacon cheeseburger that eliminates the bun in favor of two grilled glazed donuts. The Luther is now available at dozens of bars, restaurants, fairs, food stands, and ballparks around the country. Vandross, for what it's worth, died in 2005 of a stroke, after long battles with obesity, hypertension, and type 2 diabetes.
"Nutrition:" An estimated 1,000 calories

Restaurant: Applebee's
Sandwich: Quesadilla Burger
Details: Once again, no simple bread on the top and bottom—the burger ingredients are placed in between two grilled quesadillas, each of which is filled with a blend of melted cheddar and pepper jack cheeses and bacon chunks. The burger itself is smothered in lettuce, salsa, more cheese, and "Mexi-ranch sauce."
"Nutrition:" More than 1,800 calories, 60 grams of fat, and 4,410 mg of sodium, two-and-a-half times the daily recommended amount.

Restaurant: BrunchBox, a Portland, Oregon, food cart
Sandwich: The Redonkadonk
Details: The Redonkadonk takes Friendly's sandwiches-for-buns approach to the next, heart-stopping level. There is no bun, but there are two grilled-cheese sandwiches made with extra-thick and buttery Texas Toast. Between the sandwiches sits a beef patty, a slice of melted American cheese, a fried egg...and three kinds of pork: a slice of ham, two strips of bacon, and a slab of Spam.
"Nutrition:" Although BrunchBox hasn't calculated it exactly, the Redonkadonk probably packs well over the daily recommended ceiling of 2,000 calories. (So what? We hear it's *delicious*.)

* * *

FROM AN ACTUAL CRIME STORY

"An Oak Hill couple discovered a thief in their home Saturday after the homeowner told a joke and heard someone laugh upstairs."

THE ANTHRAX ATTACKS

In late 2001, just weeks after the 9-11 terror attacks, an unknown person sent letters containing the bacterium that causes the disease known as anthrax to the offices of several media outlets and to two United States senators. So began what the FBI dubbed "Amerithrax." Here's the story of the attacks, and the history of the toxin itself (which is a lot older than you might think).

INSIDER TRADING

In 2008 longtime *Washington Post* columnist Richard Cohen wrote a piece for the online magazine *Slate* entitled "How Did I Get Iraq Wrong?" The article was about Cohen's early support for the war in Iraq and how he eventually came to oppose it. But the piece was especially notable for one paragraph concerning the anthrax attacks of September 2001:

> The attacks were not entirely unexpected. I had been told soon after Sept. 11 to secure Cipro, the antidote to anthrax. The tip had come in a roundabout way from a high government official, and I immediately acted on it. I was carrying Cipro way before most people had ever heard of it.

Cipro, short for *ciprofloxacin*, is a powerful antibiotic made specifically to fight bacterial infections. Its name became a household word after the anthrax attacks because it is the drug most often prescribed to treat the disease.

OH NO, I SAID TOO MUCH...

Cohen's seemingly offhand comment raised eyebrows among those who had been following the story of the attacks for seven years. Among their questions: How did a "high government official" know there was a chance of an anthrax attack? Very few people in the U.S. were talking about it before the attacks actually occurred. Was that official questioned by the FBI after the attacks? And, most importantly, if Cohen really had been advised to secure Cipro, why on Earth hadn't he warned his readers about it? Five people died in the ensuing attacks. Could Cohen or his government connection have helped prevent one or more of them?

Cohen's comment is just one of several mysteries surrounding the anthrax attacks of 2001. And because the FBI has officially closed the investigation, most of those mysteries may never be solved.

THE FIFTH PLAGUE

The word "anthrax" comes from *anthrakis*—the Greek word for "coal"—because one form of the disease causes coal-black lesions on the skin. And anthrax itself is nothing new or unnatural—it's been around for thousands of years. Descriptions of the disease have been found in ancient Greek, Roman, and Indian texts. Some biblical scholars even suggest that the fifth of the "Ten Plagues of Egypt" in the Old Testament—the Plague of Livestock Death—may have been describing an anthrax outbreak.

Anthrax is caused by *Bacillus anthracis*, a rod-shaped bacterium found in most parts of the world in the soil, where it feeds on dead and decaying organic matter. When the bacteria use up all the matter and environmental signals tell them that conditions are becoming unfavorable, they have the ability to go into a dormant *spore* state—forming hard, almost seedlike shells. The bacteria can survive in this state without food and in extremely harsh environments, such as blazing-hot droughts or freezing cold, for decades (possibly even centuries).

In nature these spores cause periodic anthrax outbreaks among grazing mammals such as deer, cattle, and sheep that ingest them as they eat off the ground. These outbreaks are often weather-related: Wind storms or floods can expose long-buried spores that are then eaten by animals.

MICRO-TERRORIST

Most of the bacteria in the *Bacillis* genus are harmless, but *B. anthracis* is different: It's not only deadly to many mammal species (including humans), it uses their own bodies against them in devious fashion.

To learn how anthrax bacteria trick their victims'
bodies into helping them multiply and spread—
and a whole lot more—go to page 267.

Babe Ruth and Lou Gehrig homered in the same game 72 times.

MEET OMAR SHAMSHOON

If you've ever visited the Middle East, you know that when American TV programs are shown on Arab TV, culturally sensitive content is often altered or removed. Turns out some shows aren't so easy to "Arabize."

MUST–SEE TV

In late 1991, the Middle East Broadcasting Corporation (MBC) went on the air for the first time. It was the Arab world's first privately owned, independent satellite TV network, and the first to offer 24 hours of Arabic language television programming free of charge to anyone with a satellite dish.

Other networks soon sprang up, creating a huge demand for content to fill the airwaves. In the years that followed, countless American TV shows—everything from *Friends* to *The Late Show with David Letterman* to *Two and a Half Men* to *MacGyver* to *Dr. Phil* and *Oprah*—found their way onto these channels, either dubbed into Arabic or broadcast with Arabic subtitles, and with culturally offensive subject matter toned down or removed entirely.

Shows that appealed to younger audiences were especially popular. In some countries as much as 60 percent of the population was under 20 years of age, and the numbers remain high today. So it was probably inevitable that sooner or later, one of the Arab networks would set its sights on *The Simpsons*, one of most successful shows in American TV history, and try to bring it to the Middle East. In 2005 MBC did just that.

HOMER OF ARABIA

No expense was spared to prepare *The Simpsons* for the Arab market. The Arab world's best TV writers were hired to translate episodes into Arabic, and A-list actors and actresses were hired to provide new voices for the characters. To make the show seem less "foreign," Homer Simpson was renamed Omar Shamshoon, and the show itself was renamed *Al Shamshoon*—"The Shamshoons." (Marge Simpson became Mona Shamshoon, Bart became Badr, and Lisa became Beesa.) Each episode that was selected for trans-

---

A well-trained Gap employee can fold a shirt in 2 seconds flat.

lation into Arabic was carefully reviewed to remove anything that might be offensive to Muslims. For example, where Homer Simpson drinks Duff beer (Islam forbids the consumption of alcohol), Omar Shamshoon drinks Duff fruit juice. Homer eats hot dogs (which commonly contain pork, also forbidden) and donuts (which are unfamiliar to most Arabs), but Omar eats Egyptian beef sausage links and *khak* cookies, which, like donuts, are often made with a hole in the middle.

Not every episode made the cut: Those with strong religious themes were out, as were the ones where the characters spent lots of time drinking beer in Moe's Tavern. In episodes featuring shorter church and tavern scenes, they're referred to as a "mosque" and a "coffeehouse." And Ned Flanders? He became just an annoyingly perfect neighbor, not an annoyingly perfect *Christian* neighbor.

As for all that Simpsons-centric dialog like "Don't have a cow, man!" and "Hi-diddly-ho, neighbors!"…well, the writers just translated as best they could. ("D'oh!" was translated as "D'oh!")

NEITHER HERE NOR THERE

The final product was a confusing mishmash of cultural references, something not really American, not really Arab (Marge Simpson and the other female characters don't wear veils, for example)…and definitely not *The Simpsons*. It wasn't very funny, either, and with all the translations, revisions, and deletions, the storylines could be maddeningly difficult to follow.

The premiere episode of *Al Shamshoon* aired in October 2005, on the first night of the holy month of Ramadan—the biggest TV-viewing night of the year. Muslims fast from sunup to sundown during Ramadan, and after the fast is broken with an evening meal, millions of the faithful settle in for a night of watching TV. Though 52 episodes were scheduled to air that month—with MBC looking forward to "Arabizing" all 17 seasons of *The Simpsons* in the years to come—the series was pulled after only 34 shows. Why? Because not many people tuned in to watch it. *Al Shamshoon* turned out to be just too strange a show for many viewers, especially in a part of the world where cartoons were still seen as entertainment for children.

But what really killed *Al Shamshoon* may have been the very thing that brought it into being in the first place: Satellite TV

Out of the 205 bones that make up a horse's entire body, 80 are in its legs.

channels. Arabs with satellite TV dishes can pull in *non*-Arab stations, and some of these broadcast *The Simpsons* in all its original, unadulterated glory. (The show is also available on DVD.) Many of the people who tuned in to watch *Al Shamshoon* were fans of *The Simpsons* who just wanted to see how badly MBC would botch the job, and after having a few laughs at the network's expense, they went back to watching the real thing.

HOME GROWN

For Arab critics of *Al Shamshoon,* one of the most frustrating things about the show was knowing that if MBC had just taken a fraction of the money it spent on *Al Shamshoon* and hired Arab animators to create an entirely new, entirely Arab show from scratch, they might have come up with something funny and engaging that Arabs could understand and call their own.

Even as *Al Shamshoon* was falling flat on its face in 2005, work had already begun on just such a show. *Freej* ("Neighborhood"), a comedy about four grandmothers living in a quiet neighborhood of Dubai, a booming metropolis in the United Arab Emirates, was already in production. *Freej* was the brainchild of a twenty-something UAE national named Mohammed Saeed Harib, whose first exposure to animated shows came in the late 1990s when he was a student at Boston's Northeastern University and his dormmates downloaded bootleg episodes of *South Park* and other shows to watch on their computers. Hareb came up with Um Saeed, the first of his four grandmother characters, while he was still living in the dorm. By 2003 he'd developed a concept for an entire show, which he sold to the satellite channel Sama Dubai.

FULL CIRCLE

One year after *Al Shamshoon* bit the dust, the first episode of *Freej* aired in the same coveted time slot—the first night of Ramadan. Unlike *Al Shamshoon, Freej,* the Arab world's first 3-D animated series, was a hit from the very start. By the time the second season of *Freej* aired the following year, half of all television viewers in the UAE were tuning in to watch the show. Stay tuned: You may be watching one of these days, too: In 2009 Hareb entered into talks with American media companies to bring his show to the United States. (Until then, you can look for clips on YouTube.)

Mississippi's largest "crop": catfish—the state produces 150,000 tons a year.

PRODUCT FLOPS

*Don't try to make your product too new or too improved
...or nobody will know what to do with it.*

N OT-SO-INSTANT COFFEE
Since the 1960s, there have been two ways that most
Americans make coffee at home: 1) a standard Mr. Coffee-
style coffee maker, and 2) adding hot water to "instant coffee" in a
cup. The first way takes about five minutes, and the second takes
about three. In 1990 Maxwell House came up with a third option:
Maxwell House Brewed Coffee—ready-to-drink coffee in a refrigerated carton. But it had to be heated up, and the foil-lined carton
wasn't microwave-safe, so the coffee had to be poured into another
cup and *then* microwaved, making it no more convenient than
coffee-pot coffee or instant coffee. Maxwell House Brewed Coffee
lasted less than a year in stores.

FLAKING OUT

In 1998 Kellogg's noticed increased sales for fast-food breakfast
items and wanted to get in on it the action. So they introduced
Cereal Mates: a package that contained a single-serving box of
cereal, a small carton of milk, and a spoon—perfect for a break-
fast-on-the-go. Only problem: Grocers didn't know know where to
place it in the store. The milk didn't need refrigeration, but if they
put it in the cereal aisle, consumers might be repulsed by the idea
of nonrefrigerated milk. And the dairy case seemed wrong because
shoppers wouldn't look for cereal there. Ultimately, Kellogg's put
Cereal Mates in dairy cases and then spent $30 million on adver-
tising to tell people to "look in the milk section" for the product.
It didn't work; Cereal Mates didn't last a year. But what ultimately
did in this "convenience food" wasn't its placement. It wasn't
really convenient: You can't eat a bowl of cereal while you're
driving to work, like you can a Pop Tart or an energy bar.

SUNDAE WORST

In 1986 the Johnston Company, a Milwaukee ice-cream topping
maker, introduced the Hot Scoop—a hot fudge sundae that was

designed to be microwaved for 30 seconds. The ice cream was supposed to stay cold while the fudge heated up, thanks to a strategically placed heat-reflecting lining in the package. It didn't quite work—microwaves of the '80s were still full of kinks and their power and quality varied greatly by brand. The end result was that the fudge and ice cream both ended up tepid, instead of hot and cold. The product disappeared from stores by the end of the year. Amazingly, another company, Steve's Ice Cream, licensed the technology in 1987. Its microwaveable ice-cream sundaes were no more successful than Johnston's.

INTERNUTS

When General Magic launched WebTV in 1995, it was predicted to be the technology that would launch the "Information Superhighway," combining TV and the burgeoning World Wide Web into an entertainment juggernaut. Consumers wouldn't have to buy a $1,500 computer to surf the Internet—they'd just plug the WebTV console into a television. Microsoft execs thought it was such a sure thing that they bought WebTV for $425 million in 1997, when the service had only 58,000 customers. (That's more than $7,300 per customer.) Subscribers did use WebTV (rebranded as MSN TV) to surf the Internet and send e-mail, but did not, as Microsoft had hoped, create any revenue beyond their monthly $20 service fee. Microsoft incorrectly assumed that WebTV users would click on online ads or shop online (from which Microsoft would get a cut). Not only that, they actually *cost* Microsoft money in tech support. WebTV had so effectively courted technology-phobes that those customers became its bane, with more than 10,000 calls daily to tech support. WebTV peaked in 1998 with around 500,000 customers, but then began a slow and steady decline. The service and boxes still exist, but there are only a few thousand WebTV/MSN TV subscribers left. And Microsoft has stopped selling boxes to new subscribers.

*　　*　　*

"Kickboxing is my favorite sport. It combines the grace and elegance of boxing…with kicking."

—**Norm MacDonald**

WELCOME TO DRUK YUL

Isn't it odd that we call Germany "Germany," while people who live there call it "Deutschland"? Here's what we should be calling some other countries.

HUNGARY: Magyarorszag *(my-uh-YORR-sag)*

SWEDEN: Sverige *(SVERR-ee-uh)*

POLAND: Polska *(POLE-skuh)*

JAPAN: Nippon *(nee-PON)*

IRELAND: Éire *(AIR-uh)*

GREENLAND: Kalaallit Nunaat *(kuh-LAH-leet noo-NAHT)*

WALES: Cymru *(CUMM-ree)*

ESTONIA: Eesti *(ESS-tee)*

CROATIA: Hrvatska *(kurr-VOT-skuh)*

FINLAND: Suomi *(soo-OH-mee)*

GREECE: Ellas *(ELL-us)*

NEW ZEALAND, in Maori: Aotearoa *(AH-tee-air-oh-ah)*

CAMBODIA: Kampuchea *(kam-poo-CHEE-uh)*

SOUTH KOREA: Hanguk *(hahn-GUHK)*

NORTH KOREA: Choson *(cho-SAHN)*

BHUTAN: Druk Yul *(druk yool)*

THAILAND: Ratcha Anachak Thai *(RAW-tcha ah-NAH-chak tai)*

ALBANIA: Shqiperia *(shkee-PAH-ree-uh)*

GEORGIA: Sakartvelo *(sak-ART-vuh-low)*

ARMENIA: Hayastan *(HI-uh-stahn)*

MALDIVES: Dhivehi Raajje *(duh-VEH-ehh rah-JEE)*

MOROCCO: Al-Maghrib *(all-muh-GRIB)*

BELGIUM, in Dutch: Belgie *(bell-GEH)*
...in French: Belgique *(bell-JEEK)*
...in German: Belgien *(bell-GEE-in)*
(Belgium has three official languages.)

Fat chance: If you're 5'6" and weigh over 165 lbs., you can become a Sumo wrestler.

THE LOST EXPLORERS: MUNGO PARK

Veni, vidi...evanui! (*I came, I saw...I vanished!*) Here's the first article in a series on bold, intrepid explorers...who never returned.

THE WILD ROVER

Mungo Park was barely 22 years old when he left England for Sumatra in 1792 and discovered seven new species of fish. Three years later, Park ventured from the west coast of Africa into the unknown Saharan interior to become the first European to reach the Niger River and trace its course for more than 300 miles. Imprisoned by a Senegalese chieftain for four months, he escaped with only a horse and compass and somehow found his way back to the safety of the coast. Upon returning to England, he chronicled his adventures in *Travels in the Interior of Africa,* which secured his reputation as the boldest explorer of his time. Any other man might have rested on his laurels, spent his royalties (his book was a bestseller), and enjoyed life as a country squire with his wife and children. Not Mungo Park. He had the "itch"—a compulsion to wander. So when the British crown asked him to lead another expedition into the Sahara, he jumped at the chance.

RIVER OF NO RETURN

On January 31, 1805, Mungo Park and a company of 40 men sailed from Portsmouth, England, disembarked in Gambia in western Africa, and set off overland. By the time they reached the Niger River months later, only 11 men remained; fever and dysentery had killed the rest. Undaunted, they began building a 40-foot boat in which to sail down the unexplored stretch of the river to its mouth. Park dubbed the ship the HMS *Joliba,* after the native name for the river. On November 19, more than 10 months after leaving England, Park's party, now reduced to two officers, three enlisted men, three slaves, and a local guide named Isaaco, pushed off and headed downstream. Before leaving, Park sent Isaaco back to Gambia with a pack of letters to be taken home by ship. To his

England has banned bagpipes twice: in 1560 and 1746. (They were considered tools of war.)

superiors at the Colonial Office, he wrote: "I shall discover the termination of the Niger or perish in the attempt." It was the last anyone ever heard from him.

WHERE'D HE GO?

When enough time passed to convince British officials that something had gone amiss with the expedition, they made sporadic attempts to find Mungo Park, even hiring Park's guide, Isaaco, to go back to the Niger to look for him. But aside from various rumors—Park had been killed by bandits, he'd been kidnapped by slave traders, he'd gone mad and run off to live in the desert like a monk—nothing conclusive was uncovered. Then in 1810, Isaaco returned with a dramatic report of the explorer's death. Park and his companions, he said, had run the course of the Niger for more than 1,000 miles, fighting off hostile tribal attacks the entire way. Their luck ran out at the Bussa Rapids near the Guinea coast. The tribute Park intended for the local king was stolen by a go-between, and when the *Joliba* ran aground on a rock, the angry monarch sent his warriors to collect his toll. Unable to free the boat, and under a constant hail of arrows and spears, the desperate Englishmen (only Park and three others were left) jumped into the raging rapids and drowned. When pressed for proof, Isaaco admitted he had nothing to back up his story except hearsay.

IN HIS FATHER'S FOOTSTEPS

Thomas Park was only a boy when his father, Mungo Park, disappeared. Young Thomas refused to accept that his father was dead, believing instead that he must have been taken prisoner. In 1827 he led a rescue expedition from the coast of Guinea. He had traveled only a few days inland when he came down with a fever and died. As for Mungo Park, no trace of him—clothing, personal effects, skeletal remains—was ever found.

*　　*　　*

COCONUCTOPUS

A strange defense mechanism of the octopus is to wrap six of its legs around its body so it resembles a coconut. Then it uses its other two legs to slowly walk backward, out of danger.

GOVERN-MENTAL

Politicians do the strangest things.

SENDING A MESSAGE—GODFATHER STYLE

Pennsylvania Governor Ed Rendell was trying to convince lawmakers in 2010 to vote for his proposed natural gas extraction tax. When Rep. Tim Solobay, a fellow Democrat, said he was against the tax, Rendell purchased a Tim Solobay bobblehead doll, removed the head, placed it inside a small box along with a note that urged Solobay's support, and sent it to the Representative's office. Solobay got the message—and the joke—and promised to reconsider his position. He also said the gesture was a "big hit" among Democrats. Pennsylvania Republicans, however, were less amused. A spokesman for House Minority Leader Rep. Sam Smith said, "Personally I don't see the humor in sending any sort of head to anyone. I think it is kind of sickening."

BUT NOT A DROP TO DRINK

In 2003 officials in Hudson, New York, were ordered by the Americans with Disabilities Act to install handicapped-accessible water fountains in the county courthouse. Five years later, they finally got around to installing just one of the fountains...the one on the second floor. And there's no elevator in the building. County Public Works Commissioner David Robinson defended the inaccessible handicap-accessible water fountain, saying it's easier for people who have trouble bending (which makes no sense—the new water fountain is actually several inches *shorter* than the one on the first floor). Robinson pledged that there are "definite plans in the future" to install one of the new fountains on the ground floor.

EXOPOLITICS

In 2010 Kirsan Ilyumzhinov, the governor of the Russian region of Kalmykia, recounted this story on a Russian TV show: One day in 1997, he was reading a book at his Moscow apartment when a transparent tube appeared on his balcony. "Then I felt that someone was calling me." The next thing he knew, Ilyumzhinov was

---

50 light years from Earth, there is a 2,600-mile-long asteroid made of diamond.

taking a tour of an alien spaceship. The aliens spoke to him telepathically, he said, and they passed along a warning: "The day will come when they land on our planet and say: 'You have behaved poorly. Why do you wage wars? Why do you destroy each other?' Then they will pack us all into their spaceships and take us away from this place." Most people just chalked the story up as an amusing antic by the eccentric millionaire businessman. However, Andrei Lebedev, a member of Russia's parliament, didn't think it was a joke. He immediately requested that Russian President Dmitry Medvedev interrogate the governor to ensure that he didn't give the aliens any state secrets. (Results of the interrogation are unknown.)

TEXAS BANS MARRIAGE

In 2005 Texas lawmakers passed a Constitutional amendment intended to outlaw gay marriage. In 2009 Texas Attorney General Barbara Ann Radnofsky pointed out a huge flaw in a 22-word phrase in Subsection B of the amendment, which reads: "This state or a political subdivision of this state may not create or recognize any legal status identical or similar to marriage." Basically, said Radnofsky, one thing that's identical to marriage is marriage itself, so in effect, no two people of any gender are legally allowed to be married in Texas. "You don't have to have a fancy law degree to read this and understand what it plainly says," she said. Currently, there are no plans to correct the phrasing, but it does call into question whether any marriages that took place in Texas since 2005 are legal.

NICE LEGS...NOT!

Colin Hall, Lord Mayor of Leicester, England, was on a diet. He also wasn't wearing a belt. Those two factors made for an embarrassing predicament one morning in June 2010 when Hall was speaking to dozens of schoolchildren at a local library. After he was done thanking them, he stood up from his chair. His pants, however, did not. They fell down to his ankles, leaving his underpants exposed to the kids, who all laughed. After being ridiculed in the press, the portly mayor apologized, but also said that it was a great way to publicize his new diet. As a show of support, Labour MP Keith Vaz presented Lord Mayor Hall with a brand-new belt.

Odds that you will drown in a bathtub: 1 in 11,469. (In a shower: almost zero.)

NASCAR-TASTROPHIES

The Allison family has been burning rubber on the NASCAR circuit since 1965—and were involved in three of the most infamous scrape-ups in the sport's checkered past.

RACE TO THE FINISH LINE

The first complete NASCAR race ever shown live on television was the 1979 Daytona 500, the circuit's biggest annual event. Millions watched at home as star drivers Donnie Allison and Cale Yarborough headed into the final lap, neck and neck in an extremely close race. The winner, whoever it turned out to be, would probably win by a nose—if that. The lead changed between Yarborough and Allison so slightly and so often that it was just a matter of who happened to be in front when they got to the finish line. The winner? Neither. Yarborough and Allison drove so close to each other that just before the final curve, as they gunned their engines for a final push, both drivers lost control of their cars, collided, and careened into the infield. A third driver, Bobby Allison—out of contention for the win, and also Donnie Allison's brother—saw the wreckage ahead and pulled over to see if his brother was okay. (He was.) Blame it on the stress of the race or blame it on the spirit of competition, but within minutes, all three drivers were out of their cars and screaming at each other on the open raceway. Then tensions really boiled over and the screaming escalated into a two-against-one, Allisons vs. Yarborough fistfight. And as those three punched and shoved each other, another driver, Richard Petty, zoomed past the melee…and cruised across the finish line to win the race.

SEARCH AND DESTROY

Curtis "Pops" Turner was racing in the 1966 Myers Brothers Memorial, his first major event since returning to NASCAR after the league lifted a lifetime ban on him for starting a drivers' union. Turner began in fourth place, just behind Bobby Allison. On the seventh lap, Turner attempted to tightly pass Allison, but instead crashed into him and spun him out. Allison dropped a lap

---

If your cat is short-haired, its ancestors came from Egypt. Long-haired: from India.

behind Turner. But about 100 laps later, Allison finally caught up to him and was ready for vengeance. Allison smashed into Turner's bumper, then drove up alongside and bumped him again, which caused Turner to spin out. Turner then made a quick pit stop and returned to on the track, but took it slow until Allison came back around, planning to ambush him. It didn't work—Allison knew what was coming and smashed into Turner first, pinning him against a wall. Then Turner rammed Allison, and Allison rammed Turner. And so it went...for 10 full laps in what amounted to a demolition derby. It only ended when the smashed cars, dropping parts and debris onto the track in their wake, were so damaged that their engines finally sputtered out.

LAUNCH TIME
In the 1987 Winston 500, held at the Talladega racetrack in Alabama, Bobby Allison managed to get his car up to more than 200 mph, a difficult task even for world-class, high-tech racecars. Bad move. One of Allison's tires burst and ripped apart. The car (a Buick LeSabre) spun backward and then *launched into the air*. It flew about 20 feet and landed on top of the fence that separated the track from the fans. And it didn't stop there: Allison's car kept going, tearing through the protective netting as it went, for more than 150 yards. Amazingly, the car never veered into the stands, and Allison was unhurt. Flying debris, however, did hit one woman who lost her eye as a result.

Postscript: After that nearly catastrophic wreck, NASCAR decided that its racecars were *too* fast. The league then required all cars racing at superspeedways Talladega and Daytona (the fastest and most dangerous tracks) to be fitted with *restrictor plates*, which reduce the flow of air and fuel into the carburetor, making it difficult for a car to go over 200 mph...or fly.

*　　*　　*

DADDY I$$UES
Famous investor Warren Buffett's largest-ever purchase was a $26 billion acquisition of the Burlington Northern Santa Fe Railroad in 2010. Why'd he buy it? "Because my father didn't buy me a train set as a kid," said Buffett.

Water on the brain? 25% of the bottled water purchased in America is just filtered tap water.

WHAT IT COST IN 1980

In 1980 we were coming out of a gas crisis and a recession...just like today.

• A Commodore VIC-20 computer cost $299.95. It boasted a maximum of 5 KB of memory and didn't include a monitor.

• Ticket for a Los Angeles Dodgers game featuring Mexican rookie pitching sensation (and future MVP) Fernando Valenzuela: $4.50.

• Cost of one of the year's most popular novels, Stephen King's *Firestarter*: $13.95

• A 1980 Chrysler Cordoba, memorably advertised by Ricardo Montalban as being upholstered in "rich Corinthian leather," cost $6,745.

• The price of a pack of cigarettes (people still smoked in 1980): about $1.00.

• A ticket to see *The Empire Strikes Back* cost $2.75.

• A gallon of leaded gasoline, which is now banned but was still available then, cost about $1.20.

• In 1980 a new house cost, on average, just under $69,000. Barbie's Dream House cost around $100.

• This year, McDonald's expanded its menu with the first fast food chicken sandwich, the McChicken (deep fried boneless patty on a bun). Price: 80 cents.

• The Sears Catalog offered a UHF- and VHF-enabled 19-inch "big-screen" color TV with a hot feature—a wood-paneled remote control with four buttons—for just $485.

• Irene Cara's title song from the movie *Fame* won an Oscar for Best Original Song. The soundtrack LP cost about $6.

• New in the candy aisle: Big League Chew, shredded bubble gum invented by a former minor-league pitcher as a chewing-tobacco substitute. A package cost 25 cents.

• A state-of-the-art VHS machine—on which you could watch pre-recorded movies at home!—cost $699. Renting one of the few dozen titles Hollywood had released cost about $8 at one of the many new "video stores" around the country, some of which required membership fees or deposits of up to $50.

A VIRUS WITH SHOES

If you take a dim view of humanity, you're not alone…

"All men are intrinsical rascals, and I am only sorry that not being a dog I can't bite them."
—**Lord Byron**

"It's possible to love a human being if you don't know them too well."
—**Charles Bukowski**

"To really know someone is to have loved and hated him in turn."
—**Marcel Jouhandeau**

"I talk to myself because I like dealing with a better class of people."
—**Jackie Mason**

"If the devil does not exist, and man has therefore created him, he has created him in his own image and likeness."
—**Fyodor Dostoevsky**

"The human race is a virus with shoes."
—**Bill Hicks**

"What is Man? A miserable little pile of secrets."
—**Andre Malraux**

"It is no exaggeration to say that we misanthropes are among the nicest people you are likely to meet. Because good manners build sturdy walls, our distaste for intimacy makes us exceedingly cordial."
—**Florence King**

"The world is beautiful, but has a disease called man."
—**Friedrich Nietzsche**

"I wish I loved the human race, I wish I loved its silly face, and when I'm introduced to one, I wish I thought 'What jolly fun!'"
—**Sir Walter Raleigh**

"No doubt Jack the Ripper excused himself on the grounds that it was human nature."
—**A. A. Milne**

"I hate mankind, for I think myself one of the best of them, and I know how bad I am."
—**James Boswell**

"We are born crying, live complaining, and die disappointed."
—**Thomas Fuller**

185 USES FOR A PIG

Turns out that there's a lot more to a pig than just meat. The reality is that almost every part of a livestock animal is put to commercial use—from the hair and the hide to the internal organs and the bones. Don't be grossed out: This kind of recycling has been going on as long as humans have been domesticating animals. (Only now it's a little more industrialized.)

BACKGROUND
In 2004 Dutch artist and author Christien Meindertsma began researching the fate of a single pig that was slaughtered on a commercial pig farm. She spent the next three years tracking down where every piece of that animal went and how it was used. It eventually went into 185 different products, which Meindertsma details in her book, *Pig 05049*. Here are just a few of the surprising places you might find a bit of a pig.

BEER: One of the most widely used products from pigs (and other animals) is gelatin—a clear, flavorless substance made from hooves, bones, and connective tissues. In beermaking, a dry, powdered form of gelatin is mixed in near the end of the process. There it binds with and helps remove *tannins*—bitter substances found in the hulls of grains used to make beer. It does the same with agents that can make beer cloudy, such as yeast and proteins from malt.

SHAMPOO: You know how some shampoos have a very shiny, pearly look? That's often the result of adding fatty acids from pig bones. (It's also used for this purpose in paint products.)

FABRIC SOFTENER: Not only are pig by-products used in commercial fabric softeners, they're actually one of the main ingredients. Static cling is caused when fabric fibers become negatively charged. Processed pig fats are positively charged, and therefore cling to fabric surfaces—effectively coating them in pig fat, making them feel soft and slippery, so your hand or your iron glides over the fabric easily. The process also makes it less prone to wrinkling.

BRUSHES: Pig bristles are a huge business all over the world, especially in China. They're used to make brushes of every kind imaginable, including hairbrushes, coat brushes, and paintbrushes. The bristles are gathered using special machines during the slaughtering process.

BREAD: *L-cysteine* is a naturally occurring amino acid (or protein) found in meat and dairy products. It is beneficial to the human body in several ways, especially in keeping our stomach linings healthy. Bread manufacturers use it because it reacts with wheat proteins in such a way that results in softer dough. Sometimes L-cysteine is made synthetically, but it's still most often made from pigs' bristles.

HEPARIN: This widely used anticoagulant drug (it stops blood clots from forming) is derived from the mucus lining of pigs' small intestines.

CORK: Corks for wine bottles are traditionally made out of whole pieces from cork trees. But the manufacturing process generates a lot of cork waste. Rather than let all that waste go to waste, it's reprocessed and reformed into new corks using a binding agent, such as gelatin from pig bone. (Because wine is often clarified with gelatin just as beer is, there can actually be bits of pig in a wine bottle's cork—*and* in the wine itself.)

CHEMICAL WEAPONS LABS: Because of its similarity to human tissue, pig flesh—usually the ears—is commonly used to test the physiological effects of chemical weapons.

MATCHES: "Bone glue" is a type of adhesive made from proteins found in pig bones. One of its many industrial uses is in matches: The strikable heads of friction matches are a combination of flammable chemicals (like phosphorus)—held together with bone glue.

CIGARETTES: Meindertsma found that processed pig blood—yes, pig blood—is used in the manufacture of cigarette filters. In 2010 Dutch researchers confirmed this, saying, "The pig's hemoglobin was found to be a fairly effective filter for cigarettes, but this information was not on cigarette labels because the tobacco industry was not required by law to disclose the ingredients of their products." The news caused outrage, particularly among

Muslim and Jewish smokers, who are proscribed from using pig products in any form.

TRAIN BRAKES: Like those of other livestock animals, such as cattle and sheep, pigs' bones are useful, too, often in the form of *bone ash*: The bones are incinerated and processed to form a very fine powder of uniformly sized particles. Bone ash can be added to a vast number of products, including fine china, artists' paints, polishing compounds, and fertilizers. Meindertsma even tracked Pig 05049's bone ash to a factory in Germany that makes parts for train brakes.

MISCELLANEOUS: Here are some other products in which you might find gelatin, bone ash, or other parts of a pig.

safety gloves	vanilla pudding	wallpaper
beauty masks	chocolate mousse	sandpaper
energy bars	ice cream	shoe leather
licorice	pet food	china figurines
chewing gum	surgical sponge	chondroitin tablets
breath mints	paintballs	insulin
lollipops	inkjet paper	heart valves
marshmallows	X-ray film	cadmium batteries
nougat	jigsaw puzzles	injectable collagen
cupcakes	book covers	bullets

*   *   *

MYTH-CONCEPTION:
PIGS ARE FILTHY ANIMALS

Pigs are exceptionally clean animals. Yes, you might see them rolling around in the mud, but they do that only to cool themselves off because they have no sweat glands. Here's an example of pig hygiene: They typically designate one area of their pen or yard for defecation and urination—away from the area where they eat and sleep. Even piglets just a few days old will leave the nursing nest to relieve themselves.

MISSED IT BY *THAT* MUCH

You work so hard, you dedicate yourself with long hours, year after year, you get right up to the very end...and boom, you miss it.

PHILLIP K. DICK

Almost there... This American science-fiction writer published more than 120 short stories and 44 novels. He had a small following around the world, but lived most of his life in near-poverty. His later years were marred by poor health, both physical and mental, and, five days after suffering a stroke in February 1982, he died at the age of 53.

Denied: Less than three months after his death, Dick's 1968 novel *Do Androids Dream of Electric Sheep?* was adapted for the screen—becoming *Blade Runner*, starring Harrison Ford. The film was nominated for two Oscars, and it introduced the world to Dick's largely unknown work. Since then, eight films based on Dick's work, including *Total Recall* (1990), *Minority Report* (2002), and *A Scanner Darkly* (2006), have grossed more than $700 million.

ROMAN EMPEROR VESPASIAN

Almost there... Shortly after Vespasian came to power in A.D. 69, he ordered the construction of the Flavian Amphitheater (after the imperial family name). It took almost nine years to build.

Denied: In June of A.D. 79, Vespasian dropped dead after a brief illness at the age of 70. He missed the completion of his theater and its 100-day grand opening. Every day during that period, the massive arena, which was more than 150 feet high and covered six acres, was filled with more than 50,000 spectators who turned out to see boat battles (they could fill the amphitheater with several feet of water), horse races, gladiator battles, sideshows of every sort, and the slaughter of more than 9,000 animals. Vespasian's Flavian Amphitheater became the most important symbol of the power of the Roman Empire, and its ruins still stand today, better known by the name it got during the Middle Ages: the Roman Colosseum.

MADELYN LEE PAYNE DUNHAM

Almost there... Madelyn Lee Payne was born in Kansas in 1922.

One of Isaac Newton's teeth was auctioned in 1816 for $3,633. ($35,700 today.)

In 1940 she married Stanley Dunham, in 1942 they had a daughter named Ann, and in the 1950s they moved to Hawaii. There, in 1961, Ann met and married Barack Obama; Barack Jr. was born later that year. Madelyn played a big role in the boy's upbringing, even raising him for several years while his mother lived in Indonesia. In 2008 Madelyn, then 86, watched from her home in Honolulu as her grandson ran for president as the Democratic nominee. She even had a corneal transplant just so she could see the TV better.

Denied: Dunham died on November 2, 2008—just two days before Barack Obama won the historic election. Fortunately, he had visited her in late October (with only days remaining in the campaign) and was able to talk to her one last time.

FRANKLIN DELANO ROOSEVELT

Almost there... Nazi Germany's 1939 invasion of Poland marked the beginning of World War II. At first, President Roosevelt kept the United States out of it, but he was anything but uninvolved. He persuaded Congress to repeal a 1935 arms embargo, allowing the U.S. to export weapons to its European allies; he instigated a major arms buildup that helped keep England from being taken by the Nazis; and he pushed for (and got) the first peacetime draft in American history. After the Japanese attacked Pearl Harbor in 1941, the U.S. entered what had become a true "world war." For the next three-and-a-half years Roosevelt led the country through history's most devastating conflict to date.

Denied: Roosevelt was at his Warm Springs, Georgia, retreat on April 12, 1945, when he suffered a cerebral hemorrhage and died within minutes. Less than a month later, Germany surrendered. On August 14, after the U.S. dropped atomic bombs on Hiroshima and Nagasaki, Japan surrendered, and President Harry Truman announced to the American people that the war was over.

*   *   *

"I discovered I scream the same way, whether I'm about to be devoured by a great white or if a piece of seaweed touches my foot."

—Kevin James

Who hosted America's first beauty pageant? P. T. Barnum, in 1854.

SONG-WRONGERS

Politicians don't commission original campaign songs anymore.
Instead, they like to use well-known popular songs, often
without payment or permission. Here are some
of the song stealers who got caught.

Infringer: Bob Dole
Song: "Soul Man"
Story: During the 1996 presidential campaign, Sam Moore, a member of the popular 1960s R&B duo Sam and Dave (who also wrote the theme song from *Shaft*), rerecorded one of the duo's biggest hits, "Soul Man," for the presidential campaign of Bob Dole, substituting "I'm a Dole man" for "I'm a soul man." The song was originally written by Isaac Hayes and David Porter, and they were not happy with Moore's version. "People may get the impression that David and I endorse Bob Dole," Hayes told the *New York Daily News*, "which we don't." And Rondor Music International, the music publishing company that owned the song, threatened to sue for $100,000 for every unauthorized use of "Soul Man." The campaign immediately stopped using the song, and no lawsuit was filed. But the Dole campaign then tried to use the Bruce Springsteen song "Born in the USA," again without permission. Ronald Reagan had done the same in 1984, and, just as he had done with Reagan, "The Boss" (and his lawyers) forced Dole to stop. After that, Dole's aides finally *asked* a songwriter for permission, and Eddie Rabbitt allowed them to use "American Boy" as their campaign song.

Infringer: Joe Walsh
Song: "Walk Away"
Story: In January 2010, Illinois Republican politician Joe Walsh, who was running for a seat in the U.S. House of Representatives, changed the lyrics to the 1971 song "Walk Away," written by guitarist Joe Walsh in his pre-Eagles days, and used it in a campaign video on his website. Musician Walsh had his lawyer, Peter Paterno, write the campaign a letter: "Given that your name is Joe Walsh, I'd think you'd want to be extra careful about using

Joe's music in case the public might think that Joe is endorsing your campaign, or, God forbid, *is* you." Walsh the politician's response: The song was parody and therefore permitted under copyright law, and "I am not backing down on this." A month later he backed down, and the video was pulled.

Infringer: Barack Obama
Song: "Hold On, I'm Coming"
Story: In 2008 Sam Moore was back in the news when the Obama campaign used another Sam and Dave hit, "Hold On, I'm Coming," as one of its theme songs without asking permission. Although Moore didn't write the song, he sent them a letter asking them to stop, and the campaign complied. Eleven months later…Moore performed at one of Obama's inaugural balls. (He sang "Soul Man.")

Infringer: Charles DeVore
Songs: "The Boys of Summer," "All She Wants to Do Is Dance"
Story: Most unauthorized users of songs apologize and promise to never do it again, and that's usually the end of it. But sometimes they fight back. Charles DeVore's campaign to win the 2010 Republican senate primary in California used a knockoff of "The Boys of Summer" by Don Henley in a video mocking Barack Obama. (It was called "Hope of November.") Henley complained, and the video was pulled. But then DeVore did it again, ripping off Henley's "All She Wants to Do is Dance" for a song called "All She Wants to Do Is Tax" about his opponent, Democratic Senator Barbara Boxer. (DeVore actually wrote both parodies himself.) Henley had enough, and he filed a lawsuit against DeVore for copyright infringement. DeVore fought back, claiming the songs were parodies and therefore protected by free speech. In June 2010, a judge ruled that DeVore was wrong: Parody involves mocking the thing being parodied, in this case Henley's songs. DeVore's songs didn't do that; they were used to comment on something else entirely—Barack Obama and Barbara Boxer— which made them *satires*, not parodies. Henley won the case, making him the first musician to successfully sue a politician for stealing a song. (No word on how much DeVore had to pay, but he lost the election.)

More than 100 descendants of Johann Sebastian Bach have been church organists.

HAPPY WAFFLE IRON DAY!

...and other weird—but real—"holidays."

JANUARY: National Soup Month
Jan. 10: Peculiar People Day
Jan. 13: Blame Someone Else Day
Jan. 22: Answer Your Cat's Question Day

FEBRUARY: Pull Your Sofa Off the Wall Month
Feb. 9: Read in the Bathtub Day
Feb. 20: Hoodie Hoo Day
Feb. 23: International Dog Biscuit Appreciation Day

MARCH: International Mirth Month
Mar. 9: Panic Day
Mar. 28: Something on a Stick Day
Mar. 29: Festival of Smoke and Mirrors Day

APRIL: Grilled Cheese Month
Apr. 4: Hug a Newsman Day
Apr. 11: Eight-Track Tape Day
Apr. 23: Talk Like Shakespeare Day

MAY: Revise Your Work Schedule Month
May 9: Lost Sock Memorial Day
May 13: Frog Jumping Day
May 27: Cellophane Tape Day

JUNE: Dairy Alternative Month
June 1: Go Barefoot Day
June 19: World Juggling Day
June 29: Waffle Iron Day

JULY: Doghouse Repairs Month
July 3: Compliment Your Mirror Day
July 14: National Nude Day
July 15: Gummi Worm Day
July 17: Wrong Way Day

AUGUST: Foot Health Month
Aug. 12: Middle Child's Day
Aug. 20: Bad Hair Day (Don King's birthday)
Aug. 30: Frankenstein Day

SEPTEMBER: Pleasure Your Mate Month
Sept. 6: Fight Procrastination Day
Sept. 11: Make Your Bed Day
Sept. 16: Collect Rocks Day

OCTOBER: Sausage Month
Oct. 11: National Kick Butt Day
Oct. 14: Be Bald and Be Free Day
Oct. 30: Haunted Refrigerator Night

NOVEMBER: Beard Month
Nov. 2: Deviled Egg Day
Nov. 6: I Love Nachos Day
Nov. 20: Absurdity Day
Nov. 21: False Confession Day

DECEMBER: National Tie Month
Dec. 4: Wear Brown Shoes Day
Dec. 12: National Ding-A-Ling Day
Dec. 30: Festival of Enormous Changes at the Last Minute

Itchin' cousins: Mangos and cashews are both related to poison ivy.

THE MALL: A HISTORY

Modern shopping malls are so common that we forget they've only been around for 50 years. Here's the story of how they came to be…and the story of the man who invented them, Victor Gruen— the most famous architect you've never heard of.

FATEFUL LAYOVER

In the winter of 1948, an architect named Victor Gruen got stranded in Detroit, Michigan, after his flight was cancelled due to a storm. Gruen made his living designing department stores, and rather than sit in the airport or in a hotel room, he paid a visit to Detroit's landmark Hudson's department store and asked the store's architect to show him around.

The Hudson's building was nice enough; the company prided itself on being one of the finest department stores in the entire Midwest. But downtown Detroit itself was pretty run-down, which was not unusual for an American city in that era. World War I (1914–18), followed by the Great Depression and then World War II (1939–45), had disrupted the economic life of the country, and decades of neglect of downtown areas had taken their toll.

STRIP JOINTS

The suburbs were even shabbier, as Gruen saw when he took a ride in the country and drove past ugly retail and commercial developments that seemed to blight every town.

The combination of dirt-cheap land, lax zoning laws, and rampant real estate speculation had spawned an era of unregulated and shoddy commercial development in the suburbs. Speculators threw up cheap, (supposedly) temporary buildings derisively known as "taxpayers" because the crummy eyesores barely rented for enough money to cover the property taxes on the lot. That was their purpose: Land speculators were only interested in covering their costs until the property rose in value and could be unloaded for a profit. Then the new owner could tear down the taxpayer and build something more substantial on the lot. But if the proliferation of crumbling storefronts, gas stations, diners, and fleabag hotels were any guide, few taxpayers were ever torn down.

The unchecked growth in the suburbs was a problem for downtown department stores like Hudson's, because their customers were moving there, too. Buying a house in suburbia was cheaper than renting an apartment downtown, and thanks to the G.I. Bill, World War II veterans could buy them with no money down.

Once these folks moved out to the suburbs, few of them wanted to return to the city to do their shopping. The smaller stores in suburban retail strips left a lot to be desired, but they were closer to home and parking was much easier than downtown, where a shopper might circle the block for a half hour or more before a parking space on the street finally opened up.

Stores like Hudson's had made the situation worse by using their substantial political clout to block other department stores from building downtown. Newcomers such as Sears and J.C. Penney had been forced to build their stores in less desirable locations outside the city, but this disadvantage turned into an advantage when the migration to the suburbs began.

As he drove through the suburbs, Gruen envisioned a day when suburban retailers would completely surround the downtown department stores and drive them out of business.

SHOPPING AROUND

When Gruen returned home to New York City, he wrote a letter to the president of Hudson's explaining that if the customers were moving out to the suburbs, Hudson's should as well. For years Hudson's had resisted opening branch stores outside the city. It had an image of exclusivity to protect, and opening stores in seedy commercial strips was no way to do that. But it was clear that something had to be done, and as Hudson's president, Oscar Webber, read Gruen's letter, he realized that here was a man who might be able to help. He offered Gruen a job as a real estate consultant, and soon Gruen was back driving around Detroit suburbs looking for a commercial strip worthy of the Hudson's name.

The only problem: There weren't any. Every retail development Gruen looked at was flawed in one way or another. Either it was too tacky even to be considered, or it was too close to downtown and risked stealing sales from the flagship store. Gruen recommended that the company develop a commercial property of its own. Doing so, he argued, offered a lot of advantages: Hudson's wouldn't have to rely on a disinterested landlord to maintain the property in keeping with Hudson's image. And because Gruen proposed building an entire shopping center, one that would include other tenants, Hudson's would be able to pick and choose which businesses moved in nearby.

Furthermore, by building a shopping center, Hudson's would diversify its business beyond retailing into real estate development and commercial property management. And there was a bonus, Gruen argued: By concentrating a large number of stores in a single development, the shopping center would prevent ugly suburban sprawl. The competition that a well-designed, well-run shopping center presented, he reasoned, would discourage other businesses from locating nearby, helping to preserve open spaces in the process.

FOUR OF A KIND
Oscar Webber was impressed enough with Gruen's proposal that he hired the architect to create a 20-year plan for the company's growth. Gruen spent the next three weeks sneaking around the Detroit suburbs collecting data for his plan. Then he used the information to write up a proposal that called for developing not one but *four* shopping centers, to be named Northland, Eastland, Southland, and Westland Centers, each in a different suburb of Detroit. Gruen recommended that the company locate its shopping centers on the outer fringes of existing suburbs, where the land was cheapest and the potential for growth was greatest as the suburbs continued to expand out from downtown Detroit.

Hudson's approved the plans and quietly began buying up land for the shopping centers. It hired Gruen to design them, even though he'd only designed two shopping centers before and neither was actually built. On June 4, 1950, Hudson's announced its plan to build Eastland Center, the first of the four projects scheduled for development.

Three weeks later, on June 25, 1950, the North Korean People's Army rolled across the 38th parallel that served as the border between North and South Korea. The Korean War had begun.

What does the Korean War have to do with shopping malls? Turn to page 230 and mall will be revealed.

Utah's state bird: the California gull.

GUILT BY ASSOCIATION

Although they might look like it, none of the words or expressions listed below is in any way dirty, and to prove it we're giving you the correct definitions. (But use them at your own risk.)

Bed Load: Solid particles, like the pebbles in a stream, that are carried along by flowing water.

Titbits: The British spelling for the word "tidbits." *Tit-Bits* was the name of a British weekly magazine published from 1881 to 1984.

Loose Smut: A fungus that attacks wheat crops.

Oxpecker: A small bird native to sub-Saharan Africa. (Also known as tickbirds, they eat parasites that infest the hides of livestock.)

Dick Test: If your doctor suspects you have scarlet fever, you may be given this diagnostic test invented by Dr. George Dick and his wife Gladys in 1924.

Vaginicola: A single-celled organism found in pond water.

Crack Spread: The difference in value between unrefined crude oil and the products that can be made by refining, or "cracking," the oil.

F-holes: The f-shaped sound holes cut into the front of violins, cellos, and other stringed instruments.

Rump Party: In British politics, when one faction of a political party breaks away to merge with or form a new party, the faction left behind is known as the "rump party."

Urinator: A person who dives underwater in search of pearls, sunken treasure, or other riches.

Spermophile: A *genus*, or grouping, of more than 40 species of ground squirrel.

Crap Mats: The name of a mountain in the Swiss Alps.

Fucoid: An adjective that means, "having to do with seaweed."

Fucose: A type of sugar found in human breast milk and in seaweed.

Titubate: To stumble, either in step or in speech.

Dickcissel: A species of finch native to the central U.S.

In 2008 psychologists introduced a new diagnosis: Facebook Addiction Disorder.

STALLS OF TERROR

Going to the bathroom is usually a pleasant experience…
unless you happen to go in one of these bathrooms.

The Toilet: A restroom on a train in Illinois

The Setup: Julianna Mandernach was traveling from Chicago to Joliet, Illinois, in January 2009, when she used the train toilet, then flushed it.

Don't Go There: As soon as she flushed the toilet, the contents exploded all over her. She sued the Northeast Illinois Regional Commuter Railroad Corporation for an undisclosed amount, saying the exploding commode left her with injuries of a "personal and pecuniary nature." (If we didn't know better, we might think "pecuniary" was legalese for "stinky.") Oddly, the suit wasn't filed until January 2010—almost a year later. The case is still pending.

The Toilet: A portable toilet in the city of Gomel, Belarus

The Setup: A 45-year-old man popped into the toilet to do his business in June 2004.

Don't Go There: While the man was still inside the toilet, thieves wrapped a rope around it, loaded it onto a flatbed truck, and drove away. They had not only stolen a porta-potti—they had stolen an *occupied* porta-potti. The man was unable to escape until the bouncing truck jostled the rope loose enough for him to open the door slightly, after which he jumped off the moving truck and broke his collarbone. He was taken to the hospital and later reported the incident to police, who tracked down the stolen toilet to a home in the area…and arrested the poopetrators.

The Toilet: The downstairs bathroom in the home of the Bueller family of Rechlinghausen, Germany

The Setup: In November 2008, Dennis Bueller, 13, had just sprayed the bathroom with a can of aerosol air freshener. Then, being a 13-year-old, he started playing with his dad's lighter.

Don't Go There: The can ignited—and blew Dennis through the bathroom window and out into the yard. "I sprayed the toilet because it smelled," he later told Britain's *Daily Mail*. "Then I began fiddling with a lighter my dad left in there and suddenly there was this big orange *whoosh!* of flame. I woke up outside with my clothes burned off me and smelling like a barbecue." Dennis suffered burns over much of his upper body, but he recovered. "He realizes he was a bit dim," said his father.

The Toilet: A home in Iowa City, Iowa
The Setup: Nitasha Johnson, 20, was in the bathroom with her sister one evening in March 2010. They were arguing.
Don't Go There: The argument escalated—and Johnson grabbed the lid off the toilet tank and bashed her sister with it. The sister was taken to the hospital, where she was treated for injuries to her foot and finger. Nitasha Johnson was arrested on charges of domestic assault...and thrown in the can.

The Toilet: The great outdoors, near Zagreb, Croatia
The Setup: Ante Djindjic, 29, was riding his motorcycle on a rural road in September 2007 when he had to pee. So he stopped to take care of business by the side of the road. The next thing he knew, he was waking up in a Zagreb hospital.
Don't Go There: Djindjic had been struck by lightning. Doctors think the lightning bolt must have grounded itself through his urine stream. "I don't remember what happened," he said later. "One minute I was taking a leak and the next thing I knew I was in hospital." Luckily, all Djindjic suffered were minor burns on his chest and arms.

*   *   *

AUTHORS ON FILM

*The top five authors whose works have been made
into films (with the number of films made)*

Stephen King: 86
W. Somerset Maugham: 64
Ernest Hemingway: 29
John Grisham: 10
J.K. Rowling: 7

U.S. city with the most lightning: Tampa, Florida (100 "thunderstorm days" per year).

FACT-OPOLY

Thimble-size tidbits about Monopoly, one of the world's most popular board games.

• There are hundreds of versions of Monopoly, themed for sports teams, cities, movies, and TV shows, including *Seinfeld, Star Trek, The Simpsons, American Idol, Family Guy,* and *Planet Earth.* (That game's "Boardwalk," or most expensive property, is Antarctica.)

• There are also dozens of unofficial "opoly" games, including Bible-opoly, Dog-opoly, Cocktail-opoly, Dinosauropoly, Ghetto-opoly, Pot-opoly (about growing marijuana), and Make Your Own-opoly.

• A luxury edition sold by Dunhill of London in 1974 included a leather game board, nine-karat gold hotels, and silver tokens. Only one was made. It sold for $25,000.

• Longest game ever played in a moving elevator: 384 hours.

• Often-overlooked rule: If a player lands on a property and opts not to buy it, the property must be auctioned off.

• Each game comes with $15,140 in play money.

• The first sanctioned Monopoly tournament took place at the University of Pittsburgh in 1961. Four days in, all the money had been dispersed to the players. But according to the rules, the game isn't over when the bank is broke, so they wired a request for more money to Parker Brothers, the game's publisher. The company sent $1 million in Monopoly money via chartered plane and armored car.

• Only musical groups with a Monopoly version: The Beatles and KISS.

• Monopoly was popular in Cuba before the rise of Fidel Castro, who banned the capitalist game and ordered all copies destroyed.

• Neiman Marcus sold a Monopoly game made out of solid chocolate in 1978.

• In 2009 Kenneth Reppke of Fraser, Michigan, was arrested on an assault charge for hitting a friend in the head because she wouldn't sell him Boardwalk and Park Place during a Monopoly game.

Official record for the longest game of Monopoly played in a treehouse: 286 hours.

DON'T BE AFRAID...

...of these quotes about being afraid.

"To conquer fear is the beginning of wisdom."
—Bertrand Russell

"Courage is fear that has said its prayers."
—Dorothy Bernard

"Fear makes strangers of people who would be friends."
—Shirley MacLaine

"It is easy to be brave from a safe distance."
—Aesop

"Fear is a disease that eats away at logic and makes man inhuman."
—Marian Anderson

"If we let things terrify us, life will not be worth living."
—Chief Seneca

"Whatever you fear most has no power. It is your fear that has the power."
—Oprah Winfrey

"Courage is not the absence of fear, but the capacity for action despite our fears."
—John McCain

"No one is afraid of yesterday."
—Renata Adler

"Some have been thought brave because they were afraid to run away."
—Ralph Waldo Emerson

"There are times when fear is good. It must keep its watchful place at the heart's controls. There is advantage in the wisdom won from pain."
—Aeschylus

"Fear has a large shadow, but he himself is small."
—J. Ruth Gendler

"Anything I've ever done that ultimately was worthwhile initially scared me to death."
—Betty Bender

"Courage is the art of being the only one who knows you're scared to death."
—Earl Wilson

"There was never any fear of failure for me. If I miss a shot, so what?"
—Michael Jordan

JERSEY NUMBERS

*Uncle John always wore #2, for obvious reasons. Here are the
reasons some other athletes wore the jersey numbers they did.*

• **SIDNEY CROSBY**, captain of the NHL's Pittsburgh Penguins,
wears #87. Reason: His birthdate is August 7, 1987, or 8/7/87.

• **DAN MARINO** wore #13 as the Miami Dolphins quarterback,
the same number he wore as a kid in Little League baseball. His
dad, who was the coach, let the rest of the team choose their jer-
seys first. By the time Marino got to pick, all that was left was #13.

• **PENNY HARDAWAY** wore #1 when he played in the NBA—
because his first name is Penny, or one cent.

• **WAYNE GRETZKY** wore #9 in kiddie hockey leagues in tribute to his favorite player, Gordie Howe, who was also #9. When
he joined his first semipro team in 1978, #9 was taken, so he
opted for #99 and wore it throughout his NHL career.

• **JAN STENERUD**, an NFL kicker, was #3 because a team gets
three points for a field goal, and because he had a ritual of tapping
his foot on the ground three times before every kick.

• **BILL VOISELLE** pitched for three Major League baseball
teams from 1942 to 1950, and wore #96 because he was from the
town of Ninety Six, South Carolina.

• **JORDIN TOOTOO**, who plays for the Nashville Predators of
the NHL, wears #22...to match his last name.

• **DWAYNE WADE**, star of the NBA's Miami Heat, sports #3
because: 1) He's a devout Christian (so he believes in the Holy
Trinity), 2) he dribbles the ball three times before every free throw,
and 3) he played in the NCAA basketball championship in '03.

• **PAUL DADE** of the Cleveland Indians wore #00 because no
team would draft him initially.

• **JAROMÍR JÁGR**, veteran Czech-born hockey star, wears #68
to commemorate 1968, the year of the Prague Spring, a brief period of liberal reform in then-Communist Czechoslovakia.

Sammy Sosa had his swimming pool built in the shape of his jersey number: 21.

EGG ADDLERS
AND PAJAMA POLICE

*And a few other jobs that are out of the mainstream
workforce—but someone has do them.*

EGG ADDLER
If you have too many Canada geese in your yard, or in your
pond, or on the roof of your building, or for any goose over-
population problem in general, you might want to call a "goose
egg addler" to help control further growth. Here's how they do it:
First, the addler approaches a nest (when the geese aren't around)
and places the eggs in a bucket of water. If an egg sinks, he coats it
with vegetable oil, which prevents oxygen from entering and gases
from escaping. That stops the embryo from developing further.
The eggs are then placed back into the nest, which fools the
mother into thinking she's nesting on live eggs—otherwise she'll
lay more eggs. If the eggs float, it means an air sac has developed
in the egg, and the embryo has developed beyond the point where
it can be killed humanely, so those eggs are replaced in the nest
and allowed to develop into goslings. Egg addling is regulated by
wildlife services in Canada and most of the United States, and you
must have a permit to do it.

PAJAMA POLICE
Authorities in Shanghai, China, spent billions of dollars preparing
to host World Expo 2010, a cultural and trade fair designed to
show off the "new" Shanghai as one of the most modern, forward-
looking cities in the world. But the fact that a lot of Shanghainese
like to wear their PJs on the street didn't quite jibe with that
image. How did pajama-wear become the fashion of choice in
Shanghai? For years, people lived in *shikumen*—cramped commu-
nal houses with shared toilets and kitchens. The concept of personal space grew to include first the courtyard, then the street,
and finally shops beyond. In the 1970s, that led to people young
and old wearing their pajamas wherever they went. It wasn't
uncommon to see middle-aged couples in matching sleepwear

Brine shrimp can survive in water that is six times as salty as seawater.

strolling in the evening, or young housewives in Pretty Kitty prints buying produce at the market. So, in late 2009, the government began a campaign to make people get dressed. Bright red signs were posted in neighborhoods with the message, "Pajamas don't go out the door; be a civilized resident for the Expo." Pop stars appeared in TV ads warning that wearing PJs to the mall was a fashion no-no. Finally, teams of "pajama police" were dispatched to patrol the city for outlaw pajama wearers, although enforcement leaned more on shaming the scofflaw into compliance rather than with actual arrests. Did it work? Not really. There may have been fewer people in pajamas during the Expo, but there were still plenty...and the cherished Shanghai pajama tradition lives on.

AIRPLANE REPOSSESSOR

When private jet owners fall behind on their payments, somebody has to repossess their flying machines. Enter the airplane "repo" men. These people have to be certified pilots capable of flying many different types of aircraft. They also have to be courageous: Nick Popovich, president of an airplane repossession company based in Indiana, was once called to repossesses a Gulfstream jet from an airport in South Carolina. When he arrived, he was met by a group of neo-nazis, armed with shotguns, who had been hired to guard the plane. One held a pistol to Popovich's temple and told him to leave or he'd "blow his f***ing head off." Popovich told him to go ahead. Then he boarded the plane and flew it away. Pay: Popovich says he makes as much as $900,000 per job. And he's one of only a few airplane repossessors in the world.

MORE WEIRD JOBS

Monument crack filler: These workers use gallons of silicone caulk to plug the cracks in massive stone monuments like Mt. Rushmore.

Diener: In the undertaking world, a *diener* is someone who cleans and prepares a dead body for autopsy at the morgue. It comes from the German *leichendiener*, which means "corpse servant."

Hot walker: If this conjures up an image of someone tippy-toeing across a bed of hot coals, think again. A hot walker is the stable hand who cools off a horse after a race by walking it up and down the paddock. This job can be a matter of life—thoroughbreds can suffer kidney failure if they aren't "hot-walked."

World's largest democracy: India, with more than half a billion voters.

THE PEE-MOBILE

We wrote a paragraph about this in Uncle John's Unsinkable Bathroom Reader *and it fascinated us so much that we wanted to share more details. It's real science...and it could be coming to an automobile near you soon.*

BACKGROUND

Dr. Gerardine Botte is an Associate Professor of Chemical Engineering at Ohio University. She's also the founder and director of the school's Electrochemical Engineering Research Laboratory (EERL). Among its many projects, the EERL develops technology for devices known as fuel cells.

Fuel cells are devices that convert a fuel of some kind (Botte's group was working on hydrogen) into electricity. They've been around for a long time—NASA used them for the *Apollo* moon landings in the late 1960s and early '70s. But they've never been commercially viable, thanks in large part to the high costs associated with obtaining and storing the hydrogen.

STREAM OF CONSCIOUSNESS

One way to obtain hydrogen is to pass an electric current through water to separate the hydrogen atoms—the "H"s in H_2O—from the oxygen atoms—the "O"s—using a process called *electrolysis*. Because the hydrogen and oxygen atoms are bound together very tightly, it takes a great deal of electricity to break these bonds.

Another problem with this technique is that fresh water works best for the fuel-cell conversion...and it's scarce. Only three percent of the water on Earth is fresh; the rest is salt water. And very little of that three percent is available to humans for drinking, crop irrigation, and other uses. So it's doubtful that hydrogen will ever be extracted from clean, fresh water on a large scale.

But what about *dirty* fresh water? That's the idea that came to Dr. Botte several years ago when she was driving home from a conference on fuel cell technology: Why not extract hydrogen from wastewater, which is widely available, virtually free, and not in great demand? Botte soon narrowed her focus to one waste stream in particular: urine.

World's largest bowling alley: the Nagoya Grand Bowl in Japan. It has 156 lanes.

PEE 101

Urine in wastewater contains ammonia (NH_3), a compound consisting of one atom of nitrogen and three atoms of hydrogen. And as Dr. Botte confirmed when she subjected urine to electrolysis, it's a good candidate for hydrogen production because the hydrogen and nitrogen atoms in ammonia are not bound together as tightly as the hydrogen and oxygen atoms in water are.

Only five percent as much energy is needed to break the ammonia molecules apart, and because each molecule contains *three* hydrogen atoms, not two as in H_2O, more hydrogen is freed each time a molecule is split up. Less energy spent and more atoms freed makes extracting hydrogen from urine much cheaper than extracting it from fresh water—90¢ for the energy equivalent of a gallon of gas vs. $7.10 for hydrogen electrolyzed from water, Botte says. And best of all, fuel cells provide clean energy, because when hydrogen and oxygen are combined to generate electricity, the only "exhaust" created by the process is water (which could be drunk to aid in the production of more urine). No greenhouse gases are released at all.

With an estimated five million tons of ammonia entering the United States waste stream as human and animal urine each year—enough to provide electricity to 900,000 homes—the supply of "raw materials" for hydrogen production is enormous and almost completely untapped. But not for long: Botte sees a day when hydrogen extraction will be a standard function of wastewater treatment plants. "Ammonia," she says, "is our future fuel."

COMING SOON

As of the fall of 2009, Botte's pee-powered "electrolyzer" prototype was about the size of a paperback book and produced less than one watt of power, not even enough to light an incandescent lightbulb. But Botte says the technology is ready to be scaled up to car size. "With the right partnership, I believe we could have pee-powered cars capable of 60 miles per gallon on the road within a year," she told *Wired* magazine.

And if her predictions are accurate, cars powered by fuel cells will have pee tanks, just as cars today have gas tanks, because hydrogen is much easier to store as a component of wastewater than in its pure form. Pure hydrogen is a gas; it must be kept

extremely cold and stored in pressure tanks to be useful as a fuel.
Botte's design calls for the urine to be converted into hydrogen
right inside the automobile, and only as needed, eliminating the
cost and difficulty of storing hydrogen in its pure form.

But you still won't be able to pee your way to work, unless you
have a medical condition or work really close to home. A healthy
adult produces only 1½ quarts of urine a day, not enough to get
very far. "I wish we humans produced enough urine to run a whole
car," Botte says. "Maybe we could run some minor applications,
like the car stereo or something like that."

URINE GOOD COMPANY

Here are a few more waste products with the real potential to
become the fuels of the future:

• **Animal dung.** Professor Botte isn't the only person pondering
the power of pee: Scientists at Japan's Obihiro University have
developed a method of obtaining ammonia from animal urine and
dung by fermenting it in an oxygen-free environment. As with
Botte's technique, the ammonia is electrolyzed to separate out the
hydrogen, which is then fed into fuel cells to produce electricity.
The scientists estimate that one day's "output" of animal waste
from a typical Japanese farm will produce enough energy to power
a home for three days.

• **Disposable diapers.** In 2007 the British engineering firm
AMEC announced it was building a plant in Quebec, Canada,
that will use a heating process called *pyrolysis* to convert the diapers (and their contents) into a mix of synthetic diesel fuel,
methane gas, and "carbon-rich char." When the plant is up and
running it is expected to convert 30,000 tons of dirty diapers—
about a quarter of all the diapers used each year in Quebec—into
diesel fuel annually.

• **"Turkey waste."** For several years a company called Changing
World Technologies operated a plant in Carthage, Missouri, that
converted the waste from a Butterball Turkey slaughterhouse
(beaks, bones, feathers, guts, etc.) into biodiesel. Capacity: 1,200
tons of turkey parts a week. But neighbors complained about the
smell ("just like burning meat"), and in 2009 the company closed
the plant and filed for bankruptcy.

EAT MY...

Who says you can't eat bottles, boats, or shoe cream?

B ILLBOARD! On Easter Day 2007, British candy retailer Thorntons unveiled an unusual billboard in the Covent Garden district of London. The 14-by-9-foot advertisement was made entirely out of chocolate—10 large chocolate bunnies, 72 giant chocolate eggs, and 128 chocolate panels, for a total of 860 pounds of chocolate. It was eaten by passersby in less than three hours.

SHOE CREAM! If you're ever stranded in the desert with nothing but a jar of shoe cream, pray it's this kind. In 2009 London-based Po-Zu, a retailer specializing in environmentally friendly products, introduced PO-ZU Shoe Cream. It's made from organic coconut oil, and, if your shoes don't need shining, you can use it as lip balm, hair conditioner—or even cooking oil. "You can even spread it on your toast," Po-Zu says on its website.

MONA LISA! In October 2008, to mark the 100th anniversary of Tavr, a meat processing company headquartered in the Russian city of Rostov-on-Don, Russian artists completed reproductions of six classic paintings using only frames, canvas...and sausage. The works exhibited included Leonardo da Vinci's *Mona Lisa*, Vincent Van Gogh's *Sunflowers*, and Picasso's *Girl on a Ball*. And they really looked like the originals. "The biggest trouble," said artist Aleksandr Solomko, "was getting the sausages to stick to the canvas." (They used flavorless gelatin for glue.) Visitors were encouraged to use toothpicks to pick pieces of the "paintings" off the canvases and eat them, which they happily did.

QR CODE! QR codes are similar to the bar codes used to digitally encode prices on store products, but look like random patterns of square dots and blank spots. They're very popular in Japan, where advertisements using QR codes can be found in magazines, on billboards, even on buses. The codes can be read by most Japanese cell-phone cameras, which then provide links to websites where consumers can get more information about the products. In 2010 Montreal-based Clever Cupcakes decided to make the technology tastier—and began offering cupcakes topped with QR codes made of sugar. And they work: If you hold your cell phone to the cupcake, you're directed to the website of the Montreal Science Center, which helped promote the digitally enhanced cakes. Then…enjoy the cupcake!

BOAT! In 2008 the town of Eyemouth, Scotland, held a toy-boat-building contest. The winner: the one that stayed afloat the longest. The catch: All boats had to be made entirely from edible materials. Entrants included a boat made of apples, marshmallows, and strawberries; a trimaran of red pepper, carrot, and licorice root; and a canoe made from an eggplant, with two eggs as cargo. The boats were launched into the waves at Eyemouth Beach. Several hours later, a boat made from sheets of lasagna was declared the most seaworthy, and a sailboat made of chocolate cake won the prize for best overall. (Neither, however, was eaten afterward.)

SAKE BOTTLE! In 2009 officials in the town of Takahama on Honshu Island, Japan, announced the establishment of the "Committee to Reinstate the Sake Bottle Squid." They were referring to *Ika Tokkuri*, traditional Japanese sake bottles made from the skins of squid that are stuffed with rice, molded into bottle form, and allowed to dry. Not only are they edible after use—but it gives the sake a tantalizing bit of squid flavoring. (Mmmm!) The bottles can be used five or six times before eating.

LP! Peter Lardong lost his job at a brewery in Berlin, Germany, in the 1980s, and during his time off decided to make some LPs (as in long-playing records)…out of food. He tried, usually with butter, ice cream, cola, beer, and even sausages, but "none of these things quite made it." Then he tried chocolate: He made a mold of a record, melted chocolate, poured it into the mold, put it in the refrigerator overnight, and in the morning—voilà! The chocolate record actually played. Lardong now sells his chocolate LPs for about $6 apiece, and a Japanese company recently expressed interest in purchasing the patent.

*　　*　　*

"Let the beauty of what you love be what you do." —**Rumi**

UNCLE JOHN'S PAGE OF LISTS

Some random bits from the BRI's bottomless trivia files.

THE NATIONAL SAFETY COUNCIL'S 6 MOST LIKELY WAYS TO DIE
1. Heart disease (Odds: 1 in 6)
2. Cancer (1 in 7)
3. Stroke (1 in 28)
4. Car accident (1 in 85)
5. Intentional self-harm (1 in 115)
6. Accidental poisoning (1 in 139)

WORLD'S 3 MOST POPULAR SPECTATOR SPORTS
1. Soccer
2. Cricket
3. Volleyball

4 BEERS FROM TV CARTOONS
1. Pawtucket Patriot Ale (*Family Guy*)
2. Duff (*The Simpsons*)
3. Alamo (*King of the Hill*)
4. Bendërbrau (*Futurama*)

ONLY 9 MEN TO APPEAR ON THE COVER OF *PLAYBOY* (SO FAR)
1. Peter Sellers
2. Burt Reynolds
3. Steve Martin
4. Donald Trump
5. Dan Aykroyd
6. Jerry Seinfeld
7. Leslie Nielsen
8. Gene Simmons
9. Seth Rogen

THE 6 RICHEST U.S. PRESIDENTS (ADJUSTED FOR INFLATION)
1. John F. Kennedy ($1 billion)
2. George Washington ($525 million)
3. Thomas Jefferson ($212 million)
4. Teddy Roosevelt ($125 million)
5. Andrew Jackson ($119 million)
6. James Madison ($101 million)

THE 3 MOST PERFORMED HIGH SCHOOL PLAYS
1. A *Midsummer Night's Dream* (Shakespeare)
2. *Rumors* (Neil Simon)
3. *The Crucible* (Arthur Miller)

6 OFFICIAL LANGUAGES OF THE U.N.
1. Chinese
2. Russian
3. Spanish
4. English
5. French
6. Arabic

5 PLACES THAT ARE OPEN ON CHRISTMAS
1. John Deere World Headquarters
2. Greater Vancouver Zoo
3. Disney World
4. The theaters of Branson, Missouri
5. Yellowstone National Park

Sigmund Freud's daughter Anna was Marilyn Monroe's therapist.

SALEM WITCH TRIALS: THE FUNGUS THEORY

*More than three centuries after the end of the Salem witch trials,
they continue to defy explanation. In the mid-1970s, a college
undergraduate developed a new theory. Does it hold
water? Read on and decide for yourself.*

SEASON OF THE WITCH

In the bleak winter of 1692, the people of Salem, Massachusetts, hunkered down in their cabins and waited for spring. It was a grim time: There was no fresh food or vegetables, just dried meat and roots to eat. Their mainstay was the coarse bread they baked from the rye grain harvested in the fall.

Shortly after the New Year, the madness began. Elizabeth Parris, 9-year-old daughter of the local preacher, and her cousin, 11-year-old Abigail Williams, suffered from violent fits and convulsions. They lapsed into incoherent rants, had hallucinations, complained of crawly sensations on their skin, and often retreated into dull-eyed trances. Their desperate families turned to the local doctor, who could find nothing physically wrong with them. At his wit's end, he decided there was only one reasonable explanation: witchcraft.

BLAME GAME

Word spread like wildfire through the village: An evil being was hexing the children. Soon, more "victims" appeared, most of them girls under the age of 20. The terrified villagers started pointing fingers of blame, first at an old slave named Tituba, who belonged to the Reverend Parris, then to old women like Sarah Good and Sarah Osborn. The arrests began on February 29; the trials soon followed. That June, 60-year-old Bridget Bishop was the first to be declared guilty of witchcraft and the first to hang. By September, 140 "witches" had been arrested and 19 had been executed. Many of the accused barely escaped the gallows by running into the woods and hiding. Then, sometime over the summer, the demonic fits stopped—and the frenzy of accusation

---

At one point in British history, you could be hanged for "impersonating an Egyptian."

and counter-accusation stopped with them. As passions cooled, the villagers tried to put their community back together again.

UNANSWERED QUESTIONS

What happened to make these otherwise dour Puritans turn on each other with such a destructive frenzy? Over the centuries several theories have been put forth, from the Freudian—that the witch hunt was the result of hysterical tension resulting from centuries of sexual repression—to the exploitive—that it was fabricated as an excuse for a land grab (the farms and homes of all of the victims and many of the accused were confiscated and redistributed to other members of the community). But researchers had never been able to find real evidence to support these theories. Then in the 1970s, a college student in California made a deduction that seemed to explain everything.

In 1976 Linnda Caporael, a psychology major at U.C. Santa Barbara, was told to choose a subject for a term paper in her American History course. Having just seen a production of Arthur Miller's play *The Crucible* (a fictional account of the Salem trials), she decided to write about the witch hunt. "As I began research-ing," she later recalled, "I had one of those 'a-ha!' experiences." The author of one of her sources said he remained at a loss to explain the hallucinations of the villagers of Salem. "It was the word 'hallucinations' that made everything click," said Caporael. Years before, she'd read of a case of ergot poisoning in France where the victims had suffered from hallucinations, and she thought there might be a connection.

THE FUNGUS AMONG US

Ergot is a fungus that infects rye, a grain more commonly used in past centuries to bake bread than it is today. One of the byproducts present in ergot-infected rye is *ergotamine*, which is related to LSD. Toxicologists have known for years that eating bread baked with ergot-contaminated rye can trigger convulsions, delusions, creepy-crawly sensations of the skin, vomiting…and hallucinations. And historians were already aware that the illness caused by ergot poisoning (known as St. Anthony's Fire) was behind several incidents of mass insanity in medieval Europe. Caporael wondered if the same conditions might have been present in Salem.

Frank Sinatra once said rock 'n' roll was only played by "cretinous goons."

They were. Ergot needs warm, damp weather to grow, and those conditions were rife in the fields around Salem in 1691. Rye was the primary grain grown, so there was plenty of it to be infected. Caporael also discovered that most of the accusers lived on the west side of the village, where the fields were chronically marshy, making them a perfect breeding ground for the fungus. The crop harvested in the fall of 1691 would've been baked and eaten during the following winter, which was when the fits of madness began. However, the next summer was unusually dry, which could explain the sudden stop to the bewitchments. No ergot, no madness.

SHE RESTS HER CASE

Caporael continued to research her theory as she pursued her Ph.D., publishing her findings in 1976 in the journal *Science*, which brought her support from the scientific community and attention from the news media. Caporael has been careful to say that her theory only accounts for the *initial* cause of the Salem witch hunts. As the frenzy grew in scope and consequence, she's convinced that the actual sequence of events probably included not only real moments of mass hysteria but also some overacting on the part of the accusers (motivated as much by fear of being accused themselves as by any actual malice toward the accused).

OTHER POSSIBILITIES

Caporael's theory remains one of the most convincing explanations for what started the madness that tore apart the village of Salem, Massachusetts, in 1692...but there are others.

• **Encephalitis Lethargica.** Historian Laurie Win Carlson compared the symptoms of the accused in Salem (violent fits, trance or coma-like states) with those experienced by victims of an outbreak of *Encephalitis Lethargica*, an acute inflammation of the brain, between 1915 and 1926. The trials were likely "a response to unexplained physical and neurological behaviors resulting from an epidemic of encephalitis," she says.

• **Jimson Weed.** This toxic weed, sometimes called devil's trumpet or locoweed, grows wild in Massachusetts. Ingesting it can cause hallucinations, delirium, and bizarre behavior.

ONCE UPON A TIME...

*What's the most important part of a good story? The first line—
a great one will leave you anxious to read more. Here
are some great opening lines from famous books.*

"It was a bright cold day in April, and the clocks were striking thirteen."
—George Orwell, *1984*

"All happy families are alike but an unhappy family is unhappy after its own fashion."
—Leo Tolstoy, *Anna Karenina*

"In a hole in the ground there lived a hobbit."
—J.R.R. Tolkien, *The Hobbit*

"It is a truth universally acknowledged, that a single man in possession of a good fortune, must be in want of a wife."
—Jane Austen, *Pride and Prejudice*

"Once upon a time there was...'A king!' my young readers will instantly exclaim. No, children, you are wrong. Once upon a time there was a piece of wood."
—Carlo Collodi, *Pinocchio*

"It was a queer, sultry summer, the summer they electrocuted the Rosenbergs, and I didn't know what I was doing in New York."
—Sylvia Plath, *The Bell Jar*

"In an old house in Paris that was covered in vines lived twelve little girls in two straight lines."
—Ludwig Bemelmans, *Madeline*

"In our family, there was no clear line between religion and fly fishing."
—Norman Maclean, *A River Runs Through It*

"Nobody was really surprised when it happened, not really, not at the subconscious level where savage things grow."
—Stephen King, *Carrie*

"All nights should be so dark, all winters so warm, all head-lights so dazzling."
—Martin Cruz Smith, *Gorky Park*

But can it bury its poop? A zebra's night vision is about as good as a cat's.

"When I think back now, I realize that the only thing John Wilson and I actually ever had in common was the fact that at one time or another each of us had ran over someone with an automobile."
—Peter Viertel,
White Hunter Black Heart

"Ours is essentially a tragic age, so we refuse to take it tragically."
—D.H. Lawrence,
Lady Chatterley's Lover

"A throng of bearded men in sad-colored garments and gray, steeple-crowned hats, intermixed with women, some wearing hoods, and others bareheaded, was assembled in front of a wooden edifice, the door of which was heavily timbered with oak, and studded with iron spikes."
—Nathaniel Hawthorne,
The Scarlet Letter

"If you're going to read this, don't bother. After a couple of pages, you won't want to be here. So forget it. Go away. Get out while you're still in one piece. Save yourself."
—Chuck Palahniuk,
Choke

"Maybe I shouldn't have given the guy who pumped my stomach my phone number, but who cares?"
—Carrie Fisher,
Postcards from the Edge

"To the red country and part of the gray country of Oklahoma, the last rains came gently, and they did not cut the scarred earth."
—John Steinbeck,
The Grapes of Wrath

"The drought had lasted now for ten million years, and the reign of the terrible lizards had long since ended."
—Arthur C. Clarke,
2001: A Space Odyssey

"One January day, thirty years ago, the little town of Hanover, anchored on a windy Nebraska tableland, was trying not to be blown away."
—Willa Cather, *O Pioneers!*

"There was no possibility of taking a walk that day."
—Charlotte Brontë,
Jane Eyre

"All children, except one, grow up."
—J. M. Barrie, *Peter Pan*

HOW TO MAKE PRISON WINE

The bad news: You're in jail. The good news: You can
still enjoy one of the finer things in life—wine. You
just have to make it yourself. In the toilet.

W**HAT YOU'LL NEED:** several thick black garbage bags; a few slices of bread or rolls; some warm water; a straw; sugar packets or cubes; and something fruity with sugar in it, such as fruit juice, tomatoes, or Kool-Aid packets.

DIRECTIONS

Step 1. You'll start by making a double- or triple-thick brewing chamber. Do this with a plastic trash bag stuck inside another trash bag stuck inside another trash bag.

Step 2. Pour in a gallon of warm water.

Step 3. Add as much fruity material as you can muster. This can be anything from leftover fruit juice to orange rinds, raisins, tomatoes, Kool-Aid, even ketchup packets...or a little bit of each—whatever you can salvage from the limited offerings of the prison cafeteria. The fermentation process turns sugar into alcohol, so the more sugar or sugar-rich foods and liquids you have, the stronger the wine will be. Throw in about 50 sugar packets or sugar cubes, and add a new one every other day or so.

Step 4. Fermentation is triggered by the addition of yeast. Since yeast packets aren't readily available in prison, you'll have to get creative. Bread has yeast in it, but what really has a large concentration of yeast is bread *mold*. So snag some bread from the cafeteria when it's still fresh and moist and put it on a shelf for a few days until it starts to get moldy. When the mold forms, the bread is ready to go into the wine bag. Think ahead: The moldy bread should go into the chamber at the same time as the fruity material.

Step 5. Seal the bag by knotting it tightly. Run it under hot tap water every day for about 15 minutes and wrap it in a blanket to keep it warm.

Step 6. As the yeast in the bread mold ferments the sugar into alcohol, it creates carbon dioxide as a by-product, and that has to have some way to escape. So ventilate the chamber by cutting a tiny hole in the garbage bags and inserting a straw.

Step 7. Hide it. (Is there a prison anywhere in the world that lets inmates make their own liquor?) Three days will produce a slightly alcoholic wine, but wait a week and the wine will ferment into a strong—but horrible-tasting—brew of about 13 percent alcohol, the higher end of commercially available wine's alcoholic content.

Step 8. When the week is up, wait. You can't drink it quite yet. You have to "shock" the wine to stop the fermentation process. Here's how: Place the bag (careful of the straw and straw-hole) in the toilet bowl. Flush the toilet every few minutes for about an hour to allow the cold water to wash over the outside of the bag, cooling the wine and ending fermentation.

Step 9. Enjoy. (And try not to get caught.)

*   *   *

SORRY, WRONG NUMBER

In January 1971, President Miton Obote of the central African republic of Uganda learned that the head of the country's army, a former Ugandan heavyweight boxing champion named Idi Amin, was planning a coup. Obote left for a planned trip to Singapore, and while there telephoned his ministers and instructed them to remove Amin from command. Big mistake: The operator handling the call was a member of the country's Kwaka tribe—the same tribe as Amin. Obote was a member of the Lango tribe. The operator passed the information on to Amin, and on January 25, 1971, he ordered the army's mostly Kwaka troops to seize the capital city of Kampala, along with Obote's official residence. Amin ruled the country for the next eight years—all because of an ill-placed telephone call.

The backs of your knees are home to more species of microbes than your gut is.

THE #2 AMENDMENT

Now that more states are allowing citizens to carry concealed weapons in public, gun-toters face a problem that's plagued law enforcement for years: When you have to use the restroom, what do you do with the gun?

GUN OWNER: Dean Wawers, 57, a deputy with the Cass County Sheriff's Department in Fargo, North Dakota

ARMED & DANGEROUS: In January 2008, Wawers had to make a pit stop at the county courthouse, where the sheriff's department has its offices. As he prepared to answer nature's call, he removed his .40-caliber Glock semiautomatic from its holster and hung it—from the trigger guard—on a coat hook inside the stall. For those readers who do not handle firearms regularly, the trigger guard prevents the trigger from being struck by foreign objects, like, say, *coat hooks*, which might cause the gun to go off when you don't want it to. Detective Wawers was reminded of this when he reached for the gun as he was preparing to exit the stall: The trigger caught on the hook, causing the gun to fire a round into the ceiling.

WHAT HAPPENED: Thankfully, the only injury was to the detective's reputation. No charges were filed against Wawers, a 35-year veteran with the sheriff's department, but at last report an internal investigation was underway.

GUN OWNER: Dr. Richard L. Pinegar, 52, an emergency-room physician at Salem Hospital in Massachusetts

ARMED & DANGEROUS: Pinegar was working the night shift at the hospital when he had to use the bathroom. He set his .38-caliber Smith & Wesson revolver on the counter…and then when he was paged by another physician, he quickly left the restroom, forgetting to take the gun with him. Another hospital staffer found it and alerted security, who called the police.

WHAT HAPPENED: Dr. Pinegar was suspended while the incident was investigated; then he was fired. Pinegar wasn't available for comment, but his lawyer, Paul Cirel, says he wasn't aware of the hospital's anti-firearm policy. (Even hospital security guards aren't allowed to carry guns.) "He grew up in Iowa around guns,"

Cirel said. "He's a member of a sportsmen's club, and he keeps his gun locked in a gun safe. He also works crazy hours in a hospital ER and has to find his car in the parking lot at night. It's his decision to carry a gun and he's done it following the law."

GUN OWNER: Cheri Maples, captain of the Madison, Wisconsin, police department

ARMED & DANGEROUS: In February 2004, Maples attended a training session at a local community college. After the session, she went to the restroom. While there, she checked her handgun to be sure that it was properly loaded...and it went off, firing a bullet into the restroom wall.

WHAT HAPPENED: Maples was suspended for one day (without pay).

FOOTNOTE: Her punishment was similar to the one Madison Police Chief Richard Williams received in 1998 when he hid his service weapon in his oven at home, then forgot about it until he preheated the oven—BANG!—to cook a turkey.

GUN OWNER: Debra Monce, 56, of Land O' Lakes, Florida

ARMED & DANGEROUS: In July 2009, Monce was at the Clarion Hotel in Tampa, Florida, when she had to visit the ladies' room. As she was taking care of business, the gun she was carrying slipped out of her waist holster, clattered to the floor, and went off. The bullet struck the woman in the next stall, 54-year-old Janifer Bliss, in the lower left thigh.

WHAT HAPPENED: Bliss was taken to Tampa General Hospital with minor injuries. At last report the State Attorney's Office was still debating whether to file charges against Monce, who had a concealed weapons permit. "The holster was an open holster with no snaps or clips to hold the gun in place," a police spokesperson said.

❊   ❊   ❊

THE 7 EUROPEAN COUNTRIES
THAT STILL HAVE MONARCHIES

Spain, Denmark, Sweden, The Netherlands,
Belgium, Norway, and the United Kingdom.

And yours? 50% of laundry is washed in warm water, 35% in cold, and 15% in hot.

EAT THE WORLD

Have you ever noticed that a lot of the food Americans eat comes from other countries? It's almost like the entire supermarket is one big "ethnic food" aisle. Here are some examples.

KIELBASA: These sausages come from several places in Eastern Europe, primarily Poland and the Ukraine. The word *kielbasa* is Polish, and simply means "sausage." It entered the English language relatively recently—in the 1950s.

PESTO: This thick basil-and-pine-nut sauce comes from the Liguria region of northwest Italy, where it's been eaten since at least the 1600s. The earliest mention of pesto in the United States was a 1935 article about Italian food in the *Washington Post*, but the dish didn't become popular with Americans until the 1980s. *Pesto* means "crushed."

CASABA: The first of these succulent melons came to the U.S. in the 1880s from Kasaba, Turkey, hence the name.

DATES: Date palms are native to the Middle East, and were well established around the entire Mediterranean more than 5,000 years ago. The were brought to Califor-nia by Spanish missionaries starting in 1769, and are still grown there, as well as in parts of Nevada and Arizona. The name "date" comes from the ancient Greek *daktylos*—which originally meant "finger" or "toe" because of the resemblance of the date fruit to human digits.

WATERMELONS: The All-American fruit, right? Wrong. They're native to southern Africa. Watermelons were eaten by Ancient Egyptians 3,000 years ago, and by the Middle Ages, had spread to Asia and Europe. There is some disagreement as to how they first made it to the U.S. Some historians believe early Spanish explorers gave seeds to Native Americans in the Southeast in the 1500s. Others say they were brought by African slaves in the 1600s.

SALSA: Mixing tomatoes, chilis, and other ingredients has been done in Mexico since the time of the Aztecs. When the Spanish encountered the condiment in the

---

Too hard to make? 99% of all American households purchase pre-made soup.

1500s, they called it *salsa*— Spanish for "sauce." It made its way into English language in the 1840s, and today is the most popular condiment in the United States.

TORTILLA: Probably older than salsa, this cooked flatbread made from crushed corn has been used by Native Mexicans for wrapping around meats, fish, and vegetables— even insects and snails—for thousands of years. In the native Nahuatl language they were called *tlaxcalli*; the Spanish changed that to *tortilla*.

QUICHE: You may know that quiche came from France, but how many people know they got it from the Germans? It was first made many centuries ago in a German kingdom in what is now the northeastern French province of Lorraine. The name even comes from the German word for cake: *küchen*. It was first introduced to North America in the 1930s, and became popular after World War II.

BEETS: They're native to the Mediterranean region, where beet leaves were eaten and used medicinally for thousands of years. Who started eating the roots? The Romans. But beets only became popular in northern Europe in the 1700s, after German scientists discovered that sugar could be made from them. Beets were first exported to the U.S. in the 1830s, and were first grown here commercially at the farm of Ebenezer Herrick Dyer in Alvarado, California, in 1879.

MINESTRONE: Italian immigrants brought this hearty vegetable soup to the United States in the 1800s. The name means "big soup."

WALNUTS. The trees, commonly known as English walnuts, are native to the Middle East and were cultivated at least 4,000 years ago in ancient Babylon. Spanish missionaries first planted them in California in the early 1800s. Also known as mission walnuts and Persian walnuts, almost all commercially-grown walnuts in the United States are this variety, as opposed to black walnuts, which are native to North America.

* * *

"Let us all be happy and live within our means, even if we have to borrow the money to do it with."
—**Artemus Ward**

Only primate species that regularly walk on two legs: humans and gibbons.

LAST WORDS

Everybody loves reading the last words of famous people—Pablo Picasso's, for example, were "Drink to me." Not everyone is as famous as Picasso, but their last words can tell quite a story.

GILES COREY (1611–1692)

Corey was a British farmer in the town of Salem in Massachusetts Colony. In 1692 the 80-year-old man and his 72-year-old wife Martha were charged with being witches in the infamous Salem witch trials. Ordered to plead "guilty" or "not guilty," Corey refused. A person who refused to enter a plea could not be tried—but could be induced to plea via the *peine forte et dure*, which is French for "hard and forceful punishment." That meant that Corey was stripped naked and forced to lie on the ground. A board was then placed over him, and large stones were laid on it. When ordered to enter a plea, Corey would only say, "More weight," daring officials to put more stones on the board. They did. After two days of this, with more and more stones crushing his body, Corey once more cried out "More weight!"—and died. (Martha was executed by hanging two days later.)

MAJOR-GENERAL SIR WILLIAM ERSKINE (1770–1813)

Erskine was a British Army officer who fought in the Napoleonic Wars that ravaged Europe in the early 1800s, as well as a member of the British Parliament. He was also mentally unstable. One night in 1813, after having served for several years in Portugal, he jumped from a high window in a building in Lisbon. Bystanders rushed to his side and heard Erskine mutter, "Now, why did I do that?" before he fell into unconsciousness. He died three days later.

MARY SURRATT (1823–1865)

Surratt was convicted of taking part in the conspiracy to assassinate President Abraham Lincoln in 1865, and that year became the first woman ever executed by the United States government. As she stood on the scaffold and the rope was being placed around

---

Price of gold in 1969: $41 an ounce. In 2009: $972 an ounce.

her neck, she turned to the guard and said, "Please don't let me fall." But she did fall...through the trap door of the scaffold as she was being hanged.

HECTOR HUGH MUNRO (1870–1916)

H.H. Munro was a British journalist, satirist, and author better known by his pen name, Saki. When World War I began in 1914, Munro, 43 and officially too old to join, nonetheless enlisted in the British Army as a regular soldier, refusing several officer's commissions. On the morning of November 13, 1916, he was with his regiment on the front lines in France when a soldier in his group lit a cigarette. According to witnesses, Munro shouted, "Put out that bloody cigarette!" which gave his location away...and he was shot by a German sniper.

CAPTAIN LAWRENCE OATES (1880–1912)

Oates was an English explorer of Antarctica. In early 1910, he was one of four men selected to accompany Robert Falcon Scott on his Terra Nova Expedition to be the first to make it to the South Pole. They made it—but found a tent and a note from Roald Amundsen saying he'd beaten them there by 35 days. On the return trip weather conditions rapidly deteriorated and food supplies ran low. One of the four other men died on February 17. On March 16, in terrible health and fearing that he was holding the team back, Oates said to the other men, "I am just going outside and may be some time," and walked out of their tent. There was a raging blizzard outside, the temperature was about −40°F, and Oates hadn't even put on his boots. He was never seen again and was likely dead within minutes. Unfortunately, Oates's sacrifice did not save the three other men, all of whom died nine days later. This story is only known from Scott's diary, which was found by a rescue team several months later.

ROBERT FALCON SCOTT (1868–1912)

From a diary entry entitled "Message to the Public," the last thing that Robert Falcon Scott is believed to have written, which was meant to explain and defend the South Pole trip to the British people: "We took risks. We knew we took them. Things have come out against us. We have no cause for complaint."

THE DATAR FLOP

*History is full of inventions that were just a little too
far ahead of their time. Here's one of them.*

GOING UNDER

In 1948 Canadian navy engineer Jim Belyea was assigned
to worry full-time about the new Russian submarines.
There was reason to worry: These new subs were faster and able to
stay underwater for longer periods than the German U-boats the
Allies had battled just a few years earlier, and Canada's top brass
were concerned that the Russian subs could converge on a convoy
of ships for a coordinated underwater ambush. They ordered Belyea
to develop a countermeasure that would keep a lid on the Russians.
And he did.

Belyea's big idea was the "Digital Automated Tracking And
Resolving" system, or DATAR for short. It would be able to create a
visual display of the positions and movements of all attackers and
defenders in a sea battle, but it required stretching the limited capa-
bilities of 1940s computers. Not just that, he wanted to link together every Canadian navy ship and submarine so they could share
battle information instantaneously. If one ship saw a new attacker
coming, the operators could instantly give its location, speed, and
direction to the others. Every ship's sonar and radar information
would go into the mix, too, so that all ships would constantly be on
the same page. Instead of the chaotic system of radio operators
shouting over each other to report ship information, Canadian officers could instantly see every bit of known information about their
battle zone on a glowing cathode ray screen. The brass loved it.

GETTING THE BALL ROLLING

Belyea got the okay to make a prototype, with the hope that it
might someday be used on the 100 new ships the navy had just
ordered. He began working with the Canadian subsidiary of Ferran-
ti, a U.K. electronics firm, and by 1953, they had a prototype ready
for testing. It was unlike anything that had ever been seen before.
For one thing, it could store data for 500 ships on its magnetic
drum, an early form of the modern hard drive. And there was

---

another advancement: DATAR had a brand-new tool for entering data: the very first trackball, invented by engineers Tom Cranston and Fred Longstaff. (The trackball's main moving part was a small bowling ball from Canadian five-pin bowling.)

WAR GAMES

That fall Belyea's team tried out the system with a three-ship convoy on a simulated Lake Ontario battle zone. It worked exactly as planned. That success put Canada way ahead of American and British engineers, and there was more on the line than just the cost of the system—there was prestige. Canada's nascent electronics industry had a chance to lead the world in technology and sell the system to the well-financed navies of the U.S. and England, not to mention all of their NATO allies.

Canada promptly (and eagerly) demonstrated DATAR to American and British military officials, and they were duly impressed. It's been reported that one American officer was so convinced it was a fake, he crawled under the table to see if there was somebody under there manipulating the dots on the screen. But when invited to partner with Canada in financing further implementation, both countries declined. While there might have been a reluctance to admit being bested by Canada, they had other, more practical reasons as well.

BUGS IN THE MACHINE

For one, DATAR was going to be very expensive to build and debug. Worse, it was huge and heavy, making it cumbersome even on full battleships, much less on submarines. Finally, DATAR used vacuum tubes—almost 20,000 of them. That many tubes in one place require a lot of electricity, a refrigerated room to neutralize the copious heat they generate, and continuous vacuum tube replacement. The tubes burned out relatively quickly; the DATAR prototype was frequently nonoperational, sometimes for days at a time.

The Canadian navy couldn't afford to do it alone, and the Americans and British wouldn't budge. So the Canadians offered to rebuild the system using a new American invention that was proving to be much smaller, lighter, cooler, longer-lived, and less of an energy hog: the transistor. No dice. The Americans and British came, saw, and decided to build their own systems...and DATAR was shelved for good.

GODFATHER, MEET THE GODFATHER

What happens when one of Hollywood's most famous movie mobsters meets up with the genuine article? Here's the story of one of the most unusual "sit-downs" in mob or movie history. Bada-bing!

CONNECTED

Even if you've never heard of Rocco Musacchia, if you're a fan of gangster films like *Prizzi's Honor* (1985), *Donnie Brasco* (1997), and *Mickey Blue Eyes* (1999), you're familiar with his work. Musacchia works as a "technical advisor" on mob films. He teaches Hollywood actors how to act like gangsters—"how a wiseguy dresses, how he walks and talks and wears his hat," as he puts it. He grew up around such real-life characters in Brooklyn and has maintained his contacts over the years.

In the summer of 1989, Musacchia was working on *The Freshman,* starring Marlon Brando and Matthew Broderick. In the film, Brando parodies his role in *The Godfather* by playing a mobster named Carmine Sabatini, who just happens to look and even dress like *The Godfather's* Vito Corleone.

LET'S EAT

One evening after filming a scene in the Little Italy neighborhood of New York, Brando and his co-stars went to a nearby Italian restaurant to eat dinner and watch the prizefight between Sugar Ray Leonard and Thomas Hearns.

The evening got off to a bad start. Hearns was widely thought to have won the 12-round bout, but the judges scored it a draw, which drove fight fans like Brando crazy. Making matters worse, Brando was on a diet: He had to settle for a plate of broiled fish while everyone around him feasted on some of the best Italian food in the city. He was in a foul mood, but he perked up when word filtered into the restaurant that John Gotti, the infamous head of the Gambino crime family, had just walked into his headquarters, the Ravenite Social Club, right across the street.

AN OFFER HE COULDN'T REFUSE

What happened next depends on whose version of the story you believe. In his autobiography, Brando claimed Gotti sent over one of his goons with an invitation to drop by the club. "That's nice," Brando claimed he said in reply. "I was curious, and with four or five other people from the picture, I went across the street."

Musacchia remembers the event differently. He knew Gotti and offered to introduce Brando to the Dapper Don. Brando, says Musacchia, could hardly contain his excitement: "His eyes lit up. Nothing else ever impressed him. He was the biggest movie star in the world and here he was, literally star-struck."

Whichever version is true, Brando, Broderick, and a third actor, Bruno Kirby (who played the young Peter Clemenza in *The Godfather II*), were soon making their way across the street with Musacchia to meet John Gotti in his lair.

CLOSE ENCOUNTER

According to Gotti's daughter Victoria, the visit went off without a hitch. "Brando was telling jokes all night and doing magic tricks," she said. "Dad was doing what he does best, telling stories. And they just enjoyed each other's company."

Brando paints a different picture in his memoirs: According to him, the meeting was not the fun-filled encounter that one might expect. When Brando entered the Ravenite Social Club—"a shabby store-front...filled with Mafiosi," as he put it, Gotti and several of his cohorts were seated around a table playing cards. Gotti did not rise to greet Brando, though he did shake Brando's hand. Brando interpreted this to mean that Gotti did not want to lose face in front of his men by fawning over a Hollywood star, even if this was the guy who played Don Corleone. Gotti was not about to let down his guard.

The Dapper Don introduced Brando to his men, one of whom joked, "Will the real Godfather please stand up!" That got a laugh, but when Brando tried to add to the levity by joking that nobody made any money betting on the Leonard/Hearns fight, Gotti said nothing. Instead, he gestured toward the big sign on the wall that read,

THIS PLACE IS BUGGED. WHATEVER YOU SAY
WILL BE USED AGAINST YOU.

THE CARD FATHER

Brando liked to perform magic tricks and often carried a deck of cards to use as an icebreaker around awestruck fans. This room was about as tense as any he had ever been in, so he took out his cards. Gotti must have thought he wanted to play poker, because when he saw the cards he snapped, "If you wanna play in here, you don't deal."

"Take a card," Brando told him. Gotti picked a card. Brando told him to put it back in the deck and shuffle the cards. Gotti complied. Then when Brando asked for a hanky to cover the deck of cards, every goon in the joint pulled theirs out in unison and waved it at Brando. "The place looked like a washline on Monday morning," he remembered. Brando selected a hanky, used it to cover the deck of cards in his hand, and told Gotti to pull the hanky away. Gotti pulled, and when he did, the deck was gone—the only card Brando still held in his hand was the one Gotti picked.

It was a clever trick and a nice little icebreaker, but then Brando sabotaged his own efforts by joking to Gotti, "You know, you could make a living this way."

And that's when the evening screeched to a halt. "I didn't say anything more," Brando remembered, "because suddenly the whole room had become as quiet as a tomb at midnight. Suddenly I realized what everyone was thinking: Had I tried to make a fool out of the boss in front of his crew?" As Gotti stared in silence, Brando decided one brush with death was enough. He and his party said their good-nights and beat it out of the Ravenite Social Club as fast as they could.

ART IMITATES LIFE

The evening wasn't a total loss. If you ever get a get a chance to watch *The Freshman*, you'll see that in several of his scenes with Brando, Matthew Broderick has a terrified look on his face—the look that someone might have if, say, they ever met a real mobster in the flesh. According to Musacchia, that's exactly what it was. Broderick, he says, "had this totally astonished look on his face the whole time in front of Gotti, that he duplicated later in the film." (Convicted of 13 murders and other crimes in 1992, Gotti was given a life sentence and died in prison in 2002.)

...Alchemist Smurf, Finance Smurf, Mango Smurf, and Pastrycook Smurf.

IT'S A WEIRD, WEIRD WORLD

Just when we thought we'd seen all the weirdness this world has to offer, it goes and offers up some more.

WHERE THE DOORS HAVE NO KNOBS

In 2010 a building in Japan underwent a major renovation: Workers rebuilt the walls so that the doors *look* like doors, but they're really paintings. The actual doorways are hidden; the only way to enter the rooms is to find small cracks in the walls and open them up from there (one doorway splits a wall-mounted deer head in two). Other rooms are only accessible behind sliding bookcases. Making the place even more confusing are the black-and-white carpet's eye-boggling overlapping circle patterns. So what is this crazy-making building? A fun house? An eccentric millionaire's home? No, it's Clinic Akasaka, a mental-health facility in Tokyo. It was designed by a famous architect named Nendo, who explained that "the clinic aims to provide patients with something extra, a further richness in their daily lives that they did not have before starting treatment." (No word on how the mental patients took to the new floorplan.)

YOU DAMN, DIRTY SKUNK APE!

The American West has Bigfoot. Florida has Skunk Ape. Leading the search for Bigfoot's "smaller, smellier cousin" is Dave Shealy, an RV park owner in Ochopee. He's researched the elusive creature for more than a decade and even says he's got blurry video footage of it sloshing through the Everglades. Skunk Ape made headlines in May 2010 after dozens of campers reported strange shrieks emanating from the swamps at night. Shealy explained that the shrieks are the male Skunk Apes' mating calls. He also issued a warning: "Women who are in their 'time of the month' must be careful when hiking the area because the cryptoids are attracted to the scent of menstruation. They're also aroused by used lingerie, so female campers shouldn't hang their undies out to dry because that's like raising a flag and inviting them in."

A1 Steak Sauce was created for and named by King George IV of England.

REMOTE CONTROL

When multimillionaire couple Frank and Jamie McCourt purchased the Los Angeles Dodgers in 2004, they vowed to do everything they could to put a winning team on the field. They weren't kidding. The McCourts secretly hired a Russian physicist named Vladimir Shpunt who supposedly has remote healing powers he calls "V energy." Despite knowing very little about baseball, Shpunt watched the games on TV from his Boston home and sent his positive vibes toward the players. "It's very big work," he told reporters after he was outed in 2009, "but I like this team to win." In an e-mail written to team executives after the Dodgers won the 2008 N.L. West division title, the McCourts gave a "special thank you to Vlad for all of his hard work." They didn't release his salary, but according to the *LA Times*, it was "in the six figures."

IT'S AN OLD STORY

An Indonesian woman identified only as Turinah claims she was born in 1853. As of 2010, the 157-year-old's mind is still sharp—she does housework and can see, hear, and talk just fine. She even smokes clove cigarettes, a habit she said she took up before electricity was invented. According to Indonesia Statistics Bureau official Jhonny Sardjono, "There's no authentic data to prove Turinah's age, but judging from her statements and the age of her adopted daughter, who's 108 years old, it's difficult to doubt it."

DEM BONES

You have 206 bones in your body. A Danbury, Connecticut, man named Dan Aziere has a lot more than that—he suffers from a rare disease called *multiple hereditary exostosis*. "They grow around every joint," he says, "and there are a lot around my rib cage." So far, the 41-year-old auto insurance claims adjuster has undergone 19 operations, which have removed 42 of the extra bones, but he estimates that there are about a dozen more still inside him. Most people who suffer from the genetic disorder (including Aziere's father, brother, and two of his children) only have a few extra bones and aren't negatively affected. But even though Aziere has a severe case, he still does okay (his only problem is that a botched surgery left him without any feeling in one of his legs). "I can water ski," he says, "but I can't barefoot water ski."

THE MADDEN CURSE

Every year since the 1998–99 football season, the NFL star selected to appear on the cover of the popular football video game, Madden NFL, subsequently suffered devastating injuries, poor on-field performance, or really bad luck. Is that a coincidence…or is the game cursed?

MADDEN NFL 99

MThe Athlete: 49ers running back Garrison Hearst
Cursed! Hearst was selected to appear on the cover of the first Madden game, released at the beginning of the 1998-1999 football season. His previous season had been fantastic, with the third-most rushing yards in the league, and the most ever in 49ers history. In 1999-2000 he helped the San Francisco 49ers to the postseason…and in the team's first playoff game gruesomely broke his ankle. Foot surgery led to the extremely rare condition of *osteonecrosis*—the death of a bone in his foot. Hearst was sidelined for the next two seasons.

MADDEN NFL 2000

The Athlete: Detroit Lions running back Barry Sanders
Cursed! Sanders is still considered one of the best running backs of all time, and that year, at the age of only 30, was on pace to break Walter Payton's all-time rushing record in just another year or two. Yet after appearing on the *Madden NFL* cover, he retired out of the blue just before the season began. He wasn't injured, and gave no explanation for his leaving. (Years later he admitted it was because he was sick of losing with the lowly Lions.)

MADDEN NFL 2001

The Athlete: Tennessee Titans running back Eddie George
Cursed! George's previous season had been the best of his career. In the fourth quarter of the Titans' first 2001 playoff game, George bobbled what should have been an easy catch—it went right into the hands of Baltimore Ravens defender Ray Lewis…who returned it 50 yards for the touchdown that sealed the win for the Ravens and knocked the Titans out of contention. George's career went

downhill after that: He was traded two years later, and he retired in 2004.

MADDEN 2002

The Athlete: Vikings quarterback Daunte Culpepper

Cursed! Culpepper led Minnesota to the NFC Championship game the year before. Post-*Madden NFL*, he led the team to a dismal 4–7 record—then injured his knee and missed the last five games of the season.

MADDEN NFL 2003

The Athlete: St. Louis Rams running back Marshall Faulk

Cursed! Faulk injured his ankle, had his worst season in six years, and the Vikings finished a disappointing 7–9. Faulk's numbers declined after that, and he retired just two years later.

MADDEN NFL 2004

The Athlete: Atlanta Falcons quarterback Michael Vick

Cursed! Vick broke his leg in a pre-season game. He missed the first eleven games, and the Falcons finished with a record of 3–7.

MADDEN NFL 2005

The Athlete: Baltimore Ravens linebacker Ray Lewis

Cursed! Lewis—a former Defensive Player of the Year honoree and Super Bowl MVP—had a terrible season. He broke his wrist in the sixth game, and was out for the rest of the season.

MADDEN NFL 2006

The Athlete: Eagles quarterback Donovan McNabb

Cursed! In his four previous seasons, McNabb lead his team to four straight NFC Championship games. But in 2006 he tore an *anterior cruciate ligament* (ACL) in his knee, suffered a sore thumb (devastating for a quarterback) and a hernia, and played in just nine games all season, the fewest of his career.

DEN NFL 2007

The Athlete: Seattle running back Shaun Alexander

Cursed! Alexander—the previous season's NFL MVP—broke his foot and missed six games with the Seahawks. The following season he broke his wrist, the year after that he was traded, and in 2008 he quit the game for good.

MADDEN NFL 2008

The Athlete: Tennessee Titans quarterback Vince Young

Cursed! Young was injured during the fifth game of the year, and missed the sixth game, marking the first time in his career—including middle school, high school, college, and the NFL—that he'd missed a game due to injury. He still led the team to a playoff game, but they didn't even score a touchdown, and lost 17–6. The next season Young blew out his knee in the season's first game, and was replaced by quarterback Kerry Collins for the entire year.

MADDEN NFL 2009

The Athlete: Quarterback Brett Favre

Cursed! In early 2008 Favre announced his retirement from the only team he'd ever played with, the Green Bay Packers. But then he changed his mind and signed up with the New York Jets for the 2008–09 season—and made the *Madden NFL* cover, too. He started out great, leading the Jets to an 8–3 record…then injured his throwing shoulder. The team lost four of the last five games, during which Favre threw eight interceptions and just two touchdowns, and the Jets missed the playoffs.

MADDEN NFL 2010

The Athletes (there were two that year): Pittsburgh Steelers safety Troy Polamalu and Arizona Cardinals wide receiver Larry Fitzgerald

Cursed! Polamalu and Fitzgerald had faced each other in the previous season's Super Bowl. This year: Polamalu sprained a knee ligament in the first game of the season and missed four games, and later strained a knee muscle. He played in just five games all season and had the worst year of his career. Fitzgerald, on the other hand, played all year, had a great season, scored the most touchdowns of his career, and was selected for the Pro Bowl team. (So maybe the curse only works on one player at a time.)

UNLIKELY INVENTORS

None of these guys were doctors but all of them made real contributions to the field of medicine, simply because when they saw a problem, they fixed it.

ROALD DAHL

Main Claim to Fame: The British author of several classic children's books, including *Charlie and the Chocolate Factory*, *The BFG*, and *James and the Giant Peach*

Big Idea: In 1960 Dahl's four-month-old son, Theo, was struck by a car. The baby suffered head trauma, resulting in *hydrocephalus*, a buildup of spinal fluid in the brain that can lead to brain damage and death. Surgeons installed a brain shunt, a device that drains fluid and transfers it via a tube to a different part of the body, often the abdomen. Such devices have one-way valves to prevent fluid from leaking back into the brain. Unfortunately for Theo, he had blood in his brain as well as spinal fluid, and the blood was clogging the valve. Finally, after eight emergency surgeries to replace the shunt, Dahl decided his son needed better technology. He put Theo under the care of Dr. Kenneth Till, a neurosurgeon in London, and called Stanley Wade, a hydraulic engineer he'd met through their shared passion for flying model airplanes. Working together, the three designed a new type of one-way shunt valve that was more resistant to blockages. Ironically, Dahl's son made a full recovery before they were finished, so he never used it. But the WDT (Wade-Dahl-Till) valve, as it became known, was used by thousands of others until it was made obsolete by newer technology. As for Dahl and his fellow inventors, they agreed to never make any money from the device.

ROBERT GOLDMAN

Main Claim to Fame: A software engineer and one of the pioneers in the digital music movement

Big Idea: In the late 1990s, Goldman found out that his sister, Amy, had been diagnosed with cancer. Goldman decided to change careers, and dedicated his life to helping his sister. In 2002 he started a company, Vascular Designs, hoping to develop tumor

Roald Dahl created the word "gremlin" during World War II.

treatment technologies. Amy died in 2003, but Goldman pressed on. In 2009, after seven years of work, he released the IsoFlo Infusion Catheter. Here's how it works: A very thin catheter tube is threaded through the veins right to the location of a tumor. There the catheter's special design allows it to deliver chemotherapy drugs directly into the tumor. This is a huge advantage over normal chemotherapy treatment, in which the drugs are simply injected into the body and have to find their way to a tumor. The device has been called a "revolution" in cancer treatment, and has been hailed in medical journals all over the world. "I've found my agenda in life," Goldman said, "and it's about helping people."

PAUL WINCHELL

Main Claim to Fame: For 30 years Winchell was the voice of Tigger in Disney's *Winnie the Pooh* as well as other cartoon characters such as Dick Dastardly in *Dastardly and Muttly in their Flying Machines*, Gargamel in *The Smurfs*, and Boomer in *The Fox and the Hound*. He was also a ventriloquist, a TV host, an author, an acupuncturist, the owner of a shirt factory and a fish farm, and an inventor with more than 30 patents to his name.

Big Idea: Winchell often observed surgeries performed by his friend, Dr. Henry Heimlich (yes, the guy who invented the famous maneuver). When Winchell saw how difficult it was for surgeons to keep a patient's heart pumping during heart surgery, he got the idea of inventing a mechanical heart that would do the heart's work. In 1961, with Heimlich as his adviser, Winchell designed and built a prototype for the first artificial heart in history. "Odd as it may seem, the heart wasn't that different from building a dummy," Winchell later wrote in his autobiography. "The valves and chambers were not unlike the moving eyes and closing mouth of a puppet." Winchell received a patent for his artificial heart in 1963, and later donated the blueprints and model to the University of Utah Medical School. His model is considered by many experts to be the prototype for the Jarvik-7 designed by University of Utah medical researcher Dr. Robert K. Jarvik—the first artificial heart successfully implanted in a human, Barney Clark, on December 2, 1982.

The villains in *Silence of the Lambs, Texas Chainsaw Massacre,* and *Psycho* were all...

ODD SPORTS

Just when you think all the sports and games that could ever be
invented already have been, someone comes up with a weird
new one. (Is freezetagbasketball really any weirder
than hitting a little white ball with a stick?)

QUIDDITCH

Quidditch is a fabrication of author J.K. Rowling—a sport played by wizards and witches in the Harry Potter books and movies. Rules: The players fly through the air on broomsticks, trying to throw a ball through a goal. Meanwhile, one player on each team is dedicated to pursuing another ball, called a "golden snitch," which is fist-sized, yellow, and sentient. Flying broomsticks and balls that go where they want to go would seem to make real-life quidditch impossible, but in 2005 a group of students at Middlebury College in Vermont modified the game so it can be played by the non-magical. Rules: Players run down the field (a soccer field or a football field) with broomsticks between their legs as they throw foam balls (called "bludgers") into the goal. The golden snitch is portrayed by a person dressed head to toe in yellow spandex who runs around the field erratically. More than 150 colleges now boast quidditch teams (it's a club or intramural sport, so it's not technically sanctioned by the NCAA), including Yale, Vassar, Tulane, Oberlin, and Boston University. Players are not required to wear flowing wizard robes and pointy wizard hats... but most do anyway.

FREEZETAGBASKETBALL

According to their website, childhood friends Phil Anker and Dave Fisher invented this game "last weekend." A 50/50 combination of basketball and the playground game of freeze tag, the game starts off like a standard basketball game, with one major difference: One player on each team is "It." When a team has possession of the ball and is attempting to score a basket, the team on defense has to both prevent the offense from scoring and run away from It, who may tag opposing players, "freezing" them until either a basket is scored or they are "unfrozen" by the It on their own

---

...based on a real-life serial killer named Ed Gein.

team. Anker and Fisher aren't sure how many people are playing freeze tag basketball (probably not many), but they give away the rules for free to encourage its growth.

BEEP BASEBALL

The American Association of Adapted Sports Programs developed this sport in the early 1970s as a way for blind people to play baseball, which would otherwise be impossible for them. It's the same game, with a few necessary changes. Giant softballs (16 inches in diameter) are embedded with electronic beeping devices that help players determine where the ball is. Instead of bases, beep baseball uses four-foot-tall foam-rubber columns, each with a location-by-sound buzzer inside. For an added challenge, after the batter hits the ball, he or she runs to either first or third base—whichever base has been remotely activated by an off-field operator and is "buzzing." (The few seconds it takes for the batter to determine which way to run also allows extra time for fielders to locate the ball.) While a handful of sighted individuals play beep baseball, the sport is played primarily by the blind subculture, where it is very popular. There are 200 amateur teams across the United States playing in the National Beep Baseball Association, dozens of regional tournaments, invitationals, and prize matches, and even an annual World Series.

*   *   *

SPELLBOUND

"A council spelled its own name and that of several villages wrongly in a leaflet promoting cycling. Kirklees Council had 7,000 leaflets printed but they repeatedly spell Kirklees as Kirtles, Cleckheaton became Czechisation, Birstall ended up as Bistable and Kirkburton as Kirkpatrick. Even more bizarrely, an e-mail address for British Waterways was given as: *enquiries.manic-depressive@ brutalisation's.co.uk.* A spokesman for the council said the errors were the result of graphic design software used by an external printer. The leaflets have been reprinted and the £1,000 cost was reimbursed."

—*Yorkshire Post* (U.K.), August 2010

MYTH-CONCEPTIONS

"Common knowledge" is frequently wrong. Here are some examples of things that many people believe, but according to our sources, just aren't true.

Myth: If a bear is chasing you, head toward lower ground because bears can't run as fast downhill.

Fact: Bears can run about twice as fast as humans—uphill *or* down. Plus they're excellent climbers. And they can jump. So should you stay where you are and simply play dead? If it's a mother guarding her cubs, then yes—she just wants to protect them and will likely leave you alone. If it's a hungry, predatory bear, it *will* catch you if it's close enough; your best bet: Yell... and if necessary, fight back.

Myth: Air is mostly oxygen.

Fact: The air we breathe is about 21% oxygen. The rest: 0.93% argon, 0.038% carbon dioxide, trace amounts of other gases, and 78% nitrogen.

Myth: Evolution means species evolve into more complex forms.

Fact: Evolution can just as easily lead to genetically simpler forms. For example, fish species that inhabit dark caves may lose their eyes over time. Though some people refer to this as "devolution," biologists say it's a misnomer and prefer the term *degeneration*.

Myth: In Islam, a *fatwa* is a death sentence proclaimed against anyone who is deemed an infidel or a blasphemer.

Fact: A fatwa is simply a religious opinion rendered by an Islamic scholar, based on Islamic law. Rarely does that opinion conclude with a call for capital punishment. The source of this myth is probably the world's best-known fatwa, which occurred when Iran's Ayatollah Khomeini called for the death of author Salman Rushdie in response to his 1988 book *The Satanic Verses*.

Myth: The best time to learn a second language is during early childhood.

Fact: It's long been thought that kids' brains have more *plasticity*, meaning they can absorb more new information than adults can. But recent studies have found what language professors suspected all along: Plasticity remains into old age. In fact, people who have already mastered their native language are better suited to learning new ones.

Myth: People who get head lice have bad hygiene.
Fact: Clean hair is actually easier for head lice to cling to.

Myth: According to the Bible, three Wise Men, or "Magi," riding camels from the east, brought gifts to baby Jesus on the night he was born.
Fact: Nowhere in the Bible does it say there were three of them or how they got there—only that they brought three gifts. The plural use of "Magi" means that there could have been two or even ten. The names attributed to the Magi—Caspar, Melchior, and Balthasar—did not appear until 500 A.D. in Greek writings.

Myth: Vikings wore helmets with horns on them.
Fact: Vikings were buried with their helmets...and their drinking horns. When Victorians dug them up, they assumed the horns had fallen off the helmets.

Myth: Fossils are the preserved remains of animals or plants.
Fact: Very few fossils are the actual remains (such as an insect trapped in amber). Most are actually *trace fossils*: When the dead plant or animal was covered by sediment, the organic matter decayed and was slowly replaced by minerals in the groundwater. Over time, very little (if any) of the original living thing was left, except for its *cast*, or shape. Now it's basically a rock.

Myth: If you want a flat stomach, just do sit-ups or use an exercise machine that works your abdomen.
Fact: Don't let the infomercials fool you. This form of weight loss—called "spot reduction"—is impossible. Although you can build specific muscle groups via exercise, exactly *where* your body will burn off fat is determined by genetics.

*   *   *

"Myths which are believed in tend to come true." —**George Orwell**

JUST PLANE WEIRD

*If you're reading this book on a plane, you might
want to skip this chapter until your flight is
over and you're safely on the ground.*

NOT A VERY FUN GUY

The passengers on board a Ryanair flight from Budapest
to Dublin in 2008 nearly panicked when a strange liquid
began oozing from an overhead compartment. It landed on a
man (not named in press reports), whose neck began to swell up.
He could barely breathe. The plane made an emergency landing
in Frankfurt, Germany, where medics boarded and determined
that the liquid was not dangerous. The man was treated, and
after a two-hour delay, the flight took off again. A Ryanair official reassured the public that it wasn't a chemical attack and
that there was no "burning substance." Apparently, the man—
who is allergic to mushrooms—just happened to be sitting
underneath an overhead compartment where another passenger
had stored a jar of mushroom soup, which had leaked out during
the flight.

B.O. AIR

The moment that an unidentified U.S. man boarded an Air
Canada Jazz flight in Charlottetown, Prince Edward Island, in
2010 the entire plane was assaulted by his stench. "It was brutal,"
said one passenger. The smell was so bad that people started complaining to the flight attendants, but they didn't have to—the
flight crew couldn't take the smell, either. The man, described as
"unkempt," was escorted off the plane. According to reports, he
found a place to take a shower and then flew out on a later flight.

FIRE IN THE HEAD!

Pandemonium broke out on a Compass Airlines flight from Minneapolis to Regina, Saskatchewan, in May 2008 when smoke
started pouring into the rear of the main cabin. There was a fire in
the lavatory. The pilot took the plane from 30,000 feet to a runway in Fargo, North Dakota, in less than eight minutes and all 72

Crosby, Stills & Nash had played only one gig together before Woodstock.

passengers made it off safely thanks to the crew's fast action—including that of 19-year-old flight attendant Eder Rojas, who put out the flames with a fire extinguisher. Back on the ground, federal investigators discovered that the fire had been deliberately set... by Eder Rojas. Why? He was angry that he had to work that particular route. Rojas was arrested and faces up to 20 years in prison, but disappeared before his trial began. At last report, his whereabouts were still unknown.

COWBOYS & ALIENS

During a 2010 SkyWest Airlines flight from Montana to Utah with 50 people aboard, a man ran up to the cockpit door and started banging on it. "I'm a space alien!" he shouted. "And I demand to fly this human aircraft!" The plane's lone flight attendant couldn't remove the 32-year-old man, so he asked the passengers for a little help. That's when Clay Cooper, a cowboy (really), got up and forced the "alien" back into his seat. "Stay there!" said Cooper as he clicked the man's seat belt. A few minutes later, the plane made an emergency landing in Idaho Falls; the man kicked and yelled at the police officers who escorted him away. He was charged with disturbing the peace and assaulting an officer. Apparently his friend—who'd slept through most of the ruckus—was taking him home to Las Vegas because he was "acting weird."

BLOWIN' IN THE WIND

On a gusty day in April 2010, Ken Marcoux and his wife Carol drove their Toyota Prius to Colorado's Boulder Municipal Airport to watch the small planes take off and land. Sitting in their car about 250 feet from the runway, they noticed a single-engine Beechcraft Bonanza getting tossed around by the wind as it attempted to land. The plane slammed down on the runway so hard that it bounced back up, spun around in the air, and started flying uncontrollably at more than 100 miles per hour...directly toward them. "Ken!" shouted Carol. He hit the accelerator, and the Prius—not known for its pickup—moved forward just far enough that the Beechcraft's right wing clipped the car's *rear* window instead of the front, where the Marcouxs were sitting. Then the plane flew into a utility pole, lost its left wing, and crashed in

---

Mmmm! Every year, about 8 million pounds of sugar are used to make Twinkies.

a field. The pilot jumped out and ran away. "It's amazing," said Carol Marcoux. "I'm very grateful that I wasn't decapitated." A few hours later, the pilot, 67-year-old Joe Curtis, turned himself in (he said he ran away to go tend to his two dogs in his car). He described his flying skills as "rusty."

I'LL LET MYSELF OUT, THANKS

After the arriving Delta Airlines plane taxied to its gate in Phoenix, Arizona, the seat belt sign was turned off and the passengers stood up and started gathering their things. As anyone who's ever sat in the back of a plane knows, this process can take an annoyingly long time. One passenger—a 37-year-old man whose name wasn't released—didn't feel like waiting and did what most passengers only fantasize about doing: He opened the emergency exit door and climbed out onto the wing. He then scurried down to the tarmac and started looking for a way into the airport. He made it in, all right, but in police custody.

WAKING UP IS HARD TO DO

In April 2010, British law professor Kris Lines began the last leg of his long journey from England—an Air Canada flight from Calgary to Vancouver. After being awake for nearly 24 hours, Lines dozed off for the 90-minute flight. A tap on his shoulder woke him up. The plane was dark. It was inside a hangar. A mechanic stood over him. They were the only two people aboard. "Take all the time you want," said the mechanic. "The flight landed an hour and a half ago." Lines gathered his stuff and was shuttled back to the main terminal. Air Canada officials apologized and explained that the flight attendants were so busy assisting several passengers in wheelchairs that they didn't notice Griffin still sleeping in the back when they closed up the plane. "What if I'd been a vulnerable passenger?" he complained to reporters. "Or a young girl, or elderly? Or a terrorist? Then I've got 90 minutes, all by myself, in a secure area!" For his trouble, Lines was given 20% off his next Air Canada flight.

✳   ✳   ✳

"I failed kindergarten because I couldn't spell my last name."

—Zach Galifianakis

HANG UP THE PHONE!

"Distracted driving" accidents are on the rise thanks to more texting and cell phone use in cars. But as these real-life emergency room reports attest, you don't have to be in your car to have a phone-related episode.

"Nose bleed: Patient was texting on his phone, not paying attention. Ran into a door."

"Patient injured her right eye while she was walking down the hall, texting on phone. Another student ran into her eye with his head."

"Finger laceration: Patient talking on cell phone while cutting raw chicken at home."

"Patient riding horse and text messaging on cell phone same time, let go of reins. Horse took off, patient fell off."

"Fell on escalator while on phone, hit head on railing."

"Ankle sprain: 20-year-old female talking on cell phone, exiting bus. Fell down steps."

"Dirt bike accident: Patient tried to answer cell phone going 45 mph and laid bike down. Bruised chest, two fractured ribs."

"Patient fell while walking dog, talking on cell phone."

"Bruised sternum: Patient was lifting weights while talking on cell phone. Barbell fell onto chest."

"46-year-old patient riding bike, cell phone caught in spokes, patient flipped over handlebars. Fractured nose."

"Corneal abrasion: Patient got Super Glue in eye while talking on cell phone."

"Concussion, abrasions, contusion: Patient was sitting on toilet and was trying to answer pager and fell off of toilet, hitting head."

"25-year-old male was talking on cell phone when he walked over telephone guy-wire from a pole, states he might have gotten 'zapped.'"

"Concussion: Sixteen-year-old male was talking and text messaging on phone, walked into a telephone pole."

"Patient trying to get cell phone picture of squirrel. Squirrel bite to finger."

"Distracted pedestrian" accidents in the U.S. quadrupled between 2006 and 2008.

UNOBTAINIUMS

Ready to brush up on your science? Don't worry—it's fake science. Here are the names and properties of various chemicals, elements, and other substances...that exist only in books, movies, and TV shows.

Dilithium: Crystalline mineral used in the operation of the warp drive on the U.S.S. *Enterprise* on *Star Trek*. It controls the "anti-matter" used to power the warp drive, which somehow allows the ship to travel through space faster than the speed of light. Dilithium is in the "hypersonic" family of elements.

Energon: Highly radioactive and extremely unstable, this substance is found throughout the universe, but in its liquid form it's both fuel and food for the giant robots from space in the *Transformers* cartoons and movies. The search for energon is what leads the evil Decepticon robots to Earth, where the chemical is abundant.

Beerium: In Yahoo Serious's *Young Einstein* (1988), Albert Einstein turns out to have been an Australian who, in addition to his many scientific pursuits, invented rock music and beer. He invents beer by splitting the *beerium* atom, which releases carbonation.

Byzanium: In Clive Cussler's 1976 novel (and the 1980 movie) *Raise the Titanic!*, the Pentagon begins work on a secret defense system that uses sound waves to deflect missiles. But it requires tremendous power, which can only be produced by a rare, radioactive element called byzanium. And the world's only store of it is locked in a vault on board the sunken *Titanic*, requiring the book's protagonist, explorer Dirk Pitt, to go get it.

Adamantium: A metal alloy that covers the skeleton of Wolverine in the *X-Men* comics and movies. It's what allows him to have metal claws protruding from his hands.

Ice-nine: This substance drives the plot of Kurt Vonnegut's 1963 novel *Cat's Cradle*. Ice-nine has such a high melting point that any substance that comes into contact with it instantly freezes. In the novel, scientists fear that since ice-nine could freeze everything on Earth, it could bring about the end of the world.

Carbonite: A *Star Wars* substance in which living things can be frozen and suspended indefinitely. Most notably, it's how Han Solo was imprisoned for delivery to his nemesis, Jabba the Hut.

Unobtainium: In the movie *Avatar* (2009), earthlings go to the distant planet of Pandora to mine this fuel source, worth $20 million per kilogram. Writer James Cameron actually took the name from real life: Scientists have long used "unobtainium" to describe rare or possibly nonexistent materials.

Vibranium: A recurring substance in Marvel Comics, it first appeared on Earth 10,000 years ago, when a meteorite made of it crashed in Africa, causing natives to mutate. In the 1940s, a scientist named Dr. Myron MacLain obtained some while developing iron alloys for military tanks and used it to create an indestructible shield for the Nazi-fighting super-soldier, Captain America.

Eitr: According to Norse mythology, this bright-blue liquid is the source of all life, from which the first creature, the giant Ymir, first emerged.

Amazonium: In the comics, Wonder Woman's lightweight armor-like bracelets are made of this metal, found only on her native "Paradise Island." (On the TV show her bracelets are made of "feminum.")

Melange: The much sought-after "spice" from Frank Herbert's *Dune* (1965), it's a drug that can both extend life and bend time. Unfortunately, it's extremely rare and extremely addictive. Once you've started taking it, you can't stop—or you'll die.

Deutronium: Found on various planets throughout the universe on the '60s TV series *Lost in Space*, it's combustible in liquid form, making it the fuel of choice for the Robinson family's *Jupiter 2* spaceship.

Cavorite: Making appearances in novels by H.G. Wells (*War of the Worlds, First Men on the Moon*), it's a rare element that, when heated into a liquid and then cooled, can block the effects of gravity.

Nitrowhisperin: From *Get Smart*, it was invented by scientist Albert Pfitzer in an attempt to create silent fire-works. It's exactly like nitro-glycerin, except that it explodes in silence. The evil KAOS organization tries to use it to destroy the world in a 1968 episode of the TV series.

Chemical X: In the 1990s cartoon *The Powerpuff Girls*, the Professor attempts to concoct "the perfect girls" out of "sugar, spice, and everything nice," but accidentally drops in Chemical X, which gives the three little girls super-powers.

Mithril: A rare metal in J.R.R. Tolkien's Middle-earth of *The Lord of the Rings*, it looks like silver but is lighter and stronger than steel. When a cave troll stabs Frodo with a spear in the Mines of Moria, the hobbit is saved by his vest made of mithril.

Upsidaisium: From the *Rocky and Bullwinkle* cartoons, this mineral floats in the air, unbound by gravity. Its only known source: Mt. Flatten, a mountain that hovers in the sky. (Bullwinkle inherited the mine from his Uncle Dewlap.)

Flubber: In the 1961 Disney film *The Absent-Minded Professor*, Medfield College chemistry professor Ned Brainard (Fred MacMurray) botches a calculation and accidentally creates an elastic substance that absorbs energy when it hits a hard surface, causing it to bounce sky-high. He names it "flubber" (a contraction of "flying rubber"). First Brainard uses it to help basketball players jump higher, which helps them win the big game, and then he charges the flubber with radioactive particles, enabling his Model T to fly.

* * *

LIFE IMITATES ART

In May 2010, a tornado traveled down a rural Oklahoma highway and destroyed several buildings at J. Berry Harrison's farm. "It took us 50 years to build," he said, "and it blew away in 15 minutes. It was quite a wind." Thankfully, no one was injured. In 1996 Harrison's farm was featured in the movie *Twister*. The real tornado carved nearly the exact same path down the highway and across Harrison's land as the fictional one had nearly 15 years earlier.

WHY THEY DON'T SPEAK SPANISH IN RIO

Ever wonder why the official language of Mexico and nearly all of Central and South America is Spanish, but in one country in the region—Brazil—they speak Portuguese? We did too. Here's why.

THE FIRST PIRATES

The 15th century was a momentous time in world history—the beginning of the "Age of Exploration" during which European powers traveled all over the globe...and claimed large parts of it for themselves. The two biggest players: Portugal and Spain, the world's mightiest naval powers at the time.

But they weren't equal; Portugal was stronger. In 1415, under the rule of King Henry "The Navigator," the Portuguese conquered the Muslim trading center of Ceuta in North Africa. In 1420 they colonized the Madeira Islands, 500 miles off the coast of northeast Africa in the Atlantic Ocean. Seven years later they discovered and colonized the Azores, a group of islands in the middle of the North Atlantic roughly 1,000 miles west of Portugal.

And Portuguese domination might have continued into the 16th century—if their king had agreed to back a daring young explorer named Christopher Columbus. Columbus had asked Portugal's King John II for financial backing, and when the king refused him, he turned to Spain. In 1492...well, you know that story.

FRIENDS IN HIGH PLACES

Columbus's discovery of the Western Hemisphere spawned diplomatic tensions between Spain and Portugal. The Portuguese argued that the "New World" should be considered theirs—because the Azores were the closest thing to them. Spain claimed the New World was theirs, by virtue of the fact that they had discovered it. After months of bickering, King Ferdinand of Spain appealed to Pope Alexander IV, himself a Spaniard and a friend of the king, asking Alexander to issue a *papal bull* on the issue.

Most of Europe was ruled by Catholic kings and queens at the time, and the pope wielded enormous power over them. Papal

---

John Wayne said the word "pilgrim" 23 times in *The Man Who Shot Liberty Valance.*

bulls, or official letters released by the Vatican, were accepted as legally binding in every Catholic state. Any leader refusing to obey them could be excommunicated. Several papal bulls had been issued over land disputes between Spain and Portugal, and were in fact the basis for both of the counties' present claims on the newly discovered New World.

Pope Alexander agreed to his friend's request, and on May 4, 1493, issued a new bull creating an imaginary line from the North Pole to the South Pole through the Atlantic Ocean, roughly halfway between the Azores and the Caribbean islands discovered by Columbus. All lands west of that line, the bull decreed, belonged to Spain. It didn't specifically give all lands east of the line to Portugal, but the two countries made that clear when they formalized the pope's decision with the Treaty of Tordesillas in 1494.

Never mind that no one in Europe had any idea how much land they were talking about—Columbus had only explored a few Caribbean islands so far (not to mention that there were already people who called those lands home). The pope and the rulers of Spain and Portugal had effectively divided the entire world into two pieces, one half belonging to Spain and the other to Portugal. And they quickly went to work to claim all that territory.

BLAME RIO ON IT

So what does all this have to do with Brazil? Well, you might not know it, but Brazil, located on South America's great eastern bulge, actually lies to the east of the imaginary line created by the papal bull—so it was deemed to belong to Portugal. And while Spain conquered most of that continent, as well as all of Central America and much of North America, the Portuguese settled in the only place they were allowed in the New World: Brazil. They first landed there in 1500 and began colonizing it in the 1530s. Over the next three centuries, Brazil grew into a modern state under Portuguese rule. Today it's the world's fifth-largest country, both geographically and by population, and dwarfs its colonizer: Portugal has 11 million inhabitants today; Brazil has about 192 million. And the official language is still Portuguese, the one assigned to them by a 15th-century pope. And that's why they don't speak Spanish in Rio.

Almost all of South America is east of New York City.

IT AIN'T FROM THERE

Just because something is named after a place doesn't mean it came from there.

- **Outback Steakhouse,** the Australian-themed restaurant, was founded in Tampa, Florida.

- **Irish Spring** soap is manufactured by Colgate in the United States, and is not sold outside of North America.

- **Uno's Chicago Grill** pizza restaurant chain is Boston-based.

- **Texas Pete Hot Sauce,** a popular brand in the South, is made in North Carolina.

- **AriZona Iced Tea** is headquartered in New York City.

- **London broil** is a method of marinating and preparing flank steak. The dish originated in the American Midwest; it's virtually unknown in London.

- **Old Milwaukee** beer is brewed in Detroit.

- **Lone Star Steakhouse** is the name of a restaurant chain that was founded in North Carolina. In Texas, the Lone Star State, there are no Lone Star Steakhouses.

- **Hawaiian Punch** is made with Hawaiian fruits, including papaya and pineapple, but it was invented in Fullerton, California.

- **Vienna Beef** is a popular brand of hot dogs and deli meats manufactured by a Chicago-based company.

- **Arizona Jeans** clothing is produced by and sold at J.C. Penney stores, based in Plano, Texas.

- **Budweiser** beer is named after the town of Budweis in Bohemia, (now part of the Czech Republic), but it originated in Missouri.

- **Vermont Castings** manufactures wood-burning stoves and grills. The company's home offices are in Kentucky; all of its products are made in China.

- **New York Brand Texas Toast** is produced in Ohio.

In 1915 drought-ridden San Diego, CA, hired a "rainmaker." A week later, the city flooded.

LAST CONCERTS

*Quiz your friends—see if they know when and where
these famous acts played their very last shows.*

THE DOORS (WITH JIM MORRISON)

Venue and Date: The Warehouse, New Orleans,
Louisiana, December 12, 1970

The Show: In late 1970, the Doors set out on a tour to support
their upcoming sixth album, *L.A. Woman*. It lasted only two
nights. The first show was in Dallas, Texas, the second was at the
Warehouse—and that's where the increasingly drunk and drug-
addled Jim Morrison lost it. He started omitting lyrics to songs,
then slumped down on the stage, lay there for a while, got up,
tried to sing, and, according to keyboardist Ray Manzarek, "Jim
picked up the microphone stand and repeatedly bashed it into the
stage, over and over until there was the sound of wood splintering.
He threw the stand into the stunned audience, turned, and
plopped down on the drum riser, sitting motionless." Manzarek,
drummer John Densmore, and guitarist Robby Krieger met backstage after the show and agreed—the Doors were done as a live
musical act. In March 1971, Morrison moved to Paris; that July he
died there, and the Doors were done for good.

Coda: Ticket cost of the last Doors show: $5. The remaining
members actually carried on as "The Doors," released two more
albums and toured to support each one. But they weren't the same
without Morrison, and finally disbanded in March 1973.

NIRVANA

Venue and Date: Terminal 1, Munich, Germany, March 1, 1994

The Show: This concert took place less than a month into what
was supposed to be several months of touring. The band played
played 20 songs, then came out for a five-song encore, finishing
with their 1993 hit, "Heart-Shaped Box." Lead singer Kurt Cobain
was suffering from bronchitis, so the next night's show was canceled. On March 4, Cobain was hospitalized in Rome because of a
drug overdose, and the rest of the tour was canceled. On April 8,
he killed himself in his Seattle home, and Nirvana was history.

Howard Hughes based his design for a conical bra on the nose cone of an airplane.

Coda: The opening act for the show were fellow Washingtonians the Melvins, sometimes called the "Godfathers of Grunge."

STEVIE RAY VAUGHAN

Venue and Date: Alpine Valley Music Theatre, East Troy, Wisconsin, August 26, 1990

The Show: Vaughan was touring with Eric Clapton that summer, and after the night's closing set Clapton introduced the audience to "the best guitar players in the entire world." Out came Stevie, his brother Jimmy Vaughan, Buddy Guy, and Robert Cray. They played a blistering 15-minute version of the Robert Johnson blues classic "Sweet Home Chicago." Afterward, players and crew boarded four helicopters that had been reserved to take them to Chicago for their next show. Shortly after takeoff, around 12:40 a.m. and in heavy fog, the helicopter carrying Vaughan and three members of Clapton's management team crashed into a hillside. The pilot and all four passengers were killed.

Coda: The other three helicopters made it to Chicago safely, knowing nothing about the crash. They were told about it the next morning.

FRANK SINATRA

Venue and Date: The Frank Sinatra Celebrity Golf Classic, Palm Desert, California, February 25, 1995

The Show: At 79 years old, Sinatra ended his touring career with two shows at Japan's Fukuoka Dome on December 19 and 20, 1994. In 1995 he decided to retire completely, and staged one farewell performance on the final night of his charity golf tournament, singing for 1,200 invited guests. He sang a handful of the songs he made famous, including "I've Got the World on a String," "Fly Me to the Moon," "My Kind of Town," and ended his 60-year performing career with "The Best Is Yet to Come."

Coda: That was Sinatra's last *concert* appearance, but there was still one more show to come. On November 19, 1995, ABC presented an 80th birthday special for Sinatra at the Shrine Auditorium in Los Angeles. Guests included Tony Bennett, Patti LaBelle, Bruce Springsteen, Hootie and the Blowfish, Bono, and Bob Dylan. For the grand finale Sinatra joined the entire ensemble and sang the last line of the song with which he will forever

---

15,000 workers helped build the *Titanic*. Average wage: about $10 per week.

be linked—"If I can make it there, I'll make it anywhere…" Sinatra died three years later, on May 14, 1998.

QUEEN (WITH FREDDIE MERCURY)

Venue and Date: Knebworth Park, England, August 9, 1986

The Show: In 1986 Queen staged a tour of stadiums throughout Europe in support of their album *A Kind of Magic*. It was slated to end on August 5, but it was so successful that the band decided to add one more show, at Knebworth Park in Hertfordshire in southeast England. It sold out—120,000 tickets—in less than two hours. Singer Freddie Mercury led the band through a 25-song show, including a four-song encore of "Radio Ga Ga," "Friends Will Be Friends," "We Will Rock You," and the big finish—"We Are the Champions." The band went on hiatus after the tour, and seven months later, when Mercury was diagnosed with AIDS, they canceled all plans for future tours. Mercury died five years later and the Knebworth show became Queen's final performance.

Coda: Ticket cost for the final show: £14.50, or about $22. Opening acts: Status Quo, Big Country, and Belouis Some.

NICK DRAKE

Venue and Date: The Adrian Mann Theater, Ewell Technical College, Surrey, England, June 25, 1970

The Show: Drake was an English singer and songwriter who gained little fame in his lifetime, but is cited as an important influence by a huge number of artists, including REM, Lucinda Williams, Belle & Sebastian, Elliott Smith, the Cure, the Black Crowes, and many others. (His songs can be heard in the soundtracks of such films as *The Royal Tenenbaums* and *Garden State*, and in a 2010 AT&T television commercial.) He released only three albums, from 1969, when he was just 20, until 1972. He was also a very introverted person, and hated performing. His last performance came two years before the release of his last album, as the opening act for English folk legend Ralph McTell. The show did not go well. "Nick was monosyllabic," McTell later said. "He did the first set and something awful must have happened. He was doing his song 'Fruit Tree' and walked off halfway

through it." That was the last time Drake performed in public.
He died during the night on November 24, 1974, of an overdose
of the antidepressant *amitriptyline*. He was just 26.

LED ZEPPELIN
Venue and Date: Eissporthalle, Berlin, Germany, July 7, 1980
The Show: The English rockers finished off their 30th major
tour since forming in 1968 with a 15-song set. They ended the
night with four of their biggest hits—"Kashmir," "Stairway to
Heaven," "Rock and Roll," and the finale, an 18-minute version
of "Whole Lotta Love," complete with an extended John Bonham drum solo intermixed with Jimmy Page making wild sounds
on a theremin. Less than three months later, with the band in
the midst of rehearsals for their first North American tour in
three years, Bonham died after an extreme drinking binge. The
three surviving members—Page, Robert Plant, and John Paul
Jones—decided that the band could not go on without their original drummer, and Led Zeppelin was no more. (They've performed together a handful of times since Bonham's death. Almost
all of those shows have featured Jason Bonham, John's son, on
drums.)
Coda: Ticket cost: 20 Deutsche Marks, or around $9. There was
no opening act.

PINK FLOYD
Venue and Date: Hyde Park, London, July 2, 2005
The Show: Roger Waters, David Gilmour, Richard Wright, and
Nick Mason played together for what *seemed* to be the last time in
1981, after the tour for their blockbuster album *The Wall*. They
mostly went their separate ways after that: Wright left the band in
'83; Waters in '85. Then, much to the chagrin of Waters, a new
Pink Floyd era began in 1986, with only Gilmour, Mason, and
Wright remaining as original members. (Waters sued to stop them
from using the name Pink Floyd—unsuccessfully.) That version of
the band lasted until 1994, and seemed to be another end of Pink
Floyd as a live band...until July 2, 2005, when all four—Waters,
Gilmour, Wright, and Mason—walked onto the stage at London's
Hyde Park as part of the *Live 8* benefit concert extravaganza. They

performed five songs to an ecstatic audience, concluding with "Comfortably Numb." Richard Wright died in September 2008, so that remains the very last Pink Floyd show ever. Rumors that the three surviving members of the band would reunite have been swirling ever since, but so far, no go.

ABBA

Background: ABBA was made up of two married Swedish couples, Frida Lyngstad and Benny Andersson, and Agnetha Fältskog and Björn Ulvaeus. They lived atop the pop charts from 1972 until 1982—by which time both couples were divorced, and all the members were ready for something other than ABBA. They actually performed three "last shows."

Last Show #1: The last time the group officially performed as ABBA was on December 11, 1982, in a Stockholm television studio and live via satellite on the British TV show *The Late, Late Breakfast Show*. It wasn't supposed to be their final show. In fact, ABBA has never officially disbanded. They simply stopped playing together temporarily and never managed to get back together...

Last show #2: ...until January 1986, when the band recorded a video of themselves performing "Tivedshambo," the first song written by their longtime manager, Stig Anderson, who was a popular singer in his own right. The low-tech video, in which the only instruments played are an acoustic guitar and an accordion, was made for a Swedish TV show on Anderson's 55th birthday.

Last Show #3: ABBA's *last* performance came 13 years later. In 2002 Björn Ulvaeus revealed on German television that all four band members were invited to the 50th birthday of mutual friend Görel Hanser in 1999. It was held in the restaurant of the Modern Museum in Stockholm. By that time the band members hadn't seen each other in many years, but they ended up together on the restaurant's small stage, and, to a small, hushed audience, sang "Med En Enkel Tulipan," ("With a Simple Tulip"), a traditional Swedish birthday song, a cappella. That remains ABBA's last known performance (so far).

About 1 in every 10,000 snakes is born with two heads.

OTHER LEANING TOWERS

If you've already seen the Leaning Tower of Pisa in Italy and aren't crazy about going back, fear not! There are plenty of other leaning towers around the world for you to have a look at.

THE LEANING TOWER OF CHINA

Also known as the Huqiu Tower, this seven-story, 154-foot-tall brick temple in Suzhou City, west of Shanghai, was built in 960 A.D. and weighs in at more than 7,000 tons. That's a lot of weight to put on a foundation, especially one that's solid rock on one side and much softer compactible soil on the other…causing the lean. Considering that the tower is more than a thousand years old, it's a wonder that it leans only three degrees, or just over 7-1/2 feet out of line from the top of the tower to the bottom. (The Leaning Tower of Pisa is 3.99 degrees or 14-1/2 feet off center, and so is this page).

THE LEANING TOWER OF TELUK INTAN

Built in 1885, in the town of Teluk Intan, Malaysia, on what probably seemed like a solid foundation at the time. Actually, this combination water tank, clock tower, ship's beacon (and onetime Boy Scout headquarters) was unknowingly built over an underground stream. The flowing water caused the foundation to shift, which in turn caused a noticeable tilt in the building as early as 1889. The 83-foot-tall wood-and-brick tower hasn't stored water for many years (but the clock still keeps good time). It's now a tourist attraction.

THE LEANING TOWER OF NEVYANSK

Built by a Russian industrialist named Akinfiy Demidov, legend has it that the 188-foot-tall 18th-century brick tower was intentionally designed to slant in the direction of Demidov's hometown of Tula. But a study of its construction suggests that the tilt was a mistake, and that the builders took steps to correct it: The bricks higher up the tower were specially trimmed to even out the slant. As a result, the base of the tower leans about three degrees off

---

250 people have fallen off the Leaning Tower of Pisa since it was built in 1372.

center, while the top of the tower is only one degree off. (Another legend: When Demidov asked the architect if he could build anything more beautiful than the tower, the architect said yes, and Demidov had him thrown off the tower.)

THE LEANING TOWER OF SUURHUSEN

The steeple of a medieval church in northwestern Germany, this 90-foot brick tower was built in 1450 on a foundation of oak tree trunks sunken into waterlogged marshland. That may not sound like a stable foundation, but the logs supported the tower and kept it more or less vertical for 400 years. Then in the 1800s, the marsh was drained and the logs were exposed to the air for the first time. Result: The logs rotted…and the steeple was soon the most-leaning tower on Earth, with a slant of more than 5.19 degrees off of vertical (the same as this page), creating an overhang of eight feet from the top of the tower to the base.

THE LEANING TOWER OF ABU DHABI

Who says leaning towers have to be accidental? The twisting, S-shaped Capital Gate tower in Abu Dhabi, United Arab Emirates, was deliberately designed to lean a whopping 18 degrees to the west (177 feet out of line from the top of the building to the base), or more than three times the lean of the former world record holder, the Leaning Tower of Suurhusen. (Guinness World Records has since reclassified Suurhusen as the World's Most *Unintentionally* Tilted Building.) Slated for completion in late 2010, the 35-story building will contain a Hyatt hotel, 14 floors of office space, a 19th floor "outdoor" pool, and a tea lounge that hangs off the side of the leaning building more than 260 feet off the ground.

*   *   *

IF THE NAME FITS

After rock singer Jani Lane failed to show up to a March 2010 court appearance for a DUI case, the judge put out a warrant for his arrest. Lane is the lead singer of the hard rock band Warrant.

Henry Ford's first car was called the Quadricycle. It was made from bicycle parts.

DO DO THAT VOODOO!

And now the lowdown on the religion that brought you zombies.

WHAT IS VOODOO?
- It's an *animist* religion—the idea that living souls exist in all plants, objects, and natural phenomena—based on ancestor worship. In Voodoo, there is one Supreme Being and thousands of spirits, called *Loa*. Voodoo rituals center around the practitioners' relationship with the spirit world.
- The word "voodoo" comes from the West African word *vodou*, which means "invisible force."
- Haitian Voodoo is a combination of religious traditions from West Africa and the Caribbean, and Roman Catholicism.
- There are two kinds of Voodoo: *Rado* works for good; *Petro* goes to the Dark Side.

WHO DO VOODOO?
- 60 million people, mostly from the Caribbean, Brazil and Africa.
- A priest is a *houngan*; a priestess a *mambo*; a student a *hounsis*.
- Voodoo followers carry white charms called *juju* and black charms called *mojo*. *Gris-gris* are the most powerful and the most expensive. They are small leather bags filled with herbs, potions, hair and animal skin.

HOW DO YOU DO VOODOO?
- An altar is laden with candles, money, food, rum, sacred stones, saints' cards, bells, and knives. The ritual begins with the drawing of a *veve* (symbol for a specific spirit) on the floor in corn meal. Drumming and dancing begins. The dancing continues until someone is possessed by the spirit and falls. The possessed dancer is now the Loa who sees the future, gives blessings and grants wishes. Warning: anyone who touches this Loa could die.

WOO-WOO VOODOO
- According to anthropologists, Voodoo priests *do* cast spells and occasionally stick pins in Voodoo dolls. (Pinstruck.com is a website that allows you to send digital voodoo curses anonymously.)

Will their prayers be answered? A Florida church and T-Mobile have applied to build...

ART THAT POOPS

Here at the Bathroom Readers' Institute, we're always on the lookout for art that's "bathroom-themed." Here's one of the strangest items in that category that we've ever come across.

DOWN THE HATCH

Wim Delvoye, 44, is a "neo-conceptual" artist from Belgium. He's considered the *enfant terrible* of the Belgian art world, and in the fall of 2000 he lived up to expectations when he unveiled *Cloaca*, an art piece that has been described as "a room-sized intestine" and "the world's first free-standing, man-made digestive system." It's a machine that converts food into a substance approximating human waste.

If you've ever seen the original *Cloaca* or any of a number of updated versions that have made the rounds of modern-art museums, you know that the machines don't look all that impressive. They're just a series of six glass vats sitting on steel carts, connected to each other by plastic tubing, with an in-sink garbage disposal, meat grinder, pumps, and a few other pieces of hardware. But they're far more sophisticated than they appear: Delvoye, assisted by a team of plumbers, gastroenterologists, computer scientists, mechanical engineers and other specialists, spent years developing the idea. The glass vats are filled with enzymes, bacteria, acids, and other chemicals that mimic the human digestive process, from the mouth to the stomach and all the way through the small and large intestines. The vats are kept at a constant 98.6° F—just as if they were inside the human body. Delvoye controls the entire system remotely from the computer in his art studio.

MEALTIME

Watching a *Cloaca* being fed is a big part of the fun. Delvoye arranges for the finest restaurants in the area to prepare special meals for his machines, and then posts a menu next to the installation so that the public always knows what *Cloaca* is eating.

On January 24, 2002, for example, when a *Cloaca* was exhibited at the New Museum of Contemporary Art in the SoHo neighborhood of New York City, the machine dined on seared monkfish with herbs, sauteed in beer butter, with a side of baby vegetables and shrimp, plus browned French fries slathered in mayonnaise (that's how they eat fries in Belgium).

The meal, prepared and served by chef Chris Gielen of a trendy Belgian basserie called Markt, was cut into bite-size pieces and "fed" into the clear glass sink with garbage disposal that serves as *Cloaca*'s mouth. Fish, veggies, fries, and all were washed down with a bottle of Belgian beer. (*Cloaca*'s system cannot tolerate raw vegetables, spicy foods, or meat with bones. Other than that, the chefs are free to prepare any dishes they like and serve them with beer, wine, cocktails, soft drinks, water, or any other beverage that pairs well with the meal.)

It takes as little as five minutes to feed *Cloaca*, but the machine needs 22 hours to fully digest each meal. People don't need to completely digest one meal before they eat another one, and neither does *Cloaca*. It eats twice a day—breakfast and a late lunch in some museums, lunch and dinner in others—and it eats every day, even if the museum is closed. It's easy to tell when *Cloaca* is hungry: A blue light flashes when it's ready to eat.

IN ONE END...

After *Cloaca*'s garbage disposal "chews" the food, it's fed into a meat grinder for further processing, and then pumped through the six glass vats, each of which simulates a different stage of the digestive process. In most *Cloaca* models the food will travel about 33 feet—from one end of the machine to the other—in the 22 hours it takes for the meal to be digested. That distance is a pretty close approximation of the human digestive system, which if stretched end-to-end would be about 30 feet long.

Every 24 hours, *Cloaca* pumps—or poops—the remains of its most recent meals onto a rotating circular tray that could probably be referred to as the machine's toilet. What happens next depends on where the machine is being exhibited. When the first machine was unveiled in Antwerp in 2000, the *Cloaca*-doo was carefully collected and entombed in resin-filled glass flasks, which were then sold with a copy of the corresponding menu for as much as $1,000 apiece (there were plenty of takers, even at that price). In SoHo, workers just scooped up the waste and flushed it down a (real) toilet.

So make tea? The leaves of the coffee plant contain more caffeine than the beans.

CLOAC-U-LENCE

It's not easy building a machine that mimics the human digestive tract, and Delvoye's machines have had humanlike problems along the way, including constipation and diarrhea. After the first *Cloaca* was unveiled in Antwerp's Museum of Contemporary Art in 2000, it developed flatulence so severe that the museum staff went on strike until the management piped the fumes out of the building. By the time *Cloaca* arrived in SoHo, the flatulence problem had largely been solved, and the three-month visit went off without a hitch as *Cloaca* ate and excreted 188 meals without causing any visitors to lose their appetite, at least not from the smell.

FOOD FOR THOUGHT

Even so, *Cloaca* did manage to generate criticism during its stay in New York, and from a surprising source: the gourmet chefs who prepared its meals. Many came to see *Cloaca* as a tremendous missed opportunity to raise issues about contemporary eating habits, nutrition, and health. "When I heard Delvoye speak, it was odd to me, because he didn't ask questions that make us think about culture and diet," Peter Hoffman, owner/chef of Savoy restaurant, complained to *The New York Times* in 2002. "Like, if I throw in greasy food versus more healthy food, what happens? Do various diets make any difference? Does it need 2,200 calories a day, and how would it deal with 3,800?"

Delvoye says that the pointlessness of the machine *is* the point. He's a *conceptual* artist, after all, and the concept he's trying to get across has nothing to do with nutrition or food. Delvoye believes all modern life is pointless, as is all art; *that's* the point he's trying to get across. His original goal was to build the most pointless machine he could think of, and he came up with *Cloaca*: a machine that turns the finest cuisine a city has to offer into crap without benefiting anyone or anything. "I like the beauty of it doing all this work for nothing," he says.

Pointless, but not unappealing, as proven by the huge crowds who pile into modern art museums in Antwerp, Vienna, Zurich, Toronto, New York, and anyplace else where *Cloaca* is exhibited, just to watch it eat and excrete. "I think *Cloaca* is a machine that can be understood by any culture," Delvoye says. "It's a machine that poos. That's very universal."

The word most often misspelled in search engines: resturant...no, restauraunt...er, restaurant.

OL' JAYBEARD
AND BRIAN

Ol' Jaybeard likes to burst into the BRI and interrupt Brian with his strange challenges and weird word puzzles. Now we pass them on to you. Good luck! (Answers are on page 535.)

1 Ol' Jaybeard held up a *Bathroom Reader* and said, "I'll bet you I can place this book on the floor and none of you will be able to jump over it." Brian replied, "I'll take your bet, but you're not allowed to put the book underneath anything like a desk or a chair." Jay agreed to the terms. He placed the book on the floor—not under anything—and still won the bet. How?

2. Ol' Jaybeard said to Brian: "Tell me what these words have in common: hijack, coughing, astute, worst, and define." Perplexed, Brian asked for a hint. "No hints!" replied Ol' Jaybeard. "I *order* you to figure it out yourself!"

3. "Brian," said Ol' Jaybeard, "if you can tell me how much change is in my pocket, you can have it. All but three of the coins are quarters. All but three are dimes. All but three are nickels. All but three are pennies." How much money was in his pocket?

4. Ol' Jaybeard challenged Brian with a question: "What common abbreviation has three times as many syllables as an abbreviation than it does when you say the full words?" Stumped, Brian decided to look it up, which prompted Ol' Jaybeard to say, "Don't cheat and use the Google or whatever it is you kids are calling it these days!" Brian replied, "Thanks for the hint—I know the answer!"

5. Uncle John took us out to an exclusive nightclub, and wouldn't you know it—Ol' Jaybeard was the doorman. "You can't come in unless you know the password!" he barked. Then a man walked up to the door and Jaybeard said, "12." The man replied, "6," and Jaybeard let him in. Then a woman walked up and Jaybeard said, "6." The woman replied, "3," and was let in. Brian exclaimed, "This is easy!" and stepped up to the entrance. Ol' Jaybeard said,

"8." Brian replied, "4." Ol' Jaybeard yelled, "Wrong! Now go away!" While we were driving back home to the BRI, Uncle John figured out what Brian should have said. What was it?

6. "As I was speeding through Flushing," recalled Ol' Jaybeard, "the streetlights went out! And my headlights weren't on! And there was no moon in the sky! Suddenly a lady dressed all in black stepped out into the road right in front of me, but I saw her just in time to stop! How?"

7. "I'm thinking of a four-digit number," said Ol' Jaybeard to Brian. "The first digit is one-seventh of the last digit. The second digit is six times the first digit, and the third digit is the second digit plus two. What is the number?" Brian replied, "Uhh…" Ol' Jaybeard reassured him, "You don't have to be a math whiz to get this." What's the number?

8. "I placed a $50 bill between pages 57 and 58 of that *Bathroom Reader*," said Ol'Jaybeard. "The first one of you to get it can keep it." Everyone lunged for the book, except Brian, who remained in his chair. Ol' Jaybeard snarled, "What, are you too good for my money?" "No," said Brian. "I just know that you're lying." How'd he know?

9. Ol' Jaybird burst into the BRI during a winter storm. "Man, it's really coming down out there, but this stormy weather reminds me of a certain seven-letter word. Each time you remove one letter, you have another common word; remove another letter, and you have another word. You don't have even to rearrange the letters. It works all the way down until you're left with one letter, which is also a word." What is this seven-letter word?

10. "Did you know that I used to sell eggs?" asked Ol' Jaybeard. "One day, I had a total of three customers. The first one said, 'I would like to buy half of your eggs plus half an egg more.' So I sold him the eggs. Then the second customer said, 'I would like to buy half of your remaining eggs plus half an egg more.' So I sold her the eggs. Then the third customer said, 'I would like to buy half of your eggs plus half an egg more.' 'Perfect,' I said. 'That's all I have left.' How many eggs did I sell that day? And keep in mind that I didn't have to break any of the eggs."

The highest point in Florida, Britton Hill, is only 345 feet above sea level.

WEIRD ANIMAL NEWS

Strange tales of creatures great and small.

DOG GONE
"It was like something out of *The Wizard of Oz*," said Agnes Tamas, whose dog was blown away by a storm in Gesztered, Hungary, in 2010. Tamas, 57, could see the roofs being ripped from nearby houses when she ran to her cellar. She'd hoped her dog would be safe, but to her horror, she watched as his doghouse was swept up into the air and blew out of sight—with the pooch still inside! After the storm passed, Tamas searched but could find no signs of her pet. A few days later, a man found the dog...20 miles away. Tamas was reunited with her dog, whom she renamed Lucky. The dog's house, however, was never found.

CAT BURGLAR
Harry, a two-year-old Burmese cat, is notorious in his Five Dock, Australia, neighborhood for breaking into people's homes and stealing underwear, gloves, bras, and anything else he can carry. But his favorite thing to steal is footwear. "Harry has a shoe fetish," says his owner, Sue Pope.

CHEETAH SCENTS
Biologists have long known that big cats are attracted to cologne and perfume, so in 2010 they performed an experiment at the Bronx Zoo to find out which one the cats like the most. (The findings will help the scientists set scented remote camera traps.) Cheetahs were given several scents to smell, and the ferocious felines' favorite fragrance: Calvin Klein's Obsession for Men. According to zoo curator Pat Thomas, "The big cats would literally wrap their paws around a tree and just vigorously rub up and down. Sometimes they would start drooling, their eyes would half close, it was almost like they were going into a trance."

GOAT TRIP
During a DUI checkpoint in Bedford County, Virginia, in June

Goofy's original voice and laugh were provided by a circus clown named Pinto Colvig.

2010, police nabbed four drunk drivers, one drug offender…and one goat. It was heard knocking around inside the trunk of a sedan driven by 32-year-old Fiona Ann Enderby, 32, of Washington, D.C. The officers were shocked to find the animal bound in ropes and panting heavily in the 94°F trunk. Enderby, however, didn't see the problem with it. "I'm from the U.K.," she explained. "And it is acceptable there to transport goats in this manner." Enderby said she'd purchased the animal from a farmer; it was a present for the passengers in her car—four men from Kenya who live in Lynchburg, Virginia. Police gave the goat some water and had it transported to a shelter. Enderby was cited for animal cruelty. The four men never did get their goat.

COW TALE

In August 2010, a Chinese farmer from Fuijan province named Sheng Hsueh noticed that one of his cows was missing. There was no trace of theft or foul play, which left him mystified. Four days later, some of Sheng's neighbors started to hear mooing coming from the ground. Then, through an open manhole, the missing cow reared its head. Somehow, she had wandered off and gotten lost in the sewer system. Sheng retrieved her with a winch and some rope. "She didn't seem upset by her ordeal," said one villager. "As soon as they freed her, she found a patch of grass."

BEAR LEFT

Campgrounds and national parks frequently offer metal food boxes that keep out hungry bears. One night in July 2010, a bear climbed into the Story family's Toyota Corolla and went after a peanut butter sandwich that was left on the back seat. Except the Storys weren't in a national park—they were in their home in Larkspur, Colorado, a suburb of Denver. Once the bear got in the car and had a snack, he took the car for a brief spin. To be fair, the bear wasn't trying to steal the car—he just knocked the gear shift into neutral, sending the car down the Storys' driveway and into a thicket of trees. That woke up the neighborhood. Animal control authorities were summoned to remove the bear, who couldn't get out of the car. Ralph Story told reporters that the bear left "a nice pile" on the front seat as a parting gift.

Another cause of lightning: friction between ash particles from an erupting volcano.

STAND-UP FOLKS

Here's a humor break courtesy of some of the world's funniest comedians.

"Bozo the Clown. Do we really need 'the Clown'? Are we going to confuse him with Bozo the Tax Attorney? Or Bozo the Pope?"

—Jerry Seinfeld

"I must be going bald. It's taking longer and longer to wash my face."

—Harry Hill

"Studies reveal that rectal thermometers are the best way to take a baby's temperature. Plus, it really shows them who's boss."

—Tina Fey

"I can't swim. I can't drive, either. I was going to learn to drive but then I thought, well, what if I crash into a lake?"

—Dylan Moran

"Woman don't want to hear what you think. They want to hear what *they* think, in a deeper voice."

—Bill Cosby

"Kissing is just pushing your lips against the sweet end of 66 feet of intestines."

—Drew Carey

"Here's some advice: At your next job interview, tell them you're going to give 110%. Unless you're applying for a statistician job."

—Adam Gropman

"It's one of life's most memorable moments: the marriage proposal. I fantasize about it. Will he hire a plane to write, 'Will you marry me?' in the sky? And if I don't want to marry him, do I have to hire a plane to write, 'No'?"

—Rita Rudner

"I've always wanted to go to Switzerland to see what the army does with those red knives."

—Billy Connolly

"My first job was selling doors, door to door. That was tough. Ding Dong. 'Can I interest you in a…oh, you've got one already. Never mind.'"

—Bill Bailey

"I have a lot of growing up to do. I realized that the other day while sitting in my fort."

—Zach Galifianakis

WORD ORIGINS

Ever wonder where words come from? Here are some interesting stories.

HECK

Meaning: A mild exclamation of surprise or irritation

Origin: "How much truth is there to the legend that Mark Twain invented this word to spare his wife from the godless word 'hell'? None. The origin goes back several centuries to Lancashire, England. It either derives from *eck!*, an expression of surprise, or from the Lancashire imprecation *go to ecky*, meaning 'go to hell.'" (From *A Browser's Dictionary of Interjections*, by Mark Dunn)

PRUDE

Meaning: One who is excessively concerned with being or appearing to be proper, modest, or righteous

Origin: "Prude owes everything to *proud*, once upon a time the same word. It was clipped from Old French *prudefemme*, meaning a good and honorable woman, but 'prude' has long since declined into something critical and narrow." (From *The Secret Lives of Words*, by Paul West)

WIZARD

Meaning: A man skilled in the occult; a magician

Origin: "'Wizard' is formed from the adjective *wise* and the suffix *-ard*. The word originally meant a 'wise man, philosopher.' The suffix *-ard*, however, almost always has a pejorative or disparaging sense, as in the words 'coward' and 'drunkard.' 'Wizard' was therefore often used contemptuously to mean 'a so-called wise man,' and from this use it came to mean 'sorcerer' and 'male witch.'" (From *Word Mysteries & Histories*, by the *American Heritage* dictionaries)

ACNE

Meaning: A common skin condition characterized by pimples on the face, chest, and back

Origin: "It is ironic that 'acne,' which represents a low point in many teenagers' lives, comes from *acme*, 'the highest point.' The

Greeks used *akme*, which literally meant 'point,' for referring to spots on the face, but when it came to be rendered into Latin it was mistranslated as *acne*, and the error has stuck." (From *Dictionary of Word Origins* by John Ayto)

STYMIE
Meaning: To hinder or thwart
Origin: "Originally a golf term, dating from at least 1834, denoting a golf ball lying on the putting green blocking another player's ball from the hole. The root of 'stymie' is thought to be the old Scots word *stymie*, meaning 'person who sees poorly.' The logic here may be that a 'stymie' ball blocked the other ball from clearly 'seeing' the hole. What is certain is that by around 1902 'stymie' had come into general use in the 'obstruct' or 'frustrate' sense, and government agencies have been 'stymieing' their citizens ever since." (From *The Word Detective*, by Evan Morris)

MOSEY
Meaning: To stroll; walk as if not in a hurry
Origin: "This American slang word may stem from a name given to Jewish street vendors in the 1820s eastern USA who used to walk slowly under the weight of their loads. A general pejorative name applied to all Jews at one time was Moses." (From *Batty, Bloomers and Boycott*, by Rosie Boycott)

HUBBUB
Meaning: A confused sound of many voices; uproar; tumult
Origin: "It has often been remarked that the early Celtic inhabitants of Britain contributed very little to the stock of English words. This is no surprise, given the difficult relations between the Germanic and Celtic peoples of England and Ireland. It seems likely that a certain English contempt resides in the adoption of the word 'hubbub' from a Celtic source, which is probably related to *ub ub ubub*, a Scots Gaelic interjection expressing contempt, or to *abu*, an ancient Irish war cry. In any case, 'hubbub' was first recorded (1555) in the phrase 'Irish hubbub' and meant 'the confused shouting of a crowd.' 'Hubbub' was again used by the New England colonists as a term for a rambunctious game played by Native Americans." (From *The American Heritage Dictionary of the English Language, 4th Edition*)

One of the most widely recognized scents in the world: baby powder.

THE LOST EXPLORERS: PERCY FAWCETT

The second in a series on explorers who strode bravely into the face of the unknown—and never came back.

MAD DOGS AND ENGLISHMEN

Percival Harrison Fawcett (1867–1925) was a man who believed in manifest destiny—specifically, his own—and that he was born to make history. Tall and athletic, he possessed a steely will that allowed him to endure hardships that would kill most people. Among his friends were adventure writer H. Rider Haggard (*King Solomon's Mines*) and Arthur Conan Doyle, who used Fawcett's journals as inspiration for *The Lost World*. Between 1906 and 1924, Fawcett made seven expeditions to the Texas-sized unexplored region of the Amazon Basin known as the Mato Grosso. Most European expeditions into the Amazon were massive affairs—explorers venturing in at the head of small armies of bearers, guards, and heavy equipment. They stuck to navigable rivers, and rarely trekked into the jungle itself. If they encountered natives, it was considered prudent to shoot first and ask questions later. Fawcett rejected this approach. He traveled light, with only a handful of trusted men, on the assumption that natives would be less threatened by a few solitary travelers. Rather than drive the tribespeople off, Fawcett risked his life again and again by approaching them and trying to communicate (a brilliant linguist, Fawcett learned over 60 tribal languages).

THE HUNT FOR "Z"

By the early 1920s, Fawcett had become convinced that an ancient city, which he called "Z," lay buried in the Brazilian jungle. Locals had told him legends of a vanished civilization, and these reports, combined with information he gleaned from colonial archives in Peru, Bolivia, and Spain, convinced him that the ruins of "Z" were out there somewhere. This notion went completely against accepted scientific belief of the day, which held that the Amazon was too hostile an environment to support any social organization larger than the scattered villages that had already been found. Fawcett's theory was ridiculed, and soon he was considered more of a crackpot than a scientist. But Fawcett was nothing if not stubborn, and in 1925 he was able to scrape together enough money for another expedition. True to form, he decided to take only two people with him: his son Jack and Jack's best friend, Raleigh Rimell. Both were in their early 20s, athletic, adventurous, and, most important to Fawcett, trustworthy. They landed in Brazil and made their way by riverboat and mule train to the headwaters of the Upper Xingu River, in present-day Bolivia, which marked the border of the unexplored region of the Amazon. On May 29, 1925, Fawcett telegraphed his wife that they were setting off into the uncharted area and it might be some time before she heard from them again.

SWALLOWED BY THE JUNGLE

Months, then years, passed, with no word of the expedition. Finally it was assumed that either natives or disease had killed them. Whatever the cause of the trio's disappearance, it triggered a bizarre obsession to find Fawcett that lasted for decades, often with disastrous consequences. More than 100 explorers died trying to find him. Pieces of Fawcett's personal effects cropped up from time to time—a nameplate from a carrying case in 1927, an engraved compass in 1934—and every so often someone would claim to have found his bones, only to have the evidence debunked after closer examination. His fate remains a mystery.

VINDICATED

Ironically, Percy Fawcett may not have been as mad as his rivals thought. Recent excavations in the Amazon Basin, led by Michael Heckenberger of the University of Florida, have uncovered tantalizing evidence of massive earthworks believed to be the remnants of a vast irrigation system capable of sustaining a population of 50,000 or more people. Causeways, spanning hundreds of square miles, connect raised mounds containing shards of finely wrought pottery. The site, named Kuhikugu, appears to have been inhabited for 1,000 years and abandoned about 400 years ago. Heckenberger is convinced this is evidence of an advanced Amazonian civilization that rivaled "anything happening in Europe at the time." Wherever he is, Percy Fawcett must be smiling.

CYBER COWBOYS

On virtual steeds they ride into the abyss of the
information superhighway—some want to lay down
the law, and some want to break break it.

BACKGROUND
The term "hacker" dates back to 1960, when students at the Massachusetts Institute of Technology spent long hours "hacking" away at their keyboards in their Artificial Intelligence class, trying to make the computer do something it hadn't been programmed to do. Over the years, as hackers discovered they could break into all sorts of "secure" systems, they had a choice to make: Should they hack for the good of others…or for themselves? Like cowboys in Western movies, they had to choose whether they'd wear the black hat or the white hat.

BLACK HATS are the "bad guys" who break into corporate computer systems, stealing credit card numbers, bank accounts, identities, and e-mail addresses. They either use them for their own benefit or to sell or trade to other Black Hat hackers. Because of the criminal nature of their activities, the ethical hackers often call them *crackers*. Whatever you call them, they're up to no good.

WHITE HATS are the "good guys" (also known as *ethical hackers* or *penetration testers)*—security experts hired to protect companies from the Black Hats. In the era before computers, military intelligence called these experts *sneakers* and utilized them to test security systems, working in groups called Tiger Teams. The sneakers would break into a defense installation and, in prankster style, leave a cardboard sign with the word "BOMB" printed on it in an office and another with "Your codebooks have been stolen" inside the safe, then sneak away undetected. White Hat Tiger Teams do the same thing in cyberspace, only now their calling cards are virtual. They find a hole in a company's security system and show the company how to fix it. In the White Hat community there's an ethical code, inspired by the "net cowboys" of William Gibson's cyberpunk novels (*Neuromancer* and *Mona Lisa Overdrive*) and Japan's Samurai warriors: They are loyal to their employers and sneer at the greed, theft, and vandalism of Black Hats.

BLUE HATS are an offshoot of the White Hats. They're ethical hackers, but they operate outside of computer security firms and are often contracted to bug-test a system before it launches. The concept was created by Microsoft to find vulnerabilities in Windows.

GRAY HATS follow their own code of ethics. Originally coined in 1998 by a hacker group called LoPht, Gray Hats are a little bit white and a little bit black. They don't actually *steal* assets—they find a hole or a bug in a company's security system (through illegal means), but often report their findings to the company. A recent example of Gray Hat behavior occurred in 2010 when a group known as Goatse Security found a flaw in AT&T's security system that allowed e-mail addresses of iPad users to be exposed to the public. Goatse informed AT&T of the problem first, and then let the media know about their discovery. Sometimes Gray Hats aren't so altruistic. They'll alert a company to the bug in their system and offer to fix it...for a hefty fee. Or a Gray Hat might release the bug he or she's found to the public, just to embarrass a company. And then there are those Gray Hats who lean toward the Dark Side, offering to sell their knowledge of the bug to Black Hats or White Hats on the "Bug Market," an online network where computer bugs, vulnerabilities, and personal information are sold and traded.

HAT TRICKS

At the 2010 Black Hat Security Conference, security researcher Barnaby Jack wowed his audience by hacking into two different ATMs right from the stage. He used a remote connection for one and a USB port on the ATM for the other and made them both spit out money like a Las Vegas slot machine. How'd he do it? He wouldn't go into detail (otherwise we'd all become Black Hats looking for a jackpot), but he made it clear that it wasn't just ATMs that were vulnerable. Every piece of equipment that uses a standard computer, like the kind inside an ATM, can be easily hacked: cars, medical devices, televisions, you name it. Jack also pointed out that once he hacked a bank ATM, the machine's data gave him access to anyone who'd ever used it. He found that the stand-alone ATMs at convenience stores were the easiest to hack (something to think about the next time *you* go to an ATM).

It costs $100 to make a Pulitzer Prize (a gold medal), and $500 to make an Oscar statuette.

EJECTED FROM THE OLYMPICS

If you're a fan of the Olympics, you probably know that plenty of athletes have been disqualified for "doping"—using banned performance-enhancing drugs. Here are some of the more unusual reasons athletes have been shown the door.

Athlete: Arash Miresmaeili of Iran, a two-time world judo champion competing in the 2004 Summer Games in Athens, Greece

Reason for Expulsion: Too fat to fight

Details: At the weigh-in for his first-round bout with Ehud Yaks of Israel, Miresmaeili, who was favored to win the gold, was more than 11 pounds over the weight limit. He was disqualified. (Another Israeli, Gal Fridman, went on to win the gold.)

What Happened: Miresmaeili may be the only athlete in Olympic history to deliberately eat his way out of a gold medal. He reportedly went on an eating binge before the event in order to force a disqualification on technical grounds. Real reason for the binge: Iran does not recognize the state of Israel and forbids its athletes from competing against Israelis. Iran's official news agency quoted Miresmaeili as saying that he refused to fight Yaks "to sympathize with the suffering of the people of Palestine." But Miresmaeili later disavowed the statement, so his disqualification was treated as a case of an athlete simply being over the weight limit, and he was not punished. (Iran later awarded Miresmaeili $125,000, the amount it pays to gold medal winners.)

Athletes: Ibragim Samadov, a Russian weightlifter competing in the 1992 Summer Games in Barcelona, Spain

Reason for Expulsion: Awards-ceremony temper tantrum

Details: Samadov tied the silver-medal winner by lifting the same amount of weight of his closest competitor: 814 pounds. If you think that qualified him to share the silver medal, think again.

Because Samadov weighed just one-tenth of a pound more than his opponent, he was considered to have had a strength advantage, and that bumped him down to the bronze for third place. How well would *you* have handled missing the silver by one-tenth of a pound? Samadov didn't take it very well, either. At the awards ceremony, he insisted on being handed his medal instead of having it placed around his neck. Then he set the medal on the ground and stomped off in a huff.

What Happened: Did you know that refusing a medal at the Olympics is for keeps? Samadov didn't: Though he apologized for his actions, he was stripped of his medal and disqualified. And because the disqualification wasn't related to his performance in the actual events, the bronze medal wasn't awarded to the fourth-place finisher. Samadov was later banned from his sport for life.

Athlete: Angel Matos, a Cuban tae kwon do athlete competing in the 2008 summer games in Beijing, China

Reason for Expulsion: Fighting his opponent *and* the referee

Details: According to the rules of tae kwon do, if you are injured during a match you can take a 60-second break called a *kyeshi*. Matos took such a break in the second round of his bronze-medal bout with Arman Chilmanov of Kazakhstan…but he went over the 60-second limit and was disqualified. When he realized what had happened, Matos flew into a rage, pushing a judge and then kicking referee Chakir Chelbat in the face. Chelbat needed stitches to close the wound on his lip.

What Happened: One good kick deserves another. Matos was kicked out of the Olympics, and all records of his participation were erased. The World tae kwon do Federation later banned him and his coach from all sanctioned bouts for life.

Athlete: Ben Johnson, a Canadian sprinter competing in the 1992 Summer Games in Barcelona, Spain

Reason for Expulsion: Drugs and violence

Details: How many athletes have been thrown out of *two* different Games? In the 1988 Seoul Olympics, Johnson won the 100-meter sprint competition in world-record time, but three days later he was stripped of his gold medal and his world record after testing positive for performance-enhancing drugs. Four years later in Barcelona, Johnson was back, but not for long: He washed out of the 100-meter race after stumbling out of the starting blocks in his semifinal heat and coming in last. That's what knocked him out of medal contention, but it isn't what got him thrown out of the Games. That indignity came when a volunteer at an Olympic Village security checkpoint misread Johnson's credentials and refused him entry to a "restricted area"—the village restaurant. Johnson started shoving the volunteer and may have even kicked him before police broke up the scuffle.

What Happened: Johnson wasn't arrested, but his Olympic credentials were cancelled and he was thrown out of the Olympic Village. (When he tested positive for performance-enhancing drugs again in 1993, he was banned from competition for life.)

*   *   *

SEVEN DEADLY SPONGEBOBS

According to the show's creator, Stephen Hillenburg, each of the seven main characters on the children's cartoon show *SpongeBob SquarePants* is a personification of one of the seven deadly sins.

• **Sloth: Patrick Starfish.** He's so lazy that in one episode he gets an award for "doing nothing the longest."

• **Wrath: Squidward.** SpongeBob's neighbor and co-worker, who hates SpongeBob, is always angry and dissatisfied with life.

• **Greed: Mr. Krabs.** SpongeBob's boss at the Krusty Krab restaurant is obsessed with money and is always devising ways to get more.

• **Gluttony: Gary.** SpongeBob's pet snail is shown doing little more than eating, or begging for food. At one point, he runs away when SpongeBob forgets to feed him his breakfast just once.

• **Pride: Sandy the Squirrel.** She constantly talks about how strong she is, and how proud she is to have been born in Texas.

• **Envy: Plankton.** As the villain, he runs a failed restaurant and is forever trying to steal the secret recipe of the Krusty Krab's Krabby Patty.

• **Lust: SpongeBob.** He's excitable, passionate, and demonstrates what Hillenburg calls "excessive love of others."

All Africanized "killer" bees in North America are descended from 26 original queens.

AAMAZING AARDVARKS

You've got to love the aardvark. It's the first animal in Webster's Dictionary, *beating "aardwolf" by a nose. And what a nose it is.*

• Aardvarks are burrowing mammals native to sub-Saharan Africa. The name means "earth hog" in Afrikaans, but they're unrelated to pigs.

• Adult aardvarks are about two feet high at the shoulder and six feet in length (including a two-foot-long tail). They can weigh up to 180 pounds, with long, tubular snouts, and long, rabbitlike ears.

• Aardvarks are very good swimmers.

• Their arched backs and powerful tails give them a kangaroo-like appearance. They sometimes even stand up and balance on their tails like kangaroos, but they're unrelated to kangaroos.

• Aardvarks feed almost exclusively on termites and ants, but they're unrelated to anteaters —they're actually more closely related to elephants.

• Aardvarks hunt at night, clawing termite and ant mounds open, then catching the panicked insects with their foot-long, sticky tongues.

• *Cucumis humifructus* is a type of wild cucumber and is the only fruit eaten by aardvarks. In South Africa they're called "aardvark pumpkins."

• Aardvarks have powerful legs with large, spoon-shaped claws. One aardvark can out-dig several men with shovels.

• Aardvarks dig several shallow burrows throughout their home range. Once a year females dig breeding burrows that reach 40 feet in length, with several entrances.

• Several African mammal species, including porcupines and hyenas, rely on old aardvark burrows for shelter.

• Adults have no front teeth, only molars at the rear of their jaws. The molars have no roots, and grow continuously throughout their lives. Aardvark teeth are considered lucky to some African tribes.

• Some tribes hunt aardvarks for their meat.

• An unusual aardvark habit: They bury their feces like cats.

DUSTBIN OF (CARTOON) HISTORY

There are so many cartoon characters from TV, movies, comic books, and comic strips that they can't all stay popular forever. Here are some favorites you may not have thought about in a while.

CHILLY WILLY was a cute little penguin with big cheeks and huge eyes who starred in 50 theatrical cartoons for the Walter Lantz Studio from 1953 to 1972. Real life penguins live at the South Pole, but Willy lives in Fairbanks, Alaska. Real-life penguins are also adapted to the cold, but the plot of Chilly Willy cartoons usually revolved around Willy trying to get warm. (Some of the cartoons: "I'm Cold," "Operation Cold Feet," and "Hot and Cold Penguin.") Lantz Studios closed in 1972, effectively ending the runs of most of its characters, including Woody Woodpecker, Andy Panda, and Chilly Willy. The cartoons were licensed out for TV syndication, but most local stations only wanted Woody Woodpecker. Result: Willy was unknown to an entire generation of cartoon-watching kids. Nevertheless, new Chilly Willy cartoons were a part of a Woody Woodpecker revival show that aired Saturday mornings on Fox from 1999 to 2002.

FIEVEL MOUSEKEWITZ debuted in the 1986 hit animated movie *An American Tail*. Walt Disney Studios held a virtual monopoly on mainstream animated films...until mega-producer/director Steven Spielberg teamed with Universal Pictures to make this one. The plot was decidedly non-Disney, too: Fievel's family are Russian-Jewish mice who flee their homeland (cats destroy their village) and come to America. Fievel, an adorable toddler mouse in an oversize blue hat, gets lost and has many adventures before the happy ending. It looked like Universal's mouse might topple the House of Mouse—*An American Tail* grossed $47 million, more than Disney's *The Great Mouse Detective* and a re-release of *Lady and the Tramp*. Universal immediately commissioned a sequel (*Fievel Goes West*), but it didn't come out until 1991. By then, Fievel was no longer a hot commodity—the

---

In 2008 Barack Obama had 459,000 friends on MySpace. Miley Cyrus: 552,000.

sequel earned less than half as much as its predecessor, which ended the franchise.

TOP CAT was the second prime-time animated series, after *The Flintstones*. Both were produced by Hanna-Barbera and both aired on ABC. Top Cat was a con man who led a scheming gang of alley cats. And just as Fred Flintstone was based on Ralph Kramden in *The Honeymooners*, Top Cat was based on Sgt. Bilko, the shady army man on *The Phil Silvers Show*. Original episodes of *Top Cat* ran from 1961–62. After that, reruns were shown sporadically in syndication and on cable TV. In the late 1980s, several Hanna-Barbera cartoons were revived, including a *Flintstones* reboot called *Flintstone Kids* and new episodes of *The Jetsons*. A TV-movie called *Top Cat and the Beverly Hills Cats* was produced in 1987 to give Top Cat the same treatment, but it received low ratings and sold poorly on home video, scrapping any plans for a Top Cat revival.

WOODSY OWL was the mascot of the U.S. Forest Service. One of the few famous public service mascots (like Smokey Bear), Woodsy appeared in TV commercials from 1970 until around 1990, urging kids to "give a hoot, don't pollute." While that campaign was about litter prevention, Woodsy was "rebooted" in 2006 after leaving the airwaves for more than a decade, but with a broader pro-environment approach. His new slogan is "Lend a hand, care for the land."

BUSTER BROWN was one of the earliest American cartoon characters, and one that survived for decades in several media. In 1902 Richard Felton Outcault created a comic strip about Buster (he took the name from vaudeville child star Buster Keaton), a wiseacre prankster in a page-boy haircut, his sister Mary Jane, and a pit bull named Tige. The characters moved to short films in the 1920s, a radio show that debuted in 1943, and to TV in 1951. Buster and Mary Jane were hugely popular, but today they're only remembered for the shoes that bear their names. The Brown Shoe Company licensed the use of the Buster Brown characters in 1904 and has offered lines of "Buster Brown" children's shoes ever since. "Mary Janes"—now a generic term for patent leather, rounded-toe shoes with straps for girls and women—get their name from the Mary Jane of *Buster Brown*.

THE MASTER HOAXER

Here at the BRI, we have a lot of respect for people who
pull off elaborate hoaxes. Here's one of the best ever.

BACKGROUND
After graduating from Ohio State University in 1952, Alan
Abel moved to New York City, hoping to become a stand-
up comedian. When that didn't work out, he took a job answering
the customer hotline at the American Automobile Association. It
was a pretty boring job, so to entertain himself, he'd give callers
unnecessarily complicated driving instructions. Not only did that
alleviate the boredom, it was fun, which made him realize that
he'd found his niche in comedy: pulling pranks. Over the next
five decades, Abel pranked the American media repeatedly with a
series of bizarre hoaxes just believable enough to get press coverage...and get the press angry.

HOAX: The Society for Indecency to Naked Animals
STORY: While driving through Texas in 1959, Abel saw a cow and
a bull mating in the middle of a road, which held up traffic for 20
minutes. During the interlude, Abel noticed two elderly women acting horrified and covering their faces in disgust. He thought it was
absurd that anyone could consider the idea of mating animals offensive, so he took the idea a step further into absurdity and wrote a
tongue-in-cheek article for the *Saturday Evening Post* calling for the
need to *clothe* all animals. The *Post* thought he was serious (or seriously nuts) and rejected the article. But the seed for Abel's first
prank had been planted. In May 1959, he formed a phony organization called the "Society for Indecency to Naked Animals" (the
badly worded title was intentional). He issued press releases and
held press conferences for SINA, claiming he represented a large
group of people who aimed to clothe the "scandalously naked animals all over the world." SINA's slogan was "A nude horse is a rude
horse," and its logo was a horse wearing red swim trunks.

Abel recruited a young actor (and future *Saturday Night Live*
star) named Buck Henry to play SINA spokesman "G. Clifford
Prout" in radio and TV interviews, and even got him booked on

---

There are 1,500 shades of animation paint in the film *Snow White and the Seven Dwarfs*.

The Today Show. While the prank was an attempt to expose the failings of a media more interested in sensationalism than substance, many people were actually fooled, including a California woman who tried to donate $40,000 to the "cause." (Abel returned the money, explaining to her that he "couldn't accept money from strangers.") Amazingly, the organization wasn't exposed as a prank until three years later, when, after Walter Cronkite interviewed "Prout" for the *CBS Evening News*, a few network employees recognized Henry from his fledgling performing career.

HOAX: Deep Throat, Revealed
STORY: As the Watergate scandal was unfolding in 1973, *Washington Post* journalists Bob Woodward and Carl Bernstein announced that they had been getting information from a secret source, nicknamed "Deep Throat" (after the popular porno film). Speculation ran wild as to who Deep Throat really was, so when Alan Abel invited reporters to a New York City press conference to meet the legendary informant, 150 journalists showed up. What they got was a masked actor who bickered with his wife, fainted, and was quickly taken to a waiting ambulance...still incognito. Although that should have made it clear that it was a hoax, a literary agent offered Abel $100,000 to write a Deep Throat biography.

HOAX: Alan Abel is Dead
STORY: In 1979 Abel set out with a lofty goal: to force the *New York Times*, the most respected newspaper in the United States, to retract an obituary...which it had never done before. First, he had phone service installed in the trailer home of a friend in Utah and registered it to the "Wellington Funeral Home." Then he paid for a wake at All Soul's Church in Manhattan. And finally, an hour before press time on a Sunday afternoon, when he knew there wouldn't be enough time for staff to properly fact-check the story, he had his wife call the *Times*. Legendary prankster Alan Abel, she reported, had died of a heart attack while skiing in Park City, Utah. The reporter made some calls to both the "Wellington Funeral Home" and All Soul's Church to confirm the story, and the next day, the Times published an obituary detailing Abel's many high-profile pranks. Shortly after the paper hit stands, Abel issued a press release

denying his death. The following day, the *New York Times* had
to issue a retraction.

HOAX: The Donahue Fainting
STORY: In 1985 the popular talk show *Donahue* ceased taping
episodes in Chicago, opting instead to broadcast live from New
York City. Abel figured this was a good time to protest what he
considered trashy television and also make a scene on live TV. So
Abel hired seven actresses and got them all tickets to sit in the
audience for the first live *Donahue*. One by one, as the show progressed, each of the women fainted, in full view of the cameras. In
all, 10-12 people fainted, including some who weren't even in on
the prank. Although no one was seriously injured, Phil Donahue
and his producers panicked: Fearing the studio's lights were too
hot, the producers evacuated the remaining audience members
and a nervous Donahue finished his show to an empty house.
After Abel publicly came clean, he heard from a *Donahue* producer that Donahue was so mad that he tore apart his office and
kicked all the furniture around. But when it actually made the
show's ratings go up, Donahue sent Abel a Christmas card that
read, "Hope nothing causes you to feel faint in the new year."

HOAX: The KKK Symphony Orchestra
STORY: In 1991 former Ku Klux Klan grand wizard David Duke
ran for governor of Louisiana, claiming that he had abandoned his
racist ways and had broken all ties with the notorious hate group.
Abel didn't believe him. So to ensnare Duke, he created a fictitious
KKK Symphony Orchestra. Posing as "Charles Calhoun," Abel sent
out recordings of the Orchestra along with press press releases promoting a "kinder, gentler KKK" and a claim that although the
orchestra members were from different ethnic and racial back-
grounds, they'd all play while wearing white hoods. "Calhoun" even
told Julia Lobaco, a reporter from the *Arizona Republic*, that Duke
was one of the Orchestra's backers. Lobaco asked Duke, who
adamantly denied involvement, to which "Calhoun" responded,
"Well, what would you expect him to say?" Nevertheless, when Abel
invited Duke to guest-conduct the orchestra, Duke accepted the
offer...until he discovered that the "Orchestra" was a put-on. (He
lost the election, too.)

East meets West: Mary Kay Cosmetics has over 200,000 representatives in China.

"9-1-DUMB, WHAT'S YOUR EMERGENCY?"

The other day, Uncle John was thinking about how cool it is that when an emergency occurs, you can dial 911 to get help. So he dialed 911 to say thanks. Apparently, the police don't really like that. Here are some other things they didn't like.

KEEP POUNDING AWAY

James Little's voice was familiar to the 911 dispatchers in Regina, Saskatchewan. He had a long history of making frivolous emergency calls and was under a court order not to call 911 unless he had an actual emergency—or else he would go to jail. But on Easter morning of 2010, Little, 75, just couldn't help himself. He called 911 and asked the dispatcher where the pound key on his phone was located. Little spent Easter Sunday in jail.

MAMA BEER AND BABY BEER

In 2010 a 32-year-old Florida man named Charles Dennison called 911 to report that his mother had stolen his beer. The 911 operator told him that it wasn't a police matter—he should work it out with his mother. He couldn't, so he called 911 again. The operator reiterated, "Work it out yourselves." Then Dennison threatened to keep calling 911 over and over until officers came and arrested his mom. True to his word, Dennison phoned the emergency line dozens of times that night until cops came out and arrested…him.

THIS PLACE IS LIKE A PRISON!

Carly Houston, 29, was hauled into the Naperville, Illinois, police station in 2010 after she threatened a taxicab driver and refused to calm down when police attempted to reason with her. She was arrested for disorderly conduct. At the station, officers informed Houston that she could make one phone call to someone who could come in and post her bail. So who did Houston call? 911. "I'm trapped! You gotta get someone in here to get me out of here!" One more charge was added: making a false emergency call.

More than half of all items listed on eBay receive no bids.

KISS AND MAKE-UP

...and other cleverly named celebrity autobiographies.

- **The Merchant of Dennis,** by Hank Ketcham, creator of "Dennis the Menace"

- **sTori Telling,** by Tori Spelling

- **Love, Lucy,** by Lucille Ball

- **Just Farr Fun,** by Jamie Farr

- **Bunny Tales,** by Izabella St. James, ex-girlfriend of Hugh Hefner

- **Winking at Life,** by Wink Martindale

- **Breaking the Surface,** by diver Greg Louganis

- **Backstage with the Original Hollywood Square,** by Peter Marshall, host of *The Hollywood Squares*

- **KISS and Make-Up,** by Gene Simmons of KISS

- **Sly Moves,** by Sylvester Stallone

- **Out of Sync,** by Lance Bass of *NSYNC

- **To Be or Not to Bop,** by Dizzy Gillespie

- **All You Need Is Ears,** by Beatles producer George Martin

- **Priceless Memories,** by Bob Barker

- **Be My Guest,** by Conrad Hilton

- **Prairie Tale,** by Melissa Gilbert (*Little House on the Prairie*)

- **They Made a Monkee Out of Me,** by Davy Jones of the Monkees

- **My Word Is My Bond,** by Roger Moore

- **Pryor Convictions,** by Richard Pryor

- **That's Not All Folks,** by Mel Blanc

- **Between a Heart and a Rock Place,** by Pat Benatar

- **Lips Unsealed,** by Belinda Carlisle of Go-Gos (they had a hit with "Our Lips Are Sealed")

- **Landing on My Feet,** by Olympic gymnast Kerri Strug

Rule of claw: The colder the waters it lives in, the tastier the lobster.

FAMOUS FOR 15…*EWW!*

Andy Warhol once said, "In the future, everyone will be famous for 15 minutes." Let's hope that when your time comes you won't earn your 15 minutes the way this person did.

RENDEZVOUS WITH DESTINY
In August 2009, a 19-year-old British woman named Charlotte Taylor hopped a train from East Boldon, in northern England, to the city of Leeds, 75 miles away. She and some friends had tickets to the three-day Leeds Music Festival, which featured acts such as Radiohead, Vampire Weekend, the Yeah Yeah Yeahs, Kings of Leon, and the Arctic Monkeys.

Taylor made it to the festival and was enjoying the music along with thousands of other fans. Then nature called, and when she visited the portable toilets, she found her 15 minutes of fame when she accidentally dropped her purse down the hole of the toilet…and then tried to retrieve it herself.

OH, NOOOOO!

Before you pass judgement on Taylor for going after her purse, stop and think for a minute: If you were unlucky enough to drop your purse where she dropped hers, you might not go after it if all it contained was your ID, a little cash, and some credit cards that you could easily cancel. But what if the purse contained *lots* of cash—say £400 (about $650)? And your new iPhone? And your house keys and your train ticket back to East Boldon? Taylor's purse contained all this and more. "If I left it, I would have been stranded," she told a reporter.

We all have our price. Drop a purse with enough valuable stuff in it down a porta-potti and even *you* will try to get it back.

Taylor's price *was* met that day in Leeds. As she watched her purse fall down the hole, she felt she had only one option. So she reached down into the hole with one arm, then with both arms, and when she couldn't quite reach the purse, she stuck her head and shoulders down the bowl, too.

And that's when she got stuck.

World's largest phone bill: $218 trillion. The Malaysian man who…

IN A JAM

Taylor struggled to free herself, but all she managed to do was wedge herself even deeper into the bowl. Her friends waiting outside couldn't free her either, and finally the fire department had to be called. It took seven firefighters to dismantle the portable toilet and set her free; in all, she spent nearly 30 minutes wedged upside down in the john. (She did get her purse back.)

But if she hoped to escape from her situation without attracting a lot of attention, it was already too late. Even as the fire department worked to free her, word of her predicament spread through the festival, and soon a crowd formed around the porta-potti, chanting, "POO GIRL! POO GIRL!"

Fortunately for Taylor, the porta-potti was so deep that she never actually came in contact with the kinds of things you'd think a person would come in contact with deep inside a porta-potti: This was a Poo Girl who'd touched no poo. But the fire department gave her a good hosing-off anyway, and after a quick change into dry clothes, she was back enjoying the music festival with her friends.

BY ANY OTHER NAME

If Poo Girl thought her notoriety would end once the festival was over, she was wrong there, too. Her story made headlines all over the United Kingdom, and the news wire services spread it all over the world. How about the Internet? More than one concertgoer captured the incident on their cell phone cameras and posted the videos on YouTube, and when someone launched a "Poo Girl Leeds Fest 2009 Appreciation Society" page on Facebook, 22,000 people signed up. (If you wanted to order an "I Am Poo Girl" T-shirt, tote bag, or hooded sweatshirt online, those were available, too.)

It took a few weeks for Taylor's bruises to heal and her embarrassment to fade. Waiting for the notoriety to dissipate is going to take more time. Her family has tried to be supportive, but keeping a straight face around the Poo Girl has not been easy. "When Charlotte told me what happened I just laughed," her mother Chris told *The Sun*. "I felt bad for her, but you have to laugh at these things."

...received the bill said there must have been "some mistake."

PHOBIAS OF THE FAMOUS

Celebrities are just like us, if we also couldn't stand ostriches and paper.

Tyra Banks: Dolphins. Ever since she had childhood nightmares about them. On a 2006 episode of her talk show, she went to Sea World to confront the fear by petting some. (She sobbed the whole time.)

Walt Disney: The creator of Mickey Mouse was actually afraid of mice.

Meryl Streep: Helicopters.

Andy Warhol: Hospitals, after he spent two months in one after he was shot and nearly killed in 1968.

Eminem: Owls.

Pamela Anderson: Her own image startles her. She has a hard time looking in mirrors and can't bear to watch herself on television.

Matthew McConaughey: His fear of revolving doors and tunnels (a very specific form of claustrophobia) is so strong that he gets the shakes when he has to go through them.

Megan Fox: Paper. Movie scripts are sent to her either laminated or in e-book form.

Jake Gyllenhaal: Ostriches. A few were present on the set of his 2010 movie *The Prince of Persia*. Trainers warned that sudden noises could startle the birds into violent attacks, which reportedly left Gyllenhaal paralyzed with fear whenever they were around.

Woody Allen: Bright sunlight.

Madonna: She reportedly has an extreme fear of thunder.

Kylie Minogue: Clothes hangers, more specifically the terrible screeching sound they make when the loop at the top touches the closet pole.

Miley Cyrus: Fireworks.

Tom Cruise: Going bald. Insiders say he uses hundreds of dollars worth of hair tonics each month and obsessively counts the hairs he finds on his pillow.

Janet Leigh: Showers, a fear she developed after the famous murder scene in *Psycho* (which seems only fair, considering how many movie buffs developed the same fear after seeing the film).

Bestselling U.S. supermarket product: Campbell's soup. 50 cans are sold every second.

BEHIND THE RIFF

Many classic rock songs are built around memorable guitar hooks that drive them. Here are the true stories (if the musicians can be believed) behind some of the most familiar riffs in rock-music history.

Song: "You Really Got Me" (1984)
Musician: The Kinks
Story: Lead singer Ray Davies had written a jazz song based on a two-note line played on the saxophone. His brother, guitarist Dave Davies, thought it would sound better on guitar... heavily distorted. So he poked the speaker of his amplifier with needles and shredded it with a razor blade, and turned those two notes into one of the first rock songs built around a fuzzy guitar riff.

Song: (I Can't Get No) "Satisfaction" (1965)
Musician: Rolling Stones
Story: Keith Richards claims that the riff came to him in a dream, and that he envisioned it being played by a horn section. But when he played it on a guitar with some fuzz effects, he realized that the fuzzy sound provided the gritty undertone "Satisfaction" needed. (And the guitar he played it on was missing the lowest string.)

Song: "Smells Like Teen Spirit" (1991)
Musician: Nirvana
Story: This riff is played in a minor key, with Kurt Cobain's guitar tuned down to make it sound more menacing, and it drove the song that would bring alternative rock and grunge into the mainstream. But the riff came from a very mainstream source—on numerous occasions, Cobain hinted that he simply reworked the chorus riff of the 1976 Boston classic-rock radio staple "More Than a Feeling."

Song: "Crazy Train" (1980)
Musician: Ozzy Osbourne
Story: The entire song was written and arranged by Osbourne... except the opening riff. That was the creation of his lead guitarist,

---

Site of first major gold strike in the U.S.: the tiny town of Dahlonega, GA (1828).

Randy Rhoads. Rhoads listened to a looped tape of the song's drum, rhythm guitar, bass, and vocal tracks over and over for hours. While he did, he sat and composed, note by note, the intricate, rapid-fire introduction to the song.

Song: "Layla" (1970)
Musician: Derek and the Dominos
Story: It's probably Eric Clapton's most famous guitar work in a career full of memorable licks, but it was written by another major '70s rock guitarist: Duane Allman. He took the vocal melody from blues musician Albert King's "As the Years Go By," changed the key, and sped it up. That's it.

Song: "Sunshine of Your Love" (1967)
Musician: Cream
Story: Another riff that has "defined" Clapton, but that he didn't write. Bassist Jack Bruce came up with it. His inspiration: a Jimi Hendrix concert. "I love walking into a guitar shop to hear kids playing what is essentially a bass riff," Bruce said.

Song: "Misirlou" (1962)
Musician: Dick Dale and the Del-Tones
Story: "Misirlou" is an old Greek folk song, but the melody is better known as Dick Dale's blisteringly fast 1962 surf-rock instrumental (made famous again when it was used in the opening credits of *Pulp Fiction*). It came about when a fan at a show bet Dale that he couldn't play an entire song on one string. He could.

Song: "Sweet Child o' Mine" (1988)
Musician: Guns N' Roses
Story: Guitarist Slash was noodling around on his guitar one day when he struck on a high-pitched, circular melody. As he kept playing it over and over, the band's other guitarist, Izzy Stradlin, joined in, adding a chord progression. Unbeknownst to them, singer Axl Rose was upstairs, heard it, and started writing lyrics to the melody. The next day at rehearsal, Rose unveiled "Sweet Child o' Mine," written around a riff Slash and Stradlin had already forgotten.

TURTLE STORIES

*Former Harvard University president James Bryant Conant famously said,
"Behold the turtle—he makes progress only when he sticks his neck out."
Uncle John adds: "He also gives us some great bathroom reading."*

TWO FOR ONE

What has six legs, two heads, and one shell? Cheech and Chong—a star attraction at the Venice Beach Freakshow in California. Born in 2009, the conjoined red-eared slider turtles were purchased by the Freakshow when they were two months old. According to the show's owner, Todd Ray, caring for Cheech and Chong—now about the size of a fist—is a daily challenge. "Because there are two distinct personalities, they often want to go two separate ways. This can end up in a battle that causes them to flip over and they can't flip themselves back." For that reason, Ray keeps them in shallow water so they won't drown when they get upside down. Cheech and Chong aren't unique at the Freakshow—there are several other multi-headed critters, including Myrtle, Squirtle, and Thirdle, the world's only known *three*-headed turtle.

A PHOTOGRAPHIC JOURNEY

In 2010 U.S. Coast Guard agent Paul Shultz found a camera washed up on the shore in Key West, Florida. He removed it from its waterproof casing, loaded the memory card into his computer, and saw photos of various sites on the Caribbean island of Aruba. There were also some shots of two men preparing to scuba dive and some video footage of the divers exploring a shipwreck. The final file on the card was a shaky video of water, then sky, then some fish, then a sea turtle's flipper, then water, then sky, then the flipper...over and over for several minutes. "At first I thought someone was getting attacked by a sea creature," said Shultz. But then he figured out what must have happened: A sea turtle caught the camera strap on its flipper and took it for a ride. It also somehow managed to turn the camera on and record part of the camera's 1,100-mile journey. Shultz posted the photos on some travel websites along with a message asking if anyone knew who the camera belonged to. A woman in Aruba recognized one of the men—a photographer named Dick de Bruin. It turned out that he'd

---

Yale study: Having a "bad-hair day" really can negatively affect your whole day.

lost the camera six months earlier while shooting the shipwreck. The camera was returned, and the sea turtle's travel footage has become a YouTube hit, with over 2.3 million views…and counting.

DAMN THEE TO SHELL

Before the fire, Lucky looked like any other red-eared slider. But after flames tore through the A-Dora-ble Pet Shop in Frankfort, Indiana, in 2005, the palm-sized turtle was the only animal that survived. Then the store's owner, Bryan Dora, noticed something strange. Apparently, the intense heat had caused much of Lucky's shell to darken; the remaining orange markings looked just like… Satan. Complete with the horns, eyes, lips, and a goatee. "To me," said Dora, "it's too coincidental that the only thing to come out unscathed would have this image on it." (To date, Lucky hasn't been charged with arson.)

ON THE NO-FLY LIST

Ten-year-old Carly Helm's father bought her a baby turtle—her first pet—when she and her two older sisters visited him in Atlanta in 2010. After Dad dropped the sisters off at the airport for their flight home to Milwaukee, Carly and her pet turtle (named Neytiri after the princess in *Avatar*) boarded the AirTran plane with no problem. But as it was taxiing to the runway, the plane turned around and drove back to the gate. That's when Carly was informed that turtles aren't allowed to fly AirTran due to their risk of salmonella. The Helm sisters and Neytiri were escorted back to the terminal and told they could make arrangements for the turtle and take a later flight, but they couldn't wait—they had to get home. So they called Dad, who agreed to drive back to the airport to pick up Neytiri if airport workers would care for the reptile for an hour. They refused and told Carly to "get rid of it." With tears streaming down her face, she tossed Neytiri, cage and all, into a trash can. Then she reboarded and flew home. An hour later, Dad arrived at the airport but was told the trash had been emptied—the turtle was gone. Two days later, a delivery arrived at Carly's house…it was Neytiri! Apparently, a ramp supervisor had found the turtle in the trash and taken it home, and AirTran officials arranged for it to be reunited with its rightful owner. At last report, Carly and Neytiri are living happily ever after.

LA HISTORIO
DA ESPERANTO

Odds are you don't speak it, but you've probably at least heard of Esperanto. It's the most successful artificial or "constructed" language in history. Here's the story of how—and why—it came to be. Amuzigu!

BABEL

Eliezer Levi Samenhof was a Russian Jew growing up in the city of Bialystok (in modern-day Poland, then a part of the Russian Empire) in the 1870s. The majority of Bialystok's citizens were Jews, but the city was also home to large numbers of ethnic Germans, Russians, and Poles who spoke their own languages and lived in their own distinct communities within the city. There was a lot of hostility between these groups and violence was not uncommon, something that Samenhof felt acutely as he was growing up. "I was raised to be an idealist," he remembered years later. "I was taught about the brotherhood of all people. However, every time in the street and courtyard I was persuaded there are no people...only Russians, Poles, Germans and Jews. All of that tormented my spirit during childhood."

POLYGLOT

Samenhof had a knack for languages; in addition to the Yiddish and Russian he spoke at home, he picked up German and Polish in the street. When his family moved to Warsaw in 1873, he studied English, French, Latin, and Greek at the city's Secondary School of Languages. He also dabbled in Spanish, Italian, and Lithuanian.

This was a kid who spent *a lot* of time thinking about language. Not just about the languages themselves, but also about the role they played in dividing people. In a part of the world that had seen so much hostility between speakers of different languages, Samenhof wondered what the world would be like if everyone spoke the same language. Maybe, he thought, they'd come to see themselves as one single people, and the violence between communities would end.

Hailstorm capital of the United States: Tulsa, Oklahoma.

ALL TOGETHER NOW

People were never going to abandon their own native tongues; that much Samenhof understood. But what if all groups learned to speak a second language—an *international* language—in addition to their mother tongue? No such language existed, but if there was such a language, a Jew living in Bialystok wouldn't have to learn Russian, Polish, and German just to speak to his neighbors, and they wouldn't have to learn Yiddish to speak to him. Learning an international language would enable members of each group to speak with every other group.

Samenhof decided to create one. He figured he'd have to make it as simple as possible—who better to understand that than a student trying to master English, French, Latin, and Greek at the same time without confusing them with the four languages he spoke already? At first he thought a simplified version of Latin or Greek might work, but in time he decided that inventing a new language from scratch would be better.

TRIAL BY FIRE

Samenhof created his language not once, but twice. In December 1878, he was ready to demonstrate his first language—he called it *Lingwe Uniwersala* ("Universal Language")—to his high-school friends. But when he went off to medical school in Moscow the following year, his father insisted that he leave his *Lingwe Uniwersala* notes at home. Then, while Samenhof was away at school, his father burned the notes. Only four lines of *Lingwe Uniwersala* text survive today.

By 1881 Samenhof was back in Warsaw to continue his medical education, and in his spare time he began to reconstruct his international language, drawing as much from *Lingwe Uniwersala* as he could remember and improving the parts he felt needed fixing. Over the next few years he finished school, set up a medical practice as an eye specialist, and kept tinkering away. If he gave any thought to giving up, the assassination of Czar Alexander II by Russian anarchists in March 1881 must have renewed his determination to finish the job: Alexander's murder was followed by anti-Semitic riots or *pogroms* throughout the Russian Empire, including in Warsaw. If ever a universal language of brotherhood was needed, it was needed there and then.

Samenhof—soon to "Esperantize" the spelling of his name to *Lazar Ludwik Zamenhof*—finished work on his language in 1885, but it wasn't until he married into a wealthy family in 1887 that he had the money to publish the book that introduced it to the world. Perhaps because he feared being branded a crank, he published *Unua Libro* ("First Book") under the pen name *Doktoro Esperanto* ("Doctor Hopeful"). That's how the language came to be known as Esperanto.

EASY DOES IT

If you've ever struggled to learn Spanish or French, or had pity on a non-native speaker trying to master the exasperating peculiarities of English, there is much in Esperanto that may appeal to you:

• Zamenhof gave Esperanto a "one letter, one sound" alphabet: Each letter is pronounced one way and one way only. There are no silent letters, so every word is pronounced exactly as it looks.

• Words with two or more syllables are always pronounced with the accent on the second-to-last syllable.

• Forget about studying textbooks filled with grammatical rules—and long lists of exceptions to all the rules you just learned. Esperanto has only 16 rules of grammar; they take up less than two typed pages of text. Once you learn them, you're done—there are *no* exceptions to any of the rules. No irregular nouns, no irregular verbs, no irregular pronunciation. No irregular anything.

A MAN OF FEW WORDS

To cut down on the amount of vocabulary that Esperanto speakers have to memorize, words in Esperanto consist of "roots" that are modified by prefixes and suffixes. Take the word "father," for example. It begins with the root *patr*.

• Nouns in Esperanto are formed by adding *-o* to the root. To form the noun "father," add *-o* to *patr* to get *patro*.

• To make the noun plural, add *-j* to get *patroj*, for "fathers."

• Adjectives are formed by adding *-a* to the root, so "fatherly" is spelled *patra*.

• Verbs (in the present tense) are formed by adding the suffix *-as* to the root. So if you want to say "I father a child," you add the verb ending *-as* to the root to get the verb *patras*.

...signage, etc., into all 23 official languages: 1.25 billion Euros, or about $1.7 billion.

● The suffix -in denotes female. So the word for mother is *patrino*: *patr* + -in + -o (father root + feminine suffix + noun suffix.)

● There's even a prefix, do-, that denotes a relative by marriage—so the word for "father-in-law" is *dopatro*.

Whenever an Esperanto speaker comes across a word they've never seen before, the prefixes and suffixes enable them to decode what it means, which makes learning the language that much easier. By learning the 550 most-used roots, it's estimated that an Esperanto speaker learns the equivalent of more than 2,000 words of a natural language. In doing so they build a vocabulary large enough to understand more than 80% of the words they will encounter in everyday conversation with other speakers.

CHAIN LETTER

In *Unua Libro* Zamenhof provided a list of 900 word roots. And then—perhaps because he'd spent so much of his life with his nose buried in Russian, Polish, German, English, French, Latin, and Greek textbooks—Zamenhof proposed that his readers take a lighter approach: Write a letter in Esperanto, send it to a friend (he even provided sample text), and include a short note that instructs them how to translate it. Challenge them to decipher the letter and write back to you in Esperanto. Better yet, write a poem in Esperanto and send it to your girlfriend or boyfriend.

AS SIMPLE AS THAT

Encouraging people to write letters and poems was a surprisingly effective technique for spreading interest in Esperanto. Zamenhof claimed a person could master the grammar in an hour and learn to speak Esperanto in a few days; people who took him up on the challenge found that he was right. And every time a reader sent a letter off to a friend, a new person was introduced to the language. The letters and poems helped to give Esperanto an appeal similar to crossword puzzles or sudoku: It was a lot more fun than the usual drudgery associated with learning a new language, and Esperanto clubs soon began springing up all over Europe.

So why don't we all speak Esperanto?
Part II is on page 296.

Study result: Multitaskers are less productive than people who do one thing at a time.

DUMB CROOKS

Attention all criminals! Need proof that crime
doesn't pay? Read these...and weep.

NOT VERY SHARPIE

In Carroll, Iowa, two friends—Matthew McNelly, 23, and Joey Miller, 20—decided to break into the apartment of a man who was allegedly involved with Miller's girlfriend. Reason: They wanted to intimidate him and then rob him. They didn't have masks, but they did have a permanent black marker. So they scribbled black ink all over each other's faces, drove to the apartment, pulled up their sweatshirt hoods, and kicked the door several times...but couldn't get in. So they left. A neighbor who heard the racket called 911, and within minutes, the police pulled the two men over and arrested them for attempted robbery. Quipped Carroll police chief Jeff Cayler: "We're very skilled investigators and the black faces gave them right away."

NOT ALL THAT SPARKLES IS DIAMONDS

In 2009 a would-be jewel thief entered the Black Diamond Company in Salt Lake City, Utah. Armed with an ice pick, he ordered two employees: "Give me your precious gems!" The employees explained that Black Diamond doesn't sell diamonds or any other precious gems—they sell rock-climbing gear. The robber stole several computers instead.

NEXT TIME, READ THE SIGNS

In 2009 retired NYPD officer John Comparetto stepped out of a restroom stall at a Holiday Inn in Harrisburg, Pennsylvania, to find a man pointing a gun at him. "Give me your wallet and your cell phone!" said the thief. The ex-cop complied and the man ran away. Then Comparetto yelled, "Need some help!" The help came from the 300 other cops who were attending a police convention at the hotel (several signs read "Welcome Police Officers"). The cops easily apprehended the robber, 19-year-old Jerome Marquis Blanchett. Said Comparetto, "He's probably the dumbest criminal in Pennsylvania."

30% of India's population is vegetarian. Only 2.8% of Americans are.

HOOP SNAKES AND SPLINTER CATS

Were scary stories about Bigfoot part of camping trips when you were a kid? You're not the only one—it turns out that telling stories about the mythical beasts that inhabit the forest is an American tradition.

FIRESIDE FIBBIN'

In the summer of 1908, a young man named Henry Tryon took a job in a logging camp in northern Maine. One night around a campfire, another young man, who was also new to the woods, mentioned that he'd heard a strange, screeching cry that afternoon and didn't know what kind of animal had made it. "Reckon it was one o' them tree-squeaks," an older logger replied. "They're common hereabouts in July."

"What's a tree-squeak?" the young man asked—stepping right into the trap—whereupon the older lumberjacks spent the rest of the evening spinning yarns about the legendary beast. One man claimed the tree-squeak looked kind of like a weasel and was every bit as ornery. Another said it could wrap itself around a tree trunk and blend in with the bark just like a chameleon. A third claimed it could squeak like a mouse, squeal like a pig, howl like a wildcat, or give off a staccato roar that sounded like firecrackers going off. And so it went, with one logger passing the story off to the next, until the men turned in for the night.

The two greenhorns ate up every word of it. It's likely that only a day or two passed before they realized they'd been had—and by summer's end they, too, were terrorizing gullible newcomers with wild tales about "fearsome critters" that supposedly inhabited the dark and spooky forest. The tradition has been around for as long as lumberjacks have roamed the woods of North America.

ENDANGERED SPECIES

By 1908 it was already clear that at the rate the forests were being logged, lumber camps wouldn't be around forever. A handful of people, Tryon among them, began collecting the old loggers' tales and writing them down, so that this form of American folklore wouldn't vanish entirely. *Fearsome Creatures of the Lumberwoods*, by William T. Cox, Minnesota's first commissioner of conserva- tion, was one of the first books on the subject; it was published in 1910. Tryon collected his stories for more than 25 years before writing his own book, *Fearsome Critters*, in 1939.

THE FEARSOME MENAGERIE

Here are some of the more fanciful critters that Tryon, Cox, and others collected over the years. (Keep your eyes peeled for them the next time you're in the woods at night.)

• **The Will-am-alone.** A mischievous squirrel-like animal, the will-am-alone lives in the forests of Maine. It sniffs out poisonous fungus the way a pig sniffs out truffles, and when it finds a patch it rolls the stuff into tiny balls, then sneaks up on sleeping loggers and drops it into their eyes and ears. The fungus balls cause the loggers to have the most vivid and terrifying nightmares imagina- ble. "Parties well-foxed with alcohol," writes Tryon, "seem to be his special prey."

• **The Slide-Rock Bolter.** This giant, beady-eyed, drooling crea- ture resembles a large-mouthed fish, but it doesn't live in the water. The steep mountain slopes of Colorado are its home. The bolter has giant hooked fins at the end of its tail, and it uses these to anchor itself to a mountaintop. Then it lies perfectly still, often for days on end, drooling continuously as it waits for a logger to pass by in the valley below. As soon as it spots its prey, the crea- ture releases its hooked fins and roars down the mountain slope like a kid on a waterslide, its path greased by great quantities of its slippery drool. When the bolter reaches the valley floor it devours the logger in a single gulp. The momentum of its slide sends it all the way to the top of the opposite slope, where it grabs hold with its hooked fins...and waits until it is ready to eat again.

• **The Hoop Snake.** The hoop snake has a stinger at the end of its tail that's armed with venom so powerful it can kill anything it stings. But what really makes this snake dangerous is its ability to form a giant hoop by taking its tail in its mouth, and then roll along like a hula hoop at speeds of up to 60 mph. The hoop snake normally preys on jackrabbits, not loggers, but it will attack any creature if it feels threatened. The only way to get away from it is to find a fence and climb over it. When the hoop snake comes to a fence it has to un-hoop in order to climb over it, slowing it down and giving its prey a decent chance at escape. If there aren't any fences around, you're out of luck.

• **The Dungavenhooter.** This beast looks a little like a crocodile without a snout. The dungavenhooter has huge nostrils, but no mouth. It preys on loggers and is partial to drunks, especially those soused on rum. So how does it eat the loggers if it doesn't have a mouth? Easy—it hides behind a bush until a logger comes along, then it knocks him down and beats him to death with its tail. It keeps pounding away until there's nothing left of the logger except a bloody mist—which it snorts up with those huge nostrils.

• **The Hidebehind.** Another vicious man-eater, the hidebehind is a six-foot-tall creature with slender build, quick reflexes, and a thick black coat of fur. Its skinny build enables it to *hide behind* trees when sneaking up on loggers. Then, after it creeps up behind an unfortunate woodsman, it lets out a terrifying screech. If the logger doesn't drop dead from fright right then and there, the hidebehind disembowels him with a single swipe of its razor-sharp, bearlike claws. The good news: The hidebehind cannot stand the smell of alcohol and will not prey on drunks. A single swig of whisky or bottle of beer is more than adequate protection from this teetotaling timberland terror.

• **The Splinter Cat.** Harmless to humans but very destructive, the splinter cat is found in forests all over North America. It's a short, stocky feline with powerful legs and a hard, wedge-shaped head. The splinter cat feeds on honey and raccoons, both of which can be found in hollow trees. Sadly, it can't tell solid trees from hollow ones, but it makes up for this with its astonishing strength. After climbing to the top of one tree, it hurls itself against a neighboring tree with enough force to snap the top clean off. If this wedge-headed wonder finds honey or a raccoon inside the tree, it stops there and eats. If not, it hurls itself at another tree, and then another, and another, until it finally finds its dinner.

For more tall tales about the "fearsome critters" of the forest, ride your hoop snake over to page 439.

PEOPLE YOU THOUGHT WERE AMERICANS

BRI reader Christine D. recently told us that she was surprised to learn that the actor Errol Flynn wasn't from the United States. (Can you guess where he was from?) That made us wonder about other famous people that we assumed were born in America...but weren't. We were surprised by how many we found.

R ICH LITTLE. The comedian, who achieved fame on *The Tonight Show* and *The Ed Sullivan Show* in the 1960s and '70s through his impersonations of Johnny Carson, George Burns, John Wayne, and Richard Nixon, among many others, started out doing impersonations of Canadian politicians. Little was born in Ottawa in 1938 and became an American citizen in 2008—at the age of 69.

ERROL FLYNN. Flynn was born in Hobart, Australia, in 1909. He moved to England in his early twenties and to the U.S. when he was 26. He became a Hollywood star almost instantly—and didn't become an American citizen until 1942, at age 33. Flynn didn't die in the U.S., either: He had a heart attack while visiting friends in Vancouver, British Columbia. He was only 50 years old.

BOB HOPE. He was born in London in 1903, emigrated to the U.S. with his family in 1908, and became a citizen in 1920.

EDDIE VAN HALEN. The guitarist for the rock group Van Halen was born Edward Lodewijk Van Halen in Amsterdam, the Netherlands, in 1955. His family moved to Pasadena, California, when he was seven. (His older brother, Alex, the drummer for the band, is also from Amsterdam.)

DAVID BYRNE. The front man for the Talking Heads was born in Scotland in 1952, moved to Ontario, Canada, with his family when he was two, then to the Baltimore, Maryland, area when he was nine. And although he has lived in New York City for many years, he is still a British citizen.

GENE SIMMONS. The bassist and professional tongue-sticker-

First telephone area code: 201 (for northern New Jersey).

outer for the band KISS was born in Haifa, Israel, in 1949. His family moved to New York City when he was eight.

JULIAN McMAHON. Fans might know him as Cole from the series *Charmed*, or as the womanizing Dr. Christian Troy on *Nip/Tuck*. Either way, he pulls off a perfect American accent—hiding the fact that he's Australian. And he's not just any Australian: He's the son of former prime minister William McMahon, and is still an Australian citizen.

WILL ARNETT. Arnett became famous in 2003 playing George Oscar Bluth II on the Fox series *Arrested Development*. He was born in Toronto, Ontario. So was Michael Cera, who played George Michael Bluth. Portia de Rossi, who played Lindsay Bluth Fünke, is Australian.

THE ENTIRE CAST OF *TRUE BLOOD*. Okay, that's an exaggeration, but several members of the hugely popular Louisiana-set vampire series are not American. 1) The show's star, Anna Paquin, who plays Sookie Stackhouse, was born in Canada in 1982, was raised in New Zealand, and moved to the United States in 1995; 2) Stephen Moyer, who plays Bill Compton, is English; 3) Ryan Kwanten, who plays Sookie's older brother, Jason, is Australian; and 4) Alexander Skarsgård, who plays sheriff, bar owner, former Viking warrior, and vampire Eric Northman, is Swedish.

ANDREAS CORNELIS VAN KUJIK. Kujik was born in Breda, the Netherlands, in 1909. He entered the United States illegally at the age of 20 and enlisted in the army—giving the name "Thomas Andrew Parker" and claiming to be from West Virginia. He was discharged during his second two-year stint, having been diagnosed with "Psychosis, Psychogenic Depression, Emotional Instability." He worked as a carny for several years, then as a music promoter. When country singer Jimmie Davis, one of the early acts he promoted, was elected governor of Louisiana in 1944, Parker was made a colonel in the Louisiana State Militia and was henceforth known as "Colonel Tom Parker." In 1955 he became the manager of an up-and-coming singer named...Elvis Presley. He stayed with Elvis until the King's death in 1977, earning in excess of $100 million along the way. He died in 1997, never having become a American citizen.

DIED IN THE CAN

Over the course of our lives we spend a total of about one year and seven months in the bathroom. Statistically speaking, it's inevitable that some of us would have to take our final breaths in the throne room.

WENCESLAS III OF BOHEMIA (1289–1306)

Cause of death: Murder

Story: King Wenceslas III wasn't the "Good King" in the Christmas carol—that was his great-grandfather. This Wenceslas became King of Hungary at age 12 (the kingdom was a gift from his father). He added King of Bohemia to his title four years later when his father died. But there were ruthless power struggles going on in both kingdoms, and young Wenceslas could not hold on. Within a year, the teen king was stabbed to death by one of his enemies while sitting on his *garderobe*, a primitive toilet common in castles during medieval times—often just a hole that discharged into the moat below. Sixteen-year-old Wenceslas had no children, which ended his family's royal line.

JUDY GARLAND (1922–1969)

Cause of Death: Drug overdose

Story: The morning after a fight with her fifth husband, Mickey Deans, Garland was found dead of a barbiturate overdose, according to one obituary, "perched like a little bird" on her toilet. Three years earlier, comedian Lenny Bruce suffered a similar fate after overdosing on heroin in his bathroom.

THOMAS MERTON (1915–1968)

Cause of Death: Electrocution

Story: Thomas Merton was a Trappist monk and author of more than 70 books. In 1968, while attending an interfaith conference in Bangkok, Thailand, Merton had just stepped out of the shower in his hotel room, his feet still wet, and either tried to readjust the fan or slipped and fell against it. Either way, the fan's wiring was faulty. When Merton didn't show up to his scheduled events, a few of his fellow clergy broke into his room, smelled an unpleasant burning odor, and discovered Merton bruised, burned, and thor-

---

No can dew: In Canada, Mountain Dew is caffeine free.

oughly dead. One of them nearly became the fan's second victim when he tried to lift it from Merton's body. When he touched it, he was thrown across the room—still clutching the fan—by the electrical force and was unable to let go of it until another monk climbed under a bed and unplugged it.

ORVILLE REDENBACHER (1907–1995)

Cause of Death: Drowning in bathtub

Story: Before Redenbacher came along, popcorn was just popcorn. He introduced the idea of "gourmet popcorn" and charged more for it. After selling his company and retiring, the 88-year-old suffered a heart attack in his whirlpool bath. But the heart attack didn't kill him directly—he slumped down below the water and drowned.

CLAUDE FRANÇOIS (1939–1978)

Cause of Death: Electrocution

Story: François was a powerhouse in the French music business. He made a fortune translating English-language hits into French, starting with "Belles! Belles! Belles!," a cover of the Everly Brothers' "Made to Love" in 1962. He moved on to Beatles songs, Motown hits, 1970s progressive rock, disco, and early Michael Jackson. Ironically, one of his few original songs, "Comme d'Habitude (As Usual)," was rewritten into English by Paul Anka and recorded by Frank Sinatra as "My Way." One spring day at his Paris apartment, the 39-year-old singer/businessman was showering, preparing to appear on a TV show, when he noticed an electric light had burnt out above the shower. He probably should've turned off the shower and dried off before trying to change the bulb...

*   *   *

DON'T TIP THE BUCKET

After receiving hundreds of complaints about erratic driving, a bus company in China installed hanging pots of water inside each bus. If the drivers make quick turns or weave in and out of traffic, the water will spill out. Whichever driver ends the day with the most water in his bucket receives a bonus.

Elvis Presley always wore a helmet when watching football on TV.

DUMB JOCK CRIMES

*We hold our athletes to a very high standard. And perhaps because
they're so physically amazing, we think they're above doing really
stupid things...like getting their picture taken with a bag of
drugs, or offering police bribes of a billion dollars.*

POWER PLAY

In March 2000, three security guards at The Mansion on
Turtle Creek, a hotel in Dallas, responded to a noise complaint
about a guest, Dallas Stars goaltender Eddie Belfour. The caller, an
unidentified woman who was in the room with Belfour, told the
guards that Belfour had become drunk, angry, and violent, and she
feared for her safety. When three guards arrived and attempted to
subdue him, Balfour reacted as if they were charging forward on an
opposing team—he kicked two of them in the chest and spat in
the other's face. Thanks to a hefty dose of pepper spray, the guards
apprehended Balfour. By the time the police arrived, the hockey
player's violent rampage had dwindled to pathetic pleading: "If
you let me go," he slurred, "I'll give you a *billion* dollars!" The cops
rejected the bribe and placed Balfour in the back of a squad car,
where he puked all over himself. He received a $3,000 fine.

PICTURE IMPERFECT

In August 2009, Miami Heat forward Michael Beasley used his
Twitter page to show off a picture of an elaborate tattoo he'd just
gotten. The photo depicted Beasley's back, decorated with the
tattoo of angel wings and the words "Super Cool Beas" ("Beas" is
his nickname). Also depicted in the photo: a plastic baggie containing a green, leafy substance. After a few readers pressed him
on it over the next few days (he'd had frequent problems with the
NBA, and the law, over drugs), Beasley closed the Twitter account
and checked into a Houston drug treatment facility.

NAKED HUNGER

In August 2006, Detroit Lions defensive-line coach Joe Cullen
was ordering food at a Detroit-area Wendy's drive-through window. Police later pulled him over after receiving a call from

Wendy's—because Cullen was completely nude. A week later, Cullen was pulled over again by Detroit police. This time he had clothes on, but he was drunk. For the naked incident, he paid a $500 fine, for the drunk driving he paid a $300 fine, and for both he paid a $20,000 misconduct fine to the NFL. He's still a defensive-line coach in the league, now working for the Jacksonville Jaguars.

HE CAUGHT A BULLET

Plaxico Burress was a star wide receiver for the New York Giants who caught the game-winning pass in the 2008 Super Bowl. Later that year, Burress went to the New York City nightclub LQ. He brought along a large Glock handgun, which he hid by tucking it into the waistband of his jeans rather than using a holster. At one point, the gun started to slip down his leg, and when Burress went to reach for it, he accidentally pulled the trigger and shot himself in the right thigh. Burress sought medical treatment and then turned himself in to the NYPD. Not only had he injured himself, he'd committed a crime—the gun was unlicensed. Burress had a license to carry a concealed handgun, but only in Florida, and it had expired. He pleaded guilty to weapons charges and was sentenced to two years in prison.

METALHEAD

In November 2002, Portland Trailblazers star Damon Stoudamire skipped the team jet for a return trip home after a game in Seattle, opting to drive himself the 150 miles home. With teammate Rasheed Wallace in the car, Stoudamire's Humvee was stopped by police. Not only was he speeding along at more than 80 mph, he also had the windows rolled down, and marijuana smoke was billowing out of them. Stoudamire was charged with driving under the influence and speeding, and he paid a fine. In July 2003, Stoudamire was again in possession of marijuana, but had the foresight to at least try and hide it from the authorities this time. So before he boarded his flight from Tucson, Arizona, to New Orleans, he carefully wrapped his stash in tin foil and put it in his carry-on luggage. The foil set off a metal detector, and Stoudamire was detained by airport security. He paid $250,000 in fines and was suspended by the NBA for three months.

HOW TO CRACK A SAFE

Grandpa Uncle John has an old safe in his garage that he says doesn't contain any valuables, but nobody knows for sure...because he lost the combination years ago. That raises an interesting question: How do safecrackers open safes? Read on as we bust the story wide open.

COMBINATION SAFES 101

To understand how a locksmith or a safecracker opens a safe, it helps to first understand a few things about how a combination lock works:

• The numbered dial is mounted on a shaft that extends inside the door of the safe, where it connects to a mechanism called a "wheel pack."

• The wheel pack is so named because it is literally just that: a pack of free-spinning wheels, one for each number in the combination of the safe. If there are three numbers in the combination, say, 17–76–42, then there are three wheels in the wheel pack: one for the 17, one for the 76, and one for the 42.

• Imagine a cookie with a bite taken out of it. Each wheel in the wheel pack has a bite or notch taken out of it that corresponds to its number in the combination of the safe. In this example, the first wheel will have a notch at position #17, the second wheel at position #76, and the third wheel at position #42.

• Opening the safe requires rotating each of the wheels until the notches line up. That's what you're doing when you enter the combination. If you enter it correctly, the notches line up, and the safe will open. If you enter any other combination, the notches do not line up, and the safe won't open.

PLAYING IT SAFE

The first thing any skilled, experienced safecracker will try to do is find a way to *not* put their skill and experience to work. Nobody wants to find out how much it costs to have a locksmith open a safe, and one way that a lot of people try to prevent such a disaster is by writing down the combination and hiding it somewhere—

...violent weather, with 10,000 thunderstorms and 5,000 floods every year.

often in the room where the safe is located. So the first thing the locksmith or safecracker will do is search any obvious hiding places for the combination. If they're *really* lucky (and the owner of the safe is *really* dumb) the combination will be written somewhere nearby or even right on the safe.

• Another bad habit common among safe owners is to set a safe on what's known as "day lock." They enter all but the last number of the combination at the start of the day, so that when something is needed from the safe only the last number of the combination has to be entered. If a safecracker suspects that the safe has been left in day lock, they will turn the dial slowly from one number to the next, looking for the final number in the combination that opens the safe.

• Safes are sold with sample "tryout" combinations that allow customers to try the safe out in the store. After you buy the safe, you or your locksmith are supposed to change the tryout combination to something else. But not everyone bothers to do this, or even knows that they should. So the next thing a skilled locksmith or safecracker will do is try all the industry-standard try-out combinations to see if any of them opens the safe.

PLAN B

If none of the easy ways works, the locksmith has to start trying more difficult methods. One brute-force technique that works on antique safes is to knock the combination dial off the safe with a hammer, then use a tool called a punch rod to punch the wheel pack out of position. Once the wheel pack is knocked out of the way, the safe will usually open. But this technique works only on antique safes, whose value is often greater than anything that might be contained inside. Modern safe manufacturers incorporate a variety of "relocking" devices into their safes that render them unopenable if someone tries to punch their way through the lock.

So what about using stethoscopes to open
safes and all that other Hollywood stuff?
There's more on page 303.

Good news? Kids eat more Play-doh than crayons, finger paint, and paste combined.

DUSTBIN OF HISTORY: THOMAS MEAGHER

Only two things are certain in life: 1) one day you're born, and 2) one day you're going to die. How much you pack in between those two days is up to you. Here's a brief biography of a man who packed in a lot.

Thomas Francis Meagher (pronounced *mahr*) was born on August 3, 1823, in Waterford City, Ireland. He was educated at highly respected Catholic schools in both Ireland and England and became known as a gifted orator. In his twenties he became involved with the "Young Ireland" movement, a group dedicated to independence from England, and soon became one of its most eloquent voices.

In 1848 Meagher was convicted of treason after the "Young Irelander Rebellion"—a six-day uprising in southern Ireland that ended in a gun battle, during which 65 policemen were killed.

Meagher and several other rebel leaders were sentenced to death by hanging, and drawing and quartering. The sentence was commuted and the men were sent to the British penal colony of Van Diemen's Land instead, which later became Tasmania, Australia.

In 1849 he was given a "ticket of leave," meaning he was free to travel around the island…in exchange for a promise not to escape. In 1851 he saved a young woman from an overturned carriage. He later married her and they had a son.

The following year, Meagher turned in his ticket of leave and notified authorities that he planned to escape and left the island in a rowboat. After four days at sea he was picked up by an American whaling ship headed to San Francisco.

From San Francisco, he made his way to New York City, where he earned a law degree, started a newspaper, and worked the lecture circuit speaking about Irish independence. His wife came to see him in New York once, but then returned to Ireland and died a few years later. Meagher never met their son.

In the late 1850s, Meagher spent a year in Central America

People generally read an item 25% more slowly on a computer screen than on paper.

studying the possibility of building a railroad across the Isthmus of Panama, and wrote about his adventures (which included hunting jaguars) for *Harper's Magazine*.

When the American Civil War began in 1861, Meagher joined the Union Army. By 1862 he was a brigadier general and the leader of the "Irish Brigade," a hard-fighting outfit that saw action in several key battles, including Bull Run, Antietam, and Fredricksburg. He was injured twice, both times when his horse was shot out from under him. He resigned in May 1865, just after the war's end.

That September, Meagher was appointed acting military governor of the Montana Territory.

In 1867 he was aboard the steamboat G.A. *Thompson* on the Missouri River in Fort Benton, Montana, when he fell overboard. According to most reports he'd been drinking, although others say he was murdered by one of the many enemies he'd made during his time as governor.

The Irish revolutionary hero, escaped prisoner, New York lawyer, newspaper publisher, jaguar hunter, brigadier-general, and governor of Montana—was never seen again. He was 43 years old.

A statue of Meagher on horseback with a raised sword in his hand stands in front of the Montana state capitol building in Helena, and Meagher County in central Montana is named in his honor.

*   *   *

FROM THE CLASSIFIEDS

These all appeared in newspapers.

- Attorney at law: 10% off free consultation
- Braille dictionary for sale, must see to appreciate
- For you alone! The Bridal Bed Set
- Mixing bowl set. Designed to please a cook with round bottom for efficient beating
- Snowblower for sale—used only on snowy days.
- Semi-annual after Christmas sale
- Boneless bananas, 39 cents a pound

Arms race? The ant farm and Raid insecticide were both invented in 1956.

MEET THE BEATS

*The Beats were America's first hipsters. But
what were they, like, really about, man?*

THE OTHER SIDE OF AMERICA

One night in 1948, two students at New York's Columbia University, John Clellon Holmes and Jack Kerouac, were hanging out talking about what they thought was wrong with the modern world—the constant threat of nuclear war, the hollowness of suburbia, and the stifling academic mainstream. At one point, Kerouac remarked, "This really is a beat generation."

What did Kerouac mean? It was something he'd heard a few years earlier from someone he'd met in Times Square, a street hustler named Herbert Hunche. According to Kerouac, Hunche told him that "beat" meant that "you're exhausted, at the bottom of the world, looking up or out, sleepless, wide-eyed, perceptive, rejected by society, on your own, streetwise."

Holmes' and Kerouac's clique consisted of a handful of equally disenchanted artists, writers, and academics, all with (un)healthy interests in drugs, booze, and urban culture, including poet Allen Ginsberg and novelist William S. Burroughs. This was the Beat Generation, and they found their escape in the underexplored and often seedy side of American life. And they expressed it in what would come to be highly influential written works.

SEX, DRUGS, BEBOP

The Beats thought the way to enlightenment and artistic fulfillment was to go out and experience the world, especially the fringe elements. They hitchhiked around the country, befriending (and emulating) hobos and outlaws (like Hunche), and they experimented with marijuana, Benzedrine, and morphine.

The main core of the Beats ultimately settled in San Francisco's North Beach in the mid-1950s, where they congregated at jazz clubs for smokey jam sessions and in coffee houses for poetry readings. The structure of jazz—it was experimental, non-linear, free-form, often stream-of-consciousness—heavily influenced the way the Beats wrote.

The first color animated TV commercial, for Ford in 1949, was created by Dr. Seuss.

BOOKING IT

But the fact that the Beats were literary doesn't mean they were refined. Beat literature had a tendency to be raw, lurid, personal, and extremely confrontational—and that was the point. Here are some excerpts from three of the most influential pieces of Beat literature:

- **On the Road (1957).** Jack Kerouac's autobiographical novel about a road trip full of crime, shady characters, and the unseen underbelly of '50s America is considered the definitive Beat work. Kerouac reportedly wrote it in just three weeks, typing stream of consciousness-style on a 120-foot scroll of paper. It was so unstructured that before it could be published, it had to be edited (sections deemed pornographic were deleted) and reformatted with conventional punctuation and paragraph breaks. Here's a passage:

    > And for just a moment I had reached the point of ecstasy that I always wanted to reach, which was the complete step across chronological time into timeless shadows, and wonderment in the bleakness of the mortal realm, and the sensation of death kicking at my heels to move on, with a phantom dogging its own heels.

- **"Howl" (1956).** Ginsberg's furious epic free-verse poem was first performed at a poetry reading at San Francisco's Gallery Six. Published by Lawrence Ferlinghetti's City Lights Press, "Howl" was banned as obscene; Ferlinghetti was arrested, and the trial that followed brought national attention to the work. Here are the first few lines of the poem:

    > I saw the best minds of my generation destroyed by madness, starving hysterical naked, dragging themselves through the negro streets at dawn looking for an angry fix, angelheaded hipsters burning for the ancient heavenly connection to the starry dynamo in the machinery of night, who poverty and tatters and hollow-eyed and high sat up smoking in the supernatural darkness of cold-water flats floating across the tops of cities contemplating jazz...

- **Naked Lunch (1959).** William S. Burroughs' controversial novel also led to an obscenity trial. Published in Paris in 1959, it wasn't released in the U.S. until 1962. Semi-autobiographical, Naked Lunch follows the surreal adventures of junkie William Lee (Burroughs was a morphine addict). Here's a sample:

    > "Selling is more of a habit than using," Lupita says. Nonusing pushers have a contact habit, and that's one you can't kick. Agents get

it too. Take Bradley the Buyer. Best narcotics agent in the industry. Anyone would make him for junk. I mean he can walk up to a pusher and score direct. He is so anonymous, grey and spectral the pusher don't remember him afterwards.

THE BEAT LEGACY

• The Beat Generation set forth the idea that it was okay to try new avenues in art, even if (or *especially* if) they were dark, unsettling, and personal. Artists sharing this philosophy included comedian Lenny Bruce, painter Jackson Pollock, photographer Diane Arbus, and filmmaker John Cassavetes.

• Beat writers popularized spontaneous, stream-of-consciousness prose and performance art, along with abstract expressionism and postmodernism. Modern-day "slam"-style poetry is a direct outgrowth of the Beats. So was the "New Journalism" or "literary nonfiction" movement of the '60s and '70s. Writers would deliver long, narrative, true stories (in which they were active participants) about the edges of American life as if it were a novel, in a highly descriptive, free-flowing manner. Two of those writers: Tom Wolfe (*The Electric Kool-Aid Acid Test*), and Hunter S. Thompson (*Fear and Loathing in Las Vegas*).

• Blogging is a relatively new form of information delivery (often challenging mainstream media) by regular people who explore the world around them and document it in online journals, if not for an audience than for the sake of self-expression. Tech writer Tom Forenski of ZDnet.com argues that bloggers are the present-day equivalent of the Beats. "Both celebrate the written word, and both celebrate a raw and passionate literature that is largely unedited. And both are disruptive movements."

BUT SERIOUSLY

Six months after the USSR launched Sputnik, *San Francisco Chronicle* columnist Herb Caen gave the Beats their most famous nickname when he called them *beatniks* in a 1958 column. "I made fun of the Beats because they took themselves so seriously," he remembered. "I had a drink with Allen Ginsberg one night at Vesuvio and we walked across the street to Tosca. He was barefoot. The uptight Italian who owned the place kicked him out. 'But I'm Allen Ginsberg,' he shouted. The guy had never heard of him."

11 FICTIONAL DOCTORS

Is there is a doctor in the house? Yes, but he's not real.

DR. EMMETT BROWN: Inventor of the flux capacitor, which he used to travel through time. In the *Back to the Future* movies he was portrayed by Christopher Lloyd, who got the role when John Lithgow became unavailable.

DR. JOHN CARPENTER: Elvis Presley's character in 1969's *Change of Habit*, the last in the long string of Presley's musical comedies. While serving at an inner-city health clinic, Dr. Carpenter falls in love with a co-worker (Mary Tyler Moore). Elvis doesn't get the girl this time, because Moore's character is a nun. (At least he gets to sing "Rubberneckin'.")

DR. DEMENTO: The alter ego of disc jockey Barret Hansen. From 1970 to 2010, he hosted a syndicated radio show focusing on novelty songs. Claim to fame: He discovered "Weird Al" Yankovic in the late '70s when Yankovic, then an unknown college senior, started sending homemade tapes of his song parodies to the show.

DR. MARK GREENE: The main character of *ER* (played by Anthony Edwards), from its first season in 1994 until 2002. He was a divorced dad trying to raise a daughter while working his residency as an emergency room doctor. The character died from a brain tumor in season 8, after Edwards, one of the highest-paid stars in TV history, decided to leave the show.

DR. HENRY HIGGINS: In George Bernard Shaw's 1913 play *Pygmalion*, and in the Broadway musical adaptation *My Fair Lady*, the professor of phonetics bets his colleague Col. Pickering that he can turn a rough-around-the-edges Cockney flower girl into a refined, proper lady. Dr. Higgins does, but also falls in love with her. He winds up with her in the musical, but not in the play.

DR. PAMELA ISLEY: In a 1966 *Batman* comic, Dr. Isley is a botanist from Seattle who helps a criminal steal an artifact full of ancient herbs. The criminal, fearing she'll turn on him, poisons her with the herbs. They don't kill her—they make her superpowered and immune to all natural toxins. She then transforms herself into a supervillain eco-terrorist and Batman's rival, Poison Ivy (which is a corruption of "Pamela Isley").

DR. RICHARD KIMBLE: Wrongly accused of killing his wife, Dr. Kimble (David Janssen) searches for the real killer, a one-armed man, over four seasons of *The Fugitive* (1963–67). The theme of a falsely accused man trying to prove his innocence while on the run has been repeated on such TV shows as *The Incredible Hulk*, *The A-Team*, and even *Run Joe Run*, a *Lassie/Fugitive* hybrid starring a dog falsely accused of attacking its master.

REX MORGAN: The main character of the dramatic serial comic strip *Rex Morgan, M.D.* that's been running since 1948, created by real-life psychiatrist Nicholas P. Dallis. Dallis intended the strip as a means of educating the public about medical issues; more than one fan has credited the strip with helping them diagnose their own illness.

DR. BENTON QUEST: Jonny Quest's father on the '60s adventure cartoon *Jonny Quest*. He's a jet-set government scientist who conducts top-secret experiments and takes his son along on dangerous adventures around the world. The character Jonny Quest was created when the show's creators couldn't obtain the TV rights to the radio series *Jack Armstrong: The All-American Boy*.

DR. STRANGELOVE: One of three characters portrayed by Peter Sellers in the 1964 nuclear war farce *Dr. Strangelove or: How I Learned to Stop Worrying and Love the Bomb*. Serving as a scientific advisor to the U.S. President Muffley (also Sellers), Strangelove, a former Nazi, keeps accidentally referring to the president as "mein Führer," and his hand, as if it had a mind of its own, makes the Nazi salute. (The real-life neurological disorder "alien hand syndrome" is also known as "Dr. Strangelove syndrome.")

DOCTOR ZHIVAGO: A novel by Russian author Boris Pasternak, it follows surgeon and poet Yuri Zhivago as he falls in love with his muse, a girl named Lara, but then marries another woman, all against the backdrop of World War I and the Bolshevik Revolution. The 1965 film, starring Omar Sharif and Julie Christie, was a massive hit: Adjusted for inflation, it's the eighth-highest-grossing film of all time.

IRONIC, ISN'T IT?

*There's nothing like a good dose of irony to put the
problems of day-to-day life into proper perspective.*

SCARED STIFF

A 2010 Indiana University study found that anti-drinking
commercials that use scare tactics tend to bring out "feelings
so unpleasant that alcoholics are compelled to eliminate them by
whatever means possible." According to the study's respondents,
they cope by drinking. Result: "Alcoholics actually drink more
than if they hadn't been exposed to the ads in the first place."

I'VE FALLEN AND I CAN'T AVOID THE IRONY

Between 1998 and 2009, four senior citizens were killed by the
pendant cords attached to the Philips Lifeline medical alert buttons they were wearing around their necks. Cause of death: The
victims fell down and the cords became entangled with objects
such as doorknobs. (The alert buttons now come with a hazard
warning.)

ART IMITATES DEATH

After actress Brittany Murphy, 32, died of a heart attack while
taking a shower in December 2009, First Look Pictures immediately recalled and replaced the DVD cover art for her recently
released film, *Deadline*. The reason: It depicted Murphy as a lifeless
corpse lying in a bathtub.

BOOB TUBE

In 2009 the Walt Disney Company offered refunds to parents who
purchased the *Baby Einstein* educational video after a study found
that infants who watched the video actually learned fewer words
than those who didn't. Said one researcher: "The more they
watched, the less they learned."

WHERE THE WILD THINGS ARE

• An "environmental catastrophe" occurred when hundreds of
birds, reptiles, and other woodland creatures were killed and eaten

in a German forest in 2009. Who ate them? Minks—more than 4,000 of them—that had been set free from a nearby mink farm by animal activists.

• In 2009 PETA released a print ad called "Fur Free and Fabulous," featuring stock photos of Tyra Banks, Carrie Underwood, Michelle Obama, and Oprah Winfrey. Apparently no one at PETA was paying attention, because the photo of Winfrey shows her wearing a leather skirt.

BOMBS (AWAY)

Remote-controlled drones that bomb foreign targets were designed, in part, to reduce combat stress. But unlike traditional bomber pilots, a remote operator sees the target up close and observes what happens. The operator is farther away physically, but actually *sees* the destruction. The result, according to defense expert P. W. Singer of the Brookings Institution: "There are higher levels of combat stress among remote U.S. units than among units serving in Afghanistan."

FIRE IN THE SKY

In March 2010, astronomers at Arizona's Whipple Observatory complained to state authorities that bright, manmade lights were brightening the dark skies—inhibiting the astronomers' search for interstellar phenomena and, by extension, space aliens. The bright lights, it turned out, were being used by the U.S. Border Patrol in their ongoing search for *illegal* aliens.

FLYRONY

In 2001 Christian Browning, 60, and his wife were terrorized by a pair of gulls nesting near their home in Cornwall, England. "We couldn't even go into our garden," he said. Browning is the son of author Daphne du Maurier, who wrote the novella that was later adapted into Alfred Hitchcock's 1963 horror film *The Birds*.

YOU'RE KIDDING, RIGHT?

At the head offices of the National Association of Telemarketers in Fort Lauderdale, Florida, a sign is posted on the front door that reads "Absolutely NO SOLICITING."

BANK ERROR IN YOUR FAVOR

More tantalizing real-life tales from the bank vault,
to remind you to be careful what you wish for!

Customer: Louise Inger, 34, from Derby, England
Bank Error: In November 2003, Inger was down on her luck: She was off work due to illness and had only £49 (about $80) to her name. And the holidays were right around the corner. Then, on November 28, her bank deposited £24,550—just over $40,000—into her account by mistake. The money belonged to the Derby City Council and was supposed to be paid into the account of Inger's landlord, Hallmark Community Housing. But a finance officer entered Inger's information into the computer system instead of Hallmark's, causing the money to be paid into her account.

What Happened: As soon as Inger realized the money was in her account, she and her boyfriend, 32-year-old Nathan Sault, started spending it, and kept right on spending it even after the Derby City Council sent a letter, and then a bill collector, to Inger's house to get the money back. The pair managed to blow all but $650 of the council's money in just six days, buying furniture, clothing, eyeglasses, mobile phones, fine wines, a $4,400 TV, Christmas presents, and a trip to Disneyland Paris. They were arrested shortly after they returned home and before they could take a trip they'd booked to Egypt. Inger admitted to the theft immediately. "I had hardly been out this year, so I just let go and had a good time. In all honesty, it was a thrill."

Outcome: Police confiscated $10,400 worth of swag from Inger's apartment; she and Sault were both convicted of theft and each served six months in jail for their six-day spending spree. The bank sued Inger to recover the rest of the money...but decided not to sue Sault. Though prosecutors say he was present for every purchase Inger made, he was considered personally responsible for stealing only $1,000, which he used to pay off an overdraft.

World's largest school: City Montessori School in Lucknow, India, which has...

Customer: Charrise Lott, 29, an employee of Chase Home Finance in Cleveland, Ohio

Bank Error: On March 20, 2004, Lott transferred $325 from her Chase savings account into her Chase checking account. But the bank deposited $32,500 into the account, not $325.

What Happened: Prosecutors say Lott immediately transferred $10,000 into her savings account, went on a $6,000 spending spree, and then wrote $14,000 worth of checks, including $7,500 that she gave to relatives and $5,907 that she spent on a motorcycle.

Outcome: At last report, Lott was under indictment by a grand jury on fraud charges.

Customer: An unidentified Brazilian man

Bank Error: In 1997 the man received a letter from his bank, the state-owned Banco do Brasil, informing him that his bank account had a balance of one billion reals (approximately $560 million).

What Happened: The man did the honest thing—he notified the bank of the error. But rather than correct the mistake, some of the bank's employees hatched a plot to withdraw the money, launder it through local currency exchanges, and deposit it in bank accounts abroad. The schemers offered to pay the man a 5% share, or $28 million, in exchange for his cooperation. He agreed.

Outcome: The conspirators spent a decade trying to figure out how to get the one billion reals out of the man's account without alerting the bank. By the time the plot was broken up in 2007, the scheme had grown to include more than 150 people, including several government employees in three different Brazilian states. And in all that time, the plotters never did manage to withdraw any money from the man's account. (It's not even clear that the money ever really existed; it may have been nothing more than a typographical error on the letter the man received from the bank.)

Customer: Linda Parish, a 50-year-old grandmother living in Lower Earley, England

Bank Error: In June 2001, Parish, who works as a chauffeur, sold a home she owned for a £47,000 profit (about $67,000). On the advice of managers at her Lloyd's TSB branch, she transferred the money into a high-interest savings account. But when Lloyd's

transferred the money into the new account, it neglected to subtract the same amount from the old account, giving Parish two
accounts containing £47,000 instead of one.

What Happened: Parish promptly notified the bank of the error,
but Lloyd's TSB insisted that nothing was amiss. "The bank does
not make mistakes," an employee told her. Parish returned to the
bank four more times to report the error, but was rebuffed each
time. Her "little problem," as bank employees called it, became a
bit of a joke at the branch. When an internal review found that
no mistake had been made, an exasperated bank employee told
Parish, "Look, it's your money, my dear. Spend it!"

So Parish spent it.

She used the money to pay off a mortgage on another property.
That's when Lloyd's TSB realized they had indeed made an error...
and that's when they had Parish arrested for theft. And on top of
demanding the £47,000 back, the bank wanted her to pay them
an additional £25,000 (about $36,000) in interest, legal fees, and
other costs.

Outcome: The judge threw out the criminal case after prosecutors
decided "it was not in the public interest" to prosecute Parish, but
she still had to pay back the £47,000 with interest, which she did
by remortgaging her property. Lloyd's waived its legal fees as a
"gesture of goodwill," but at last report the bank was still refusing
to apologize for its mistake. "Mrs. Parish was aware the money in
her account belonged to the bank but proceeded to withdraw the
funds knowing they were not hers to spend," says a Lloyd's
spokesperson. (Parish no longer banks with Lloyd's TSB.)

*　　*　　*

SHUSH!

"It's funny that we think of libraries as quiet demure places where
we are shushed by dusty, bun-balancing, bespectacled women. The
truth is libraries are raucous clubhouses for free speech, controversy,
and community. Librarians have stood up to the PATRIOT Act,
sat down with noisy toddlers and reached out to illiterate adults.
Libraries can never be shushed."

—Paula Poundstone

DON'T CALL ME LIZ

In 2009 a lobbyist from JP Morgan Chase e-mailed the office of Rep. Jim McDermott (D-WA) requesting a meeting. The recipient was Elizabeth Becton, the congressman's scheduler. After a week, she still hadn't responded. So the lobbyist wrote her again, and made one crucial mistake. Here's the exchange.

From: [Name redacted—we'll call him "Chase Lobbyist."]
Hi Liz, Just checking in on whether the Congressman is available next week. Thank you! Best, Chase

---

From: Elizabeth Becton
Who is Liz?

From: Chase Lobbyist
Hi Elizabeth, I thought you went by Liz, apologies if that's incorrect. Best, Chase

---

From: Elizabeth Becton
I do not go by Liz. Where did you get your information?

From: Chase Lobbyist
Hi Elizabeth, I'm so sorry if I offended you! I thought you'd gone by Liz at Potlatch [a paper company]. My mistake. Best, Chase

---

From: Elizabeth Becton
NEVER. I hate that name.

From: Chase Lobbyist
Hi Elizabeth, I'm so sorry if I offended you! I must have mis-heard. My mistake! Best, Chase

---

From: Elizabeth Becton
Chase, if I wanted you to call me by any other name, I would have offered that to you. I think it's rude when people don't even ask permission and take all sorts of liberties with your name. This is a real sore spot with me. My name has a lot of "nicknames" which I don't

---

Third caller to talk to Bill Clinton after he won the '92 election: Whoopi Goldberg.

use. I use either my first name or my last name because I row with a lot of other women who share the same first name. Now, please do not ever call me by a nickname again.

From: Chase Lobbyist
Hi Elizabeth, I'm so sorry I offended you! My mistake! Best, Chase

From: Elizabeth Becton
Chase, sounds like you got played by someone who KNOWS I hate that name and that it's a fast way to TICK me off. Who told you that I go by that name? They are not your friend...

From: Chase Lobbyist
Hi Elizabeth, Again, I am sincerely sorry for offending you. I don't want to cause trouble as I clearly must have mis-heard the person. It was in no way my intention to make you upset. Best, Chase

From: Elizabeth Becton
I REALLY want to know who told you to call me that.

From: Chase Lobbyist
Hi Elizabeth. Again, I am sincerely sorry. I don't recall who I overheard. It was in no way my intention to upset you. Best, Chase

From: Elizabeth Becton
Let me put it this way, they don't know me and perhaps they were PRETENDING to know me better than they do and pretended that I go by Liz. They did YOU a disservice. In the future, you should be VERY careful about such things. People like to brag about their connections in DC. It's a pastime for some. It's also dangerous to eavesdrop, as you have just found out. Quit apologizing and never call me anything but Elizabeth again. Also, make sure you correct anyone who attempts to call me by any other name but Elizabeth. Are we clear on this?

EPILOGUE: After the e-mail exchange was leaked to the press, McDermott's spokesperson apologized for Becton's behavior: "This is not reflective of the way we do business in this office." (There were no reports on whether the meeting ever took place.)

AMAZING ANAGRAMS

An anagram is when you rearrange the letters in a word or phrase to get a new word or phrase. Sometimes, the new phrase is a fitting commentary on the original phrase; sometimes it's just funny.

UNITED STATES OF AMERICA *becomes...*
DINE OUT: TASTE A 'MAC, FRIES

TWENTY THOUSAND LEAGUES UNDER THE SEA becomes... **HUGE WATER TALE STUNS. END HAD YOU TENSE.**

THE SILENCE OF THE LAMBS becomes... **THE CON BITES MALE FLESH**

THE AMERICAN DREAM becomes... **MEET A DEAR, RICH MAN**

RUDOLPH, THE RED-NOSED REINDEER *becomes...*
DEPLORED, HE IS THE ODDER RUNNER

WALTER CRONKITE *becomes...*
NETWORK RECITAL

THE IRS *becomes...* **THEIRS**

MADAME CURIE *becomes...*
ME? RADIUM ACE

NEW YORK YANKEES *becomes...*
SNEAKY OWNER KEY

RICHARD MILHOUSE NIXON *becomes...*
HIS CLIMAX RUINED HONOR

ROMEO AND JULIET becomes...
ONE JILTED AMOUR

MICKEY AND MINNIE MOUSE *becomes...*
KID MICE MEAN MONEY IN U.S.

THE GREAT DEPRESSION *becomes...* **OH, DO I SEE GDP SHATTERER?**

THE PILLSBURY DOUGHBOY *becomes...*
HI! BEHOLD BURLY GUY'S POT!

SLURPEE *becomes...* **REPULSE**

SPAM LUNCHEON MEAT *becomes...* **MEANS CHUM ON PLATE**

ACT YOUR AGE

There are many reasons why casting directors hire older actors to play teenagers. They might want more-experienced performers, or they may want to avoid child labor laws, for example. But sometimes they go a little bit too old.

MOVIES
• *Grease.* The four main characters in the 1978 movie were all supposed to be 18 years old. Actual ages of the actors: John Travolta (Danny) was 23, Olivia Newton-John (Sandy) was 29, Jeff Conaway (Kenickie) was 27, and Stockard Channing (Rizzo) was 33—nearly twice the age of the character she was playing.

• *Sorority Boys.* Stand-up comedian Harland Williams co-starred in this 2002 college comedy. His character is supposed to be around 21. Williams was 40.

• *Ferris Bueller's Day Off.* Ferris Bueller was an iconic teenage character, still in high school...portrayed by 24-year-old Matthew Broderick. (For the 1990 *Ferris Bueller* TV series, the role went to 24-year-old Charlie Schlatter.)

• *Joan of Arc.* Ingrid Bergman starred in husband Roberto Rossellini's 1954 film about Joan of Arc, *Giovanna d'Arco Al Rogo.* Her age at the time: 39. Joan of Arc's age in the movie: 14.

• *Harry Potter.* In the film series, Moaning Myrtle is a depressed ghost who haunts a girl's school bathroom. Why is she so depressed? Because she was murdered at age 14. Myrtle was first portrayed by actress Shirley Henderson, who was 36.

TELEVISION
• *Happy Days.* In 1974 Henry Winkler portrayed 17-year-old Fonzie on *Happy Days.* Winkler was 29.

• *Beverly Hills, 90210.* Gabrielle Carteris was 29 when she took on the role of 14-year-old Andrea Zuckerman.

• *The Beverly Hillbillies.* This show did the opposite, casting an actress *younger* than the character she was portraying. Irene Ryan was 60 when she played Granny in 1962. How old was Granny? She mentions once that she'd taken part in a beauty contest as an 18-year-old in 1897, which would mean she was 83 in 1962.

- **Hannah Montana.** Jason Earles portrayed the title character's brother, Jackson, whose age was never explicitly stated, but he was a teenager. Earles was born in 1977, making him 33 years old during the filming of the show's final season in 2010.
- **24.** Every season of *24* takes place in real time over the course of a day, but that timing doesn't explain why the Kim Bauer character ages by nearly two decades over the show's run. Kim was 16 when the show began, and 34 in the seventh season. Elisha Cuthbert, the actress who played her, was 19 when Kim was 16, and 26 when Kim was 34.
- **LazyTown.** This Nickelodeon fantasy show for toddlers starred Julianna Rose Mauriello as Stephanie. When the show began, Stephanie was 8, portrayed by a 13-year-old Julianna. By the end of the program's three-year run, Stephanie had aged just one year: she was 9…and Julianna was still playing her at age 16.
- **The Golden Girls.** Estelle Getty played 86-year-old Sophia Petrillo. Getty was 62 when the show first aired, a year younger than 63-year-old Bea Arthur, who portrayed her daughter.

REPEAT OFFENDERS

- **Gary Burghoff** was 29 when he reprised his movie role as Radar O'Riley for the TV adaptation of M*A*S*H in 1972. Radar was 18 years old—part of the reason Radar usually wore a cap was to conceal Burghoff's receding hairline. And since M*A*S*H's Korean War lasted 11 years (compared to the three years the Korean War really lasted), Burghoff was playing 18 *throughout* his 30s.
- **Antwon Tanner** was 20 years old when he played a high school basketball player in the 1996 movie *Sunset Park*. Eight years later, at age 28, he took a role on the prime-time soap *One Tree Hill*…as a high school basketball player.
- Sure, the movies were about time-traveling, but **Michael J. Fox** was 24 when he played 17-year old Marty McFly in *Back to the Future*…28 when he played 17-year-old Marty in *Back to the Future Part II*…and 29 when he played 17-year-old Marty in *Back to the Future Part III*.
- **Kevin Bacon** was an appropriate 20 years old when he played a college student in 1978's *Animal House*. Six years later, at age 26, he starred in *Footloose*, playing a high-school student.

BIG BROTHER 2.0

Uh-oh. Looks like a big road block ahead on the information superhighway.

Y OU DON'T OWN ME
Until recently, when you bought a song from the Apple
iTunes Store, it wasn't your property to do with as you
pleased. Because of music piracy concerns, Apple embedded mp3s
with "Digital Rights Management" code, or DRM, which prevents
the song from being played on more than five devices. That means
that you can't share DRM-coded songs with friends. It also means
that if you copy downloaded songs to a CD, they won't play on
many stereos, such as a car CD player. Apple now sells DRM-free
music, but any music purchased before 2009 is still restricted. (You
must pay Apple 30 cents per song to remove the DRM.)

SOME DAY MY PRINTS WILL COME
Do you work in an office with one of those big printer/fax/copiers?
If it was manufactured after 2002, it's digitally enabled, meaning
it has a computer hard drive, and on that hard drive is an image
of every single document ever scanned, faxed, or copied on it. So
if you made a photocopy of your tax return, Social Security card,
passport, credit card bill, paystub, or any other sensitive document—it's still on the copier. There are about 25 industrial printer
resalers in the U.S., where anyone can buy a used printer for
about $400. With some easily obtained software and a screwdriver,
that sensitive information can be unlocked—and potentially
exploited by identify thieves—in just a few hours.

YOUR SEARCHES LIVE FOREVER
Ever searched Google for something you wanted to keep secret,
like a medical issue or a surprise birthday present? No problem.
You can always just delete the search history on your computer
and it's gone, right? Wrong. That just deletes it from your browser's history. Google still has a record of *everything* you (and everyone else) has ever used its service to research online. Everything
from "burning sensation" to "stylish adult diapers" is stored on
Google's electronic servers along with information that shows
exactly what computer made the embarrassing search. (Ouch.)

First movie star to live in Beverly Hills: Douglas Fairbanks.

DON'T DRINK AND _____

Actual emergency room reports involving people who had too much to drink.

Exercise. "Injured shoulder in cartwheel race, admits drinking alcohol."

Target practice. "Patient was drinking when friends shot him in back of head with BB gun. Has lump on head; thinks BB is still in his head."

Sit near a pool table. "Patient fell off a bar stool and hit head on a pool table in a bar."

Play golf. "Patient was intoxicated in golf cart, flipped out of the cart onto head."

Practice martial arts. "Patient drinking, practicing karate. Kicked in the mouth."

Do home repairs. "Laceration rt. index finger: Patient was working on his toilet while drinking alcohol."

Skateboard. "Patient, intoxicated, fell skateboarding down stairs."

Water ski. "Drinking while water skiing; ran into a dock in the river."

Poop. "Elbow fracture: Patient was sitting on the toilet, reached for a glass of wine she was drinking and fell off toilet."

Travel. "Patient was intoxicated on his mobility scooter, trying to cross the street. Fell off."

Fly. "Knee pain: Patient was flying a kite when kite lifted him 15 feet off the ground and then dropped him. Intoxicated."

Ride. "Patient was riding his bike and texting on his cell phone and crashed the bike— also had been drinking."

Sit. "Drinking 6 beers a day, unable to get off couch."

Lose things. "Patient was looking for his cell phone and fell into some brush; lacerated right knee. Smells of alcohol."

Eat. "Patient found intoxicated at McDonald's, pant leg on fire."

Walt Disney World goes through about 194,871 miles of toilet paper each year.

A HISTORY OF THE SHOPPING MALL, PART II

*Love 'em or hate 'em, it's hard to deny the role that shopping malls
have played in American life over the past 50 years. Here's
Part II of our story. (Part I is on page 99.)*

WORST-LAID PLANS

Though Victor Gruen is credited with being the "father
of the mall," he owes a lot to the North Korean Communists for helping him get his temples of consumerism off the
ground. He owes the Commies (and so do you, if you like going to
the mall) because as Gruen himself would later admit, his earliest
design for the proposed Eastland Center was *terrible*. Had the
Korean War not put the brakes on all nonessential construction
projects, Eastland might have been built as Gruen originally
designed it, before he could develop his ideas further.

Those early plans called for a jumble of nine detached buildings organized around a big oval parking lot. The parking lot was
split in two by a sunken four-lane roadway, and if pedestrians
wanted to cross from one half of the shopping center to the other,
the only way to get over the moat-like roadway was by means of a
scrawny footbridge that was 300 feet long. How many shoppers
would even have bothered to cross over to the other side?

Had Eastland Center been built according to Gruen's early
plans, it almost certainly would have been a financial disaster.
Even if it didn't bankrupt Hudson's, it probably would have
forced the company to scrap its plans for Northland, Westland,
and Southland Centers. Other developers would have taken
note, and the shopping mall as we know it might never have
come to be.

ALL IN A ROW

Shopping centers of the size of Eastland Center were such a new
concept that *no* architect had figured out how to build them well.
Until now, most shopping centers consisted of a small number of
stores in a single strip facing the street, set back far enough to

allow room for parking spaces in front of the stores. Some larger developments had two parallel strips of stores, with the storefronts facing inward toward each other across an area of landscaped grass called a "mall." That's how shopping malls got their name.

There had been a few attempts to build even larger shopping centers, but nearly all had lost money. In 1951 a development called Shoppers' World opened outside of Boston. It had more than 40 stores on two levels and was anchored by a department store at the south end of the mall. But the smaller stores had struggled from the day the shopping center opened, and when they failed they took the entire shopping center (and the developer, who filed for bankruptcy) down with them.

INSIDE OUT

Gruen needed more time to think through his ideas, and when the Korean War pushed the Eastland project off into the indefinite future, he got it. Hudson's eventually decided to build Northland first, and by the time Gruen started working on those plans in 1951, his thoughts on what a shopping center should look like had changed completely. The question of where to put all the parking spaces (Northland would have more than 8,000) was one problem. Gruen eventually decided that it made more sense to put the parking spaces around the shopping center, instead of putting the shopping center around the parking spaces, as his original plans for Eastland Center had called for.

WALK THIS WAY

Gruen then put the Hudson's department store right in the middle of the development, surrounded on three sides by the smaller stores that made up the rest of the shopping center. Out beyond these smaller stores was the parking lot, which meant that the only way to get from the parking lot to Hudson's—the shopping center's biggest draw—was by walking past the smaller shops.

This may not sound like a very important detail, but it turned out to be key to the mall's success. Forcing all that foot traffic past the smaller shops—increasing their business in the process—was the thing that made the small stores financially viable. Northland Center was going to have nearly 100 small stores; they all needed to be successful for the shopping center itself to succeed.

SUBURBAN OUTFITTER

Northland was an outdoor shopping center, with nearly everything a modern enclosed mall has…except the roof. Another feature that set it apart from other shopping centers of the era, besides its layout, its massive scale, and the large number of stores in the development, were the bustling public spaces between the rows of stores. In the past developers who had incorporated grassy malls into their shopping centers did so with the intention of giving the projects a rural, almost sleepy feel, similar to a village green.

Gruen, a native of Vienna, Austria, thought just the opposite was needed. He wanted his public spaces to blend with the shops to create a lively (and admittedly idealized) *urban* feel, just like he remembered from downtown Vienna, with its busy outdoor cafés and shops. He divided the spaces between Hudson's and the other stores into separate and very distinct areas, giving them names like Peacock Terrace, Great Lakes Court, and Community Lane. He filled them with landscaping, fountains, artwork, covered walkways, and plenty of park benches to encourage people to put the spaces to use.

NOVELTY STORES

If Northland Center were to open its doors today, it would be remarkably *un*remarkable. There are dozens, if not hundreds, of similarly-sized malls all over the United States. But when Northland opened in the spring of 1954, it was one-of-a-kind, easily the largest shopping center on Earth, both in terms of square footage and the number of stores in the facility. *The Wall Street Journal* dispatched a reporter to cover the grand opening. So did *Time* and *Newsweek*, and many other newspapers and magazines. In the first weeks that the Northland Center was open, an estimated 40-50,000 people passed through its doors each day.

DON'T LOOK NOW

It was an impressive start, but Hudson's executives still worried. Did all these people really come to shop, or just look around? Would they ever be back? No one knew for sure if the public would even feel comfortable in such a huge facility. People were used to shopping in one store, not having to choose from nearly 100. And there was a very real fear that for many shoppers, finding their way back to their car in the largest parking lot they had ever parked in would be too great a strain and they'd never come back. Even worse, what if Northland Center was *too* good? What if the public enjoyed the public spaces so much that they never bothered to go inside the stores? With a price tag of nearly $25 million, the equivalent of more than $200 million today, Northland Center was one of the most expensive retail developments in history, and nobody even knew if it would work.

CHA-CHING!

Whatever fears the Hudson's executives had about making back their $25 million investment evaporated when their own store's sales exceeded forecasts by 30 percent. The numbers for the smaller stores were good, too, and they stayed good month after month. In its first year in business Northland Center grossed $88 million, making it one of the most profitable shopping centers in the United States. And all of the press coverage generated by the construction of Northland Center made Gruen's reputation. Before the center was even finished, he received the commission of a lifetime: Dayton's department store hired him to design not just the world's first *enclosed* shopping mall but an entire planned community around it, on a giant 463-acre plot in a suburb of Minneapolis.

For Part III of the story, go past the food court, up the escalator, right after Spencer's Gifts, and on to page 399.

*　　*　　*

EASY RIDER

"A 40-year-old man was stopped by police and charged for not wearing a helmet while riding his motorcycle this past weekend in Hamilton. He also wasn't wearing pants, or underwear. Police tried to stop the nearly-nude motorcyclist—he was wearing a T-shirt—around 4 a.m. Sunday. When he spotted the officers, he lost control of his bike, managed to steady himself and then took off. Authorities managed to catch up with him a short time later. 'It is kind of bizarre,' said Staff Sgt. David Hennick."

—*City News*, Toronto, August 2010

Cars didn't have gas gauges until 1922. Before that you had to dip a stick in the tank.

SHEETHEADS

For some fans, being a "fanatic" isn't enough—they want a title, too.

• Rush Limbaugh adherents so completely agree with every opinion expressed by Limbaugh that they just say "Ditto," and refer to themselves as **Dittoheads.**

• Die-hard fans of *American Idol* singer Clay Aiken are **Claymates.**

• Devotees of the series of *Twilight* vampire novels and movies are known as **Twi-Hards.**

• The early days of the Internet coincided with the popularity of TV show *The X Files*. People who discussed the show online called themselves **X-Philes.**

• Singer-songwriter Tori Amos coined a term for her highly loyal fan base, which they then adopted: **Ears With Feet.**

• Playing off the state's endless wheat fields, fans of the classic rock band Kansas call themselves **Wheatheads.**

• The American sitcom *The Office* takes place at a small paper company called Dunder Mifflin. *Office* fans are thus **Dunderheads.**

• *Glee* is a musical comedy TV show, for which its fans are "geeks." *Glee* + geeks = **Gleeks.**

• Serious fans of *The Daily Show* call themselves **Stoned Slackers.** Why? That's what Fox News pundit Bill O'Reilly derisively called *Daily Show* viewers when he appeared on the show in 2003.

• The fans of the Broadway musical *The Phantom of the Opera* are known as **Phans.**

• Grateful Dead fans are well known to be **Deadheads.** Phish, a band heavily influenced by the Dead, has fans called **Phish Heads.**

• Are you a big fan of the TV show *The West Wing*? Then you're a **Wingnut.** (Secondary meaning: In the real world of politics, left-wing or right-wing extremists are also referred to as wingnuts.)

• Devoted users of Microsoft's computer spreadsheet program Excel gave themselves this nickname: **Sheetheads.**

First person featured on a Wheaties box: animal trainer Maria Rasputin (1934).

A TOY IS BORN

Even when all hope seems lost, don't give up...because
you just might get that random phone call from
your sister-in-law in New Jersey.

WHEN LIFE GIVES YOU LEMONS...

In the 1930s, a Cincinnati soap company called Kutol Products expanded their line to include wallpaper cleaner. Their doughy detergent mixture was the best way to remove the soot from walls caused by coal-burning stoves—you just formed a handful of Kutol into a ball and rolled it over the soot.

But after World War II, fewer people had coal-burning stoves, and more people had easy-to-wash vinyl wallpaper. Result: Kutol's sales plummeted. In 1949 the company's owner was killed in a plane crash. His widow inherited the business, and she hired her 25-year-old son, Joe McVicker, to run it. Not long after, young McVicker was diagnosed with Hodgkin's disease, a type of blood cancer. He was dying, he had a factory full of products that hardly anyone needed, and Kutol was on the verge of folding.

...MAKE LEMONADE

In December 1954, McVicker got a phone call from Kay Zufall, his sister-in-law, who ran a nursery school in New Jersey. She told him that because the clay her kids were using to sculpt Christmas tree ornaments was too hard for their little hands to manipulate— and it stained—she went to a hardware store and bought a tub of Kutol Wallpaper Cleaner. It was softer than clay, nontoxic, and didn't stain. And it worked great. So McVicker sent a few tubs to the Cincinnati School District. Again, it was a hit.

Then, after receiving experimental radiation treatment, McVicker's cancer went into remission. With a renewed sense of purpose, he had the detergent removed from Kutol Wallpaper Cleaner, added coloring and an almond scent, and decided to market it as Kutol's Rainbow Modeling Compound. "Don't call it that!" said Zufall. McVicker asked her what they should call it. "It's dough you play with," she replied, "so how about Play Dough?" Since 1955 two billion cans of Play-Doh have sold.

The Navy ship USS *New York* was built with recycled World Trade Center steel.

IT'S GREEK TO US

The meanings have changed a bit, and they weren't originally in English, of course, but many of today's most common words and phrases are literally ancient, dating back to the heyday of ancient Greece.

BITE THE DUST
Meaning: To die suddenly
Origin: Homer's epic poem the *Iliad*. Written around the 8th century B.C., it's a tale about the legendary Trojan War, which erupts when Troy kidnaps the Greek queen Helen. The Greeks invade Troy to retrieve Helen, and in one pre-battle passage, the Greek warrior Agamemnon prays to Zeus to make sure that the Trojans are absolutely slaughtered. "Do not let the sun go down until thousands who share in this quarrel fall headlong in the dust and bite the earth." In other words, Agamemnon wanted his opponents dead, face-down in the dirt. In an 1898 English-language translation of the *Iliad*, "bite the earth" was changed to "bite the dust," which is when it entered the vernacular.

DRACONIAN
Meaning: Brutally strict
Origin: In ancient Greece, administering punishment for murder (and other crimes) wasn't the concern of government—it was a private issue, left up to the family of the victim. In 640 B.C., an Olympic champion named Cylon and a band of followers from the neighboring city-state of Megara attempted to take over Athens. The invasion was thwarted, but so many people were involved that the Athenian government, trying to avoid a bloodbath of Athenians killing Megarans and Megarans exacting revenge by killing Athenians, set up trials for Cylon and his followers. It worked so well that in 621 B.C., Athens gave a legislator named Draco full authority to enact a law requiring that murder charges be heard in state-sponsored trials. This is both the foundation for present-day justice...as well as for the death penalty. Draco meted out death sentences for many crimes—not just for murder—leading to the English adjective *draconic*, used to describe anything severe or strict. It became *draconian* in the late 1800s.

A cursed year: The "f-word" was first printed in English in 1475.

SWAN SONG

Meaning: A triumphant final performance before death or retirement

Origin: It first appears in *Phaedo*, Plato's transcript of conversations between the philosopher Socrates and his students (including Plato himself) during Socrates' final days—just before a death sentence for corrupting Greek youth (his students) was carried out against him. In one section, Socrates declares that he has to come to terms with his impending death and is at peace with it to such a degree that he can actually enjoy his final days. He tells his friends that he has "as much of the spirit of prophecy as do the swans. For they, when they perceive that they must die, having sung all their life long, do then sing more, and more sweetly, than ever, rejoicing in the thought that they are about to go away." Socrates was revered, and after he died the quote was frequently repeated in documents by such philosophers and writers as Aeschylus, Aristotle, Cicero, Chaucer, and Shakespeare. That's why we still say it today. Only problem: Swans don't really sing—they honk.

MENTOR

Meaning: A person, usually older, who offers wisdom, advice, and guidance

Origin: In Homer's *Odyssey*, Mentor is the name of an older man who remains loyal to King Odysseus even after the king has been missing for 10 years and is presumed dead. All of Ithaca, Odysseus' kingdom, believes that Odysseus' wife, Penelope, should marry one of her many suitors...except Mentor, who has held out all along that Odysseus was still alive, and is ultimately proven right. The word came to mean not just a loyal friend but a wise one with the 1699 publishing of the novel *Telemaque* by Fenelon of Cambrai, a retelling of the *Odyssey* in which Mentor is the central character—a wise figure of near superhuman goodness.

IN A NUTSHELL

Meaning: A complicated concept or experience expressed succinctly

Origin: The ancient Greek historian Pliny the Elder was known

---

The Statue of Liberty is 20 times taller than an average woman.

to stretch the truth a bit, especially when it came to the poems of Homer, which themselves were historical epics that embellished the truth. In *Natural History*, Pliny claims that a copy of Homer's *Iliad*, written entirely on a piece of parchment, had once been found inside a nutshell. (There's no way this be true—the *Iliad* is 15,690 lines long.) This amusing boast later became a Latin proverb, *in nuce Ilias*, or "the *Iliad* in a nutshell," which expresses the same meaning it holds today. The 16th-century English writer Stephen Gosson was the first to use the phrase without mentioning the *Iliad*, but it was popularized by frequent usage in the works of 19th-century writers Charles Dickens and Robert Browning.

*   *   *

I'M SO AFRAID!

There's a lot to be afraid of. Do you have any of these phobias?

Automatonophobia: fear of robots

Nephophobia: clouds

Vestiphobia: clothes

Pedophobia: children

Podophobia: feet

Ouranophobia: heaven

Cnidophobia: insect bites

Barophobia: gravity

Sciophobia: shadows

Oneirophobia: dreams

Caligynephobia: beautiful women

Rhytiphobia: wrinkles

Mycophobia: mushrooms

Pteronophobia: getting tickled (by feathers)

Cyclophobia: bicycles

Defecaloesiphobia: painful bowel movements

Xanthophobia: things that are yellow, or even the word "yellow"

Toursiphobia: pickles

Sinapiphobia: mustard

Dendrophobia: trees

Rothakinophobia: peaches

Achondroplasiaphobia: little people

Bambagiaphobia: cotton balls

Catheterphobia: balloons

Eel blood is toxic to humans.

THE NAME'S FAMILIAR

You already know the names—here are the people behind them.

L AURA ASHLEY
Welsh-born Laura Mountney left school at 16, became a
secretary and, at 24, married engineer Bernard Ashley.
Inspired by Victorian textiles, in 1953 the Ashleys invested £10 in
supplies and began producing printed fabrics in their kitchen.
That same year, while vacationing in Rome, they noticed a new
fashion trend among young women, sparked by Audrey Hepburn's
appearance in the film *Roman Holiday*: colorful headscarves. So
Ashley designed a line of scarves—and that proved to be her first
success. Within a few years, Ashley added home furnishings and
clothing to the line. By 1970 business was brisk—in a single week,
one London shop sold 4,000 Laura Ashley dresses. Laura died in
1985, Bernard in 2009, but the brand—synonymous with pastels
and floral prints—still generates $600 million annually.

DINTY MOORE

In the 1910s comic strip *Bringing Up Father*, Dinty Moore is the
name of a tavern owner who serves corned beef and cabbage to
the strip's main character, an Irish immigrant named Jiggs. Author
George McManus's inspiration for Dinty was a real-life New York
restaurant owner named James Moore, who capitalized on the
popularity of the strip by legally changing his first name to Dinty
and opening a chain of diners. His specialty: corned beef. Moore
didn't start the line of Dinty Moore canned products (notably beef
stew) available today; Hormel Foods licensed the name and introduced the product in 1935, using Jiggs in early advertising. Dinty
Moore Beef Stew is still the bestselling canned stew in the U.S.

BURT SHAVITZ

In 1983 an unemployed single mom named Roxanne Quimby met
a beekeeper named Burt Shavitz on the side of a road in Bangor,
Maine. The two struck up a friendship: Quimby had a knack for
crafts, and Shavitz had more beeswax and honey than he knew
what to do with, so they began selling honey at local craft fairs,

---

Oranges that grow higher on the tree have more vitamin C than the lower fruit.

along with candles and other products made from Burt's leftover beeswax. Then, using a 19th-century book of homemade personal-care recipes, they began producing lip balm, and after selling thousands of tubes of it throughout New England, they founded a company—Burt's Bees—in 1989. Quimby bought out Shavitz's share of the company for $130,000 in 1993. She later sold 80% of the business for $141.6 million. Burt's Bees is now owned by Clorox, but still produces more than 150 products made from honey, beeswax, and other natural sources.

FRANK NICHOLAS MEYER

Born Frans Nicholas Meijer in 1875, he became a gardener's assistant in Amsterdam at age 14. Always a wanderer, he set off on foot to study plants and gardens all over western Europe, then emigrated to the U.S. in 1901, where he was hired by the Department of Agriculture as a "plant explorer." Preferring to travel alone, Meyer gathered and studied plants in Mexico and Cuba and eventually made several trips to Asia. All told, he introduced more than 2,500 plant species to the West, including soybeans, Ginkgo biloba, Chinese cabbage, and a deep-yellow Chinese ornamental fruit thought to be a cross between a sweet or mandarin orange and a lemon—today known as the Meyer lemon. Unfortunately, Meyer didn't live to see his namesake: In 1918, on his way to Shanghai on a commercial Japanese riverboat, he fell overboard into the Yangtze River and drowned.

MAX KOHL

Factory worker Max Kohl, a Polish immigrant, saved enough money to buy a Milwaukee corner grocery store in 1927. He transformed it into the city's first modern supermarket, and 40 years later he had a chain of 50 stores. Then Kohl expanded the business out of the grocery sector, opening six Kohl's department stores. In 1972 he sold a controlling interest in the operation to the Brown & Williamson tobacco company, which sold off the grocery stores to A&P and focused on opening more Kohl's department stores. Some Kohl's executives bought the chain in 1986, and it now has more than 1,000 stores in 49 states. Kohl maintained an executive position in the company until his retirement in 1979. He died two years later. His son, Herb Kohl, is currently a Wisconsin senator and owns the NBA's Milwaukee Bucks.

George Washington, Thomas Jefferson, and John Adams all played marbles.

CITY LIGHTS

Anyone can request to have a particular color scheme displayed in lights on the top third of New York City's Empire State Building at night (which is usually lit up in white). Here are some recent examples of special lighting.

Aug. 14–16, 2009: Orange (spire and base), white (upper floors), green (lower floors), the colors of the Indian flag, in honor of India Day, which commemorates the Aug. 15, 1947, independence of India from the British empire.

Aug. 31, 2009: All yellow lights—the color of a tennis ball—to celebrate the first night of the U.S. Open.

Sept. 8, 2009: All orange, commemorating the 400th anniversary of Henry Hudson's exploration of what is now called the Hudson River. The lights were orange because it's the Dutch royal family's color.

Sept. 9, 2009: The day is an annual breast cancer awareness event called City in Pink, so the lights were pink, the color of breast cancer awareness ribbons and bracelets.

Sept. 11, 2009: Red, white, and blue to honor the victims of the 9-11 attacks.

Sept. 20, 2009: The lights were green, the traditional color of Islam. This day was Eid-al-Fitr, the final day of the Muslim holy month of Ramadan.

Sept. 24, 2009: All red, or "ruby," to honor the 70th anniversary of the film premiere of *The Wizard of Oz.*

Oct. 9–12, 2009: For Columbus Day weekend, the building was green, white, and red—the colors of the Italian flag. (Columbus was Italian.)

Oct. 19, 2009: The NY Historical Society was having a Grateful Dead exhibit, so the Empire State Building provided "psychedelic colors": Green, yellow, red, purple, and white lights were lit on all four sides of the skyscraper.

Oct. 30–31, 2009: Black and orange for Halloween.

Nov. 5–8, 2009: Blue and white, the team colors of the New York Yankees, who'd just won the World Series.

Dick Van Dyke and Gordon Lightfoot are members of the Barbershop Harmony Society.

Nov. 25–29, 2009: The traditional autumn colors of yellow, orange, and red were used over Thanksgiving weekend.

Dec. 11–20, 2009: Blue represents the divine in Judaism, and it appears on the Israeli flag. For the Jewish holiday of Chanukah, the lights on the Empire State Building were turned to blue and white.

Dec. 23, 2009–Jan. 6, 2010: Green and red, for Christmas. They stayed lit for the 12 days of Christmas.

Jan. 15–17, 2010: Green and white, the colors of the New York Jets, who made the NFL playoffs (a rare occurrence). They won, so the color scheme was repeated for the next playoff game. (They lost.)

Feb. 5, 2010: The lights were all red for the American Heart Association's heart disease awareness campaign, National Wear Red Day.

Feb. 8, 2010: The New Orleans Saints won the Super Bowl, so its team colors of yellow and black were lit up.

Feb. 15, 2010: Red, white, and blue, used for all patriotic holidays, including President's Day (this day), Memorial Day, Flag Day, Independence Day, Labor Day, Election Day, Veterans Day, and on Sept. 11.

Feb. 26–28, 2010: For the Winter Olympics' closing weekend, the building was lit in three of the Olympic ring colors: black, blue, and yellow.

March 17, 2010: All green for St. Patrick's Day. The green theme was repeated on Earth Day (April 22), and Rainforest Awareness Week (May 13).

Apr. 1, 2010: The advocacy group Autism Speaks encourages supporters to wear blue every April 1 to raise awareness of the condition. The Empire State Building was lit in blue on this day, too.

Apr. 2–4, 2010: The pastel colors of yellow, pink, and green were used for Easter.

May 7, 2010: All blue lights for "the boys in blue," honoring Police Memorial Week.

June 16, 2010: On this day in 1860, a Japanese diplomat visited New York for the first time. For the 150th anniversary of that event, the building was lit up in white and red, the colors of Japan.

July 11–12, 2010: Spain won soccer's World Cup, so red and yellow—Spanish flag colors—were used for the lights.

World's worst-smelling cheese: French Vieux Boulogne—it smells like "a barnyard."

SUPERHERO FLOPS

At the top of the superhero list, you've got your Superman, your Batman, and then way, way down on the list, you've got these.

Shamrock. In 1982 Marvel Comics told staff artists to create an Irish superhero. They created the most stereotypically Irish superhero possible. Shamrock (real name: Molly Fitzgerald) is the daughter of a militant IRA member, has long red hair, and her superpower is having extremely good luck.

Madame Fatal. In this 1940s title, Richard Stanton is an actor whose world goes into turmoil when his daughter is kidnapped. To get her back, he uses his "acting skills": dressing up like an old lady. The disguise fools the kidnappers; he beats them up and rescues his daughter. But he likes it all so much that he decides to become Madame Fatal, the butt-kicking old lady who is really a man.

Dazzler. In 1980 Casablanca Records, primarily a disco label operating in a world that had moved on from disco, commissioned Marvel Comics to create a comic book about a disco singer-superhero. The plot: Alison Blaire is a law student who quits to become a disco singer, aided by her newly discovered abilities to generate light, to transform sound into pure energy...and to roller skate.

U.S. Archer. Ulysses Solomon Archer is a trucker who fights evildoers on the highway system, avenging the death of his brother who was murdered by an evil trucker known only as the Highwayman. Archer has the ability to track his nemesis through a metal plate in his skull that can pick up CB transmissions. 10-4!

Wundarr the Aquarian. Premiering in 1973, this Marvel character was the first "New Age" superhero. Wundarr's goal isn't to rid the streets of crime—it's to enlighten all of humanity with universal consciousness. To that aim, his superpower is the ability to negate any kind of energy, from nuclear to gravity.

Arm Fall Off Boy. This 1940s DC Comics character came here from the 30th century, and his name says it all: He has the ability to detach and re-attach at will his own arms and legs, a power gained in an antigravity mishap. (When AFOB removes an arm, it makes a "plorp" sound, which seems exactly right.)

In Poland, the day after Easter is called Dingus Day. It's celebrated with water fights.

POLI-TALKS

Politicians say the darnedest things...

"His mom lived in Long Island for 10 years or so. God rest her soul. Wait, your mom's still alive? Your dad passed. God bless her soul."
—**Vice President Joe Biden, to Irish PM Brian Cowen**

"Of course their current lodgings are a bit temporary but they should see it like a weekend of camping."
—**Silvio Berlusconi, Italian prime minister, on earthquake refugees**

"What a bizarre time we're in, when a judge will say to little children that you can't say the Pledge of Allegiance, but you must learn that homosexuality is normal and you should try it."
—**Rep. Michelle Bachmann**

"What the hell do I want to go to a place like Mombasa? I just see myself in a pot of boiling water with all these natives dancing around me."
—**Mel Lastman, Toronto mayor, before going to Kenya to support his city's bid for the 2008 Olympics (the bid failed)**

"I believe in natural gas as a clean, cheap alternative to fossil fuels."
—**House Speaker Nancy Pelosi (unaware that natural gas *is* a fossil fuel)**

"You must obey the law, always, not only when they grab you by your special place."
—**Vladimir Putin, Russian president**

"You may have noticed that Senator Obama's supporters have been saying some pretty nasty things about Western Pennsylvania lately. And you know, I couldn't agree with them more. I couldn't disagree with you. I couldn't agree with you more than the fact that Pennsylvania is the most patriotic, most God-loving, most, most patriotic part of America, and this is a great part of the country."
—**Sen. John McCain**

"A showgirl and a bottle of Bombay Sapphire gin."
—**Oscar Goodman, Las Vegas mayor, to school-children who asked what he'd like on a deserted island**

California penal code bans the scattering of "cremains" from the Golden Gate Bridge.

"Fat rednecks try to shove food down my face. I know I'm the people's senator, but do I have to hang out with them?"
—**Sen. John Edwards, to an aide at the North Carolina state fair**

"To our seniors, I have a message for you: You're going to die sooner if the healthcare bill passes."
—**U.S. Sen. Tom Coburn**

"When the stock market crashed, Franklin Roosevelt got on the TV and didn't just talk about the, you know, the princes of greed. He said, 'Look, here's what happened.'"
—**Vice President Joe Biden, unaware that FDR wasn't president in 1929 (nor was there TV)**

"It's now a very good day to get out anything we want to bury. Councillors' expenses?"
—**Jo Moore, British special adviser, in an e-mail to her boss just minutes after the 9-11 attacks (both resigned)**

"I believe marriage should be between a man and a woman, and a woman, and a woman."
—**Mass. Gov. Mitt Romney, a Mormon (he was joking)**

"Hunger can be a positive motivator."
—**Missouri State Rep. Cynthia Davis, speaking against a program that feeds poor children**

"We need to uptick our image with everyone, including one-armed midgets."
—**Michael Steele, RNC chairman, on a GOP "hip-hop makeover"**

"Well, you know, God bless him, bless his heart, the President of the United States, a total failure."
—**House Speaker Nancy Pelosi, on President George W. Bush**

"Come on! I just answered, like, eight questions!"
—**Barack Obama, putting an end to a press conference**

* * *

TWO REAL COMBINATION BUSINESSES

- Aves Taxidermy & Cheese (Wisconsin)
- Dentist & Thai Restaurant (Australia)

MISSING LINKS
WORD GAME

BRI members Jack Mingo and Erin Barrett invented this game. Here's how you play: Each group of words below has a "missing link"—a word that can be added to the beginning or end of each word to form a familiar phrase. For example, if we listed "roll, splitter, Lincoln, captain's, cabin, yule," the answer would be "log." Bonus: The answers from 1 through 7 make another "missing link" puzzle. Get the idea? Now try these. (The answers are on page 536.)

PUZZLE #1

1. Summer, Vacation, Rainy, Sun, Work, End, of Our Lives

2. Shooting, Fish, Power, North, Dark, Dwarf, Movie, Crossed

3. Down, Over, Low, DMC, Home, Bank, in My Stocking, Marathon

4. Potato, Pepper, Red, Chocolate, Seat, Box, Not so, Flash

5. Big, Band, Gingerbread, Cat, Keeping, Hold, Playing, Maxwell

6. Ring, Wig, Canal, Plug, Corn, Inner, Rabbit

7. Level, Bass, Black, Red, Dead, Slug, Salt

PUZZLE #2

1. Steam, Dixie, Pea, Dog, Slide, Train, Blower, Police, Penny

2. Here, Post, Off, Danger, In, Open, Up, Zodiac

3. Arm, Coal, Bull, Boss, Orchestra, Viper, Peach, Barbecue

4. Caught, Fall, Order, Supply, Sell, Circuit, Cake, Hand, Wave

5. Wave, Moon, Year, Fire, Head, Weight, Bulb

6. Ear, Hurried, Law, Product, Myself, Stand, Appointment, Golly

7. Leader, Job, Profit, Appetite, Prevention, Hair, Incalculable, Weight

---

Including the attic, there were 11 rooms in the *Brady Bunch's* TV house.

I STINK, THEREFORE I AM

Thank goodness you only have to read these stories of horrible
odors instead of experiencing them first hand. (Of course,
if you're in the bathroom right now...)

OH, DEER

The unfortunate neighbors of Randy Good in North Buffalo Township, Pennsylvania, complained to authorities in late 2008 about a smell coming from Good's yard. "You can barely go outside," said neighbor Dallas Bryan. "The last couple days, it's been so bad you can't even stay *inside*." Cause of the smell: hundreds of deer carcasses piled up in Good's yard. Good has a contract with the Pennsylvania Department of Transportation to remove dead deer from roads in five counties—and he picks up 50 to 100 a day. Normally he takes them to a landfill, but one of his trucks had recently broken down, and the landfill was closed on the weekend, so Good just started dumping the excess carcasses in his yard. After numerous complaints and the intervention of a local congressional representative, embarrassed state officials finally sent in DOT workers, who hauled all the dead deer away.

EAU DE DUMP

In 2010 the Chinese government announced that they had figured out how to deal with the stench emanating from the enormous, overflowing landfills around the city of Beijing: They installed 100 high-pressure "deodorant cannons" at one site and plan to install more at other sites in the future. The cannons can shoot fragrance sprays up to 170 feet. So instead of the unpleasant odor of rotting garbage, residents will now smell the unpleasant odor of rotting garbage...mixed with the sweet fragrance of industrial deodorant.

THAT NEW DRUG SMELL

In March 2010, police were called to investigate a strange odor in a Fairview, New Jersey, neighborhood. They were able to trace it to one house where four men were using lighter fluid to burn the labels off of prescription medication bottles. And they were trying to mask the odor it created by boiling water with cinnamon in it.

At 72 years of age Alexander Graham Bell set a world water-speed record of over 70 mph.

Police discovered almost 15,000 pill bottles of several different kinds of medication, mostly painkillers, and more than $5 million worth of pills. The four men were arrested.

WALFART

A 51-year-old Seattle-area man was questioned by police after they were called to a Walmart in South Kitsap, Washington, in early 2010. The man had been seen dumping vials of liquid on the floor, and the liquid smelled. *Bad.* The store had to be evacuated, and several people reported getting severe headaches immediately after taking a whiff of the foul substance. The man initially told police that he was shopping in the store with his girlfriend, but later admitted that he'd dumped the liquid—which he called "stink bombs"—and that he had also dispersed the contents of a can called "Super Fart Spray" in the store. He said he thought it would be funny. The man wasn't arrested, but he is banned from Walmart for life.

*　　*　　*

THE WORLD'S MOST VALUABLE VIDEO GAME

Stadium Events was a track-and-field game released by Bandai in 1987 to go with its Family Fun Fitness Mat, a soft vinyl mat. When you hooked it up to the Nintendo console, it allowed you to control characters by walking and jumping. In 1988 Nintendo bought the rights to the Family Fun Fitness Mat and rebranded it as the Power Pad. Then it changed the name of *Stadium Events* to *World Class Track Meet* and recalled and destroyed all unsold *Stadium Events*. But 200 had already been sold, of which only 10 to 20 are believed to exist today.

• In 2010 a North Carolina woman found her kids' old Nintendo games in her garage and put them up for sale on eBay...including *Stadium Events.* Expecting two or three bucks for each game, she got $13,105 for *Stadium Events.*

• A Kansas man heard about the rare game and found a sealed copy he was about to donate to Goodwill. (It was sealed because he'd bought the game in 1987 but never found a fitness mat to make it work.) He sold it on eBay for $41,300.

HUH?

Sometimes you read a news story and you can only say, "Huh?"

NEWS ITEM: Two doctors at Cape Fear Valley Medical Center in Fayetteville, North Carolina, induced labor on a woman in November 2008 when she was having difficulty giving birth. When the baby still didn't come, they performed a caesarean section on her.

HUH? They performed the caesarean…but found no baby. It turns out the woman wasn't pregnant. After a yearlong review of the case, the North Carolina Medical Board determined that the woman was actually experiencing *pseudocyesis*, or "false pregnancy," a real ailment, but one more common in dogs and mice than in humans. The doctors were issued "letters of concern."

NEWS ITEM: In March 2010, Joan Higgins, 66, owner of Majors Pet Shop in Sale, England, was fined £1,000 ($1,506) and ordered to wear a tracking device on her ankle for two months for the unlawful sale of an animal.

HUH? The unlawful sale for which Ms. Higgins was being punished: She sold a goldfish to a 14-year-old boy. (An animal welfare law passed in the U.K. in 2006 makes it illegal to sell pets to anyone under the age of 16.) Ms. Higgins was also given a curfew—she had to be inside her house from 7:00 p.m. until 7:00 a.m. every day for seven weeks. And the boy who bought the fish? He'd been sent into the store as part of a police undercover investigation of pet-shop sales.

NEWS ITEM: A 32-year-old Croatian soccer player was penalized for taking a dive—meaning he faked being knocked down by an opposing player—during a match in May 2010. Goran Tunjic had fallen to the ground and was approached by a referee with a yellow card, which signifies that a player has been penalized.

HUH? Tunjic hadn't taken a dive—he was dead. Tragically, he'd suffered a heart attack during play. Medical attendants immediately attempted to revive him, but it was no use. "Doctors tried to help him but there was nothing they could do," a league spokesman said. "He just fell dead on the spot."

NEWS ITEM: In April 2010, Robert K. Cheruiyot, 21, of Kenya won the 114th Boston Marathon, shattering the course record with a time of 2 hours, 5 minutes, and 52 seconds.

HUH? The previous course record was held by four-time winner...Robert K. Cheruiyot. *That* Robert K. Cheruiyot is also from Kenya. He's not related to the Robert K. Cheruiyot who won in 2010—the two record-breaking Boston Marathon runners just happen to have the same name.

NEWS ITEM: In 1990, 18-year-old Kendall Gibson was convicted of robbery, abduction, and gun charges and sentenced to 47 years in the Greensville Correctional Center in Virginia. And for more than 10 years he's been in a 8-by-10-foot isolation cell reserved for the most violent prisoners. He spends 23 hours a day in the tiny cell and gets to spend one hour per day outside.

HUH? Gibson hasn't spent a decade in isolation because he's violent—he's there because he refuses to cut his hair. And it's for religious reasons. Gibson is a Rastafarian; he wears the religion's trademark long dreadlocks. But according to a prison rule implemented in 1999, Gibson's refusal to trim them means he has to live in isolation. At least 40 other prisoners were so confined when the law went into effect. Nobody knows how many there are today—prison officials refuse to divulge that information.

NEWS ITEM: In March 2010, a security guard walking around a parking lot in Ilford, East London, England, when he saw a chicken drumstick on the ground. He kicked it around for a while. Then he noticed that the "drumstick" had an unusual feature.

HUH? The unusual feature was a nail—and the drumstick wasn't a drumstick—it was a human thumb. Even weirder, a surveillance video showed that it had fallen from the sky. Tests determined that the thumb belonged to kebab shop worker Mahmood Ahmad, 41, who had disappeared three days earlier. Several people were arrested in connection with the case over the following months, but the rest of Mr. Ahmad still hasn't been found. Just how his thumb came to be removed from his hand, not to mention how it fell from the sky, has not yet been explained.

In 2006 the Hell's Angels sued Disney for using their logo in the movie *Wild Hogs*.

SUPER BOWL I

*The Super Bowl is more than just a football game—it's a cultural event
with weeks of advance media coverage, a full day of TV programming,
and a third of America tuned in. Even the commercials are considered
news. But the first Super Bowl in 1967 was a lot different.*

• **NAME:** The first Super Bowl wasn't called Super Bowl I. Officially, it was the "1967 AFL-NFL World Championship Game."
The two major leagues, the American Football League and the
National Football League, had merged in 1966, and this was the
first interleague title game.

• **PLACE:** Today, the location of the game is announced two or
three years in advance so the city can prepare stadium renovations
and make sure there are enough facilities, primarily hotel rooms.
The location of the 1967 game—the Los Angeles Memorial Coliseum—was decided on by the league about six weeks before the
big game.

• **DATE:** Nowadays, the game date is known well in advance—
it's always the first Sunday in February, by decree of the NFL and
TV broadcasters. But the date for the 1967 game wasn't locked
down until December 1966, when the league decided to delay the
final AFL playoff game (set for December 26) and the NFL playoff
(set for January 1) in order to present them back to back on the
same day—January 8, 1967—in an unprecedented TV double-
header (standard practice today). The championship would then
take place the following week on January 15, 1967.

• **TV BROADCAST:** The Super Bowl now generates millions
in advertising revenue. It's so lucrative that it actually rotates
between the four major broadcast networks each year, whether
they regularly air NFL games or not. In 1967 the Super Bowl aired
on two networks. Reason: CBS had a contract to air NFL games;
NBC had one to air AFL games. The championship was technically an NFL game *and* an AFL game, so both networks aired it,
each with its own sportscasters. However, only CBS's camera crew
and live feed were used, because it was held in the Los Angeles

---

U.S. sport with the most viewers: Pro football. Second-most: NASCAR.

Memorial Coliseum, home to the Los Angeles Rams of the NFL—CBS territory.

- **TECHNICAL PROBLEMS:** A halftime ad ran too long and NBC missed the second-half kickoff. The network actually talked officials into redoing the kickoff once they were back on the air (which confused viewers watching the game on CBS).

- **COMMERCIALS:** Because the Super Bowl is almost always the most-watched single TV show of the year (the 2010 game was the most-watched American TV broadcast *of all time*), the networks can command huge fees for advertising. A 30-second spot at Super Bowl I cost $40,000, the equivalent of about $245,000 in today's money. A 30-second spot at Super Bowl XLIV in 2010: $2.8 million.

- **POST GAME:** One of the spoils for each year's broadcasting network is the opportunity to launch a new show or expose an existing show to a huge audience immediately after the game, and win a lot of new viewers. *Family Guy* and *Undercover Boss* both debuted after Super Bowls, and post-game episodes of *Friends*, *House*, and *The X Files* were those series' most-watched ever. What aired after Super Bowl I? On CBS, it was a regularly scheduled episode of *Lassie*. NBC aired *Walt Disney's Wonderful World of Color*. That night's episode: part 2 (of 3) of "Willie and the Yank," about a young Confederate soldier who befriends a Union soldier during the Civil War.

- **ATTENDANCE:** Super Bowl I is the only Super Bowl that wasn't a sellout. The official attendance number for the game: 61,946...well under the 100,000-plus that regularly attended USC football home games in the same stadium.

- **TICKET PRICE:** The face value of a 2010 ticket was around $500, with scalpers and ticket brokers charging tens of thousands. Cost of a ticket to the 1967 game, of which there were more than 30,000 still available at game time: $12.

*　　*　　*

"Why do they lock gas station restrooms? Are they afraid someone will clean them?"

—George Carlin

FLYING BLIND

Imagine you're driving your car down the highway and you suddenly lose your eyesight. Now imagine that same scenario—only you're flying a plane.

THE PREDICAMENT

On a bright November day in 2008, Jim O'Neill, a 65-year-old Cessna pilot, was flying solo from Scotland to Sheffield, England. All was going fine until about 40 minutes into the flight. Cruising at 5,000 feet over the English countryside, everything started to get blurry. At first O'Neill thought he'd been blinded by the sun. He rubbed his eyes, but the feeling didn't pass. In fact, it was getting worse. He started to panic and immediately radioed for help: "Mayday! I can't see the dials! It's all a blur!"

Controllers at Full Sutton Airfield, near North Yorkshire, attempted to guide O'Neill to the runway. He flew right past it. Growing more stressed each minute, he sounded confused and his speech was slurred. That and the sudden blindness pointed to one thing: O'Neill had suffered a stroke.

THE WING MAN

The U.K.'s Royal Air Force overheard the mayday call and offered to send help. A few minutes later, Wing Commander Paul Gerrard, the chief flying instructor from nearby Linton-on-Ouse Base, flew his Tucano T1 turboprop plane to within a few hundred feet of the Cessna. "Mr. O'Neill," he said over the radio, "I'm going to take you back to my base." Gerrard then kept in constant contact with O'Neill for the 20-mile trip, giving him course corrections along the way: "Left a bit, right, descend, level, left." (Gerrard had to fly in a zigzag pattern to keep from zooming past the much slower Cessna.) By the time the two planes reached Linton, O'Neill was having trouble keeping his composure. He kept apologizing for all the trouble he was causing and worried that he'd crash onto people on the ground. "Everything's going to be fine, Jim. Just keep listening to me. Now, you're above the airstrip, can you see it?"

"No," replied O'Neill. "I'm sorry, sir, I just can't see."

Of the two choices available—try to talk him down, or send

Ancient Egyptians shaved their armpits and used citrus-cinnamon deodorant.

him to a secluded area to crash where no one else could get hurt—Gerrard and the base personnel never even mentioned the latter choice. "We're going to get you down safely, Mr. O'Neill. You just have to follow my instructions to the tee."

THE APPROACH

Once O'Neill aligned his plane with the runway, he was able to begin his descent. In order to land safely, however, a pilot must have visual contact with the ground. O'Neill couldn't even see his instruments, let alone the ground, so he pulled up at the last second. "No worries," said Gerrard. "Let's turn around and we'll try again." And they did—six more times. On a couple of the attempts, the plane bounced off the runway; on others O'Neill pulled up early, apologizing each time. Gerrard was patient, though, as both planes had enough fuel to remain up there for a long time. But O'Neill was the wild card: No one knew how much longer he could keep flying. What they did know was that a second stroke near the base and neighboring village could mean disaster, so they had no choice but to keep trying.

Finally, on the seventh attempt, more than 45 minutes after Gerrard took O'Neill's wing, the Cessna hit the runway hard and bounced back up. O'Neill was able to keep it steady; the plane bounced again on the runway and started veering to the right, then hit ground a third time—and stayed down. O'Neill engaged the brake and the Cessna rolled to a stop in the grass…without a scratch. When paramedics met him at the plane, he was confused and disoriented but otherwise uninjured.

THE REUNION

O'Neill spent several weeks at the hospital and several months recovering. By the following April, his vision started slowly improving. He still couldn't fly a plane or even drive a car, but a friend flew him—in the very same Cessna—to Linton so he could finally meet (and see) his rescuers. Gerrard was humble about the ordeal: "I was glad to help a fellow aviator in distress, but I was just part of a team. There were 12 people working at the base that day that helped get Jim safely back on the ground."

"I owe my life to the RAF," said O'Neill, "as well as the lives of those dozens of people I could have crash-landed on."

HOW TO TICKLE A TROUT

Here's an intriguing "art" that dates back to the days when most
Americans lived in rural areas: catching trout with your bare hands.
(And to learn how to hypnotize a chicken, turn to page 371.)

S**TEP 1.** Figure out where the trout are hiding. When trout
are startled or need to rest, they seek shelter in areas that
offer protection from predators, such as underneath submerged rocks or logs. Or, on stretches of a river or stream bank,
the bank may be "undercut"—there may be a recessed area
beneath the bank where trout hide. If the water is brimming with
trout, the easiest way to find their hiding places may be to simply
follow them. Walk along the bank, keeping an eye out for movement. The trout are also keeping an eye out for you, and when
they see you, they will head for shelter.

STEP 2. When you find a spot where the trout may be hiding,
approach slowly and carefully to avoid scaring them out of their
hiding place. Position yourself so that you can reach down into
the water and touch the fish. In the case of an undercut bank, you
can lie down on the bank with one arm in the water.

STEP 3. Slowly and carefully feel around for trout. If you do
make contact with one, slowly tickle its underside, just forward of
the tail fin, with your forefinger. This will start to calm the fish.

STEP 4. Slowly tickle your way forward along the underside of the
trout. This will calm the fish further, putting it into a trance-like
state. When you've tickled your way up to the gills, you should be
able to grab the trout without much trouble. Toss it on the bank.
(If you're strictly tickle-and-release, throw it back in the water.)

FISHY BUSINESS

Trout tickling is a surprisingly effective technique once you get
the hang of it. So effective, in fact, that it's considered a form of
poaching in the U.K. and punishable by a fine equivalent to about
$4,000. Why so high? Tickle-poachers fish without equipment,
and that makes them difficult to catch. They have to be caught
"wet-handed," while they're lying at the water's edge with one
hand in the water.

BIRD BRAINS, PART II

In Part I, we told you about some really intelligent birds. But most of them are lame ducks compared to these avian Einsteins. (Part I is on page 44.)

CAWS AND EFFECT

The world's most intelligent bird: According to ornithologists, it's the common crow. Surprised? As we noted earlier, eagles and vultures use rocks to break open hard-shelled eggs. Urban crows do kind of the same thing to open hard walnut shells, only they utilize cars. At busy intersections in cities around the world, they've been observed standing on the sidewalks alongside pedestrians, waiting for the light to change. When it does, the crows hop to the middle of the street and drop a few walnuts. Then they hop back to safety, wait for the light to turn green, and watch as the cars drive over the nuts, cracking them open. When the light turns red again, the crows hop back into the street and collect their meals.

BY HOOK OR BY ROOK

All members of the corvid family—crows, ravens, rooks, magpies, jackdaws, and jays—are intelligent, but none more so than crows and ravens. Much of what we know about these birds comes from two of the world's leading corvid researchers, Nathan Emery and Nicky Clayton. Their most famous experiment took place in 2002 when they studied New Caledonian crows, native to the South Pacific. The researchers placed a small canister full of insects inside a slim glass beaker and challenged a crow named Betty to get it out so she could eat the insects: There was a little wire loop on top of the canister, but Betty couldn't reach it with her beak; next to the beaker was a straight piece of wire. She picked it up and stuck it inside the beaker, but couldn't lift up the canister. What Betty did next stunned the scientific community: She pressed the piece of wire against the tabletop a few times and bent it into a small hook. Then she used the hook to remove the canister.

Clayton and Emery concluded, "Some corvids are not only superior in intelligence to birds of other avian species, but also rival many nonhuman primates."

If all the freight trains in the U.S. were lined up, they'd cross the country six times.

WINGING IT

It's impressive that Betty taught herself how to bend that piece of wire, but it's not *that* much of a stretch—crows regularly construct tools in the wild. Like chimpanzees, for example, they remove leaves from twigs to scoop up insects. But another sign of intelligence is whether an animal can be taught to do something it *doesn't* do in the wild. Mammals are good at this. (Think of a bear riding a bicycle.) Rooks, another species of corvid, don't use tools in the wild. Could they be taught to do so in a lab?

In 2009 Emery and another researcher, Christopher David Bird (really), put one of Aesop's fables to the test: In "The Crow and the Pitcher," the crow throws stones into a pitcher until the water level is high enough for him to take a drink. They set up the same scenario for the rooks and demonstrated how it worked. The rooks observed and, according to Emery, "All four subjects solved the problem with an appreciation of precisely how many stones were needed." Three of the rooks figured out pretty quickly that large rocks work better than small ones. These findings showed that rooks have a "flexible ability" to use tools—they can improvise and learn from their mistakes, both signs of higher intelligence. "Clayton and Emery's work has opened up ways of looking at the role of learning from experience," said Uta Frith, a neuroscientist at University College London. "Birds are providing an imperfect but extremely revealing mirror to us. They let us see the behaviors we most treasure as part of being human in a new light."

OUT OF SIGHT, NOT OUT OF MIND

One of those human behaviors is *mental time travel*—the ability to call on memories of past experiences to guide future actions. Dr. Clayton observed mental time travel in corvids one day while she was outside having lunch at the University of California, Davis. Scrub jays (smaller cousins of the crow) would battle each other for food scraps and then hide them in *caches*—storage places such as small holes in the ground and under shrubs. But after all the jays flew away, a few returned by themselves and re-hid their scraps in new caches. Did the birds come back because they knew they were previously being watched by other birds who wanted to steal their food? If so, that would qualify as mental time travel.

About 1 out of every 20 people with asthma are also allergic to aspirin.

Clayton and Emery decided to test this theory in the lab. The jays who knew they were being watched by other birds when they hid their food returned later and re-hid it. The control group that wasn't watched left the food in the original hiding places. The scientists' conclusion: "Since re-caching is not dependent on the potential thief being present, the experienced jay must be using some cognitive ability to perform this behavior." Again, this is a behavior that, until recently, was thought to only occur in mammals.

Here are two more examples of higher thinking in crows.

• Crow hunters have reported that if three hunters enter a hunting blind, the crows will fly away and won't return to the area until not one, not two, but all three hunters have left. That puts the bird in a very exclusive animal kingdom club: those that can count.

• Another trait thought to be uniquely mammalian is the ability to enjoy things for pleasure. Crows have been witnessed collecting bright objects such as coins and hiding them away. Biologists can find no evolutionary or survival motive for this action except that the birds just seem to like shiny things.

SCARY CROWS

To say that crows have adapted to living alongside humans is an understatement. They thrive in rural areas, cities, and suburbs. And to many people—and other animals—they're a nuisance.

• For millennia, farmers have been trying to scare crows away from their fields. Here's an excerpt from an 1881 book, *Household Cyclopedia of General Information*, by Henry Hartshorne:

> Machinery of various kinds, such as wind-mills in miniature, horse rattles, etc., to be put in motion by the wind, are often employed to frighten crows; but with all of these they soon become familiar. The most effectual method of banishing them from a field is the frequent use of the musket.

• In their quest to find food and nesting materials, urban crows are smart, creative, and relentless. They empty trash cans, terrorize pedestrians, and have even knocked out high-speed Internet networks by stealing wires from control boxes. In one case in Japan, a crow was blamed for shutting down a bullet train. Since 2000, game officials in Tokyo have killed more than 100,000 crows, but they remain a daily problem.

What are *murmets*, *hodmedods*, and *tattie bogles*? Different names for scarecrows in England.

• In Cape Cod, Massachusetts, endangered piping plovers nest on the beaches, but crows eat their eggs. Conservation officials built protective cages over the plover nests, expecting that the cages would keep out the crows but allow the smaller birds to come and go. The officials might as well have painted big bull's-eyes on the nests. Now the crows simply land hard on top of the cages and rattle them until the spooked plovers abandon their nests...and become easy crows' meals themselves. In 2010 the U.S. Department of Agriculture announced a plan to set up fake plover nests (without cages) that contain poisoned hard-boiled eggs. They're counting on the crows being intelligent enough to make the connection that eating the plovers' eggs will kill them. The question yet to be answered: Are the crows smart enough to discern between the real nests and the fake nests?

QUOTH THE RAVEN

All birds use complex forms of communication, but crows and ravens may actually use rudimentary forms of language. When you hear that cacophony of caws in the morning, that's the group of crows or ravens discussing where to go look for food. However, deciphering the subtle differences between corvid alarm calls, assembly calls, distress calls, and their other vocalizations has proven difficult. According to the University of Vermont's professor emeritus of biology Bernd Heinrich, who authored several books about ravens: "Our research has been something like that of aliens from outer space who make sonograms of human vocalizations. Certain differences noted in frequency, intonation, and loudness are correlated with feelings and emotions. But human sounds convey much more, and perhaps ravens' do, too." One particular behavior that has led scientists to believe that ravens may use language is their distinctive regional dialects. When ravens from different areas meet, it takes some time for them to learn each other's calls.

A few ravens have even learned to mimic the human voice. Of course, there's one bird order known for this skill: the *Psittaciformes*, or "true" parrots, which include lories, cockatoos, and parakeets. And their intelligence level ranks close to corvids.

To read about the world's most learned parrot, as well as some other amazing avian abilities, migrate on over to page 416.

WEIRD CRIME

*This year's surreal selections of scurrilous scofflaws features sausages,
superheroes, a snake, and the seeds of a dandelion.*

THE MISSING LINKS

After a 23-year-old man named He finished his meal at a restaurant in the Chinese city of Benxi, he grabbed the owner's daughter, pulled out a knife, and demanded all the cash from the register. Some of the other patrons overpowered He and held him until help arrived. When the police came, He opened his shirt to reveal what looked like a belt of tube-shaped bombs around his chest. Officers rushed He outside and called the bomb squad. "When they arrived," said an officer, "they laughed out loud as they quickly realized the explosives were actually sausages." He later explained that he came up with the idea when he looked in his refrigerator: "The sausages looked liked bombs, so I decided to try it."

SAVE THE LAST TRANCE

"You are getting sleepy." That's the last thing the women told police they could remember before they regained their senses and discovered their cash registers were empty. The strange crime spree took place at several banks and supermarkets in northern Italy in 2008, and so far the suspect has eluded capture. Although experts say that this kind of hypnotism is impossible—you can't just walk up to someone and with a single command and get her to do your nefarious bidding—surveillance footage clearly shows the man (who police say "bears a striking resemblance to Saddam Hussein") talk to the women and then simply reach into the register and take the money. In each case, the svengali walked out with a wad of cash and a smile on his face.

A SEEDY NEIGHBORHOOD

In 2010 police in Hittfeld, Germany, received an emergency call from a boy who said that his eight-year-old friend had just been abducted by a man driving a Porsche. The cops put out an all-points-bulletin and began a city-wide search. A few minutes later, the Porsche driver (age 47, name not released) walked into the police station dragging the kid behind him. The man said the boy had vandalized his Porsche. How? He was blowing dandelion seeds into the air and some of them "hit" the sports car. The boy was freed; the man was arrested and faces up to two years in prison.

JOE UNCOOL

"This has got to rank as one of the worst attempted jailbreaks ever," said a prison official in Albany, Isle of Wight, England. The first problem: The perpetrator tried to break into the wrong prison (his cousin was incarcerated at a prison in a neighboring town). Second, the man's weapon was a squirt gun. Third, the man—who tried to no avail to kick down a door—was wearing a Snoopy costume. "He wasn't too conspicuous," said the official.

SNAKE ATTACK!

In 2010 a guest in a Rock Hill, South Carolina, motel knocked on his neighbor's door and asked the occupant, 29-year-old Tony Smith, to please turn down the music. Smith complied, and the other guest thought that was the end of it. It wasn't. A few hours later, he stepped out of his room and saw Smith quickly walking toward him carrying a four-foot-long python. Then, according to police reports, "Smith hit him in the face with the snake's head." Smith was charged with assault and lost custody of the snake.

IT'S A JUNGLE OUT THERE

On April 21, 2010, police in Stevens Point, Wisconsin, received a strange call: A woman said she was walking through town when she felt a sharp pain in her chest. She looked down and saw a tiny dart sticking out of her blouse. A little while later, a similar call came in from another person, and then another, and then another. Then it dawned on police that they were probably dealing with a serial tiny-dart shooter. Thankfully, the darts weren't poisonous. And the cops had a lead: One of the victims saw a small tube sticking out of the window of a black minivan, which sped away. Police found the minivan; sitting inside was 41-year-old Paula Wolf...and her blow darts. Why did she do it? "I like to hear people say 'ouch.'"

BUMPER STICKERS

We keep thinking that we've seen every clever bumper sticker that exists, but every year readers send us new ones.

Never do anything you wouldn't want to explain to the paramedics

To err is human.
To arr is pirate.

I've got a God-given right to be an atheist

Free airbag test: come a little closer

If you're not supposed to eat animals, how come they're made of meat?

EVEN IF THE VOICES AREN'T REAL, THEY HAVE SOME GOOD IDEAS

If it weren't for physics and law enforcement, I'd be unstoppable

Drive it like you stole it

I'm great in bed: I can sleep all night

Look out! I drive just like you

Eliminate and abolish redundancy

I missed winning the lottery by only six numbers

I STARTED WITH NOTHING, AND I STILL HAVE MOST OF IT LEFT

Lord, give me patience... but hurry!

I beat up five hippies and all I got was this lousy VW bus

Warning: driver applying makeup

Help! I Farted and can't roll down my windows!

THIS IS NOT AN ABANDONED VEHICLE

Even though this is a stupid sticker, you're squinting to read it.

Hello, officer. Put it on my tab.

IF GOD IS YOUR CO-PILOT, PLEASE SWAP SEATS

My other bumper sticker is funny

On *Star Trek*, Spock's blood type was T-negative.

VOLCANO MOON

Using any half-decent telescope, you can easily view Jupiter and its four largest moons. The moon closest to the gas giant—called Io—may look like any other point of light, but don't be fooled: Io is perhaps the strangest, and certainly the most volatile, celestial body in our solar system.

IO'S CONTENTIOUS DISCOVERY

In 1610 Galileo Galiei claimed he discovered four moons around Jupiter. So did one of his chief rivals, fellow astronomer Simon Marius. But because Galileo published his findings a few days earlier than Marius, Galileo got the credit.

• It was Marius, however, who named Jupiter's moons. Based on a suggestion from Johannes Kepler that he name them after Jupiter's illicit lovers in Greek and Roman mythology, Marius chose Io, Europa, Ganymede, and Callisto. Galileo hated those names and simply called the moons Jupiter I, II, III, and IV. Those names stuck until the 20th century, when several more moons were discovered, and Marius's original names became official. (To date, 63 moons have been discovered orbiting Jupiter.)

LAND OF EXTREMES

• For centuries Io was assumed to be similar to the other moons in the solar system—an inactive rock speckled with impact craters. But in the last 50 years, more-powerful telescopes and several unmanned flybys revealed a different picture: Io is a volcanic world. Only a handful of moons and planets have volcanic activity, but none are anywhere near as active as Io.

• Io owes its violent nature to the extreme forces constantly affecting it. About the same size as our moon, Io is actually closer to Jupiter than our moon is to Earth. (Picture a BB floating a few inches above a beach ball.) So on the near side, Jupiter's gravity is pulling tremendously on Io. At the same time, Io's far side is being pulled on by the gravity of Europa and Ganymede.

• This tug-of-war results in what's called "tidal heating." Io's surface bulges in and out an average of 328 feet each day. Compare that to Earth's tides, which at their maximum reach about 60 feet.

• This creates an incredible amount of friction *inside* Io, which heats it up—sort of like the way kneading dough makes it warm. That heat gets released in the form of more than 400 active volcanos, including the most powerful one in the solar system, called Loki, which spews lava several hundred miles above Io's surface. At any given time, dozens of Ionian volcanoes are erupting, creating huge umbrella-shaped plumes that cover vast areas.

• Another record: Io's solid iron core makes it the densest moon in the solar system. In that respect, Io is more similar to the four inner planets—Mercury, Venus, Earth, and Mars—than it is to the other large *Jovian* moons, which are mostly made of water ice.

ASSAULT ON THE SENSES

• A trip to Io would be amazing…and treacherous. Viewed from afar, Io resembles a giant pizza, complete with tomato sauce, melted cheese, and black olives. These colors are created by sulfur and sulfur dioxide in their various states—liquid, gas, and solid. If you flew closer to Io (avoid the massive plumes!), you'd see enormous sulfur icebergs floating in bubbling sulfur lakes, volcanic craters the size of Texas, raging rivers of molten lava, and mountains twice as high as Mt. Everest.

• Please remain in the safe confines of your spacecraft…or at least hold your nose when you venture outside. Because it literally snows sulfur dioxide, Io smells like a really, really, *really* bad fart. If you do want to get out, wear layers. Io boasts some of the most extreme temperature differences ever recorded: The surface temps are about -200°F; the areas surrounding volcanoes can top 3,000°F. Only one place in the solar system is hotter than that: the sun.

• But that's assuming you could even fly close enough to observe these phenomena. Io's thin sulphur dioxide atmosphere is sucked away at about one ton per second by Jupiter. This creates an intense radiation belt known as the *Io plasma torus*, a doughnut-shaped ring of ionized sulfur, oxygen, sodium, and chlorine around Io. Between the ionized field, the radiation, and the bad weather, it's best to observe Io from a safe distance. (Bring a camera.)

*   *   *

"I've loved the stars too fondly to be fearful of the night."

—Galileo

Stomach ulcers aren't caused by spicy foods or stress—they're caused by bacteria.

NO FINALE

The finales of popular TV shows like M*A*S*H or Friends are big media events, wrapping up the series neatly and bringing in huge numbers of viewers. But some shows tape their final episodes without knowing it's the final episode, or that the show's about to get canceled.

Show: *Married...With Children* (Fox)
On the Air: 1987–1997
The End: An offbeat, cynical, and often crude take on the traditional family sitcom, *Married* was one of the first-ever shows on the Fox Network. It remained on the air through its 11th season, getting renewed well in advance of the season's end each year. In early 1997, Fox was noncommittal about another year of the show, but the producers filmed the 11th-season finale as planned—a regular episode in which Al Bundy (Ed O'Neill) prevents daughter Kelly (Christina Applegate) from marrying a jerk. A few weeks later, Fox canceled the show. O'Neill got the news that he was out of a job when a couple of fans bumped into him in a parking lot and expressed their condolences.

Show: *My Name Is Earl* (NBC)
On the Air: 2005–2009
The End: *Earl* was the most popular new sitcom of the 2005–06 season and finished the year at #40 in the ratings with 11 million viewers. The original premise appealed to audiences: Earl (Jason Lee) was a redneck petty thief who won the lottery and tried to turn his life around by righting every wrong he'd ever committed. But the show took a lot of weird turns (example: Earl spent half of season three in a coma with an imaginary 1950s sitcom playing in his brain, in which he was the star and the other characters were his friends and family) and lost nearly half its viewers, dropping to #85 in the fourth season. Creator Greg Garcia knew the show was slipping and asked NBC what their plans were so he could produce either a wrap-up final episode or an end-of-season cliffhanger in which Earl finds out he may be the father of his ex-wife's child. NBC told him to go with the cliffhanger. After it aired, the network canceled the show. (And Earl never found out if he was a dad.)

What do Henry Ford and Paul Revere have in common? They both made clocks.

Show: *All in the Family/Archie Bunker's Place* (CBS)
On the Air: 1971–1983
The End: *All in the Family*, the satirical show about a loud-mouthed, blue-collar bigot named Archie Bunker (Carroll O'Connor) and his "dingbat" wife Edith (Jean Stapleton), was one of the biggest hits in TV history—it was the #1 show for five years. Then, in 1979, the actors who played Archie's daughter and son-in-law (Sally Struthers and Rob Reiner) quit the show, necessitating a format change away from the "family" setting. So producers changed the name to *Archie Bunker's Place* and moved most of the action to the bar that Archie bought in season eight. The new show continued to draw viewers and was a top-20 hit, although it wasn't as popular as *All in the Family*. Then Stapleton left. With none of the original characters in the cast except Archie, the ratings plummeted, and CBS canceled *Archie Bunker's Place* without a proper ending to the 13-year Archie Bunker story. Instead, the last episode is about the bar's co-owner trying to win back an old girlfriend. Writer Fred Rubin said that if he'd been given advance notice, he would have written an ending that reunited Archie with his WWII army buddies in Italy.

Show: *Gunsmoke* (CBS)
Years: 1955–1975
The End: *Gunsmoke* debuted in TV's early black-and-white days, outlasted more than 100 other Western shows, and was still popular in 1975, when sitcoms like *Happy Days*, *Sanford and Son*, and *The Mary Tyler Moore Show* dominated and it was the *only* Western on the air. For 15 of its 20 years, *Gunsmoke* was a top-10 show, and no prime-time TV show has ever produced as many episodes—635 in all. (*The Simpsons* is a distant second, with over 460 and counting.) Despite all that, *Gunsmoke* was simply pulled off the air in April 1975, a few weeks after a forgettable episode—the sharecropping Pugh family struggles to get their crops planted before they're evicted; lead character Marshal Dillon barely appears. The show had slipped to #23 in the ratings, but no one from CBS had ever mentioned to anyone in the cast or on the production staff that the end was even a possibility. James Arness, the star of *Gunsmoke* for 20 years, had planned to retire after another three years. Instead, he read about the show's cancellation in *Variety*.

THE ANTHRAX ATTACKS, PART II

For Part I of the story of the 2001 anthrax attacks, go to page 75.

HOW THE DISEASE WORKS

The method by which anthrax disables its victims is like something out of a horror movie. Once spores enter the body, either through a cut on the skin or via food or inhalation, the body's immune cells capture and ingest them. Normally invaders are broken down and taken to the nearest lymph nodes, where antibodies against further infestation are produced. But that's just what anthrax wants: The spores have a protective coating that prevents them from being broken down, but being ingested by immune cells induces them to *germinate*, or "wake up," so to speak, from their spore state and become fully active bacteria. Then they begin to multiply incredibly rapidly, quickly killing and bursting out of their host immune cells to enter the bloodstream. They continue multiplying in the blood, which carries them throughout the body. That's bad, but it gets worse: The bacteria now begin producing and releasing the deadly anthrax toxin.

Anthrax toxin is made up of three proteins that work together to chemically "trick" the body's cells into allowing the proteins to enter them—a big cellular no-no—then induce them to produce inflammation-causing fluids. Inflammation is a normal immune response and is usually a good thing. But this is a *massive* response, and toxic levels of fluids quickly build up in the body, leading to tissue damage, decreased blood pressure, organ failure, and, in the worst forms of the disease, death in just a few days.

Result: The little *B. anthracis* bacteria have what they wanted all along: something dead to feed on. And when they're all done, and there's no food left, they go back into their spore state. And wait.

TRIPLE WHAMMY

There are three different forms of anthrax disease, each one corresponding with how the bacteria enter the body.

• *Cutaneous anthrax*, caused when anthrax spores enter through a cut or abrasion on the skin, accounts for about 95 percent of all known human cases. It begins as a small, itchy sore at the site of contact, then a blister that eventually bursts and dries into a very black scab, all of this accompanied by flulike symptoms. Cutaneous anthrax is easily treatable with antibiotics and is fatal in only about one percent of cases. People most likely to get it: those who work with wool and cow hides. (Anthrax is also known as *woolsorter's* and *ragpicker's disease.*)

• *Gastrointestinal anthrax* is caused by ingestion of the spores, most commonly through eating infected meat. It is extremely rare, and no cases have ever been reported in the United States. (It is, however, the most common form in animals.) Symptoms include abdominal pain, fever, and severe inflammation. It is often fatal in livestock, but is treatable with antibiotics.

• *Inhalational anthrax* is caused by inhaling airborne spores, and it's the worst form of the disease. Characterized by fever, flulike symptoms, and fluid buildup in the lungs, it causes death within days in nearly 75 percent of all cases—even with treatment. It's also extremely rare: Before the 2001 attacks, the last death in the United States due to inhalation anthrax occurred in 1976, when a 31-year-old weaver in California died after working with spore-infested yarn imported from Pakistan.

FROM MEDICINE TO WEAPON

For all the bad press that anthrax gets, it actually holds an important place in the history of advances against infectious diseases: It's the very first disease positively linked to a particular bacterium. That discovery was made by German physician Robert Koch in 1876. (He did the same with cholera and tuberculosis, for which he won the Nobel Prize in Medicine.) Five years later, French scientist Louis Pasteur developed an anthrax vaccine, which is still used on livestock around much of the world today.

Unfortunately, the discoveries also led to less-than-humane pursuits, and it wasn't long before the anthrax bacterium (as well as many other microorganisms) was being studied for possible use as a weapon.

• During World War I, the German government reportedly sent agents supplied with anthrax bacteria to several Allied countries in order to kill livestock. One agent, Dr. Anton Dilger, a German-American physician, set up a lab in his basement in Washington, D.C.—just miles from the White House—in 1916. There's little evidence to suggest that he and the other agents were successful.

• In the 1930s, several nations—including Germany, the United States, the U.S.S.R., Canada, and Japan—conducted extensive research into weaponizing anthrax, though it's unclear whether it was ever used in battle.

• In 1942 the British military exploded the first known "anthrax bomb" in a test on Gruinard Island off Scotland. It released a cloud of anthrax spores that killed 60 sheep and made the island uninhabitable for the next five decades.

• The British also produced five million "anthrax cakes" intended to be dropped over Germany and eaten by cattle, but never deployed them. They were safely incinerated after the war.

• In 1943 the United States began producing anthrax-based and other biological weapons at Fort Detrick in Frederick, Maryland.

• In 1969 President Richard Nixon ended America's biological weapons program, but studies, including work on human anthrax vaccines, continued. The FDA approved a human vaccine a year later.

• In 1979 an unknown amount of anthrax spores in aerosol (airborne) powder form was accidentally released at a bioweapons plant near the Ukrainian city of Sverdlovsk. At least 68 people in the area died in the days that followed, as did livestock as far as 30 miles away.

• In the 1980s, the Iraqi government developed an extensive biological-weapons program and produced large amounts of anthrax bacteria. For this reason, American and allied soldiers were inoculated with anthrax vaccine before the Persian Gulf War in 1991. No biological weapons are believed to have been used in the war.

So how were the deadly bacteria used to terrorize a nation in 2001? Turn to page 424 to find out.

KURT'S CUTS

*Kurt Vonnegut is one of our favorite authors here at the BRI. He wrote
science fiction, but he was all about humor and what it means to be human.*

"All persons, living and dead, are purely coincidental."

"If people think nature is their friend, then they sure don't need an enemy."

"Who is more to be pitied, a writer bound and gagged by policemen or one living in perfect freedom who has nothing more to say?"

"I urge you to please notice when you are happy, and exclaim or murmur or think at some point, 'If this isn't nice, I don't know what is.'"

"Nobody will stop you from creating. Do it tonight. Do it tomorrow. That is the way to make your soul grow, whether there is a market for it or not."

"It is exhausting, having to reason all the time in a universe which wasn't meant to be reasonable."

"Life happens too fast for you ever to think about it. If you could just persuade people of this, but they insist on amassing information."

"There is a tragic flaw in our precious Constitution: Only nut cases want to be president."

"Earth, should it find a voice and a sense of irony, might now well say of our abuse of it, 'Forgive them, Father, They know not what they do.' The irony would be that we know what we are doing."

"Everybody wants to build and nobody wants to do maintenance."

"I fully expected that by the time I was 21, some scientist would have taken a color photograph of God Almighty and sold it to *Popular Mechanics* magazine. Scientific truth was going to make us so happy and comfortable. What actually happened was that we dropped scientific truth on Hiroshima."

"The two real political parties in America are the Winners and the Losers."

"Enjoy the little things in life, for one day you'll look back and realize they were big things."

WEIRD CANADA

Canada: land of beautiful mountains, clear lakes…
and some really odd news stories.

YOU WANT THE TOOTH, OFFICER?

Outside Sarnia, Ontario, in June 2010, a driver flagged down a police officer on Highway 402 to warn him of a semi truck meandering all over the road. The officer caught up to the truck and pulled it over. The driver's explanation for his erratic driving: He was attempting to pull out one of his teeth. No longer able to deal with a toothache, he tied one end of a piece of string to the bad tooth and the other to the roof of his cab. "One good bump" and it would come right out, he told the officer. As it turned out, he was right—the officer could tell by the bloody tooth on a string sitting on the seat.

BEEFY VINO

In Japan, Wagyu cattle are fed beer and massaged with sake each day. The result is the richly flavored and expensive (more than $100 a pound) Kobe beef. Seeking to create his own specialty beef market, Bill Freding of Southern Plus Feedlots in Oliver, B.C., has developed his own booze-based method: wine-fed cows. Like the cattle at other high-volume beef producers, Freding's cattle eat a diet of primarily grain. But they also drink a liter of wine every day for 90 days prior to slaughter. The red wine is from wineries in the Okanagan Valley of British Columbia, and Freding claims the beef tastes "sweeter."

ANIMAL ACT

Wildlife officials in Deer Lake, Newfoundland, had to put down a moose in 2009, after someone reported the animal collapsing from exhaustion in their backyard. Witnesses reported seeing three teenage boys chasing the moose for hours and hitting it with sticks. The teens were quickly caught, brought up on animal cruelty charges…and acquitted. Why? One of the boys' fathers testified that they couldn't have been abusing the moose, because at the time they were busy vandalizing a local church.

What's Mt. Lee's claim to fame? It's the hill that the famous "HOLLYWOOD" sign stands on.

PLEASE KNOCK FIRST

For Valentine's Day 2010, the Toronto restaurant Mildred's Temple Kitchen pulled out all the stops for romantic diners—serving intimate meals for two…and openly encouraging couples to "couple" in the restrooms. A handful of concerned citizens reported the Mildred's promotion to the Toronto Public Health office. The agency investigated and found nothing wrong with the idea, as long as frisky patrons stayed out of food-preparation areas.

THE LAW IS THE LAW

In June 2010, Marika De Florio's five-year-old neighbor was driving her crazy, riding his battery-powered four-wheeler past her Seeley Bay, Ontario, house over and over again all afternoon. She asked the boy's grandparents several times to keep it down, but to no avail. So De Florio went outside and, in full view of the boy, took off her shirt. That, she reasoned, would convince the boy's grandparents to bring him inside. Indeed, Mike and Nancy Berry quickly hustled their grandson inside and then called the police on De Florio. No charges were pressed, however—it's legal in Seeley Bay for women to be topless in public.

DIRTY YOUNG MEN

Professor Simon Louis Lajeunesse of the University of Montreal's social work department began a project in December 2009 investigating how pornography affects the way men view and relate to women. Part of that research required a "control group" for comparison, so Lajeunesse advertised around Montreal to recruit 20 young men who did not view pornography. He received zero responses.

BAN-ADA

In the 1910s, Toronto police had full authority over movies, including the right to ban films they considered offensive. The criteria: Any movie that showed a pro-America attitude, murder, or an extramarital romance could be banned. *Any* movie. In 1911, an inspector reported, "I witnessed a moving picture show of *Hamlet*, written I think by Shakespeare. That's all very well to say it's a famous drama, but it doesn't keep it from being a spectacle of violence." A few weeks later, the same inspector banned a film version of *Romeo and Juliet*.

Bees fly at about 12 mph.

FAMILY BUSINESS

It's hard to become famous. One thing that often helps: having a famous parent. Some of these may surprise you.

RASHIDA JONES. She co-stars on the sitcom *Parks and Recreation* and has a role on *The Office.* Her mother is *The Mod Squad* star **Peggy Lipton**; her father is music producer **Quincy Jones.**

MITT ROMNEY. The former Massachusetts governor and 2008 presidential candidate is the son of Michigan governor and 1968 presidential candidate **George Romney.**

JOSS WHEDON. He has created four TV series with low ratings and rabid cult fan bases—*Buffy the Vampire Slayer, Angel, Firefly,* and *Dollhouse*—but got his start as a staff writer on *Roseanne.* He's also the first third-generation television writer: His father, **Tom Whedon**, wrote for *The Golden Girls*, and his grandfather, **John Whedon,** wrote for *The Donna Reed Show.*

NORAH JONES. She's the daughter of classical sitarist **Ravi Shankar.** (He didn't raise her, though, and they've had long periods of estrangement.)

PAUL GIAMATTI. The Oscar-nominated actor (*Sideways, American Splendor*) is the son of **A. Bartlett Giamatti**, a president of Yale University before becoming president of baseball's National League in 1986, and then commissioner of Major League Baseball in 1989. He was in the position for only a few months before he died, but it was long enough to ban gambler Pete Rose from baseball for life.

FRANCIS FORD COPPOLA. He directed *Apocalypse Now* and *The Godfather.* His father, **Carmine Coppola**, a film-score composer long before his son became one of the most important directors of his generation, composed the music for many of his son's films. Francis's daughter, **Sofia Coppola**, also became a director, winning an Oscar for her second film, *Lost in Translation.*

WHITNEY HOUSTON. Her, mother **Cissy Houston**, is primarily a gospel singer but once paid the bills as a backup singer for

Elvis Presley and Aretha Franklin. (And Dionne Warwick is Whitney's aunt.)

ELVIS COSTELLO. He's one of the most influential rock musicians of the last 30 years, but *his* biggest influence was his father, bandleader and trumpet player **Ross MacManus.**

ZAK STARKEY. He's the current drummer for the Who. It's not easy to fill in for Keith Moon, the band's legendary drummer, who died in 1978. But Starkey has a decent resume: He was once the drummer for the band Oasis...and his father is **Ringo Starr.**

DUNCAN JONES. He's the winner of the 2010 BAFTA Award (the British Oscar) for best first-time British director for his film *Moon.* He's also the son of rock legend **David Bowie,** and was better known as Zowie Bowie during his childhood.

GEORGE W. BUSH. President Bush is the son of another president Bush, **George H. W. Bush,** who is the son of banker, Wall Street executive, and U.S. Senator **Prescott Bush.** And Prescott Bush was the son of **Samuel Bush,** one of the most prominent and powerful business tycoons of the early 20th century.

GRANT HILL. Hill was one of the biggest stars of the NBA in the 1990s, being named the Rookie of the Year and playing in five all-star games. His father, **Calvin Hill,** was also a star athlete, but in professional football, not basketball. He played from 1969 to 1981, winning a Super Bowl with the Dallas Cowboys in 1972.

KRISTIN GORE. Like many comedy writers, she went to Harvard, was the editor of the humor magazine the *Harvard Lampoon,* and parlayed that into writing jobs for TV shows such as *Futurama* and *Saturday Night Live.* A guest star on both those shows during Gore's stints: her father, former vice president **Al Gore.**

LISA MURKOWSKI. She has served as a U.S. senator from Alaska since 2002. Her predecessor: her father, **Frank Murkowski,** who left Congress after 21 years to become the governor of the state and appointed his daughter to finish out his Senate term. She was reelected to a full term in 2004.

STELLA MCCARTNEY. She's one of the world's most famous and top-earning fashion designers. Her father is **Paul McCartney,** of the '70s rock band Wings (and the Beatles).

KNOCK-KNOCK JOKES

We used to think limericks were the lowest form of humor. (We were wrong.)

A: Desdemona.
Q: Desdemona who?
A: Desdemona Lisa still hang in Paris?

A: Wayne.
Q: Wayne who?
A: Wayne dwops keep falling on my head.

A: Amaryllis.
Q: Amaryllis who?
A: Amaryllis state agent. Wanna buy a house?

A: Shelby.
Q: Shelby who?
A: Shelby comin' 'round the mountain when she comes…

A: Esther.
Q: Esther who?
A: The Esther Bunny!

A: Venue.
Q: Venue who?
A: Venue vish upon a star…

A: Tarzan.
Q: Tarzan who?
A: Tarzan stripes forever!

A: Yule.
Q: Yule who?
A: Yule never know until you open the door.

A: Zeus.
Q: Zeus who?
A: Zeus company, three's a crowd.

A: Interrupting cow
Q: Interrupting c-
A: MOO.

A: Dwayne.
Q: Dwayne who?
A: Dwayne the tub, I'm dwowning!

A: Macho.
Q: Macho who?
A: Macho do about nothing.

A: Marcus Welby.
Q: Marcus Welby who?
A: I Marcus Welby dead for all you care.

A: Sam and Janet.
Q: Sam and Janet who?
A: Sam and Janet evening…

A: Somber.
Q: Somber who?
A: Somber over the rainbow.

A: Cat gut.
Q: Cat gut who?
A: Cat gut your tongue?

A: Hair comb.
Q: Hair comb who?
A: Hair comb trouble.

A: Amish.
Q: Amish who?
A: Amish you when you go away!

A: H.
Q: H who?
A: Gesundheit!

A: Control freak.
 (Okay, now you say "Control freak who?")

A: Police.
Q: Police who?
A: Police stop telling me these awful knock-knock jokes!

Average SAT score: 1,520 out of a possible 2,400 points.

JOE STALIN VS. JOHN WAYNE

After World War II, the U.S. and the Soviet Union engaged in a "cold" war: an ideological conflict that was waged through political rhetoric, military posturing, espionage, and an arms race. Would it lead to WWIII? It didn't, but at the time people weren't so sure. Here's an incredible story from that era.

THE PEACE CONFERENCE

In the late 1940s, Joseph Stalin, dictator of the Soviet Union, ordered a prominent Russian film director named Sergei Gerasimov to go to New York to attend a left-wing gathering called the Cultural and Scientific Conference for World Peace.

Gerasimov dutifully attended the conference, and that's pretty much all there was to the story for the next 50 years. Then in 2003, British film critic Michael Munn wrote a book entitled *John Wayne: The Man Behind the Myth*, in which he tells a more sinister tale of Gerasimov's trip to the United States and its aftermath. Munn says he got the story from actor/director Orson Welles, who heard it through contacts in the Soviet film industry.

MARKED MAN

According to Munn, while Gerasimov was in New York he learned of the leadership role that John Wayne, one of America's biggest movie stars, was playing in driving communists out of Hollywood. Wayne was the president of the Motion Picture Alliance for the Preservation of American Ideals, a right-wing group dedicated to compiling a "blacklist" of communists working in the film industry. That blacklist was used to destroy the careers of hundreds of actors, screenwriters, and directors, either because of alleged communist sympathies or simply because they refused to testify before Congressional investigating committees.

When Gerasimov returned home and reported the havoc that Wayne was wreaking on communist efforts to infiltrate the film industry, Munn's story goes, Stalin became so angry that he dispatched a team of KGB hit men to California. Their orders: Kill John Wayne.

BACKLOT JUSTICE

The KGB killers really did come to California, Munn writes, and they even made it onto the Warner Brothers lot, where "Duke" Wayne had an office. Disguised as FBI agents, they checked in at the front gate and were given directions to Wayne's office. (This part of the story, says Munn, was told to him by Yakima Canutt, a Hollywood stuntman and one of Wayne's closest friends.)

Luckily for the Duke, FBI informants had already learned of the plot. As the fake FBI agents made their way across the studio lot, *real* FBI agents hid in the back room of Wayne's office while he and a screenwriter named James Grant sat in the front room, pretending to be working. When the hit men entered, the FBI agents pounced, disarming and handcuffing the killers before they could harm Wayne.

Those G-men must have been *big* John Wayne fans, because they let him deal with the killers his own way: At Wayne's direction, the FBI men loaded the KGB agents into cars and drove them to a secluded beach north of Los Angeles. At the beach the KGB men, still handcuffed, were marched down to the surf and made to kneel in the wet sand. Then, as the FBI agents looked on approvingly, Wayne and Grant drew pistols and aimed them at the heads of the KGB men. "On the count of three," Wayne told Grant. "One…two…THREE!"

HOLLYWOOD ENDING

Both Wayne and Grant fired their guns, but the KGB men didn't die. It took a moment for them to realize they were still alive; when they opened their eyes, Wayne held up his gun and exclaimed, "Blanks!" The Duke had never killed a man (except in the movies), and he wasn't about to start now. "I just wanted to scare the living s*** out of them," Munn says Wayne told him.

The KGB men's lives were spared, but probably not for long, and they knew it: If the FBI deported them back to the U.S.S.R., Stalin would surely have them executed. The KGB men decided to defect to United States right then and there, and tell the FBI everything they knew. "Welcome to the land of the free," Wayne told them. Then he and Grant got into their car and drove off.

Wayne was safe, but would the commies try again? To guard against future attempts on Wayne's life, Yakima Canutt and his

---

In one study, spiders given marijuana started to spin webs but quit halfway through.

stuntmen friends organized themselves into a private intelligence-gathering force for Wayne and began infiltrating communist cells operating in southern California. On the basis of the information they gathered, Munn writes, the stuntmen were able to break up at least two more attempts on Wayne's life, the first one in the summer of 1953, while Wayne was in Mexico filming *Hondo*. They thwarted a second attempt in 1955 by storming the communists' hideout in the back room of a Burbank printing company and beating them to a bloody pulp.

Those would-be assassins didn't fare as well as the two that Wayne and Grant "killed" on the beach after the first attempt, Munn writes: The stuntmen bought them tickets on the next plane to Russia...and they were never seen or heard from again.

A DICTATOR MEETS THE DUKE

Wayne didn't learn that the threat to his life had abated until 1959, when Stalin's successor, Nikita Khrushchev, visited the United States. (Stalin died in 1953.) The Duke met him at a reception hosted by Twentieth Century Fox. It was there, according to Munn, that Wayne pulled Khrushchev aside during a quiet moment and asked through an interpreter why the Soviets were trying to kill him. "That was the decision of Stalin during his last five mad years," Khrushchev supposedly told the Duke. "When Stalin died, I rescinded the order."

That took care of the threat posed by *Soviet* communists, but Khrushchev warned him that Mao Zedong, leader of Communist China, had been in on the plot to assassinate him, and was likely still trying to do so.

ONE LAST TRY

Wayne learned how serious Mao's threat was when he made a three-week goodwill tour of Vietnam in the summer of 1966. Munn claims that during a visit to one village, Wayne was nearly shot by a sniper, who was later caught by U.S. troops. The sniper wasn't Vietnamese, he was *Chinese*—and he said that he'd been sent to the village on Mao's orders, specifically to kill John Wayne.

Part II of the story, turn to page 515, pilgrim.

Ouch! Roman emperor Hadrian toured his entire empire on foot.

HIP-HOP LAWSUITS

We were going to do "lite jazz" lawsuits, but we couldn't find any.

The Plaintiff: "Freeway" Ricky Ross, a Los Angeles gangster and drug kingpin in the early 1980s

The Defendant: Rick Ro$$, a rap star from Miami

The Lawsuit: Freeway was sentenced to life in prison in 1996. Ten years later, a young Miami rapper named William L. Roberts II signed with Def Jam records using the name Rick Ro$$, an homage of sorts to the convicted drug kingpin. And in addition to taking his name, Ro$$ adopted Freeway's persona. Freeway was furious. His lawyers sent Def Jam several cease-and-desist letters, but they were ignored. Meanwhile, Ro$$ made a string of successful albums that glorified "his" drug-dealing past. As soon as Freeway got out on parole in 2010 (his sentence was reduced to 20 years), he filed suit against Ro$$, claiming that the rapper was profiting off his name and image. Not only that, he says, he planned to start a program to keep troubled youths out of prison, and Ro$$ is hindering that effort by tarnishing his reputation. Freeway is suing the rapper for $10 million plus half of his royalties.

The Verdict: Pending.

The Plaintiff: 50 Cent

The Defendant: Taco Bell

The Lawsuit: In 2008 Taco Bell's president, Greg Creed, wrote an open letter to 50 Cent asking him to change his name to 99 Cent and star in a commercial, rapping his order for items from Taco Bell's value meal. "We know that you adopted the name 50 Cent years ago as a metaphor for change," Creed wrote. "We at Taco Bell are also huge advocates for change. We encourage you to 'Think outside the bun' and hope you accept our offer." Creed's open letter ran in several publications, which 50 Cent claims led his fans to believe that he was in on the deal. He wasn't. He filed a lawsuit against Taco Bell, alleging that "Taco Bell was, in effect, using his name in advertisements with his permission." According to 50 Cent's lawyer, "Taco Bell has used this infringing tactic before, issuing press releases using other celebrities' names, such as Rihanna, Chris Brown, Fergie, and Paris Hilton." According to 50 Cent, "When my legal team is finished with them, Taco Bell is going to have a new slogan: 'We messed with the bull and got the horns!'"

The Verdict: The case was settled out of court for an undisclosed sum. Don't expect to see 50 Cent rapping in a Taco Bell ad.

The Plaintiff: Richard Monroe Jr., a 25-year-old hip-hop fan

The Defendant: Snoop Dogg, The Game, Kurupt, Daz Dillinger, Soopafly, and several of Snoop Dogg's bodyguards

The Lawsuit: At a 2005 concert in Seattle, Washington, Snoop Dogg was performing when Monroe ran onto the stage and put his arm around Snoop's shoulder. Bad idea: Snoop's bodyguards, along with several other rappers, pounced on Monroe. "They beat me like a slave," he later told reporters. In the melee, Monroe suffered bruised ribs, a broken nose, and a split lip. He also claimed that his diamond earrings were ripped out of his ears and his wallet and cell phone were stolen. No criminal charges were filed, so Monroe filed a $22-million civil suit, naming Snoop as the chief defendant. According to Monroe's lawyers, Snoop invited him onto the stage. According to Snoop's lawyers, Snoop only invites women on stage. In the video footage of the incident, there are so many fists and feet flying that it's tough to tell who is doing what to whom, but it appears that Snoop was whisked away to safety while the beatdown occurred.

The Verdict: The jury ruled that the response to Monroe jumping onstage was excessive, but that Snoop Dogg wasn't involved. Instead of receiving $22 million, Monroe was awarded $449,400.

❈   ❈   ❈

LIFE IMITATES A BOARD GAME

In the 1970s, British Petroleum released a board game for kids called "BP Offshore Oil Strike." The goal: Find oil in the sea, build a rig, and get rich. The first player to make $120 million wins. But beware of the hazard cards, such as this one which reads: "Blow-out! Rig damaged. Oil slick cleanup costs. Pay $1 million."

REAL TEST ANSWERS

Sometimes, when knowledge is lacking, cleverness takes over. These are actual answers to questions on students' tests submitted to education websites by frazzled teachers.

Q: What type of force or bond holds the sodium ions and chloride ions together in a crystal of sodium chloride?
A: James Bond

Q: What is hard water?
A: Ice

Q: What happens during puberty to a boy?
A: He says goodbye to his childhood and enters adultery.

Q: Name six animals which specifically live in the Arctic.
A: 2 polar bears and ~~3~~ 4 seals

Q: What was Sir Walter Raleigh famous for?
A: He invented cigarettes and started a craze for bicycles.

Q: Briefly explain why breathing is important.
A: When you breathe, you inspire. When you do not breathe, you expire.

Q: What is a fossil?
A: A fossil is an extinct animal. The older it is, the more extinct it is.

Q: Explain why phosphorous trichloride (PCl_3) is polar.
A: God made it that way.

Q: Name the wife of Orpheus, whom he attempted to save from the underworld.
A: Mrs. Orpheus

Q: Name one measure that can be put into place to avoid river flooding in times of extensive rainfall.
A: Flooding may be avoided by placing a number of dames into the river.

Q: Why do mushrooms have their distinctive shapes?
A: Mushrooms always grow in damp places and so they look like umbrellas.

Q: Name one of the Romans' greatest achievements.
A: Learning to speak Latin.

Q: Expand $(a+b)^n$
A: $(\quad a \quad + \quad b \quad)^n$

Q: Where was the Declaration of Independence signed?
A: At the bottom.

POOP THAT'S ART

Some artists are known for creating magnificent masterpieces
like David (Michelangelo), the Mona Lisa (Da Vinci), or
The Starry Night (Van Gogh). Others are known for,
well, taking a more "earthy" approach to art. Like
Italian artist Pietro Manzoni, for example.

THE OUTSIDER

Piero Manzoni (1933–63) decided early on that he wanted to be an artist, but was pressured by his parents to be more practical and become a lawyer instead. He tried studying law but soon washed out, and he didn't fare much better when he switched to philosophy and literature. Finally, in 1955, the 22-year-old returned to his first love and began creating art full-time.

Manzoni's early landscape paintings were fairly conventional, but his work didn't stay that way for long. Perhaps it was because he felt alienated from his controlling parents, or because he'd been born into a family of aristocrats and was used to seeing himself as superior to other people. Or maybe it was because he was largely self-taught. Whatever the case, Manzoni never identified with the European art establishment. He saw himself as an outsider, forgoing paints, plaster, and other traditional art materials in favor of things like bread rolls, petroleum, rabbit fur, and cotton balls. He used them to create art that purists did not consider art at all.

In 1959, for example, he exhibited a series of inflated balloons attached to bases inscribed with the words "Piero Manzoni—Artist's Breath" in Italian. The following year, in a show titled "Consumption of Dynamic Art by the Art-Devouring Public," he decorated hard-boiled eggs with his thumbprint, then fed them to the people who came to the show.

CAN–DOO ATTITUDE

Manzoni's most famous work of art was *Merde d'Artiste* ("Artist's Sh*t"), a series of 90 cans that he filled with his own excrement, then numbered, signed, and labeled with the words "ARTIST'S

SH*T, CONTENT 30 GR., FRESHLY PRESERVED, PRODUCED AND TINNED IN MAY 1961" in Italian, English, French, and German. Manzoni pegged the price of his poop to the value of gold at the time, about $34 a can.

FOOL'S GOLD

Manzoni apparently intended *Merde d'Artiste* as a commentary on the foolishness of the art-buying public, which valued even the excrement of an artist more than gold.

If you were one of the people "foolish" enough to trade gold for poop when the *Merde d'Artiste* cans went on sale in the summer of 1961, you're probably a happy fool today. Why? Because Manzoni never issued a second series of cans, and he dropped dead from a heart attack in his Milan studio when he was only 29. The value of the remaining cans (he only made 90 of them) has been rising faster than the price of gold for nearly 50 years.

When the Tate Gallery, home to the Great Britain's collection of modern art, plopped down £22,300 (about $33,000) of taxpayer money to buy can #4 in 2000, many art critics (not to mention taxpayers) howled. "Why is the art world so much more absurdly gullible than, say, the world of books, or the world of music?" the London *Daily Telegraph* complained. "No concert hall would ever think of forking out £22,300 for an 'incredibly important international composer' to defecate live on stage."

FOOL'S POOP

Ever since the *Merde d'Artiste* cans first went on sale on 1961, a lot of people have wondered if they really do contain Manzoni's excrement as advertised, or were filled with some other substance. None of the cans has ever been opened by its owner—that would destroy the art and rob the can of most of its monetary value. All anyone could do was guess what the contents really were...until one of Manzoni's collaborators, Agostino Bonalumi, admitted in 2007 that the cans actually contained...plaster.

So did the revelation that the poop cans contain no poop hurt their value? Not at all—if anything, the publicity made them even more valuable: In 2007 can #19 sold at auction for $80,000.

Biggest balloon in the Macy's Thanksgiving Day Parade: a 100-foot-long Superman (1939).

OTHER POOP ARTISTS OF NOTE

- **Robert Wyndam Bucknell** (Miami). In his 2004 show "Why I Am So F***ing Special: It's All About Me," the 27-year-old Bucknell parodied Manzoni's work by displaying in glass jars the stool samples of a realtor, a pharmacist, and an art gallery owner alongside a jar of what he said was his own excrement. (His jar actually contained purple toy dinosaurs.) The jars were displayed beneath a sign paraphrasing F. Scott Fitzgerald's *The Great Gatsby*: "Let me tell you about the very talented: they are different than you and I."

- **Buster Simpson** (Seattle). "Among many other projects, Simpson offered a recycling solution to waste in the urban core: portable potties on the edges of sidewalks, with wastes falling into pre-dug and prepared holes," Regina Hackett wrote about the environmental artist in the *Seattle Post-Intelligencer* in 2008. "When enough fertilizer falls in, the potty moves on and a tree takes its place." Simpson's goal: raise awareness of environmental issues without "spoon-feeding the manifesto" to the public, he explained.

- **Sarah Lucas** (Great Britain). In 1996 London's Institute for Contemporary Arts (ICA) showcased Lucas's piece *The Great Flood*, a working toilet that she autographed with a gold marker. "Is it a step beyond Duchamp's *Fountain* [a urinal that Marcel Duchamp entered in an art show in 1917], a laconic metaphor for the body, or just a plain piece of plumbing?" read a sign near the toilet. ("I'd go with the latter," wrote the London *Independent's* art critic.) A German art collector paid $20,000 for the toilet, and when it was put on display in a Berlin gallery, two art lovers made use of the facilities—something the ICA described as "the ultimate involvement of the audience."

- **Susan Robb** (Seattle). In 2008 The Lawrimore Project gallery showcased Robb's one-woman exhibition "The Challenge Nature Provides," which included a piece of artwork called *DIGESTER*— a contraption made from three 55-gallon barrels that extracted methane from human waste "provided" by the gallery's owner, Scott Lawrimore. The methane gas was then used to fuel a campfire that was also part of the piece. "At the show opening, gallery-goers could toast marshmallows on the flames."

Fred MacMurray (*My Three Sons*) was the model for the face of superhero Captain Marvel.

NOT COMING TO A THEATER NEAR YOU

*You'd be surprised by how many films in Hollywood are started…
but not finished. Here's a look at a few fascinating could-
have-beens and almost-wases that never were.*

THE BREAKFAST CLUB 2 (2006)

Shortly after the influential teen-oriented dramedy *The Breakfast Club* was released in 1985, writer-director John Hughes mentioned to a reporter that he planned to make a new *Breakfast Club* film every 10 years or so, checking in on the lives of the five characters who meet in high-school detention in the first film. That plan never worked out. In 1999 Hughes started writing a sequel, but as a novel. He never finished it. In 2005 he tried again, letting the original cast know that he was writing a screenplay for *The Breakfast Club 2* in which the characters would be "nontraditional college students" in their late 30s, all in detention again. The twist was that all the characters had turned out the opposite of how they'd been in high school. The rebel (Judd Nelson) would now be conservative, the jock (Emilio Estevez) would have turned into a nerd, and so on. Hughes never managed to finish a script he liked, and *The Breakfast Club 2* will probably never happen—Hughes died in 2009.

FROM RUBEN TO CLAY (2004)

When *American Idol* debuted in 2002, it unleashed a pop-culture juggernaut—winners such as Kelly Clarkson and Carrie Underwood have become huge stars, and an annual *Idol* tour takes place every summer. Did you know that the pop-culture onslaught was supposed to include *Idol* movies too? The show's production company planned to make a movie after the conclusion of each season, starring that year's winner and runner-up. One movie was actually produced and released in 2003. *From Justin to Kelly*, a cheesy beach romance set during spring break, starred first-season winner and runner-up Kelly Clarkson and Justin Guarini. It was panned by critics and made only $4.9 million, hitting theaters just

---

Sideshow lingo: When an audience member faints, it's called a "falling ovation."

a few weeks after the *Idol* second-season finale, in which Ruben Studdard edged out Clay Aiken. The film's abysmal performance led to the cancellation of all future *Idol* movies, including *From Ruben to Clay*, which was going to be a modern-day version of the Bing Crosby/Bob Hope "Road" movies of the 1940s, such as *Road to Singapore* and *Road to Morocco*.

BATMAN TRIUMPHANT (1999)

The fourth Batman movie, *Batman and Robin* (1997) made $100 million at the box office—a lot, but far less than the previous three Batman movies. It was also critically lambasted for being campy and cartoonish (critics especially singled out the fact that there were nipples on Batman's costume), a far cry from the dark and gothic feel of 1989's *Batman*. While *Batman and Robin* was still in movie theaters, Warner Bros. called off the planned fifth Batman movie, *Batman Triumphant*. George Clooney was set to return as the title hero, and it was reportedly, ironically, going to be a return to the dark feel of the first movie. The plotline included the murder of Robin (Chris O'Donnell), and villains Harley Quinn (to be played by Madonna) and the Scarecrow (Jeff Goldblum and Howard Stern were both being considered for the part) teaming up to terrorize Gotham City and cause Batman to go insane by poisoning him with a chemical gas that would make him think he was fighting the Joker, who'd died in the original *Batman* movie. A new, darker Batman movie finally emerged in 2005 under new director Christopher Nolan—*Batman Begins*.

GRAYSKULL: MASTERS OF THE UNIVERSE (2010)

Mattel Toys commissioned a line of He-Man and the Masters of the Universe toys in the early 1980s. They had originally planned to produce *Conan the Barbarian* action figures (to go along with the Arnold Schwarzenegger movie), but changed their minds because of the film's kid-unfriendly R-rating. Good move. The He-Man toys went on to become the bestselling line of the '80s, buoyed by the *Masters of the Universe* TV cartoon show, which followed He-Man, a muscular warrior on a distant planet, who battled an army of monsters led by the evil Skeletor. The toys' popularity had diminished by 1987, but that's when Cannon Films released a live action *Masters of the Universe* starring Dolph Lundgren. It was a low-budget production, and to save costs, it took place on Earth (He-Man fell into a time-space portal), not in the familiar He-Man world, and it was a box office bomb. Twenty years later, screenwriter Justin Marks was hired by Warner Bros. to write a new script that stayed truer to the source material. He turned in *Grayskull: Masters of the Universe*, a "reboot" in the style of the newer *Batman* and *Star Trek* films. Reportedly, the script was a dark-and-gritty He-Man "origin story" like *Batman Begins*, and thoughtful and serious enough that Warner Bros. thought it could be an epic on par with the *Lord of the Rings* trilogy. Nevertheless, every director offered the project turned it down, including Doug Liman (*Mr. and Mrs. Smith*) and Bryan Singer (*X-Men*). But what really killed the He-Man movie: Between 2007 and 2009, the handful of Warner executives who approved the movie were all fired…and the prospect for a big-budget He-Man film died. For now.

*   *   *

THE SANDWICH ARTIST STRIKES BACK

Have you ever given any grief to the person who's making *your* sandwich? You may want to think twice next time. A Subway employee who identified himself only as "Chris" sent in this letter to *The Consumerist*:

> I've been working at Subway for about a year and a half, and it always amuses me when people complain about me not "tessellating" their cheese [ie., place the triangles in such a way that there's cheese in every bite]. Now, merely to amuse myself, not only do I *not* tessellate the cheese, but I also leave gaps in the cheese placement so that an indeterminate amount of your bites will be cheeseless. Also, I put a really small amount of dressing on your sandwich whenever you ask for it. Then when you ask for more, I squirt out a large quantity before you can say stop so that your sandwich has far too much dressing. Then, when I cut the sandwich in half, I only cut it 3/4 of the way through so that you have to messily tear the rest of the sandwich yourself.
>
> Cheers! —Chris

IT'S A CONSPIRACY!

If you know anybody who believes in these wacky theories, please send them our way. (We have a bridge we'd like to sell them.)

CONSPIRACY THEORY: The NFL fixed the 2001–02 season so that the New England Patriots could win the Super Bowl. Reason: The league wanted to use the "Patriots" to cash in on a post-9/11 wave of American nationalism.

THE STORY: The Patriots finished the 2000–01 season with a dismal 5–11 record. The following year, they somehow improved to 11–5 and won their division. With two minutes left in their first playoff game, they trailed the Oakland Raiders 10–13. The Pats had the ball…and quarterback Tom Brady fumbled it. But the referees had instructions to make sure the Patriots won, so they ruled that because Brady tucked the ball into his body and his arm was moving forward, it was an incomplete pass, not a fumble. The Patriots retained possession. A few plays later, Patriots placekicker Adam Vinatieri made a game-tying field goal from 50 yards out…aided by a helium-filled ball that the NFL provided to enhance the ball's flight. The Pats won the game and went all the way to the Super Bowl, which they won with another helium-assisted field goal.

THE TRUTH: Although it is rarely invoked, the "tuck rule" is real. As for the lighter-than-air football, tests show that helium-filled balls don't travel any farther than air-filled balls. The real reason for the Pats' rapid turnaround? Tom Brady improved after his rookie year in 2000. He led the Patriots to two more Super Bowl titles.

CONSPIRACY THEORY: Singer Bob Marley was a voice for political change in Jamaica. But when he opposed a puppet government, he was murdered…by George H.W. Bush's son Neil Bush.

THE STORY: In 1980 the U.S.-backed International Monetary Fund was offering loans to Third World governments. Jamaican president Michael Manley turned it down because he thought it would make him a puppet of American business interests and the CIA. The CIA was furious, so it worked with American-born Jamaican politician Edward Seaga to force Manley out of office. But an outspoken critic of the IMF plan was Jamaica's *other* most influ-

---

"Dord" appeared in the dictionary for 5 years before anyone realized there is no such word.

ential voice: Bob Marley. One night as Marley slept, two of Seaga's goons went to the singer's home in Kingston and shot him. But he didn't die—he went to a mountain retreat to recuperate, where he was interviewed by a reporter from *Rolling Stone*. When Marley's manager called the magazine a few days later, editors told him they hadn't sent a reporter. So who *had* been there? Neil Bush, CIA operative and son of former CIA director George Bush. While Marley was asleep, Bush injected him with a syringe of "something," and a few months later, in May 1981, Marley died at age 36 of cancer.

THE TRUTH: Manley rejected the IMF loan, but he wasn't overthrown—his party simply lost power in 1980. As for Marley, he was diagnosed with cancer far earlier, in 1977, and died four years later. He was never shot and never went to a mountain retreat, so he never had a chance to "get" cancer from Neil Bush.

CONSPIRACY: Matt Damon and Ben Affleck didn't write the Oscar-winning script for their career-launching film *Good Will Hunting*. Oscar-winning screenwriter William Goldman did.

THE STORY: In 1996 two out-of-work actors, Damon and Affleck, wrote a violent, action-packed screenplay about a poor Boston kid who's really a math genius and gets caught up in a spy ring. It was terrible, but Miramax producers realized that a movie written by two handsome and charismatic lead actors, even if they were unknown, was marketing gold. So Miramax hired William Goldman to anonymously write a new script—a quiet, sensitive piece about a poor, troubled math genius who worked as a janitor at Harvard. *Good Will Hunting* made more than $100 million for Miramax and won the Oscar for Best Original Screenplay for Damon and Affleck. (And Goldman was paid millions in hush money.)

THE TRUTH: Damon and Affleck wrote the script with parts for themselves because they couldn't get acting work. The first draft *was* action-oriented, but it also contained most of the math subplot and emotional torment that ended up in the film. The source of the Goldman rumor: Producer Rob Reiner, who had the rights to the script before Miramax, asked Goldman to read the script and offer his opinion. He suggested dropping the spy stuff and concentrating on the human drama. So they did. Goldman himself denies he's the author, saying, "People just don't want to think those two cute guys wrote it."

NEOLOGISMS

The term neologism *comes from the Greek* neo *("new") and* logos *("word"). Here are some recent additions to English, and where they came from.*

DOWNSIZE: The term was adopted by companies in the early 1980s, but it was actually coined during the energy crisis of 1975, when U.S. automakers were forced to curtail the manufacture of giant gas guzzlers and "downsize" their cars.

WIKI: In 1994 programmer Ward Cunningham was developing new Web software that would allow anyone to edit a site's content. While on a Hawaiian vacation, he took a *wiki wiki* shuttle bus. *Wiki wiki* means "quick," so he called the software "WikiWikiWeb." Wiki software now powers scores of wiki websites. "Wiki" entered the dictionary in 2007.

GAYDAR: It's unknown who coined this term for the supposed ability to discern whether a person is homosexual, but it first showed up in print in a 1982 article in the *Village Voice*.

BLING: Rapper Lil Wayne claims he invented this term for "gaudy jewelry," but it predates him. In the early 1990s, comedian Martin Lawrence often made fun of 1970s Ultra Brite toothpaste commercials which promised to "give your smile (ping!) sex appeal!" Lawrence substituted "bling" for "ping." The term went mainstream thanks to a popular 1999 song called "Bling Bling" by New Orleans rapper BG. "Bling" was added to the dictionary in 2003.

BLOGOSPHERE: Coined as a joke in 1999 by blogging pioneer Brad Graham: "Oy! That name! 'Blog'!" he wrote in his blog. "Goodbye, cyberspace. Hello blogiverse! Blogmos? Blogosphere?"

CRINGEWORTHY: This adjective for a person or action that causes extreme embarrassment was invented in 1972 by Leo Baxendale in his popular British comic strip *The Bash Street Kids*. A new student in class, Cuthbert Cringeworthy, was such a know-it-all that none of the other kids wanted to be near him.

DUH: First uttered in a 1943 Bugs Bunny cartoon, "Jack Wabbit and the Beanstalk," when the dimwitted giant announces, "Duh! Well, he can't outsmart me, 'cause I'm a moron!"

ODD MUSICALS

For every great idea that gets turned into a musical (fiddlers on roofs, poor girls transformed into fair ladies, wagons getting painted), there are a bunch of nutty ideas that also get turned into musicals.

MUSICAL: *High Fidelity* (2006)
DETAILS: The 1997 Nick Hornby novel and the 2000 movie version are both about an immature, obscure-record-collecting music store owner who learns what it takes to be a man and have a serious relationship with a woman. Naturally, *High Fidelity* is a cult classic among young men and the obscure-music-obsessed. But these are generally not the kind of people who like show tunes or who are willing to pay $100 to see them performed on Broadway. And ironically, all the characters in *High Fidelity* are obsessive fans of obscure music who abhor mainstream pop music, including show tunes from musicals. The main character even throws a customer out of his store because he wants to buy "I Just Called to Say I Love You." People who do like musicals hated this one, and so did the critics. Result: *High Fidelity* opened on Broadway in December 2006... and closed just ten days later.

MUSICAL: *Taboo* (2003)
DETAILS: In 2002 talk show host and musicals aficionado Rosie O'Donnell saw a show in London called *Taboo*. It was a minor hit there, but O'Donnell loved it, and immediately went to work on staging a production in the U.S. She financed it herself, putting up $10 million to bring it to Broadway, where it opened in late 2003. *Taboo* is set in the gay London club scene of the early '80s and the "New Romantic" pop music fad. One problem: The New Romantic style never really hit it big in the United States, except for Culture Club, the band fronted by Boy George, who co-wrote *Taboo*. Culture Club hadn't had a hit in 20 years, but to attract their aging fans, Boy George was billed as the star of *Taboo*. Another problem: He played only a minor role; the character of "Boy George" was played by someone else. One more problem: Nearly all characters wore bondage-inspired costumes, and

engaged in explicit sex, lurid violence, and overt drug use. *Taboo* barely stayed open for three months. O'Donnell lost every penny of her $10 million investment.

MUSICAL: *The Fields of Ambrosia* (1996)

DETAILS: It's a love story set against the backdrop of post-World War I anti-German hostility. And two characters are executed on stage. And it's a *comedy!* The plot: Gretchen, a German immigrant, is sentenced to death for a murder she probably didn't commit. Jonas, the state executioner, falls in love with her and destroys the electric chair, hoping to delay the execution. No matter—they hang her instead. A few months later, the electric chair gets repaired and Jonas gets fried for trying to save Gretchen. End of play. The London *Daily Mail* called it "the biggest turkey, the floppiest flopperoo, the greatest slice of ham to hit the West End stage in years." (If that wasn't bad enough, a show about capital punishment is a very odd choice for England, a country where they don't have the death penalty. It lasted for just three weeks.)

MUSICAL: *Moby Dick* (1992)

DETAILS: A dense novel that takes place largely in the thoughts of one character, who is far out at sea, chasing after a giant whale? Seems like a hard thing to put on a stage. But if anyone could do it, it was Cameron Mackintosh, the British producer best known for ultra-lavish productions based on classic literature. His two biggest hits: *Les Miserables* and *The Phantom of the Opera*. *Moby Dick*, however, wasn't really based on the Herman Melville novel. It was about a group of wild Catholic school girls who try to save their school from bankruptcy by staging a performance of *Moby Dick* in a swimming pool. The show was not an epic, grand spectacle like Mackintosh's other work. It was really a raunchy, awkwardly funny burlesque show. The mostly-female cast wore swimsuits most of the time, the dialogue was loaded with dirty puns built around the words "Moby Dick," and the Captain Ahab character, written for a woman, was played by a male actor in drag. *Moby Dick* closed after four months on the London stage.

Knights who died during the Crusades were buried with their legs crossed.

"MIND OVER MATTRESS"

Jane Ace is one of the unsung stars of the golden age of radio. From 1930 until 1945 she appeared in Easy Aces, *a comedy about a real estate agent and his wife. Much of the show's humor revolved around the crazy situations Jane got into, and her unparalleled gift for mangling the English language. She may be largely forgotten today, but some of the malaprops she made famous on the show are still in use.*

"Hopefully we'll be more combatable."

"Neatness is next to cleanliness."

"I was sound awake all night."

"You're making a mountain out of Mohammed."

"I must get her out of my cistern."

"I'm a member of the weeper sex."

"We're living in squander."

"I don't drink, I'm a totalitarian."

"You've got the cards before the horse."

"He talks with a Western drool."

"You can't judge a book by its lover."

"I am his awful wedded wife."

"Where've you been? Long face no see!"

"That used car wasn't what it was jacked up to be!"

"Get thee behind me, satin!"

"I couldn't do it of my own violation."

"He went off half-crocked."

"Here's the whole thing in a nut-house."

"I don't like to cast asparagus."

"Stop shouting yourself horse in the face!"

"Be it ever so hovel, there's no place like home!"

"I don't like your altitude!"

"You look ravenous in that sweater."

"I want your candied opinion."

"She got rid of all her exhibitions."

"He told her what makes her thick."

"Time wounds all heels."

"Truth is stranger than friction."

"You're as pale as a goat!"

"Birds of a father flock together."

"Make up a story out of whole wheat."

"The word 'birthday' is tattoo around here!"

Over tall buildings? Superman's birthday is February 29th, Leap Day.

HIS ROTUNDITY

Recently, we've had "Tricky Dick," "Slick Willie," "Shrub," and "Nobama," which are pretty tame compared to some of these other mean nicknames for American presidents.

Little Jemmy: James Madison was the shortest president, just 5'4" (average height of a male American at the time: 5'8"), which explains the "little." "Jemmy" was a nickname commonly given to children and babies named James (like Jimmy). The name implied that Madison was a toddler, and not a man.

General Mum: Gen. William Henry Harrison, hero of the Battle of Tippecanoe, was elected in 1840 and died after only a month in office. He caught a cold while delivering a three-hour inaugural address in freezing temperatures; the cold developed into pneumonia, which killed him. Ironically, his nickname during the election campaign was "General Mum" because, like any savvy politician, he avoided addressing any definitive opinions on controversial issues.

His Accidency: When William Henry Harrison died, Vice President John Tyler ascended to the presidency.

The Negro President: Given to Thomas Jefferson following the election of 1800, which he won thanks to "the three-fifths compromise," which counted slaves as ⅗ of a human being for population purposes. That, in turn, gave greater representation to slaveholding states in determining electoral vote distribution, allowing Jefferson to defeat New Englander John Adams.

The Fainting General: While fighting in the Mexican-American War in 1848, future president Franklin Pierce was on a horse when it was startled by exploding artillery. The horse tossed him forward onto the pommel of his saddle, which was driven into his groin. The injury was so painful that Pierce fainted and remained passed out, lying on the battlefield for the rest of the day.

Queen Victoria in Riding Breeches: Rutherford B. Hayes, and his wife "Lemonade" Lucy Hayes, were ardent teetotalers. It wasn't very macho for a man to abstain from alcohol—or smoking, as

---

Lowest governor's salary: Maine ($70,000). Highest: California ($206,500).

Hayes also did—earning him this emasculating nickname. (The "riding breeches" are because he was a horseback soldier in the Civil War.)

The Walrus: Chester Alan Arthur sported a large handlebar mustache, and he was fairly overweight, both of which made him look like...a walrus.

Uncle Jumbo: It's a fat joke. By the time he was running for reelection in 1892, Grover Cleveland's weight had risen to 250 pounds. Some newspapers called him "Uncle Jumbo." Others favored "The Stuffed Prophet" and "The Elephantine Economist."

His Rotundity: Another fat joke. It's what detractors called the overweight second president, John Adams, who was also accused of being pompous. (When Washington was president, Adams proposed calling him "His Majesty" or "His High Mightiness.")

Ronnie Raygun: President Ronald Reagan proposed the multibillion dollar weapons defense system called the Strategic Defense Initiative, which would use orbiting structures in space to shoot down Soviet-launched nuclear missiles. SDI was perceived as so bizarre and impractical that it was called "Star Wars," earning Reagan this sci-fi nickname.

President Hardly: A play on the name of Warren G. Harding, and his work ethic—he reportedly left most of the day-to-day work of his office to advisers.

Kid Gloves: Benjamin Harrison suffered from various skin problems, particularly infections on his hands, and often wore gloves during the frequent outbreaks. Other nickname: "The Human Iceberg" because, although he was a gifted orator, he tended to be cold and aloof in person.

That Man in the White House: Some of Barack Obama's loudest opponents suggested he wasn't actually born in the U.S.; George W. Bush's opponents labeled him "Commander-in-Thief" after the disputed 2000 election. Similarly, some Republicans referred to Franklin Roosevelt as "that man in the White House" because they were so disgusted with his social-welfare agenda that they couldn't even bring themselves to say his name.

ESPERANTO, PARTO DU

Esperanto—the most successful made-up language in history—is much easier to learn than most "natural" languages. So why don't more people speak it? Here's Part II of the story. (Part I is on page 195.)

TALK SOUP

When L. L. Zamenhof's *Unua Libro* introduced Esperanto to the world in 1887, the time seemed ripe for what the language had to offer. Railroads, steamships, the telegraph, transatlantic cables, and other inventions of the Industrial Revolution were remaking the world and bringing people closer together. A person who might otherwise have lived their entire life without ever leaving their village could now travel the world in ease and comfort, at a price that was within reach of just about everyone.

Standardization was also the order of the day: Many countries around the world had already abandoned their traditional systems of weights and measures in favor of a new international standard, the metric system. They would soon begin setting their clocks according to a single standard, too: Greenwich Mean Time. To many people it seemed like just a matter of time before the world adopted a single international "auxiliary" language that people could speak when traveling or conducting business abroad, to save the trouble of having to master German, Swedish, Arabic, Hindi, Cantonese, and Swahili. Why not Esperanto?

GOING GREEN

Zamenhof saw his language as much more than just a language of convenience for tourists and businessmen. For him it was a means to a very important end: stopping violence between communities by encouraging peace and understanding through a shared language. Without this as a goal, Esperanto had little or no value as far as he was concerned. The most dedicated Esperantists shared his vision, and over time an Esperanto "culture" of sorts began to develop. Esperantists wore green clothes. They pinned green five-pointed stars on their lapels to identify themselves to other speakers they might meet on the street. They went on trips together. They attended Esperanto conferences and theater performances.

They had their own flag, with a single, giant five-pointed green star on a white background against a field of solid green. They had their own hymns and their own Esperanto anthem, "La Epero," which they sang at every gathering. People met each other through Esperanto, fell in love, married, and had kids that they raised as native Esperanto speakers. In time Esperanto culture began to overshadow the language itself, as people learned the language to join the community, and not vice versa.

CULTURE CLASH

But as Esperanto spread beyond the Russian Empire into western Europe and other parts of the world where ethnic unrest was not (yet) as acute as it was in Warsaw and Bialystok, many people who were intrigued by Esperanto's practical potential weren't interested in the movement's culture and values at all. They were repelled by it: All that talk about peace, brotherhood, and universal understanding came to be seen as, well...flaky. Esperantists were like turn-of-the-century hippies.

Add to that the fact that while Zamenhof had a knack for languages, he was an eye doctor, not a professionally trained linguist. There were things about Esperanto that drove language experts crazy. When an organization called the Delegation for the Adoption of an International Language began meeting in Paris in 1901 to choose an auxiliary language, they agreed to consider Esperanto as a candidate...provided that Zamenhof and his followers toned down their goofy green-shirt idealism and fixed the "problems" that the critics had identified in Esperanto.

CANON FODDER

Zamenhof, a man who had literally seen blood running in the streets, would have none of it. He had a lot more in mind for his language than simply making it easier for tourists to say "I'd like to buy a train ticket" and "Where is the bathroom?" He wasn't about to temper his idealism—not one bit.

Furthermore, Zamenhof understood something about artificial languages that his critics apparently didn't, namely that they needed to have a central core of unchanging grammar and vocabulary if they were going to survive over time. In natural languages like English, this is such a given that we hardly think about it.

Billionaire philanthropist George Soros (b. 1930) is a "native" Esperanto speaker.

The word "elephant," for example, is spelled only one way: e–l–e–p–h–a–n–t, and it's pronounced "EH–luh–funt," not "EEL–uh–fint." or "eh–LEE–funt." Questions are indicated by a question marks, not by ampersands or asterisks. And the question mark is placed at the end of the sentence, not at the beginning. These rules are inviolate; not obeying them probably doesn't even occur to English speakers.

TINKER TOY

With artificial languages, however, everything is up for grabs. And once the tinkering starts, it's hard to stop. Soon there are multiple "reformed" versions of the language, each with its own unique grammar, vocabulary, and spelling conventions. Once that happens, how is a prospective language learner supposed to know which version to study? More than one artificial language has been killed this way. Esperanto itself owed much of its popularity to the failure of another constructed language, called Volapük. After its adherents splintered into several warring factions in the 1880s, many Volapük clubs abandoned the language and remade themselves as Esperanto clubs. (For more on Volapük, see page 429.)

MAN CRAZY

Zamenhof's critics had a long list of things they didn't like about Esperanto. They took umbrage, for example, at the fact that Esperanto had no word for "mother," other than the word "father" with the feminine suffix *–in* attached. Most family words in Esperanto are masculine by default and are feminized this way.

They also resented the fact that Zamenhof used the letter *–j* to indicate plural nouns, not the letter *–i*, which would have resembled Latin and not made Esperanto so foreign-looking.

The Esperanto alphabet was another object of scorn: Zamenhof had eliminated the letters Q, W, X, and Y entirely. Even worse, he added special marks called *diacritics* to the letters C, G, H, J, S, and U when he wanted them to represent a second set of sounds. U had a special curved diacritic over it that looked like a small u; the rest had ^ marks. And neither diacritic could be reproduced on a typewriter—one more thing that drove Esperanto's critics crazy.

Part III of the story is on page 373.

Q & A:
ASK THE EXPERTS

*More answers to life's burning questions from
some of the world's top trivia experts.*

NOT 2 SHORT 4 U

Q: *Why are text messages capped at 160 characters?*
A: "In the late 1980s, 45-year-old Friedhelm Hillebrand
sat at his typewriter, tapping out random sentences on a sheet of
paper. He counted the number of letters, numbers, punctuation
marks, and spaces on the page. Each blurb ran on for a line or two
and nearly always clocked in under 160 characters. That became
Hillebrand's magic number—and set the standard for text messaging. He and others had been laying out plans for a standardized
technology that would allow cell phones to transmit and display
text messages, and because of tight bandwidth constraints, messages had to be as short as possible. Two decades later, to avoid the
need for splitting text messages into multiple parts, the creators of
Twitter capped the length of a tweet at 140 characters, keeping
the extra 20 for the user's unique address." (From the *Los Angeles
Times*, "Why Text Messages Are Limited to 160 Characters," by
Mark Milian)

BEE WARM

Q: *Bees can live for years, so how do they survive during winter?*
A: "Unlike other insects, bees do not go into diapause (dormancy)
and become inactive. Instead, they keep themselves warm by producing heat. When the temp drops to about 55°F., all the workers
in a nest form a cluster that surrounds the queen, the brood, and a
store of honey. The workers at the periphery crowd closely together to form a living blanket that is two bees thick. Bees within the
cluster are less densely packed and can move about. Bees move
back and forth between the periphery and the inner cluster. Those
in the inner cluster eat honey and convert its calories to heat by
vigorously vibrating their wing muscles without moving their
wings. Even when the outside temps are below freezing, the bees

---

...attaches to your surfboard and emits an electrical field that supposedly repels sharks.

can keep the cluster at a comfortable 68 to 86°F." (From *The Handy Bug Answer Book*, by Dr. Gilbert Waldbauer)

TIME DOESN'T HEAL ALL WOUNDS

Q: *If skin is always renewing itself, why don't scars completely heal?*

A: "The outer part of your skin, the *epidermis*, renews itself once every 28 days. It's made up of cells that keep pushing up towards the surface, where they die and are rubbed off by your clothing or in the shower. A scar forms when the epidermis and the layer of skin just below it are injured and replaced by scar tissue. This scar tissue is much tougher than normal, and doesn't produce new cells like the surrounding tissue. That means the scar never changes and never gets rubbed off like other used-up skin cells." (From *Owl Magazine's You Asked—Over 300 Great Questions and Astounding Answers*, edited by Katherine Farris)

GUILTY MINUS THE GUILT

Q: *What does pleading "no contest" in a trial mean? Is it the same as pleading guilty?*

A: "When someone is charged with a crime, he can respond in one of three ways: he can plead not guilty, guilty, or *nolo contendere*, which means 'no contest.' A guilty plea is not automatically accepted by the court, however. The judge must be convinced that the person is actually guilty, as opposed to, say, covering for a loved one. A no contest plea in effect says, 'I'm not saying I committed the crime, but I recognize that I may be convicted anyway, so I'll take the punishment.' A person entering a no contest plea may feel that the costs of a trial—financial, emotional, or time-related—are greater than the costs of the plea. Especially if the punishment is relatively minor, like a fine or community service, a defendant may enter a no contest plea rather than chancing conviction, and possibly a harsher penalty, at a trial." (From *Clear Answers for Common Questions*, by Joellen Barak)

*   *   *

TWO STRANGE (BUT REAL) SIGNS

- "Please be aware that the balcony is not on ground level."
  - "If door does not open do not enter"

If you're average, you'll spend 5 1/2 weeks of your life brushing your teeth.

THE FLORIDA WHITE SOX

Sports teams often threaten to move to a new, more interested city, usually as a way to get the city to build them a new stadium. The strategy works, too, as evidenced by these big franchise moves that never quite came to fruition.

O**ld Team:** Chicago White Sox
New City: Seattle
Not So Fast: In 1970 Milwaukee businessman Bud Selig bought baseball's Seattle Pilots after a single season of play and moved them to Milwaukee, where they became the Brewers. Even though the team moved because Seattle's stadium was falling apart, Chicago White Sox owner John Allyn considered moving his team there because Chicago's stadium, Comiskey Park, was even older (built in 1910) and in worse repair. Ultimately, he decided to sell the Sox to businessman Bill Veeck, because selling a team is a lot easier than moving one. Veeck kept the team in the Windy City.

Old Team: Chicago White Sox
New City: St. Petersburg, Florida
Not So Fast: In 1988 the White Sox once again tired of the crumbling Comiskey, and then-owner Jerry Reinsdorf told the city of Chicago that if the Sox didn't get a brand-new stadium, he'd move the team to St. Petersburg, Florida, which wanted a big league team so badly that it had already built a 50,000-seat tax-payer-funded stadium. Chicago residents, horrified at the prospect of losing one of the oldest teams in American sports, wrote thou-sands of letters to Illinois lawmakers (and sent pairs of dirty white socks in protest to St. Petersburg mayor Robert Ulrich). Result: Lawmakers approved $167 million to build a new stadium next door to Comiskey Park.

Old Team: St. Louis Cardinals (NFL)
New City: Baltimore
Not So Fast: In 1960 the NFL's Chicago Cardinals moved to St. Louis, where they played for 37 middling seasons (three playoff

appearances, no championships). In 1987 owner William Bidwill thought a fresh start was in order, and announced plans to relocate the team. The city of Baltimore, having lost the Colts a few years earlier, began aggressively courting the Cardinals. They presented plans for new training facilities and allocated millions of dollars for a domed stadium. Bidwill met with business and community leaders in other major American cities, but Baltimore was clearly the frontrunner. That's why it sent shockwaves through the league when Bidwill announced that the Cardinals would be moving to...Phoenix. (They offered a bigger stadium.)

Old Team: Cleveland Indians
New City: New Orleans
Not So Fast: Vernon Stouffer (of the Stouffer's frozen-food family) bought baseball's Indians in 1966 at a period of low on-field success, as well as low attendance and low revenues. Stouffer bought the team as an investment, so he immediately began scouting out places to move the Indians where they could make money. In 1971 New Orleans extended an offer for the team to play 30 games there, essentially a test run to see if moving the team there permanently the following season would be a good idea. But as with the White Sox, it's a lot simpler just to sell a team. Before the New Orleans deal could be finalized, Stouffer sold the team to Cleveland Cavaliers owner Nick Mileti, who kept the team in Ohio.

Old Team: St. Louis Blues
New City: Saskatoon
Not So Fast: Pet food/cereal manufacturer Ralston-Purina acquired the NHL's St. Louis Blues in 1977, but by 1983, had lost millions on the team...and were still bleeding money. Solution: RP planned to simply wait it out— the team would fold and the company could write it off as a loss. That's when an investment group led by businessman Bill Hunter, a one-time owner of the Edmonton Oilers, offered to buy the Blues, under the condition that he could move them to Saskatoon, Saskatchewan, whose population of less than 200,000 would have made it the NHL's smallest market...which is exactly why the league blocked the move and made plans to fold the team for good. At the last minute, Los Angeles businessman Harry Ornest bought the team, and kept it in St. Louis.

HOW TO CRACK A SAFE, PT. II

Can't remember where you hid the paper that you wrote the combination to your safe on? Here's Part II of the story. (Part I is on page 209.)

IF AT FIRST YOU DON'T SUCCEED...

There really is a way to open a safe using an ordinary stethoscope, but it's much more tedious and complicated than it's usually depicted in the movies. And because modern safes are much quieter than older models were, stethoscopes have given way to electronic listening devices that are much more sensitive.

So what are safecrackers listening for when they put their headphones on? If you thought they were trying to hear the tumblers tumbling, think again:

• There's a piece of hardware in the wheel pack called a drive cam. It, like the wheels in the wheel pack, has a notch in it.

• By turning the dial on the safe, the safe cracker can find the location of this notch by listening for two clicks. The first click indicates where the notch begins, and the second indicates where it ends. Let's say the dial is numbered from 0 to 99: The two clicks might be heard at number 15 and 25 on the dial.

• It turns out that when the dial is turned a certain way, the spacing between the two clicks will shrink ever so slightly, say from 15 and 25 on the dial to 18 and 22. But—and this is important—the space between the clicks shrinks only when you begin the procedure from certain numbers on the dial. The trick is finding out *which* numbers, because each one is a number in the combination.

• The only way to find all the numbers in the combination is by repeating the procedure over and over again, using every third number on the dial as a starting point. If the dial is numbered from 0 to 99, for example, you start the procedure at 0, then 3, 6, and so on, until you reach 99 on the dial (that's 33 times in all).

• This trick doesn't reveal the *order* of the numbers in the combination, but in a three-number combination there are only six possibilities. Once the numbers are revealed, opening the safe is easy.

So you'd rather just bust open the safe? Turn to page 485.

World's longest-running reality TV show: *Cops.* (It debuted in 1989.)

ODD-PHRODISIACS

Don't have any Barry White CDs to get your partner in the mood?

• Bat meat is a folk aphrodisiac in parts of Indonesia and Malaysia. Bats are a fairly common food item there, so they're inexpensive in markets. Bats are served up like a Western romantic dinner—whole, like a lobster.

• In Nepal, some people believe that drinking rhinoceros urine increases sexual desire and male virility. It may be difficult to collect rhino pee, but it's so commonly regarded as an aphrodisiac that you can actually buy it in the gift shop of the Kathmandu Zoo—collected and bottled fresh daily by the staff.

• You may have heard that soup made from the male organ of a tiger is considered an aphrodisiac in some cultures, and that *sort of* makes sense. A little more confusing: unhatched sea turtle eggs. It's unclear why, but they're consumed raw in Mexico. Their popularity (they're frequently stolen from American coastal areas) is thought to be one reason many sea turtle species are endangered.

• The *Atta laevigata*, a species of ant nicknamed "the big-bottomed" ant due to its wide mid- and end sections, is eaten as an aphrodisiac in Colombia. But only if it's a queen, and if its appendages are removed, and if it's roasted. It's believed to be so effective that it's a traditional wedding gift to Colombian newlyweds.

• *Extracto de rana* has been sold for over a century in the outdoor markets of Lima, Peru. What is it? Frog juice, believed not only to increase sex drive, but also to relieve asthma and fatigue. Here's how it works: A customer picks a live frog from a tank (like a lobster); the proprietor then kills, skins, and blends it with a mixture of white beans, honey, aloe vera, and *maca*, a plant-based stimulant (which is probably the real source of the increased virility).

• Not all aphrodisiacs are edible. One ancient Arabian formula calls for a man to catch and kill a vulture, chop up the meat, and mix it with honey and amalaka juice (an Asian berry). Rubbing the entire body with the meaty paste is said to enchant women.

One version of the video game *Grand Theft Auto* includes a hidden X-rated scene.

EAT THE WORLD, PART II

*With international foods like these, it's no wonder that
America's considered a culinary "melting pot." But what
are these tasty dishes, and how did they get here?*

GENERAL TSO'S CHICKEN: The sweet-and-spicy
deep-fried chicken dish is credited to Peng Chang-kuei, a
chef from Hunan, China, who named it after a Qing
Dynasty military hero from Hunan. Peng first made it in Taiwan
in the 1950s. He opened a restaurant in New York City in the
early 1970s, and the dish has been a Chinese restaurant staple
ever since.

FRANGIPANE: This almond-based pastry filling was imported
to America from Belgium in the 1800s. The name is traced to
16th-century Italian nobleman Mutio Frangipani, who created a
perfume which included oils from the flowers of the plumeria tree,
now commonly known as the frangipani tree. The almond pastry
was said to have a similar scent, so it got the name too.

JERK CHICKEN: Also called "Jamaican" jerk chicken, this spicy
dish combines the influences of the island's native, Spanish, and
African populations. The cooking process known as "jerking"
involves marinating meat or fish in a mix of spices—the key being
pimento berry (Americans call it "allspice") and habanero chili—
and then slowly cooking/smoking it. "Jerk" comes from the word
charqui, Spanish for dried meat, from which "jerky" is also derived.

YAKITORI: Most commonly yakitori is skewered and barbecued
chicken (the word means "grilled bird" in Japanese), but other
meats and fish are often substituted. They're flavored with either
salt or a mix of soy sauce, sugar, and *mirin*—sweet rice wine. Yakitori has been a luxury item since the 1600s, became extremely
popular after World War II, and it made its way from Japan to the
U.S. in the 1960s.

HIBACHI: The word has been part of the English language since
the 1860s, but the mini-barbecues didn't become popular until the

iHave (money): The iDiamond Ear is a $6,400 set of diamond-studded earphones.

1970s. A Japanese *hibachi*, meaning "fire bowl," is a round container, often made from clay, in which charcoal was burned—but they were used to heat rooms, not cook food. The Japanese grill that most Americans would recognize as a hibachi is called a *shichirin*. It's been suggested that shichirin was too hard for English speakers to say...so they were called "hibachis" instead.

OXTAIL SOUP: A type of "soul food" still popular in parts of the American South, this is a stewlike soup based around beef tails. Similar stews have been eaten around the world for many centuries; the American variety most likely has its roots in an English dish of the same name.

UDON NOODLES: You're probably familiar with the thick, chewy wheat noodles commonly served in Japanese restaurants. They're actually Chinese in origin, and, according to legend, were brought to Japan by a Buddhist monk in the 8th century. They were introduced to Americans when the country's first Japanese restaurants opened in San Francisco in the 1880s.

❇   ❇   ❇

REVIEWS OF THE BEATLES ON
THE ED SULLIVAN SHOW, FEBRUARY 1964

"They wear sheep-dog bangs. The sound of their music is one of the most persistent noises heard over England since the air-raid sirens were dismantled. It's high-pitched, loud beyond reason, and stupefyingly repetitive."

—*Newsweek*

"The Beatles are 75 percent publicity, 20 percent haircut, and five percent lilting lament."

—*New York Herald Tribune*

"Their musical talent is minimal. Their weird hairstyle is merely a combination of the beehive and the 'little moron' hair-do."

—*Washington Star*

"Imported hillbillies who look like sheepdogs and sound like alley cats in agony."

—*Washington Post*

Fat fact: The average American gains one pound during the holiday season.

GUILT BY ASSOCIATION

More words that only seem naughty…but are actually quite nice.

Titration: The practice of gradually adjusting the dose of a medication until the desired affect is achieved.

Organ meat: The internal organs (eyes, lungs, brain, etc.) of a butchered animal. Depending on the animal, the organ, and the culture, it's either considered a delicacy or tossed out in the trash.

Barfi: An Indian dessert made from condensed milk cooked in sugar, and often flavored with fruit. It's also known as "Indian cheesecake."

Pista Barfi: Barfi flavored with pistachio nuts.

Drip Dickey: A brand of "wine collar" that fits over the neck of an opened bottle to prevent the wine from dribbling down its side.

Cockaleekie: A soup from Scotland. The two main ingredients: 1) a game bird, or *cock*, and 2) an onion-like vegetable called a *leek*.

Homogamy: A marriage between people who are culturally similar to one another.

Shittah: A species of acacia tree that features prominently in the Old Testament: The Ark of the Covenant is said to be made of *shittim*, or wood harvested from a shittah tree.

Decocker: The part of a firearm that allows you to uncock the weapon safely, without risk of it going off.

Great Tit: The largest member of the tit family of songbirds, native to Asia and Europe.

Assiette: French for "dinner plate." It can also mean a selection of cold cuts served on a just such a plate.

Horny-handed: Someone whose hands are calloused from physical labor is said to be "horny-handed."

Spanker: The rear-most sail on a square-rigged sailing ship. (Modern racing sailboats have a spanker called a "blooper.")

Laywoman: A woman who is training to become a Catholic nun, but who has not yet completed the process.

Crapulent: Sick from eating or drinking to excess.

Gun control: In 1882 a Texas cattle association banned cowboys from having six-shooters.

THE PORTMANTEAU MOVIE QUIZ

A portmanteau is a word that results from two other words being combined. (Example: WALL-E + E.T. = WALL-E.T.) So, here's a wordplay game we came up with: We took two movies and made portmanteaus of their titles. Can you guess the movies, and their combined titles, based on these combined plots? Answers are on page 536.

1. A ragtag group of Midwestern teenagers (Jennifer Gray, C. Thomas Howell) band together, get their dads' guns, and fight off a surprise aerial attack from Russian Communist zombies who want to eat their delicious teenage braaaaaains.

2. A corporate axeman (George Clooney) spends most of his time flying around the country from one office to another, terminating redundant employees. Disenchanted, he thinks he might want to settle into a life of more permanence, when he falls in love with a golden retriever that plays basketball.

3. Stuck in both a dead-end telemarketing job and a loveless marriage with a career-driven wife (Annette Bening), a suburban man (Kevin Spacey) has a midlife crisis and falls in love with a fur-covered, animated monster (voice of Robby Benson) who lives in a castle full of talking candlesticks and teapots, and just may be a kind-hearted prince under that gruff exterior.

4. Billionaire industrialist Tony Stark (Robert Downey, Jr.) builds a metal suit that gives him superhuman powers, and uses it to create a new identity for himself: Don Quixote, an elderly knight who wanders the medieval Spanish countryside in search of adventure (while singing "The Impossible Dream").

5. A little girl (Abigail Breslin) and her eccentric family pile into an old Volkswagen microbus to attend a beauty pageant three states away. The surprising "talent" she shows off in the contest: the ability to quickly and efficiently clean up a room after deaths and homicides.

Barbie's first car: A pink 1962 Austin-Healey.

6. A young assassin (Uma Thurman) is left for dead on the eve of her wedding, and after emerging from a coma, she begins a mission of revenge against those who tried to kill her, and claim the daughter she's never met. First up: two dumb, metal-head teenagers (Alex Winter, Keanu Reeves). Can she catch them as they travel through time trying to find historical figures who will help them write the term paper they need to graduate?

7. Grotesque alien beings crash land in South Africa and are detained in a walled, prison-like ghetto of Johannesburg until one night when a few violently break out to enjoy a sexually charged series of romantic encounters with Mickey Rourke.

8. A suburban mother (Jamie Lee Curtis) and her daughter (Lindsay Lohan) magically trade bodies and experience life through the other's eyes, before they put on hockey masks and team up to murder amorous teenagers at a summer camp.

9. A 1960s rock and roll band called the Wonders rises to fame on a single hit, but break up when they are forced to play a concert in the Bedford-Stuyvesant area of Brooklyn on the hottest day of the year, getting caught in racially-fueled riots and arsons.

10. A man (Ben Stiller) tries to win the heart of his true love (Cameron Diaz), competing with a sleazy private investigator and an NFL quarterback. He's assisted by a British nanny (Julie Andrews) who is practically perfect in every way.

11. An army of Spartan soldiers marches into battle to defeat their sworn enemy: a horde of adorable black-and-white spotted puppies.

BONUS THREE-MOVIE QUESTION: The head of a New York organized crime family (Marlon Brando) must contend with a son who does not wish to enter the family business, all the while having to deal with the many mishaps in the lead-up to the wedding of his daughter (Elizabeth Taylor) to a monster (Boris Karloff) that was made by a German scientist out of reanimated corpse pieces.

SHORT STORY: THE MINI

For more than 40 years the Mini was one of the most recognizable cars on Earth.
But because it wasn't sold in the U.S. after 1969, few Americans were familiar
with it. That changed in 2001, when BMW introduced a modern version to
the U.S. market. Here's the story of the little car that started it all.

OUT OF GAS

In July 1956, Egyptian President Gamal Abdel Nasser nationalized the Suez Canal. Though the canal is on Egyptian soil, in 1956 it was controlled by Britain and France. Four months later, Britain, France, and Israel tried to regain control of the canal by invading Egypt. But the invasion was opposed by both the United States and the U.S.S.R., and it failed. Even worse for Britain and France, Saudi Arabia cut off oil supplies to the two countries to punish them for the invasion. The resulting shortages sent the price of gasoline soaring in the United Kingdom, forcing the British government to ration supplies. Many drivers were limited to just 12 gallons, about a single tankful, *per month.*

THINKING SMALL

That sent the British auto industry into a slump, and consumers switched to tiny gas-sipping vehicles, many of them imported, which were derisively called "bubble cars." The Messerschmitt Kabinenroller ("Cabin Scooter"), for example, was just that: A three-wheel enclosed scooter with a one-cylinder, two-stroke engine like a lawn mower's. The BMW Isetta, described by one critic as resembling an "egg on roller skates," was built like a refrigerator: The entire front end served as the car's only door—you opened it just like a refrigerator, and climbed in.

Bubble cars drove purists crazy. Leonard Lord, head of the British Motor Corporation—the parent company of Austin, Morris, MG, and other makes—was outraged that motorists should be forced to drive such cheap, uncomfortable vehicles. He told his engineers to drive those "bloody awful bubble cars" off the road by building "a proper miniature car" that motorists would be proud to drive.

Lord wanted the car, soon to be called the Mini, to be no more than 10 feet long, 4 feet wide, and 4 feet in height—the minimum amount of space he judged would be necessary to hold four passengers plus a small amount of luggage. He wanted it to have a "proper" four-stroke, four-cylinder engine, and the "proper" number of wheels—four. Adding to the challenge, he wanted it built entirely out of existing mechanical parts, since there was no money available to design new ones.

LITTLE BIG MAN

The man that Lord put in charge of the Mini, Alec Issigonis, may have been the only British auto executive who would even have had a chance at pulling off such a feat. The son of Greek refugees from Turkey, in the late 1940s Issigonis led the design team that created the hugely successful Morris Minor, a car already well on its way to becoming the first British car to sell a million units.

The Minor was a fairly small car by the standards of the day, but it was surprisingly roomy inside, which was one of Issigonis's trademarks as a designer—he had a knack for squeezing the maximum amount of interior space out of any car he worked on.

Safety was another important part of his design philosophy: "I make my cars with such good brakes, such good steering, that if people get in a crash it's their own fault," he liked to say. Considering how tiny the Mini was expected to be, roominess and safety were going to be very high priorities indeed.

SIDEWAYS

Working out of a special studio set apart from the rest of the company, Issigonis, an automotive engineer named Jack Daniels, and seven other staffers set to work. Issigonis and Daniels had worked together on the Minor, and as they developed the design for the new car, they drew heavily from a prototype they'd built a few years earlier. That car had front-wheel drive and a "transverse" engine—the engine block was rotated 90° to give it a left-to-right orientation, instead of the standard front-to-back of the time.

Front-wheel drive improved the car's performance, and it also eliminated the need to run a driveshaft the length of the car from the engine (in front) to the rear wheels, which saved space, weight, and cost. The transverse engine also saved a lot of room—because the engine was installed sideways, it could be squeezed into just a few feet of space under the hood.

...to speed up the car in front of them.

Back when Issigonis and Daniels first proposed their sideways-engined, front-wheel drive Minor, their superiors rejected such an unconventional and seemingly risky design. But now that reducing space, weight, and cost were so important in making the new car a success, suddenly the design didn't seem so risky after all.

PUTTING IT TOGETHER

The Mini team managed to squeeze the transverse engine and a 4-speed manual transmission into just 18 *inches* of space, which left 8½ feet for the passenger compartment, if Lord's goal of keeping the car under 10 feet in length was to be met. (The Volkswagen Beetle, by comparison, was just under 13½ feet long.)

Because interior space was at such a premium in so tiny a car, Issigonis gave it a very boxy shape to provide the driver and passengers with as much room as possible. To limit the wheel wells' intrusion into that space, he pushed the wheels out to the four corners of the car. And to keep those wells as small as possible, he used the tiniest wheels ever used in a production automobile: just 10 inches in diameter, smaller than a dinner plate. In such tight confines there was no room for a standard spring suspension, either, so small rubber cones called "doughnuts" were used instead, which gave the car a very stiff ride.

The car windows did not roll up and down—you slid them open and closed by hand, which saved on the weight and expense of window hardware. No radio was installed, and neither were seat belts (few cars of the era had them). But Issigonis, a chain-smoker, made sure the car had an ashtray.

SMALL WONDER

Issigonis wanted the Mini to have a 948cc engine that would have given the car quick acceleration and a top speed of more than 90 mph. But he worried that it might be too powerful for ordinary drivers to handle, so he had a couple of engineers take the car for a test drive. They flipped the car. Issigonis replaced the engine with an 848cc engine. New top speed: 72 mph. That might not sound like much, but the Mini was faster than just about any other small car of the day, including the VW Beetle, which had a top speed of 68 mph. That, combined with the stiff suspension and the placement of the wheels at the four corners of the car, gave it go-kart-like handling that was absolutely thrilling. BMC head Leonard Lord realized it the first time he took the prototype out for a test drive in July 1958: He was gone only five minutes before he roared back to the plant at top speed, braked sharply, and jumped out of the car. "Build it!" he ordered. The first production Minis rolled off the assembly line in early 1959.

LITTLE INTEREST

As fun as the Minis were to drive, it took them a while to catch on. They were, after all, *tiny*. Compared to ordinary British cars, they looked pretty silly. They were also noisy, spartan, and underpowered by big-car standards. Even the car's low price—£500, or about $1,400—may have put buyers off. How good could a car that small and that cheap really be?

But as more people experienced the thrill of driving one, word of mouth began to spread and demand surged. BMC sold 116,000 Minis in 1960, not bad for the car's first full model year, and sales climbed quickly from there, passing 157,000 in 1961. The introduction of the Mini Cooper, a suped-up racing Mini designed by Formula One racing legend John Cooper in July 1961, followed by the even sportier Mini Cooper S in 1963, generated even greater interest, pushing sales past the 240,000 mark for 1964. (John Cooper was paid £2—around $5.40—for every Mini Cooper sold, just for the use of his name.) Sales remained strong through the rest of the decade, finally peaking in 1971, when more than 318,000 Minis were sold.

NO CLASS

Within just a year or two of its introduction, the Mini became *the* car to be seen in for British film stars, the London "in crowd," and celebrities around the world. Peter Sellers bought one, so did Mick Jagger, Paul Newman, Steve McQueen, Bridget Bardot, all four of the Beatles, and at least one of the Monkees. King Hussein of Jordan owned one, so did Princess Grace of Monaco. Prince Charles learned to drive in his, and he wasn't alone—in the years to come more British subjects would learn to drive in a Mini than in any other car. In this most class-conscious of societies, here was Britain's first (and probably last) truly *classless* car—everybody wanted to own one, and almost anybody could afford to buy one.

All domestic chickens are descended from *Gallus gallus*, the Red Junglefowl.

No British car before or since has had the Mini's widespread appeal. Few cars have enjoyed the long life that it had: There were plenty of improvements over the years to be sure (roll-up windows were standard after 1969, heaters after 1974), but the same basic car stayed on the market from 1959 until the year 2000. In that time it sold more than 5.3 million cars—that's an average of nearly 2,500 cars a week, *every* week, for 41 years.

THINKING BIG

The Mini was by far the most successful British car in history; no other model has ever come close to selling 5.3 million units. But the success of the tiny car also contributed to the decline of the British auto industry, as Issigonis tried to repeat the Mini's formula in much larger cars and failed.

When customers pay $1,400 for a car, they're willing to settle for one that offers only the bare essentials, but when they pay full price, they want a little luxury. Issigonis understood this, but because he thought he understood car buyers better than they understood themselves, he would not budge. "I know there are such people, but I will not design cars for them," he said.

FOLLOW THE MONEY

Later cars designed by Issigonis, including the full-sized Austin Maxi, were sales disappointments that helped force the flailing British Motor Corporation into a shotgun merger with other troubled British automakers in 1968. The resulting conglomerate, British Leyland, lost so much money that the British government nationalized it in 1975, keeping it from going under.

The remnants of British Leyland were renamed the Rover Group in 1986. BMW bought Rover in 1994 and spent millions trying to make it profitable. But BMW finally gave up in 2000 and sold the company off in pieces—every piece, that is, except for the Mini division. BMW has since built Mini into a thriving company, one that owes much of its success to nostalgia for Issigonis's original tiny car of dreams. In April 2007, 11 years after they bought the company, BMW sold its one millionth Mini—about the same amount of time it took the British Motor Corporation to sell its millionth Mini. If sales remain strong, the new Mini should outsell the old Mini sometime in the late 2030s.

Dutch winemaker Ilja Gort insured his nose for $8 million.

GROSS COCKTAILS

Culled from bartenders and bar guides from around the world, most of these drinks had to have been created—and consumed—on a dare.

Buffalo Sweat
3 parts bourbon
1 part Tabasco

Liquid Steak
1.5 oz rum
Drizzle of Worcestershire
    sauce
(The end result supposedly
tastes like grilled meat.)

Smoker's Cough
1.5 oz Jägermeister
A dollop of mayonnaise

Relishious
1.5 oz Jägermeister
A spoonful of pickle relish

Prairie Oyster
1.5 oz bourbon
Dash of Tabasco
1 raw egg

Hot Sauce
1.5 oz pepper-flavored
    vodka
1 oz olive juice
1 oz tomato juice
3 oz Guinness
Dash of Worcestershire sauce
Dash of Tabasco
(Garnish with blue-cheese-
stuffed olives.)

Green Monster
4 oz Red Bull energy drink
12 oz Mountain Drew
6 oz cognac

Eggermeister
1.5 oz Jägermeister (or
licorice-flavored liqueur)
1 pickled egg
(Drink the booze while
chewing the egg.)

Beergasm
1 part beer
1 part whole milk

Black Death
1 part vodka
1 part soy sauce

Ranchero
2 parts tequila
1 part Tabasco
1 part ranch dressing

Cement Mixer
1.5 oz Irish cream
A lime wedge
(The drinker sucks the wedge
and holds the juice in their
mouth while consuming the
Irish cream. The acidity of the
lime juice makes the creamy
liqueur instantly curdle.)

Active ingredient in Planet brand anti-aging face cream: snake venom.

PRANKELANGELO

*Michelangelo's paintings and sculptures are beautiful,
timeless...and full of secret messages.*

The massive mural on the ceiling of the Sistine Chapel in
Rome contains hundreds of images. The work was commissioned by Pope Julius II, who Michelangelo reportedly
thought was corrupt due to his aggressive schemes to obtain new
lands for the church. So he painted Julius II ("The Fearsome
Pope") into the mural: The depiction of the prophet Zechariah
has Julius' face. But behind Zechariah is an angel holding his thumb
between his index and middle finger—a gesture known as "the
fig." It meant to Renaissance-era Italians what the middle finger
does to present-day Americans—the angel is flipping off the pope.

• Another part of the Sistine mural is "The Creation of Adam,"
in which God and Adam touch fingers, representing the creation
of human life. Upon closer inspection, writes Dr. Frank Meshberg-
er in the *Journal of the American Medical Association*, the "heaven"
in which God and angels float is shaped like a human brain. The
different parts of the organ are distinct, including the cerebellum,
optic nerve, and pituitary gland. God's green sash, for example, is
the vertebral artery. What does it mean? Michelangelo believed in
a philosophy called *Neoplatonism*, which attests that intellect is a
divine gift, so the painting may be his expression of that idea. Or,
as he believed the Church was corrupt, it might have been a suggestion that God was the creation of a human brain (i.e., not real).

• Michelangelo's *David* is one of the world's best-known statues,
and represents the artist's ideal human form—even though critics
have long wondered why the "ideal human form" would have such
disproportionately small "private parts." *David* is 13 feet high and
placed on a pedestal so admirers have to look up at it. But according to Pietro Bernabei, writing in the Italian journal *Il Giornale
dell'Arte*, viewing David's face head-on, his blank expression
changes to one of fear and worry. This makes sense—the statue
depicts David just before his fight with the giant Goliath. And in
a bit of dark humor, it explains the figure's "shrinkage": Male geni-
tals typically recede when the body is under stress.

Most dangerous food to consume while driving, according to one study: coffee.

PUN-LINERS

*They say puns are the lowest form of humor. Just who are "they,"
and why are "they" trying to rain on our pun parade?*

"Putting your hands in the earth is very grounding."
—**John Glover**

"Two Dallas women opened up a marina. They ran the best little oarhouse in Texas."
—**Richard Lederer**

"Sometimes I pray to Cod for the veal-power to stop playing with my food words, but I fear it's too bread into me."
—**Mark Morton**

"I made a killing on Wall Street a few years ago. I shot my broker."
—**Groucho Marx**

"Dunkin Donuts…Just move the 'D' to the end and you get 'Unkind Donuts,' which I've had a few of in my day."
—**Merl Reagle**

"The advantages of simple origami are twofold."
—**Tim Vine**

"What did the carrot say to the wheat? Lettuce rest, I'm feeling beet."
—**Shel Silverstein**

"My wife's a water sign. I'm an earth sign. Together we make mud."
—**Rodney Dangerfield**

"This concerto was written in four flats because Rachmaninoff had to move four times while he wrote it."
—**Victor Borge**

"Double negatives are a no-no."
—**Zac Hill**

"The safest place in an earthquake is a stationary store."
—**George Carlin**

"Why is a martini without an olive or lemon twist called a Charles Dickens? No olive or twist."
—**Martin Gardner**

"I've always wanted to make an impact on the world. I've also always wanted to go sky diving. I just hope I don't to both at the same time."
—**David Brandenburg**

"It was so quiet, you could hear a pun drop."
—**Bugs Baer**

Uncle John is a *paronomasiac*—one who is addicted to puns and wordplay.

THE #2 AMENDMENT

*More examples of what can happen when a
pistol-packin' person makes a pit stop.*

GUN OWNER: Deputy Robert Greek of the Plymouth County Sheriff's Department in Massachusetts
ARMED & DANGEROUS: In November 2005, nature called while Deputy Greek was at a Dunkin' Donuts. He popped into the restroom and set down his service weapon while he attended to the matter at hand. Then, when it was time to leave, he forgot to take his gun with him. Nearly an hour passed before he realized his gun was missing. He immediately returned to Dunkin' Donuts to get it, but by then, it was long gone.
WHAT HAPPENED: Luckily for Deputy Greek, the gun was found by a responsible citizen, who dropped it into a Post Office letter box and then notified the police where they could find it. Deputy Greek's carelessness cost him his firearm license, and that in turn cost him his job. "Because he was unable to be certified to carry a firearm, we were unable to retain him as a deputy," a Sheriff's Department spokesperson told reporters. (Greek did notify the department as soon as he realized his firearm was missing: "He deserves some credit for that," said the spokesperson.)

GUN OWNER: An unidentified 52-year-old woman living in Hoover, Alabama
ARMED & DANGEROUS: On election day in June 2000. the woman went to her polling station to vote. Unfortunately for her, the polling station was located in the chambers of the Hoover City Council, and no handguns are allowed in there. (The woman was packing a loaded .45-caliber Beretta semiautomatic.) Apparently she didn't realize that guns weren't permitted until she saw the warning sign next to the metal detectors. Instead of leaving the premises, the woman simply hid the Beretta in the ladies' room while she went in and voted. She couldn't have hidden it very well, because by the time she got back, a city employee had already found the gun and turned it over to the police.

WHAT HAPPENED: When the woman asked if anyone had seen her gun, the police arrested her...at which point the woman began complaining of chest pains. Rather than file charges, the police called paramedics. (She received a clean bill of health and was released from the hospital two hours later; the police did not attempt to file charges again.)

GUN OWNER: Steve Schmulbach of Belleville, Missouri

ARMED & DANGEROUS: In July 1990, Schmulbach, his wife, and another couple were visiting Union Station in St. Louis when Schmulbach had to use the restroom. Not long after he got down to "business," he was confronted by two robbers who poked their heads over the bathroom stall and pointed a gun at him.

WHAT HAPPENED: What are the odds that the robbers would have picked a bathroom stall occupied by an off-duty police officer? An *armed* off-duty police officer? Schmulbach, a 12-year veteran of the Belleville, Missouri, police department, grabbed for his .38-caliber service revolver and fired off a shot, missing both men but so startling them that the one with the gun dropped it (it didn't go off) as he fled the restroom. At last report, a 19-year-old suspect was in custody and police were still looking for his 21-year-old accomplice.

GUN OWNER: Sergeant Nicole Girardi of the Boca Raton, Florida, police department

ARMED & DANGEROUS: In March 2006, the Secret Service asked the Boca PD to assist in securing a local country club in advance of a GOP fundraiser headlined by Vice President Dick Cheney. Sgt. Girardi was assigned to the detail. When she took a bathroom break at the country club, she put her gun down in the restroom and forgot to take it with her when she finished. Police officers conducting a security sweep found the gun a short time later.

WHAT HAPPENED: Luckily for Girardi, the gun was found before Vice President Cheney arrived. That kept the incident a local police matter rather than a federal case. Girardi received an official reprimand, but no other disciplinary measures were taken. (Although she has been warned that if she misplaces her gun again, she could lose her job.)

The words "stereotype" and "cliche" both originated as French book-printing terms.

HOW _____
GOT TO JAPAN

See if you can guess the blank before the end of the article.

Clue #1: In 1897 the German government was able to coerce the Chinese government into giving them a 99-year lease to the city of Tsingtao, on Kiautschou Bay in East China. The bay and surrounding region soon became a German colony, and a large naval fort was built in its harbor.

• **Clue #2:** In July 1914, World War I officially began. In August the British—and their allies, the Japanese—attacked Tsingtao, and by November they had taken it from the Germans. The Japanese captured about 4,000 German prisoners in Tsingtao and transported them to POW camps in Japan.

• **Clue #3:** In 1915 several hundred of those prisoners were transferred to the newly built Narashino camp, east of Tokyo. Among those prisoners was one Karl Jahn, an expert in a field that had been mastered by Germans centuries earlier.

• **Clue #4:** In 1918 Jahn and a handful of other POWs taught the secrets of their skill to Yoshifusa Iida, a Japanese government official. Yoshifusa, who happened to be in the midst of experiments with the processing of a certain kind of food, was impressed.

• **Clue #5:** Yoshifusa subsequently taught the process to manufacturers all across Japan, marking the beginning of a new industry in the country.

• **Clue #6:** As the years passed, the story of how the Japanese learned to produce this product was almost completely forgotten. Then, in 2008, a collection of photos of Narashino camp was discovered—including images of Yoshifusa Iida, Karl Jahn, and the other prisoners making it.

Have you guessed the mystery German product?
Turn to page 534 for the answer.

Los Angeles has 24-hour vending machines for marijuana.

READY...SET...HURL!

We've done hundreds of "weird world" articles over the past two decades. This, we believe, is the first one that's focused on vomiting. (Warning: not for the squeamish.)

Ready: Police in Winona, Minnesota, were called to the scene of an automobile accident in April 2010. **Set:** They found a car that had been driven into a utility pole. Witnesses said they saw a young man walking a dog leave the scene. Four hours later, 18-year-old Michael Allen Butler called police and confessed.

HURL! Butler told police he had crashed into the pole...because his dog had puked on him. Deputy Police Chief Tom Williams was skeptical at first, but after investigating the scene said he believed the young man...because they found dog puke all over the inside of the car. Butler was ticketed for driving without a license.

Ready: Matthew Clemmens, 21, of Cherry Hill, New Jersey, and a friend were at a Philadelphia Phillies-Washington Nationals baseball game in 2010. They were both drinking. They started yelling obscenities and acting like jerks.

Set: Clemmens and his friend were sitting behind off-duty Police Captain Michael Vangelo. When the two wouldn't stop swearing, Vangelo asked an usher to call the cops. Result: Clemmens and his friend were expelled.

HURL! As they were being escorted out of the stadium, Clemmens leaned over the railing between the seat rows, stuck his finger down his throat, and purposely puked on Vangelo...and his 11-year-old daughter. He also managed to puke on a security officer. Bad idea: Clemmens was arrested on charges of aggravated assault, harassment, resisting arrest, and other offenses. "It was the most vile, disgusting thing I've ever seen," Vangelo said. "And I've been a cop for 20 years." Clemmens was sentenced to a month in jail, two years' probation, and 50 hours of community service...and he had to reimburse the Vangelo family for their tickets to the game.

Ready: Twenty-six-year-old Justin Krohmer, an off-duty sheriff's

---

Cloudiest city in the U.S.: Astoria, Oregon, which averages 240 cloudy days a year.

deputy in Fargo, North Dakota, was at a Kenny Chesney concert in the Fargodome in June 2009. (He was with his mom.)

Set: He was drinking. (So was his mom.)

HURL! At one point during the show, Krohmer—now drunk—threw up on the people in front of him. Then he was told by Fargodome security that he had to leave—but he refused. Police were called, and Deputy Krohmer was arrested for disorderly conduct.

Extra: Krohmer's mother, 47-year-old Susan Krohmer, was also arrested and taken to jail, after allegedly screaming profanities at the officers and trying to prevent them from removing her son. Mrs. Krohmer is the wife of the local police chief.

Ready: In July 2008, the town of Builth Wells, Wales, hosted their annual Mountain Bike Marathon race. More than 650 showed up to participate.

Set: The starter fired the starting gun…the race began…and the bikers finished the race without incident.

HURL! Then they all started puking. Well, not all of them, but over the next few days more than 160 of the racers suffered severe bouts of vomiting. The U.K.'s National Public Health Service issued a report and England's *Sunderland Echo* newspaper ran a story about it. Headline: "Sheep poo caused mountain bike vomit carnage." Explanation: Some of the mud that the racers had ridden through was contaminated with *Campylobacter*—a bacteria found in sheep feces—which caused the bikers to become ill. The situation had been exacerbated, the report said, by heavy rain before the races, which made for an abundance of liquid mud that could easily fly into the participants' mouths. (Yum!)

*　　*　　*

PRIORITIES?

A 2010 poll asked British adults to rank the 100 greatest inventions of all time. Coming in at #1 and #2: the wheel and the airplane. Coming in at #8 was the Apple iPhone, which is apparently a more important invention than the flush toilet (#9), the internal combustion engine (#10), hot tap water (#29), and the wristwatch (#59).

"9-1-DUMB, WHAT'S YOUR EMERGENCY?"

More real stories of ill-conceived 911 calls.

MULTITASKING

In 2008 two Sarasota, Florida, police cars were following a suspicious vehicle when they received a 911 call that an armed robbery was in progress a few blocks away. The lead cop went to check it out, but the other one kept following the vehicle until it stopped in a parking lot, at which point the officer ordered the driver to exit the vehicle. It turned out that the 28-year-old driver had a gun, and he was a convicted felon and, therefore, not allowed to own a gun. After the robbery call turned out to be bogus, the cops checked the felon's phone records and their suspicions proved correct: He'd made the fake 911 call about the robbery while the cops were following him. His ruse almost worked.

NO SHRIMP FOR YOU!

A woman in Haltom City, Texas (name not released), ordered a takeout meal from A&D Buffalo's in 2009: shrimp fried rice with extra shrimp. She left with her order, but 20 minutes later she was back, complaining that she didn't get the extra shrimp. She demanded that they either give it to her or refund her $1.62. The cashier told the woman that the extra shrimp *was* added to her order, but because she took it out of the restaurant, there was nothing they could do about it. Irate, the woman called 911: "Yeah, I always get the shrimp fried rice, so I said I'm going to get extra meat this time. But he didn't put extra shrimp in there! I'm just saying, to get a police officer here, what has to happen?" Making a frivolous 911 call, that's what. An officer showed up and cited the woman for misuse of the 911 system.

BAR NONE

Late one night in December 2009, a 911 operator in Oldsmar, Florida, received a call from 37-year-old Gregory Oras. He said that several men attacked and shot at him outside a bar. "My nose is broken and my ears are bleeding!" When officers rushed to the scene, they found Oras—and his nose wasn't broken nor were his ears bleeding. Appearing quite intoxicated, he informed them that he just wanted a ride to another bar, and thought dialing 911 was the fastest way to make that happen. The police ticketed Oras for the frivolous call, but he put up a fight and kicked one of the officers in the knees. They tazed Oras and took him to jail.

PROFESSOR 911

Here's an actual exchange between a little boy and a 911 operator:

911: 911 Emergency.

Johnny: Yeah, I need some help.

911: What's the matter?

Johnny: I need help with my math.

911: With your mouth?

Johnny: No, with my math. I have to do it. Will you help me?

911: Sure. (pause) What kind of math do you need help with?

Johnny: I have take-aways.

911: Oh, you gotta do the take-aways?

Johnny: Yeah.

911: All right, what's the problem?

Johnny: Okay. 16...

911: Yeah.

Johnny: ...take away 8. Is what?

911: You tell me. How much do you think it is?

Johnny: I dunno. 1?

911: How old are you?

Johnny: I'm only four.

911: Four?

Mom (yells in the background): Johnny, what are you doing?

Johnny (to mom): This policeman's helping me with my math!

Mom: What did I tell you about playing on the phone?

911: Listen to your mother.

Johnny: You said when I need help to call somebody!

Mom: I didn't mean *the police!*

Bestselling postcard image in the 1970s: the World Trade Center.

THEY MIGHT BE FED UP

One of our favorite bands, They Might Be Giants, issued this "things you may no longer say" list of overused phrases to their friends and crew. So if you roll with them, don't go there, or they'll throw you under the bus.

- Too much information
- Off the hook
- That's what she said
- My bad
- Game changer
- I can't work under these conditions
- Playing the (whatever) card
- Throw someone under the bus
- Drinking the kool-aid
- LOL
- Phone tag
- Don't go there
- Crackberry
- It's all good
- It is what it is
- Talk to the hand

- Think outside the box
- Off the reservation
- Oh no you didn't
- I threw up a little in my mouth
- Give one-hundred and ten percent
- IMHO (short for "In My Humble Opinion")
- No worries
- Jumped the shark
- Voted off the island
- (Anything) on acid
- (Anything) from hell
- (Anything) on steroids
- Literally (unless it's used in the correct context)
- That's how we roll
- (The list itself is now on the list too.)

FUNNY BUSINESS

Big corporations sometimes make strange business decisions.

TACOS! In the early 1990s, Taco Bell opened three stores in Mexico City. That seems like a natural fit, but Mexican customers weren't buying it, and the stores had to close. The reason? The Taco Bell menu is so Americanized that Mexicans didn't know it was "Mexican food." In 2007 the company tried again, but this time positioning itself as an *American* food restaurant. For example, the crunchy "tacos" are called "tacostadas" in Mexican Taco Bells, so as not to confuse them with traditional tacos—soft tortillas filled with seasoned meat and onions, not ground beef, cheese, and sour cream. The menu also includes standard American fare like soft-serve ice cream and french fries.

COFFEE! Starbucks' sales have declined in the last few years—the recession has forced many consumers to cut back on expensive coffee. But sales are up at *independent* coffeehouses, most of which sprang up after Starbucks became popular. In an attempt to cash in on the anticorporate shift, Starbucks redid three Seattle stores as generic coffee bars with no Starbucks signage whatsoever. The experiment did not go well—word got out on the Internet almost immediately that "15th Avenue Coffee and Tea" was still a Starbucks. And if the company was actually trying to keep it a secret, they didn't help themselves by posting "Your neighborhood coffeehouse is getting a makeover!" signs in stores while they were still operating as Starbucks.

CAMERAS! One side effect of the availability of affordable digital cameras: It killed sales for Polaroid's instant-print cameras. In 2008 Polaroid announcing that it was ending production of the cameras and focusing on digital photography products. One of those new products: a portable photo printer that hooks up to any digital camera (essentially the same thing you got with a Polaroid camera). The printer sold poorly, and Polaroid's revenues continued to decline. Meanwhile, Fuji bought the instant-camera technology from Polaroid, and its new line of instant-film cameras were the most popular new cameras in Japan in 2009.

Thanks! The male strawberry poison dart frog keeps its mate's eggs warm by peeing on them.

THE CUBICLE

Audiences cheered when the hero of the 1999 movie Office Space *unscrewed the walls of his cubicle and watched them come crashing down. Yet 30 years earlier, when the very first cubicle walls went up, employers and workers alike cheered them as the "workplace of the future."*

SEA OF DESKS

"Today's office is a wasteland. It saps vitality, blocks talent, frustrates accomplishment. It is the daily scene of unfulfilled intentions and failed effort."

That may read like a critique of the modern corporate office, but it was written by an inventor named Bob Propst in 1960. Propst went to work in post-World War II America, just after the majority of the U.S. workforce had shifted from factory jobs to office jobs—"pencil pushers," as they were called. Their typical workplaces were giant rooms full of rows of desks laid out in a grid, all facing the same direction. The average pencil pusher's view: the back of a fellow worker's head. No one had any privacy, but that didn't matter too much, because workers were discouraged from talking to each other. They had few places to store work papers and personal items, other than an inbox on top of their desk and maybe a drawer or two below. "Here were large numbers of intelligent people working on complex tasks," said Propst about an aviation company he'd worked at in the 1950s, "acres of them hunched over their desks, trying to create."

SYSTEMS INTEGRATION

As a sculptor, designer, and former college art professor, Propst specialized not so much in inventing new things but in revamping entire systems (he'd previously designed new quality controls for manufacturing concrete and a more ergonomic cockpit for super-sonic jet pilots). Setting his sights on creating a better workplace, in 1958 Propst signed on as head of research and development at the Michigan-based office furniture company Herman Miller Inc.

How could Propst and his design team give office workers more privacy and autonomy, yet still maintain the open environment that he felt would facilitate interaction and communication? First,

---

Nerd king: Electrical engineer Hurley Smith invented the pocket protector in 1943.

Propst had to find out what made workers tick, so he interviewed hundreds of them and their bosses, as well as doctors, psychologists, anthropologists, architects, and mathematicians.

Propst also studied a new kind of workplace gaining popularity in Germany called *Bürolandschaft*, or "office landscape." Based on socialist principles that encouraged working together as a group, this system eliminated the grid and—depending on the workers' duties—turned some desks to face each other, placed others side by side, and put still others in a circle. In addition, the file cabinets and bookshelves, usually set along the office's perimeter, were pulled away from the walls and put in the middle of the room, creating makeshift privacy dividers. Potted plants were strategically placed throughout the room to complete the "landscape" motif. Propst borrowed elements of *Bürolandschaft* and improved on it to create what Herman Miller called the "Action Office."

BUILDING BLOCKS

The first design, released in 1964, was a single, freestanding piece of furniture that included bins and a few shelves on each side. The biggest selling point: Employers could place these units anywhere they saw fit. Sales were slow at first, but Propst and his team kept working on the full version—which would feature the floor units attached to partition walls that could be joined to each other in different configurations. In 1968 Herman Miller released the complete Action Office, touted as "the world's first open-plan office system of reconfigurable components."

• The entire workroom floor consisted of both common and private spaces. Workers were urged to move from one to the other several times throughout the day. Potted plants and bright walls spruced up the mood even more.

• Each desk was surrounded by three attachable dividers, or walls, which were high enough to give some privacy but not so high that the worker couldn't stand up and see the rest of the workroom (a practice that would later be called "prairie dogging").

• These walls didn't connect at 90-degree angles: The angles were much wider, allowing for a more open space. This irregular geometry was designed to facilitate "organic circulation patterns" that would keep movement—and productivity—flowing.

• The old desktop inbox was replaced with slanted wall slots

From 1968 to 2000, the International Olympic Committee required all female competitors...

allowing files for several different projects to be off the desk but still within arm's reach.

• Soft boards and plenty of thumbtacks let employees personalize their spaces and keep important papers in full sight.

• The height of the desktops varied in places, which encouraged workers to change their posture frequently and even stand up while they worked in order to keep their blood flowing. (Though Propst was a big proponent of this practice, it never really caught on.)

• Perhaps most important of all: Action Office allowed managers to customize their constantly changing workplaces for a fraction of the cost (and downtime) that would have been required by hiring architects and contractors to do the job.

ACTION OFFICE[3]

In 1968 Intel, a new technology company in Santa Clara, California—located in the heart of what would later be called Silicon Valley—became one of the first to incorporate Propst's system. Hundreds more companies (both startups and established ones) placed orders for Action Offices, and Herman Miller raked in over $25 million in corporate sales in the first two years alone. As the 1970s ensued, workplaces across the United States steadily switched from rows of desks to partitioned walls. By the end of the decade, the average workspace area was 12 feet by 12 feet.

Then, in the 1980s, the Digital Revolution took hold. The Action Office system (and the dozens of copycats that followed) could easily fit a computer, monitor, and printer. Sure, those early computers were much larger than today's sleek PCs and Macs, but the Action Office was spacious enough to handle them. At least that's how it was supposed to work. But as office rents skyrocketed in the 1990s (nowhere more than in Silicon Valley), employers were forced to accommodate more workers in smaller areas. Ironically, the feature that made it so easy to give these workers more space—adjustable walls—also gave bosses an easy way to cram more and more cubicles together. Result: The wide angles of the Action Office closed up and became squares, and the area of the average workspace was reduced to 8 feet by 8 feet. (It's even smaller today.) The grid of desks had returned, only now they had fabric-covered walls between them.

Only 20 years after partitioned offices ushered in a new era of comfort and productivity, cubicles (as they were being called) came to symbolize everything that was wrong with the American workplace. The nation's 40 million or so cubicle workers spent their days in "cube farms" with seemingly no escape from their neighbors' chit-chatting, keyboard-tapping, radio-blaring, Dorito-crunching, perfume-wafting, gas-passing...

NOT-SO-PROUD PAPA

Just as Alfred Nobel came to regret inventing dynamite, and Robert Oppenheimer lamented the atomic bomb, Bob Propst was demoralized by what his grand idea turned into. He didn't blame himself, though: "The dark side of this is that not all organizations are intelligent and progressive. Lots are run by crass people who take the same kind of equipment and create hellholes. They make little bitty cubicles and stuff people in them. Barren, rat-hole places." The research backed him up, too: The International Workplace Studies Program concluded that "cubicles can inhibit teamwork by separating workers via artificial walls."

By the time Propst passed away in 2000, he'd obtained 120 patents, including ones for a vertical timber harvester, an electronic tagging system for livestock, a mobile office for quadriplegics, and a new workflow chart system for hospitals. But today, he's mostly remembered as the "father of the cubicle"—even though his original design consisted of no cubes at all.

But Propst's dream of a better workplace didn't die with him.
For the future of the office, fast-track over to page 435.

For the future of the office, fast-track over to page 435.

*   *   *

IRONY, R.F.D.

Actress Betty Lou Lynn, 83, played Thelma Lou on *The Andy Griffith Show* in the 1960s. In 2007 she decided to move away from Beverly Hills after twice being mugged. So Lynn moved to Mount Airy, North Carolina. What could be safer than the town that inspired Mayberry in the first place? Not long after, she was mugged outside of a shopping center.

Marilyn Monroe tried out 9 different shades of blonde before settling on platinum.

MYTH-CONCEPTIONS

"Common knowledge" is frequently wrong. Here are some
more examples of things that many people believe...but
that, according to our sources, just aren't true.

Myth: Front-line troops are nicknamed G.I.s, which stands for "general infantry."
Truth: They are called G.I.s, but it doesn't stand for general infantry. The term dates to World War I, when American troops referred to German artillery shells as "G.I. cans" because they were made of galvanized iron. Over time, the "G.I." came to refer to the people who made up the abbreviation.

Myth: Cranberries are grown underwater.
Truth: Farmers grow them in bogs near waterways, which they use to flood the bogs during harvesting. The individual berries float to the surface, where they're easily collected.

Myth: During the Civil War, all slaveholding states seceded from the United States.
Truth: Kentucky, Missouri, Maryland, and Delaware were slave states, but remained in the Union. Slave owners in those states kept their slaves until the 13th Amendment to the U.S. Constitution was ratified in 1865 and the practice was outlawed.

Myth: It was illegal to drink alcohol during Prohibition (1920–33).
Truth: It was only illegal to produce, sell, or transport alcohol, although home brewing of up to 20 gallons of wine and cider (but not beer) was legal. And if you had any alcohol left over from before 1920, it was legal to consume that.

Myth: In his 1859 book *On the Origin of Species*, Charles Darwin theorized that humans evolved from chimpanzees—the basis for the theory of evolution.
Truth: Darwin never asserted that humans came from chimps. Rather, he claimed that humans and chimpanzees both descended— separately—from the same ancestral hominid, called the *Sahelanthropus tchadensis*, about seven million years ago. (Humans and chimps share 94 percent of their DNA.)

Only some shark species, such as the Great White, must swim constantly to breathe.

OMENS

Can you tell a good omen from a bad one? Here's a handy guide.

Good Omen: If ants have built a nest by your front door, you'll be coming into money soon.
Bad Omen: If you hear the tapping of a deathwatch beetle, someone in your house is going to die within the year.

Good Omen: A bird flying through your house means important news is coming.
Bad Omen: But if that bird can't get out, the news will be about the death of someone you know.

Good Omen: If the first butterfly you see in the New Year is white, good luck will be yours throughout the year.
Bad Omen: A black moth in your home means death will come calling within the year.

Good Omen: Wearing a jade ring on your little finger will bring you wealth. Men should wear the ring on their left hand. Women on their right.
Bad Omen: Wearing a ring on your thumb isn't just a bad fashion statement; it will make you lose all your money and any chance of future success.

Good Omen: Having a bent or crooked little finger means you're lucky with money.
Bad Omen: A white spot on the nail of your middle finger means you have an enemy.

Good Omen: If your right ear is ringing, someone is saying nice things about you.
Bad Omen: If your left ear is ringing, someone is trashing you.

Good Omen: It's good luck if you make a rhyme by accident. If you make a wish before you say another word, it will come true.
Bad Omen: If you drop the comb while combing your hair, misfortune will visit you.

Good Omen: Finding a spider in the evening is good luck.
Bad Omen: Seeing a spider in the morning will bring bad luck for the rest of the day.

Good Omen: Got itchy feet? Pack your bags—you're going on a trip.
Bad Omen: Start a trip on Friday and disappointment will follow wherever you go.

That's not nice: In the 1300s, the word "nice" meant "lazy, lecherous, and strange."

ARCADE IRE

Here's a handful of the biggest controversies involving video games.

LOVE ON THE ROCKS

In 2009 Courtney Love, widow of Nirvana frontman Kurt Cobain, licensed her husband's image to Activision for use in its latest *Guitar Hero* music simulator game, *Guitar Hero 5*. She thought Cobain's image would only be seen on-screen playing guitar along with the Nirvana songs in the game, but was shocked when she saw a YouTube clip of "Cobain" playing a song by the '80s hair-metal band Bon Jovi—something Cobain would have loathed. Love sued Activision for misappropriating Cobain's image. Activision CEO Dan Rosensweig responded in public, saying Love's contract clearly permits the use of Cobain's image, and that Love "happily cashed the check." The suit is still pending.

NO WAY, JOSÉ

In April 2000, Jose Rabadan Pardo of Madrid murdered his parents and his sister with a *katana*, a Japanese sword. Afterward, police investigating the case suspected that Pardo's crime may have been triggered by delusions stemming from round-the-clock video game play. Pardo, they said, believed that the video game *Final Fantasy VIII* was real and that he was a character in it—"Squall Leonhard," a sword-toting mercenary on a mission of revenge. Just as Leonhard avenged his "enemies" in the game by killing them with a sword, so did Pardo in real life. But further investigation revealed that Pardo may have been faking his delusions to avoid prison. Evidence showed that he'd been planning the murders for two weeks, and that immediately after the killings, he dumped his bloody clothes far away from home, something a noble warrior in the feudal world of *Final Fantasy* (or a mentally ill person) probably wouldn't do. He was sentenced to eight years in a Spanish psychiatric hospital...and was released in 2008.

PLAYING DIRTY

Video games took off in 1982, with arcade and home consoles like

---

Study: Only 50% of emergency-room personnel wash their hands during their shifts.

Atari earning billions. The games were purchased and played primarily by children and teenagers, leading to a moral crusade over the negative effects of video games, namely that they were a waste of time and that video-game arcades attracted juvenile delinquents. So when a company called Mystique began releasing sexually explicit video games for the Atari 2600 home console in 1982, it generated even more negative attention. The most infamous was *Custer's Revenge*, in which the player controlled a naked General George Custer as he dodged arrows while attempting to reach, and then rape, a nude Native American woman tied to a post. *Custer's Revenge* drew outrage from numerous women's and Native American groups and was banned in Oklahoma City (where there is a large Native American population). But it sold nearly 80,000 copies nationwide before Mystique finally bowed to pressure and pulled the game from stores. Mystique went on to release more potentially offensive games (including *Bachelor Party* and *Philly Flasher*), and then attempted to reap the benefits of the free publicity from the resulting controversy. It didn't work—Mystique went out of business in 1983.

JOE LIEBERMAN, ZOMBIE KILLER

Connecticut senator Joe Lieberman has frequently spoken out against violent pop culture that he finds offensive and believes is harmful to young audiences. He once called for sweeping censorship of the Internet, and he supported Tipper Gore's mid-1980s crusade to label music. In 2005 he publicly criticized the Xbox game *Stubbs the Zombie in Rebel Without a Pulse*. He called it "cannibalistic," with the capacity to "harm the entirety of American youth." He may have been a little off base. With all of the violent video games on the market (*Grand Theft Auto*, *Metal Gear Solid*, *Halo*, for example), Lieberman decided to go after one that was fairly tame. *Stubbs* wasn't a gorefest—it was a comic adventure set in the 1950s, featuring a bumbling zombie who isn't very good at hunting for brains. Further, the kids that Lieberman claimed would be corrupted by the game couldn't even buy it. The game had a rating of "M," meaning gamers under the age of 17 couldn't buy or rent it. Before Lieberman decried it, *Stubbs* was just another video game. Thanks to Lieberman's rant, it became "controversial" (which probably helped sales).

There are more than 120 Boy Scout merit badges (including one for dentistry).

PILOT (T)ERROR

When you're on a plane, do you wonder about the "professional"
sitting in the cockpit? Is he a suicidal nut? A war criminal?
Is he even a real pilot? If you never wondered
before, you will after you read these.

HIGH ANXIETY

"Imagine your adrenaline is being excited by the roar of the 747 engines as you thunder down the runway. Just after lift-off, there's a sudden hush from those massive engines. Your heart is in your mouth, pumping as it had never done before." Those are the opening lines from a book called *One Obsession, Two Obsession, Three Obsession, Four*, written by a former Qantas Airlines pilot named Bryan Griffin. Hired in 1966, the Australian pilot developed a compulsive urge to crash a plane, and it grew worse and worse as the years passed. A few times he even had to grab his own hand to keep it from shutting off the engines. "It's like it wasn't even my arm," he said. In 1979 Griffin finally informed his bosses of his urges but, amazingly, they cleared him to fly. Then a psychiatrist diagnosed him with severe obsessive compulsive disorder, anxiety, and depression. But still, Qantas cleared him to fly. Fortunately for passengers, in 1982 Griffin quit. He spent the next 28 years working odd jobs, seeing psychiatrists, writing his book, and filing lawsuits against Qantas. In 2010 a judge finally ruled that airline officials had "exacerbated" Griffin's condition by continuing to let him fly and awarded him $160,000 for loss of earnings, medical expenses, and legal costs.

ON-THE-JOB TRAINING

A Boeing 737 carrying 101 passengers was about to take off in Amsterdam in March 2010 when police boarded and walked into the cockpit. A few minutes later, they returned with the pilot in handcuffs and took him off the plane. When a passenger asked a flight attendant what was going on, he responded, "He wasn't a real pilot, but we have one coming on to replace him." Technically, the 41-year-old man (name not released) was a pilot, but he

---

was certified to fly only very small planes. Thirteen years earlier, he had meticulously falsified his pilot's license so it said he could operate passenger jets as well. He then logged more than 10,000 flying hours with several airlines, never having earned a valid license. Dutch police said the man, from Sweden, actually seemed relieved when they finally caught him: He tore off his flying stripes and handed them to the officers.

STOP DRAGGING YOUR TAIL AROUND

Prior to takeoff in Wellington, New Zealand, in 2001, the first officer of a Singapore-bound 747 entered the plane's weight into the flight computer, and the captain confirmed the numbers. Unfortunately, the first officer's estimate was short by 110 tons. When the 747 attempted to lift off with nearly 400 people aboard, it was traveling much too slowly. The nose lifted off the ground, but the rest of the aircraft did not, causing the tail to drag on the runway for 1,600 feet. By the time the plane became airborne, the tail was engulfed in flames. The pilots made a hasty turnaround and landed safely. The investigation revealed some disturbing facts: The pilot had little experience flying 747s and was accustomed to taking off at much slower speeds; the first officer also had little experience in 747s; and the third pilot, who did have experience and *should* have noticed, had been distracted by an argument with the ground crew over whether the plane was carrying enough fuel. All three pilots were reprimanded.

THE SCENIC ROUTE

Forty-five minutes into their flight, the 40 passengers aboard Hawaii's go! Mokulele Airlines jet became concerned when they looked out and saw only ocean. The September 2008 flight from Honolulu to Hilo should have already landed. Air Traffic Control was wondering the same thing: They'd radioed the two pilots, Scott Oltman and Dillon Shipley, but received no response. Finally, after nearly 20 minutes and a dozen calls, Shipley answered, "Yeah, we're here. Switching off auto-pilot and turning around for final approach." The plane landed safely, but during questioning both pilots admitted to having fallen asleep. Their licenses were suspended; they were later fired by the airline.

THE UNFRIENDLY SKIES

An Argentina-born Dutch pilot named Julio Poch, 57, was arrested moments before his Transavia flight was set to take off from Spain in 2009. His past, it seemed, had finally caught up with him...because he bragged about it. In the 1980s, Poch had served in Argentina's military dictatorship and, according to the Argentinian Human Rights Secretariat in 2007, "he boasted of having been a pilot of the aircraft that threw live prisoners into the sea after the military coup." According to his colleagues, Poch was unrepentant, explaining, "It was war." He was extradited to Argentina and charged with 950 crimes against humanity. (After an eight-hour delay, the flight took off with a new crew; the passengers were never told why the pilot was led away in handcuffs.)

BRB

Only a few hundred feet from touching down in Singapore in May 2010, an Australian Jetstar Airbus carrying 167 passengers was forced to abort the landing and circle the airport for another attempt. Why did the plane have to abort? Because the landing gear wasn't down. Why wasn't the landing gear down? Because the pilot whose job it was to pull the landing gear lever was distracted. Why was he distracted? According to SkyNews, he was sending a text message on his cell phone. The plane landed safely and the pilot was suspended pending an investigation. OMG!

*　　*　　*

THE LAW SURE DID KETCHUP WITH HER

Officials and patrons at the Ada County Library in Boise, Idaho, were perplexed by a bizarre series of crimes in 2009 and 2010: Someone was dumping ketchup, mustard, mayonnaise, and even syrup into the book drop box. After dozens of books had been damaged, police staked out the drop box and busted Joy L. Cassidy, 74, with a jar of mayonnaise in her car. Her motive is still unknown, but police did say that she was mentally competent enough to stand trial. (We assume they'll throw the book at her.)

THE NANNY STATE QUIZ

The British government has been accused of filling their law books with nitpicky regulations covering the details of everything from public safety to energy consumption. Result: a legal system that critics say treats its citizens like babies unable to think or care for themselves without help from the government, hence the nickname "the Nanny State." How much truth is there to the charge? Take this quiz and find out. (Answers on page 537.)

1. On orders from the British government, between 2007 and 2009 local governments ("councils") spent £1.65 million ($2.5 million) addressing which of the following threats to public safety:

a) Unsafe tire pressure. The money was spent issuing tire gauges to "traffic wardens" (meter maids) to enable them to check tire pressure on parked cars and issue tickets to "at-risk offenders."

b) Wobbly tombstones. As many as a million tombstones in cemeteries all over the U.K. were subjected to a device called a "topple tester" to see if they were in danger of falling over. Unsafe grave markers were strapped and propped up with stakes, then flagged with large yellow stickers to warn mourners of the danger.

c) "Dangerously hot" beverages. The money was used to develop a cup lid that seals shut when a beverage is too hot. Fine for not using the "locking lid" while driving: £50 (about $78).

2. In 2008 the West Sussex County Council in southern England proposed a £20 fine for which of the following offenses:

a) Leaving your engine running while stuck in traffic.

b) Drying underwear on washlines within 150 ft. of a school.

c) Cursing within earshot of public officials or the Queen.

3. In 2007 the British government made which of the following changes to the criminal justice system:

a) Persons convicted of soccer hooliganism must attend mandatory "sports fan etiquette and anger control" courses.

b) Instead of arresting shoplifters, police now issue £80 ($125) "penalty notices," similar to parking tickets, for thefts under £200 ($312). They do not appear on the thief's criminal record.

c) Motorists with five speeding offenses in a two-year period must have a speed-limiting device called a "speed guv" (short for "governor") installed in their vehicle "to prevent repeat offenses."

4. The public pool owned by the Hackney (East London) Council is closed to swimmers whenever which of the following occurs:

a) It rains—the pool is closed when it becomes "too wet to swim."

b) A swimmer is seen entering the pool without showering first.

c) 45 minutes have elapsed since the last urine test. (The pool is closed for 15 minutes every hour and tested for the presence of urine; if the pool is found to be pee-free, swimmers may re-enter.)

5. At least 2.6 million British households have had a microchip installed in which of the following items by their local government councils:

a) TVs, to supervise the viewing habits of families with children.

b) Washing machines, to monitor which households waste water.

c) Trash cans, to monitor how much garbage people throw away.

6. In 2008 the British government caused a public uproar when it made plans to publish which of the following:

a) The income of every citizen in the United Kingdom (to discourage tax fraud).

b) The names of every citizen treated for a sexually transmitted disease within the past ten years (enabling people to find out whether their partners are infected).

c) Guidelines for the safe consumption of alcohol by children.

7. In 2009 the British government launched a pilot program to pay British citizens to do which of the following:

a) Turn off the TV and read a book. Reward: £1 ($1.50) for every hour spent reading a book on the "approved reading list."

b) Lose weight. The fattest Britons who lose the most weight (and keep it off for six months) receive up to £425 ($665).

c) Pick up after their dogs. Dog owners are paid £1 for each pound of poop they turn in to the local animal control office. (Title of the program: P3—"One Pound per Pound at the Pound").

First movie Steven Spielberg ever saw: *The Greatest Show on Earth,* at age 4.

MMM...WORDS

The Simpsons *has been on the air for more than 20 years, and in that time the show's writers have invented dozens of words (some of which have actually made it into common usage). Here's a sampling.*

MEH: An expression of indifference, first uttered by Lisa when Homer wanted to take the family to a Legoland-like theme park.

YOINK: In a 1993 episode, Homer yanks a wad of money right out of Marge's hand and says "yoink" as he does so. It's since been said by other characters when they're stealing something, and has become part of the vernacular—half slang for "stealing," half sound effect.

KWIJIBO: To wrap up a game of Scrabble, Bart puts all his letters on the game board to form the imaginary word *kwijibo*, which he defines as "a big, dumb, balding North American ape with no chin and a short temper" (i.e., Homer).

ZAZZ: Lisa is told by a TV producer that Bart, unlike her, has plenty of "zazz," which means flair and charisma.

SMARCH: In a 1995 episode, Springfield Elementary receives misprinted calendars that include an extra month called Smarch. (Smarch is almost always included in *Simpsons* calendars.)

EMBIGGENS: Springfield town founder Jebediah Springfield coined the town's motto, "A noble spirit embiggens the smallest man."

CROMULENT: Lisa questions whether the founder of Springfield ever really said the town motto, especially the made-up sounding *embiggens*, but is reassured by her teacher that embiggens is a "perfectly cromulent word."

GLAVEN: An interjection used by the wacky scientist Professor Frink to express any grand emotion, from joy to wonder to terror. The character is based on Jerry Lewis's *Nutty Professor*, and *Simpsons* writers thought the sing-songy "GLAY-ven" sounded like something Lewis would've said.

VELOCITATOR: The speech of the evil, extremely

Sharks can hear lower frequencies than humans can....

old tycoon Mr. Burns is characterized by words that seem antiquated, but were really made up by *Simpsons* writers. A velocitator, for example, is what Mr. Burns calls a car's accelerator pedal.

SENSELESS DUNDER-PATE: Another Burns word, it means "a stupid person."

SUPERLIMINAL: *Subliminal* communication is the delivery of information via secret or undetected means. *Super*liminal communication is a blatant, direct message. Navy recruiter L.T. Smash demonstrates the technique by yelling out his window to a man: "Hey, you! Join the Navy!"

UNPOSSIBLE: Ralph Wiggum isn't a very smart kid. When told he's failing English class, he gasps and says, "Me, fail English? That's unpossible."

BOLOGNIUM: Springfield schools are so cash-strapped that they use periodic element charts provided by Oscar Mayer. One of the elements listed is *Bolognium*. (Its atomic weight is "snacktacular.")

FORFTY: In a 1994 episode called "Homer the Vigilante," Homer dismisses statistics with a claim that "forfty percent of all people" know that statistics can be easily manipulated.

TRAUMEDY: A combination of the words "trauma" and "comedy," it's used by town doctor Julius Hibbert to describe hilarious pratfalls that end in brutal injuries.

*　　*　　*

THE GRANDPA SIMPSON LEXICON

Abraham Simpson—Homer's father on *The Simpsons*—frequently talks about the good old days, especially what things were supposedly called back then. Examples:

• Bananas were once known as *yellow fatty beans*.

• Turkeys were called *walking birds*.

• A *Swedish lunchbox* was a slang term for suitcase.

• He claims that during World War II, anti-Japanese sentiment led America to change the name of sushi to *liberty logs*.

• Grandpa uses the word *dickety* instead of "twenty," because when he was young, "the Kaiser had stolen our word 'twenty.'"

TATT-OOPS!

*A few stories that may make you want to rethink
that new tattoo you're planning to get.*

BAD SUIT. In 2003 Michael Machetti sued Riverside, California, tattoo parlor Bullseye Tattoo. Misspelled tattoo? No—Machetti went in to have his "F*** YOU" neck tattoo altered into "666." He charged that in the process of making the alteration, the shop somehow infected him with a rare disease called *necrotizing fasciitis*, better known as "flesh-eating bacteria," which he claims cost him $580,000 in medical bills. The suit was thrown of court.

BAD CAREER MOVE. Stephen Baldwin, a member of the Baldwin acting family, had been in a career slump since the mid-'90s, and by 2008 he seemed willing to do just about anything to land a major role. That year he met Miley Cyrus, teen star of the popular Disney Channel sitcom *Hannah Montana,* and the two made a pact: If Baldwin got an "HM" tattoo (for *Hannah Montana*), Cyrus would get him a cameo on her show. Baldwin got the tattoo in late 2008 and showed it to Cyrus, but she never was able to get him the promised role before the show was cancelled in 2010. (Baldwin now says he "regrets" the tattoo.)

BAD PRODUCT PLACEMENT. Steven Smith was a devout fan of Microsoft products. ("The Apple community can kiss my a**," he says.) In 2007, when Microsoft announced the release of its Zune MP3 player, Smith got three Zune-related tattoos: 1) the helix-like Zune logo on his upper arm, 2) a line drawing of a man and a rabbit, taken from a Zune TV commercial, on his other arm, and 3) the Zune slogan, "Welcome to the Social" on his back. Pictures of Smith and his tattoos became an Internet phenomenon, and Smith received a free Zune from Microsoft. But the company backed out of the free trip to company headquarters he claims they promised him...even after he nearly had his name legally changed from Steven Smith to "Microsoft Zune." Smith, feeling cheated, covered up his Zune logo with a giant image of Vice President Dick Cheney as the devil.

In Mesopotamian myth, the god Enlil flooded the Earth because humans were too noisy.

DUSTBIN OF HISTORY: THE PEARL HARBOR SPY

*The Japanese attack on Pearl Harbor on December 7, 1941, remains
one of the most infamous events in U.S. history. Yet the spy who
played a key role in the sneak attack is a forgotten man,
unknown even to many World War II buffs.*

UNDER COVER

On March 27, 1941, a 27-year-old junior diplomat named Tadashi Morimura arrived in Honolulu to take his post as vice-consul at the Japanese consulate. But that was just a cover—"Morimura" was really Takeo Yoshikawa, a Japanese Imperial Navy Intelligence officer. His real mission: to collect information about the American military installations in and around Pearl Harbor.

Relations between the United States and Japan had been strained throughout the 1930s and were now deteriorating rapidly. In 1940, after years of Japanese aggression in China and Southeast Asia, Washington froze Japanese assets in the U.S., cut off exports of oil and war materiel, and moved the headquarters of the U.S. Navy's Pacific Fleet from southern California to Pearl Harbor, bringing it 2,400 miles closer to Japan.

The fleet was in Pearl Harbor to stay. But if Japan wanted its funds unfrozen and the crippling economic embargo lifted, the United States insisted that all Japanese troops had to leave China and Southeast Asia. This was a demand that Japan was unwilling to meet. Instead, it began preparing for war, and by early 1941, the eyes of Japan's military planners had turned to Pearl Harbor.

THE AMERICAN DESK

Yoshikawa had become a spy in a roundabout way. He'd been a promising naval academy graduate, but his career hopes were dashed in 1936 when, just two years after graduation, stomach problems (reportedly brought on by heavy drinking) forced him out of the Japanese Navy. The following year he landed a desk job with Naval Intelligence, where he was put to work learning all that he could about the U.S. Navy.

From 1937 until 1940, Yoshikawa pored over books, magazines, newspapers, brochures, reports filed by Japanese diplomats and military intelligence officers from all over the world, and anything else he could find that would give him information about the U.S. Navy. "By 1940 I was the Naval General Staff's acknowledged American expert," he recounted in a 1960 article in the journal *Naval Institute Proceedings*. "I knew by then every U.S. man-of-war and aircraft by name, hull number, configuration, and technical characteristics. I knew, too, a great deal of general information about the U.S. naval bases at Manila, Guam, and Pearl Harbor."

MISSION IMPLAUSIBLE

In August 1940, Yoshikawa was ordered to begin preparing for a spy mission in Pearl Harbor. And he was probably surprised by what his superiors told him next: He wasn't going to receive any training in the art of espionage—none at all. He wasn't going to receive any support from Japan's Hawaiian spy network, either, because there wasn't one. He would be the only Japanese spy in Hawaii, posing as one Tadashi Morimura, a low-level diplomat assigned to the consulate in Honolulu, and only the consul general would know his true identity and mission. The job paid $150 a month, plus $600 every six months for expenses. In March 1941, Yoshikawa arrived in Honolulu.

A MAN WITH(OUT) A PLAN

Now what? Yoshikawa had received very little guidance on how to go about his job, but his worries ended when the consul general, Nagao Kita, took him to dinner at the Shuncho-ro, a Japanese restaurant on a hill overlooking Pearl Harbor. From a private dining room on the second floor of the restaurant, Yoshikawa could see both the Navy base and the nearby Army Air Corps base at Hickam Field laid out below. The Shuncho-ro was the perfect location for studying the flow of ships and aircraft in and out of the harbor, and it even had telescopes. It also happened to be owned by a woman who came from the same prefecture in Japan as Yoshikawa, and she happily made the private dining room (and

---

What is *enuresis*? The scientific term for bed-wetting.

telescope) available to the up-and-coming young diplomat whenever he requested it.

THE NATURAL

Yoshikawa quickly discovered that he could accomplish much of his spying without attracting attention, and without even breaking any laws. After all, Pearl Harbor was no isolated military installation; it was part of Honolulu, the Hawaiian Islands' capital city and largest commercial port. Civilians, foreigners, and sightseeing tourists were everywhere. Even if the military had tried to shield Pearl Harbor's operations from prying eyes, it would have been virtually impossible.

Yoshikawa collected a lot of useful information from his observations at the Shuncho-ro, and also by hiking the hillsides that overlooked Pearl Harbor. He could even rent planes at a nearby airport whenever he wanted to take aerial photographs of the ships at anchor. He blended in easily with the large Asian-American population, and he was careful to vary his routine, never visiting any one place too frequently, and never staying any longer than necessary. Sometimes he posed as a laborer; other times he put on a loud Hawaiian shirt and masqueraded as a tourist. When he felt conspicuous traveling alone on, say, a visit to a military air show or a plane or boat ride around the harbor, he'd take one of the geisha girls who worked at the Shuncho-ro or one of the female consular staff on a "date," always being careful not to reveal his true identity or mission to his companion. An experienced long-distance swimmer, Yoshikawa also made many swims around the harbor to study its defenses. By breathing through a reed, he could swim underwater when needed to avoid detection.

NICE TO MEET YOU

After a long day of spying on land or in the water, Yoshikawa passed many an evening picking up hitchhiking U.S. soldiers or buying drinks for servicemen in bars, prying as much information out of them as he could without arousing suspicion. (Soldiers who were tight-lipped around *male* foreigners often happily spilled the beans to the geishas at the Shuncho-ro, so Yoshikawa made sure to question them, too.) After the restaurants and bars closed, he would pose as a drunken bum and scour the dumpsters outside of military installations for any documents he could get his hands on.

Yoshikawa rarely took photographs, and he never drew diagrams or wrote anything down while making his rounds. He never carried a notepad: Instead, he relied on his photographic memory to record every detail—locations and numbers of ships and aircraft, the timing of their arrivals and departures, the depths of water in different parts of the harbor, everything—so that if he was stopped or questioned, there would be no evidence on him that suggested he was a spy. He never even carried binoculars for fear they would call too much attention to him or arouse suspicion.

PACKING A PUNCH

If Japan had planned its attack on Pearl Harbor without the data Yoshikawa gathered, it's quite possible that it would have been merely a glancing blow, one that damaged the Pacific Fleet but did not knock it out of commission. But the information Yoshikawa provided was devastating:

• When he reported that air patrols rarely watched the waters north of Oahu (where the seas were thought to be too treacherous for an enemy to mount an attack), the Japanese military planners decided to attack from that direction.

• When he told them the water in the harbor wasn't deep enough for ordinary torpedoes, they devised a torpedo with special fins that would work in shallow water.

• When Yoshikawa told them that the ships along "Battleship Row" were moored in pairs to protect the inboard ships from torpedo attacks, the planners decided to attack those ships with armor-piercing bombs dropped from dive-bombers.

• When he reported that ships commonly left the harbor for maneuvers on Monday and returned to port at the end of the week, the planners set their attack for the weekend.

• When they asked Yoshikawa which day of the weekend the most ships were likely to be in the harbor, he replied simply: "Sunday."

Part II of the story is on page 477.

Water isn't colorless—it's actually very slightly blue.

BRAIN POWER

Pay close attention—there's a lot going on in that skull of yours.

• The human adult brain weighs about three pounds—the same as a bag of sugar.

• 100,000 years ago, our ancestors' brains weighed just one pound.

• Your brain is three percent of your body mass, but consumes more than 20 percent of the oxygen your body uses.

• The brain has no pain receptors so it registers no pain. Brain surgery can actually be conducted while you're awake. (Except for the part where they drill through your cranium—that can hurt.)

• The brain is the fattiest organ in the body.

• The brain is made up of *gray* matter (mostly on the surface) and *white* matter (mostly the inner brain). They're both actually pinkish, and are so-named for the color they become in formaldehyde.

• Studies show that the areas of the brain that process vision "turn off" when you blink. That's why we don't notice our blinks.

• Worried about brain research? No problem. Harvard maintains a "brain bank" of 7,000 brains for study.

• It takes about 25 years for your brain to become fully developed.

• Your brain is so soft it can be cut with a butter knife.

• The *cerebral cortex* is the folded, "wrinkly" surface of the brain. It's about 1/16 of an inch thick. The "wrinkles" appeared as our brains evolved and grew larger over the ages. More folds means more surface area—and more brain power—in less space.

• Other animals that have "wrinkled" brains: cats, dogs, monkeys, and dolphins. One that doesn't: the rat, which has a smooth brain.

• Recent studies have shown that people who learn a second language, especially at a young age, have increased gray matter density in the left hemispheres of their brains.

• The Chinese pictogram for "brain" translates to "fleshy contents of the skull."

UNCLE JOHN'S STALL OF SHAME

It is with heavy hearts that we bring you these true stories of stinkers who seem to have forgotten that each and every bathroom is a hallowed place—it should never be used for nefarious purposes.

Dishoneree: Michael O'Leary, CEO of Ryanair
Dubious Achievement: Charging to go where no airline has charged to go before
True Story: Even though the British discount carrier is known for charging extra for checked baggage, carry-on items, food, and drink (even water), most people thought O'Leary was joking when he announced in 2010 that he would install pay toilets on 168 planes. He wasn't joking: On each plane, O'Leary planned to remove all the restrooms except for one...to be shared by 189 people, including the flight crew. That way, Ryanair can add six more seats. And charging for that lone toilet, he explained, "will change passengers' behaviors so they will do their business before and after they get on the plane." O'Leary's announcement brought jeers from thousands of prospective customers. Still, he held firm with the plan...until Boeing, the company that manufactures Ryanair's fleet, refused to refit or build planes with only one bathroom.

Dishonerees: David and Deanne Elsholz, a married couple from Wesley Chapel, Florida
Dubious Achievement: He missed; she didn't
True Story: The details are a bit hazy (news reports say the couple's trailer was littered with Natural Lite beer cans). Apparently, late one night in February 2010, David, 50, got out of bed and went to the bathroom. Deanne, 44, awoke to the noise of David urinating all over the bathroom floor. "What are you doing?" she yelled. David didn't answer; he just wanted to go back to sleep, he said later. But Deanne says that when she pressed the matter, he "smacked me in the head with a towel." So she threw a glass at him. It hit him in the nose; he started bleeding. Then, according to the police report, "Deanne ran into the bathroom and slipped

on David's urine." She called 911, but after officers questioned them, she—not he—was arrested for domestic battery.

Dishoneree: Joshua Nelson, of Lincoln, Nebraska
Dubious Achievement: Using TP on the wrong end...of the law
True Story: Before cops caught up with him, Nelson, 29, was simply known as the "Toilet Paper Bandit" (TPB). In April 2010, he wrapped some Charmin around his head (like a mummy), went into Kabredlo's convenience store, pulled out a knife, and demanded all the money from the safe. The clerk complied and the TPB ran away. Officers called to the scene found a trail of toilet paper leading away from the store, but they were unable to track down the TPB. A week later, a prescription bottle with Nelson's name on it was found near the store, along with discarded coin roll wrappers. The Toilet Paper Bandit was arrested and confessed to his crime, which has been added to his...rap sheet.

Dishoneree: Curtis Jones, 31, incarcerated at the Howard County Jail in Missouri on burglary charges
Dubious Achievement: Using a roll to go on the lam
True Story: Jones took the empty cardboard TP roll from his cell toilet and jammed it into the door just before lockdown. Then, while the night guard was on the other side of block, Jones opened his cell door and escaped. He was free for a week before an anonymous tip led police to his whereabouts. He was recaptured and placed in a higher-security area of the jail.

Dishoneree: Calvin Robinson, a 19-year-old homeless man from Spokane, Washington
Dubious Achievement: Using a public restroom to make...money
True Story: In 2008 Robinson paid $100 for a color copier so he could make $90 in counterfeit money and buy a bag of marijuana. But being homeless, Robinson had no place to plug in his copier, so he used a public restroom in the River Park Square shopping mall. His plot unraveled when mall workers alerted the police that someone had been in the locked restroom for more than an hour. The cops broke in and found Robinson sitting on the floor with his copier and his poorly copied $10 bills. "I don't believe he's going to be recruited by NASA," said the arresting officer.

DO YOU SPEAK DOG?

Many dog owners believe their special relationship with their pet includes an ability to understand what the dog "says" and does. We've been reading up on the subject and talking to canine behavior experts. Not all of these tricks work with all breeds, but you won't know unless you try.

PROBLEM: You have to repeat commands over and over before your dog obeys. Almost anyone who has owned a dog has gone through it: You want your dog to sit, so you say, "Sit." The dog doesn't sit, so you say "Sit" again...and again. Now you're SHOUTING!...and the dog finally sits.

EXPERTS SAY: You're falling into a bad habit. Your dog may actually be learning that the command for "Sit" is the multisyllabic word "Sit...sit...sit...SIT!" (maybe with a few dirty words thrown in). When you get frustrated and start yelling commands at your dog, you also may be teaching it to ignore any command that *isn't* shouted.

SOLUTION: Call the dog by name to get its attention, then give your command just once, in a firm but not loud voice. Wait. If the dog doesn't respond, call it by name again and repeat the command. Repeat again if you need to, but if you get frustrated, take a break—it's better than teaching the dog bad habits.

PROBLEM: Your dog barks whenever someone comes to the door or walks past your house.

EXPERTS SAY: The dog sees these people as threats to the security of its "den." That much you know already. But yelling at a dog for barking at strangers not only doesn't work, it may even reinforce the undesirable behavior. That's because you're responding to the threat the dog has called to your attention by making loud noises of your own, which the dog hears as "barks." It interprets your barking to mean that it has done the right thing in alerting you to the danger, and will probably continue barking as long as you do, to help you drive the threat away.

SOLUTION: Respond calmly and quietly to whatever your dog is calling to your attention, then calmly say "okay," or "thank you," give it a pat, and call it back to your side. The dog interprets this

---

A Maryland community college offers a 12:00 a.m. psych class called "Midnight Madness."

to mean that you evaluated what it has called to your attention, and decided it's not a threat. No further barking is required.

PROBLEM: Your puppy pees whenever it greets someone.

EXPERTS SAY: One of Uncle John's friends has a border collie named Bijou that used to pee every time she greeted a person, regardless of whether it was a threatening stranger, a familiar visitor, or even her owners returning home. This is a behavior trait that begins in the litter, when a mother dog stimulates her pups into "eliminating" on command by nudging their genital area. When the pups become old enough to see, all the mother has to do is give her pups a certain look and they pee or poop. Young dogs, therefore, come to associate authority figures with elimination, which is why they pee during greetings. (Uncle John has a similar relationship with the IRS.)

SOLUTION: Puppies grow out of this behavior naturally, but until then, you can lessen its occurrence by making your greetings as calm and non-authoritative as possible. Don't approach the puppy; let it come up to you. Avoid eye contact, speak softly or remain silent, and rub the puppy under the chin instead of stroking it on the head and back.

PROBLEM: Your dog engages in behavior it clearly understands is bad, just to get your attention.

EXPERTS SAY: A dog doesn't distinguish between good attention and bad attention the way humans do, so any action that gets attention, even if it makes the owner mad, is a good thing to the dog and will likely be repeated.

SOLUTION: To a dog, eye contact is a form of attention, so when your dog does something that annoys you, look away, leave the room, or cover your eyes with your hands until the dog stops the bad behavior; then resume eye contact and praise the dog's good behavior. Keep it up even if the dog increases the bad behavior for a time. All this means is your efforts are paying off.

NOTE: Unfamiliar dogs will also study your eyes. Don't stare—a dog will interpret this as a challenge and may become aggressive. It may even bite.

For more tips, turn to page 472.

LAST CONCERTS, PART II

On page 155, we told you the stories of the final
concerts of some of the greatest musical acts
in history. Here are a few more.

TALKING HEADS

Last Concert: The Waldorf-Astoria Hotel, New York City, March 18, 2002

What Happened: The Talking Heads stopped playing together in 1988 on less-than-friendly terms, and officially disbanded in 1991. Rumors of a reunion swirled in 1996, but eventually fizzled when frontman David Byrne said "no." The rumors returned in 2002...and this time they came true, when Byrne, bassist Tina Weymouth, drummer Chris Frantz, and guitarist Jerry Harrison took the stage at the Waldorf-Astoria Hotel in New York for the ceremony inducting them into the Rock and Roll Hall of Fame. They played just three songs: "Life During Wartime," "Psycho Killer," and "Burning Down the House," but it remains the last Talking Heads performance in history.

Coda: Rumors of another reunion surface every few years, but Byrne has always refused. "The only reason to get back together," he told Australia's *The Age* in 2005, "would be to do one of those 'sound like you used to sound' tours. And who wants to do that? I've already sounded like that once. And I don't need the money."

ROSEMARY CLOONEY

Last Concert: Honolulu, Hawaii, November 16, 2001

What Happened: In 2001 Clooney, a music and screen star since the 1950s, was diagnosed with lung cancer. That November she took a vacation in one of her favorite places, Hawaii, and while there agreed to perform with the Honolulu Symphony Pops. She did the show—sang, cracked jokes with the audience, told stories, and by all reports had a great time. And that was that. She returned to her home in Beverly Hills, where she died seven months later.

Coda: Nobody connected with Clooney knew it at the time, but

Parking lot: Automobiles take up about 24% of the total land area of Los Angeles.

the concerts had been recorded. The Honolulu Symphony Pops had been trying to get a record deal with orchestral specialists Concord Records for some time. Concord said they'd need to hear samples—so the Pops had been recording all their 2001 shows. That news eventually got to Clooney's longtime manager, Allen Sviridoff, he took the recording to Concord—and Rosemary Clooney's very last performance became her first live record in 45 years—*Rosemary Clooney: The Last Concert* (2002). "As it turns out, this show was one of the best performances Rosemary had done," Concord vice president John Burk said. "It was just one of those magical moments that came together. No one knew it would be her last show."

THE RAMONES

Last Concert: The Palace, Hollywood, California, August 6, 1996

What Happened: The groundbreaking punk rockers announced beforehand that the August 6 show at the Palace would be their last. They played 31 songs—nonstop—for 70 minutes. The show featured several special guests, including bassist Dee Dee Ramone, who'd left the band years earlier, and Pearl Jam's Eddie Vedder, who came onstage during the last song, wearing a rubber mask. He ripped it off in time to join in the final chorus on the final song, the Dave Clark 5's "Anyway You Want It."

Coda: Once inside the arena, every member of the audience was given a special numbered ticket reading, "Adios Amigos. Ramones. The 2263rd Show. Billboard Live. August 6, 1996." Only problem: The show was held at the Palace, not the Billboard Live club. It was *supposed* to be at the brand-new Billboard Live, but had to rescheduled at the last minute when the club was prevented from opening due to building code problems.

JOHNNY CASH

Last Concert: The Carter Ranch, Hiltons, Virginia, July 5, 2003

What Happened: A black Mercedes ambled up to a rustic old amphitheater on a hillside in rural Virginia. About 700 people were there, and they got the shock of their lives when Johnny Cash was helped out of the car and into a wheelchair. He'd been been in increasingly deteriorating health since being diagnosed

---

Whale oil was used as a lubricant in car transmissions as recently as 1973.

with a degenerative nerve disorder in 1997. Cash was rolled into the theater, and physically carried onto a chair on the stage. "Hi," he said, "I'm Johnny Cash." Backed by a small band, he played seven songs: "Folsom Prison Blues," "I Walk the Line," "Sunday Morning Coming Down," "Ring of Fire," "Angel Band," "Big River," and finished with one he said he hadn't sung in 25 years, "Understand Your Man." He was then carried back to his chair, rolled out to the car, and was gone.

Coda: Cash made the difficult trip to the old Carter family home in tribute to June Carter Cash, his wife of 40 years, who had died less than two months earlier. Cash himself wasn't far behind: He died three months later, on September 12.

THE POLICE

Last Concert: Madison Square Garden, New York City, August 7, 2008

What Happened: The Police broke up in 1984, but got back together briefly in 1986, played at Sting's wedding in 1992, and at their induction into the Rock and Roll Hall of Fame in 2003. Then in May 2007, after 21 years apart, the original three—Sting, Andy Summers, and Stewart Copeland—kicked off a worldwide 30th anniversary reunion tour. A whopping 151 shows later (and after grossing roughly $358 million), they finished off at Madison Square Garden on August 7, 2008. They started the final show with Cream's "Sunshine of Your Love," then brought up the New York City *Police* Department's band to help them on "Message in a Bottle" (the usual show opener), played 11 more of their biggest hits, and then left the stage. The crowd watched on the big screens as backstage Sting had his beard shaved off while getting a manicure and massage. The band then returned for a five-song encore, left again, and came back for the big finish, an amped-up version of "Next to You"—the very first song on their very first album, *Outlandos d'Amour* (1978).

Coda: As the Police left the stage for the last time, the "That's All Folks" Looney Tunes theme was played on the house speakers. As far as the chances of a reunion go—don't count on it. According to Sting: "There was no new energy on the tour. Who really wants to go and live with the wife you divorced? I won't do it again."

Gallup poll results: 49% of Americans don't know white bread is made from wheat.

THE STRANGE FATE OF BIG NOSE GEORGE

"Big Nose" George Parrot got his nickname from the fact that he had a very large proboscis, but his real claim to fame comes from something much stranger than a prodigious schnoz.

THE (NOT SO) GREAT TRAIN ROBBERY

In the late 1870s, a band of Wyoming outlaws called the Sim Jan gang decided to try their hand at robbing Union Pacific trains. Most banking was done by cash in the 19th century, and much of the cash moved by rail. This made trains very tempting targets for criminals looking for big scores.

Some gangs, the James-Younger and Hole-in-the-Wall gangs among them, became quite adept at train robbery. Sim Jan and his gang never did: When, for example, they tried to derail a train outside of Medicine Bow, Wyoming, by loosening a length of rail, a railroad crew on a handcart came by and discovered the damage to the track. After repairing the track, the crew sped off to report the incident to the sheriff, all in plain sight of the gang, who were hiding in bushes nearby. The next day the gang shot it out with the two lawmen sent to find them, Deputy Sheriff Robert Widdowfield and railroad detective Henry Vincent, killing them both. They were the first Wyoming lawmen killed in the line of duty.

FRONTIER JUSTICE

Frank Tole was the first member of the gang to pay for his crime; he was killed a few weeks later while trying to rob a stagecoach. Then came "Dutch" Charlie Burress, who was arrested for the murders and put on a train bound for Rawlins, Wyoming, where he would have gone on trial had he lived long enough to see a trial. He didn't: when his train made a stop in the town of Carbon, which was Deputy Widdowfield's hometown, an angry mob pulled him from the train and hanged him from a telegraph pole.

Next up for justice: "Big Nose" George Parrot. His turn might never have come at all, had he not gotten drunk in Montana two years after the killings and been overheard boasting of his involvement in the crimes. He, too, was arrested and put on a train bound for Rawlins; when the train pulled into Carbon, history seemed about to repeat itself, because once again a lynch mob was waiting. But Big Nose George managed to talk the mob out of the hanging by admitting guilt and promising to tell all if they let him live to face trial. Had he known what fate awaited him, he probably would have preferred being lynched.

DOPE ON A ROPE

Big Nose George lived long enough to be sentenced to death by hanging, to be carried out in 3½ months' time. But he *didn't* live long enough to see the sentence carried out, because when he nearly killed a guard trying break out of jail, the lynch mob decided that a speedier, *un*official hanging would do just fine. On March 22, 1881, a crowd of about 200 people dragged Big Nose George from the jail and hanged him from the crossarm of a telegraph pole.

Twice.

The mob had to hang him twice because the first rope broke. After a sturdier rope was found, Big Nose George, still very much alive, was hanged again. By now, however, George had managed to untie his hands from behind his back without anyone noticing. Then, when he was strung up the second time, he swung himself —*by the noose around his neck*—over to the telegraph pole, wrapped his flailing arms around it, and held on for dear life.

Big Nose George had no sympathizers in the crowd. The mob was happy to wait for gravity and muscle fatigue to finish the job. Over the next several minutes, he slowly lost his grip and died what must surely have been a slow and painful death.

(According to legend, George's namesake beak was so big that when he was finally cut down hours later and laid out in a coffin, the undertaker had trouble nailing down the lid because the dead man's nose was pressing up against it.)

AND NOW THE GRUESOME PART

When no next of kin arrived to claim the body, two local doctors, Dr. Thomas Maghee and Dr. John Osborne, claimed it in the name of medical science. Dr. Maghee had a personal interest in the case: His wife was criminally insane, the victim, it was thought, of head injuries sustained from falling from a horse.

Blueprints for the Eiffel Tower required a third of an acre of drafting paper.

Maghee wanted to examine Big Nose George's brain for any signs of abnormality that might explain his criminal behavior, then use what he learned to try and help his wife. With the assistance of Lillian Heath, his 15-year-old apprentice, he sawed off the top of the skull, removed the brain, and studied it, but found nothing unusual. Perhaps in a macabre gesture of thanks, he let Lillian keep the top of the skull as a souvenir.

NEXT OF (S)KIN

Dr. Maghee would probably have been better off examining Dr. Osborne's brain for signs of abnormality. Osborne's interest in Big Nose George was anything but scientific (he may have been motivated by revenge; according to one account, he was on one of the trains robbed by the Sim Jan gang and the delay caused him to miss a party). After making a plaster death mask of the deceased, a common practice at the time, Maghee removed the skin from Big Nose George's chest and thighs (but not his nose), and mailed the human flesh to a tannery in Denver, Colorado, where it was made into human "leather"—definitely *not* a common practice at the time. Osborne then had the leather made into a coin purse, a doctor's bag, and a pair of shoes.

Well, not the entire shoes. They were made from a combination of 1) leather taken from the shoes Big Nose George was wearing the day he died and 2) Big Nose George's own skin. If you're ever in the Carbon County Museum in Rawlins, where the shoes are on display to this day, you'll see that it's easy to tell where the ordinary cowhide ends and Big Nose George begins: Most of the shoes' leather is an ordinary dark brown, but the leather on the front of the shoes over the toes is much paler—the color of Big Nose George's own Caucasian hide.

Dr. Osborne loved to wear his Big Nose George shoes. He wore them while practicing as a country doctor, and when he diversified into ranching, banking, and politics in later years, he kept wearing them. When he was elected the first Democratic governor of Wyoming in 1892, in what some claimed was a stolen election, he wore the shoes to his inauguration—which must surely make him the only elected official in U.S. history to be sworn into office while wearing another man's skin.

Let's hope so, anyway.

Physician Amynthas of Alexandria performed the first known nose job in the 3rd century B.C.

WHERE'S THE REST OF ME?

The remainder of Big Nose George's remains did not fare much better: Drs. Maghee and Osborne kept them in a whiskey barrel filled with saltwater for about a year; then, when Dr. Maghee decided he'd learned everything he could (or Osborne decided one pair of shoes was enough), Maghee buried the barrel, with Big Nose George still in it, in the yard outside his medical office.

The remains, long since forgotten, were still there in 1950 when Dr. Maghee's office building was torn down and the site cleared for new construction. It was then that workmen found the whiskey barrel containing a human skeleton—a human skeleton with the top of its skull sawed off.

Luckily for the medical examiners called in to investigate, someone remembered that many years earlier a young woman named Lillian Heath had been presented the top of the skull of an outlaw named Big Nose George as a gift. She had gone on to become the first female doctor in the state; now in her eighties, she was still very much alive. She still had the top of the skull, too. Over the years she had used it as a pen holder and a doorstop; her husband had used it as an ashtray. When the skull top was brought to where the barrel had been found, it fit the rest of the skull perfectly. A DNA test later confirmed the match.

REST IN PIECES

Today, the lower portion of Big Nose George's skull is on display in the Carbon County Museum alongside "his" shoes, his death mask, and other related artifacts. But if you want to see the top of the skull, you have to go to Iowa—Dr. Heath held on to it for another decade or so, then donated it to the Union Pacific Museum in the city of Council Bluffs.

That leaves the coin purse and the doctor's bag, also made from Big Nose George's hide. They haven't been seen in ages. Who knows? Maybe they're still out there somewhere, waiting to be discovered, perhaps on a future episode of *Antiques Roadshow*. How about you—do you have an old, pale-leather coin purse or doctor's bag collecting dust in your attic?

They may tell a stranger tale than you realize.

Study result: People who smile in their high school yearbook photos live happier lives.

WORD ORIGINS

Ever wonder where everyday words come from?
Here are some more interesting stories.

ADULTERY

Meaning: The act of having sexual relations with someone other than a spouse

Origin: "You may be surprised to hear that there's no 'adult' in 'adultery.' That's because the word goes back to the Latin term *adulterare*, 'to pollute, corrupt, or defile.' (This in turn comes from *alterare*, 'to alter.') Having extramarital relations was seen as defiling—or adulterating—the marriage vows, and the verb eventually turned into the noun 'adultery.' 'Adult' traces back to the Latin *adultus*, a form of the verb *adolescere*, 'to grow up,' which was the source of the word 'adolescent.'" (From *The Complete Idiot's Guide to Weird Word Origins*, by Paul McFedries)

AVATAR

Meaning: An electronic image that represents a computer user

Origin: "From the Sanskrit *avatra*, meaning 'descent,' 'avatar' first appeared in English in 1784 to mean an incarnation or human appearance of a deity, particularly Vishnu. It entered the computer world via Randall Farmer and Chip Morningstar, who created the 1986 video game *Habitat*. Said Farmer: 'Chip came up with the word because back then, pre-Internet, you had to call a number on the telephone and then put the handset into the cradle of a modem. The avatar was the incarnation of a deity, the player, in the online world. We liked the idea of the puppet master controlling his puppet, but instead of using strings, he was using a telephone line.'" (From *The New York Times Magazine* "On Language," by Aaron Britt)

EUNUCH

Meaning: A castrated male; an ineffectual person

Origin: "'From the Greek *eunoukhos*, 'a castrated person employed to take charge of the women and act as chamberlain.' The Greek

---

Like cats, pigs also get hair balls...but they can't cough them up.

word is derived from *eune,* 'bed,' and *ekhein,* 'to keep.' For obvious reasons, a eunuch was ideally suited to guard the bedchamber of women." (From *Word Mysteries & Histories,* by the editors of the American Heritage dictionaries)

PUPPY
Meaning: A young dog
Origin: "Etymologically, a puppy is a 'toy' dog. The word was borrowed from Old French *popee,* meaning 'doll,' hence 'toy,' which went back via Vulgar Latin to *puppa* (source of English 'puppet'). The shift from 'toy dog' to 'young dog' happened at the end of the 16th century. (The Middle English word for 'puppy,' incidentally, was *whelp.*)" (From *Arcade Dictionary of Word Origins,* by John Ayto)

PLATONIC
Meaning: The description of a close relationship between two people—usually a man and a woman—that does not involve sex
Origin: "Named after Plato, the great Athenian philosopher (420–348 B.C.), to whom we owe almost all our knowledge of Socrates. In his *Symposium,* Plato lauds not the sexless love of a man for a woman but rather Socrates' love of young men, which was entirely without sexual implications." (From *Batty, Bloomers and Boycott,* by Rosie Boycott)

UNCANNY
Meaning: Weird, mysterious, strangely coincidental
Origin: "The word is Scottish in origin, and in the 16th century meant 'malicious.' In the 17th century, a meaning of 'careless' developed, this in turn coming to mean 'not safe to deal with' a century later. The last sense implies that the person who is uncanny is believed to have supernatural powers. The modern meaning evolved in the 19th century, and was particularly common from about 1850 on. All but the earliest sense above are still current." (From *Dunces, Gourmands and Petticoats,* by Adrian Room)

POT-TASTROPHES

Here's hoping that your next visit to the throne room doesn't land you in the emergency room like these folks. Here are some actual notes taken from real-life E.R. case files.

"Patient strained abdomen when lightning came through bathroom ceiling while patient was on toilet, causing patient to fall to floor."

"Fell in bathroom while sleep-walking."

"Cut hand: Patient in a public restroom urinating when his cell phone started to ring. He reached for it and struck right hand on a glass ashtray."

"Patient was fixing toilet and son slammed lid on patient's hand. Bruised right hand."

"Patient was at KFC, leaned over while sitting on toilet, toilet broke. Patient fell on floor, cutting left knee."

"Patient painting toenails sitting on toilet, fell, hitting head on floor."

"20-year-old male punched a porcelain toilet in the street. Laceration right hand."

"Spider bite to buttock. Patient saw spider on toilet."

"51-year-old male fell asleep on the toilet and fell off, hitting tile wall and trash can."

"Patient sat on the toilet for about 30 minutes and legs became numb. Could not move."

"Patient using restroom at Lowes, flushed toilet with foot, lost balance and fell. Dislocated kneecap."

"Right shoulder fracture. Using Port-a-Potti, wind blew it over."

"Patient caught web of hand (between thumb and forefinger) in toilet handle. Abscess right hand."

"Toilet in house flooded, ankle deep. Now ill. Gastroenteritis."

"Patient drank half a gallon of rum and took Xanax last evening; today while sitting on the toilet felt dizzy and fell off, bumping head."

"Patient sat on the end of a plunger left in toilet."

There are 40,000 toilet-related injuries annually in the U.S.

THE SUPER BOWL CAN KILL YOU

Do you think you have to play in the Super Bowl to be injured by all the action on game day? Think again. You may not be as safe as you think.

DYING TO WATCH THE GAME

In 2008 the *New England Journal of Medicine* published a German study of cardiac emergencies on the days Germany played in the 2006 World Cup soccer championships. The results were surprising: The number of cardiac emergencies among German men more than tripled, and the number among German women nearly doubled. The researchers attributed it to the excitement and stress of game day, and speculated that lack of sleep, overeating, overconsumption of alcohol, and excessive smoking, all common on game days, were contributing factors. Could the Super Bowl have a similar effect on American sports fans? Dr. Gerhard Steinbeck, one of the study's authors, thought so. "I know a little bit about the Super Bowl," he told reporters. "It's reasonable to think that something quite similar might happen."

L.A. STORIES

In 2009 researchers at the University of Southern California's Keck School of Medicine decided to find out. They studied a different, more gruesome statistic, that of death rates for Los Angeles county on Super Bowl Sunday during the two most recent years that Los Angeles sent a team to the big game: 1980, when the L.A. Rams lost to the Pittsburgh Steelers 31–19; and 1984, when the L.A. Raiders defeated the Washington Redskins 38–9. The researchers studied the death statistics for game day, and for two weeks after each game. They compared these figures to similar periods in 1980–83 and 1984–88, when Los Angeles didn't have a team in the Super Bowl, and to periods after the end of football season, when there were no games at all.

Their findings for 1980: "The Super Bowl-related days during L.A.'s losing game were associated with higher daily death rates in

L.A. County for all deaths, circulatory deaths, deaths from ischemic heart disease, and deaths from acute myocardial infarctions (heart attacks)."

That was for the year that the Rams lost the Super Bowl. What about 1984, when the Raiders won it? "By contrast," the study's authors write, "the Super Bowl-related days during the winning 1984 game were associated with a lower rate of all-cause death." In other words, when an L.A. team *won* the Super Bowl, the death rate in L.A. County not only didn't rise, it *dropped.*

AVOIDING MYTH-UNDERSTANDINGS

It would be easy to conclude from these findings that when a team loses the Super Bowl, fans die, and when it wins, fans gain a new lease on life, even if only for a couple of weeks. But there's another possibility: The critical factor in determining whether fans live or die may not be whether a team wins or loses, but rather how exciting or stressful the game is to watch.

The 1980 Super Bowl was one of the most dramatic in history, with the lead changing from one team to the other *seven* times, a record for the Super Bowl. The Rams were leading 19–17 at the end of the third quarter, but the Steelers scored two touchdowns in the fourth quarter to win the game. It was a stressful game to watch, no matter which side fans were on.

THE BORING BOWL

The 1984 Super Bowl, by comparison, was a blowout: The Raiders scored their first touchdown just five minutes into the game and built on their lead from there. An impressive win, but one with very little drama. (And besides, the Raiders only moved to Los Angeles in 1982, so the Southern California fans' emotional ties to the team weren't very strong to begin with.) The decline in death rates in L.A. County in 1984, therefore, may be attributable not so much to the victory, but rather to the lack of drama, plus the fact that so many people were safe at home watching the game on TV, instead of out and about where they'd be more likely to get into some kind of trouble. "In conclusion," the study's authors wrote, "the emotional stress of loss, *and/or* the intensity of a game played by a sports team in a highly publicized rivalry such as the Super Bowl, can trigger total and cardiovascular deaths."

PILING ON

These and other studies have found that people with a prior history of heart disease, or coronary risk factors like high cholesterol, high blood pressure, diabetes, or a history of smoking, are at greatest risk for experiencing cardiac problems during the Super Bowl. When you're under stress during the game, your body can release adrenaline and other hormones into your bloodstream. These, along with small proteins released by an overstimulated nervous system, can cause atherosclerotic plaques in diseased arteries to rupture, causing irregular heartbeats, heart attacks, and even death. The danger increases when at-risk fans gorge themselves on sugary and fatty foods, the staples of many a Super Bowl party, and wash it all down with too much beer.

SUPER BOWL BATHROOM DEFICIT DISORDER

But what if you don't have a history of heart problems or coronary risk factors? Can you watch the game without fear of ending up in the emergency room? Maybe not. There's another illness specifically associated with the biggest game of the year, and it has to do with the fact that Super Bowl commercials have become as popular as the game itself.

During ordinary football games, fans take advantage of the commercial breaks to go to the bathroom. During the Super Bowl, however, a lot of people want to see the commercials. They put off pit stops until their bladders become so full that the muscles they use to relieve themselves aren't strong enough to generate a urine stream. "Most of the time the commercials are the best part of the Super Bowl," says Dr. Jeff Kalina, associate director of emergency medicine at the Methodist Hospital in Houston, Texas. "We have seen people who have to come in and have a catheter put in to relieve themselves." The lesson here: *Go to the bathroom.*

*   *   *

"I stand up and a button falls off. I pick up my briefcase and the handle falls off. I'm afraid to go to the bathroom."
—Rodney Dangerfield

THE ONLY TIME...

Some things are so unique that they've only happened once.

...a book was arrested: Just before its scheduled publication in 1961, Russian author Vasily Grossman's government-critical book *Forever Flowing* was seized and actually arrested by the Soviet government. (It wasn't published until 1989, in censored form.)

...a band held the #1 spot on both the singles and albums charts in both the United States and England: In August 1964, the Beatles held the top spot on the American and British singles charts with "A Hard Day's Night." The band also topped the album charts in both countries with *A Hard Day's Night.*

...an American pro football team played a Canadian Football League team: On August 8, 1961, the Buffalo Bills played the Hamilton Tiger-Cats in Hamilton, Ontario. The Tiger-Cats won, 38–21.

...a disease was said to be completely eliminated: In 1980 the World Health Organization declared that smallpox had been eradicated worldwide (though laboratory samples still exist).

...a Congressman was killed on the job: In 1979 Rep. Leo Ryan (D-CA) flew to Guyana to investigate the activities of Jim Jones's Peoples Temple cult. He visited the cult's compound and offered to take anyone who wanted to go back to the U.S. At the airport, he was ambushed and shot by group members.

...one democracy declared war on another democracy: Great Britain declared war on Finland, a German ally, on December 6, 1941.

...the House of Representatives cancelled sessions: Severe weather has forced closure several times, but it's only been intentionally closed once: on October 24, 1877, so members could go to nearby Pimlico racetrack to watch a championship horse race.

...the U.S. government was debt-free: For a few months in 1835, during the presidency of Andrew Jackson, the federal government's debts were paid in full and it didn't owe any money to anyone.

Aw, horse spit! An adult horse produces 10 gallons of saliva every day.

FLAKES ON A PLANE

You think flying commercially is a pain for us nobodies? Imagine how difficult it was for these celebrities (whose private jets must have been at the shop) when they had to tough it out in the main cabin with the rest of us.

THE SOCIALITE

The day after Christmas 2009, a Delta Airlines flight was preparing to depart from Palm Beach, Florida, to New York. Sitting in first class was 60-year-old socialite Ivana Trump, famous for once being married to billionaire Donald Trump. She was already in a bad mood when she arrived (a few days earlier she'd divorced her fourth husband, 37-year-old Rossano Rubicondi, who'd been philandering in Europe). Making matters worse, Trump was upset with her seat assignment, a baby was crying, and a bunch of kids were running in the aisle. According to witnesses, Trump went ballistic on them, shouting, "Sit down you little f*ckers!" When nearby passengers told her to calm down, Trump swore at them, too. When flight attendants attempted to calm her down, she swore at them, too. She did the same thing to police as they cuffed her and removed her from the plane. No charges were filed, but the incident led to Trump losing her job as an advice columnist for the supermarket tabloid *Globe*.

THE DIRECTOR

Actor/director Kevin Smith made headlines in 2010 when he was kicked off a Southwest Airlines flight from Oakland to Burbank for being too fat to fit in one seat. Just before takeoff, a flight attendant told Smith, "Captain Leysath has deemed you a safety risk." Smith refused to deplane, pointing out that he could put both armrests down (a requirement for flying Southwest). The attendant held firm, and Smith begrudgingly went to the terminal and started typing angry messages for his 1.6 million Twitter followers to read: "Southwest Air, go f*** yourself. I broke no regulation, offered no 'safety risk' (was I gonna roll on a fellow passenger?)" Allowed on board a later Southwest flight, Smith took a picture of himself with his cheeks puffed out and posted it with this message: "Hey SouthwestAir! Look how fat I am on your

---

Burning wood in a fireplace can actually make it colder in the house.

plane! Quick! Throw me off!" After dozens more angry tweets from Smith (and a few YouTube videos), the airline responded on its blog. An excerpt: "Our pilots are responsible for the safety and comfort of all customers on the aircraft and therefore, made the determination that Mr. Smith needed more than one seat to complete his flight." So who had the last laugh? Smith: "Free Publicity! = 200 articles declaring I'm fat. Yay, me. Epic win!"

THE SINGER

Choosing style over comfort for an eight-hour flight from London to New York in February 2010, eccentric pop singer Lady Gaga wore a black-and-yellow striped dress made out of tightly wound police tape and matching 10-inch-high-heeled shoes. As the hours wore on, Gaga grew uncomfortable. A flight attendant advised her to remove the shoes, but Gaga refused. "I would rather die than have my fans not see me in a pair of high heels," she said. But when her legs started swelling up (a potentially fatal condition known as *deep vein thrombosis*), it took two flight attendants to remove the shoes and cut her out of the dress. Gaga changed into a black dress, furry boots, and a veil, which airport security asked her to remove (the veil, not the dress and boots) when she arrived in New York. She refused. After questioning, the cops let Gaga go.

THE SUPERMODEL VS. THE PILOT

While the plane was still on the tarmac at London's Heathrow Airport in 2008, British Airways captain Miles Sutherland took the unusual step of personally informing a passenger that one of her three bags had gone missing. That passenger was tantrum-prone supermodel Naomi Campbell. She cut Sutherland off mid-sentence and called someone on her mobile phone, saying, "They have lost my f***ing bag! Get me another flight! Get the press! Get my lawyer!" Sutherland tried to inform her of her options, but was again cut off: "How dare you tell me what my options are," she said. "You are not leaving until you find my f***ing bag!" (It contained her favorite pair of jeans.) Sutherland walked away while Campbell shouted, "You are a racist! You wouldn't be doing this if I was white!" When police came to get her, she spat at and kicked them. According to a witness, "Campbell was wearing formidable platform boots with stiletto-style heels." She was

---

The Fatburger fast-food chain sells "Hypocrites"—veggie burgers topped with bacon.

convicted of assaulting an officer and disorderly conduct, fined
£2,300 ($3,500) and ordered to perform 200 hours of community
service.

THE RAPPER VS. THE POLITICIAN

Former Massachusetts governor Mitt Romney and Grammy-nomi-
nated rapper Sky Blu (real name: Skyler Gordy, nephew of
Motown founder Berry Gordy) were on the same Air Canada
flight, returning to Los Angeles after attending the 2010 Winter
Olympics in Vancouver, British Columbia. While they were still
at the airport, Sky Blu reclined his seat back. Romney was sitting
behind him. The plane had pulled away from the gate and was
rolling toward the runway, which meant the seats were supposed
to be in the upright position. According to Sky Blu, Romney
sternly ordered him to put up his seat-back. Sky Blu ignored him.
Romney asked again, and then grabbed his shoulder in a "Vulcan
grip." Sky Blu stood up, turned around, and raised his fists. "I
didn't take it any further than that," he later told reporters. "The
man assaulted me. I was protecting myself." But according to a
spokesperson for Romney, the rapper actually took a swing at the
politician. Whether he did or not, Romney's wife screamed, the
flight crew intervened, and the plane returned to the gate, where
police took Sky Blu into custody. Romney didn't press charges;
Sky Blu was released and caught a later flight home. He later said
that if Romney had simply asked him nicely, he would have put
his seat-back up.

*   *   *

PARENTAL ADVISORY: DICK VAN DYKE

In October 2008, a technical glitch in Apple's iTunes Music Store
led to unintentional censorship of song titles without regard to
context. For example, Dick Van Dyke's novelty song "The Dick
Van Dyke Song" was listed as "The D**k Van D**e Song," and
Danny Kaye's "I Thought I Saw a Pussy Cat" became "I Thought I
Saw a P***y Cat." The errors occurred when Apple ran an internal check for explicit song titles...and the software automatically
censored the titles.

Sacramento Kings forward Lionel Simmons missed two games in 1991. Reason:...

BAD NEWS / GOOD NEWS

*More proof that not every cloud has
a silver lining...but some do.*

CALL ME

Bad News: One night in March 2010, Dan Oien, 62, began suffering seizures in his Indianapolis, Indiana, home. Oien, who had been fighting brain cancer for some time, tried to call for help. Unfortunately, he didn't have enough control of his muscles to dial the right number, and he accidentally called a local college student named Aquarius Arnolds. Arnolds didn't recognize the number on her caller ID—and she doesn't answer such calls.

Good News: *Normally* she doesn't answer such calls, but this time, for some reason, she did. "I couldn't understand anything the caller was saying," Arnolds said. "It seemed like he was in distress, so I just said, 'Do you need help?' and he belted out 'Yes.'" Arnolds quickly called 911 and gave them the caller's phone number. Minutes later paramedics busted down Oien's door and rushed him to a hospital. "He dialed one phone number, and it just happened to be the right person," said Sherry Proctor, Oien's girlfriend. "I thank God for that." She added that Arnolds's actions allowed the terminally ill man's out-of-town siblings to visit him before he passed away. (And Arnolds herself became a regular visitor to Oien's bedside in the months before he died.)

EASY STREET

Bad News: In the early 2000s, Tommy Larkin of Newfoundland, Canada, began looking for his younger brother; they had been adopted into different families when they were kids in the early 1980s. Unfortunately, despite years of trying, he'd had no luck and was close to resigning himself to the fact that he was never going to find his brother.

Good News: In 2010 Larkin, now 30 years old, got a call from the adoption agency that had been helping him. They'd found his brother. The woman at the agency, Larkin said later, gave him his brother's name—Stephen Goosney—"and asked four or five times

---

...tendinitis from playing too much Game Boy.

if I knew him. I said I didn't, and she kept asking me if I was sure I haven't met him." Why was she being so insistent? Because Goosney lived across the street from him. It turned out that the long-lost brothers had lived on the same street for more than two years and had lived across the street from each other for the previous seven months. Not only that, Stephen Goosney had been looking for *his* lost brother all that time, too. "It was a good feeling," Goosney told reporters, "knowing there was actually someone looking for me," adding that he and his newfound brother were now "just hanging out and trying to catch up."

SHOP AROUND

Bad News: For several years, social worker Dan Coyne did all his grocery shopping at the same Jewel-Osco store in Evanston, Illinois. And his favorite checkout clerk was Myra de la Vega. "Whenever I saw her working there I'd intentionally go to her line," Coyne, 52, told CNN, "because she's one of those rare employees that treats everybody with respect and kindness." One day de la Vega, 57, didn't look so good. Coyne asked her what was wrong, and she told him that she'd been diagnosed with renal failure, which required her to undergo nearly eight hours of dialysis every night. She needed a kidney transplant but couldn't find a donor. Not even her own sister was the right blood match.

Good News: Coyne went home and talked to his wife about it and, a few days later, offered de la Vega one of his kidneys. She was understandably shocked—she only knew Coyne from the store. But Coyne was serious. He got tested and—against 4,000-to-1 odds—was a perfect match. Finally, two years after Coyne made his offer, on March 26, 2010, he and de la Vega walked together into Northwestern Memorial Hospital's Kovlar Organ Transplantation Center in Chicago. Several hours later, Coyne's favorite checkout clerk had one of his kidneys. "It was an easy decision," Coyne said. "All I have to do is fall asleep on a table, and then the doctors take over." De la Vega was, of course, a bit more impressed. "I think he is an angel living on Earth," she said. "You can say I'm corny but that's how I regard him." Both patients made full recoveries—and de la Vega is no longer on dialysis.

HOW TO HYPNOTIZE A CHICKEN

When Uncle John learned that it was possible to do this, his first thought was, "Why would anyone want to hypnotize a chicken?" Good question. As Sir Edmund Hillary would say, "because it's there." (And it's a lot easier than climbing Mt. Everest.)

YOUR CHICKEN IS GETTING SLEEPY...

It wasn't very long ago that most Americans lived on farms, and lots of people knew how to hypnotize chickens. Not anymore—how many people can say they know *anything* about chickens, let alone how to hypnotize one? But if you ever get a chance to place a chicken under your spell, give it a try—it's fascinating to watch, harmless and painless for the chicken, and it provides an interesting insight into animal intelligence and behavior. (Who knows—you might even win a bar bet.)

STEP BY STEP

1. Techniques vary widely from place to place. Some methods call for laying the chicken gently on its side, with one wing under its body, holding it in place with one hand so that your other hand is free. Others say that turning the chicken upside down, lying on its back with its feet up in the air, is best. Either way, the disoriented bird will need a second to regain its bearings, but once it does it will not be bothered by being in this unfamiliar position.

2. Some hypnotists advocate placing a finger on the ground at the tip of the chicken's beak and drawing a line four inches long in the dirt extending out from the beak and parallel to it (picture Pinocchio's nose growing). Trace your finger back and forth along the line for several seconds. Other practitioners say that drawing a circle, not lines, in the dirt around the chicken's head works best. Still others say all you need to do is stroke the chicken on its head and neck with your index finger. If one method doesn't seem to work, try another.

3. Whichever method you try, keep at it for several seconds.

That's about how long it takes for a chicken to go into a trance. Its breathing and heart rate will slow considerably, and its body temperature may even drop a few degrees.

4. You can now let go of the chicken. It will lie perfectly still in a trancelike state for several seconds, several minutes, or even an hour or more before it comes out of the trance on its own. You can also awaken the chicken yourself by clapping your hands or nudging it gently. (The unofficial world record for a chicken trance: 3 hours, 47 minutes.)

5. If holding a chicken in one hand while hypnotizing it with the other proves too difficult, another technique calls for putting the chicken in the same position it goes into when it's asleep—with its head under one wing—and rocking it gently to induce a trance.

CHICKEN SCIENCE

Just as there are different theories as to which method of chicken hypnotism is best, so too are opinions divided as to what exactly is going on with the chicken when it is being hypnotized:

• The trance could be a panic "freeze" response, similar to a deer stopping in the middle of the road when it sees headlights.

• It may also be an example of *tonic immobility*, a reflex similar to an opossum's ability to go into a trancelike state when it feels threatened. Chickens roost in the branches of trees or other high places at night; the trance reflex, if that is indeed what it is, may help the chicken to remain perfectly still, silent, and (hopefully) unnoticed as foxes, raccoons, and other predators prowl below.

*　　*　　*

SPORTS MEDICINE

"In a development that could one day score a touchdown for better health, chemists in Australia have created a 'Super Bowl' molecule that shows promise for precision drug delivery. Shaped like a miniature football stadium, the molecule is capable of delivering a wide range of drugs—from painkillers to chemotherapy cocktails —to specific areas of the body, potentially resulting in improved treatment outcomes and perhaps saving lives."

—*Journal of the American Chemical Society*, January 2005

A normal breath takes five seconds: two to inhale, three to exhale.

ESPERANTO, PARTO TRI

So why isn't this chapter written in Esperanto instead of English?
Because while Esperanto has its fans, it never really caught on
as an international language. Why not? Here's Part III
of our story. (Part II is on page 296.)

HERE, THERE, CIULOKE

By 1905 Esperanto had become a worldwide movement, with speakers on every continent except Antarctica. Speakers had 27 different Esperanto-language magazines to choose from and thousands of books to read, many of them original works of Esperanto literature. More of the world's great works of literature were translated into Esperanto every year.

1905 was also the year that the Esperanto movement held its first World Congress, in Boulogne-sur-Mer, France. With the exception of the World War I and World War II years, a congress has been held every year since. The single most important piece of business ever conducted by the Esperantists was transacted at that very first conference in Boulogne: They voted to establish Zamenhof's early works, known collectively as *Fundamento de Esperanto,* as the permanent and immutable basis of the Esperanto language. This "Declaration of Boulogne" remains in force to this day.

WIN SOME, LOSE SOME

The Declaration of Boulogne spared Esperanto from the fate that had befallen Volapük and other constructed languages: With the basis of Esperanto set in stone, the movement would never splinter into a hundred different factions, each believing its own version of Esperanto was best.

But the Declaration of Boulogne also set the Esperanto movement on a collision course with the Delegation for the Adoption of an International Language, which was still trying to pick a single international auxiliary language. The advantages of adopting Esperanto were obvious—it was the most successful constructed language in history, it already had an established base of tens of thousands of speakers all over the world, and it was growing rapidly.

A pitched baseball slows by about 8 mph by the time it reaches home plate.

But Esperanto was the language of linguistic *amateurs*, as far as the French intellectuals at the Delegation were concerned. It was still burdened with Zamenhof's silly diacritical alphabet, and it still had no word for "mother" other than "father-feminine-noun." To the Delegation, Esperanto wasn't so much a language as it was a scandal, one popular with—gasp!—*ordinary* people. The Delegation refused to endorse it.

ESPERANTO JR.

Not *as is*, anyway. Esperanto wasn't going to change—the Declaration of Boulogne made that clear. But the language did have much about it that was desirable, so in the end, the Delegation decided to build a new language out of Esperanto by fixing or getting rid of everything they hated about it. They called their new language *Ido*—Esperanto for "Offspring"—and in 1907, they proclaimed it the world's new international auxiliary language. They probably assumed that the great unwashed Esperanto masses would see the error of their ways and come over to Ido, which was close enough to Esperanto to make it easy for them to switch.

They were wrong. Ido flopped: Though many university professors and other high-profile leaders in the Esperanto movement defected to Ido, the overwhelming majority of rank-and-file Esperantists stayed put. They had no interest in a language without a culture, even if the eggheads thought Ido was better.

And just as Zamenhof had feared would happen to Esperanto, once Ido opened its own door to tinkering, it was doomed. One reformer after another split off from Ido to create their own "improved" version of the language, each of them sapping Ido's strength without any of them catching on. Only an estimated 2,000-5,000 people speak Ido today, and if it weren't so similar to Esperanto, the number of speakers would likely be smaller still.

WAR AND PEACE

Esperanto's best chance for becoming a truly universal language came in the early 1920s, following the end of World War I. An estimated nine million solders died in the war—*far* more than had died in all the wars fought in the previous 100 years—and six million civilians were killed as well. (Zamenhof himself died of natural causes in April 1917, at the age of 57.)

First white man scalped by Indians: Simón Rodriguez, in what is now Florida, in 1540.

The astonishing scale of the carnage helped to reignite interest in establishing an international language as a tool for peace. Attempts were made to win official support for Esperanto at the League of Nations, which, had they succeeded, might have led to Esperanto being made a part of elementary and high-school curricula worldwide. But France and other countries saw Esperanto as a threat to their own national languages, and they withheld all but token support for it.

THE ENEMY WITHIN...AND WITHOUT

The League of Nations was set up to prevent a repeat of World War I. It failed, of course. After World War II ended in 1945, yet another attempt was made to promote Esperanto as an international language with the United Nations, the successor to the League of Nations. The leaders of the postwar Esperanto movement made repeated attempts to tone down the eccentrics among the Esperantist community, at least when they were out among the general public. These efforts were not particularly successful, but it didn't really matter. The real challenge that Esperanto faced in the postwar era wasn't its own eccentricities: It was English.

ESPERINGLISH

By the end of World War II, English was well on its way to becoming the new international language. It, not Esperanto, had become a mandatory part of the educational curriculum in schools all over the world. Numerous attempts were made to boil English down to a more simplified or "controlled" form that non-native speakers could adopt as a first step to learning the full language.

In 1959, for example, the U.S. Government's Voice of America foreign broadcasting service inaugurated broadcasts in what it called "Special English" that used a limited vocabulary of about 1,500 words, simplified grammar, and a slow, careful delivery to make broadcasts targeted at non-native speakers easier to understand. Making English simpler—more like Esperanto, in other words—has proven a lot more effective than trying to teach the whole world to speak Esperanto.

ESPERANTO TODAY

When L. L. Zamenhof introduced Esperanto in 1887, he included in *Unua Libro* a printed pledge form that the reader could tear out, sign, and send in—a commitment to learn Esperanto if 10 million other people made the pledge. Each book contained four copies of the pledge, so that the reader's family and friends could also sign up.

Esperanto has been around for more than a 120 years now, and in all that time it's doubtful that 10 million people ever learned to speak it. It never did become a universal language. It didn't end violence. It didn't prevent World War I or World War II. It didn't save the world. It didn't even save Zamenhof's own children: All three were killed in the Holocaust, singled out for murder by the Nazis, who viewed Esperanto as a tool of the international Jewish conspiracy. (Zamenhof's grandson Louis did narrowly escape; as of 2008, Louis, alive and well at age 83, was still attending the annual Esperanto World Conferences.)

Esperanto has never been endorsed as an official language of any country anywhere on Earth. In 1908 the tiny one-square-mile territory of Neutral Moresnet, consisting only of one village and a zinc mine in what is now eastern Belgium, tried to adopt Esperanto as its "national" language. That effort failed too.

STILL KICKING

But Zamenhof also placed great importance on the values and culture that grew up around his language. The *language* may never have fulfilled the high hopes that Zamenhof had for it, but Esperanto *culture*, though small, is still alive, its proponents still communicating in an artificial language invented by a schoolboy more than a century ago. Esperanto remains the most successful constructed language in history: Estimates vary as to how many people speak it today; the number could be anywhere from 100,000 to more than 2 million people in 80 countries around the world. The Internet has made learning it even easier, and has helped aspiring Esperantists to meet and get involved with each other. Esperanto will never replace English as an international language, but considering how long it's been around, it's likely to be around for a long time to come.

Templar Motor Co.'s 1919 roadster offered an odd option: a Kodak camera mounted on the exterior.

LET'S SPEAK ESPERANTO

Thinking of joining an Esperanto group near you? Bone!
Here's a list of phrases to get you started. (For the
origin of Esperanto, go to page 195.)

Saluton! "Hello!"
- **Mi volas iri al la kavoj.** "I would like to go to the caves."

- **Kioma estas la horo?** "What time is it?"

- **Kiel vi fartas?** "How are you?"

- **Bone, dankon, kaj kiel fartas via edzino?** "Fine, thanks, and how is your wife?"

- **Mi ne komprenas.** "I don't understand."

- **Kiel vi povas fari tion al mi?** "How could you do it to me?"

- **Ni devas rapidumi.** "We're in a hurry."

- **Kafon kun sukero kaj lakto-polvoro, mi petas?** "May I have coffee with sugar and non-dairy creamer?"

- **Kiu diris tion?** "Who told you that?"

- **Mi iras al florejo.** "I'm going to the florist."

- **Mankas varma akvo.** "There is no hot water."

- **Konsentite:** "It's a deal!"

- **Lasu min trankvile!** "Leave me alone!"

- **Pardonu.** "Excuse me."

- **Mi bezonas keksojn.** "I need cookies."

- **Jen** (passing the cookies): "Here you are."

- **Ne faru tion.** "Don't do that."

- **Kion vi faris?** "What did you do?"

- **Kion vi diris?** "What did you say?"

- **Mi amas vin!** "I love you!"

- **Ripetu, bonvole.** "Please repeat."

- **Mi estas okupata.** "I'm busy."

- **Bonvolu ne fumi, mi petas.** "Could you please not smoke?"

- **Mi ne fumas.** "I don't smoke."

- **Sanon!** "Gesundheit!"

- **Voku la policon!** "Call the police!"

Why were treadmills invented? So that prison inmates could use them to grind grain.

- **Ni dancu.** "Let's dance."

- **Kio estas la problemo?** "What's the matter?"

- **Mi estas edzino** (female): "I'm married."

- **Kiel oni diras tion en Esperanto?** "How do you say that in Esperanto?"

- **Mi havas kapdoloron.** "I have a headache."

- **Mi estas de Usono.** "I'm from the U.S."

- **Ne gravas.** "Never mind."

- **Kie estas mia mono?** "Where is my money?"

- **Mi soifas.** "I'm thirsty."

- **Mi devas pisi.** "I need to pee."

- **Vi estas freneza!** "You're crazy!"

- **Irlandan viskion kun glacio, mi petas.** "Irish whiskey on the rocks, please."

- **Mi preferas legomojn.** "I prefer vegetables."

- **Hola, Moe!** "Hey, Moe!"

- **Certe!** "Soitenly!"

- **Kie mi estas?** "Where am I?"

- **Multan dankon.** "Thank you very much."

- **Ne dankinde.** "You're welcome."

* * *

KNOW YOUR LANDS

Archipelago: a chain of islands grouped or clustered close to each other.

Isthmus: a narrow stretch of land that connects two large landmasses, and with water on either side. The Isthmus of Panama, for example, connects North America to South America and is bordered by the Pacific Ocean and Caribbean Sea.

Atoll: an island in an ocean or sea that was formed out of a ring of coral.

Mesa: generally occurring in dry areas (like a desert), it's a raised area of flat land atop steep walls. If it's a vast, miles-spanning area, it's a **plateau.** If it has a pointed top or summit instead of a flat top, it's a **butte.**

Cape: a piece of land that juts out into a water body.

COMPLAINTS DEPT.

Just a page of people whining about this and that.

"Insincere people compliment you, but they don't mean it. The worst was Ray Charles. He said he liked my dress."
—**Joan Rivers**

"The Pope is single, too. You don't hear people saying *he* has commitment problems."
—**Garry Shandling**

"You want me to *be* great, but you don't ever want me to *say* I'm great."
—**Kanye West**

"Girls scream for Edward, not Robert. I still can't get a date."
—**Robert Pattinson, who played Edward in *Twilight***

"I can't stand when people say, 'Don't hate me because I'm beautiful.' OK, how about I hate you because you said that?"
—**Tia Carrere**

"Sometimes I'm so sweet even I can't stand it."
—**Julie Andrews**

"Moses dragged us through the desert to the one place in the Middle East where there's no oil."
—**Golda Meir**

"Abstract art? A product of the untalented, sold by the unprincipled to the utterly bewildered."
—**Al Capp**

"There's no such thing as soy milk. It's soy juice."
—**Lewis Black**

"Just standing around looking beautiful is so boring, really boring, so boring."
—**Michelle Pfeiffer**

"You know why the French hate us? Thay gave us the croissant. And you know what we did with it? We turned it into a croissandwich."
—**Denis Leary**

"It is clearly stated in Article 5 of the U.N. Universal Declaration of Human Rights that 'No one shall be subjected to torture or to cruel, inhuman or degrading punishment.'"
—**Lindsay Lohan, on being sentenced to 90 days in jail**

"The people who live in a golden age usually go around complaining how yellow everything looks."
—**Randall Jarrell**

The photographic effect called "red-eye" is most visible in people with blue eyes.

THE WORST MOVIE OF ALL TIME?

If you're a fan of cheesy films like Manos: The Hands of Fate, Plan 9 from Outer Space, *and* Troll 2, *you'll love this one. Uncle John saw it last year when our local Bad Film Society screened it, and as he was watching, it occurred to him that it actually gave new meaning to the word "bad."* *(But somehow he couldn't stop talking about how great it was.)*

THE SIX MILLION DOLLAR MAN

In June 2003, a film called *The Room* premiered in a handful of Los Angeles theaters. It's the story of a love triangle between Johnny, a banker; Lisa, his girlfriend; and Johnny's best friend Mark. The film was the brainchild of Tommy Wiseau, the actor who plays Johnny. Wiseau also wrote, directed, produced, and distributed the film. He financed *The Room*, too, shelling out $6 million of his own money to make it, plus thousands more on print and TV ads and a single giant billboard overlooking busy Highland Avenue in Los Angeles.

The Room was Wiseau's first feature film. He hoped to use it to launch a Hollywood career...but all he succeeded in doing was blowing $6 million in record time. *The Room* played to nearly empty theaters for just two weeks before it was yanked from the screen; in that time it grossed only $1,900, not enough to cover even one month's rent on the Highland Avenue billboard. Put another way, for every million Wiseau spent, *The Room* earned less than $320, making it one of the worst box-office flops in history.

CITIZEN PAIN

Is there anything about *The Room* that isn't bad? The acting is stunningly incompetent—none of the actors had ever had a major film role before, and Wiseau was incapable of providing decent direction. And the love scene between Johnny and Lisa is *creepy* (picture a Troll doll having its way with a seat cushion, except that Lisa is the cushion). Wiseau recycles the footage in a *second* love scene 20 minutes after the first, so you get to watch it twice.

As a screenwriter, Wiseau was even worse. New characters

appear out of nowhere and aren't properly identified, so it's never clear who they are. A number of subplots—such as drug abuse, unrequited love, and bad real estate deals—are introduced, then quickly abandoned. ("I got the results of the test back. I definitely have breast cancer," Lisa's mother tells her, and the subject never comes up again.) And though the thickly-accented Wiseau refuses to this day to say where he comes from, English is clearly not his first language. *The Room* is full of clunky, confusing, and unintentionally funny dialog: When a (never-identified) character catches Lisa and Mark kissing at Johnny's birthday party and confronts them, Mark yells, "Leave your stupid comments in your pocket!"

PATRON ZERO

The movie likely would have died a quick and unmourned death had an aspiring young screenwriter named Michael Rousselet not happened to see the film near the end of its two-week theatrical run. As Rousselet sat alone in the empty theater, he was stunned by what he saw—bad lighting, out-of-focus scenes, dubbed dialog out of sync with the lip movements onscreen, poorly designed sets (it's never clear which room is *the room*, or why the room is so important), one wooden, sophomoric acting performance after another, and much, much more. Whenever Rousselet thought *The Room* had given all that it had to give, it would cough up some wonderful new chunk of mediocrity and incompetence for him to savor. It was unlike any film he'd ever seen. Sure that such a flop would never make it onto DVD, Rousselet sat in the empty theater (while the movie was still running) and called everyone he could think of on his cell phone, telling them they *had* to see *The Room* for themselves before it vanished forever.

MISERY LOVES COMPANY

That theater didn't stay empty for long. Though *The Room* died at every other venue where it was shown, Rousselet's promotional work paid off at this one. A small crowd of friends joined him at the next showing, and as these people phoned *their* friends, the numbers grew steadily at each remaining screening. "We saw it four times in three days, and on the last day I had over 100 people there," he told *Entertainment Weekly* in 2008.

By the time *The Room* ended its theatrical run, a small but

The Romans had heated swimming pools as far back as 1 B.C.

dedicated fan base had already begun e-mailing Wiseau to thank him for his efforts and ask him to screen the film again. Wiseau received dozens more e-mails in the months that followed, and in June 2004 he booked a small theater in West Hollywood for a single midnight screening. That event was a hit—so many people turned out to see the film that Wiseau booked another midnight showing a month later, then another, and then another.

As the crowds continued to grow like lookie-loos at a traffic accident, he expanded to two screens at the multiplex, then three, then four, and then five. Strong word of mouth among a steadily growing fan base of "Roomies," as they call themselves, led Wiseau to schedule screenings in cities up and down the West Coast, then in other parts of United States and Canada, and eventually in Great Britain. And with foreign-language editions reportedly in the works, *The Room* may soon have fans all over the world.

SPOONING

Have you ever been to a showing of the 1975 film *The Rocky Horror Picture Show*? As was the case with that cult film, *The Room*'s fans have created audience participation rituals all their own. Roomies attend screenings dressed as their favorite characters, shout out their favorite bad lines at the appropriate moments, yell "FOCUS!" during blurry scenes, march out "in protest" during the troll doll/seat cushion love scenes, and throw plastic spoons whenever the spoon photograph in Johnny's apartment appears. There's no question that the Roomies are there to laugh at Wiseau and his masterpiece, but he says he doesn't mind. "As long as they laugh or enjoy themselves, I enjoy with them," he says.

NO ROOM AT *THE ROOM*

If you're ever in L.A. on the last Saturday of the month, go see *The Room*. Buy your tickets early—even when the film is being shown on five screens, *The Room* sells out quickly, especially when Wiseau or other stars appear in person. Wisseau's fabulous flop has been reborn as the hottest cult film phenomenon in decades, and at an estimated gross of more than $1,000 per screening, *The Room* is on track to break even sometime in the year 2504, maybe sooner if you consider the profits from *The Room* T-shirts, CDs, DVDs, movie posters, and talking Johnny bobblehead dolls.

MODERN WORDS...NOT!

Here are a few terms that you might think were recent additions to English, but have actually been in the language for quite some time.

POLITICALLY CORRECT: Dates back to a 1793 U.S. Supreme Court decision in *Chisholm v. Georgia*. Justice James Wilson wrote that the people, not the states, held the real power in the country: "To 'The United States' instead of to the 'People of the United States' is the toast given. This is not politically correct."

SMASH HIT: The entertainment trade magazine *Variety* began using this accolade to describe a successful movie in the 1920s.

SPORK: The term for a spoon/fork has been around since at least 1909, when it appeared as an entry in the *Century Dictionary*. The utensil itself has been in use since the mid-1800s.

BUNK: This word for "empty talk" or "nonsense" originated in 1820 when Congressman Felix Walker, who was from Buncombe, North Carolina, talked at length about whether Missouri should be admitted to the Union as a free state or a slave state. Politicians subsequently adopted the phrase "talking from Buncombe." That was shortened to "bunkum" and finally to "bunk" by humorist George Ade, who wrote in his 1900 book *More Fables*, "History is more or less bunk."

TRUTHINESS: Popularized by satirist Stephen Colbert in 2005, it's been listed in the *Oxford English Dictionary* since 1824 as an alternate form of "truthfulness." When told that it was already a word, Colbert retorted, "You don't look up 'truthiness' in a book, you look it up in your gut!"

NOT!: Loudly proclaiming "Not!" at the end of an assertion to negate that assertion was popularized in the late 1980s in *Saturday Night Live*'s "Wayne's World" sketches, but the joke first gained popularity in the early 1900s by, among others, humorist Ellis Parker Butler, who wrote in *Pig is Pigs* (1905), "Cert'nly, me dear friend Flannery. Delighted! *Not!*"

Today 15% of U.S. workers belong to unions, down from over 40% in the 1950s.

THE LOST EXPLORERS: LUDWIG LEICHHARDT

The third installment in Uncle John's look at explorers who should have known better than to "boldly go where no one has gone before."

CRAZY LUDWIG

The Australian Outback is one of the harshest environments on Earth—a sun-blasted wasteland stretching thousands of miles across the continent. That made it one of the great exploration challenges of the 19th century, and the lure of being the first white man to cross the Outback drew adventurers from around the globe. Among them was a quirky German scientist named Ludwig Leichhardt. He came to Australia in 1842 to study the peculiar animals and rock formations of this strange new world, but quickly shifted his focus to exploring the uncharted interior. Leichhardt's first expedition barely got off the ground—the arrogant, socially awkward Prussian had difficulty finding backers and he spoke little English. Furthermore, he knew nothing about the bush or how to plan an expedition, and didn't care to learn. He just went.

LUCKY LUDWIG

If some people are just born lucky, Ludwig Leichhardt was one of them. On his first expedition, in 1842, the 29-year-old explorer made his way along 1,500 miles of desert following the northeast coast, filled in some blank spaces on the map, wrote a book about it, and became an overnight sensation. London's Royal Geographical Society even awarded him a medal. Suddenly the doors to wealthy patrons (and their checkbooks) flew open. Success fueled his ambition, and Leichhardt set his sights on becoming the first European to cross the continent. Many had tried; none had succeeded—yet. On Leichhardt's first attempt, in 1846, he set out with a small contingent from Brisbane, on the continent's east-central coast, for Perth, on the west—a distance of about 2,800 miles. They'd traveled about 500 miles before torrential rain, hunger, and malaria sent them limping back to Brisbane. In March 1848, Leichhardt assembled a new team—this time of five European men, two Aboriginal guides, seven horses, 20 mules, and fifty bulls—and again headed west into the interior. He never made it.

LOST BUT NOT FORGOTTEN LUDWIG

Australian authorities waited almost four years before sending out a rescue party. They found no trace of Leichhardt's expedition except for one curious bit of evidence at a campsite: a tree with an "L" carved into its trunk above the letters "XVA." In 1868 another search party was sent out, but aside from finding a few more trees marked with a carved "L," it too came up with nothing. Leichhardt's case was labeled "Unsolved" and stayed that way for the next 138 years. Then in 2006, a small brass nameplate found in a box of memorabilia in the back room of a district office in the Western Territories was determined to have belonged to Leichhardt. An aborigine stockman had discovered the plate 100 years earlier, but a local clerk had filed it away and forgotten about it. Tracing the story back to its source, investigators found that the nameplate had been pulled from the stock of a badly burned rifle found hanging from the trunk of a baobab tree with an "L" carved into its trunk. The tree was located between the Tanami and Great Sandy deserts, almost two thirds of the way along Leichhardt's planned route. "We still don't know how much further he got," says Matthew Higgins of the National Museum of Australia, where the nameplate is now on display, "but at least we know he got that far, and that's a massive achievement for a European at the time."

*   *   *

A MOUSE JOKE

The Mouse family was making their way across the kitchen floor when the family cat rushed toward them. Daddy Mouse yelled, "BOW-WOW!" And the cat ran away. "That," said Daddy Mouse to his kids, "is why it's important to learn a second language."

WEIRD FISH STORIES

Read one and you'll be hooked.

THAT BITES. Brian Guest, 51, of Perth, Australia, was a longtime and controversial advocate for the protection of sharks. In December 2008, he was snorkeling at a beach not far from his home…when he was attacked and killed by a shark. Guest's son Daniel, 24, said the attack was a random event, and that it shouldn't make people afraid of sharks.

SHAD SHAM. Every April the town of Grifton, North Carolina, holds the Grifton Shad Festival in honor of the Atlantic shad, a herringlike fish that migrates through the state's coastal waters each spring. The festival includes a "Shad Parade," a 5K "Spring Shad Run," a "Shad Shack" that sells shad-based souvenirs, and, of course, a fish fry. Only problem: The Grifton Shad Festival fish fry has no shad. The fish's numbers have dropped so drastically due to overfishing in recent decades that festival organizers removed it from the menu. They serve catfish instead. "They don't eat mules at the mule festival," explained festival secretary Janet Haseley. (The Benson Mule Days festival takes place in nearby Benson, North Carolina, every September.)

THE COST OF FREEDOM. In 2006 animal activists broke into a fish farm near the town of Oban, Scotland, and opened its huge underwater cages, freeing 15,000 halibut. Over the next few weeks thousands of the "freed" fish washed up dead on nearby beaches. Biologists said that because the fish had been raised on commercial pellet feed, they didn't know how to find food in the wild.

HEADS UP! In April 2010 a man was leaving a restaurant parking lot in Melbourne, Florida, when a fish fell from the sky and landed on his windshield. Seeing that the fish was still alive, he picked it up, ran back into the restaurant—and dropped it in their large aquarium. The fish had the odd fortune to have fallen from the sky right in front of Chameleon's…a sushi restaurant. Workers there said the fish, which is believed to have fallen from the talons of an osprey, would not be eaten, as it was a "lucky fish." (They also said it had a "dent" in its head from the fall.)

Late bloomer: Mae West was over 40 when she began her acting career.

POP-CULTURE ALPHABET

*One day Uncle John saw the movie Z on TV, and during
an ad starring Mr. T, he wondered what other pop-
culture things were known by just a single letter?
Here's a look at pop culture...from A to Z.*

A The title of a 1980 album by the British rock band Jethro
Tull. The group's 13th overall, it was intended to be a solo
release by lead singer/flautist Ian Anderson (A is for Anderson),
but Chrysalis Records thought it would sell better if it was billed
to the whole of Jethro Tull. It didn't work—A was the group's lowest selling album in a decade and marked the beginning of the
band's decline in popularity.

B -list. A movie industry and entertainment term that means
"second-rate." The A-list comprises the biggest, most successful, most popular stars of the moment—currently box-office draws
like Sandra Bullock and Will Smith. B-listers are well-liked but
not quite the theater-fillers of their A-list counterparts—someone
like Steven Seagal, Ashton Kutcher, or Megan Fox. This is all
purely subjective, and unofficial, but such status is taken very seriously in Hollywood. That means it can be mocked, too: Stand-up
comedian and former sitcom star Kathy Griffin self-effacingly
titled her reality show *Kathy Griffin: My Life on the D-List.*

C One of the major computer programming languages, first
developed in the 1970s at Bell Labs. It's not used much today,
but its successor, the language C++, is one of the most widely used
of all time.

D This interactive, horror-themed puzzle video game for the Sony
PlayStation went on sale in 1995. The player controls a
character named Laura, whose father has gone on a killing spree.
Laura gets stuck in an alternate reality as she attempts to find clues
and solve puzzles that will help her understand why her father did
what he did. Ultimately, Laura discovers that she and her father
are vampires—direct descendants of Dracula (that's where the
game gets its cryptic title). D was one of the first home video
games to feature full-motion live-action video as part of game play.

$127 billion per year of Italy's GDP (about 7%) is attributed to organized crime.

E The stage name of experimental rock musician Mark Everett, who released two albums: *A Man Called E* (1992) and *Broken Toy Shop* (1993). When he formed a band in 1996, he extended his stage name slightly, to Eels, which became a popular alternative rock group with the hits "Novocaine for the Soul" and "Last Stop, This Town." One benefit of picking the name Eels, according to E: Eels albums directly follow the E albums in record-store bins.

F-1 Also known as Formula One, an auto racing circuit. Most teams are based in Europe, where it's one of the most popular spectator sports, second only to soccer. Each major race is called a Grand Prix and is held on specially built courses, or sometimes on public roads (unlike American NASCAR or IndyCar). Each car contains one seat and is individually built, often by sports car producers. Top speed of a typical F-1 car: over 200 mph.

G. A novel by British writer and art critic John Berger about a sex-obsessed lothario who becomes politically aware and involved as Europe plunges into World War I. G. won the 1972 Booker Prize, England's national book award.

H An absurdist French sitcom (1998–2002) set in a hospital. (It was very similar to the American sitcom *Scrubs*.)

i-zone The last major instant-film camera produced by Polaroid. An inexpensive (under $50), easy-to-use camera marketed to kids and teenagers, the i-Zone instantly printed tiny photographs—about one square inch each—on paper, with colorful or decorated borders and removable paper backs, so the photos could be stuck onto any surface. The widespread consumer shift from film cameras to digital cameras hurt i-Zone's sales, but in 2001, it was the bestselling film camera in the United States. The film was pulled off the market for good in 2006; Polaroid stopped making instant-film cameras shortly thereafter.

J, K, L The main characters in the *Men in Black* movies, portrayed by Will Smith, Tommy Lee Jones, and Linda Fiorentino, respectively. The movies were based on a 1990 underground comic book series about the conspiracy theory that the U.S. government really does have an alien-invasion-coverup agency. (They don't, do they?)

M James Bond's superior and assignment giver—the nickname of the head of MI6, the British spy agency (real name: Miles Messervy). The role has been portrayed by five actors in the Bond film series: Bernard Lee, Robert Brown, John Huston, Edward Fox, and, most recently, Judi Dench.

"N." A novella by Stephen King, published in 2008 in King's short-fiction collection *Just After Sunset*. The plot: A woman tries to figure out why her brother, a psychiatrist, killed himself. As it turns out, he and one of his patients (named N.) were driven to suicide after seeing a monster named Cthun. Before it was published, *N.* was adapted into a series of twenty-five 90-second animated films to promote *Just After Sunset*. The films were available only as online "webisodes" on iTunes and video-enabled cell phones.

O A 2001 film version of William Shakespeare's *Othello* set against the backdrop of a high school basketball team. The lead character, Othello, was called Odin, the only African-American student at a prep school. The coach's son Hugo (originally Iago) is jealous of his on-court skills, and also covets his girlfriend, Desi (Desdemona). The film starred Mekhi Phifer, Josh Harnett, and Julia Stiles. *O* was filmed in 1998, part of a spate of teen movies based on Shakespeare plays, such as *William Shakespeare's Romeo + Juliet* starring Leonardo DiCaprio, and *10 Things I Hate About You*, a retelling of *The Taming of the Shrew*, which also starred Stiles. The film was scheduled for an April 1999 release date, but after the shootings at Columbine High School in Colorado, studio Lions Gate Entertainment shelved the film for two years because its final scenes depict high-school violence.

P The name of a band formed in the early '90s by movie star Johnny Depp and singer Gibby Haynes of the Butthole Surfers. Featuring Depp on guitar and bass, P had minor radio hits with covers of ABBA's "Dancing Queen" and Wings' "Jet."

Q James Bond's gadget-master. (His real name is Major Boothroyd; Q stands for "Quartermaster.") In the first Bond film, *Dr. No* (1962), the part was portrayed by British actor Peter Burton. Bad luck: Burton had a scheduling conflict for the next movie, *From Russia With Love*, so filmmakers cast Desmond Llewelyn, who went on to play the part in 17 films until his death

---

The *Mona Lisa* is insured for about $670 million.

in 1999. Some of the gadgets Q developed include a garrote-wire wristwatch, a poison-dagger shoe, a cigarette-lighter grenade, binocular glasses, a whistle-activated stun-gas-emitting key ring, a camera rocket launcher, a grappling-hook gun, an underwater jet pack, a rocket belt, a ring camera, a cigarette-case safecracker, a surfboard that contains C-4 explosives, a mini computer, a combat knife, a small satellite GPS transmitter, and radioactive lint.

R. The title of R&B superstar R. Kelly's third album, released in 1998. It sold more than 10 million copies in the United States and peaked at #2 on the album chart. It included an unlikely #1 hit—a duet with soft-rock superstar Celine Dion called "I'm Your Angel."

S Club 7 was a British teen pop band, formed in 1999 by Spice Girls creator Simon Fuller. He auditioned more than 10,000 singers for the prefabricated group, narrowing it down to seven singers—four girls and three boys. Fuller launched the group with a 13-episode Monkees-like TV series called *Miami 7*, in which the group cavorted around the beach and performed their songs. The show was a moderate hit when shown in the U.S. on the Fox Family Channel, but the group's musical success in America was limited to a single top-40 hit, "Never Had a Dream Come True," which hit #10 in 2000. It didn't really matter, though, because S Club 7 sold 17 million albums in Europe and Asia, and scored four #1 hits in the United Kingdom. S Club 7 broke up in 2003, but regrouped in 2008 as S Club 3, because that's how many members were interested in getting the band back together. What does the letter S stand for? According to the band, nothing.

T—as in **Mr. T,** the mohawked 1980s icon most famous for co-starring in *Rocky III* (1982) and the action-adventure TV series *The A-Team* (1983–1987). In the former he was Rocky's rival, boxer James "Clubber Lang"; in the latter, he was B.A. Baracus. Although the initials stood for "bad ass," B.A. was afraid to fly, which is why the A-Team went everywhere in a van. Born Lawrence Tureaud, Mr. T was a bouncer before he was an actor, and after *The A-Team* ended in 1987, his star faded. In 2006 he hosted a reality show called *I Pity the Fool,* in which he helped real people solve their problems, and he most recently appeared in commercials for title-loan company.

U A 1970 double album by the influential Scottish psychedelic/ folk group the Incredible String Band, commemorating and named after the band's 1969 concert tour.

V A 1983 TV miniseries (remade in 2009) about humanoid aliens who arrive on Earth to befriend humanity…before revealing that they are actually reptiles who just want to eat us.

W. The title of Oliver Stone's 2008 biopic about the life of ◆ President George W. Bush (Josh Brolin). It's Stone's third film about a president, following *Nixon* and *JFK*, but the only to take on a comic tone, characterizing Bush's early adulthood as aimless, reckless, and alcohol-soaked. Stone deliberately released the film just a few weeks before the Obama/McCain presidential election, hoping it would have an anti-Republican sway, but *W.* was a box-office bomb, earning just $29 million. (McCain, the Republican, lost the election anyway.)

X Also known as *The Man With the X-Ray Eyes*, it's a 1963 science-fiction film directed by Roger Corman about a scientist (Ray Milland) who conducts experiments with X-ray technology until it goes horribly wrong, mutating him and giving him X-ray vision. Being able to see through humans and ultimately *past* humans into only shades of light and what he believes is an all-knowing eye at the center of the universe, the man with the X-ray eyes obtains relief by plucking out his own eyes.

"Y" After the Baby Boomers, there was Generation X. The next generation—people born between around 1980 and 2000—is known as Generation Y or, sometimes, the Millennials. Generation Y is characterized by technological savvy (they are voracious users of the Internet and adapt easily to new gadgets). There are currently about 80 million Gen-Y-ers in the United States—outnumbering Baby Boomers by about five million.

Z The title of a 1966 novel by Vassilis Vassilikos, but better known as a 1969 movie directed by Costa-Gavras, it's a political thriller about the ruling military dictatorship in power in Greece at the time. The film version was the first movie not in English to be nominated for the Academy Award for Best Picture. (It lost; *Midnight Cowboy* won. But it did win the award for Best Foreign Language Film.)

Country with the world's highest fertility rate: Niger, with 7.1 children per mother.

DUMB CROOKS

More proof that crime doesn't pay.

THE TWO STOOGES

Regan Reti was facing jail time. Tiranara White was facing sentencing. The two men—handcuffed together after their respective hearings—were awaiting transport back to the Hastings, New Zealand, jail when they decided to make a break for it. The connected convicts darted across the street and encountered a lamppost. One man went to the right, the other to the left...and they slammed into each other on the other side. Each man blamed the other for going the wrong way. Both were returned to the jail.

DUMMIES

Thieves broke into a cell phone store in Moriela, Mexico, in 2009 and made off with some hollow plastic cell phone replicas that were on display. Employees told police that the burglars passed up dozens of real cell phones just a few feet away and stole the fake ones.

BUT THEY SEEMED SO NORMAL

In 2009 Christopher Gray of Quincy, Massachusetts, posted an ad on Craigslist that read "420 help is here!" (420 is stoner-subculture code for smoking marijuana...so we hear.) A man called the phone number, and Gray arranged to meet him in a nearby parking lot. The man showed up with a friend. "Are you guys cops?" asked Gray. "No," they replied. "Okay, I trust you. You look normal." Gray then sold them a $45-bag of marijuana. (They were cops.) Said the arresting officer: "It goes without saying that we will continue monitoring Craigslist."

HE GOT CARDED

A chef from Mexico (name not released) arrived at the Manchester, England, airport in 2010. Customs officials routinely asked what he was doing in the U.K. "I'm visiting a friend who's opening a restaurant," he replied. "I'm just staying for a few days." But while searching his bag, the agents discovered a greeting card that

---

Who says it's not a real sport? The average heart rate of a NASCAR driver...

read "Good luck with your new life in the U.K.!" That prompted a confession from the chef: He was planning to work—illegally—at the restaurant. He was deported the next day.

DON'T FENCE ME IN

One night in March 2010, a Cleveland police officer tried to pull over a car for a minor traffic violation, but the driver sped off. The ensuing chase reached speeds of 90 mph before the car stopped at an intersection and four men jumped out. They all ran toward a tall chain-link fence with thickly wound barbed wire lining the top. Two of the men were captured right away; another was tased while climbing the fence. The driver, Ricky Flowers, actually made it all the way over, despite severely cutting his arms on the barbed wire. He got away? No, he landed in the yard of a women's prison. Flowers received several stitches at the hospital before being taken to jail (a men's jail). And why didn't he pull over when the cops told him to? Because, he told officers, he had a suspended license and "didn't want his mom to know he was driving."

MMM...PIZZA

In May 2009, police responded to a robbery call at an Italian restaurant in Osijek, Croatia. The cops entered and asked the employees which way the suspect went. One of the workers pointed to a man named Ante Baranovic, who was sitting in a booth gobbling up a slice of pizza. "I know I should have run," he said as the officers arrested him, "but this pizza is good!"

*   *   *

A SIT-DOWN COMEDIAN

"Dogs are gross. They drink out of the toilet. But when you're going to the bathroom, maybe your dog is thinking, 'Hey, I drink out of that thing! Why don't you just go in my dish, save yourself a walk down the hallway.'"

—Garry Shandling

I BURP, THEREFORE I AM

As once said by that famous philosopher, René Descaaaaartes.

CAN'T STOP BURPING YOU. Jean Driscoll, 72, of Chelmsford, England, started burping constantly (and loudly) in 2006…and has been unable to stop ever since. She's been to several doctors, taken numerous medications, had acupuncture and hypnotherapy, and has even had her digestive tract examined with a tiny camera—but the loud, spontaneous burping won't stop. "I don't go out anymore because I'm too embarrassed," Ms. Driscoll said, "People laugh and stare at me." At last report, she's still trying to find a cure.

JAILHOUSE BURP. In February 2010, Thomas Scott Vandegrift of Roanoke, Virginia, filed suit against several police officers for $6 million each—because they beat him up for burping. Vandegrift claims he was physically assaulted by the officers when they misread his acid-reflux-caused burping as deliberate and disrespectful.

SLAP MY BURP UP. Chinese newspapers reported in April 2007 that a man in the northeastern province of Liaoning had tried to cure his constant belching by slapping himself in the face—hard—several times. Good news: He cured his belching. Bad news: He also broke one of his eardrums. His doctors told reporters that people should not try to cure medical problems by slapping themselves in the face.

DRY YOUR BURPS. In June 2007, Frederick Cronin was arrested for drunk driving in Stratham, New Hampshire. He lost his driver's license but appealed. According to police rules, officers must observe people arrested for drunk driving for 20 minutes before giving them a breathalyzer test. If the person burps during that period, the officer has to start over. Cronin and the arresting officer agreed that Cronin burped during his waiting period, but the officer insisted it wasn't a real burp—it was a "dry burp." At a state Department of Motor Vehicles hearing, Cronin argued that it was indeed a "wet" burp and that the police officer had broken the rules. The hearing officer's ruling: The "gaseous mix that flowed out of Cronin's mouth had not emanated from his stomach and contained nothing but air." Cronin the Burparian did not get his license back.

EVERY BURP YOU TAKE. In July 2006, Bryan S. Jeanfreau of Natchez, Massachusetts, was issued U.S. Patent Number 7070638 for a Burp Gas Filtering Device. It's about six inches long and cylindrical, with a large opening at one end and several small openings on the side, near the other end. When you feel a burp coming on and you're afraid it's going to be a foul-smelling one, you put the end with the large opening in your mouth, and the gases released with the burp go through a filter of activated charcoal before being released. Bonus: It's also a pen. (We don't know why.)

THE WAY WE BURPED. Have you ever wanted to burp, but couldn't? For some people it's a lifelong reality. Normally when gases build up in the stomach or the esophagus, the *belch reflex* allows them to be released through the upper esophageal sphincter (UES), a one-way valve below your voice box that is chiefly used to let food into the esophagus while you eat. (The vibration of the UES is what makes burps sound the way they do.) But for people with a disorder called "dysfunction of the belch reflex," that valve doesn't work properly—and they can't burp. Ever. The condition can cause severe bloating of the stomach and esophagus, and excruciating pain. What causes the disorder is unknown, and so far there is no cure.

TINY BURPLES. Do fish burp? Many fish species have *swim bladders*, baglike organs that they can fill with air in order to maintain buoyancy at different depths in the water. They can also expel air from the bag, and they do this by belching it out of their gills. You can see little fish burp bubbles when they do.

*   *   *

"I come from a very big family. Nine parents." —**Jim Gaffigan**

BEHIND THE LOVE SONGS

*What's every songwriter's favorite topic? Love. Only problem: They
can't seem to agree on love's true nature. Either it's strange, it's
all around, it hurts, it's crazy, or it's a battlefield. Here are
the stories behind some well-known "love" songs.*

The Song: "Love Is All Around" (1967)
The Artist: The Troggs
The Story: The Troggs were a British garage-rock band
best known for the raw 1966 hit "Wild Thing." But when Troggs
singer Reg Presley saw a Salvation Army band play an old, senti-
mental folk song on a TV variety show—he can't remember the
song or the show—it inspired him to write a gentle song about
love. (Presley claims he wrote it in just a few minutes.) By the end
of 1967, "Love Is All Around" had reached the Top 10 in America
and the U.K. More than 25 years later, the song became a hit
again when the band Wet Wet Wet covered it for the 1994 film
Four Weddings and a Funeral, taking it to #1 for 15 weeks. (Presley
donated his songwriting royalties from the Wet Wet Wet version
to crop-circle research.)

The Song: "Love Is Strange" (1957)
The Artist: Mickey & Sylvia
The Story: In 1956 blues legend and early rock 'n' roll influence
Bo Diddley wrote this blues song about the intricacies and exas-
peration of being in love. He had to publish it under the name of
Ethel Smith (his wife) because of a legal dispute with his record
label, Chess Records. Diddley performed and recorded the song,
and it was a minor success. But it didn't register much with the
public until it hit #11 as a cover by the married duo Mickey &
Sylvia (Mickey Baker and Sylvia Vanderpool), who turned the
song into a sexy, purring love duet. The most famous part, the
call-and-response portion of Diddley's song, became a spoken
interlude between Mickey and Sylvia. ("How do you call your
loverboy?" "I say, 'Come here, loverboy.'") The song has been used
in a number of movies, including *Badlands, Deep Throat*, and *Dirty
Dancing*. It was Mickey & Sylvia's only major hit. Baker returned

---

Between 1934 and 1955, there was not a single bank robbery in Hawaii.

to session guitar work—he'd played on dozens of classic rock 'n' roll songs, including "Shake Rattle & Roll" and "Whole Lot of Shakin' Going On." Vanderpool went on to found Sugarhill Records, which released some of the first-ever rap singles in the '80s, including "Rapper's Delight" by the Sugarhill Gang and "The Message" by Grandmaster Flash and the Furious Five.

The Song: "Love Hurts" (1976)
The Artist: Nazareth
The Story: Boudleaux and Felice Bryant got their first big breaks as songwriters with a series of hits for the Everly Brothers in the early '60s, including "Bye Bye Love" and "All I Have to Do Is Dream." In 1960 Boudleaux wrote "Love Hurts," a familiar "woe is me" country-music heartache song. It wasn't a single or a hit, but it appeared on the Everly Brothers' 1961 album *A Date With the Everly Brothers.* Musicians seemed to love it, though—Roy Orbison, Gram Parsons, and Emmylou Harris all recorded the song. The British hard-rock band Nazareth often played "Love Hurts" for fun during warm-ups and tunings. It was a joke...until they heard Harris's version and thought it could be a hit for them. Nazareth recorded the song in 1974, and it became their only Top-10 hit in the United States.

The Song: "Love is a Battlefield" (1983)
The Artist: Pat Benatar
The Story: Mike Chapman had been a top-level pop songwriter for years when rock superstar Pat Benatar called in 1982 and asked him to write a song for her. Chapman extended the offer to his protégé, Holly Knight. She played him a three-chord electric guitar riff she'd come up with; Chapman thought the riff was catchy and "very commercial," but to "make it special," he thought they should make the lyrics really weird. He came up with "Love Is a Battlefield," comparing the uncertainty and risk of falling in love and being in love with being bombarded by bombs and bullets in war. They actually wrote it as a ballad, but Benatar sped it up to make it an up-tempo rock song. Appearing on her *Live from Earth* album, "Love is a Battlefield" peaked at #5 on the pop chart.

Famous foot fact: Dorothy's ruby slippers were size 5 1/2.

The Song: "Crazy in Love" (2003)
The Artist: Beyoncé
The Story: In the summer of 2002, Beyoncé starred in and recorded the theme song for *Austin Powers in Goldmember*, taking a two-pronged approach to the launch of her solo career after a decade in the R&B group Destiny's Child. Her debut solo album, *Dangerously in Love*, was finished and set to be released in October 2002. But when "Hey Goldmember" bombed on the pop chart, and another member of Destiny's Child, Kelly Rowland, scored a #1 hit with "Dilemma," Columbia Records decided to delay the release of *Dangerously in Love* until 2003 in order to focus on Rowland's success for a bit longer, and to give Beyoncé time to make sure she had a hit the next time. Seeking to add one more track to *Dangerously in Love*, Beyoncé asked R&B songwriter/producer Rich Harrison to pitch something. He played her a sample of the 1970 Chi-Lites song "Are You My Woman" and accompanied it on the bongos. Beyoncé liked the hook (Harrison had been holding on to it for months, in search of the right project) and asked him to write a song around it…and gave him only two hours to do it. He was up to the challenge. Remembering an offhand comment Beyoncé had made about her harried appearance that day— "I'm looking so crazy right now"—Harrison wrote "Crazy in Love" in less than two hours. Beyoncé recorded it that night (her boyfriend, Jay-Z, came in at 3:00 a.m. and improvised his rapped section) and took it to #1, where it stayed for seven weeks in the summer of 2003, successfully launching her solo career.

The Song: "Love Story" (2008)
The Artist: Taylor Swift
The Story: Swift was 19 when she wrote this song, in tandem with a later hit, "White Horse." Both are about the same boyfriend, and each expresses a different side of young love—fairy tale romance …and disillusionment. Swift's inspiration: *Romeo and Juliet*. Like the play, "Love Story" is about teenage lovers whose parents don't approve, but her song doesn't end with suicide—it ends with Romeo asking Juliet's dad for her hand in marriage. "Love Story" was the first single from Swift's second album *Fearless*, which propelled her from country star to pop superstar. The song hit #1 on the country, adult contemporary, and pop charts.

A HISTORY OF THE SHOPPING MALL, PART III

Tired of shopping at the mall? Try reading about one instead—it will forever change how you look at malls. (Part II of the story is on page 230.)

N UMBER TWO
Southdale Center, the mall that Victor Gruen designed for Dayton's department store in the town of Edina, Minnesota, outside of Minneapolis, was only his second shopping center. But it was the very first fully enclosed, climate-controlled shopping mall in history, and it had many of the features that are still found in modern malls today.

It was "anchored" by two major department stores, Dayton's and Donaldson's, which were located at opposite ends of the mall in order to generate foot traffic past the smaller shops in between.

Southdale also had a giant interior atrium called the "Garden Court of Perpetual Spring" in the center of the mall. The atrium was as long as a city block and had a soaring ceiling that was five stories tall at its highest point. Just as he had with the public spaces at Northland, Gruen intended the garden court to be a bustling space with an idealized downtown feel. He filled it with sculptures, murals, a newsstand, a tobacconist, and a Woolworth's "sidewalk" café. Skylights in the ceiling of the atrium flooded the garden court with natural light; crisscrossing escalators and second-story skybridges helped create an atmosphere of continuous movement while also attracting shoppers' attention to the stores on the second level.

GARDEN VARIETY

The mall was climate controlled to keep it at a constant spring-like temperature (hence the "perpetual spring" theme) that would keep people shopping all year round. In the past shopping had always been a seasonal activity in harsh climates like Minnesota's, where frigid winters could keep shoppers away from stores for months. Not so at Southdale, and Gruen emphasized

---

Only bone never reported broken in a ski accident: the *stapes*, found in the inner ear.

the point by filling the garden court with orchids and other tropical plants, a 42-foot-tall eucalyptus tree, a goldfish pond, and a giant aviary filled with exotic birds. Such things were rare sights indeed in icy Minnesota, and they gave people one more reason to go to the mall.

INTELLIGENT DESIGN

With 10 acres of shopping surrounded by 70 acres of parking, Southdale was a huge development in its day. Even so, it was intended as merely a retail hub for a much larger planned community, spread out over the 463-acre plot acquired by Dayton's. Just as the Dayton's and Donaldson's department stores served as anchors for the Southdale mall, the mall itself would one day serve as the retail anchor for this much larger development, which as Gruen designed it, would include apartment buildings, single-family homes, schools, office buildings, a hospital, landscaped parks with walking paths, and a lake.

The development was Victor Gruen's response to the ugly, chaotic suburban sprawl that he had detested since his first visit to Michigan back in 1948. He intended it as a brand-new downtown for the suburb, carefully designed to eliminate sprawl while also solving the problems that poor or nonexistent planning had brought to traditional urban centers like Minneapolis. Such places had evolved gradually and haphazardly over many generations instead of following a single, carefully thought-out master plan.

The idea was to build the Southdale Center mall first. Then, if it was a success, Dayton's would use the profits to develop the rest of the 463 acres in accordance with Gruen's plan. And Southdale was a success: Though Dayton's downtown flagship store did lose some business to the mall when it opened in the fall of 1956, the company's overall sales rose 60 percent, and the other stores in the mall also flourished.

But the profits generated by the mall were never used to bring the rest of Gruen's plan to fruition. Ironically, it was the very success of the mall that doomed the rest of the plan.

LOCATION, LOCATION, LOCATION

Back before the first malls had been built, Gruen and others had assumed that they would cause surrounding land values to drop, or

---

at least not rise very much, on the theory that commercial developers would shy away from building other stores close to such a formidable competitor as a thriving shopping mall. The economic might of the mall, they reasoned, would help to preserve nearby open spaces by making them unsuitable for further commercial development.

But the opposite turned out to be the case. Because shopping malls attracted so much traffic, it soon became clear that it made sense to build other developments nearby. Result: The once dirt-cheap real estate around Southdale began to climb rapidly in value. As it did, Dayton's executives realized they could make a lot of money selling off their remaining parcels of land—much more quickly, with much less risk—than they could by gradually implementing Gruen's master plan over many years.

From the beginning Gruen had seen the mall as a solution to sprawl, something that would preserve open spaces, not destroy them. But his "solution" had only made the problem worse—malls turned out to be sprawl *magnets*, not sprawl killers. Any remaining doubts Gruen had were dispelled in the mid-1960s when he made his first visit to Northland Center since its opening a decade earlier. He was stunned by the number of seedy strip malls and other commercial developments that had grown up right around it.

REVERSAL OF FORTUNE

Victor Gruen, the father of the shopping mall, became one of its most outspoken critics. He tried to remake himself as an urban planner, marketing his services to American cities that wanted to make their downtown areas more mall-like, in order to recapture some of the business lost to malls. He drew up massive, ambitious, and *very* costly plans for remaking Fort Worth, Rochester, Manhattan, Kalamazoo, and even the Iranian capital city of Tehran. Most of his plans called for banning cars from city centers, confining them to ring roads and giant parking structures circling downtown. Unused roadways and parking spaces in the center would then be redeveloped into parks, walkways, outdoor cafés, and other uses. It's doubtful that any of these pie-in-the-sky projects were ever really politically or financially viable, and none of them made it off the drawing board.

HOMECOMING

In 1968 Gruen closed his architectural practice and moved back to Vienna...where he discovered that the once thriving downtown shops and cafés, which had inspired him to invent the shopping mall in the first place, were now themselves threatened by a new shopping mall that had opened outside the city.

He spent the remaining years of his life writing articles and giving speeches condemning shopping malls as "gigantic shopping machines" and ugly "land-wasting seas of parking." He attacked developers for shrinking the public, non-profit-generating spaces to a bare minimum. "I refuse to pay alimony for these bastard developments," Gruen told a London audience in 1978, in a speech titled "The Sad Story of Shopping Centers."

Gruen called on the public to oppose the construction of new malls in their communities, but his efforts were largely in vain. At the time of his death in 1980, the United States was in the middle of a 20-year building boom that would see more than 1,000 shopping malls added to the American landscape. And were they ever popular: According to a survey by *U.S. News and World Report*, by the early 1970s, Americans spent more time at the mall than anyplace else except for home and work.

VICTOR WHO?

Today Victor Gruen is largely a forgotten man, known primarily to architectural historians (and now bathroom readers). That may not be such a bad thing, considering how much he came to despise the creation that gives him his claim to fame.

Gruen does live on, however, in the term "Gruen transfer," which mall designers use to refer to the moment of disorientation that shoppers who have come to the mall to buy a particular item can experience upon entering the building—the moment in which they are distracted into forgetting their errand and instead begin wandering the mall with glazed eyes and a slowed, almost shuffling gait, impulsively buying any merchandise that strikes their fancy.

It's true—big things come in mall packages.
Part IV of the story on page 458.

Some San Francisco bakers still make sourdough bread from dough started in 1849.

COLLEGE RIVALS

Sis-boom-bah! Which is the most hated college football team ever?
Whichever one happens to be your school's rival. Here are
a few of the most famous annual college battles.

THE APPLE CUP: University of Washington vs. Washington State. It's named for the state's huge apple crop. The winner is awarded an actual golden apple trophy.

THE FRIENDS OF COAL BOWL: West Virginia University vs. Marshall University. Coal mining is a major industry in West Virginia, where both schools are located, and the game is sponsored by a coal industry trade association.

THE CIVIL WAR: University of Oregon vs. Oregon State. These two teams have been playing each other since the 1880s. The trophy awarded to the winner is called the Platypus Trophy because the animal has characteristics of both school's mascots: the Duck and the Beaver. The 1983 game was such a dismal affair that its still referred to as the "Toilet Bowl." After eleven fumbles, four missed field goals, and five interceptions, in a game played in the pouring rain, the Ducks and Beavers, both mediocre teams, slogged to a 0–0 tie.

THE EGG BOWL: Ole Miss vs. Mississippi State. A trophy has been awarded to the winner since 1927, and almost immediately it was nicknamed "the Golden Egg." That's because it's polished brass (which looks like gold), and it's shaped like an early-20th-century football (which looks like an egg).

THE RED RIVER SHOOTOUT: University of Oklahoma vs. University of Texas. Part of the boundary between the states of Oklahoma and Texas is a naturally occurring one—the Red River. A similarly named rivalry: the "Battle of the Brazos" between two other Texas schools—Baylor University and Texas A&M, which are less than 90 miles apart, separated by the Brazos River.

THE IRON BOWL: University of Alabama vs. Auburn University. Until 1989 the annual 'Bama/Auburn game was held in

---

There are more than 85,000 possible drink combinations available at Starbucks.

Birmingham, Alabama, a neutral city with a big stadium. In the early 20th century, Birmingham was the nation's second-biggest iron-producing city (behind Pittsburgh), so the game was nicknamed the "Iron Bowl."

THE HOLY WAR: University of Utah vs. Brigham Young University. More than 50 percent of Utah citizens are Mormons, giving rise to the "holy" wordplay for the game between the state's two biggest universities.

THE BLACK AND BLUE BOWL: Southern Mississippi vs. University of Memphis. The name is taken from the color of each team's uniforms—black for Southern Mississippi, and blue for Memphis. But it has a double meaning: The teams play so aggressively that the players are bruised "black and blue."

THE BATTLE FOR THE VICTORY BELL: USC vs. UCLA. These two schools are crosstown Los Angeles rivals, and the winner of their annual football game gets to keep the Victory Bell, an actual bell mounted on a metal cart, for a year. And they get to paint it their school color: blue for UCLA and cardinal red for USC. But wait! There are two more rivalries that have an annual Battle for the Victory Bell: University of North Carolina vs. Duke University, who have been battling for an old railroad bell since 1948, and Miami University vs. University of Cincinnati, who have been going at it for their own Victory Bell since 1888.

* * *

FIVE TOASTS

- *May we all come to peaceful ends,
  and leave our debts unto our friends.*

- *Here's to you, and here's to me, may we never disagree.
  But if we do, to Hell with you…and here's to me!*

- *May we never flatter our superiors or insult our inferiors.*

- *What shall we drink to? About three in the morning.*

- *Here's to a clear conscience—or a poor memory.*

If the name fits: One of the founders of CNN was named William Headline.

BEHIND THE MAGIC 8-BALL

Can a plastic orb connect you to the spirit world and lift the future's filmy veil? OUTLOOK NOT SO GOOD. *Can it at least give good advice?* REPLY HAZY, TRY AGAIN. *Can a toy company make money selling it?* SIGNS POINT TO YES!

A SEEKER BORN EVERY MINUTE

Wartime has long been a boom time for spiritualists, mostly because people long for *any* news about loved ones at the battlefront. In the 1940s, a woman named "Madame" Mary Carter was capitalizing on that opportunity, plying her trade as a professional clairvoyant in Cincinnati. Her best séance stunt was one she called the Psycho-Slate, consisting of a chalkboard inside a box, with a lid covering it. When a client asked a question, Carter would close the lid, and after a short interval of muffled chalkboard scratching, she would dramatically flip open the lid to reveal the spirit world's answer, written with chalk in a ghostly scrawl. (How she did it remains a mystery.)

TELL A FORTUNE, MAKE A FORTUNE?

Mary Carter had a son named Albert who had little use for any spirits that couldn't be drunk straight from a bottle. When sober, however, he fancied himself an inventor, and seeing the success of his mother's Psycho-Slate, Albert Carter came up with his best idea ever: a portable fortune-telling device that any spiritual seeker could use at any time or place.

It took some time for Carter to work out the details. It had to look mysterious, it had to offer a variety of answers and, because he had no capital to work with, it had to be cheap to build. He went to work using what he knew best—murky liquids in cans and bottles—and developed what he called the Syco-Seer Miracle Home Fortune Teller—a seven-inch can-shaped device with a glass window on each end. The inside of the can was divided in two; each half contained a six-sided die floating in a dark, viscous liquid (according to some accounts, molasses from his mother's

---

When the 13th Dalai Lama died in 1933, he was buried sitting up in a bed of salt.

kitchen) and each of the die's six sides was inscribed with a short answer. His reasoning for having two compartments isn't clear, but perhaps it was for efficiency: You could get an answer from one end, then turn it over and get the next answer with little lag time. In 1944 Carter filed for a patent, made a prototype, and began showing it around Cincinnati's toy and novelty shops.

YOU WILL MEET A HELPFUL STRANGER

One of the storekeepers, Max Levinson, not only wanted to stock Syco-Seers, he was very interested in helping Carter produce and market them. Levinson brought in his brother-in-law, Abe Bookman, an engineer from the Ohio Mechanical Institute, who suggested improvements to Carter's design—adding ridges inside the chamber to make the die spin and better randomize the answers. He also hired a designer to give the Syco-Seer's outer label a mystical appeal.

In 1946 the three men formed a partnership, which—in a nod to his two creative partners' first names—Levinson called the Alabe Crafts Corporation. Bookman arranged for a manufacturer and planned for the retail release of the Syco-Seer in 1947. At just about the same time, Albert Carter's alcoholism and self-neglect had finally caught up with him and he died. "When he was sober, he was a genius," Bookman recalled to a *Cincinnati Post* reporter a few years later. "He stayed in flophouses and he was always broke. But I bought every idea he ever had, and that gave him enough to keep going."

I SEE A PATENT IN YOUR FUTURE

Carter's patent came through the following year, and luckily for Bookman and Levinson, he had signed rights over to the partnership before he died. Given new creative freedom to experiment with the design, Bookman began making changes that Carter had resisted.

First, while the Syco-Seer was attracting curious browsers in stores, it wasn't generating sales, and Bookman was convinced that it was priced too high. To bring down the price, Bookman reduced costs by cutting Carter's double-chambered design in half, using only one chamber, one die, and one window. He also decided that Carter's mother was a good judge of product names.

He borrowed her chalkboard gimmick's name, calling his 3½-inch single-chambered device "Syco-Slate, the Pocket Fortune Teller." Next, he decorated it with the 12 zodiac signs and an illustration of a gypsy fortune-teller.

In stores, models dressed as gypsies demonstrated how to use the device. But demonstrations weren't really needed. On the top of the cylinder were the instructions:

> Place left hand on this end. Ask a "yes or no" question about the future, wait 10 seconds and turn SYCO-SLATE over. Answer will appear on "Spirit Slate" in the window.

ON THE BALL

Although the price of the new incarnation was lower, the Syco-Slate didn't sell much better than the Syco-Seer had. Why? It looked like a can of peas. Bookman racked his brain—what did people expect when they had their fortunes read? Then it came to him: a crystal ball. Late in 1948, Bookman began encasing Syco-Slates in a translucent, iridescent ball. Then he changed the six-sided die to a 20-sided one, and even hired a University of Cincinnati psychology professor named Lucien Cohen to come up with answers for each of its 20 faces. Bookman was sure he had a winner this time.

He didn't. The crystal ball flopped too.

CONCENTRATE AND ASK AGAIN

Bookman was out of ideas. He'd put a lot of money, time, and sweat into this thing. He was sure it was going to strike it big, yet nothing seemed to work. Then something strange happened, almost as if it had been preordained by the stars: Bookman got a message from beyond—just beyond Ohio's western border. A representative of the Brunswick Billiards Company of Chicago called to say that Brunswick needed a unique promotional item—would it be possible to change the skin of Alabe's crystal ball and make it look like a billiard ball?

It was a strange request, and it didn't make sense. Who ever heard of an 8-ball that tells fortunes? But Bookman, looking for a way to make some money and reduce his surplus stock, agreed to do it.

Mr. Bigglesworth, the hairless cat in the *Austin Powers* movies, was played by Ted Nude-Gent.

OUTLOOK GOOD

Even Madame Mary Carter couldn't have foreseen that a fortune-telling billiard ball would strike a chord with the public. Maybe it was because the absurd 8-ball design stripped away that phony gypsy fortune-teller aura, making the object clearly designed as a fun toy instead of an occult item. By 1950 most Americans were planted firmly in the material world. They might enjoy reading fortune cookies and newspaper horoscopes, but they weren't trying to get genuine answers or relief from war anxieties. Most saw fortune-telling as something offbeat to laugh about with friends.

It turned out that a "Magic 8-Ball" fit right in. The Brunswick Billiards Company quickly distributed their supply, but people were contacting Alabe Crafts asking for more. Abe Bookman was smart enough to recognize that he had a good thing going. Albert Carter's invention finally found its market.

RANDOM FACTS AND QUICK ANSWERS

• Half of the 20 answers on a Magic 8-Ball are positive. Five are noncommittal, and the remaining five are negative.

• What's inside a Magic 8-Ball? First of all, there's a cylinder that's very much like Carter and Bookman's original Syco-Seer / Syco-Slate design. It's filled with a blue dye dissolved in alcohol. The 20-sided die has raised white letters and openings for the liquid to enter. This makes the die just barely buoyant, which accounts for the way it slowly floats to the top, making the answer gradually emerge from the gloomy dark liquid.

• There is one recent addition to the original Magic 8-Ball design. When Ideal Toys bought Alabe Crafts in 1971, their designers tackled a problem that had vexed users for decades: annoying bubbles appeared in the message window, making it hard to see the answers. In 1975 Ideal patented the solution—the "Bubble-Free Die Agitator," consisting of an inverted funnel that routes air into an internal bubble trap. The BFDA has been part of the Magic 8-Ball ever since.

• Some users seem to think they're supposed to shake the 8-Ball when they ask their questions. That's wrong. Agitating an 8-Ball is likely to release bubbles from the bubble catcher, obscuring the words in the inky blue window into the future.

- If you wanted to get every one of the 20 possible answers, it would take an average of 72 questions.

- The 20-sided shape of the Magic 8-Ball die is an *icosahedron*. In the natural world, it's a shape that shows up in viruses, amoebas, crystals, and a form of carbon called fullerene. In the *un*natural world, it's a shape found in dice made for role-playing games and in Buckminster Fuller's "Fuller Projection Map," a nearly round globe that can be opened up and laid flat on a table with very little distortion of the land area's sizes and shapes.

- About a million Magic 8-Balls are sold annually.

- A coincidence? A look into the future? In a wartime short film called *You Nazty Spy* (1940), the Three Stooges parody Hitler and his henchmen's proclivity for seeking occult guidance. In the film, a psychic named Mati Herring tells their future with what she calls "the Magic Ball"—an oversized 8-ball that looks exactly like the well-known toy-to-be.

- Is the 8-Ball cursed? See if you can follow the bouncing Magic 8-Ball through its various owners: In 1971 Ideal Toys bought the Magic 8-Ball from Alabe Crafts. In 1982 Ideal was acquired by CBS for its new CBS Toys Company. Three years later, in 1985, the broadcaster got out of the toy business and sold its Ideal division (including the 8-Ball) to Viewmaster. Four years after that, Viewmaster was acquired by Tyco Toys, itself having been acquired by Consolidated Foods 20 years earlier. In 1997 Consolidated—now called the Sarah Lee Corporation—sold the remains of Tyco, including the 8-Ball, to Mattel Toys. Since 1997 Mattel has owned the Magic 8-Ball. However, if the curse is real, it's probably just a matter of time before Mattel reads the writing on the ball:

"OUTLOOK NOT SO GOOD."

*   *   *

"We are well advised to keep on nodding terms with the people we used to be, whether we find them attractive company or not."

—Joan Didion

A teenager using a cell phone while driving has the reaction time of a 65-year-old.

KNOW YOUR BUTTS

*Lots of things that have nothing to do with rear ends are known as butts.
Here's a whole load of non-butt butts for you to ponder. (Special
thanks to BRI reader Seymour Butts for sending them in.)*

Butt Roast: A particular cut of pork taken from the pig's...shoulder.

Boston Butt: This variation on the butt roast originated in Boston.

Butt Rubbing: The practice of rubbing spices and other dry seasonings into a butt roast. (For Boston butts, the practice would be known as Boston butt rubbing.)

Major Butt: A military aide to presidents Teddy Roosevelt and William Howard Taft, Archibald Butt was present when Taft threw out the first presidential baseball in 1910. He was also present when the *Titanic* struck an iceberg on April 14, 1912, and he went down with the ship.

The Butt Memorial Bridge: A bridge in Augusta, Georgia, built in 1914 and dedicated to the memory of Major Butt.

Butt Log: A log cut from the lowest, widest part of a tree trunk, just above the stump, or "butt."

Buttle: A verb that describes what butlers do: They "buttle."

Water Butt: The British name for a rain barrel.

Sackbut: A style of trombone popular during the Renaissance and Baroque eras.

Butt Rot: When the butt of a living tree suffers from a fungal infection, it's said to have "butt rot."

The Butt Report: A secret World War II report critical of British bombers for an inability to hit their targets. The Butt Report spurred changes in tactics and technology that vastly improved bomber accuracy.

Buttlegger: A person who smuggles cigarettes. (Get it? Cigarette butts!)

Alfred Mosher Butts: The unemployed American architect who invented the board game Scrabble in 1938.

David Bensusan-Butt: A wartime British civil servant and author of the Butt Report.

THE PHYSICS OF BREAKFAST CEREAL

*Americans eat nearly three billion boxes of cereal every year.
And yet few of us know how Rice Krispies, Corn Pops, or
any other cereal is made. Here's a look at the science
behind some of our favorite breakfast foods.*

NATURAL-BORN POPPER

Popcorn for breakfast? It's not the first thing most people think of eating in the morning, and it's not marketed as a breakfast food. But popcorn does have many of the qualities that cereal manufacturers look for in a breakfast food: It's light and airy, it's crispy, and it crunches when you eat it. If you put some popcorn in a bowl and poured milk over it, it would probably stay crunchy at least as long as your favorite breakfast cereal does.

But what about foods that don't pop naturally the way that popcorn does? Quite a bit of the technology used in the manufacture of breakfast cereals is employed specifically to make those foods "poppable"—to produce desirable, popcorn-like qualities in foods that don't normally have them. Foods like whole-grain rice and wheat, for example. Or grains that have been milled into flour, then mixed with other ingredients to make dough that is then baked into individual pieces of cereal.

POPCORN 101

To understand how whole grains and dough end up as Puffed Wheat, Cheerios, and Kix, it helps to understand what makes popcorn pop in the first place.

• A kernel of popcorn consists of a hard shell that surrounds a dense, starchy center, and there's a lot of moisture in the starch. When you place a bag of unpopped popcorn in a microwave oven, the microwave "cooks" the popcorn by heating the moisture in the starch. The starch softens and develops a consistency similar to gelatin as it cooks.

• When the moisture is heated to the boiling point, it converts into

---

In winter, the air in the average American home is twice as dry as the Sahara Desert's.

steam and begins to expand. Or at least it wants to: What makes popcorn different from most other grains is that its hard outer shell does not allow the steam to escape. Instead, the kernel of corn becomes like a tiny pressure cooker: The steam pressure builds up until the outer shell can no longer contain it, and it ruptures.

• If you've ever opened a bottle of champagne or a shaken bottle of soda, or squirted a dollop of shaving cream into your hand, it's easy to understand what happens next: When the shell cracks, the pressure drops and the moisture in the starch instantly converts from a liquid state to a gaseous state, creating air bubbles in the cooked, gelatinous starch that cause it to froth up into a foamy mass, expanding it to 30 or 40 times its original size. The steam escapes, leaving behind the dried, crunchy, styrofoamy starch that we know as popcorn.

POP! GOES THE CEREAL

Wheat and rice don't have external shells that trap steam the way that corn does, so if you want to obtain popcornlike results with these grains, *you* have to provide the pressure cooker. When cereal companies want to make puffed wheat, puffed rice, or puffed dough, they do just that, using a process known as "gun puffing" developed by Quaker Oats researchers at the turn of the 20th century. Why is it called gun puffing? Because the process was perfected using an actual Army cannon—one that saw action in the Spanish American War—that was converted into a pressure cooker. (Corn kernels can also be gun puffed. That's how Kellogg's Corn Pops are made.)

Corn Pops, Puffed Wheat, and Puffed Rice

• Whole grains are steam cooked in a pressure cooker (or cannon) until the pressure builds to about 200 pounds per square inch (psi), or about 13.6 times the normal atmospheric pressure (at sea level).

• When the grains have been properly cooked, the pressure inside the pressure cooker is released all at once, just like when popcorn pops. There's even a loud POP! when the pressure is released.

• The sudden drop in pressure causes the moisture in the grains to flash into steam, puffing up the grains just like popcorn.

• The puffed grains are baked dry, and in the case of puffed-wheat cereals like Kellogg's Honey Smacks and Post Golden Crisp, *lots* of sweeteners are added to make them more appealing to kids.

"Extruded" Gun-Puffed Cereals Made From Dough

How do they make Kix, Trix, Cheerios, Alpha Bits, Cocoa Puffs, and other "extruded gun-puffed" cereals?

• Various combinations of corn, oat, wheat, and rice flours are mixed with sugar, water, coloring, flavoring, and other ingredients to make a sweet dough, which is then fed into a machine called a *forming extruder*.

• The extruder forms the dough into the desired shape just like you might have done if you played with Play-Doh when you were a kid: To create a star shape, you squeeze, or *extrude*, the dough through a star-shaped hole. If you want a round shape, you squeeze the dough through a round hole. If you're making Cheerios, you punch a hole in the middle to get a donut shape, and if you're making Alpha Bits, you use letter-shaped holes.

• As the extruded dough emerges from the hole in the proper shape, rotating blades cut it into individual cereal pieces.

• The freshly extruded dough pieces have too high a moisture content to be suitable for gun puffing, so they are dried until their moisture content drops from as high as 24% down to a more desirable 9% to 12%. (Unpopped popcorn kernels, by comparison, have a moisture content of 13.5% to 14%.)

• The dried pieces are fed into a gun puffer. The puffed cereal is then toasted dry.

RICE KRISPIES

If you've ever watched cookies bake in the oven, you know that the dough puffs as it cooks. Rice Krispies are made the same way, in a process that's called "oven-puffing."

• First, rice is pressure cooked at a low 15–18 psi (vs. the 200 psi used in the gun-puffing process) with water, sugar, salt, flavoring, and other ingredients.

• The cooked rice is then dried to reduce the moisture content from 28% to 17%; then it is "bumped," or fed through rollers to flatten the grains slightly and create small cracks in the rice, which will aid puffing.

• The cooked, bumped rice is dried a second time to bring the moisture content from 17% down to around 10%, which is ideal for oven-puffing. The grains are then fed into a rotating oven and baked at 550°–650°F for about 90 seconds to give them their distinctive puffy appearance and crunchy texture.

• So what causes the famous Snap! Crackle! Pop! sound? The walls of the puffed Rice Krispies kernels are so thin and brittle that many of them collapse when they come into contact with milk.

CORN FLAKES AND BRAN FLAKES

Looking into a bowl of Corn Flakes or Raisin Bran, it's easy to imagine that all those flakes started out as one single sheet of cereal that was crumbled into a thousand individual flakes. But that's not how they're made.

• It turns out that it's much easier to make each flake separately. In the case of corn flakes, kernels of corn are processed to remove the hard outer shell and the *germ*, the part of the kernel that would have grown into a corn stalk if the kernel had been planted as a seed. What's left after the shell and the germ are removed? Chunks of starch, each of which will become an individual corn flake.

• The chunks are cooked in a solution of water, sugar, salt, flavoring, and other ingredients until the hard, white starch has become soft, translucent, and a light golden brown in color.

• The cooked corn is fed into "de-lumping" equipment to break up any clumps; then it's dried in a hot-air dryer and fed through giant rollers to flatten the chunks of corn into flakes.

• The flakes are toasted until they reach the proper golden color and have a moisture content of 1.5 to 3 percent.

• Bran flakes are made pretty much the same way, except that whole grains, not chunks, are used to make the flakes. Flaked cereals can also be made from rice or from dough.

*　　*　　*

"People will accept your ideas much more readily if you tell them somebody famous said them first."

—Benjamin Franklin

Study: Kids who eat high-sugar cereals eat twice as much as kids who eat low-sugar cereals.

CEREAL FACTS

A few more golden nuggets for you to savor.

- First athlete to appear on the front of a box of Wheaties: Olympic pole vaulter Bob Richards, in 1958. Athlete with the most Wheaties box appearances: NBA star Michael Jordan, with 18. Tiger Woods has appeared 14 times.

- Most unusual cereal premium of the 1980s: actual $1 bills, stuffed into 1 out of every 20 boxes of Cheerios in General Mills' 1986 "Treasure Hunt" sales promotion.

- In 1960 Post cereals sponsored *The Danny Thomas Show*, set in New York City, but the big-city show didn't appeal to rural Americans. When the company decided it wanted a homier showcase for its traditional Grape-Nuts cereal, which had been on the market since the 1890s, an episode was created in which Danny Thomas' character, a nightclub singer, makes a trip to a small town in North Carolina and has a run-in with the local sheriff. The episode was a hit; the spin-off *Andy Griffith Show* was born.

- How did Kellogg's Product 19 get its name? The advertising executive assigned to come up with a name for the product in 1966 couldn't think of one...until he noticed that it was the 19th product developed by Kellogg that year.

- First slogan used by the Trix Rabbit: "Rabbits are supposed to like carrots. But I hate carrots. I like Trix." (It was later changed to "Silly rabbit, Trix are for kids.")

- Why was Franken Berry cereal temporarily pulled from store shelves shortly after it was introduced in 1971? According to the character's designer, graphic artist Bill Tollis, "When kids went to the bathroom, their stools were pink from the food coloring."

- In 1937 Wheaties held a contest to find the most popular baseball announcer in the country. First prize: an all-expenses-paid trip to Hollywood. Winner: a 26-year-old Iowa sports announcer named Ronald "Dutch" Reagan. While in Hollywood, Reagan took the screen test that launched his movie career and set him on his path to the Presidency.

President Eisenhower damaged the floor of the Oval Office with his golf spikes.

BIRD BRAINS, PART III

Caw! Caw! 256! Caw! Caw! Caw! Caw! Caw! Caw! Caw!
(Translation: On page 256, you learned that crows and ravens
are really smart. Here's our final installment of brainy birds.)

POLLY WANNA DOCTORATE

Have you ever seen a talk show where an animal expert comes out with a parrot and they perform tricks? The handler asks, "What sound does a pig make?" The parrot replies, "Oink. Oink." This isn't as impressive as it may seem. Using treats as rewards, the bird was simply trained to give that response to that question. It would be much more impressive if the bird could give a vocal response that required actual thinking.

An African grey parrot named Alex could do just that. But Alex wasn't a genius among birds, he was just one of several young parrots at a Chicago pet store, selected at random by a college student named Irene Pepperberg for an experiment in 1977. After watching a TV show about gorillas that use sign language, Pepperberg wanted to see if a parrot could also learn to converse with a human. So for the next 30 years, she and Alex—whose name is short for **A**vian **L**anguage **EX**periment—worked together in a lab at Boston's Brandeis University. By the time Alex died of natural causes in 2007, he had learned more than 100 words, could identify 35 objects by recall, and understood the words "yes" and "no" as well as relative adjectives such as "bigger," "smaller," "different," and "same."

WHAT A BLOCKHEAD

In one test, Dr. Pepperberg held up a tray of objects and asked, "How many green blocks?" There were several blocks on the tray, not all of them green. There were also several green objects that weren't blocks. To come up with the answer, Alex needed to know how to differentiate between colors, how to differentiate between objects, and how to count. He inspected the tray for a moment and then answered, "Two." He was correct. Alex even understood the concept of zero, something that humans don't really pick up on until about age three. Dr. Pepperberg showed him a tray with three triangles, four squares, and five circles, and asked him, "How many are six?" His reply: "None."

But Alex's abilities went beyond using words and numbers; he understood emotions, too. When Dr. Pepperberg was stressed out, Alex would say, "Calm down." When Alex himself was getting a little tired of answering questions, he'd say, "I want dinner" or "I want to go back" (to his cage). According to Pepperberg, he displayed the emotional equivalent of a two-year-old child and the intellectual equivalent of a five-year-old child. In fact, several of the cognitive tests that were created specifically to teach Alex—and now his successors, Griffin and Arthur—are being used by developmental therapists to teach learning-disabled children how to talk and count. "This kind of research is changing the way we think about birds and intelligence," said Dr. Pepperberg, "but it also helps us break down barriers to learning in humans—and the importance of such strides cannot be underestimated."

COMING HOME TO ROOST

The more that scientists discover about parrots, crows, and other birds, the smarter they get (the birds *and* the scientists). Yet because the field of avian psychology is only a few decades old, there's still a lot about bird behavior that we don't know. For example, how does a flock of thousands of starlings seem to move as a single organism? And how exactly does a migrating Swainson's hawk find its way from Brazil to the same tree in Oregon year after year? Does it have a built-in magnetic homing device? Or can it actually *see* Earth's magnetic field? Biologists and psychologists alike are pecking away at these mysteries—trying to gain more insight into the avian condition in the hope of better understanding the human condition.

SMARTER THAN THE AVERAGE BIRD

Want more evidence of avian intelligence? While researching this article, we learned about so many birds with amazing abilities that our gooses would be cooked if we didn't include just a few more.

• **Herons:** Displaying a behavior that may have been learned by watching humans, the striated heron uses bait to catch fish. It lands on a riverbank and tosses an object into the water—an insect, berry, twig, people food, or even a fisherman's discarded fly. It waits until a hungry fish swims by, and then dives in and grabs it. Not all striated herons catch their fish this way, but it's been observed that those who do yield more fish than those who don't.

- **Honeyguides:** These African birds eat beeswax, but to get at it, they must pierce tough beehives and survive the onslaught of angry bees. Two honeyguide species get around the problem by finding a honey badger and leading it to the hive. The badger gets the honey and the birds get the wax. But if a honeyguide doesn't find a badger, it flies to a village and starts pestering people, who know exactly why it's there. The bird leads the villagers to the hive and awaits its sweet reward.

- **Cowbirds:** Brown-headed cowbirds are like mob enforcers. Females don't incubate their own eggs; instead, they wait until a female of another species, say, a warbler, lays her eggs. Then the cowbird flies in and lays her own eggs among the warbler's. If the warbler throws out the cowbird's eggs, the cowbird comes back and destroys the warbler's eggs. Over time, the warblers—and more than 200 other host species—have come to understand that if they want to raise their own chicks, they must raise the cowbirds' as well...or else.

- **Owls:** Ironically, "wise" owls rank quite low on the avian intelligence scale. Who needs tools when you have such keen nocturnal senses and silent flying abilities? But a recent discovery shows that burrowing owls do indeed use stools...er, tools. They collect animal dung and spread it out near their burrows. The dung then attracts beetles—an important part of the owls' diet.

- **Snowball:** A pet cockatoo named Snowball is believed by ornithologists to be the "first non-human animal that's conclusively demonstrated to be capable of beat induction." In other words, he can dance. After his dancing videos became famous on YouTube, scientists at Harvard University studied the bird, along with other animals, to see if they could dance. Snowball proved his abilities by keeping perfect time even when the music was slowed down and sped up. (Dogs, cats, and chimps were found to have no sense of rhythm whatsoever.) So the next time you're on the Internet, type "snowball" and "cockatoo" into a search engine. And while you're tapping your toes to the video, appreciate all of the brainpower it takes for that little ball of feathers to come up with such incredible dance moves.

Researchers say: New Zealand kea birds drop stones onto roofs just to watch people run outside.

INVENTORS, U.K.

*You may not be familiar with these British people's names—
but you know the things they invented.*

INVENTOR: Bryan Donkin (1768–1855)
STORY: In the early 1800s, Donkin, an engineer by trade, ventured into the pursuit of a cutting-edge invention. In 1812 he acquired the patent of British merchant Peter Durand: an idea for preserving meat in cans made of tin. Durand never actually made tin cans, but Donkin made the concept a reality when he developed a method of sterilizing meat inside sealed cans by heating them very slowly, and in 1813 opened the world's first canning factory in London. Apart from the exclusion of lead soldering used in the original tin cans, and the change from tin-coated iron to tinned steel in the 1860s, the product has changed little since then and is still being produced by Crosse and Blackwell—the company that took over Donkin's original business—to this day.

INVENTOR: Stephen Perry (dates unknown)
STORY: In 1839 Charles Goodyear of New Haven, Connecticut, invented the process of *vulcanization* of rubber, in which natural rubber, made from the sap of rubber trees, is heated and mixed with sulfur. This made the normally fragile raw rubber very tough, durable, and elastic, and led to its many uses in the modern world, not least of which are the tires that bear Goodyear's name. Just a few years later, an English businessman named Stephen Perry had a vulcanized-rubber factory up and running in London, and one day found himself with a small, thin, stretchy loop of vulcanized rubber, which he used to bind a bunch of letters. On March 17, 1845, he was issued the very first patent for the rubber band.

INVENTOR: George William Manby (1765–1854)
STORY: In 1807 Manby was an army captain serving on the east coast of England when he witnessed a ship sinking in a storm just 60 yards offshore. Many people died as Manby and others looked on helplessly. He went on a mission after the event, it seems, because over the next 15 years he developed several lifesaving

---

According to Guinness, each year 200,000 pints of beer are lost to beards and mustaches.

devices, including a way to shoot a rope to distressed ships via cannonball; a device for catching people jumping from burning buildings; and yet another device for rescuing people who'd fallen through ice. But he invented his most famous lifesaver by far in 1819. It was a capped copper cylinder filled with compressed air and potassium carbonate, a fine white powder known as "pearl-ash." The pearl-ash could be shot from the "Extincteur," as it was named, through a narrow hose at a fire, smothering the flames in the process. Manby's creation: the first portable fire extinguisher.

INVENTOR: James Henry Atkinson (1849-1942)

STORY: Atkinson was an *ironmonger*, meaning he sold goods made from iron, in a shop in Leeds in the north of England. In 1897 he received a patent for what he called the "Little Nipper." Today it's known as the common mousetrap.

INVENTOR: Frank Pantridge (1916-2004)

STORY: Pantridge was a cardiologist at a hospital in Belfast, Northern Ireland, in 1961, when he started working on a prob-lem: Too many heart attack victims arrived at the hospital dead. If they had made it to the hospital sooner, a defibrillator might have saved them. (Defibrillators are the "paddles" that deliver an electric shock to people having *ventricular fibrillations*, or rapid, uncontrolled heart contractions, the most deadly heart attack symptom. The electricity causes the contractions to cease.) But what if a defibrillator could be brought to the vic-tims? Pantridge received little support from his colleagues, who believed that only doctors like themselves were qualified to operate a defibrillator—not lowly emergency personnel. He kept at it anyway, and finally tested a device of his own design in 1965. It weighed 150 pounds and was powered by car batteries. Pantridge had it installed in an ambulance—and over the next 15 months successfully defibrillated 10 people. It took several years for the device to catch on, but today there are portable defibrillators in ambulances worldwide, not to mention at fire stations, on airplanes, and in many other public places. The number of people saved by Pantridge's invention may literally number in the millions.

Survey says: 57% of British kids think Germany is the most boring country in Europe.

(M)AD MEN

These quotes about advertising will leave you feeling fresh and clean.

"It is unnecessary to advertise food to hungry people, fuel to cold people, or houses to the homeless."
    —John Kenneth Galbraith

"A good advertisement is one which sells the product without drawing attention to itself."
    —David Ogilvy

"Advertising is the modern substitute for argument; its function is to make the worse appear the better."
    —George Santayana

"Advertising is the rattling of a stick inside a swill bucket."
    —George Orwell

"Ads are the cave art of the twentieth century."
    —Marshall McLuhan

"When executing advertising, think of yourself as an uninvited guest in the living room of a prospect who has the magical power to make you disappear instantly."
    —John O'Toole

"You *can* fool all the people all the time if the advertising is right and the budget is big enough."
    —Joseph E. Levine

"Advertising nourishes the consuming power of men. It sets up the goal of a better home, better clothing, better food for himself and his family. It spurs individual exertion and greater production."
    —Winston Churchill

"An advertising agency is 85 percent confusion and 15 percent commission."
    —Fred Allen

"Advertising is selling Twinkies to adults."
    —Donald R. Vance

"Good advertising does not just circulate information. It penetrates the public mind with desires and belief."
    —Leo Burnett

"Marketing is what you do when your product is no good."
    —Edwin Land

Pop quiz: How many spikes of hair are on Bart Simpson's head? A. Nine.

OOPS!

More tales of outrageous blunders.

UNFRIENDLY FIRE

In July 2009, a French Foreign Legion commander ordered his troops to engage in target practice on a field near Marseille, in southern France. Bad idea: It was a hot, dry, and windy day, and the guns fired tracer rounds—which burn, so the soldiers can see where their shots land. Each round started a little fire…and all the little fires became one big fire (France's largest in three years, forcing the evacuation of 300 homes in a nearby neighborhood). The Foreign Legion apologized and explained that there are rules in place *not* to use incendiary devices on hot days, but for some reason, the commander ignored that rule. (Reportedly, the same thing nearly happened the year before.) Said one homeowner: "I've lost my home, my car, and all my possessions. My family is now living in a gym, and it's all because of these ridiculous soldiers."

READ ALL ABOUT IT!

In the November 2, 2009, edition of the *Philadelphia Inquirer*, Macy's ran a ¾-page ad in big, bold type: "Congratulations Phillies! Back-to-Back Champs!" Below the banner was a photo of a Phillies World Series Championship T-shirt, "on sale now at Macy's!" Only problem: When the ad ran, the Phillies and the New York Yankees were *still playing* the Series—and the Phils were down three games to one. After they lost the next game, ending the Series, the *Inquirer* ran an apology for the mixup. And even though Macy's received hundreds of requests for the erroneous shirts (thousands were printed), none ever went on sale. Instead, they were all donated to disaster relief efforts in Indonesia.

IT'S AS GOOD AS GUANO

Several times over the course of five years, a British doctoral student named Daniel Bennett traveled to Indonesia to search for an endangered tree-dwelling lizard called a Butaan. (They're so hard to find that they were thought to be extinct.) Unable to locate any actual lizards, Bennett collected their droppings from the jungle floor and brought them back to his lab at Leeds University. One day in early 2009, he returned to the school to find that all 70 pounds of the poop was gone—and with it the only dietary record of the species in existence. What happened? A lab technician thought it was garbage and incinerated it. Bennett was livid—he refused the £500 ($756) the university offered him as compensation, saying, "I will see them in court."

(NOT) HOME ALONE

A family in Israel was moving to France in 2010. Gathering all five kids and their luggage put them behind schedule, but they made it to the airport in Tel Aviv on time. Although Mom and Dad had to sit in different sections of the plane, they were happy to finally have all of their children on the plane...or so they thought. Back at the airport, a police officer discovered a three-year-old girl crying in a gift shop. Luckily, the toddler was able to say her name. A quick check revealed that the rest of her family was halfway to France. Neither parent knew the other didn't have their youngest daughter until the pilot told them. The little girl was put on a later flight (with supervision) and her relieved parents retrieved her in Paris.

A CLOSE SHAVE

In March 2010, a Ford Thunderbird rear-ended a pickup truck on Highway 1 in the Florida Keys and then sped off. When Highway Patrol officers pulled over the Ford, Megan Barnes, 37, was sitting in the passenger seat; her ex-husband was in the driver's seat. But when trooper Gary Dunick noticed that the man's face had injuries consistent with the passenger-side airbag, he pressed the pair for the truth. Barnes reluctantly admitted that she'd been driving when the accident happened, and they'd switched seats afterward because she didn't have a license. (She'd lost it the day before due to a DUI conviction.) What caused the wreck? "She said she was meeting her boyfriend in Key West and wanted to be 'ready for the visit,'" said Dunick. So while her ex-husband steered from the passenger seat, Barnes was shaving her bikini line...and never even saw the slow pickup truck ahead of her.

THE ANTHRAX ATTACKS, PART III

Here's the next installment of our story on the 2001 anthrax scare. (Part II is on page 267.)

THE ROAD TO TERROR

Anthrax entered the modern era of bioterrorism in 1993, just two years after the Persian Gulf War, via an unexpected—and very scary—source: That year the Japanese religious cult Aum Shinrikyo secretly paid scientists to produce thousands of gallons of anthrax bacteria in liquid aerosol form...and over the course of several months released it from a chimney atop their headquarters in a Tokyo neighborhood. (The plan was to cause a global war and, in the ensuing mayhem, to take over the world.) Fortunately, they didn't hire very good scientists: The strain of anthrax they were using was very weak, and the aerosol spray they attempted to release turned out to be more of a goop that dribbled down the side of their building. Nobody was killed, though several people were sickened. In any case, it's the first known time in history that anthrax was a used as a weapon of terror.

The second time came eight years later.

DEADLY STRIKE

On October 2, 2001, Bob Stevens, a 63-year-old photo editor for American Media, a publisher of supermarket tabloids based in Boca Raton, Florida, was hospitalized with a high fever and severe lung infection. Infectious disease specialists in Florida believed they recognized the rod-shaped anthrax bacteria in Stevens's spinal fluid, and sent samples to the Centers for Disease Control (CDC) in Atlanta, Georgia. On October 4, the CDC publicly confirmed that Stevens had inhalation anthrax. A day later, he was dead.

Coming so soon after 9-11, the news set off a media firestorm. Officials tried to allay fears, saying it was a one-off event unrelated

---

The *Harry Potter* and *Twilight Saga* books are in the prisoners' library at Guantanamo Bay.

to terrorism. Health and Human Services Director Tommy Thompson told reporters that Stevens may have contracted the disease by drinking from a stream on a recent visit to North Carolina. (The problem with this explanation: You cannot contract inhalation anthrax by drinking water.) But all efforts to quell people's fears were useless.

ATTACK!

Two days after Stevens's death, one of his coworkers, Ernesto Blanco, 73, who had been in the hospital with "pneumonia-like" symptoms for days, was diagnosed with inhalation anthrax. (He was treated and survived.) American Media's building was immediately quarantined; more than 1,000 employees and regular visitors were tested and given antibiotics. On October 10, a third employee, 36-year-old Stephanie Dailey, tested positive for exposure to the spores, though she did not become ill. The Justice Department announced that a criminal investigation had begun... and that they believed the anthrax spores had been sent to American Media through the mail. The "anthrax attacks" were now a reality.

Investigators had a real challenge on their hands: How many people were sick and, like Blanco, already hospitalized without knowing that they had anthrax? And should they check for possible attacks at other media companies? They got their answers in a hurry: On October 12, Erin O'Connor, Tom Brokaw's assistant at NBC News in New York, tested positive for cutaneous anthrax, the less dangerous, skin-based form of the disease. (O'Connor had been in the hospital several days earlier with a rash and a fever.) And this time they had evidence.

WAIT A MINUTE, MR. POSTMAN

O'Connor was confirmed to have handled a letter that was addressed to Brokaw, and luckily she still had it. It arrived at NBC on September 19 or 20, and was first opened by an entry-level employee named Casey Chamberlain. When Chamberlain opened it, Brokaw wrote later, "a lot of granular material spilled out of it. She swept it into a wastebasket with a plastic lining and then sent the letter on to my assistant." Inside was a threatening note:

09-11-01

THIS IS NEXT

TAKE PENACILIN NOW

DEATH TO AMERICA

DEATH TO ISRAEL

ALLAH IS GREAT

The letter sat on O'Connor's desk for days—Brokaw actually picked it up and looked at it once (threatening letters were not uncommon, he said). Then, in late September, both O'Connor and Chamberlain fell ill. After Stevens's death on October 4, Brokaw became worried that the two women had contracted anthrax, but it took until October 12 to find out. When both O'Connor and Chamberlain tested positive for cutaneous anthrax, the letter was also tested—and it was confirmed to contain anthrax spores. Now things began to move very quickly:

October 15: A letter addressed to Senator Tom Daschle of South Dakota was opened by an aide…roughly 20 feet from the Senate chamber in the United States Capitol. It contained a fine, powdery substance that tested positive for anthrax.

October 18: An assistant to Dan Rather at CBS News in New York and a postal worker in New Jersey were both diagnosed with cutaneous anthrax.

October 19: An employee at the *New York Post* and a second New Jersey postal worker were diagnosed with cutaneous anthrax.

October 21: A 63-year-old Washington, D.C., postal worker named Thomas Morris Jr. died. The next day his coworker, Joseph Curseen Jr., 47, also died. Tests confirmed that both had suffered inhalation anthrax.

October 25: A 59-year-old State Department mailroom worker in Sterling, Virginia, was diagnosed with inhalation anthrax.

October 31: Kathy Nguyen, 61, a New York City hospital worker, died of inhalation anthrax.

November 16: Hazardous-materials experts sorting through letters addressed to Capitol Hill found a letter containing anthrax spores intended for Senator Patrick Leahy of Vermont.

November 21: Ottilie Lundgren, 94, of Oxford, Connecticut, died of inhalation anthrax. Hers was the fifth and final death.

1,100 horses were used in the filming of *Gone With the Wind*.

November 23: A letter sent to a doctor in Santiago, Chile, from Zurich, Switzerland, was confirmed to contain anthrax spores. It was the last letter known to be linked to the anthrax attacks.

Roundup: In less than two months, 22 people contracted anthrax and five of them died. At least 31 more were exposed to spores but did not get sick, and more than 10,000 people were prescribed Cipro as a cautionary measure. Thirty-five post offices and commercial mail centers, 26 buildings around Capitol Hill, and several other sites, including the American Media building in Florida and the NBC and CBS offices in New York, were known to have been contaminated. Some of the facilities remained closed for years.

THE LETTERS

Investigators believe that a total of seven or eight letters containing anthrax spores were sent on two different dates, though only four of the letters were ever found.

• Two were addressed to NBC and the *New York Post,* and were postmarked September 18, 2001, in Trenton, New Jersey. Both contained photocopies of the same handwritten threatening note. Neither had return addresses. It is believed that three more letters were sent the same day to ABC and CBS in New York and American Media in Florida, but were later lost.

• The letters to the offices of Senators Daschle and Leahy were postmarked October 9, also in Trenton, New Jersey. Both had handwritten, fictitious return addresses—4th Grade, Greendale School, Franklin Park, NJ 08852—and both contained photocopies of a different message:

> 09-11-01
>
> YOU CAN NOT STOP US.
>
> WE HAVE THIS ANTHRAX.
>
> YOU DIE NOW.
>
> ARE YOU AFRAID?
>
> DEATH TO AMERICA.
>
> DEATH TO ISRAEL.
>
> ALLAH IS GREAT.

• All the letters were later traced to a spore-contaminated sidewalk postal-service mailbox not far from Princeton University.

Totally Tattoos Barbie came with stick-on tattoos, including a lower-back "tramp stamp."

THE ANTHRAX SPORES

The anthrax samples mailed on the two different dates were of very different quality. The first batch, which went to the media outlets in Florida and New York, was described as a brown "granular" substance, and was relatively weak, being made up of only about 10% anthrax spores—although it was still obviously very dangerous. The substance sent in October to the two senators was described as a fine white powder...and was nearly 100% pure. (Each of those letters contained trillions of spores, theoretically enough to kill millions of people.)

For investigators, one of the most fortunate pieces of the anthrax puzzle was that you can actually identify anthrax spores the same way you can identify people: via DNA. (Bacteria have DNA, too.) There are only 89 known genetic strains of anthrax bacteria in the world, and markers identifying each strain are on record. That meant investigators could test all the spore samples collected and compare them to the known strains. And from early on, investigators knew exactly what they were working with and exactly where it came from. The spores were cultured from what is called the "Ames strain," which produces a particularly powerful form of the anthrax toxin. There were just 16 government, commercial, and university labs around the country that had Ames-strain bacteria, and further testing narrowed the spores used in the attacks to a particular batch known as RMR-1029.

That batch existed in only one place in the world: the U.S. Army Medical Research Institute of Infectious Diseases (USAMRIID) at Fort Detrick in Maryland—the military's primary biological weapons lab. The 2001 anthrax attacks, it seemed, came not only from inside the United States, it looked like they had been done by someone working for the government.

But even though this was known very early on, it didn't stop federal investigators—and the media—from looking for blame elsewhere.

For Part IV of the story,
turn to page 489.

When people in Sweden have their picture taken, they say "omelet," not "cheese."

DO YOU SPEAK *LÁADAN*?

You've heard of Esperanto (page 195) and you can probably speak a little pig Latin. Here's a look at some other "constructed languages" that have been created over the years. Appy-hay eading-ray!

SOLRESOL ("Language"): A "musical language" created by François Sudre, a French author, in the mid-1800s.
Features: Sudre based his entire language on the musical scale: "do," "re," "mi," "fa," "sol," "la," and "ti." Each word in Solresol is composed of one or more of these syllables. It's probably the only language in the world that can be translated directly into music, and vice versa. And not just music: Any system you can think of that has seven different components—seven hand signals, seven whistles, seven colors, etc.—can serve as a medium for communicating in Solresol.

Sample Words:

dodomi: season	*ladoti*: book	*fadore*: corrupt
reredo: July	*tiremido*: deaf	*sollamifa*: sculpture
midofasol: orphan	*dofafado*: Easter	*laremila*: blue
fafadosol: surgeon	*remitisol*: stairs	*tilamido*: police

Fatal Flaw: Sudre drew huge crowds at demonstrations where language students translated his violin playing into speech. But as much as the public enjoyed the show, most thought of Solresol as nothing more than a novelty act. It never caught on.

VOLAPÜK ("World Language"): Invented by a Bavarian Catholic priest named Johann Martin Schleyer in the 1870s, Volapük was inspired by a dream: God told Schleyer to invent a single, universal language that people of all nations could speak.

Features: To make Volapük easier to pronounce, Schleyer left the "th" sound out of the language entirely. He also kept the use of the letter "r" to a minimum, to make it easier for native Chinese speakers to pronounce. These and other efforts at simplification paid off: By the late 1880s, there were nearly 300 Volapük societies around the world. More than two dozen magazines were printed in or about Volapük, and textbooks of Volapük language

---

Unlike humans, whales and dolphins have to actively decide when to breathe.

instruction were available in 25 different languages. Three international Volapük conferences were held, in 1884, 1887, and 1889; the last one, in Paris, was conducted entirely in Volapük.

Sample Words:

nenomik: abnormal	*rolatridem*: escalator	*yebafel*: lawn
sanavik: medical	*niblit*: pants	*sasenan*: murderer
delagased: newspaper	*paänakek*: pancake	*geböfik*: ordinary
släm: mud	*jipal*: mother	*adyö!* goodbye!

Fatal Flaw: Schleyer was very protective of Volapük, and that proved to be its downfall. When a group of reformers tried to fix what they felt were flaws in his language, he blocked them. The movement then split into several factions, each of which then created their own version of Volapük. The entire point of a single universal language having been defeated, the movement collapsed. Today there are fewer than 30 Volapük speakers on Earth.

INTERLINGUA ("Between Language"): Since English, Spanish, French, Italian, German, and Russian are all cousins, they have many words with common roots that look and sound similar to one another. Why not use these words as a basis for creating a universal language? That was the thinking behind Interlingua, a language started in 1937 by a group called the International Auxiliary Language Association. The project was delayed by World War II, but by 1951 Interlingua was ready to go.

Features: Basing Interlingua on existing languages made it a lot easier to learn. You don't have to be a fluent Interlingua speaker to guess what words like *fragile*, *politica*, *rapide*, and even *disveloppamento* mean.

Sample Words:

in flammas: ablaze	*abbreviar*: abridge	*condemnar*: convict
ris: rice	*salon*: living room	*cisorios*: scissors
escaldar: scald	*inseniar*: teach	*legumine*: vegetable
servitor: waiter	*vinia*: vineyard	*juvene*: young

Outcome: Interest in Interlingua peaked in the 1950s and 1960s, when more than 30 scientific and medical journals published article summaries in Interlingua. Interest has dropped off considerably since then, but Interlingua remains the second-most popular constructed language after Esperanto.

LÁADAN ("Perception Language"): The world's first feminist language. Invented by science-fiction author Suzette Haden Elgin in 1982, Láadan was an experimental language created to test a theory that was popular with feminists: namely, that modern languages had a male bias that restricted feminine thought and perception.

Remember the old saw that Eskimos have a hundred different words for "snow" while English has only "snow"? If having only one word for "snow" limits how English speakers think about snow, the feminist theory went, then a male bias in modern languages, if it existed, would similarly restrict the perceptions of women. Elgin theorized that if women embraced Láadan within 10 years, or were at least inspired by it to create a better feminist language, that would support the theory of a male bias in modern languages. If Láadan flopped, that was evidence of little or no bias: Women had no need for Láadan because they were well served by the languages they already spoke.

Features: Láadan had five words for "joy," five words for "anger," four words for "it" (three female and one male), and six words for "alone." It also had 13 words for "love," including *ab*, "love for one liked but not respected"; *ad*, "love for one respected but not liked"; and *éeme*, "love for one neither liked nor respected." (Curiously, Láadan also has a word for "sewage plant"—*waludal.*)

Sample Words:

with: adult (female)	*withid*: adult (male)	*héeya*: fear
lub: chicken	*oba*: body	*sheb*: change
miwith: city	*miwithá*: city dweller	*yob*: coffee
oma: hand	*wíi*: alive	*óol*: moon

Outcome: Láadan never attracted more than a handful of enthusiasts, some of whom are still contributing new words and grammar to this day. But as Arika Okrent writes in *In the Land of Invented Languages*, "After 10 years passed, and women still had not embraced Láadan or come up with another language to replace it, Elgin declared the experiment a failure, noting, with some bitterness, that Klingon (a hyper-male 'warrior' language) was thriving."

SHOW STOPPERS

The show must go on! Or, well, um, no. It doesn't, really.

PERFORMER: John Cale, Welsh singer-songwriter and a founding member of the highly influential rock band the Velvet Underground. He was also quite a strange person.
SHOW: Cale was performing with his own band at a club called The Greyhound in Croydon, England, in April 1977. During a long and very dark version of the Elvis Presley classic "Heartbreak Hotel," Cale brought a dead chicken onto the stage (it had been killed backstage a short time earlier) and started swinging it around his head.
STOPPER: Then he pulled out a meat cleaver and decapitated it—and threw the head and body into the dancing crowd. Everyone immediately stopped dancing. Cale later called it "the most effective showstopper I ever came up with." But it didn't stop with the audience: The band's drummer, Joe Stefko, and bass player, Mike Visceglia, were vegetarians. They'd actually discussed the chicken routine with Cale before the show, and told him that if he did it, they'd leave. He did it...and they left. Not just the stage—they both left the band. (Stefko went on to play with Meat Loaf; Visceglia with Suzanne Vega.) Cale's next album, titled *Animal Justice*, contained a track that, so the story goes, was about the two quitting bandmembers. Title: "Chickensh*t."

PERFORMER: Cate Blanchett, Oscar-winning actress
SHOW: Blanchett was playing Blanche DuBois in *A Streetcar Named Desire* at the Sydney Theater in Australia in 2009.
STOPPER: In the middle of a fight scene with Joel Edgerton, playing Stanley Kowalski, Edgerton was supposed to pick up a large, 1960s-style radio and, in a fit of rage, throw it out a window. He missed the window and nailed Blanchett right in the head. The audience gasped as Blanchett dropped to her knees, and blood started dripping down her face and neck. Somehow, the actress managed to get up and continue the scene, but about 30 seconds later the lights went out and the curtain came down. After 10 more minutes went by, a producer came out and

---

James Earl Jones, Ray Liotta, and Susan Sarandon all got their start on soap operas.

announced that the show was canceled. (Fortunately, Blanchett was only slightly injured and returned to the show the next evening.)

PERFORMER: Cat Power, a singer/songwriter whose real name is Chan Marshall

SHOW: In November 2000, just as she was beginning to gain national attention, Power did a show at Irving Plaza, a music hall in New York City. She was also becoming known for her bizarre onstage antics. That night she started—but didn't finish—several songs on both the guitar and the piano, mumbled apologies to the crowd, *asked* them to talk during her songs, and constantly interrupted songs to make requests or complaints to the soundman.

STOPPER: An hour or so into the show, Power jumped off the stage and ran through the crowd and out the front door. She wasn't seen again that night. Power later blamed the antics on a drinking problem. She's now sober and not nearly as erratic onstage as she used to be. But before that, she once mooned an audience, told them all to go away, and said that if they didn't like it they could sue her. Another time, at an outdoor show, she ignored the crowd altogether for 15 minutes...while she talked to a squirrel.

PERFORMER: Idina Menzel, a Tony Award-winning actress

SHOW: In January 2005, Menzel was performing in the Stephen Schwartz musical *Wicked*, playing the part of Elphaba, the misunderstood, green-skinned girl modeled after the Wicked Witch of the West from the L. Frank Baum story *The Wizard of Oz*.

STOPPER: Near the end of the play, the character Dorothy throws a bucket of water on Elphaba...and she "melts." Here's how the effect is done: a trapdoor in the stage floor opens, exposing a platform; Menzel steps onto the platform, which is then lowered while Menzel wails and flails her robes, giving the appearance of melting. But that night someone lowered the platform too early and when the trapdoor opened, the Wicked Witch of the West fell into the hole and broke several ribs. The curtain was dropped, actors and crew rushed to help the actress, and she was taken to the hospital. The show was stopped for 45 minutes—but did eventually go on, as Menzel's understudy got into costume and finished out the performance. Unfortunately, the following day's performance was slated to be Menzel's final show—after a 14-month run—and for her, the show did not go on. What was supposed to be Menzel's grand finale was, in fact, performed by her understudy.

PERFORMERS: The Who
SHOW: On the night of May 16, 1969, the Who played the Fillmore East in Manhattan.
STOPPER: A few songs into their set, a disheveled-looking, heavy-set man climbed up on stage and grabbed the microphone out of singer Roger Daltrey's hand, right in the middle of a song. Daltrey stood there stunned, while bassist John Entwistle and one of the band's roadies grabbed the guy. Then guitarist Pete Townshend walked up and kicked the interloper right in the "bollocks." Then they threw him off the stage and finished the song. (Drummer Keith Moon hadn't stopped playing at all…and possibly hadn't even noticed what was going on.)

A minute later, Pete Townshend said, "I smell smoke." Someone walked out from backstage, whispered in his ear, and the band quickly left the stage. Why? The five-story apartment building and supermarket next door were on fire. The audience was asked to exit the theater quietly (which they did). Unbeknownst to the band, the man who had jumped onstage was a plainclothes cop trying to tell everyone about the fire. The NYPD nearly charged Townshend with assault; he eventually paid a fine and the matter was dropped.

BONUS. We didn't have to read a rock 'n' roll history book to research this item. Why? Because a very young Uncle John was there that night. And—amazingly—he remembers it! (But we researched it anyway, just to be sure.)

*　　*　　*

TWO RANDOM FACTS

• In an early draft of *Raiders of the Lost Ark*, Indiana Jones's weapon of choice was brass knuckles, not a whip.

• Gustave Eiffel, designer of the Eiffel Tower, had a fear of heights.

THINKING OUTSIDE THE BOX

As anyone who works in a large office knows, the corporate workplace is dominated by little boxes called cubicles. On page 327 we told you the history of the cube. Here's what you have to look forward to.

A NEW WORKDAY IS DAWNING
However flawed it may be, the office cubicle is still a very flexible and economical way for an employer to give workers a bit of privacy, easy access to their equipment and files, and a place to put up Dilbert posters. So don't expect cubicles to be "made redundant" anytime soon. But new designs are being tested with the knowledge that the workplace is different than it was in 1980, and different than what it will be in 2020. Workers aren't the same, either. Due to a combination of factors—improved technology, cheaper outsourcing, corporate downsizing, and the changing economy—there are fewer low-level positions such as receptionists and data entry personnel, and more specialists, middle managers, salespeople, and creative types. All of them must multitask more than ever before, and very few will get an office of their own.

What does this mean for cubicles? The goal is still the same: They should keep out distractions and encourage interaction, but not make the workers feel "oppressed." To accomplish this, several design firms are working on what many refer to as "Cubicle 2.0." Here's a bit of what looms on the horizon both inside and outside of the box.

NEWBICLES

• **No more squares:** Many new personal workspaces are circular, like pods. A company called StrongProject sells S-shaped cubicles. High-tech cubicles resemble the command center of a sci-fi spaceship.

• **Lighting:** Because studies have shown that fluorescent bulbs cause eye strain and fatigue, some new cubicles include their own incandescent lighting systems. "My Studio Environment," made by Herman Miller, the company that released the first partitioned office system in 1968, comes with translucent plastic walls, which still give workers privacy but let in more light. (Most revolutionary, My Studio Environment actually comes with a sliding door.)

• **Noise:** After a lack of privacy, cube dwellers' biggest complaint is that they overhear co-workers' conversations. One solution is a device called the "Babble," a white-noise generator that broadcasts garbled recordings of the user's voice. If you can't decipher your neighbor's actual words, the thinking goes, the talking will be less distracting. (There's also the tried-and-true method for blocking out unwanted noise—headphones.) Three other noise reduction ideas:

1) Soundproof phone booths called "Cell Cells." Located throughout an office floor, they come with cell-phone reception boosters so workers can talk on their phones in private.

2) A 2-person soundproof pod called a "Dyadic Slice." Two co-workers can sit inside it and gossip all they want (or work, or settle their differences) without the rest of the office overhearing them.

3) And for loud brainstorming meetings, there's the larger, but also soundproof, "Digital Yurt."

WAY OUTSIDE THE BOX

• **Studio 53:** In the 1970s, New York City's Studio 54 was *the* premier disco club. Studio 53, made by Steelcase, recreates that feeling with shag carpeting, velvet walls, and plush pillows...in an eight-foot by eight-foot cubicle. When it was unveiled at a trade show in 2006, it wasn't meant to be taken seriously (for one thing, it cost thousands of dollars), but according to James Ludwig, Steelcase's director of design, "Not only were people connecting to its high-concept message of 'Don't Hate Me Because I'm a Cubicle,' but designers were unrolling blueprints to discuss how we could include some of the workstations in their projects." Much to Ludwig's surprise, Steelcase received several orders on the spot.

• **Dilbert's Ultimate Cubicle:** In 2001 *Dilbert* creator Scott Adams realized that "somehow, accidentally, I'd become a leading authority on what's wrong with the cubicle." Spurred on by his readers, Adams partnered with the design firm IDEO to build "Dilbert's Ultimate Cubicle." Though most features were intended as a spoof (the hammock and the "boss monitor"), a few have since been incorporated into actual cubicle designs, including lighting that changes in accordance with the time of day.

50% of American men wear briefs, 40% wear boxers, and 10% wear boxer-briefs.

TEAR DOWN THE WALLS

As innovative as these new cube farms are, they're still cube farms—and employers pay a lot of rent and other overhead costs just so workers can show up and sit inside their boxes all day. Solution: Many offices of the future may not be offices at all.

In 1993 Jay Chiat, chairman of the ad agency Chiat/Day, sent shockwaves through the corporate world by removing all of the cubicles and desks from his Venice, California, office building. He replaced them with lounge chairs, couches, floor lamps, and low tables. Chiat's aim was to create the relaxed yet productive atmosphere he'd witnessed in coffee shops. When his staff arrived at work, they'd store their belongings in lockers, check out a laptop computer, pour a hot cup of joe, find a comfy place to sit, and get to work. The idea bombed. Most employees stopped showing up, opting to work from home instead. Productivity plummeted, and Chiat was ridiculed by the industry.

Two decades later, however, many are calling him a visionary. His idea was good, but the technology simply wasn't yet advanced enough to make it work. Today, thanks to high-speed Internet access, Wi-Fi, versatile handheld devices, and powerful laptop computers, "hoteling" is becoming more common. Now many workers can perform most of their tasks at home or on the road. They have a desk at the main office but only use it for a few days per week. On other days, it's used by someone else.

VIRTUAL REALITY

Proving the merits of a cubicle-free workplace, in 2009 Rich Sheridan, CEO of Menlo Innovations, a Michigan software company, removed all of his office's partitioned walls, stating, "Cubicles kill morale, communication, productivity, creativity, teamwork, energy, spirit, and results." Now no one at Menlo has their own desk. Instead, they do what Chiat had attempted in 1993—show up, grab a seat, turn on their laptops, and start working. Executives work alongside designers...if they're not working from home. In contrast to Chiat's virtual failure, according to Sheridan, Menlo's costs are way down and productivity is way up.

So expect to see improved cubicles of all shapes and sizes, and a lot more virtual offices in the near future. For now, though, it's time to get back to work! (Is it six o'clock yet?)

Terminal velocity—the top speed at which an object on Earth can fall—is about 120 mph.

CAUSE OF DEATH

How do you determine how someone died when they died hundreds of years ago? You do a little research, find a few clues—and make a guess.

Alexander the Great died in 323 B.C. He was only 32. Greek historians later wrote that a few weeks before his death people witnessed ravens acting strangely...and that some birds even died at Alexander's feet. After that he became ill, suffering a high fever and severe headaches. Several possible causes for Alexander's death have been guessed at over the centuries, including poisoning, malaria, and typhoid fever, but in 2003 researchers at the Centers for Disease Control in Atlanta put forth a new diagnosis: He died of West Nile virus. Ravens, they said, are especially susceptible to the disease, and can spread it via mosquitoes to humans, who usually die within a few weeks...after suffering primarily from fever and headaches.

Herod the Great was the king of ancient Judea from about 36 B.C. until his death in 4 B.C. Jewish historian Flavius Josephus, who lived shortly after Herod, wrote that leading up to his death the king had suffered excruciating pain in his sides, intense itching, and gangrene—or tissue death—of the genitalia. In 2002 Professor Jan Hirschmann of the University of Washington concluded that Herod's symptoms indicate that he died from a combination of kidney disease, which causes side pain and intense itching, and a rare condition called Fournier's Gangrene, which causes swelling, itching, intense pain, and tissue death in the genitalia.

King Henry VIII died in 1547 at the age of 56. Surviving pieces of his clothing and armor indicate that his waist and chest both measured more than 50 inches, so Henry weighed roughly 300 pounds. Paintings show him with a very round face, and it's known that at the time of his death his legs and feet were covered in ulcerated sores—some of which he had endured for many years. In 2006 British historian Robert Hutchinson theorized in his book *The Last Days of Henry VIII* that the king may have died from a rare hormone disorder called Cushing's Syndrome. Major symptoms of Cushing's: upper-body obesity, a rounded "moon" face, and impaired wound-healing ability—fitting Henry to a tee.

Why did Teddy Roosevelt denounce Christmas trees? "A waste of good timber."

WHOPPERKNOCKERS AND SAND SQUINKS

*A few more mythical beasts to keep terrified campers
awake at night. (Part I is on page 200.)*

The Whirling Wumpus. The wumpus is similar to the Tasmanian Devil of cartoon fame, except that he's about seven feet tall and has a face like an ape, giant forelegs, and front paws that are as big and hard as boat oars. It has been known to station itself by a bend in a trail, and then, when a logger happens along, it rears up on its powerful hind legs and spins so fast that it becomes nearly invisible. In this state it emits a low humming drone. As the logger wanders up to investigate the strange sound and steps within striking distance of those giant boat-oar paws, he is instantly beaten to a meaty pulp and sprayed all over the surrounding trees and vegetation. When this happens, the whirling wumpus spins to a stop and slurps up all the goo.

• **The Rumtifusel.** This strange and deadly creature has a body that's as flat as a griddle cake and beautiful fur—which is what makes it so enticing to the loggers. When the rumtifusel sprawls itself over a tree stump, it looks exactly like a mink coat that someone has abandoned. Who can resist that? When a logger comes up for a closer look, no doubt hoping to snag the prize for a lady friend, the rumtifusel strikes, leaping up and instantly wrapping itself around the logger. The thousands of squid-like suction cups on the rumtifusel's underbelly can reduce the logger to a pile of bones in mere seconds.

• **The Columbia River Sand Squink.** Found in British Columbia, Washington, and northern Oregon, the sand squink has the body of a fox, the head and long ears of a jackrabbit, and the bushy tail of a squirrel. It feeds on electric eels and gold prospectors, and always in that order. Normally a timid creature, when the sand squink eats the eels it gains both courage *and* an electric charge; then, when it spots a prospector walking alone, it touches its bushy tail to one ear and then the other, creating an electric light show the prospector finds irresistible. The sand squink

---

Studies show: Americans are much more likely to be killed by a car than by a gun.

then leads the prospector deep into the forest...and he is never seen again.

- **The Whopperknocker.** A woodland critter with lightning-fast reflexes and what must be the best eyesight of any animal in the forest, the whopperknocker cannot be shot: It can see the sparks in the chamber of the hunter's rifle even before the bullet has left the barrel. As soon as it sees the sparks, it moves out of the bullet's path and makes a clean getaway (which doubtless explains why so few specimens have been recovered from the wild).

- **The Ball-Tailed Cat.** This wildcat is found in some parts of Pennsylvania and Oregon and nowhere else. The male cat's distinguishing feature: a heavy, bony ball about the size of a cantaloupe at the end of its tail. The cat uses the tail to kill its prey: lumberjacks. It hides in tree branches over logging trails and other places where loggers are likely to come along. When one passes underneath, it drops on the logger and beats him to death with the ball. During mating season the male also beats the ball against hollow logs to attract females.

- **The Snow Wasset.** One of the few creatures that hibernates in summer and is active in winter, the snake-like snow wasset is green in color during the summer months, with tiny legs that enable it to move around just enough to stay in the shade. As soon as the first snow falls, the creature sheds its legs and turns a snowy white. For the rest of the winter it prowls beneath the surface of the snow like a submarine stalking ships, sneaking up on wolves and other prey and devouring them at will.

*   *   *

MOST-WANTED FACTS

- Since 1950, there have been 494 fugitives on the FBI's "Ten Most Wanted" list. Of those, 463 have been captured.

- Shortest amount of time on the list: two hours (Billy Austin Bryant, in 1969). Longest: armored-car-facility robber Victor Gerena was put on the list in 1984; he still hasn't been captured

- Minimum reward for information leading to the arrest of a fugitive on the Top Ten list: $100,000.

Back to basics: *Martha Stewart Living*'s most-requested recipe is macaroni and cheese.

RESIGNED IN PROTEST

Throughout history there have been people who have stood up and said
"I quit!"—and it just makes you feel all warm and fuzzy inside.

WHO: William Pitt the Younger, Prime Minister of Great Britain

BACKGROUND: In 1800 Pitt introduced the Emancipation of Catholics Bill, which would have ended discrimination against Catholics (they could not, for example, hold public office at the time) and strengthened Great Britain's union with Ireland.

RESIGNATION: King George III refused to accept the bill, saying it would violate the oath he took to protect the Church of England. Pitt felt equally strongly about making concessions to Catholics, so on February 16, 1801, after 18 years in power (the second-longest term in British history), he resigned in protest. He remains the only prime minister in British history to resign the position in such a way. (Unfortunately, Pitt's resignation did little to help Catholics, as the issue was effectively squashed for decades. They weren't allowed to hold elected office until 1829.)

WHO: Eleanor Roosevelt, First Lady, and a member of the Daughters of the American Revolution

BACKGROUND: The DAR is a historical preservation society open to women who can prove ancestral lineage to someone who aided the American Revolution. (Roosevelt had ancestors who fought in the war.) In 1939 the DAR was caught in a controversy when legendary music impresario Sol Hurok tried to book singer Marian Anderson into the organization's concert venue, Constitution Hall in Washington, D.C. DAR officials refused to allow it because Anderson was African American, and the DAR had a "whites only" performer policy.

RESIGNATION: Roosevelt very publicly resigned her DAR membership in protest. Then she used her influence to arrange for Anderson to perform on the steps of the Lincoln Memorial. More than 75,000 people attended. Chastened DAR officials apologized, and Anderson was later allowed to perform. (The "whites only" policy, however, wasn't officially rescinded until 1952.)

U.S. death rates rise 15% in winter due to influenza, pneumonia, and hypothermia.

WHO: James A. Bayard Jr., United States Senator from Delaware

BACKGROUND: In 1864, in the midst of the Civil War, Congress passed a law requiring its members to take a greatly expanded loyalty oath, hoping to root out supporters of the Confederacy. The new oath required them to swear that they had never taken up arms against the government or supported such action in the past, and would never do so in the future.

RESIGNATION: Senator Bayard, who'd been in office since 1850, took the oath—then immediately resigned his seat. It was an insult, he said, to long-serving members of Congress. Even worse, it would make it impossible to reunite the country after the war, as no senator from the South could honestly take such an oath, given its "in the past" provision.

ON SECOND THOUGHT: When Bayard's successor died in office in 1867, Bayard was appointed to finish out the term...and he took the expanded loyalty oath. (The wartime oath was finally repealed and replaced with a much milder oath in 1884.)

WHO: Edvard Beneš, President of Czechoslovakia

BACKGROUND: In 1938 Adolf Hitler demanded that Czechoslovakia cede to Germany their western border land, known as the Sudetenland, which was home to many ethnic Germans. Beneš, assured that he had the backing of France and the Soviet Union, refused. In September 1938, leaders of Nazi Germany, France, Britain, and Italy met in Munich—without the Czechs—and agreed that Hitler could have the Sudetenland.

RESIGNATION: On October 5, Beneš resigned in disgust. Within months, the Nazis had taken all of Czechoslovakia. Beneš formed a Czechoslovak government-in-exile in London, and in 1945, at war's end, returned to be elected the president of the country. That lasted until the takeover by communists allied with the Soviet Union in 1948—at which point Beneš resigned again. He died later that year at the age of 64.

WHO: Einar Hovdhaugen and Helge Rognlien, members of the Norwegian Nobel Prize Committee

BACKGROUND: The 1973 Nobel Peace Prize was awarded jointly to U.S. National Security Advisor Henry Kissinger and North Vietnamese general Le Duc Tho for having negotiated a

cease-fire between North and South Vietnam in January 1973.
RESIGNATION: Hovdhaugen and Rognlien, both longtime
Norwegian politicians, were so disgusted with the choice that they
resigned from the Nobel committee. Why? For starters, the cease-
fire had been signed in January, and the war was still raging at the
time the prize was awarded—10 months later. General Tho, in
fact, refused to accept his prize for just that reason. (The war actually continued for another two years.) Need another reason?
Kissinger, having been the main force behind America's bombing
campaigns in Cambodia, seemed unworthy of a "peace" prize.
BONUS FACT: When South Vietnam fell to the North in 1975—
rendering the earlier "cease-fire" meaningless—Kissinger tried to
give the prize back, but the committee refused.

WHO: Jerald terHorst, Press Secretary to President Gerald Ford
BACKGROUND: Vice President Ford became president on
August 9, 1974, after the resignation of Richard Nixon, and made
terHorst, a veteran reporter for the *Detroit News*, his press secretary the same day. Rumors began swirling almost immediately that
Ford was going to pardon Nixon for any crimes he may have committed in relation to the Watergate scandal. TerHorst assured
reporters that there were no such plans.
RESIGNATION: A month later, Ford pardoned Nixon. An
appalled terHorst turned in his resignation the same day. "I cannot
in good conscience support your decision to pardon former President Nixon even before he has been charged with the commission
of any crime," he wrote in his letter of resignation. He was
replaced by NBC reporter Ron Nessen. TerHorst stood by his
decision to leave the post until his death in 2010 at the age of 87.

WHO: U.S. Secretary of State Cyrus Vance
BACKGROUND: On November 4, 1979, hundreds of Iranian
students stormed the U.S. embassy in Tehran, taking dozens of
Americans hostage. President Jimmy Carter's aides advised him to
try a rescue operation. Vance advised against it, insisting it was too
risky to the hostages, rescuers, and American-Iranian relations.
Carter went against Vance's advice and authorized "Operation
Eagle Claw." It was a disaster. Eight American servicemen were
killed, several aircraft were lost, and no hostages were rescued.

Bite me! Researchers have recently discovered two species of frogs that have fangs.

RESIGNATION: Vance was so opposed to the rescue plan that he actually resigned on April 21, 1980, three days before the attempt (although it was kept from the public for the sake of the mission). "I know how deeply you have pondered your decision on Iran," he wrote to the president, "I wish I could support you. But for reasons we have discussed I cannot." The 52 American hostages were held for 444 days, until January 20, 1981—the day after Jimmy Carter's presidency ended. Vance served in several diplomatic positions with the United Nations over the following decades, and died in 2002 at age 84.

WHO: Bruce Boler, a water quality specialist with the EPA

BACKGROUND: Boler was assigned to southwest Florida in 2001 to assess the impact of development in and around the area's wetlands. In the course of his work he refused several permits for golf course developments because of the amount of pollutants the developments would discharge into sensitive wetland areas. Outraged developers funded their own "scientific" studies, which determined that developments such as golf courses were actually better for the environment...than natural wetlands. Amazingly, in 2003 the EPA accepted the studies.

RESIGNATION: Boler immediately resigned, calling the findings "absurd," and went public with the information. (He now works at Florida's Everglades National Park.)

WHO: Larry Ramsell, Historian for the National Fresh Water Fishing Hall of Fame in Hayward, Wisconsin

BACKGROUND: In 2005 the Illinois-based World Musky Alliance (a "musky" is a type of fish) filed a protest with the Fishing Hall of Fame. The problem: They listed a musky caught in 1949 by one Louis Spray in Wisconsin as the largest ever caught, at 63.5 inches—and it was a lie! The Musky Alliance claimed they had photographic proof that the fish in question was only about 56.3 inches long. That meant that a 60.25-inch fish caught by Mr. Cal Johnson, also in 1949, was really the largest. In January 2006, the Hall of Fame announced that, after a long investigation, they had determined that the record would stand.

RESIGNATION: Ramsell resigned in protest. Almost nobody noticed.

BASIC INSTINCT, STARRING JODIE FOSTER

More films that required a lot of trial and error before casting the actors we've come to know in the roles. Can you imagine, for example...

CHRISTIAN BALE AS GEORGE W. BUSH (*W.*, 2008) After he was hired by director Oliver Stone, Bale (*Batman Begins*) spent months studying the president, but then dropped out just before filming began because he felt that his prosthetic makeup didn't make him look enough like Bush. Stone hastily cast Josh Brolin instead. (Coincidentally, his father, James Brolin, had played Ronald Reagan in a 2003 TV movie.)

JULIA ROBERTS AS CATHERINE TRAMMELL (*Basic Instinct*, 1992) Jodie Foster, Julia Roberts, and Kim Basinger were each offered the role of the seductive crime novelist, but all declined due to the graphic sex scenes. So director Paul Verhoeven cast Sharon Stone after seeing her play a seductive killer in 1990's *Total Recall*. The male lead was turned down by Sylvester Stallone, Wesley Snipes, Denzel Washington, Kurt Russell, Mickey Rourke, Alec Baldwin, Don Johnson, Tom Cruise, and Patrick Swayze. Michael Douglas finally signed on, but only after producers agreed to have his part rewritten as less "wimpy."

JAKE GYLLENHAAL AS JAKE SULLY (*Avatar*, 2009) James Cameron's first choice was the little-known Australian actor Sam Worthington, but because 20th Century Fox was spending nearly half a billion dollars on the film, they told Cameron to audition Gyllenhaal and Matt Damon, both of whom were bigger box-office draws. "Honestly, did I go out and try to woo them? No," admitted Cameron. "I had my heart set on Sam. Maybe Jake and Matt sensed my lack of 100% commitment." Neither Damon nor Gyllenhaal wanted the role, so Cameron got Worthington, and Fox still made its half a billion back...and then some.

ROB LOWE AS REN McCORMACK (*Footloose*, 1984) Tom Cruise and John Travolta both turned down the role of the high-school kid who dares to dance in a town where dancing is banned, so Rob Lowe was cast. When Lowe injured his knee while dancing and had to quit, the producers asked Kevin Bacon to audition, based on his work in *Diner*. Bacon said no—he'd already accepted the lead in the Stephen King horror movie *Christine*. "If you get *Footloose*," they told Bacon, "it will make you a star." One minute into the audition, Bacon got the part (and it did make him a star).

FRANK SINATRA AND ANTHONY PERKINS AS JERRY AND JOE (*Some Like It Hot*, 1959) Named by the American Film Institute as the "best comedy of all time," this classic stars Jack Lemmon and Tony Curtis as musicians who dress in drag and join an all-girl orchestra to hide from the Mob. Director Billy Wilder wanted Lemmon and Curtis, but the studio wanted bigger stars. Sinatra didn't show up to a lunch meeting, and Perkins just "wasn't right." (Jerry Lewis declined because he didn't want to wear women's clothes.) Wilder got his first choices. A year later, Perkins starred in Alfred Hitchcock's *Psycho*, the AFI's "best thriller of all time."

SANDRA BULLOCK AS MAGGIE FITZGERALD (*Million Dollar Baby*, 2004) Bullock tried for several years to get this short story made into a film so she could star in it, but no studio wanted to finance a movie about a female boxer. Bullock gave up due to a contractual obligation to film *Miss Congeniality 2*. Director Clint Eastwood took over the project and secured some financing, but had to come up with half of the money himself. With Bullock unavailable, he hired Hilary Swank and shot the film on a shoestring budget in just 37 days. Result: The movie that no studio wanted ended up winning four Oscars, including Best Picture.

KEVIN KLINE AS SAM WHEAT (*Ghost*, 1990) Writer Bruce J. Rubin told director Jerry Zucker (*Airplane!*) that Patrick Swayze should star. "You mean the *Dirty Dancing* guy?" asked Zucker. Zucker's first choice was Kevin Kline, who declined. So did Tom Hanks, Tom Cruise, Kevin Bacon, Al Pacino, Bruce Willis, Harrison Ford, Nicolas Cage, Mickey Rourke, David Duchovny, Johnny Depp, Chevy Chase, and Alec Baldwin. None of them believed in the ghostly love story. But Swayze did: "The script made me cry." So Zucker reluctantly gave him an audition. Swayze got the part, and *Ghost* became 1990's top-grossing movie worldwide.

More than 125 women are known to have posed as men and fought in the Civil War.

THE LLOYDS BANK TURD

It may sound gross, but it's real and it's considered a national "treasure." And although we might wish we did, we didn't make up the name—that's really what it's called. Get ready to learn about bathroom archaeology.

BEAUTY, SKIN DEEP
If you've ever been to the English city of York, you already know that it's one of the most beautiful cities in the United Kingdom. Situated at the junction of the Ouse and Foss rivers, this onetime capital of the kingdom of Northumbria is home to picturesque cobblestone streets, elegant Tudor architecture, and York Minster Cathedral, one of the finest churches in England. York was one of the nation's largest cities until the Industrial Revolution, when it was eclipsed by manufacturing centers like Sheffield and Birmingham. That may not have been good for the local economy, but it did preserve the city's charm.

Alas, York wasn't always the sparkling jewel that it is today. In the Middle Ages it was positively filthy, something King Edward III observed when he visited in the 14th century. He ordered that the streets be cleaned at once, noting that the "abominable smell abounding in the city...from dung and manure and filth and dirt," was worse "than any other city in the realm."

DOWN UNDER

Edward's observation wasn't unfounded. There have been settlements at York for more than 2,000 years, and one result of the continuous occupation of the site is that the modern city sits on a layer of densely compacted rubbish and filth that archaeologists estimate is about 10 feet deep.

Portions of this mass are remarkably well preserved, thanks to the fact that the soil in some parts of the city is waterlogged and largely oxygen free, preserving for more than 1,000 years things like wood, leather, cloth, and bone, most of which normally would have biodegraded completely in just a decade or two. Modern archaeologists got their first inkling of how much lay beneath York in 1972, when the foundation for a Lloyds Bank branch was dug on Pavement Street and artifacts from the city's Viking period were discovered in the muck. (Viking raiders captured York—then known as Jorvik—in 866 A.D. and held it for nearly a century before they were finally driven off in 954.)

HERE, THERE, EVERYWHERE

An even bigger discovery of Viking artifacts was made down the road in 1976, when an old candy factory on Coppergate Street was torn down to make way for a shopping center. There excavators discovered the remains of a cluster of Viking buildings, complete with animal enclosures, wells, refuse pits, and latrines. Working from 1976 until 1981, archaeologists sifted through 36,000 individual layers of debris—more than eight tons of material in all—to recover more than 40,000 objects, including glass beads, knives, combs, shoes, bowls, keys, locks, dice, fish hooks, even a leather ice skate with a blade carved from bone. Many of these items had been discarded by the Vikings in their rubbish pits.

The artifacts recovered from the Coppergate site were impressive enough that a Viking museum was added to the shopping center so that the artifacts could be displayed right where they'd been found, in a reproduction of the Viking village unearthed at the site. The Jorvik Viking Center opened in April 1984; since then, more than 20 million people from all over the world have passed though its doors.

But many visitors come not to see the treasures unearthed at Coppergate Street—not the Viking coins, shoes, or jewelry, or the dice, the knives, or even the leather-and-bone ice skate. They come to see a much more humble and earthy "treasure" recovered from a lowly Viking latrine at the Lloyds Bank site on Pavement Street. The crowds come to see the 1,200-year-old Lloyds Bank *Coprolite*—or Lloyds Bank Turd, as it is affectionately known—one of the oldest, largest, most intact fossilized pieces of human excrement ever found on Earth.

It's the only artifact that visitors ask for by name.

A DIFFERENT KIND OF BANK DEPOSIT

The Lloyds Bank Turd isn't valued just by naughty schoolchildren, either: Serious scientists assign great weight to the discovery, because finding a single, intact human turd from a thousand years ago is so unlikely.

Picky eaters: Of the 5,400 known mammal species, humans have domesticated only 16 for food.

Finding large deposits of biodegraded human waste at a settled site like Jorvik isn't unusual; indeed, it's estimated that a third of the entire 10-foot-deep mass of debris beneath York is made up of human and animal waste. Scientists can distinguish between the human poop and the animal poop, which makes it possible to look for clues about the diet and health of the populations that created it.

But such waste is usually found only in large masses, such as at the bottom of latrine pits, and archaeologists can draw only general conclusions about the people that used the latrines, since it's nearly impossible to distinguish one pooper's poop from another's. The value of a single, fossilized poop like the Lloyd's Bank Turd is that it provides a snapshot of a single person at a single point in time.

GETTING TO KNOW YOU

So what do we know about the anonymous Viking who made the most famous deposit that Lloyds Bank is ever likely to see? His or her diet consisted largely of meat and grains, but not much in the way of fruits or vegetables, which may help explain why the sample is nine inches long and weighs half a pound. "Whoever passed it probably hadn't 'performed' for a few days," says student conservator Gill Snape. Considering the large number of fruit pits and vegetable seeds found at the site but *not* in this particular Viking's stool, this was likely not the healthiest or the most regular person in the village.

Like a lot of Vikings, this one suffered from at least two types of intestinal parasites: The remains of hundreds of whipworm and maw-worm eggs were found in the stool. The presence of worms in the stool is indicative of the filthy conditions and poor hygiene in Viking settlements. Wells were dug too close to latrines, making the availability of clean, uncontaminated water a hit-or-miss (usually miss) proposition. The dirt floors of the Viking dwellings teemed with fly larvae (maggots) and mouse and rat droppings, with plenty of dog, pig, cow, and horse droppings just outside the door. It was virtually inevitable that residents of such settlements would be infested with intestinal parasites.

HISTORICALLY ACCURATE (MOSTLY)

If you get a chance to visit York, be sure to go to the Jorvik

Viking Center and view the Lloyds Bank Turd in all its glory. Take the entire tour. The Viking village was painstakingly created using the most up-to-date information available when it was built in the early 1980s. And in 2001, when the exhibit underwent a $7.5 million facelift, 25 years of studying the artifacts was used to make the exhibit even more historically accurate. How accurate? The Lloyds Bank Turd was chemically analyzed to create a "fecal odorgram"—a best-guess estimate of what it smelled like when it was first created 1,000 years ago, and that smell has been artificially reproduced to give the latrine display a level of olfactory authenticity unheard of—and unsmelt of—in other museums.

About the only thing that isn't accurate about the latrine display is that the Viking figure depicted in mid-squat is partially hidden behind a screen. That's to protect the *visitors'* modesty, not the Viking's. According to the best available evidence, a real Viking latrine wouldn't have had such a screen. Vikings of that period had little or no squeamishness regarding bathroom functions. They were perfectly comfortable pooping out in the open, even when there were other people around.

THE CROWN STOOLS

So how much is a treasure like the Lloyds Bank Turd worth? More than 20 years ago, Dr. Andrew Jones, the director of the Jorvik Viking Center and a leading "paleo-scatologist" (a scientist who studies ancient fecal matter), had the turd appraised for insurance purposes. The verdict: It was valued at $39,000, an amount that Jones said was *way* too little. "It's insulting, really," he told *The Wall Street Journal* in 1991. "This is the most exciting piece of excrement I've ever seen. In its own way it's as irreplaceable as the Crown jewels."

Irreplaceable, but not *irreparable*, as the world learned in 2003 when a teacher on a class trip to the Viking Center dropped the poop and it broke into three pieces. So did the center cash in its insurance policy? Nope—they just had student curator Gill Snape glue the poop back together and put it back out on display.

"I heard I may be doing some unusual things while I was here," Snape says, "but I never imagined it would include this."

SMART AND TALENTED

Many people have dedicated their lives to a trade, science, or art to the point of mastery. But even geniuses need a hobby.

JEAN AUGUSTE DOMINIQUE INGRES

Genius: Nicknamed "the Napoleon of Painting" for his dominance of the French art world in the 19th century, Ingres's talent emerged fully formed at age nine and didn't change much after that. He was a neoclassicist who painted primarily portraits, including Napoleon's.

He had a hobby, too: Ingres was a master violinist. His father started him on lessons almost from birth, and he studied under some of the greatest violinists in Europe. By his 14th birthday, he was already the second violinist for the Orchestre du Capitole de Toulouse, a major French orchestra. Today, "Ingres' Violin" is a French expression for a secondary talent totally unrelated to one's true calling in life.

CLAUDE SHANNON

Genius: In his 1937 graduate thesis at the Massachusetts Institute of Technology, 21-year-old Shannon proved that electrical circuits could be used to solve any complex algebra problem. Later, he proposed that these same circuits could be used to store and transmit information—essentially the basis for the technology behind the modern computer. For this, and other work, Shannon is referred to as "the father of information theory."

He had a hobby, too: Shannon taught at MIT and was known as an eccentric who traveled around campus on a unicycle, sometimes juggling as he rode. Shannon amassed a collection of exotic unicycles from around the world, a passion that overlapped with his technological genius: He devised a juggling robot as well as several mathematical proofs for an ideal juggling method.

H.G. WELLS

Genius: Wells is best known for writing the science-fiction novels *The War of the Worlds*, *The Time Machine*, and *The Island of Dr. Moreau.* He was one of the first writers to take sci-fi seriously, using it to express complex philosophical concepts about world peace and human potential. Wells was a great visionary, foreseeing the United Nations, the military use of the airplane, and space travel. He also coined the terms "Martian" and "time machine."

He had a hobby, too: Wells enjoyed designing (and playing) military simulation games, notably one called "Little Wars." While the game was made for children, it included complex rules for maneuvering infantry (mass-produced tin soldiers) and artillery (working miniature cannons that shot wooden dowels, popular in an age before safety regulations). "Little Wars" was the first modern tabletop game, and inspired hundreds of others. While games like "Warhammer" are now much more popular, Wells's game was so well designed that it's still played today.

ISAAC NEWTON

Genius: Newton, the father of modern physics and originator of the theory of universal gravitation and three laws of motion, was also the warden of Britain's royal mint, responsible for regulating the coinage of the British Empire.

He had a hobby, too: He liked to disguise himself as a drunkard. Reason: In 17th-century England, counterfeiting was a serious crime, equivalent to treason and punishable by death. However, counterfeiters were almost impossible to catch due to Britain's complex legal code and stratified class system. So Newton occasionally took drastic measures, hanging out in bars and brothels— where counterfeiters gathered—to collect the evidence he needed firsthand. He was, by all accounts, pretty good at this, and managed to catch more than 20 big-time counterfeiters.

TYCHO BRAHE

Genius: Brahe was one of the 16th century's most prominent scientists. Together with his student Johannes Kepler, he made observations which led to Galileo's groundbreaking theory that the sun, rather than the Earth, was the center of the solar system. Brahe was an excellent businessman too, and could afford to build and staff his own personal research facility for astronomical studies.

He had a hobby, too: Brahe had a bad temper, which he relieved through fencing. On one occasion, he was involved in a duel with another intellectual of the Early Modern period, the Danish mathematician Manderup Parsbjerg. Unable to resolve a bitter dispute about who was the better mathematician, they decided to settle the matter with a duel. Brahe may have been good, but Parsbjerg was better: Brahe lost the bridge of his nose to a well-timed sword stroke. For the rest of his life, he wore a prosthetic nose made of metal (gold, silver, or perhaps copper—accounts vary) and held in place with paste.

RICHARD FEYNMAN

Genius: Theoretical physicist Feynman was the very *definition* of a genius. His first job after graduating from Princeton and MIT: nuclear physicist in the Manhattan Project, which developed the first atomic bombs. Later, he made several groundbreaking contributions to particle physics, and even won a Nobel Prize.

He had a hobby, too: Feynman had numerous interests that occupied his time: painting, Meso-American history...and the bongo drums. Feynman's drumming talents were overshadowed by his achievements as a physicist, but in some circles he was known only for his musical abilities. As Feynman himself said, "On the infrequent occasions when I have been called upon in a formal place to play the bongo drums, the introducer never seems to find it necessary to mention that I also do theoretical physics."

He had *another* hobby, too: As if that wasn't enough, Feynman was also an expert safecracker. He was particularly adept at solving combination locks, and was so good that, amazingly, he could often deduce combinations to safes from the psychology of their owners. Feynman earned his reputation while working at Los Alamos National Laboratory during the Manhattan Project, where he easily—and routinely—cracked the safes containing classified nuclear secrets.

*   *   *

ASIA IS LARGER THAN THE MOON

The surface area of the moon is about 14,645,750 square miles. The area of the continent of Asia: about 17,212,000 square miles.

THE OTHER OLYMPICS

Every country loves to root for its hometown heroes, hoping they'll win the gold. But the real joy of the Olympics is watching the world's finest compete in a politics-free atmosphere. Right? Well, not necessarily.

BACKGROUND
In December 1979, the Soviet Union invaded Afghanistan in an attempt to bolster that country's faltering communist government. The spread of Communism and a Soviet Union that aggressively perpetuated it were the two biggest fears of the West. The Afghanistan invasion both concerned and infuriated United States President Jimmy Carter. He condemned it in the United Nations, and made a bold statement in his 1980 State of the Union address: If Soviet troops remained in Afghanistan past February 20, the United States—and many of its allies—would boycott the upcoming Summer Olympics, scheduled to be held in Moscow.

Soviet troops did not budge. And so, on March 21, 1980, Carter announced that the United States would not participate in the 1980 Summer Olympics. Soon, 62 more countries, including Canada, West Germany, and Japan, followed suit, supporting the boycott by pledging that they wouldn't send any athletes to Moscow either. (A few of those 62 countries probably couldn't really afford to send Olympians, and adding themselves to the boycott roll was a great way to both save face and earn American favor.)

American athletes—some of whom had been training their whole lives to reach the Olympics—were devastated, and Carter personally addressed 150 of them to explain his difficult decision. While the U.S.S.R. didn't succumb to the political pressure of the boycott (it didn't withdraw from Afghanistan until 1988), the Olympics definitely suffered. With nearly half the industrialized world refusing to compete, the Games were not a full picture of world-class sports... and besides that, the loss of vital Olympics- and tourism-generated revenue was costing Moscow billions.

THE LIBERTY BELL CLASSIC
But from something bad came something good. After Carter failed to rally international support for a full alternative Olympics in the

Ivory Coast, the U.S. Track & Field organization decided to step in and create an alternative competition for the track-and-field athletes who'd been shut out because of politics. (Athletes competing in other events were out of luck.) On July 16, 1980, three days before the opening ceremonies of the Moscow Olympics, athletes from 29 boycotting nations met on the campus of the University of Pennsylvania in Philadelphia for the Liberty Bell Classic, more popularly known as the Olympic Boycott Games.

LET THE GAMES BEGIN

The United States, Canada, China, West Germany, Egypt, Thailand, the Bahamas, Kenya, and Sudan, among others, competed in 33 track-and-field events over the course of a week—19 for men and 14 for women. The results of the Liberty Bell Classic (LBC) indicate that had there been no boycott, there would have been some truly exciting Olympic events. For example, American runner Renaldo Nehemiah completed the 110m hurdles in 13.31 seconds, which was a faster time than the actual Olympic gold medalist, East German runner Thomas Munkelt. The United States dominated the LBC, taking 20 gold medals, 23 silver, and 14 bronze; Canada took 5 gold, 5 silver, and 4 bronze; and Thailand, China, Kenya, and the Bahamas also took home multiple gold medals.

SECOND BOYCOTT

As the 1984 Summer Olympics approached, the world wondered how the Soviet Union would respond to the boycott of its 1980 games, especially since they would be held in Los Angeles. Not surprisingly, on May 8, 1984, the U.S.S.R. announced that it would not send athletes to the United States. Joining them were 13 other communist, Eastern Bloc, and Soviet-influenced nations: East Germany, Poland, Hungary, Bulgaria, Czechoslovakia, Cuba, Afghanistan, North Korea, Vietnam, Mongolia, Angola, Ethiopia, and Laos. Iran and Libya, not communist, but anti-America for other reasons, joined in the boycott.

And just as the United States had done in 1980, the Soviet Union planned an alternate Olympics for its athletes. But unlike the track-only Liberty Bell Classic, the 1984 alternate Olympics was huge in scope, nearly on par with the real Olympic games that were taking place on the other side of the world.

Saddam Hussein's favorite American foods: Raisin Bran and Doritos.

DRUZHBA-84

The Druzhba ("Friendship") Games featured events in 23 sports, including track and field, basketball, field hockey, rowing, swimming, weightlifting, gymnastics, boxing, water polo, archery, handball, judo, pentathlon, tennis, and equestrian events. More than 2,300 athletes competed in the two-monthlong games.

Unlike the Olympics, usually held in and around a single city, "Druzhba-84" spread events around 17 cities in nine countries, in order to demonstrate the unity of the communist world...and also to share the cost. It even looked like the Olympics. The opening ceremonies took place in the packed Grand Arena of the Central Lenin Stadium in Moscow where the Olympic cauldron from the 1980 games was, once again, reverently lit with a torch.

As in the 1980 alternate games, the nonparticipation of hundreds of the world's greatest athletes cast a shadow on the results of the "real" Olympics. For example, Mary Lou Retton was the star of the 1984 Olympics when she became the first American woman to score a perfect 10 and win an individual gold medal. While Retton may have been a stellar athlete, no American woman had yet won a gold medal in gymnastics because the Soviet Union had, up to that point, completely dominated the sport. Had she competed against Soviet gymnasts, Retton may not have made history.

Retton wasn't the only example. Of the 41 track and field events and 29 swimming competitions that were held at both the 1984 Olympics and Druzhba-84, the communists outperformed their Olympic counterparts in 20 track events and 11 swimming events.

SPIRIT OF THE GAMES

There have been no significant boycotts or alternate Olympics since. Relations between the United States and the Soviet Union improved in the late 1980s, and the Soviet Union (as well as communism in Europe) collapsed in 1991. There are still communist countries, of course, and they still compete in the Olympics—Cuba and North Korea, for example, and China, which even hosted the 2008 games. After the two boycotts, nations have put aside their political differences to compete in friendly sports... which, after all, is the entire point of the Olympics.

Hippocrates believed that constipation was caused by the north wind.

13 FACTS ABOUT THE WITCH HAZEL TREE

An amazing product from the pharmacy of Mother Nature.

• It's actually more of a shrub, usually reaching just 10 to 20 feet in height. It grows in the eastern U.S. and Canada, China, and Japan.

• The witch hazel sold in drugstores is a distillation of the plant's branches combined with alcohol. It's an *astringent* (it shrinks body tissue) with a variety of modern uses, but it had ancient uses, too.

• Native Americans brewed curative teas and medicines from its leaves and bark.

• The Cree called their brew "Magic Water" and used it for colds, coughs, and dysentery.

• The Osage put *shemba*, a poultice of the leaves, on sores, ulcers, boils, and tumors.

• The Potawatomi treated backaches and sore muscles with a liniment made from witch hazel bark.

• The Mohegan concocted remedies from its leaves and stems to treat insect bites, bruises, and cuts.

• English settlers named it the "wych hazel" tree in the 1600s. *Wych* is a Middle English term meaning "flexible" or "pliable," and it referred to the plant's branches, which were used as *dowsing rods* to locate water underground.

• It was named wych *hazel* because its leaves resemble those of the hazelnut tree.

• In 1846 Theron Pond of Utica, New York, and an Oneida medicine man sold a witch hazel skin cream called Golden Treasure. It became Pond's Vanishing Cream, which is still sold today.

• Witch hazel tincture shrinks hemorrhoids, varicose veins, and bags under the eyes. (Grandpa Uncle John swears by it as an aftershave lotion.)

• It also soothes diaper rash, razor burn, and sunburn and takes the itch out of poison ivy and poison oak.

• Witch hazel seeds are said to taste like pistachios.

A HISTORY OF THE SHOPPING MALL, PART IV

The shopping mall has been such a central part of American consumer culture for so many years that it's hard to believe their days could be numbered. But that's what some retailing experts think. Here's Part IV of our story; Part III is on page 399.

FINISHING TOUCHES

Victor Gruen may well be considered the "father of the mall," but he didn't remain a doting dad for long. Southdale Center, the world's first enclosed shopping mall, opened its doors in the fall of 1956, and by 1968 Gruen had turned publicly and vehemently against his creation.

So it would fall to other early mall builders, people such as A. Alfred Taubman, Melvin Simon, and Edward J. DeBartolo Sr., to give the shopping mall its modern, standardized form, by taking what they understood about human nature and applying it to Gruen's original concept. In the process, they fine-tuned the mall into the highly effective, super-efficient "shopping machines" that have dominated American retailing for nearly half a century.

BACK TO BASICS

These developers saw shopping malls the same way that Gruen did, as idealized versions of downtown shopping districts. Working from that starting point, they set about systematically removing all distractions, annoyances, and other barriers to consumption. Your local mall may not contain all of the following features, but there should be much here that looks familiar:

• It's a truism among mall developers that most shoppers will only walk about three city blocks—about 1,000 feet—before they begin to feel a need to head back to where they'd started. So 1,000 feet became a standard length for malls.

• Most of the stairs, escalators, and elevators are located at the ends of the mall, not in the center. This is done to encourage

---

In 1968 Steven Spielberg and George Lucas took a directing class taught by Jerry Lewis.

shoppers to walk past all the stores on the level they're on before visiting shops on another level.

• Malls are usually built with shops on *two* levels, not one or three. This way, if a shopper walks the length of the mall on one level to get to the escalator, then walks the length of the mall on the second level to return to where they started, they've walked past every store in the mall and are back where they parked their car. (If there was a third level of shops, a shopper who walked all three levels would finish up at the opposite end of the mall, three city blocks away from where they parked.)

• Another truism among mall developers is that people, like water, tend to flow down more easily than they flow up. Because of this, many malls are designed to encourage people to park and enter the mall on the upper level, not the lower level, on the theory they are more likely to travel down to visit stores on a lower level than travel up to visit stores on a higher level.

THE VISION THING

• Great big openings are designed into the floor that separates the upper level of shops from the lower level. That allows shoppers to see stores on both levels from wherever they happen to be in the mall. The handrails that protect shoppers from falling into the openings are made of glass or otherwise designed so that they don't obstruct the sight lines to those stores.

• Does your mall's decor seem dull to you? That's no accident—the interior of the mall is designed to be aesthetically pleasing but not particularly interesting, so as not to distract shoppers from looking at the merchandise, which is much more important.

• Skylights flood the interiors of malls with natural light, but these skylights are invariably recessed in deep wells to keep direct sunlight from reflecting off of storefront glass, which would create glare and distract shoppers from looking at the merchandise. The wells also contain artificial lighting that comes on late in the day when the natural light begins to fade, to prevent shoppers from receiving a visual cue that it's time to go home.

A NEIGHBORLY APPROACH

• Great attention is paid to the placement of stores within the mall, something that mall managers refer to as "adjacencies." The

---

The Pentagon has 14 fast-food restaurants, including McDonald's, KFC, and Dunkin' Donuts.

price of merchandise, as well as the type, factors into this equation: There's not much point in placing a store that sells $200 silk ties next to one that sells $99 men's suits.

• Likewise, any stores that give off strong smells, like restaurants and hair salons, are kept away from jewelry and other high-end stores. (Would *you* want to smell cheeseburgers or fried fish while you and your fiancé are picking out your wedding rings?)

• Have you ever bought milk, raw meat, or a gallon of ice cream at the mall? Probably not, and there's a good reason for it: Malls generally do not lease space to stores that sell perishable goods, because once you buy them you have to take them right home, instead of spending more time shopping at the mall.

• Consumer tastes change over time, and mall operators worry about falling out of fashion with shoppers. Because of this, they keep a close watch on individual store sales. Even if a store in the mall is profitable, if it falls below its "tenant profile," or average sales per square foot of other stores in the same retail category, the mall operator may refuse to renew its lease. Tenant turnover at a well-managed mall can run as high as 10 percent a year.

HERE, THERE, EVERYWHERE
Malls have been a part of the American landscape for so long now that a little "mall fatigue" is certainly understandable. But like so much of American culture, the concept has been exported to foreign countries, and malls remain very popular around the world, where they are built not just in the suburbs but in urban centers as well. They have achieved the sort of iconic status once reserved for airports, skyscrapers, and large government buildings. They are the kind of buildings created by emerging societies to communicate to the rest of the world, "We have arrived." If you climb into a taxicab in almost any major city in the world, be it Moscow, Kuala Lumpur, Dubai, or Shanghai, and tell the driver, "Take me to the mall," he'll know where to go.

KILL 'EM MALL
America's love-hate relationship with shopping malls is now more than half a century old, and for as long as it has been fashionable to see malls as unfashionable, people have been predicting their demise. In the 1970s, "category killers" were seen as a threat.

Stand-alone stores like Toys "R" Us focused on a single category of goods, offering a greater selection at a lower price than even the biggest stores in the mall couldn't match. They were soon followed by "power centers," strip malls anchored by "big box" stores like Walmart, and discount warehouse stores like Costco and Sam's Club. In the early 1990s, TV shopping posed a threat, only to fizzle out…and be replaced by even stronger competition posed by Internet retailers like Amazon.com.

By the early 1990s, construction of new malls in the United States had slowed to a crawl, but this had as much to do with rising real estate prices (land in the suburbs wasn't dirt cheap anymore), the savings and loan crisis (which made construction financing harder to come by), and the fact that most communities that wanted a mall already had one…or two…or more.

Increasing competition from other retailers and bad economic times in recent years have also taken their toll, resulting in declining sales per square foot and rising vacancy rates in malls all over the country. In 2009 General Growth Properties, the nation's second-largest mall operator, filed for bankruptcy; it was the largest real estate bankruptcy in American history.

FULL CIRCLE

But mall builders and operators keep fighting back, continually reinventing themselves as they try to keep pace with the times. Open-air malls are remade into enclosed malls, and enclosed malls are opened to the fresh air. One strategy tried in Kansas, Georgia, and other areas is to incorporate shopping centers into larger mixed-use developments that include rental apartments, condominiums, office buildings, and other offerings. Legacy Town Center, a 150-acre development in the middle of a 2,700-acre business park north of Dallas, for example, includes 80 outdoor shops and restaurants, 1,500 apartments and townhouses, two office towers, a Marriott Hotel, a landscaped park with hiking trails, and a lake. (Sound familiar?)

In other words, developers are trying to save the mall by *finally* building them just the way that Victor Gruen wanted to in the first place.

CHILDREN OF THE CORN

There are an estimated 35 million teenagers in the United States today, and they are a lucrative target for merchandisers because they have lots of disposable income (more than $100 a week, on average). Believe it or not, a lot of the social science that marketers use to spot teenage trends and cash in on them comes from a farm study done in the 1920s.

THE FARM REPORT

In 1928 an improved strain of hybrid corn seed became available to farmers in Green County, Iowa. Around that same time, a pair of University of Iowa sociologists named Neal C. Gross and Bruce Ryan began a study of how the new seed was being adopted by farmers in the area. Gross and Ryan tracked 259 farmers in all, and the study they published, "The Diffusion of Corn in Two Iowa Communities," laid the groundwork for a theory of consumer behavior that describes when, how, and why human beings embrace new products and ideas. It turns out that some of the concepts they developed apply as much to modern teenagers as they did to Iowa corn farmers 80 years ago.

FOLLOW THE LEADERS

The new hybrid corn seed offered greater resistance to drought and disease, and it increased crop yields by as much as 20%. Even so, it took almost 15 years for all of the farmers to switch to the new seeds. Gross and Ryan divided them into several groups:

• **Innovators:** The handful of farmers—less than 5% of the total—who took a chance on the new seed in the first few years.

• **Early Adopters:** A somewhat larger group of farmers, but under 15% of the total, who switched to the hybrid seed in the early to mid-1930s after seeing the success of the Innovators. The Early Adopters were some of the most respected farmers in their communities. They were what sociologists call "opinion leaders."

• **Early and Late Majority:** Only after the Early Adopters had success with the corn did the great majority of farmers follow their example; by 1939 more than 90% of the farmers had switched.

• **Laggards.** The handful of farmers who were the most resistant

---

John Wayne smoked 5 packs of cigarettes a day. (He quit when he got lung cancer.)

to change and the last to try the new seeds. (As late as 1941, there still were two farmers who had not switched to the better seeds.)

FROM CORN TO KIDS

Consumer research firms may use different terms to describe how today's teenagers respond to new trends, but these modern groupings are surprisingly similar to the ones in Gross and Ryan's study.

• **Edgers.** The risk-taking nonconformists of the teenage world, Edgers create their own styles to suit themselves, without caring or often in spite of what other people think. They are like the Innovators in Gross and Ryan's study: They eagerly try new things.

• **Influencers.** The attractive, socially confident kids that other teenagers look up to, the Influencers are teenage Early Adopters. They copy Edger styles, and it is their star power that makes out-of-the-mainstream styles socially acceptable and desirable. (Which of course makes them *un*acceptable to the nonconformist Edgers, who respond by inventing even newer and edgier styles, in a cycle of innovation that never ends.)

• **Conformers.** About half of all teenagers are considered Conformers, analogous to the Early and Late Majority groups in Gross and Ryan's study. Conformers don't have the rebellious, innovative style of the risk-taking Edgers, and they aren't as popular or as self-confident as the Influencers. But they *want* to be cool like the Influencers, and they copy Influencer styles in an attempt to be more like them. This makes them a gold mine for companies that market clothing, athletic shoes, and other products to teenagers.

Using surveys and focus groups, or even by sending "spies" into the field to study what the Edgers and the Influencers are up to, consumer research companies try to spot trends as they emerge. They communicate their findings to shoe companies, clothing manufacturers, and other clients, who adjust their offerings in response. With good timing and a little luck, a company that catches a trend as it's beginning can make a fortune selling cool merchandise to needy, free-spending Conformers who hope to use the goods as leverage to improve their fragile social standing.

• **Passives.** The Passives are the Laggards of teenage culture. They either don't know or don't care what's cool, so it's hard to sell things to them. For that reason, they are largely ignored by the marketers and merchants of "cool."

Ancient nerds: The Romans wore socks with their sandals.

THE FEARLESS WONDERS

How Mohawk "skywalkers" came to build New York's skyscrapers.

THE FEARLESS WONDERS

In 1886 the Dominion Bridge Company (DBC) of Canada was hired to build a cantilever railroad bridge across the St. Lawrence River near Montreal. The north end of the bridge lay in the village of Lachine; the south end fell on the preserve of a Mohawk band called the Kahnawake. In order to get permission to build the bridge on Indian land, DBC agreed to employ as many Mohawks as possible as laborers. As work progressed, the bridge builders noticed something unusual about the Mohawks: They were fascinated by the bridge. In fact, the company couldn't keep them off it. They walked all over it, scrambling along the narrow spans hundreds of feet above the river with a grace and agility that wowed DBC's seasoned riveters, most of whom were former sailors, used to working high above the ground on flimsy ropes. Word quickly spread that the Mohawks had something special—no fear.

DO THE "SHUFFLE UP"

As an experiment, one of the foremen decided to train some of the local boys as riveters. Riveting was the most dangerous job in high steel construction, and good riveters were hard to find. He hired 12 Mohawks, all teenagers, and began teaching them the job. As the foreman recounted later, "Putting riveting tools in their hands was like putting ham with eggs." The Mohawk teens were naturals—so good, in fact, that they became known as "The Fearless Wonders." When the bridge was completed, the Fearless Wonders were split into three teams, or "gangs," and hired to work on another bridge, the Soo, spanning Lake Superior between Ontario and Michigan.

Each Mohawk gang arrived with a young apprentice. As soon as the gang trained the new recruit, another new one would be summoned from the reservation. When there were enough men to create a new gang, the Mohawks had what they called a "shuffle-up": Old hands were pulled from the existing gangs to buddy up with the new guy, creating a new gang. The demand for Mohawk gangs grew, and by 1907 there were more than 70 skilled Mohawk bridgemen working all across Canada, or, as they called it, "booming out."

DISASTER

On August 29, 1907, while building the Quebec Bridge across the St. Lawrence River near Quebec City, 84 bridgemen died when a span collapsed. Thirty-five of the dead were Kahnawake. It was a horrifying blow to the band, and builders feared that the Mohawks would abandon steelwork forever. Instead, young Mohawk men *wanted* to boom out with the gangs working the high steel. Why? It was the appeal of danger itself. A Mohawk man's place in his community was determined by the respect he earned for acts of bravery. Traditionally those moments had occurred during hunting or in battle. With those avenues largely taken away from them, young men had no way to prove their manhood. But now Mohawk men were wanted by the world for precisely the thing they valued most: their courage. That's what really attracted the Mohawks to "skywalking." The idea that they had no fear of heights was a myth; they were as frightened as anyone else. But by mastering their fear, the Mohawks earned the respect of their community and the entire world. Best of all, they were paid handsomely for their skills. As a white bridgeman observed, "Men who want to do it are rare, and men who *can* do it are even rarer."

However, there were changes after the disaster. The Kahnewake women insisted that the gangs no longer work together on one single project. From then on they had to split up to spread the risk of widowhood. The men agreed and went back to work. And the work kept coming, fast and furious. The skywalkers decided to boom out across the border, where the skyscraping phase of American architecture was just getting under way in New York City.

FALLING DOWN

The first attempt by Mohawk bridgemen to work in Manhattan ended in tragedy. John Diabo, known as "Indian Joe" to his Irish coworkers, worked on the Hell Gate Bridge in 1915. He soon formed his own gang with three fellow tribe members. They'd been on a job for only a few weeks when Diabo fell off a scaffold

Half of the city of Istanbul, Turkey, is below sea level.

and plummeted hundreds of feet to his death in the East River below. When asked what happened, one of the other Mohawks said tersely, "He got in the way of himself." The Mohawks quit and went back to the reservation in Canada, and that was it for almost a decade.

CLIMBING BACK UP

By 1926 New York was experiencing a frenzy of steel construction, and high-flying riveters were in hot demand. That's when a few Kahnewake gangs came down from Canada to work on the George Washington Bridge, followed by more teams to build Rockefeller Center, the Chrysler and Empire State buildings, and every other significant high-rise and bridge. The Mohawk gangs joined the Brooklyn branch of the International Association of Bridge, Structural and Ornamental Steel Workers, and settled their families in the North Gowanus neighborhood. Other Mohawk bands joined the original Kahnawake, and together they created the legend of the fearless Mohawk skywalkers, one that has endured for more than 80 years.

A RIVETING JOB

Skywalkers building a bridge or skyscraper during the heyday of high steel construction (1920–1950) fell into three groups:

• **Raising Gangs.** Buildings were (and still are) put together like gigantic Erector sets—girders, beams, and columns arrived at the construction site with pre-bored holes labeled with chalk marks indicating where each piece went. The raising gang hoisted the steel piece up to the right spot with a crane, and then attached it to the framework with temporary bolts.

• **Fitting-up Gangs.** This unit was split into *plumbers* and *bolters*. The plumbers worked with guy wires and turnbuckles to align the girders and beams into perfect position. The bolters added extra bolts to secure the piece more firmly.

• **Riveting Gangs.** These gangs had four workers: a *heater*, a *sticker-in*, a *bucker-up*, and a *riveter*.

Setting up: The heater was responsible for the small coal-fired stove that heated the rivets. He'd lay a few boards across some beams near the piece to be riveted, set the stove on it, and put the rivets in the stove. While the rivets heated, the other three team members hung a plank scaffold—ropes looped over the beam that was to be worked on, with wooden planks for the men to stand on either side. Then they'd grab their tools and climb onto the scaffold, an unnerving prospect at any height but especially several hundred feet above the ground. There was very little room to move: Any misstep meant almost certain death.

Preparing for the rivet: The sticker-in and bucker-up would get on one side of the beam, the riveter on the other. Once the rivets were red-hot, the heater grabbed one with a pair of metal tongs and tossed it to the sticker-in, who'd catch it in a metal bucket. The bucker-up had already unscrewed one of the temporary bolts, which was about to be replaced with the rivet.

Putting the rivet in place: The sticker-in took the hot rivet out of his bucket with his own set of tongs and slid it into the empty hole (at this point the rivet looked like a mushroom, with a round "buttonhead" and a stem). The sticker-in then stepped out of the way (carefully), and the bucker-up slipped a backing brace called a *hold-on* over the buttonhead.

Riveting: The stem of the red-hot rivet protruded through the hold-on and out the other side, where the riveter placed the cupped head of a pneumatic hammer against the stem and smashed the almost-molten metal into a matching buttonhead. The team then walked down the scaffold, repeating the process until they ran out of beams. Then they moved the scaffold and repeated the process until every hole was riveted. Every man on the team knew how to do each other's jobs, and they switched often because the pneumatic hammer was a bone-jarring tool to use. As for the heater, he stayed put, tossing hot rivets with (hopefully) unerring accuracy anywhere in a 30-foot radius from his platform.

Riveting is no longer the preferred method of assembling pieces of structural steel—advances in welding and bolting made those techniques safer and equally effective—so the Mohawk skywalkers simply learned the new skills and stayed at work high over the city. More than 100 Mohawks were aloft at construction sites across lower Manhattan when the World Trade Center came down in 2001. They were among the first rescuers at the scene and worked for months to help clear away the rubble of the great towers they had helped erect.

DEFUNCT MAGAZINES

*Of the hundreds and hundreds of magazines published, very few
rise to the top and become cultural icons. But when they do,
they become such a part of our collective consciousness
that it's shocking when they go out of print.*

McCALL'S

To promote his sewing patterns, Scottish tailor James McCall founded a four-page fashion journal in 1876. That evolved into a full-scale women's magazine, featuring articles on health, beauty, travel, and homemaking (and sewing patterns), and underwent a series of name changes, from *The Queen of Fashion*, to *McCall's Magazine*, and finally, in 1897, to *McCall's*. Popular throughout the 20th century, *McCall's* published high-end fiction by writers such as Willa Cather, John Steinbeck, and Kurt Vonnegut, and from 1949–1962, featured a column written by former First Lady Eleanor Roosevelt. Circulation peaked at 8.4 million in the 1960s, but dropped to 4.2 million by 2000 and was still falling. So that same year, talk show host Rosie O'Donnell was hired as editorial director. (Why O'Donnell? Because fellow talk show host Oprah Winfrey's O magazine had been one of the biggest new magazines of the 1990s). *McCall's* then underwent its final name change, to *Rosie*, in 2001. By June 2002, sales were down to 3.5 million, less than before O'Donnell arrived; *Rosie* was one of the least-read homemaking magazines on the market. O'Donnell left the magazine in September 2002 in a widely publicized dispute with publisher Gruner + Jahr over editorial control. But not even the publicity helped the magazine's falling numbers, and it ceased publication under any name in late 2002.

PHOTOPLAY

One of the first "fan magazines," *Photoplay* was founded in 1911 during the infancy of the motion picture industry, and it became the prototype for the "celebrity news" genre dominant today in print (*People, Us Weekly*) and on TV (*TMZ, Entertainment Tonight*). *Photoplay* created celebrity culture by publishing stories not just about movies—then known as "photoplays"—but also about the stars who appeared in them. One of the first issues featured the star of the 1911 silent movie *Little Red Riding Hood*. Thousands of letters poured in from readers who wanted to know more about the actress, Mary Pickford, who soon became one of the most popular stars of the silent era. It worked the other way, too: In the 1930s, *Photoplay* dubbed Katharine Hepburn "box office poison" after a string of bombs, and her career took a two-year dip. The magazine awarded an annual Medal of Honor (a gold medal created by Tiffany & Co.) to the movie its readers voted the best film of the year, a concept that inspired the creation of the Academy Awards. *Photoplay* merged with two other fan magazines—*Movie Mirror* in 1941 and *TV-Radio Mirror* in 1977—but by that time it had been supplanted by other gossip/fan magazines. When *Photoplay* stopped publication in 1980, most of its staff transferred to *Us Weekly*.

GEORGE

The conventional speculation was that presidential son and tabloid fixture John F. Kennedy Jr. would eventually go into politics. He didn't—in 1995 he went into publishing instead. That year, Kennedy founded *George*, named after George Washington. Kennedy aimed for a literate mix of political topics with humor and celebrity profiles thrown in. (The first cover depicted model Cindy Crawford dressed up as Washington.) Kennedy's celebrity certainly helped the magazine's popularity: In 1996 it was the #1 political magazine in the country, but by the time Kennedy died in 1999, circulation had dropped by half, to 400,000. For six months after Kennedy's death, interest resurfaced and circulation jumped by a third. But the boost was only temporary. Despite contributions from popular political, humor, and fiction writers such as Ann Coulter, Al Franken, and Norman Mailer, without Kennedy's leadership the magazine flailed and folded in 2001. *George*'s legacy can be seen today, however. The mix of politics with humor and culture was a precursor to shows like Comedy Central's *The Daily Show* and *The Colbert Report*.

NATIONAL LAMPOON

Launched in 1970, *National Lampoon* was a for-profit spinoff of the revered collegiate humor magazine *Harvard Lampoon*. *National*

Lampoon became popular by presenting cutting, sometimes surreal, parody and satire of cultural institutions, politicians, and celebrities in the Vietnam and Watergate eras. A few examples: a cover illustration of Lt. William Calley, court-martialed for his role in the My Lai massacre, made to look like *Mad* mascot Alfred E. Neuman; and a cover photo of a dog with a revolver pointed at its head and the caption, "If you don't buy this magazine, we'll kill this dog." The magazine was so successful that "National Lampoon" was used as a brand for TV specials, books, a radio show, and films, notably *Animal House* and *Vacation*. *National Lampoon* signed up its one-millionth subscriber in 1974, and circulation remained steady until the end of the decade, but as the counterculture spirit of the '70s gave way to the optimistic upward mobility and conservatism of the 1980s, readership dropped drastically. The print version was kept alive at a financial loss, as a flagship/brand name to support the other media projects until 1998, when *National Lampoon* finally folded.

PLAYGIRL

Founded in 1973, *Playgirl* cashed in on the feminist movement, offering beefcake to women as a response to the cheesecake in men's magazines such as *Playboy*. Featuring nude male centerfolds, Playgirl was marketed to heterosexual women, but before long, research indicated that its audience was predominantly gay males. *Playgirl*, however, refused to alter its content or advertising to reflect that readership. Circulation peaked at about half a million in the late 1990s. As other forms of pornography, both softcore and hardcore, became more available in print and online, *Playgirl*'s sales softened. The last printed issue appeared in January 2009. **But wait!** In 2010 it relaunched to a lot of publicity (but poor sales) when it featured a seminude spread of Levi Johnston, the teenage father of Alaska governor Sarah Palin's grandchild.

MORE HIGH-PROFILE MAGAZINES THAT FOLDED

• **Vibe** (1993–2009). A major pop-music magazine (surpassed in readership by only *Rolling Stone* and *Spin*) that covered hip-hop and R&B music. Owned by Quincy Jones, *Vibe* spun off a late-night talk show and a televised music awards ceremony. After peaking at 800,000 subscribers in 2007, readership dropped off sharply and the magazine folded in 2009. The brand name was then sold to a private equity firm; they turned *Vibe* into a pop culture website.

- **Talk** (1999–2002). It got a lot of publicity before its launch because it was a joint project between the behemoth Hearst Publications and the Miramax film studio (*Pulp Fiction*, *Good Will Hunting*), and because its first editor was former *New Yorker* and *Vanity Fair* chief Tina Brown. Consisting of in-depth interviews with celebrities and politicians, *Talk* never turned a profit.

- **Cracked** (1958–2007). A crude humor magazine for kids—a blatant knockoff of *Mad*, even poaching several *Mad* artists and writers in the 1980s, but its circulation numbers never came close to *Mad*'s, so in 2005 it was revamped as a humor magazine for adult men (similar to *Maxim* or *FHM*). That didn't work either, and the magazine shut down after three issues. Today it's a trivia website.

- **Omni** (1978–1995). Created by *Penthouse* magazine publisher Bob Guccione and his wife Kathy Keton, *Omni* was a magazine that blended science fiction and science fact. It combined reporting on legitimate, cutting-edge science with science fiction from top writers in the genre such as William Gibson and Stephen King, plus a healthy dose of articles on fringe pseudoscience and paranormal topics. The magazine went to a web-only format in 1996 and then shut down completely two years later. (General Media, the company that publishes *Penthouse*, filed for bankruptcy in 2003.)

- **Weekly World News** (1979–2007). When the *National Enquirer* switched to full color in 1979, the magazine's founder, Generoso Pope, didn't want to let his black-and-white press machine go to waste. So he created the *WWN*, a highly successful supermarket tabloid featuring stories about Bigfoot sightings, two-headed lizard boys, and presidents meeting with aliens. The magazine's circulation peaked at 1.2 million in the 1980s, but dropped to just 83,000 by 2007, when publication ceased. Why did it go defunct? Because, after 20 years, readers simply grew tired of stories about Bigfoot sightings, two-headed lizard boys, and presidents meeting with aliens. It's now an online-only magazine.

DO YOU SPEAK DOG?

More tips and tricks to help you better understand what your dog is thinking and doing. (Part I is on page 350.)

PROBLEM: Your dog "greets" your guests by jumping up on them.

EXPERTS SAY: Dogs do this as a natural part of play with other dogs, but it can be upsetting or even dangerous if they do it to small children, senior citizens, or anyone who's afraid of dogs.

SOLUTION: You can discourage jumping on guests by teaching the dog a new command for sit. Raise both hands, palms up and facing the dog, whenever you tell your dog to sit. Then, when it's used to the new command, stop saying "Sit," so that it learns to sit when only the hand gesture is given. This gesture is the same defensive motion that people make when they fear that an approaching dog is going to jump on them. So when your dog sees a guest making this defensive movement, it will interpret that as a command to "sit."

PROBLEM: When you take your dog for a walk, it pulls against the leash until it chokes, and just keeps on pulling.

EXPERTS SAY: This can be difficult behavior for dog owners to understand, because the dog could easily relieve the choking by not pulling so hard on the leash. *You* know this intuitively, but a dog may not. Dogs that pull continuously on the leash do so because they have come to see walking on a leash as an inherently asphyxiating experience, and they're trying to escape it.

SOLUTION: This problem can be controlled easily—and gently—with head collars, no-pull harnesses, and other training tools that discourage your dog from pulling during walks.

Problem: Your dog has accidents in the house.

EXPERTS SAY: Dogs do this when they haven't been completely house-trained, or when they have to wait too long for the opportunity to go outside.

SOLUTION: If you catch a dog "eliminating" inside the house, just interrupt it and take it outside without yelling or punishing it.

Punishing a dog that is peeing or pooping in the house just teaches it to do its business in out-of-the-way places that are harder for you to find…and clean up.

CLEANING TIP: If your dog does have an accident in your house, deodorize the spot with white vinegar, rubbing alcohol, or a commercial odor eliminator after you've cleaned up the mess. The lack of an odor will make the dog less likely to go there again. Whatever you do, *do not* clean it with any cleaning products that contain ammonia. When urine breaks down in the air, it gives off ammonia, and your dog associates this smell with urine. Adding more ammonia smell to a spot that has already been peed upon may be telling your dog, "this is the place to pee."

PROBLEM: Your dog suffers from "separation anxiety"—it gets very upset when you leave the house. It chews furniture, barks incessantly, has accidents in the house, or engages in other forms of undesirable behavior.

EXPERTS SAY: Adolescent dogs in the wild eventually reach an age where they can leave the den and hunt with the adult dogs. When your dog reaches that age, it will want to go with you when you leave the den. Not being able to go can be very stressful.

SOLUTION: One trick that can be effective in reducing separation anxiety is de-emphasizing the significance of your comings and goings by being as quiet and undemonstrative as possible. Don't say goodbye to your dog before you leave—a farewell may give *you* comfort, but all it does for the dog is emphasize your departure. Then, when you return home, let a few minutes pass before you greet the dog. Put away your stuff, get a drink or a snack from the fridge, sit in your favorite chair, and when the dog has calmed down, say hello. Another trick: Leave a radio on while you're gone. It can lessen the distinction between an empty house and one with you in it. And drawing curtains over windows through which the dog can see passersby may help your pet feel less threatened when it is defending the den all by itself.

OTHER DOG BEHAVIORS EXPLAINED

• **Yawning.** Dogs yawn when they're tired just like people do, but not only when they're tired: They also yawn when they are feeling timid or under stress—a dog may yawn to calm itself or other dogs, reducing the threat they pose.

• **Tail Wagging.** When a dog wags its tail it can mean either of two things: 1) the dog is happy, or 2) the dog is in an excited, aggressive state. If you don't know the dog, don't let the tail fool you! Many dog-bite victims report they were bitten by a dog that was wagging its tail. Greet a strange dog *very* carefully before trying to pet it, even if it is wagging its tail.

• **Licking Your Face.** In the days when dogs lived in the wild, when the mother returned to the den after hunting for food she fed her young pups by vomiting up whatever partially digested prey she'd caught for them to eat. Experts say that puppies learned they could trigger Mom's barf reflex by licking her face. So when your dog licks your face, it may really be more interested in what you had for dinner than in showing how much it loves you. But not necessarily: A lick may really mean "I love you," after all, because dogs continue to greet their mothers this way long after they've learned to hunt for their own food.

• **Poop-Eating.** Easily one of the most disgusting spectacles a dog owner has to witness, poop eating actually served an important purpose when dogs lived in the wild: A mother dog ate all the poop produced by her pups to remove the strong smell from the den. This helped the defenseless pups remain hidden from predators while she was away from the den hunting for food. The good news: Poop eating teaches pups that their sleeping area is a place that needs to be kept clean; that, in turn, can sometimes speed up the house training.

*   *   *

SYA HWAT?

Aoccdrnig to a rscheearch at Cmabrigde Uinervtisy, it deosn't mttaer in waht oredr the ltteers in a wrod are; the olny iprmoetnt fatcor is taht the frist and lsat ltteres be at the rghit pclae. The rset can be a total mses and you can sitll raed it wouthit a porbelm. Tihs is bcuseae the huamn mnid deos not raed ervey lteter by istlef, but the wrod as a wlohe. Petrty amzanig, huh?

Zebras can be trained to pull carts, but they've never been fully domesticated.

DEAD TV

When an actor on a TV show dies, producers are left with a dilemma: What do they do with the actor's character? Say they moved away? Pretend they never existed? Or make the character die too?

Actor: Will Lee
Show: *Sesame Street* (1983)
Story: Lee had played Mr. Hooper, the grandfatherly candy store owner, from the show's inception in 1969 until his death of a heart attack in 1982. *Sesame Street* writers decided to have Mr. Hooper die as well, in order to teach kids about death—that it's forever, and that it's okay to feel sad. On a highly publicized episode that aired on Thanksgiving Day in 1983 (so parents would be home to answer their children's questions), Big Bird can't find Mr. Hooper anywhere, and the human characters tell him that "Mr. Hooper died"—the writers didn't want to use a euphemism like "passed away." When Big Bird asks when he'll be coming back, he's told that he won't. "But it won't be the same," Big Bird pleads. "No, it won't," says Bob, who goes on to assure Big Bird that they will always have memories of Mr. Hooper, and that David, the new candy shop owner, will make Big Bird his birdseed milk shakes.

Actor: Phil Hartman
Show: *NewsRadio* (1998)
Story: Hartman's death was a sudden and violent one—in May 1998, his mentally ill wife shot him, and then herself. The sitcom had finished taping for the season, so the first episode that aired after Hartman's death was the September 1998 season premiere. Plot: the staff of the news radio station deals with the sudden death of Hartman's character, the arrogant news reader Bill McNeal. The actors choke back real tears as they read a letter found in Bill's desk to be opened upon his death, "If Dave is reading this to you, I have either been fired or I have passed away. Since my formidable talent would preclude the former, I'll have to assume that the latter is true." Hartman's former *Saturday Night Live* castmate Jon Lovitz joined *NewsRadio* as a replacement, but the show was cancelled at the end of the 1998–99 season. Hartman was also a voice actor on

---

The Simpsons, playing two recurring characters: washed-up B-movie actor Troy McClure and the terrible lawyer Lionel Hutz. *Simpsons* producers opted to simply retire those two characters.

Actor: John Ritter
Show: 8 *Simple Rules for Dating My Teenage Daughter* (2003)
Story: Ritter suddenly fell ill on the set in September 2003 and was rushed to a hospital, where he died later that day of an undiagnosed heart ailment. It was early in the show's second season, and ABC wasn't sure what to do about 8 *Simple Rules*, a family sitcom that was also a starring vehicle for Ritter. Ultimately deciding that the show could continue with the other characters (James Garner and David Spade were later added to the cast), producers transformed the show into one about a family trying to put their lives back together after the death of the patriarch. It ran for two more seasons.

Actor: Nicholas Colasanto
Show: *Cheers* (1985)
Story: Colasanto was primarily a director of TV drama series episodes, but in 1982 he was cast as bartender Ernie "Coach" Pantusso on *Cheers* as Sam Malone's (Ted Danson) absent-minded former baseball coach. While at home after completing his work on the third season of *Cheers* in early 1985, Colasanto died of heart failure. His death was acknowledged as part of the plot in the fourth season premiere that September—Coach had died, and the bar needed to hire a new bartender to replace him. Colasanto, however, was remembered in more subtle ways by the cast and crew. Colasanto had kept a picture of Geronimo in his dressing room as a good-luck charm, and after his death it was placed on the *Cheers* set. In the last scene of the very last episode of *Cheers* in 1993, Sam straightens the Geronimo picture, turns off the lights, and the show ends.

*   *   *

"If you make people think they're thinking, they'll love you; but if you really make them think, they'll hate you."
—Don Marquis

THE PEARL HARBOR SPY, PART II

From Uncle John's Dustbin of History, here's the final installment of our story about the person most responsible for making Japan's attack on Pearl Harbor in 1941 as devastating as it was. (Part I is on page 343.)

BEFORE THE STORM

On the evening of Saturday, December 6, 1941, Yoshikawa sent what would turn out to be the last of his coded messages to Tokyo:

VESSELS MOORED IN HARBOR: NINE BATTLESHIPS;
THREE CLASS-B CRUISERS; THREE SEAPLANE TEN-
DERS; SEVENTEEN DESTROYERS. ENTERING HARBOR
ARE FOUR CLASS-B CRUISERS; THREE DESTROYERS.
ALL AIRCRAFT CARRIERS AND HEAVY CRUISERS HAVE
DEPARTED HARBOR....NO INDICATION OF ANY CHANGES
IN U.S. FLEET. "ENTERPRISE" AND "LEXINGTON"
HAVE SAILED FROM PEARL HARBOR....IT APPEARS THAT
NO AIR RECONNAISSANCE IS BEING CONDUCTED BY
THE FLEET AIR ARM.

Though Yoshikawa provided much of the intelligence used to plan the attack on Pearl Harbor, he did not know when—or even if—it would occur. ("To entrust knowledge of such a vital decision to an expendable espionage agent would have been foolish," he later explained.) He learned the attack was under way the same way that Hawaiians did: by hearing the first bombs go off as he was eating breakfast, at 7:55 a.m. on the morning of the 7th.

INFAMY

Yoshikawa had been feeding the war planners in Japan a steady stream of information for eight months, and his efforts had paid off. The Japanese military accomplished its objective with brutal effectiveness: The naval strike force, which included nine destroyers, 23 submarines, two battleships and six aircraft carriers bristling with more than 400 fighters, bombers, dive-bombers and torpedo planes, had managed to sail more than 4,000 miles across

---

There are 42 gallons in a barrel of oil.

the Pacific undetected and then strike at the home base of the U.S. Pacific Fleet while its ships were still at anchor and the Army Air Corps planes were still on the ground.

Twenty American warships were sunk or badly damaged in the two-hour attack, including the eight battleships along Battleship Row, the main target of the raid. More than 180 U.S. aircraft were destroyed and another 159 damaged. The destruction of the airfield on Ford Island, in the very heart of Pearl Harbor, was so complete that only a single aircraft managed to make it into the air. More than 2,400 American servicemen lost their lives, including 1,177 on the battleship *Arizona*, and another 1,178 were wounded. It was the greatest military disaster in United States history.

The Japanese losses were miniscule in comparison: 29 planes and 5 midget submarines lost, 64 men killed, and one submariner taken prisoner—the first Japanese P.O.W. of the war—when his submarine ran aground on Oahu.

INVISIBLE MAN

The FBI raided the Japanese consulate within hours, but by then Yoshikawa had burned his code books and any other materials that would have identified him as a spy. He was taken into custody with the rest of the consular staff, and in August 1942 they were all returned to Japan as part of a swap with American diplomats being held in Japan.

Yoshikawa worked in Naval Intelligence for the rest of the war. When Japan surrendered in August 1945, he hid in the countryside, posing as a Buddhist monk, fearful of what might happen to him if the American occupation forces learned of his role in the Pearl Harbor attack. After the occupation ended in 1952, he returned to his family. In 1955 he opened a candy business.

By that time Yoshikawa's role in the war had become widely known, thanks to an Imperial Navy officer who identified him by name in a 1953 interview with the newspaper *Ehime Shimbun*. If Yoshikawa thought the exposure would bring him fame, fortune, or the gratitude of his countrymen, he was wrong on all counts. Japan had paid a terrible price for starting the war with the United States: On top of the estimated 1.6 million Japanese soldiers who died in the war, an additional 400,000 civilians were killed, including more than 100,000 who died when atomic bombs were dropped on Hiroshima and Nagasaki. Few people wanted anything to do with the man who helped bring such death and destruction to Japan. "They even blamed me for the atomic bomb," Yoshikawa told Australia's *Daily Mail* in 1991, in one of his rare interviews with the Western press.

The candy business failed, and Yoshikawa, now a pariah in his own land, had trouble even finding a job. He ended up living off of the income his wife earned selling insurance. He never received any official recognition for his contribution to the war effort, not a medal or even a thank-you note, and when he petitioned the postwar government for a pension, they turned him down. By the end of his life he had returned to the same vice that supposedly landed him in the spying business in the first place: alcohol. "I drink to forget," he told a reporter. "I have so many thoughts now, so many years after the war. Why has history cheated me?" He died penniless in a nursing home in 1993.

FINAL IRONY

Yoshikawa was the only Japanese spy in Honolulu before the outbreak of war; only the consul general knew his true identity and purpose, and with the exception of the geishas, his driver, and others who assisted him without fully realizing what he was up to, he worked alone.

And yet it was the Roosevelt administration's fear that other Japanese spies might be out there, both in the Hawaiian Islands and on the West Coast of the United States, that prompted the federal government to round up 114,000 Japanese Americans and incarcerate them in internment camps for the duration of the war. Many were given only 48 hours to put their affairs in order and as a consequence lost everything they owned.

Not a single internee was ever charged with espionage, and no one understood better than Yoshikawa that they were innocent. He knew because he *had* tried to recruit Japanese Americans, sounding them out about their loyalties without revealing his purpose, and had failed. "They had done nothing. It was a cruel joke," he admitted to the *Daily Mail*. "You see, I couldn't trust them in Hawaii to help me. They were loyal to the United States."

THE MONTY HALL PARADOX

Remember Monty Hall, the host of the TV game show Let's Make a Deal? *Monty (and the show) may be gone, but his name lives on in a fascinating probability puzzle that was inspired by one of the "deals" on his show.*

DOOR PRIZE

Imagine you're a contestant on *Let's Make a Deal*, standing in front of three giant doors labeled "1," "2," and "3." Behind one of the doors (you don't know which one, but Monty does) is a new car. Behind the other two doors are booby prizes: live goats. Monty Hall invites you to choose a door; you'll win whichever prize is behind it. You pick a door—say, Door #1. But before Monty tells you what you've won, he opens one of the doors you *didn't* pick, say Door #3, to reveal...a goat. Then he asks you, "Do you want to switch to Door #2?" Well, do you? Will switching from Door #1 to Door #2 improve your chances of winning the car? This puzzle, originally called the "Monty Hall Problem," was first proposed by a statistician named Steve Selvin in 1975.

THINK AGAIN

If you think the odds are the same whether you stick with Door #1 or switch to Door #2, you're not alone. That's what most people would say, because that seems to make sense. After all, if there's one car and three doors, the odds of it being behind Door #1, Door #2, or Door #3 are are exactly the same: 1-in-3. But that's the wrong way to look at the problem. According to Selvin, you have to think of it in terms of the one door you *picked* versus the two doors you *didn't pick*: The odds that the car is behind the door you picked are 1-in-3, and the odds that the car is behind one of the two you didn't pick are 2-in-3. The odds don't change when one of the doors is opened because the prizes haven't moved. Sure, once Door #3 is opened to reveal a goat, the odds of the car being behind that door drop to zero. But there's *still* a 2-in-3 chance that the car is behind one of the two doors you didn't pick. That means there's now a 2-in-3 chance that the car is behind Door #2. Switching from Door #1 to Door #2 actually *doubles* your odds of winning the car—from 1-in-3, to 2-in-3. So switch doors!

Ataullah Durrini, the creator of Minute Rice, was a cousin of the king of Afghanistan.

THE MISSING-CHILDREN MILK CARTON PROGRAM

If you were around in the 1980s, you undoubtedly remember them: black-and-white photos of missing children printed on the sides of cardboard milk cartons. Here's the story of how it all started.

ABDUCTED

On Sunday morning, September 5, 1982, 12-year-old Johnny Gosch set out from his West Des Moines, Iowa, home before dawn on his *Des Moines Register* newspaper route. His father often went with him on Sundays, but this time the boy did his route alone, taking only the family Dachshund with him. By 6:00 a.m. the Gosch home was getting phone calls from neighbors: Where were their newspapers? John Gosch, Johnny's father, got out of bed and went to look for his son. Two blocks from their home he found Johnny's wagon, full of papers, and the Dachshund standing nearby. Johnny Gosch was nowhere to be found.

Almost exactly two years later, on Sunday, August 12, 1984, an eerily similar tragedy struck the city: 12-year-old Eugene Wade Martin left his home before dawn to deliver the *Register*. His older brother normally went with him, but not that day. At 7:30 a.m. the route manager called the family to say that Eugene's newspapers were found at a corner on his route. Eugene Martin had been abducted, and he hasn't been seen since.

HELPING HANDS

The story of a second boy being kidnapped shook the small Iowa city, and people there did what they could to find them: The *Register* ran full-page ads with the boys' pictures and information, and a local trucking company put poster-size images of the boys' faces on the sides of their trucks. Then, in September 1984, a month after the second abduction, an employee of Anderson-Erickson Dairy asked company president Jim Erickson if there was some way they could help, too. Erickson said yes and, influenced by

---

The braille edition of *Harry Potter and the Deathly Hallows* weighs 12 lbs.

what both the newspapers and the trucking company had done, he decided to run photos and short bios of the missing boys on the sides of the dairy's half-gallon milk cartons. That, he figured, would get the boys' faces onto kitchen tables in thousands of homes in the area every morning. A week later, Prairie Farms Dairy, also in Des Moines, decided to do the same. Tragically, Johnny and Eugene were never found, but Jim Erickson's idea gave the issue of missing and abducted children a big publicity boost in Des Moines—and it wasn't long before it became a national phenomenon.

TO THE WINDY CITY

In November 1984, Walter Woodbury, vice president of Hawthorne Mellody Dairy in Whitewater, Wisconsin, one of the biggest milk distributors in Chicago, saw one of Anderson-Erickson's cartons while on a trip to Iowa. "I thought we could do it in Chicago," he told a newspaper at the time. "I talked to Commander Mayo [of the Chicago Police Department's youth division], and he was very enthusiastic. The police thought it was a heck of an idea." Using the same format as Anderson-Erickson, the dairy's half-gallon cartons would carry photos and short descriptions of two of the city's missing children. The photos would be chosen by the police department and approved by parents, and would be changed monthly. Best of all, they would appear on roughly two million cartons every month. Shortly after Chicago's first missing-children milk cartons appeared in January 1985, the program got the national attention it needed. *Good Morning America*, *The Today Show*, and CBS *Morning News* all covered the story, as did the Associated Press.

GO WEST, YOUNG PROGRAM

Near the end of 1984, Steven Glazer, chief of staff for California state assemblyman (and future governor) Gray Davis, read a newspaper article about the Chicago milk carton program. He thought it was a great idea, and he talked Davis into promoting it as a statewide program. Glazer contacted dairies around the state, and dozens signed up. The program kicked off in early 1985, and photos of missing kids began appearing on tens of millions of milk cartons every month.

California's program produced results. Glazer says that in just the first few months at least 12 children, most of them runaways, returned home as a result of the campaign. One of the first was a Los Angeles teenager who'd run away to live with friends in Sacramento; she saw a local news report about the program—and saw her own photo on one of the cartons. She decided to go home the next day. And a *Los Angeles Times* news story on May 23, 1985, reported that of the 14 missing kids from the Los Angeles area who appeared on milk cartons, seven were returned home.

Having a state as large as California take on the program earned it national and even international press, and it was about to get even bigger.

FROM SEA TO SHINING SEA

In late January 1985, the National Child Safety Council (NCSC), a non-profit organization that had been working with police and schools around the country to promote child safety issues since the 1950s, announced that they were launching their own Missing Children Milk Carton Program nationally. The NCSC already had 100 dairies signed up and would soon begin printing information about missing children, along with a national toll-free telephone number, on cartons distributed all across the country. By March more than 700 dairies were involved—and an incredible 1.5 billion milk cartons with images of missing kids on them were being distributed nationwide. In April the NCSC announced that reported sightings of missing children had increased by more than 30 percent.

The success of the program led to many other items being used to display missing kids' faces over the next few years, including shopping bags, soda bottles, billboards—even bills from power and gas companies.

MOVING ON

But as big as the Missing Children Milk Carton Campaign was (and as big a piece of American culture as it remains), it was actually pretty short-lived. A combination of factors, including the fact that many parents complained that seeing the pictures of missing kids everyday was scaring their own children, led to the end of the program after just a few years. "The milk-cartons program ran its course," said Gaylord Walker, NCSC vice president.

"They had a tremendous impact and they did a great job of creating public awareness." But how successful was the program in helping with the return of abducted kids? Nobody knows for sure—because nobody kept any hard, verifiable numbers on the program as a whole. What we do know is that many runaways and at least *some* abducted children were returned to their families as a result of the milk cartons—and that, most would argue, made it all worthwhile.

And the idea behind it didn't go away: The NCSC, along with organizations such as the government-funded National Center for Missing and Exploited Children (NCMEC), continued using a variety of programs to teach parents and kids how to avoid trouble in the first place, what to do if the worst happens, and especially how to get information about missing kids to police agencies and the public as quickly as possible. One of the best-known programs is an electronic version of the milk carton program: the NCMEC's "Amber Alert" system, implemented nationally in 2002 and named for 9-year-old Amber Hagerman, who was abducted and killed in Arlington, Texas, in 1996. It allows for extremely rapid public outreach on abduction cases via TV and radio stations, e-mail, electronic traffic-and-road condition signs, electronic billboards, and more. So although pictures of missing kids no longer appear on milk cartons, the spirit of the program lives on.

EXTRAS
• Missing-children programs are still being implemented worldwide. As recently as 2008, the British organization Missing People launched a campaign with a supermarket chain to put the faces of missing people on milk cartons.

• On March 2, 2009, a three-year-old girl was abducted from her bed in Yreka, California, in the middle of the night. Her father managed to get a look at a car speeding off. Yreka residents, each with Amber Alert posters with photos of the girl and descriptions of the car, started their own search the next morning. An hour later, three volunteers spotted tire tracks in the mud near a railroad track. They followed them, saw the car—and found the little girl. She was unharmed, and was quickly back home with her parents. The car's owner, Kody Lee Kaplon, 22, was arrested and is facing felony charges.

HOW TO CRACK A SAFE, PT. III

So you can't find the combination to your safe, and you don't have the time, patience, or skill (or the electronic listening device) to try the method on page 303. Fear not: You can still drill, burn, or blow the safe open.

DRILL, BABY, DRILL
If a safecracker can't figure out the combination to the safe he's trying to open, the next step is often to drill into the safe. The safecracker's assessment of how the safe is constructed will help determine whether to drill through the door, the rear, or one of the sides.

• Drilling through the door is the most direct method. The safecracker may try to drill directly into the locking mechanism in order to defeat or destroy it. Or they may drill a peephole over the wheel pack that allows them to see the notches in the wheels. Once the wheel pack is visible, all the safecracker has to do is turn the dial until the notches line up, and the safe is unlocked. A special fiber-optic instrument called a *boroscope* can be inserted into the peephole to make the wheel pack easier to see.

• The problem with drilling through the door is that safe manufacturers *expect* you to drill through the door, and many pack the door with extra security features to discourage an attempt. The area around the dial and locking mechanism, for example, may be protected by special layers of hardened steel or other materials that are very difficult to drill through. The door could be filled with ball bearings (also difficult to drill through) or even a pane of glass that incorporates one or more spring-loaded relocking devices. Drilling into the glass will cause it to shatter, tripping the devices and making the safe *much* more difficult to open.

ON THE SIDE

• One simple way to get at the contents of the safe is to drill not one hole in the side or the rear of the safe, but several, in a close square or circular pattern. The safecracker can then use a sledge hammer to punch out the square or circle, resulting in a hole big enough to reach through to remove the contents of the safe.

• Another technique is to drill two holes—a peephole and a second hole—in the rear of the safe, directly opposite the locking mechanism in the door. Because many models of safes are designed to make changing the combination easy (when the safe door is open), the locking mechanism may only be covered by a panel that's fastened to the inside of the door with ordinary screws. Breaking into the wheel pack may be as simple as inserting a long screwdriver through the hole drilled in the back of the safe and unscrewing the panel.

KABOOM!

• Of course, it's also possible to drill a hole large enough to insert a stick of dynamite or TNT, then light the fuse and blow the door off the safe, just like in the movies. Or you could pour nitroglycerine into the gap between the door and the rest of the safe and ignite it with a blasting cap and an electric charge.

• A safecracker can also burn into the safe using an acetylene blowtorch, which burns at 4,000–4,500°F, or something called a *thermic lance*, which burns at 7,000°F, hot enough to melt through six inches of hardened steel in just 15 seconds.

• The problem with these techniques, of course, is that they can easily destroy the contents of the safe. Paper burns at 451°F, and the steel in the safe is an excellent conductor of heat. If you try to burn your way into a safe filled with cash, all you may have to show for your trouble is ash that *used* to be cash.

LUCKY BREAK

• The good news—for you, if you're the legitimate owner of a safe that you cannot open—is that there isn't much of a market for safes that can never be opened again once the combination is lost or the relocking mechanisms have been triggered. Because of this, safe manufacturers incorporate flaws into the designs of their safes that enable locksmiths to drill them open again. All the locksmith has to do is obtain a special drilling template from the manufacturer that shows where and how to drill the safe open.

• These templates are some of the most closely guarded secrets of the safe manufacturing industry; they're made available only to approved professional locksmiths. So if you're a burglar trying to open a safe, it'll be just about impossible to get your hands on one.

POSTMORTEMS

No, it's not a breakfast cereal made from dead people. It's a collection of bizarre stories about things that happened to people postmortem, *or "after death."*

MISSED-EM

In October 2006, a landlord in Vienna, Austria, checked the apartment of a tenant who hadn't responded to several letters regarding a rent increase. He found the tenant, 93-year-old Franz Riedl, in the apartment, dead. And he'd been like that for at least four years. The landlord said he had no idea there was anything amiss with Riedl, explaining that Riedl had always been a recluse, so he'd seldom been seen, and that his rent had always been paid on time. (It was paid automatically from the same bank account that received his pension payment.) And nobody had ever reported an odor coming from the apartment. Police said they were able to determine the approximate date of death only because they found Austrian schillings in the apartment. The schilling was taken out of circulation and replaced by the euro in January 2002. Officers added that Riedl's body appeared to be "mummified."

TEXTED-EM

In October 2009, police in Miramar, Florida, were investigating the case of a missing 35-year-old woman. In the first days after she disappeared, the woman sent her family text messages saying she'd moved, but the family didn't believe it, telling police they had never received text messages from her before. They also said that she had been trying to leave her abusive boyfriend, Paul Edwards, 44, for some time. After the woman had been missing for almost a month, police decided to see how Edwards would react to a message…from his missing girlfriend. They received court permission to transfer her old cell phone number to a new phone, and then sent Edwards a text message: "Just wait 'til I get better." It worked. Edwards left his house and drove to several different locations—and eventually led police to the woman's body. Thanks to her "ghostly" text message, Edwards is now in jail, facing a charge of first-degree murder.

In Japan, builders use bubble wrap as insulation and soundproofing in houses.

RECYCLED-EM

Gene Wilford Hathorn was convicted of capital murder in Huntsville, Texas, in 1985, and has been on death row ever since. In 2008 he was contacted by Danish-based artist Marco Evaristti, who asked Hathorn if he could have Hathorn's body after the execution, when and if it ever happens. If that wasn't weird enough, he told Hathorn what he wanted to do with it. "My aim is to first deep freeze Gene's body," Evaristti said, "and then make fish food out of it." Hathorn agreed. Evaristti plans to stage an "art" exhibit—where visitors will have the opportunity to feed fish with the food made from Hathorn's body. "It's the last thing he can do for society and he views it as positive," says Evaristti. Texas officials permit prisoners to choose whoever they want to care for their remains, and Hathorn has made the artist the legal heir to his body, so this may actually happen some day. (We'll be sure to let you know if it does.)

SMOKED-EM

A mummified human body was found in the chimney of a Finnish industrial building as it was being demolished in 2010. The corpse still had clothes on, and had a wallet with identification in one of the pockets. It identified the body as that of a man born in 1953 who had gone missing in 1991. Exactly how and why the man ended up in a chimney is still under investigation.

TOWED-EM

In March 2010, police in New York City towed a mini-van that was illegally parked in front of a funeral home. Funeral director Paul DeNigris had illegally parked the van in front of the building for a few minutes while he picked up some paperwork and took a call. When he came out and found it gone, he was aghast: There was a corpse in the van. He raced to the police impound yard and spent the next hour-and-a-half trying to get it back. He finally did, and raced to the airport: The corpse was bound for Miami, Florida, where it was scheduled to be cremated. The impound lot waived its usual $185 towing fee because of the "special circumstances" involved in the incident. (But he still had to pay $115 for the parking violation.)

What do Steve Jobs, Faith Hill, and Rev. Jesse Jackson have in common? All were adopted.

THE ANTHRAX ATTACKS, PART IV

Here's the final installment of our story on the 2001 anthrax scare. (Part III is on page 424.)

IGNORE THE EVIDENCE

The first suspect in the anthrax attacks of 2001 was Iraqi dictator Saddam Hussein. It seemed plausible: The letters at least *seemed* to come from a Muslim source (they all said "Allah is great"). Hussein once had large stores of anthrax-based weaponry and he'd had a beef with the United States since the Persian Gulf War. But the evidence being presented in the media didn't add up.

The first stories linking Iraq to the anthrax attacks appeared in October 2001 in several newspapers, including the *New York Times* and the London *Times*. They reported that an Iraqi intelligence agent had met with al-Qaeda member and 9-11 ringleader Mohammad Atta in Prague in April 2001. There, according to the reports, they discussed the attacks of 9-11—and the Iraqi gave Atta a vial of anthrax spores. The story had the effect of linking Iraq to both the anthrax attacks *and* the 9-11 attacks, and it increased the panic already felt by Americans. The only problem: Both the FBI and the CIA said there was no evidence such a meeting ever took place.

BAD PRESS

The next bit of "evidence" that Iraq was involved was reported by ABC News' Brian Ross on October 26, 2001. Citing "three well-placed but separate sources," Ross said that government tests on the anthrax powder used in the attacks showed that it contained a chemical called *bentonite*, and that the only country in the world known to use bentonite in its biological weapons...was Iraq. The problem with this story: There was no bentonite in the anthrax. Both the White House and Homeland Security Director Tom Ridge immediately said it wasn't true. (And Ross never revealed who had given him the bogus information.)

While stories like these were making headlines, the FBI had a

---

Iraq war fact: Water-soaked (unused) disposable diapers are good for sponge baths.

real investigation to carry out. That turned into about as much of a fiasco as the sketchy news stories.

THE WRONG SUSPECTS

The investigation of the FBI's "Amerithrax" case was the biggest (and the most expensive) in the agency's history. According to the FBI:

> Efforts involved more than 10,000 witness interviews on six different continents, the execution of 80 searches, and the recovery of more than 6,000 items of potential evidence during the course of the investigation. The case involved the issuance of more than 5,750 grand jury subpoenas and the collection of 5,730 environmental samples from 60 site locations.

Over the course of the investigation more than 1,000 people were viewed as possible suspects. Here are the most significant:

Dr. Ayaad Assaad. The Egyptian-born microbiologist worked at USAMRIID at Fort Detrick from 1989 to 1997. On October 2, 2001—two days before the first confirmed case of inhalation anthrax—the FBI received an anonymous letter saying Assaad was planning a bioterror attack. "The letter-writer clearly knew my entire background, my training in both chemical and biological agents, my security clearance, what floor where I work now, that I have two sons, what train I take to work, and where I live," said Assaad. The FBI later cleared him of any connection to the attacks. The letter writer was never identified. Assaad believes it was a coworker, and quite possibly the attacker.

Dr. Philip M. Zack. In December 2001, Connecticut's *Hartford Courant* newspaper reported that although Zack, a retired army lieutenant colonel and a microbiologist, had been fired from the Fort Detrick lab in 1991, video surveillance tapes showed him being let in by a coworker, Dr. Marian Rippy, months later—when he should not have had access to the site. (Zack had been fired for harassing Dr. Assaad, the story said.) This was right around the time that anthrax bacteria samples were reported missing from the lab. The FBI said little publicly about Zack, and despite the fact that the *Courant* ran this story just a few months after the attacks, he was almost completely ignored by the press over the entire course of the investigation.

Dr. Steven J. Hatfill. The one person who was not ignored by the press was Hatfill, a medical doctor, virologist, and bioterror expert who worked at Fort Detrick from 1997 until 1999. He was first implicated in early 2002 by Don Foster, a linguistics professor hired by the FBI to study the letters and other classified documents connected to the case. According to Foster, there were too many odd clues pointing to Hatfill to ignore.

• Hatfill had studied medicine in Rhodesia (now Zimbabwe) in the 1970s, when one of the largest anthrax outbreaks among humans in modern history occurred.

• The Rhodesian medical school Hatfill attended was near a suburb named "Greendale"—the name of the fictitious school listed as the return address on the letters sent to the Senate.

• Hatfill had authored an unpublished novel years earlier. The subject: a bioterror attack on Washington, D.C.

• He'd taken Cipro in the days before the attacks.

The FBI initially told Foster he was wrong—no matter what the evidence said, Hatfill had a solid alibi. But under intense pressure to solve the case, in August 2002, the agency named him as a "person of interest" anyway. And for the next three years, Hatfill's life unraveled as the FBI trailed him 24 hours a day, questioned his friends, family, and co-workers, and repeatedly searched his home, all the while leaking seemingly incriminating information about him to the press. Hatfill was in the news constantly, sometimes being named outright as the attacker. He ended up losing his job, many of his friends, and nearly his mind. "You might as well have hooked me up to a battery," he told *The Atlantic* magazine in May 2010. "It was sanctioned torture." During the investigation Hatfill sued the Justice Department for ruining his reputation. In 2008 they quietly settled for $5.82 million, and soon afterwards the department fully exonerated him of any wrongdoing.

THE FINAL SUSPECT

On August 6, 2008, the FBI announced for the first time that they believed that just one person was responsible for the 2001 anthrax attacks, and that they knew who that person was: Dr. Bruce Ivins, one of the leading researchers at Fort Detrick—and someone who had actively helped them in the investigation into the attacks.

Homer Simpson, John Cleese, and Mr. T have each been the voices of GPS systems.

One big problem for anyone looking for true closure in the case: Ivins had committed suicide a month earlier. He would never face the trial that might have answered at least some of the many questions that remained. There was, however, a lot of compelling, if circumstantial, evidence against him:

• Ivins worked in the lab at Fort Detrick from 1990 until his death in 2008, and had easy access to the Ames strain of anthrax bacteria.

• In the weeks before both the September and October attacks, he worked several late nights alone in the lab.

• Ivins had twice—once in December 2001 and again in April 2002—performed unauthorized cleanups of anthrax spills at Fort Detrick. He did not report the events to authorities at the time.

• While working on developing an anthrax vaccine, Ivins not only had access to the RMR-1029 batch of the Ames strain—he had been its sole custodian since it was first cultured in 1979. (Hatfill did not have access to RMR-1029.)

• Just days after being informed by the FBI that he was going to be indicted in the anthrax attacks, Ivins committed suicide.

CASE CLOSED?

In February 2010, a year and a half after first naming Ivins as their sole suspect, the Justice Department and the FBI officially closed the case of the 2001 anthrax attacks. Many people believe there are still far too many mysteries to justify ending the investigation. Among them: The government never showed any evidence that Ivins had been to the New Jersey post office box used to mail the letters—seven hours from his Maryland home; Jeffrey Adamovicz, Ivins's onetime supervisor at Fort Detrick, said Ivins didn't have the skill necessary to process anthrax liquid into concentrated powder form; and no traces of anthrax were ever found at Ivins's home or on any of his belongings.

Questions not involving Bruce Ivins also remain unanswered: How did Kathy Nguyen, 61, the New York City hospital worker, and Ottilie Lundgren, 94, of rural Connecticut, come into contact with anthrax spores? (The only explanation ever given was that their mail must have been cross-contaminated while in the postal system, but no contaminated letters were ever found at their

Two of the 14 actors who played the "Marlboro Man" died of lung cancer.

homes or at Nguyen's workplace.) Why did the FBI focus on Hat-fill for so long when evidence pointed to Ivins at least as early as 2002? And, going back to the start of this story—who was the "high government official" who warned columnist Richard Cohen to take Cipro before the attacks even occurred?

Those questions will likely remain unanswered for years to come.

A FEW SPORE FACTS

• The anthrax spores in the letter sent to Chile were not from the Ames strain. Whether it was related to the attacks in the U.S. is still unknown.

• The name "Ames strain" was based on an error: The strain was grown from a bacteria sample taken from a cow that died of anthrax in Texas in 1980. The Army lab at Fort Detrick acquired the strain in 1981, and a researcher there dubbed it "Ames" because he thought it came from the National Veterinary Services Laboratories, a government lab where cattle diseases are studied, in Ames, Iowa. He was wrong—but the name stuck.

• According to the American Medical Association, at least 2,500 anthrax spores have to be inhaled to cause an infection.

• Cats, dogs, pigs, and birds can contract anthrax, but rarely do. Cold-blooded creatures such as frogs and snakes cannot contract the disease.

• Seven people in Scotland and one in Germany died of anthrax after injecting contaminated heroin in late 2009 and early 2010.

• It's believed that only the United States and Russia have developed the technology to convert anthrax spores to powder form.

• The bacteria used in the anthrax-based weapons that Iraq developed in the late 1980s were created from strains Iraq bought from the American Type Culture Collection, a private, not-for-profit company based in Manassas, Virginia, that sells cell cultures.

• No letter was ever found at American Media, workplace of the first victims, but several employees said they remembered a letter that had come to the company in early September that contained a "soapy, bluish powder." They said all three victims had handled the letter, and that it was a "weird love letter to Jennifer Lopez."

BASEBALL CONTRACTS

Uncle John's contract grants him use of the BRI's toilet-shaped car (the Pot Rod). Here are some weird contract stipulations from the world of baseball.

Charlie Kerfeld. In his rookie season with the Houston Astros in 1986, pitcher Kerfeld amassed an impressive 11-2 record and 2.69 earned-run average. That meant when it came time to negotiate his 1987 contract, Kerfeld could make some strange requests. So he asked for a salary of $110,037.37 (because 37 was his jersey number) and 37 boxes of orange Jell-O (because orange was the main color in the Astros uniform).

• **Mark Teixeira.** His 2007 contract with the Atlanta Braves included a $100,000 bonus should he be named that year's American League Most Valuable Player. What's so odd about that? The Braves play in the National League. (The contract had been negotiated when Teixeira played for the Texas Rangers, of the American League.)

• **Bobby Bonilla.** Bonilla signed with the New York Mets in 1999. After a subpar season, the team released him, but still owed him $5.9 million. The team had to get him off their books so they could sign another player, so they worked out a deal: If Bonilla would defer payment for a decade, they'd pay him an annuity worth far more than the $5.9 million. Offer accepted. Result: From 2011 until 2035 Bonilla will receive a yearly check for $1.19 million.

• **George Brett.** In renewing the All-Star third baseman's contact in 1984, the Kansas City Royals gave him a strange perk: partial ownership of a Tennessee apartment complex. Team co-owner Avron Fogelman owned several in Memphis, and offered Brett a 10 percent stake in a 1,100-unit complex, which guaranteed him $1 million a year for however long he owned it.

• **Rollie Fingers.** Oakland Athletics owner Charlie Finley conceived a bizarre promotional gimmick in 1972: He promised $300 cash to any player who grew a mustache. Fingers took Finley's offer and grew a curvy handlebar one—perhaps the most famous in baseball history. The next year, Fingers' contract included a $300 "mustache bonus," plus another $100 to buy mustache wax.

In a year, the Disneyland train will travel 20,000 miles...just circling the park.

NUMBERS ON THE RADIO

*A mechanical voice cuts through the shortwave static, repeating
sets of numbers endlessly into the night: "8, 6, 7, 5, 3...
4, 5, 7, 8, 9." You've tuned in to a "numbers station,"
one of the great mysteries of the airwaves.*

STRANGENESS IN THE NIGHT

If you've ever spent time turning the dial of a shortwave
radio, you may have found a station on which a voice—
usually a woman's—slowly enunciates long strings of numbers,
five at a time. It may go on for only a few minutes, or for many
hours. And the voices, sometimes punctuated by tones or music,
might recite their numeric codes in English, but they might use
German, Chinese, Spanish, Arabic, or a Slavic language. It's
almost hypnotic to listen to, but it's also disquieting, even down-
right creepy. What's it all about? You've stumbled upon what
shortwave listeners call a "numbers station."

Aficionados have recorded the signals, looked for clues and
patterns, and tried to decode what the numbers mean. Their websites keep logs of times, languages, transcripts, and frequencies of
transmissions, but all their efforts have yielded only a little bit of
solid data...and a lot of conjecture. Their conclusion: The numbers stations are being used to communicate with spies and covert
operatives. Even though no country has officially admitted to
using numbers stations for espionage, enough tantalizing information has leaked out to support that theory.

OLD-FASHIONED

Numbers stations on the shortwave channels have been broadcasting for decades, at least as far back as World War II. (One expert
claims to have evidence that the first one began during World
War I.) But if they are being used as spycraft, why? Shortwave may
seem like a remnant of the time when secret radio transmission
was state-of-the-art for spies. After all, we've got encrypted tele-
phones and e-mail, secure Internet sites, and miniature storage
media that are easily hidden and can store millions of images and
documents. Yet despite all these high-tech options and the fact

---

In 2005 German scientists succeeded in creating a material harder than diamond.

that the Cold War has ended, there may be more shortwave numbers stations now than ever before.

HANDLE WITH CARE

Intelligence agents in deep cover can't risk making regular contact with their handlers. And even when mail, phone, and computer messages can't be decoded, they *can* be detected. In fact, many agents have been caught by what's called a "traffic analysis" of their outgoing and incoming messages, with spy-hunters looking for patterns, phone numbers, and addresses that suggest something suspicious. That's what makes shortwave transmissions so useful.

Unlike AM or FM, shortwaves bounce off outer layers of the atmosphere. Result: Any modest transmitter can cover the entire world and obscure the broadcaster's origin. Not that obscurity matters much: Even if the transmitter's location is known, the receiver's location isn't. Anybody with an inexpensive shortwave radio can pick up the signals without anybody else being the wiser. If they know the code, they can get a secret message anonymously using just an everyday radio, a pad of paper, and a pencil. It's simple and effective, and it saves the agent from being caught with an incriminating array of sophisticated communication devices.

But what about security? If *everybody* can receive these messages, aren't the senders worried that somebody out there will figure out the code? The answer, it turns out, is that a few simple codes are, for all practical purposes, unbreakable if you use what's called a "one-time pad." (We'll explain this later.)

QUIRKY FORMATS

How can spies be sure they're tuning in to the right station? The broadcasters add distinctive trademarks to their transmissions. Hobbyist monitors have given informal names to the stations, based on some peculiar eccentricities. For example:

• **"Yosemite Sam,"** a station that appeared in 2004, is called that because its broadcast begins with the voice of the Looney Tunes character saying, "Varmint, I'm-a gonna blow yah to smithereens!"

• **"Tyrolean Music,"** reportedly from East Germany, started and ended with several minutes of "oom-pa-pa" music—complete with

---

Technically speaking, the "fly" on a pair of pants is the cloth flap covering the zipper.

yodeling—before a voice came on saying "*Achtung! Achtung! Achtung!*" and then numbers in German.

- **"Lincolnshire Poacher"** station, thought to be run by England's supersecretive MI6, punctuates its broadcasts with a few bars of an English folk song (it's called "Lincolnshire Poacher") played over and over again on a calliope. Another quirk: It's also the only numbers station with inflection; its voice generator delivers the last number in each five-number string with an upward lilt.

- **"Magnetic Fields"** divides its Arabic-language number messages with snippets of the album *Les Chants Magnétique* by French composer Jean Michel Jarre.

- **"Czech Lady,"** also known as "Bulgarian Betty," opens with an unidentified synthesizer tune. The nervous-sounding voice delivers numbers in Czech. (Or maybe it's Bulgarian.)

- **"Atencion"** begins with the Spanish command "*¡Atención!*" In the early 2000s, the station was publicly implicated as a Cuban broadcaster in American cases against Cuban agents.

- **"NATO Phonetic Alphabet"** uses lists of letters from the phonetic alphabet ("Alfa, Bravo, Charlie...") instead of numbers. Israel is said to be the source of this station.

- **"Wunderland bei Nacht,"** believed to be a German station, starts with two songs by 1960s pop instrumentalist Bert Kaempfert, "Wonderland by Night" and "Dreaming the Blues."

- **"Swedish Rhapsody"** begins its broadcast with part of Hugo Alfven's "Swedish Rhapsody" as if played by an ice cream truck, and its numbers are read in a young girl's voice.

(Don't worry that there's a real woman or child locked up in a broadcasting booth, being forced to read numbers all day. Nowadays, numbers stations use the same recorded voices and technology as automated messages from telephone service providers.)

THEY LIVE AMONG US

Cracks occasionally appear in the wall of secrecy: Some governments have admitted that *other* governments use numbers stations for espionage. A British government spokesperson even told the *Daily Telegraph* that numbers stations "are what you'd suppose they are. People shouldn't be mystified by them. They are not for, shall we say, public consumption."

In 1941 Winston Churchill had a heart attack while opening a window in the White House.

In 2010, though, numbers stations became a part of a news story when 10 Russian spies were discovered living suburban American lives. Court documents revealed that a raid on an apartment in Seattle found a shortwave radio and spiral notebooks "which contain apparently random columns of numbers," with the explanation that "the spiral notebook contains codes used to decipher radiograms as they came in." And that wasn't the first time numbers stations got a mention in U.S. espionage cases. In four separate cases between the 2001 to 2009, agents were said to have "received instructions through encrypted shortwave transmissions from Cuba." Using code pads found in a break-in leading up to the arrests, the U.S. government said it was able to decode a handful of messages, including "Prioritize and continue to strengthen friendship with Joe and Dennis," and "Congratulations to all the female comrades for International Day of the Woman."

GOING MAINSTREAM

For many years, numbers station broadcasters who wanted theme songs simply used music without crediting or paying the artists and composers. Since then, musicians have turned the tables by incorporating recordings of numbers stations into their work and thus dragging them into the sunlight.

The musicians' awareness of the stations is mostly due to a four-CD set called *The Conet Project: Recordings of Shortwave Numbers Stations*, released in 1997 by the Indial label. The spooky weirdness of the recordings began attracting the attention of recording artists such as the indie group Wilco, whose album *Yankee Foxtrot Hotel* got its name from a phrase heard repeatedly on Disc 1, Track 4. Wilco used that cut in the song "Poor Places." At least a dozen other bands have also used *Conet Project* recordings, including the Submarines, We Were Promised Jet Packs, Boards of Canada, and Stereolab. Expect to hear more: Indial has made the out-of-print CD available as a free online download.

AN EASY, UNBREAKABLE CODE

Given enough time and computer crunching, most codes can be broken. For example, if you simply replace letters with numbers, it's not hard to figure out the patterns, as anybody who has done cryptogram puzzles knows. But what if the code changes randomly

---

PEZ flavor flops: yogurt, eucalyptus, and chlorophyll.

with every letter? That's the idea behind a one-time pad system.

For example, start with a very simple pattern of 1=A, 2=B, 3=C, and so on. When your handler wanted to send you a HELLO, he'd first convert the letters to the simple 1=A system, getting 8-5-12-12-15. Easy, right? But what if, before you left the homeland for your spy assignment, you were given a cleverly concealed pad of paper with computer-generated numbers on every page, and your handler kept an identical pad at his transmitter?

Now, make it obscure

To make the message impenetrable to eavesdroppers, he'd take out his pad and read the first five random numbers there—say they're 7, 15, 1, 8, 3. He'd add the first number of his message to the code pad's first number and get 15. He'd add the message's second number to the second number on the pad, and so on, eventually ending up with 15-20-13-20-18.

When he broadcasts the message on his numbers station, you write down 15-20-13-20-18. To anybody else, the five numbers could mean anything. You, though, have the only pad that's identical to the sender's. You can subtract exactly the same random numbers he added and figure out the message. Since nobody else has a pad, every single number could literally be any letter—even the repeated number 20 offers no clue, because it happens to mean E the first time and L the second time.

Just to be safe...

After you translate the message, you destroy that page of numbers. The next time he sends a message, he'll use the next page on the pad with a new set of random numbers. That way, no one can figure out your ever-changing code—unless they get ahold of one of your pads. That's the only weakness of the system, so spy agencies have gone to great trouble to keep the pads secure. The U.S.S.R., it's said, issued a powerful magnifying glass to spies because its code pads were made small enough to hide inside a walnut shell. Spy lore holds that the Russians also printed the pads on flash paper—self-igniting paper that stage magicians use to produce flames from their fingertips—so the pads could be destroyed in (literally) the snap of a finger. What about the United States? Rumor has it that the CIA accomplished the same result by printing its code pads on flattened pieces of chewing gum.

Technically, bears don't hibernate—they just go "dormant" and sleep all winter.

FALSELY ACCUSED

You're just living your life, doing your thing, and then—boom!—someone
accuses you of a crime you didn't commit. Everything goes topsy-turvy
and nothing is ever the same again. It happened to these people.
(Warning: Some of the allegations are disturbing.)

THE ACCUSED: A.J. and Lisa Demaree, of Peoria, Arizona
BACKGROUND: In 2008, after the Demarees and their three daughters, aged 5, 4, and 1, returned from a trip, A.J. took his camera's memory card to Walmart to have prints made.
STORY: A few of the 144 photos showed the girls playing at bathtime. "They're typical pictures that 99% of families have," A.J. said. A Walmart employee, however, thought the photos were pornography and called the cops. Result: Child Protection Services went to the Demarees' home and took the girls away. A.J. and Lisa were questioned by police, who wouldn't even let them see their kids. No criminal charges were filed and the parents were granted supervised visitation rights, but the girls were remanded to the state until an investigation was completed. After officials interviewed the couple's friends and coworkers, Lisa was suspended from her teaching job, and both parents were put on a list of sex offenders. A month later they still didn't have their children, so they asked that a judge review the case. He looked at the pictures and determined that they were *not* pornographic, and ruled the kids be returned immediately. But the investigation dragged on for a year.
OUTCOME: The Demarees are suing Walmart for not displaying its "unsuitable print policy." They're also suing the state of Arizona, who they claim slandered them by telling their friends and co-workers that the couple were "child pornographers." In all, the family is seeking $8.4 million for "emotional stress, headaches, nightmares, shock to their nervous system, grief, and depression."

THE ACCUSED: Francis Evelyn, 58, a custodian at Brooklyn's Public School 91 in New York City
BACKGROUND: Having spent nearly 20 years in the job, Evelyn was well respected at work and in his neighborhood. The native

---

October 30 is "National Candy Corn Day."

Trinidadian described himself as "happy-go-lucky," had no criminal record, and was less than two years from retirement.
STORY: On March 19, 2007, police officers arrived at P.S. 91, arrested Evelyn, cuffed him, and took him away for questioning. Police commissioner Raymond Kelly announced that Evelyn was accused of the "heinous rape of an eight-year-old student on multiple occasions." Detectives told Evelyn that if he didn't confess, they'd make sure he got a life sentence in the "worst kind" of prison, where he'd likely be raped and possibly killed. If Evelyn did confess, they said, he'd get a lesser sentence. They even said they had DNA evidence against him. "How?" replied Evelyn. "I didn't *do* anything!" Then the police took the unorthodox step of locking him up in Rikers Island Prison with actual murderers and rapists.

OUTCOME: Three days later, police finally interviewed the accuser. It turned out that she was known as a "troubled child" who had lied about being abused on previous occasions. (The principal knew this, but failed to tell the police.) Worse still, the girl described her attacker as a bald, white man, yet cops arrested Evelyn, who is black. The charges were dropped immediately, and Evelyn was free. But the story had already gained worldwide attention. "On the bus home," Evelyn said, "a woman was reading the paper with my picture on the cover. The headline said 'The Rapist.'" He couldn't walk down the street without people pointing at him or insulting him. He was given his job back, but was unable to go near the school for months because he'd "start shaking." At last report, Evelyn was suing the city of New York for $10 million. "They ruined my life. I don't want those charges just to be sealed," he said. "I want them to be washed away!"

THE ACCUSED: Richard Jewell, a security guard at the 1996 Olympic Summer Games in Atlanta, Georgia
STORY: Jewell was patrolling Centennial Park, the "town square" of the Olympics, at 1:00 a.m. when he noticed a suspicious bag under a bench, only a few feet away from where thousands of people were enjoying a concert. Inside the bag were three pipe bombs surrounded by a bunch of nails. Jewell called the bomb squad and immediately started evacuating people. A few minutes later, the

bombs exploded. Although two people were killed and dozens more were injured, it could have been much, much worse.

The press called Jewell a hero as the manhunt for the bomber began. President Bill Clinton announced: "We will spare no effort to find out who was responsible for this murderous act. We will track them down. We will bring them to justice." Suddenly, the FBI was under a lot of pressure, which may be why they leaked a "lone bomber" criminal profile, with a note that Jewell was a "person of interest." The next day, *The Atlanta Journal Constitution* ran this headline: "FBI suspects hero guard may have planted bomb." For the rest of the summer, the FBI and the press followed Jewell wherever he went. Editorials called him a "failed cop" who planted the bomb and then called it in just so people would think he was a hero. News cameras were there when the FBI searched his apartment and special reports broke into regular programming to broadcast the searches live.

OUTCOME: In October 1996, the FBI announced that they had no evidence linking Jewell to the bombings and that he was no longer a suspect. So did he return to being regarded as a hero? No. "No one wanted anything to do with him," said his lawyer. Jewell sued four news outlets for libel (but not the FBI). "This isn't about the money," he said in 2006. "It's about clearing my name." CNN, NBC, and the *New York Post* all agreed to settle their lawsuits, but the *Atlanta Journal Constitution* would not. That case was dismissed a few months after Jewell died in 2007 of heart failure at age 44.

SO WHO DID IT? In 2003 the FBI arrested Eric Rudolph, who had also bombed an abortion clinic and a lesbian nightclub in Atlanta. Investigators were able to link him to the Olympic bombing because of similarities among the three bombs.

THE ACCUSED: Abu Bakker Qassim, a Chinese citizen

BACKGROUND: Qassim is a Uighur Muslim (pronounced WEE-gur) living in northwestern China. Uighurs are a Turkic ethnic group that the Chinese government considers terrorists, so they are persecuted and also highly taxed. With little possibility of work and his wife pregnant with twins, Qassim fled the country in 1999, hoping to join a Uighur community in Turkey, make some money, and then send for his family. He never made it.

STORY: His journey led him to the wrong place at the wrong time: Afghanistan in September 2001. When the United States retaliated for the 9-11 attacks, the village where Qassim was staying was bombed. Along with several other people, he hid in caves in the Tora Bora mountains. Known as a terrorist stronghold, the caves were bombed relentlessly. Qassim wasn't a terrorist, but he'd learned how to use a machine gun at a Uighur village. He escaped to Pakistan in late 2001, where his group met some people who promised to take them to the city. But instead they were led into a trap. The people were bounty hunters, receiving $5,000 from the American government for every terrorist they turned over. Because Qassim had received weapons training, he was considered an enemy combatant. He was incarcerated in Afghanistan, and six months later, along with several other Uighers, he was transported to the U.S. military prison at Guantanamo Bay.

OUTCOME: Three and a half years after their arrival, Qassim and four of his countrymen were listed as "NLEC"—No Longer Enemy Combatants. A federal judge ruled that the men be set free. But they weren't. They spent another year in Guantanamo—not because the U.S. wanted to keep them, but because no other country would take them. "After four years at Guantanamo Bay," he explained, "you earn the title 'terrorist.' And the Chinese strongly believe it." Had Qassim been returned to China, he said, he would be tortured. American officials agreed, but also denied him entry to the United States. The governments of Canada and several European countries rejected him as well. Only one country opened its borders to him: Albania. Even though there were no other Uighurs there and he didn't speak Albanian, he went there and worked hard to make a life. Six years after he left his wife, he was finally able to phone her for the first time. At last report, Qassim was working at an Italian restaurant in Albania and was close to raising enough money to retrieve his wife and the 10-year-old twins he's never met. He's also petitioning the U.S. government to release 16 other Uighurs who are still being held at Guantanamo, all of whom he says are innocent.

THE ACCUSED: Eric Nordmark, 35, a homeless man in Garden Grove, California

STORY: In May 2003, Nordmark was walking down the street when two police officers told him to sit down on the curb. Nord-mark explained that he was an "army vet looking for work." A few minutes later, the cops brought him to the station and took his mug shot. Then he was released. A few days later, he found a job setting up rides at a carnival. After his first day, he went to a store to buy some beer and cigarettes. When he walked out, the police were waiting for him. They cuffed him and arrested him. The charge: the assault of three 11-year-old girls. A few days earlier, the girls had claimed they were attacked by a homeless man on the way home from school, and escaped when one of them kicked the man in the groin. Nordmark's disheveled appearance matched their description, and two of the three girls identified him in a photo lineup. Bail was set at $50,000, but Nordmark didn't even have $50, so he was forced to remain in jail until his trial began... eight months later. Although Nordmark repeatedly denied attack-ing or even ever meeting the girls, several witnesses were set to testify that the local kids were afraid of him. On the second day of the trial, one of the accusers took the stand. "He started choking me," she testified. "And then I turned purple...I couldn't breathe, and I felt like I was going to black out." That night, Nordmark told his lawyer that if he was convicted, he'd kill himself before he ever got to prison—he'd heard how child molesters are treated in jail.

OUTCOME: The following day, Nordmark was brought back into the courtroom. Only the lawyers, the judge, and one of the girls were there. The judge told him, "All charges have been dis-missed. You're free to go." The girl apologized and explained that they made up the story because they got home late from school that day and didn't want to get in trouble. The following week, all three girls were arrested at their school for the false accusation and led away in handcuffs. Two were given 30 days in detention. The girl who committed perjury got 45 days. Nordmark told reporters he wasn't really angry with the accusers. "Kids are kids. They do bonehead things." What upset him most was that the police didn't perform a thorough investigation at the beginning. All they had to do, he said, was interview the girls individually and the truth would have come out. But they interviewed them as a group, and Nordmark ended up spending eight months in jail for a crime he didn't commit.

IT'S A WEIRD, WEIRD WORLD

More proof that truth can be stranger than fiction.

BOY IN THE HOOD

A 31-year-old man named Chris Jarvis walked into a Job-centre in Essex, England, in 2010 wearing a sweatshirt with the hood pulled up over his head. He was there to pick up his disability check (he fractured both ankles in 2008). A security guard told Jarvis to put down his hood, but Jarvis refused, so the guard threw him out. Jarvis later complained that he was discriminated against; he wears the hood for religious purposes. "Muslims can walk around in whatever religious gear they like, so why can't I?" Jobcentre apparently agreed, because they sent Jarvis a letter of apology. But what's his religion? According to Jarvis, he's a Jedi knight—a "religion" practiced by thousands of *Star Wars* fans all over the world.

PEEK-A-BOO!

In 2010 three fisherman were boating about four miles off the coast of Hollywood, Florida, when the boat's owner, Ryan Danoff, spotted something strange sticking up out of the water. As he got closer, he saw that it was a periscope. And then, as if it knew it had been spotted, the periscope started speeding away at about 20 knots (which is pretty fast) and disappeared below the surface. And then a huge burst of bubbles rose up out of the water, as if a submarine had just released its ballast. Then the sea was calm again. "It was crazy," said Danoff. "If it was just myself out there I wouldn't believe what I saw." He reported the incident to the Coast Guard, but never heard anything about it after that. Though no official explanation was given, it was most certainly a submarine. But whose sub it was—and what it was doing so close to the U.S. coast—remains a mystery.

THE MOST HAZARDOUS OF MATERIALS

One day in June 2010, police in Destin, Florida, received an emergency call from a man who said that he was inspecting a house that was for rent, but as soon as he walked in, a noxious odor sent him fleeing. Then his eyes started burning, and he was having trouble breathing. Fearing the worst, the police sent a HAZMAT team to the neighborhood. The road was closed, nearby homes were evacuated, the 911 caller was placed in quarantine, and then the HAZMAT team entered the house. Meanwhile, neighbors watching from the end of the street suspected that the empty home was being used either as a meth lab or by a terrorist cell creating biological weapons. After several tense minutes, the HAZMAT team exited the house. So what was all the hubbub about? Mayonnaise. A five-gallon jug of the stuff had been left there "some time ago" by the former tenants—the lid was off, it wasn't refrigerated, and as a result, it had become rancid.

WHATEVER

In September 2008, Framingham State College in Massachusetts sent a fund-raising letter to alumni. Here's an excerpt:

> With the recent economic downturn and loan crisis, it has become even more important for Framingham State College to receive your support. Blah, blah.

Was it a goof? Did an incomplete draft get sent by mistake? No. The 312-word letter—which had 137 "blah"s—was supposed to be funny. However, many of the 6,000 recipients contacted the school and said they were insulted. Framingham's VP of Admissions, Christopher Hendry, admitted that it was a "misguided and embarrassing attempt to connect with alumni in a different way." Or as one graduate commented: "The fundraising letter was impudent and childish. Blah, blah, blah, blah, blah."

*   *   *

"Do first things first, and second
things not at all." —**Peter Drucker**

"Inches make champions."
—**Vince Lombardi**

PEOPLES AND THEIR DISEASES

Uncle John said to Thom one day, "Write an article about 'steeples and their freezers,'" but Thom must have misheard him.

MOM GENES

There are about 4,000 known inherited genetic diseases today—disorders caused by a mutation to a single gene, passed from parents to children. Many of these diseases occur in much higher frequencies among certain ethnic or demographic groups than others. Reason: Those groups, for one reason or another, intermarried primarily among themselves for a significant part of their history, thereby passing along the mutation that causes the disease. That fact has helped scientists better understand genetics over the past few decades, and much progress has been made in treating many of these disorders. Here is a look at just a few of these diseases, and their stories.

Disease: Hereditary hemochromatosis (HH)

Cause and Symptoms: More commonly known as "iron overload," it's caused by a mutation in a gene that produces a protein whose job it is to regulate iron absorption from food. The mutation allows overabsorption, which can lead to toxic iron levels and a wide variety of disorders, including type 2 diabetes, cirrhosis of the liver, and heart failure.

Who Gets It: People with ancestry from Northern Europe (especially Scandinavia and the British Isles) are many times more likely than any other group to develop HH. Genetic studies say this is because the disease has its origins in a single Northern European ancestor who had the gene mutation about 40,000 years ago. The disorder spread throughout the population via that one person's descendants, all the way to the present.

Extra: According to geneticists, the disease became so prevalent because it actually had a plus side: Too much iron is harmful when you've got plenty of food, but when you haven't got enough it's

---

actually helpful, because we need at least some measure of iron for our bodies to function properly. That means that people with HH were more likely to survive when food was scarce—a common occurrence in ancient times—and, therefore, were more likely to live long enough to have children and pass on the mutation.

Disease: Sickle cell disease (SCD)

Cause and Symptoms: This disease is caused by a mutation to a gene that aids in the production of a type of hemoglobin (red blood cells), the oxygen-carrying component of blood. Normally these cells are disk-shaped and soft; the mutation causes them to become sickle- or c-shaped, rigid, and prone to rupture. This results in a variety of health problems, including severe anemia, clogging of the body's capillaries, tissue and organ damage, and early death.

Who Gets It: SCD is especially prevalent in people who live in or are descendants of people from sub-Saharan Africa. African Americans, for example, are 10 times more likely to have the disease than Caucasian Americans. And in parts of Central Africa it affects as much as 30 percent of regional populations. (It's also found in people of Middle Eastern and Indian descent.) Recent genetic studies have determined that the original gene mutation that causes SCD didn't happen just once to one person, but occurred independently at various times in different parts of Africa, and also in Saudi Arabia and possibly India. These original mutations, geneticists say, showed up between 70,000 and 150,000 years ago.

Extra: SCD, like hereditary hemochromatosis, is so prevalent today because it also has a positive side. The disease thrives in tropical regions where malaria outbreaks are common—and people with certain forms of the disorder are actually resistant to malaria. (The malaria virus works by infecting the body's red blood cells, and the red blood cells of people with SCD break down when infected—thereby preventing the virus from becoming established.)

Disease: Tay-Sachs

Cause and Symptoms: This devastating genetic disease is caused by mutations to a gene that normally helps produce an enzyme that breaks down certain types of fatty acids. That leads to a buildup of these fatty acids in cells, especially brain nerve cells, beginning in the fetus. That results in severe mental and developmental disabilities, and is always fatal, usually by age five. (A much more rare form occurs in adults.) Tay-Sachs was named for Warren Tay, a British ophthalmologist who discovered a defining characteristic of the disease in 1881 (a "cherry red spot" in the retina of afflicted children), and American neurologist Bernard Sachs, who first noticed the prevalence of the disease among Jews in 1887.

Who Gets It: Overall about 1 in 250 people carries the Tay-Sachs gene. In Ashkenazi Jews—1 in 27 carries it. (Ashkenazi Jews are those descended from the Jewish communities that lived in Northern and Eastern Europe since medieval times, and make up about 80% of the world's Jewish population.) Geneticists say the mutation first occurred about 1,000 years ago, and has spread through the population since. Some have suggested that people with the mutation were more likely to survive tuberculosis outbreaks, but this has not been firmly established.

Extra: Tay-Sachs also strikes 1 in 25 Cajuns in southern Louisiana. Geneticists have been able to trace the origin of that local occurrence to a single couple—believed to be non-Jewish—who lived in France in the 1700s. Oddly, the disease is also prevalent among French Canadians in southeastern Quebec, caused by a completely different mutation event to the same gene.

Disease: Cystic fibrosis (CF)

Cause and Symptoms: CF is caused by a mutation in the gene that regulates the makeup of fluids such as sweat, digestive juices, and mucus. It results in the formation of thick, sticky fluid that clogs the lungs and obstructs the function of the pancreas, preventing pancreatic enzymes from breaking down and absorbing nutrients in food. Victims usually die by the age of 40.

Who Gets It: Cystic fibrosis occurs in about 1 in 3,000 Caucasian newborns in the United States—and only about 1 in 17,000 African Americans and 1 in 31,000 Asian Americans. It's believed that the original CF gene mutation may have occurred as long as 50,000 years ago, probably in Northern Europe.

Extra: Cystic fibrosis is one of the most common inherited genetic diseases among people of European descent, with 30,000 people affected in the United States alone. Just why such a deadly disease became so common is unknown, although some researchers believe people with CF may have some kind of protection from diseases like cholera and typhoid fever.

Disease: Scleroderma

Cause and Symptoms: This disease causes a hardening of the skin and/or internal organs. Scleroderma is very painful, can last for years, and can be fatal. It most commonly strikes people in their 40s or 50s, and affects more women than men. Exactly what causes the disease is unknown, but recent studies suggest that a mutation to a specific gene (known as *fibrillin-1*) is at the very least related to the disorder.

Who Gets It: Scleroderma affects people of all races around the world, but for reasons unknown, occurs in especially high numbers among Choctaw Indians from Oklahoma. Researchers have traced the disease to five Choctaw families that lived in the 1700s, and postulate that the original mutation probably occurred hundreds of years earlier.

Extra: The Choctaw are divided into several different tribes in various states today—but only the Oklahoma Choctaw have the high prevalence of the disease. This leads scientists to believe that the disease may be caused by a combination of genetic *and* environmental factors.

Disease: Machado-Joseph disease (MJD)

Cause and Symptoms: People with this rare disease have a gene mutation that results in abnormally long copies of a protein called *ataxin-3*. These proteins accumulate in brain cells, and, beginning anywhere from the late teens to the 50s, cause a loss of muscle control. This results in symptoms such as arm and leg weakness, a staggering gait often mistaken for drunkenness, difficulty in swallowing, and bulging eyes. The disease progresses slowly over the course of 5 to 30 years before resulting in death.

Who Gets It: MJD is found almost exclusively in people with Portuguese ancestry, and especially those from the Azores—a chain of islands in the Atlantic Ocean controlled by Portugal. In the United States about 1 in 4,000 Portuguese Americans has MJD. On the Azorean island of Flores the number skyrockets to 1 in 140.

Extra: The disease was only discovered in 1972, when Massachusetts doctors diagnosed it in members of a Portuguese-American family named Machado. They called it "Machado disease." A few years later doctors found a similar disease in a California family named Joseph, also from Portugal, and named it "Joseph disease." It took until 1981 for researchers to realize they were the same disease. It has been known as "Machado-Joseph disease" ever since.

RANDOM FACTS

• All the diseases mentioned here (except MJD) are *recessive* genetic disorders. That means that you have to receive a copy of the mutated gene from both of your parents to develop the disease. People with just one copy of the mutated gene, along with a normal copy (we have two copies of all of our genes—one from each parent), are simply *carriers*. If two carriers have children, they have a one in four chance of each of them passing the mutated copy to a child, in which case the child will contract the disorder.

• Machado-Joseph disease, on the other hand, is *dominant* rather than recessive. This means that receiving just one copy of the mutated gene from either parent will lead to the disease.

• Two famous people with sickle cell disease: jazz musician Miles Davis and pro football player Tiki Barber.

• The introduction of genetic testing has reduced the numbers of many genetic diseases drastically over the last few decades. In the 1970s, for example, a simple blood test was developed to determine whether someone carries the Tay-Sachs gene mutation. Since then, prospective parents have been able to determine whether they are carriers, and the number of Tay-Sachs cases worldwide has decreased by more than 90%.

✳   ✳   ✳

LOONEY LAW

In Hong Kong, wives who've been cheated on may legally kill their two-timing husbands, but only with their bare hands.

43% of women want their boyfriends to "commit" before they sign "love" on a card.

CROSSED PATHS

*Take note of who's near you right now—you may
meet again later in life, as these people did.*

NOW: William Rehnquist was appointed to the U.S.
Supreme Court in 1971, where he served until his death
in 2005. Sandra Day O'Connor was named to the Court
in 1981, the first female justice in the court's 200-year history.

THEN: Rehnquist and O'Connor knew each other long before
they served on the Supreme Court. They attended Stanford Law
School together and graduated at the top of the class—Rehnquist
was #1, O'Connor was #2. While students, they even dated.

NOW: In 2010 filmmaker Kathryn Bigelow's movie *The Hurt
Locker* won the Oscar for Best Picture, and Bigelow won the
Best Director prize, the first woman ever to do so. Her main
competition: the blockbuster film *Avatar,* and its director, James
Cameron.

THEN: Bigelow and Cameron were married from 1989 to 1991.
They divorced when Cameron left her for actress Linda Hamilton,
whom he met on the set of his movie *The Terminator.*

NOW: In the 2010 NBC "late night wars," Conan O'Brien was
forced out of his job as host of *The Tonight Show* and his contract
bought out so the network could give the show to Jay Leno, from
whom O'Brien had taken over just seven months earlier. The
NBC executive who orchestrated the squeeze-out of O'Brien:
NBC Universal president Jeff Zucker.

THEN: In the mid-1980s, at Harvard University, O'Brien was the
president of the *Harvard Lampoon,* the university's famous humor
publication. Zucker was the president of the *Harvard Crimson,* the
sedate daily college newspaper. The publications had been rivals
for decades and frequently pranked each other. In 1985 O'Brien's
staff stole an entire print run of the *Crimson.* When Zucker found
out about it, he knew exactly who'd done it and sent police to the
Lampoon's office. "My first meeting with Jeff Zucker was in handcuffs," O'Brien later told a reporter.

THE LOST EXPLORERS: SALOMON ANDRÉE

Our final installment on lost explorers looks at a screwball Swede who flew off into the wild blue yonder—and stayed there.

FLY ME TO THE POLE

Another quixotic quest of 19th-century explorers was to be the first man to the North Pole. Geographers knew as early as the 16th century that the North Pole was probably just a spot on the open ocean covered with pack ice. How would anyone get there? The earliest expeditions tried to *sail* to the top of the world. None succeeded. Then teams of explorers using dogsleds and sledges tried to *slog* across the pack ice to the pole—the great Norwegian explorer Fridtjof Nansen even tried it on cross-country skis—but to no avail. After more than half a century of attempts, the North Pole remained unconquered. Then in 1896, a 43-year-old Swedish engineer came up with a novel alternative: He'd *fly* to the North Pole in a balloon. Salomon August Andrée was an experienced balloonist, having already made several crossings of the Baltic Sea, so he had little trouble convincing wealthy backers and the Swedish public that a balloon was the easiest way to the pole. Armed with reports that a steady wind blew northward from Spitzbergen all the time, Andrée was convinced the stiff Arctic breeze would carry his balloon over the pole all the way to Alaska.

"WE CANNOT FAIL"

His first attempt, from Spitsbergen, was such a failure that Andrée went from being Sweden's biggest hero to Sweden's biggest fool overnight. The extreme temperature variations in the Arctic—something Andrée hadn't considered—had caused the seams of the balloon to crack and leak, bringing the airship down almost immediately. Stung by scathing criticism in the media, Andrée worked furiously to mount another expedition. His spirits and reputation lifted when famous inventor Alfred Nobel became his chief financer, and on July 11, 1897, the *Örnen* (Eagle) lifted off from Svalbard, part of an archipelago of islands off the northwest coast of Norway and close to the Arctic Circle. The balloon was huge—97 feet high and 68 feet in diameter. The silk alone weighed a 1 ½ tons. The basket carrying Andrée and his team, fellow engineer Knut Fraenkel and photographer Nils Strindberg, was a double-decker affair made of wicker and wood. The upper level served as an observation platform, the lower as sleeping quarters and darkroom (Andrée brought along 36 homing pigeons to send back photographs and reports of the expedition's progress and ultimate success). The small crowd of Swedish naval officers and sailors cheered as the balloon rose into the air and drifted off to the north and out of sight forever.

A GRIM DISCOVERY

The disappearance of the Örnen became one of the great mysteries of the Arctic. Only 1 of the 36 pigeons made it home, and that one was released only hours after takeoff with a scrawled note that everything was going well. After that there was no word, no sign, nothing—until 33 years later. In 1930 a Norwegian sealing ship hunting the coast of White Island, just off the northeastern tip of Svalbard, made a grim discovery: two skeletons, one propped against a rock, the other curled up on the ground. Both still wore fur parkas. A third skeleton was found in a shallow grave nearby. The man sitting up held a diary. It was Andrée, and the journal in his dead hands told all. The balloon had crashed on July 14, just three days into the flight and only 160 miles north of takeoff.

WRONG-WAY ANDRÉE

It took the men a week to make a sledge of their basket and load it with supplies. Then they started walking—the wrong direction. Two weeks and 60 miles of slogging later, they realized their mistake. Then the ice pack began to break up around them, and they converted the sledge to a boat. For weeks they drifted, finally sighting land—White Island—on September 17, and reaching the island two weeks later. They had enough food to last out the winter, but they were physically spent and suffering from food poisoning caused by eating raw polar bear meat. Strindberg was the first to go, apparently from a heart attack. On October 17, Frankel died in his sleep. Andrée made a final note in his diary and died soon after. Another 12 years passed before Robert Peary, Matthew Henson, and four Inuit guides became the first humans to reach the North Pole. They arrived on April 6, 1909...on foot.

During Robert Peary's trek to the North Pole (1909), he lost eight toes to frostbite.

JOE STALIN VS. JOHN WAYNE, PART II

*Conspiracy theorists take heart: Here's Part II
of the story. (Part I is on page 276.)*

STRANGER THAN FICTION

The tale that Michael Munn tells in his book *John Wayne: The Man Behind the Myth* is more exciting than the plots of many of Duke Wayne's own films. And it raises some interesting questions. Did Stalin really send KGB agents to kill Hollywood's most outspoken enemy of communism? And if so, how did all of the Duke's other biographers miss the story?

One thing that makes Munn's story difficult to verify is the fact that it's based entirely on circumstantial evidence. Wayne died in 1979, a quarter-century before Munn's book was published, so he can't vouch for any of the things that Munn claims he said and did. All the other firsthand witnesses to the events described—Orson Welles, Joseph Stalin, Nikita Khrushchev, stuntman Yakima Canutt, and others—have been gone for many years as well. Another problem: Wayne's 48-page FBI file, made public as a result of the Freedom of Information Act, makes no mention of *any* communist conspiracies against him, let alone a KGB hit ordered by Stalin and thwarted by FBI agents.

THE DICTATOR

Munn's story does seem to fit with what historians know about Joseph Stalin's personality, his interests, and the bizarre way in which he ruled the Soviet Union after World War II. Stalin turned 70 in 1948, and although Soviet propaganda still presented him as a vigorous man with an iron constitution, his health was failing and he had just five more years to live. He never really recovered from the strain of waging war against Nazi Germany from 1941 to 1945, and within weeks of the war's end he suffered what was either a heart attack or a stroke. More attacks soon followed, and by 1948 visitors to the Kremlin began to notice what one described as "conspicuous signs of his senility." By then, Nikita Khrushchev wrote in his memoirs, the Soviet government had "virtually ceased to function" at the highest level as the failing Stalin lost interest in the day-to-day business of governing. He almost never convened meetings of the Politburo, the Central Committee, or any other formal organs of government. Instead, Stalin hosted informal gatherings of his cronies several nights a week in the Kremlin movie theater.

SHOWTIME

Movies, not affairs of state, were the first order of business at these gatherings. What little work that could be done had to be done between the film screenings, or at the drunken dinners Stalin hosted at his country house after the movies were over.

Stalin liked Soviet films and had a large collection of European and American films, many of which were seized from the collection of Nazi propaganda minister Joseph Goebbels at the end of WWII. Among his favorites: detective films, boxing films, and any Charlie Chaplin comedy (except *The Great Dictator,* which he despised). He also liked Clark Gable and Spencer Tracy, and was a big fan of James Cagney gangster movies.

But most of all, said Khrushchev, Stalin liked cowboy movies. "He used to curse them and give them a proper ideological evaluation and then immediately order new ones." Stalin especially liked Westerns by director John Ford, who gave John Wayne his breakthrough role in 1939's *Stagecoach.* Ford cast Wayne in more than 20 films, eight of which were released during Stalin's lifetime, and though few records of the Kremlin screenings survive, it's a pretty safe bet that he'd seen at least a few of the Duke's films and knew who he was.

NO WONDER THEY CALL HIM MARSHAL

Stalin identified with the characters in Western films. He saw himself as the Soviet equivalent of a town sheriff or U.S. Marshal, biographer Simon Sebag Montefiore writes in *Stalin: The Court of the Red Tsar.* "Stalin regarded himself as history's lone knight, riding out, with weary resignation, on another noble mission, the Bolshevik version of the mysterious cowboy arriving in a corrupt frontier town."

Stalin's contemporaries reported that he had trouble distin-

TASER is an acronym for "Tom Swift's Electric Rifle." (The A was added later.)

guishing between reality and life as it was depicted in the movies. Soviet filmmaker Grigori Kozintsev learned this when he was invited to a Kremlin screening in the 1930s: "Stalin didn't watch movies as works of art," he wrote in *Sight and Sound* magazine, "he watched them as though they were real events taking place before his eyes, the real actions of people—beneficial or destructive—and he immediately gave vent to his irritation if the people on the screen didn't work well, and praised them when they acted correctly."

CECIL B. DE STALIN

For years Stalin had been, in all but name, the head of the entire Soviet film industry as well as its chief censor. He personally assigned film projects to directors and actors, instructed screenwriters on the ideologically "correct" means of presenting historical events, made editorial changes to screenplays, and even composed lyrics for songs used in films. He had the final say on everything. If there was something he didn't like about a film, it was done over. Period. No film was released to the public without Stalin's personal approval.

Even foreign films—which were almost never shown outside the Kremlin walls—had to meet Stalin's approval: Once when Minister of Cinema Ivan Bolshakov showed a foreign film containing a brief nude scene, Stalin pounded the table and yelled, "Are you making a brothel here, Bolshakov?" then stomped out of the theater. Bolshakov was luckier than his two predecessors— when they displeased Stalin, they were taken away and executed. (Bolshakov *never* showed Stalin a nude scene again. From then on he previewed every film before showing it to Stalin and cut out any scene containing even a hint of nudity.)

WHITE HATS VS. RED HATS

It's conceivable that Stalin could have ordered John Wayne killed. After all, Stalin was nuts—"not quite right in the head," as Khrushchev put it. He certainly had no hesitation when it came to killing people: Stalin is believed to have murdered as many as 20 million of his fellow citizens during his 30 years in power, and he wasn't shy about reaching beyond the borders of the Soviet Union to kill them, either. In 1940, for example,

Stalin dispatched KGB assassins to kill his rival Leon Trotsky in Mexico.

John Wayne was one of the most popular film stars in Hollywood, but he was an outspoken opponent of communism—an anticommunist cowboy who publicly and vehemently opposed everything that Stalin stood for. He was someone Stalin could not control—a "black hat," or villain, perhaps, in the crazy Western movie that was playing in Stalin's failing, paranoid mind. And what does a sheriff do when a villain arrives in town? It's conceivable that U.S.(S.R.) Marshal Joe Stalin could have decided, as the Western cliché goes, that "this town ain't big enough for the both of us" and ordered John Wayne killed.

STAR TREATMENT

The pieces might seem to fit...until you learn more about Michael Munn, who turns out to be the weakest link in his own chain. Had Munn stopped with the Wayne biography in 2003, he might have retained the credibility he had when the book was first published. But he didn't stop: In 2008 he wrote a biography of actor Richard Burton, and it, too, is filled with claims that are hard to believe and harder to prove. Munn writes, for example, that Burton had affairs with Lana Turner and Marilyn Monroe (he'd never been linked to them before) and was once caught in a brothel with actor Errol Flynn. ("Sensationalist nonsense," a Burton family member told the South Wales *Evening Post*. "We've read his diaries and he never mentions Errol Flynn. I don't think they met.")

Then in 2009, Munn published a biography of British actor David Niven. In it, Munn claims he was at the dying Niven's bedside in 1982 when Niven confessed to attempting suicide after his first wife died in a freak accident. Munn says Niven also confessed to having affairs with Grace Kelly and Princess Margaret, the sister of Queen Elizabeth II. As if that were not enough, he says Niven also claimed that his second wife contracted a venereal disease after sleeping with John F. Kennedy.

HERE COME THE SONS

Niven's sons had never heard any of these stories before, and they'd never heard of Munn, either, even though Munn billed himself as an intimate family friend. Even more puzzling: Niven's sons couldn't figure out how Niven would have even been able to tell Munn any of these stories. Niven died from Lou Gehrig's disease, which by 1982 had robbed him of the ability to *speak*—and that would have made such "confessions" very difficult. (Munn says he taped his conversations with Niven. So why doesn't he just produce the tapes and put the controversy to rest once and for all? Because, he says, the tapes got "chewed up" by his tape recorder and he threw them all away.)

So why would Munn wait until 2009 to publish things that Niven supposedly told him 25 years earlier? Niven's son, David Jr., has a theory that could apply to all three of Munn's biographies: "Everyone featured in these stories is rather conveniently dead, so we can't ask them to verify them," he says.

*   *   *

PRESIDENTIAL CAMPAIGN SONGS

- William Henry Harrison (1840): "Tippecanoe and Tyler Too." Harrison was a hero in the Battle of Tippecanoe during the War of 1812; his running mate was John Tyler.
- Abraham Lincoln (1864): "Battle Cry of Freedom," a Union rallying song written during the Civil War by George F. Root. More than 700,000 copies of the song's sheet music were sold, making it one of the bestsellers of the 19th century.
- Franklin D. Roosevelt (1932): "Happy Days Are Here Again." Originally written for the movie *Chasing Rainbows*, the song came to be known as the unofficial Democratic Party theme song.
- John F. Kennedy (1960): "High Hopes," written by Jimmy Van Heusen and Sammy Cahn a year earlier for the film *A Hole in the Head*. (It won an Oscar.) Cahn wrote new lyrics for JFK's campaign.
- Lyndon Johnson (1964): "Hello, Lyndon," a parody of "Hello, Dolly."
- Jimmy Carter (1976): "Ode to the Georgia Farmer," by K.E. and Julia Marsh, written to sound like a Civil War ballad.
- George W. Bush (2000): "We the People," performed by Billy Ray Cyrus.
- John McCain (2008): "Raisin' McCain," performed by John Rich of the country music duo Big & Rich.

Humphrey Bogart and Princess Diana were distant relatives.

VIOLET PRECIPITATION

In the puzzle below, we've substituted synonyms into the titles of popular books, movies, TV shows, landmarks, etc. See if you can identify the items we're talking about. (Answers on page 538.)

1. Joined Commonwealths of the Western Hemisphere (country)

2. *Birthed to Travel* (album title)

3. Jesus-believing Bundle (actor)

4. A *Wind-Up Citrus Fruit* (novel and movie)

5. Bestride, Increasing the Frequency With Which You Hurry (American landmark)

6. *Woman and the Vagrant* (animated movie)

7. *Violet Precipitation* (album title and movie)

8. Check Turnstile (software company founder)

9. *Angry Males* (TV drama)

10. The Enormous Barricade of the Orient (landmark)

11. Circuit of Gaul (sporting event)

12. English Crude Oil (company)

13. *The Big Cat, the Sorceress, and the Bureau* (book and movie)

14. *The Shadowed Section of Earth's Satellite* (album title)

15. "Praise the lord, it's the last day of the work week!" (common phrase)

16. Insignificant Quest (board game)

17. Officer Engines (corporation)

18. *Determination and Elegance* (TV sitcom)

19. *The Nobleman of the Jewelry* (book and film series)

20. Global Drinking Container (sporting event)

21. *Banishment on Central Ave.* (album title)

22. *The Book of Maps Gesticulated* (novel)

23. Dad's Brother Toilet (important person)

UNCLE JOHN'S ANTS

One day Mrs. Uncle John said, "How come there isn't ever anything about aunts in Uncle John's Bathroom Reader? and Uncle John answered, "Hey! An article about ants! That's a great idea!"

THE ANT-CESTOR

One day around 150 million years ago, a small wasp went through an evolutionary change—and poof! it became the very first ant on Earth. Okay, it wasn't quite like that, but evolutionary biologists claim that all evidence shows ants evolved from a primitive species of wasp between 130 and 160 million years ago. It happened just once, they say, in just one location, and all ants alive today are descended from those very first ants.

Wasps are indeed the creatures genetically most closely related to ants today. Ants, along with bees—which also evolved from wasps—are the only members of a suborder of insects known as *Apocrita.*

HIGH HOPES

Fossil records reveal that ants weren't very numerous for the first several million years of their existence. It wasn't until the explosion of the *angiosperms*—the flowering trees and plants—around 100 million years ago, and the subsequent creation of friendly new habitats (like leafy forest floors), that ants began to diversify into hundreds, then thousands, of species. Today there are more than 14,000 known species spread around the planet so thoroughly that there are only a few places *without* native ant populations— Antarctica, Greenland, Iceland, and some remote islands in the Pacific Ocean.

Ants range from just $\frac{1}{25}$ of an inch to more than an inch in length. They can live in an enormous variety of habitats—underground, inside fallen trees, and even in treetops where they never touch the ground. They're able to communicate a huge amount of information to each other through a combination of touch and *chemoreception*—the use of pheromones to send and detect messages. And they live in highly organized, very complex societies. They are without question among the most successful animals in

---

"Choose to be optimistic. It feels better." —the Dalai Lama

the history of life on Earth and, according to *myrmecologists* (scientists who study ants), they number in the quadrillions. That's millions of millions of ants. So many that, combined, they not only outnumber, they actually *outweigh* all six billion humans on Earth.

ANT-I-MATTER

With so many different kinds of ants out there, just what is it that distinguishes them from insects? First, the basics: Ants are insects and, like all insects, they have three body parts (head, thorax, and abdomen), three sets of jointed legs, a pair of antennae on their heads, and a hard exoskeleton (as opposed to the internal skeleton that humans have) that supports and protects their bodies. They are also *holometabolous* insects, meaning they go through four distinct life stages: egg, larva, pupa, and adult.

A trait ants share with only their closest relatives, wasps and bees, is the *petiole*, that narrow "waist" between the thorax and abdomen, which allows them to bend their bodies and navigate through their twisty nest tunnels. Also, like wasps and bees, females of many ant species can release a potent cocktail of poisons through a stinger on the end of their abdomen. Why only females? Because the stinger is actually an evolved version of an *ovipositor*, an organ used to lay eggs, found in many insect species.

One characteristic that is unique to ants: *metapleural glands*. These two tiny glands, one on either side of the thorax, produce and secrete an antibiotic concoction that protects ants and their nests from fungus, bacteria, and other infestations—a huge plus in the warm, moist world of ant nests. No other animal is known to have metapleural glands, which, experts say, may play a large part in their overwhelming success.

ANT CASTES

Myrmecologists divide ant society into three major *castes*: queens, males, and workers.

Queens: The fertile egg-producing members of ant society, they are born with two sets of lacy wings, mate once, lose their wings, and spend the rest of their lives inside their nests, doing little else but laying eggs. An ant colony can have one queen or several; some have hundreds.

Males: In nearly all ant species, the males are fertile (meaning they can fertilize eggs) and, like queens, they have two sets of wings. They have only one job—to mate with queens, after which they die. There are no other males in a typical ant colony.

Workers: Making up the largest part of a colony's population by far, worker ants are wingless, sterile females. The workers of a single colony can be many different sizes, creating sub-castes that have different jobs, including nurses, scouts, foragers, and soldiers.

Which caste are you? One of the most interesting things about ant castes is how they're produced. In most species, queens create the castes by producing different kinds of eggs. They can make unfertilized eggs by laying them without bringing them into contact with the sperm they have stored in their bodies; these always become males. A queen can also lay fertilized eggs by using that stored sperm; these all become females. Most of the females will be the sterile workers, but some will become fertile and, potentially, new queens. The exact details of how this happens are still unknown, but what *is* known is that young, larval ants that are fed a "normal" diet become sterile workers, and those fed more nutritious food become potential queens.

COLONY FOUNDING

You've no doubt heard of the ant's famous cooperation and social organization skills. To help illustrate how this works, here's a look at the life cycle of a typical ant colony. There are many different types of colonies, and many different ways that ants behave in those colonies, but this is a good, basic look at the most common way a new colony is formed. It's called *swarming*.

• Usually in spring, a mature ant colony starts producing fertile males and females. Because they have wings, they're commonly referred to as "flying ants."

• As soon as they're able, the males fly away and gather with males from other colonies in "swarms" 70 to 1,000 feet in the air. Females from several colonies soon follow. During these "nuptial flights," the females will mate with 1 to 10 males, usually from other colonies, storing the sperm they acquire in special sacs. That sperm will last each female the rest of her egg-laying life. The males, having done their sole job, soon die.

- Each mated female flies a few miles, lands, uses her legs to break off her wings, uses her mandibles (jaws) to dig a cavity in the ground a few inches deep, and then closes herself inside it. Her bulky wing muscles, now unnecessary, begin to disintegrate inside her body. The nest she has dug will serve as the basis for a new colony.

- She lays her first tiny, shiny, white eggs. After several weeks they hatch into pale, grublike, legless larvae. They are voracious, and the new queen feeds them with salivary secretions derived primarily from her disintegrated wing muscles.

- After a few more weeks the larvae *pupate*: They enclose themselves in a cocoonlike covering and go through *metamorphosis*, changing from larvae to the body shape we know as ants. A few weeks later they hatch, all of them sterile female worker ants.

- Immediately upon hatching, the workers open the nest and begin foraging for food, caring for new eggs, digging new tunnels and chambers, and bringing food to the new queen, who now presides over the beginnings of a brand-new colony.

DIVIDE AND CONQUER

As an ant colony grows in size, it naturally develops more complex needs—better food gathering and defense, for example. To meet those needs, the colony begins producing different types of workers. This is accomplished through larval diet (just as it was with the fertile females).

- Some larvae are fed a small amount of food and emerge from the pupal stage as very small ants. These often become *nurses*, whose primary job is to stay in the nest and care for the young.

- Others are fed a bit more and become larger ants. These might become *scouts*, who leave the nest to find food and return to notify *foragers*, even larger (and better-fed) ants who carry the food back to the nest.

- Some larvae are fed large amounts of very nutritious foods—perhaps protein-rich insect parts (liquefied, as ants must liquefy all their food). These larvae emerge as massive ants with huge heads and stout, powerful mandibles. These are the *soldiers*, and their primary job is to crush and kill whatever threatens, or appears to threaten, the colony. In some species soldiers can be more than 200 times the size of their smaller sisters.

Not just peanuts: George Washington Carver invented 75 uses for pecans.

- The colony continues to grow, sometimes for years, and can eventually include many nests. When it is firmly established and if food is plentiful, one spring the queen will begin to produce fertile males and females. Upon maturing, they fly off and mate, the females create new colonies...and the process starts all over again.

- Another way colonies are commonly founded is *budding*. This occurs in species that have more than one queen, and entails one or more queen simply taking hundreds (or thousands) of workers and eggs from an established colony and moving out to form another.

- Recently mated females of some species do not form their own colonies, but return to the nest and become egg-laying queens alongside their mother queen. Others travel to established colonies and kill the queen (or queens) and take over the colony. Still others lay their eggs in colonies of competing ant species and, using pheromones, trick the ants there into caring for their young. Those young are all fertile, and upon reaching adulthood they fly off and mate.

HOME MAKERS

Ants are one of a very few animal groups that, like us humans, significantly modify their surroundings to suit their needs. Many ants do it in amazing ways. Here are some examples.

Wood ants are common in forests in southern England. Using pine needles and other debris, they build mounds that can reach 3 feet in height and more than 10 feet in diameter, and can extend many feet underground. Like the nests of most ant species, the chambers inside are climate-controlled: Vents around the nest can be opened or closed to attain the perfect temperature for the development of ant eggs.

Weaver ants are arboreal ants (they live in trees) found in Africa, India, Australia, and the Solomon Islands. To build a nest, rows of workers use their legs and mandibles to form chains between two leaves, which they then pull together. Other workers bring developing larvae to the site—and squeeze them with their mandibles. This causes the larvae to secrete a sticky substance, similar to spider silk, that the workers use to "sew" the leaves together. They do this again and again, eventually forming large, ball-shaped nests.

One colony can have hundreds of nests in several adjacent trees. (The young survive the mandible squeezing and are taken to safety in the new nests.)

Some driver and army ants form "bivouac" nests, made out of... ants. Hundreds of thousands of them converge around a queen and her brood, linking legs and forming a living nest more than three feet across. There are tunnels throughout the mass, and chambers inside are kept at just the right temperature by adjusting the space between the ant bodies. These are migratory ants, and they sometimes construct and deconstruct their ant-nests every day as the colony moves across the terrain.

TRIUMPH-ANTS

We've already mentioned several incredible ant species, but here are some more that we just couldn't leave out.

Leafcutter ants. There are about 40 species of true leafcutter ants, all of them native to the Americas. They're named for their practice of going on foraging missions for leaves, but that's not what's so amazing about them. Once back at the nest, the ants masticate (chew) the leaves into mulch. The mulch is then added to "gardens" that are used to grow fungus—the only food leafcutter ants give to their larvae. In some species, the fungus and the ants are totally dependent on each other for their survival. Leafcutters are the only animal on Earth besides humans known to cultivate their own food in this way.

Leptothorax minutissimus. These ants have been found in only four spots—all in the eastern United States—and were only discovered in 1942, in Washington, D.C. They have evolved to the point where there are no workers—only queens. They survive by invading colonies of other ant species and setting up shop. Why they aren't killed by the other species is still unknown. And they're tiny, just a few millimeters in length: An entire colony, along with their hosts, can live in one hollowed-out acorn.

Mycocepurus smithii. Found primarily in South and Central America, this is another species of leafcutter. Queens reproduce asexually through a process called *parthenogenesis*, so all the ants in a single colony are clones of the queens.

Driver ants. In this species found in central and east Africa, the males are more than an inch long. Rather than mate in the air, these males are drawn to the scent of long columns of roving workers from other driver ant colonies. Once discovered by those super-aggressive workers, the male is immediately swarmed, his wings are cut off, and he is carried back to the nest. There he serves as a sperm donor for new, virgin queens.

Honey pot ants. These ants are found in the American Southwest, Mexico, South Africa, New Guinea, and Australia, and feed on flower nectar, some of which they store in sacs in their bodies. Back in the nest they feed it to their larvae—and they also force-feed it to a special caste of workers. These special workers become so engorged with the stuff that their abdomens swell to the size of grapes. From then on, they're kept deep in the nest as prisoners—and when food is scarce, other ants in the nest come and feed from their swollen "honey pots."

WE ANT DONE YET

Here are some more random facts about these amazing creatures.

• About 100 ant species have no queens. All the workers in these species are wingless, fertile females, and one usually takes on the dominant egg-laying role. To mate, she leaves the nest, performs a mating dance of sorts, releases pheromones, and attracts a male. She then copulates with him and, in some species, carries him into the nest and bites off his genitalia. The genitalia will continue supplying her with sperm for an hour or more. The male dies.

• The name "ant" traces its roots to the ancient Germanic word *amaitjo*—which means "the biter."

• Ants were known to the Romans as *formicae*. Formic acid, the substance that some species produce as their "sting" chemical, gets its name from this. It's also why ants are classified in the taxonomic family *Formicidae*.

• The sting of the inch-long South American bullet ant is considered the most painful of all ant, bee, and wasp stings. It is said to feel like a gunshot wound (which is why they're called *bullet* ants). As part of an initiation rite, the Brazilian Satere-Mawe people make mittenlike pouches from leaves and fill them with hundreds of bullet ants. Boys undergoing the initiation have the mittens

---

German folk remedy: To quiet a teething baby, rub its gums with sheep brains.

tied to their hands. Then they must keep the mittens on for about 10 minutes—during which they can be stung hundreds of times—and are not allowed to cry out. Their arms are often paralyzed for days afterward.

• During floods, fire ant colonies will gather together and form large balls with their bodies, with the queen and her brood at the center. They become living ant rafts that can float this way for miles until they make it back to land, where they set up a new nest.

• Queens of some ant species can live for as long as 30 years and can produce hundreds of millions of eggs over a lifetime.

• Some ant species build *supercolonies* comprising millions of separate nests, millions of queens, and billions of workers. These supercolonies can cover a few acres—or many thousand square miles.

• Aphids are tiny bugs that feed on sugar-rich plant fluids and poop a substance called *honeydew*, which is also sugar-rich. Several ant species survive on honeydew and actually "farm" aphids to get it: They protect the aphids from predators and take aphid eggs into their nests during the winter. Some ants have even learned to induce aphids to excrete honeydew by stroking them with their antennae, essentially "milking" them. Some aphid species have even lost the ability to poop...if they're not stroked by ants.

• In 2009 it was reported that Argentine ants (*Linepithema humile*), native to South America but accidentally spread around the world, now inhabit several massive supercolonies in the United States, Europe, and Japan, and are now part of an interrelated *megacolony* of ants...that is literally taking over the ant world.

*　　*　　*

EXPAND YOUR VOCABULARY

• A *gynotikolobomassophile* is someone who likes to nibble on women's earlobes.

• The fuzzy frame of mind between sleep and consciousness is technically referred to as a *hypnopompic state*.

According to the CDC, food allergies cause only 11 fatalities per year in the U.S.

FROM AUDI 5000 TO ZUNNDAPP JANUS

An A-to-Z of the weirdest, wildest, and most wonderful motor vehicles ever made.

A **is for Audi 5000,** the car that gave us the phrase "sudden unintended acceleration" in the 1980s. The phrase refers to defects that make a car suddenly speed up without pressing the accelerator. It was believed to have caused hundreds of crashes and even some deaths. Audi was forced to recall millions of the 5000 models due to the problem...but it was never really proven that the cars had any defects—and a class-action suit by owners of the cars is still in court. The phrase resurfaced in 2009 when several Toyota models were recalled for the same reason.

B is for Bugatti Veyron, a French high-performance "supercar" first produced in 2004. It has 16 cylinders, can go from 0–180 mph in 14 seconds, and has an astounding 1,001 horsepower. The Veyron EB model has a top speed of just over 265 mph—making it the fastest production car in the world. Cost: about $1.7 million.

C is for Chevrolet 6700-series bus—the model used in the 1970s TV classic, *The Partridge Family.* Painted in brightly-colored blocks (inspired by the work of Dutch painter Piet Mondrian), the bus appeared in the pilot in 1970 and remained on the show until it was canceled in 1974. It was abandoned after that, and sat behind Lucy's Tacos on Martin Luther King Boulevard in Los Angeles until 1987, when it was taken to a junk yard.

D is for Divco, founded in 1926. Divco—an acronym for **D**etroit **I**ndustrial **V**ehicles **Co**mpany—made delivery vehicles, and if you're old enough, you may remember one of them: They made the iconic milk delivery trucks that were used all over the country until the 1970s. Divco made the milk trucks for 60 years (until 1986) giving them the distinction of being the company that made the same model vehicle longer than any other in the world...after the Volkswagen Beetle.

When Antarctica's Mt. Erebus erupts, its lava contains pieces of pure gold.

E is for Edsel, the name that still means "FAILURE!" Ford made about 115,000 of them from 1959 until 1962—and lost an astounding $350 million along the way. The unfortunate car was named after Henry Ford's only son, Edsel Bryant Ford.

F is for Fisker, a California-based hybrid luxury sportscar manufacturer named after owner Henrik Fisker. They debuted their first prototype, the Karma, in 2008. Features: solar panels on the roof to run minor electrical systems; leather interiors made from the hides of free-range cattle that were never branded; wood trim from "non-living" trees (such as wood taken from trees long submerged in lakes); an "animal-free" model that uses bamboo-based cloth instead of leather; and a center console inlaid with fossilized leaves. Cost: from about $80,000 to $106,000.

G is for Gumpert, a German street-legal supercar made by Roland Gumpert. Our favorite thing about the Gumpert: the name. (We really hope they have a "Forrest" Gumpert model.) The car first appeared in 2005, and became known around the world in 2008 when the popular British television show *Top Gear* raced one on their test track—and it ran the best time in the show's history.

H is for Horsey Horseless Carriage, invented by Battle Creek, Michigan, inventor Uriah Smith in 1899. Smith thought he had come up with the design for the first car that wouldn't scare horses. It looked like a small horse-drawn carriage, except that it had a small engine…and a wooden facsimile of a horse's head jutting out from its front. "The live horse would be thinking of another horse," Smith wrote, "and before he could discover his error and see that he had been fooled, the strange carriage would be passed!" The Horsey Horseless is known only from advertisements; no examples survive.

I is for Isuzu, named after the Isuzu River, located in Mie Prefecture on the east coast of Honshu Island, Japan. The name means "50 bells" and was first used in 1934 for a truck made by the Automobile Industries Co., Ltd., in Tokyo. In 1949 the company changed its name to Isuzu.

J is for John Steinbeck's Camper Truck. In 1960 the Nobel Prize-winning author bought a brand new, dark green, GMC pickup and ordered a customized camper for it from Wolverine

Camper of Gladwin, Michigan. Steinbeck told them he wanted a "little house, built like the cabin of a small boat," and that's what he got: The camper had a double bed, a four-burner stove, a heater, a refrigerator, and a chemical toilet. Calling his drivable home "Rocinante" (after Don Quixote's horse), Steinbeck took his French poodle, Charly, on a three-month trip across America, and chronicled the journey in his 1963 classic, *Travels With Charly*. You can see Rocinante yourself; it's in the National Steinbeck Center in Salinas, California.

K is for King Midget, the first product offered by Midget Motors Supply of Athens, Ohio, in 1946. The founders wanted to build cars that anyone could afford—so they decided to *not* build them. The King Midget was a kit: It came in a box in pieces—frame, axles, springs, steering mechanism, sheet metal for the body, and instructions—and you had to put it together yourself. Cost: $250. But you also had to get your own engine. King Midgets were sold until 1970.

L is for Le Car, otherwise known as the Renault 5. It's on virtually every list of the worst cars in history. In the words of Tom and Ray Magliozzi, "Click and Clack, the Tappet Brothers" of NPR's *Car Talk* radio show: "Like any French restaurant in America, it was overpriced, noisy, moody, and would put you in mortal danger if you had an accident with anything larger than a croissant."

M is for Mack, the company founded by John, Augustus, and William Mack in 1890. They made carriages and covered wagons at the time, but in 1900 John Mack had a "vision," according to the Mack website, and in it saw the Macks making the world's best heavy-duty work trucks. Their commercial trucks are known today for their signature bulldog logo, adopted in 1922. Ten years later, Alfred Fellows Masury, Mack's Chief Engineer, was recovering from surgery when he carved a bulldog out of wood. He received a patent for the design, and the bulldog hood ornament has been on every Mack truck ever since.

N is for Nike ONE, an imaginary car dreamed up by Nike designers in 2004 to promote the release of the driving simulator game, *Gran Turismo 4*. One physical model was made; it looked like a giant, futuristic roller skate. According to the concept, the driver puts on a "Spark Suit," a specially-designed suit that converts muscle movement into electricity, lays down inside the low, teardrop-shaped glass body, and the Spark Suit provides all the power needed for the HEP ("Human Energy Potential") drive system. Top speed: 230 mph. (We hope it becomes real some day.)

O is for Ol' Yeller, the name given to nine bright yellow racecars built by legendary Hollywood car builder Max Balchowsky from 1956 to 1963. Balchowsky mixed parts from different cars and put them together himself in his shop—he called them "junkyard dogs," hence "Ol' Yeller"—and actually beat the best-known racecar makers in the world, including Ferrari and Jaguar. You may have even seen one of his cars: Elvis Presley drove Ol' Yeller VIII in the 1964 film *Viva Las Vegas*.

P is for Porter, the fictional make of automobile from one of the dumbest TV shows of all time, *My Mother the Car*. The show starred Jerry Van Dyke as David Crabtree, who, while shopping for a used car, hears an old car talking to him. It turns out to be the reincarnated spirit of his dead mother. (Did we mention it's regarded as one of the dumbest TV shows of all time?) The actual car was made from pieces of several different models, including a Ford Model T, a Maxwell, and a Hudson, with a custom radiator case that had the word "Porter" on it. It was blown up after the show was cancelled. (We wish. It's actually at the Star Cars Museum in Gatlinburg, Tennessee.)

Q is for Queen, manufactured from 1904 to 1907 by Detroit automaker Carl H. Blomstrom. About 2,500 of these two- or four-person runabouts were made. Although the engine was under the seat, Blomstrom was going for the European style, so he added a "faux hood" to the front. (There was nothing under it.) Company slogan: "Big Power. Few Parts."

R is for Rinspeed iChange, a futuristic concept car designed by Swiss manufacturer Rinspeed. Every year the company produces a new concept model for the Geneva Auto Show, and this was 2009's model. The iChange is an electric car that looks sort of like a stylized shoe. It has no doors—the roof tilts up to allow passengers to get in it—and though it's normally a one-seater, the back expands to reveal two additional seats. And there's no key—it's controlled by an iPhone.

S is for Shall We Join Us?, which—question mark and all—is the actual name of a car sold in Japan by Mitsubishi. Other great Japanese car names include the Toyota Deliboy, the Mitsubishi Chariot Grandio Super Exceed, the Daihatsu Naked, the Yamaha Pantryboy Supreme, and, our favorite, the Isuzu Light Dump.

T is for Trabant, possibly the most drab, unstylish car in history, made in one of the most drab, unstylish countries ever, East Germany. Trabants were made from 1957 all the way until the fall of the Soviet Union in 1991, and barely changed in all those years. They came in just two styles, two-door sedan and two door wagon, and were equipped with a two-stroke engine, meaning you had to add oil to the gas every time you filled the tank. Best of all: For the average East German who ordered one, it took about 15 years to be delivered.

U is for Used Car Salesmen. Thanks for the Ford Econoline Van you sold Uncle John in 1973, Used Car Guy. He loved being stuck on the New Jersey Turnpike in that lemon so much that he did it three times!

V is for VW Golf—which sounds like it's named after a sport, but it's based on the German word for the Gulf Stream, and references the winds associated with it. The company has named several cars after winds—*Scirocco* (Mediterranean winds from the Saharan Desert), *Passat* (German for "trade wind"), and *Jetta* (for "jet stream"). And the VW Polo—which isn't yet sold in the U.S., but won the coveted "World Car of the Year" in 2010—is named after the Marco Polo ocean current and the winds it generates.

W is for White Bus Model 706, which wasn't white and wasn't a bus. It was a large, open-topped 14-passenger coach made by the White Motor Company (now better known for their long haul trucks) in the 1930s. They were made specifically for National Parks, including Yellowstone, Yosemite, and Glacier National Park, to take visitors on tours. Several are still in use today.

X is for X-Hawk Flying Car, the "car of the future" we've been promised since the 1950s. It's being developed by Urban Aeronautics in Tel Aviv, Israel, and will be powered by rotors that can can be pivoted, giving it VTOL (Vertical-Take-Off and Landing) capability like a helicopter, but with much more maneuverability.

It also has four wheels, so it can be driven like a car. Company owner Rafi Yoeli says the X-Hawk will be a perfect rescue vehicle, as it will be able to fly right up to windows of burning buildings and hover there while picking up trapped people. Yoeli says the flying cars will be on the market by 2012.

Y is for Yugo, first made in 1978 in the former Yugoslavia. In 1986 Yugo America started selling the cars in the U.S. for $3,999. More than 150,000 of the small, nondescript hatchbacks sold before people figured out that $3,999 was *way too much money* for them. They were poorly built cars, prone to numerous mechanical problems—including broken timing belts—which destroyed engines. Yugo folded in 1992, but the cars continued to be made in Serbia until 2008.

Z is for Zunndapp Janus, a car made entirely out of *zunndapp,* a superlight material derived from asteroids, making it invisible in direct sunlight. Just kidding. It's a microcar that was made by German motorcycle maker Zunndapp in 1958. It had a 14-horsepower engine and a top speed of 50 mph. Best feature: It had two bench seats. One faced forward, where the driver sat, and one faced backward, where the terrified passenger sat. (It was named for the two-faced Roman god Janus.)

✳   ✳   ✳

ANSWER TO "HOW _____ GOT TO JAPAN"
(page 320)

The answer is…sausage. Jahn and his fellow prisoners were sausage makers, and Yoshifusa was a government engineer experimenting with new ways to process meat. The photos show the prisoners slaughtering, butchering, and smoking pigs, and then stuffing the minced pork into pig intestines. Sausage making is an especially effective way of preserving meat without refrigeration, and Japanese meat processors eagerly adopted it—which is why there are still sausage and hot dog stands all over Japan today. We probably (we hope) fooled you, because Tsingtao is a fairly well-known brand of Chinese beer—and the Germans are, of course, expert beer makers. But beer had actually been in Japan since the 1870s, when Dutch traders first introduced it.

ANSWER PAGES

OL' JAYBEARD AND BRIAN
(Answers for page 166)

1. Ol' Jaybeard placed the *Bathroom Reader* on the floor up against the wall in a corner of the room.

2. Each word contains three consecutive letters as they appear in the alphabet: **hij**ack, cou**ghi**ng, a**stu**te, wo**rst**, **def**ine.

3. 41 cents. Ol Jaybeard was holding four coins, one of each denomination.

4. "World Wide Web" has three syllables, whereas "WWW" has nine.

5. The password is the amount of letters in the spelled-out number that Ol' Jaybeard said, so the password for "8" was "5."

6. It was daytime.

7. 1,687.

8. Brian knows that the odd pages of a book are on the right-facing pages, and the evens are on the left, so there's no way Ol' Jaybeard could have hidden the cash between pages 57 and 58 because they are on the opposite sides of the same sheet of paper.

9. SNOWING
SOWING
SWING
SING
SIN
IN
I

10. Ol' Jaybeard sold seven eggs that day. Here's how it worked out: He sold four eggs to the first customer, which was three-and-a-half—or half of seven—plus one-half. That left him with three eggs, so he sold two to the next customer: one-and-one-half plus one-half equals two. That left him with one egg. Half of that plus one-half equals one.

It figures: Soda drinkers have more CO_2 in their farts than non-soda drinkers.

MISSING LINKS WORD GAME
(Answers for page 246)

ANSWERS TO #1
1. Days; 2. Star; 3. Run; 4. Hot; 5. House; 6. Ear; 7. Sea
BONUS: Dog

ANSWERS TO #2
1. Whistle; 2. Sign; 3. Pit: 4. Short; 5. Light; 6. By; 7. Loss
BONUS: Stop

PORTMANTEAU MOVIE QUIZ
(Answers for page 308)

1. *Red Dawn* (1984) + *Dawn of the Dead* (1978) = *Red Dawn of the Dead*

2. *Up in the Air* (2009) + *Air Bud* (1997) = *Up in the Air Bud*

3. *American Beauty* (1999) + *Beauty and the Beast* (1991) = *American Beauty and the Beast*

4. *Iron Man* (2008) + *Man of La Mancha* (1972) = *Iron Man of La Mancha*

5. *Little Miss Sunshine* (2006) + *Sunshine Cleaning* (2008) = *Little Miss Sunshine Cleaning*

6. *Kill Bill* (2003) + *Bill and Ted's Excellent Adventure* (1989) = *Kill Bill and Ted's Excellent Adventure*

7. *District 9* (2009) + *9 1/2 Weeks* (1986) = *District 9 1/2 Weeks*

8. *Freaky Friday* (2003) + *Friday the 13th* (1979) = *Freaky Friday the 13th*

9. *That Thing You Do!* (1996) + *Do the Right Thing* (1989) = *That Thing You Do the Right Thing*

10. *There's Something About Mary* (1998) + *Mary Poppins* (1964) = *There's Something About Mary Poppins*

11. *300* (2007) + *101 Dalmatians* (1961) = *301 Dalmatians*

It takes 300 gallons of water to produce a loaf of bread. A pound of beef: 3,500 gallons.

BONUS: *The Godfather* (1972) + *Father of the Bride* (1950) + *Bride of Frankenstein* (1935) = *The Godfather of the Bride of Frankenstein*

THE NANNY STATE QUIZ
(Answers for page 338)

1. b) The tombstone program was halted in 2009, in part because the taxpayer-funded topple-testing made cemeteries *more* hazardous, not less. "If you look at the cemetery now, it's in a dangerous state with all the stakes stuck out for people to trip over," said Mavis Fields, whose husband's marker was damaged by topple-testing.

2. a) The fine was proposed as a means of saving gas and reducing air pollution, but the idea was abandoned in the face of vehement public opposition and fears that it would increase traffic and air pollution. "The danger of everyone switching off in a jam is that some may not start up again," says a spokesman for the British Automobile Association.

3. b) "The average shoplifter makes off with £149 worth of goods every time they steal. It is nonsense to think a repeat offender is going to be put off by an £80 fine," complained Kevin Hawkins, a spokesperson for an association of U.K. retailers. "It's a license to walk into shops and take things."

4. a) According to the council, the splashing of raindrops clouds the surface of the water, making it harder for lifeguards to spot anyone drowning at the bottom of the pool. "It was difficult to believe what I was hearing," one swimmer told the *Daily Mail* newspaper. "The idea that it could be too wet to swim seems almost incredible, but that was what they were actually saying."

5. c) Cans are weighed as they are lifted into garbage trucks; the information is collected in a database that lets officials monitor whether households are recycling.

6. c) In the U.K., the legal drinking age for alcohol consumed in the home is five years of age. "Health department officials point out that current guidance on safe drinking levels exist only for those over 18. They argue that this is a gap which is a cause for concern," *The Independent* newspaper reported in 2008. "The Government is also reviewing whether the current age at which it is legal to drink should remain at five."

7. b) The U.K.'s National Health Service spends £1 billion treating obesity related diseases each year. But health experts warn the program could encourage yo-yo dieting, which increases the risk of heart attack and stroke and may actually *increase* health costs. The plan has also been criticized for consuming the resources of an already overburdened NHS. "When people who are ill through no fault of their own are struggling to get appointments and drugs, it is unfair for money to be allocated to people who simply need to choose to exercise more and eat less," says Mark Wallace, a spokesperson for a British taxpayer watchdog group.

VIOLET PRECIPITATION
(Answers for page 520)

1. United States of America

2. *Born to Run*, by Bruce Springsteen

3. Christian Bale

4. *A Clockwork Orange*, by Anthony Burgess

5. Mount Rushmore

6. *Lady and the Tramp*

7. *Purple Rain*, by Prince

8. Bill Gates

9. *Mad Men*

10. The Great Wall of China

11. Tour de France

12. British Petroleum (B.P.)

13. *The Lion, the Witch, and the Wardrobe*, by C.S. Lewis

14. *The Dark Side of the Moon*, by Pink Floyd

15. "Thank God it's Friday!"

16. Trivial Pursuit

17. General Motors (G.M.)

18. *Will and Grace*

19. *The Lord of the Rings*, by J.R.R. Tolkien

20. World Cup

21. *Exile on Main St.*, by the Rolling Stones

22. *Atlas Shrugged*, by Ayn Rand

23. Uncle John

In 50 mph winds, the Statue of Liberty can sway back and forth as